D1478795

THE LOGIC OF MODERNITY

THE LOGIC OF MODERNITY

MODERNITY

GERALD J. GALGAN

NEW YORK UNIVERSITY PRESS
New York *and* London
1982

B
791
.63
1982

Copyright © 1982 by New York University

Library of Congress Cataloging in Publication Data

Galgan, Gerald J., 1942–
The logic of modernity.

Bibliography: p.
Includes index.
1. Philosophy, Modern.   I. Title.
B791.G3   190   82-2181
ISBN 0-8147-2983-5   AACR2

Manufactured in the United States of America

ACKNOWLEDGMENTS

I wish to thank the following publishers for granting me permission to quote from their publications.

Permission to quote from Jasper Hopkins' translation of Nicholas of Cusa's DE DOCTA IGNORANTIA has been granted by The Arthur J. Banning Press, 305 Foshay Tower, Minneapolis, Minnesota 55402.

Permission to quote from Lewis White Beck's translation of Kant's CRITIQUE OF PRACTICAL REASON has been granted by The Liberal Arts Press, Inc., a division of The Bobbs-Merrill Company, Inc.

Lines from "The Second Coming" are reprinted with permission of Macmillan Publishing Company, Inc. and A. P. Watt Ltd. from COLLECTED POEMS of William Butler Yeats. Copyright 1924 by Macmillan Publishing Company, Inc., renewed 1952 by Bertha Georgie Yeats.

Permission to quote from T. S. Eliot's "Little Gidding," in THE COMPLETE POEMS AND PLAYS, has been granted by Harcourt Brace Jovanovich, Inc., and Faber and Faber, Ltd.

Permission to quote from HEGEL'S SCIENCE OF LOGIC, translated by A. V. Miller, has been granted by George Allen and Unwin Ltd.

Permission to quote from HEGEL'S LOGIC, translated by William Wallace, has been granted by Oxford University Press.

CONTENTS

PREFACE   xi

1. THE MEDIEVAL CONTEXT FOR MODERNITY   1
   The Ancient "Mythos"   3
   The Medieval "Mythos"   9
   Nicholas of Cusa: The Herald of Modernity   14

2. THE BIRTH OF THE MODERN COSMOLOGY   21
   Copernicus and Kepler: The Charting of a New
       Universe   22
   Galileo: Apologist for the New Scientific Method   30
   Bruno: Probing the Ethical Implications of the New
       Universe   43

3. THE MATURATION OF MODERN SCIENTIFIC
       METHOD   50
   Descartes: The Metaphysical Foundations of Modern
       Science   53
   The Newtonian Revision of Modern Scientific Method   74
   The Leibnizian Postscript to Modern Scientific
       Method   85

4. THE EMERGENCE OF THE MODERN
       PROBLEM OF KNOWLEDGE   95
   Locke: Psychology as a Modern Science   96
   Berkeley: An Attempt to Overcome Cartesian
       Dualism   109
   Hume: The Breakdown of Certitude   118

5. THE ENLIGHTENMENT: MODERNITY MADE
       SELF-CONSCIOUS   137
   The Anti-Christian Polemic   143

The Redefinition of Human Nature 156
The Enlightenment as Heritage 175

6. THE SYSTEMIZATION OF THE MODERN
   MEANING OF MAN 193
   Rousseau: The Rudiments of a Modern Philosophical
   Anthropology 193
   Kant: The Metaphysical Foundations for the Meaning
   of Man in the Modern Universe 220
   1. INTRODUCTION 220
   2. THE METAPHYSICS OF NATURE 227
   3. THE METAPHYSICS OF MORALS 246
   4. THE UNITY OF THE KANTIAN METAPHYSICS 258
   5. THE SIGNIFICANCE OF KANT'S PROJECT 268

7. THE COMPLETION OF THE LOGIC OF
   MODERNITY 274
   Hegel: History as the Modern "Cosmos" 275
   1. INTRODUCTION 275
   2. THE HEGELIAN METHOD AND ITS LOGIC 281
   3. HEGEL'S LOGIC AND ITS METHOD 284
   4. THE PHILOSOPHY OF NATURE 297
   5. PHILOSOPHY OF SPIRIT 307
   6. THE SIGNIFICANCE OF HEGEL'S PROJECT 338
   Nietzsche: The Struggle with Faith in the Logic of
   Modernity 350

8. REFLECTIONS ON MODERNITY AND THE
   PRESENT AGE 369
   A Profile of Modernity 369
   An Exercise in Thinking about the Present Age in the
   Light of Modernity 389

LIST OF WORKS FREQUENTLY CITED 402

NOTES 404

INDEX 465

PREFACE

FAR from being a history of modern philosophy, this book is intended as the beginning of a philosophical reflection on the meaning of the present age. "Philosophy too," says Hegel, "is its own time apprehended in thoughts."[1] But how great a *compre*hension of times that are not one's own is required for such *ap*prehension!

This book proceeds from the premise that there is a "uniquely intimate relationship between the modern philosophical sources and our contemporary act of philosophizing"[2]—that we today "are what we are as functionaries of modern philosophical humanity," as "heirs and cobearers of the direction of the will which pervades this humanity."[3] This work attempts, therefore, to be philosophical about the modern philosophical past in order to appropriate that past for the sake of understanding the unique way in which the meaning of man has manifested iteself in the present age.

The point of departure for this venture can best be expressed in the words of Edmund Husserl.

Our task is to make comprehensible the *teleology* in the historical becoming of . . . modern philosophy, and at the same time to achieve clarity about ourselves, who are the bearers of this teleology.[4]

In place of "teleology," however, the "logic" of the title is proposed. Logic is *not* to be understood in its usual sense as a method for examining thought in its purely formal character; rather, it is to be understood in a sense more akin (but not rigidly confined) to that of Hegel, that is, as an exhibition of philosophical thought in terms of its necessary self-development throughout modern history.[5]

The logic of modernity, then, denotes a developmental unity of thought underlying philosophical positions that oppose each other in a dynamic co-operation. Since this unity is developmental, it cannot, by and large, be verbalized by the modern philosophers. In its attempt to verbalize the logic of their modernity, this book makes an effort to understand these philosophers "in a way that they could never have understood themselves."[6] Here, the attempt of the book to verbalize this logic can only be summarized in barest outline.

The modern philosophical past (Chapter 8) has made possible the present understanding of the meaning of man. Technology— the unique way in which the meaning of man is manifested in the present age—is a programmatic implementation of a temporal way of man's being in the world. Contemporary technology is the fruit of the modern philosophical view of time. But this view of time is a coming to self-awareness, beyond the confines of theology, of a more-than-natural consciousness wherein the infinite is brought into relation with the human subject. The modern philosophical view of time, therefore, is itself the outcome of medieval theological thinking about a Divine Being who mediates His presence to (and absence from) creation temporally and who valorizes temporal particulars. Contemporary technology, in short, presupposes the medieval thought-world that made modern consciousness possible. And so the significance of the present age and its uniqueness reduce, in the final analysis, to whatever novelties may be found in the world-unifying otherworldliness first presented by medieval Christianity.

Ancient philosophy (Chapter 1) presents a hierarchical, finite cosmos in which time is cyclically repetitive and divinity is the immanent consciousness of a finished and eternal world. Nature (as older and larger than man) appoints proper limits to all things. With the advent of thinking about the Christian God in the Middle Ages, however, the essence of things is now derived from a more-than-natural being. Infinity is present to, and spills over into the realm of nature; infinity discloses its meaning in time—a time that can no longer be cyclically confined. Modernity is heralded, but philosophy will assimilate these implications of Christian doctrine only gradually.

The process of assimilation begins with the birth of a new cosmology (Chapter 2) in which a homogeneous, abstract or mathematicized space is substituted for the heterogeneous, hierarchical cosmos of the ancients. Descartes (Chapter 3) then initiates the transformation, in metaphysics, of the medieval notion of nature—as a presentation of divine creativity—into the (modern) notion of nature as a representation of man's rationality. Nature becomes an object-ified framework that exists as a network of relationships set up by the human subject and *meant* to be mastered by his knowledge and production. With the completion of this transformation in Newton and Leibniz, the focus of philosophy shifts (Chapter 4) from *how* man knows in the modern universe to the problem of the *limits* of his knowledge within this universe. Hume transmutes Locke and Berkeley's theory of knowledge here into a skeptical program in which the extrarational dimensions of human nature are accorded primacy. Then, bringing the focus of modern philosophy to rest in the problem of human nature, the Enlightenment (Chapter 5) makes modernity self-conscious by means of its perception of history as an autonomous human creation freed from Divine Will.

Kant provides the metaphysical foundations (Chapter 6) for the meaning of man in the modern universe by conjoining the modern science of external nature with the Enlightenment's exploration of the (inner) nature of man. The highest employment of reason is now seen to be practical and moral rather than speculative. Metaphysics no longer examines the being of the things that *are* but the ground of their being-for-man. Hegel (Chapter 7) attempts to locate Kant's metaphysical foundations for the human subject in a cosmic perspective. The energies of reason no longer operate as a schematism in individual consciousness but as a continual process of canceling out the past of history and at the same time preserving the essence of that past in a higher synthesis. The result is that the Enlightenment's portrayal of history as an autonomous human creation freed from Divine Will is transformed by Hegel into a synthesis where the infinite autonomy of modern moral selfhood is referred back to the truths of Christian revelation. Hegel thus completes the logic of modernity by returning it to an awareness of its source. This completion is tacitly confirmed by Nietzsche, who strives to look upon modernity in as unmodern a way as possible. Self-proclaimed "firstling" of the twentieth century,[7] Nietzsche can announce the withering of Christianity only by imitating unconsciously and in reverse the critique of the ancient cosmos provided by early medieval Christian thinkers.

Modern philosophy thus remains informed by the Christian faith from which it proceeds (Chapter 8), even when this faith is viewed as a pretense. And the meaning of contemporary consciousness, wherein technology becomes the unique way in which the meaning of man appears, must be ultimately sought in modern philosophy's developmental incorporation of originally theological categories that were "dissolved and transformed into philosophy"[8] and that were elaborated by and for medieval Christianity. This, in fact, is the task this book proposes for philosophy in the late twentieth century.

Whatever may be the virtues, therefore, of the following account, it must perforce fall short of its aim, namely, to verbalize at last the logic of modernity. "Our powers become known to us through the performance of our tasks, and it is better to fail nobly than to succeed basely."[9] But if this book can find its readers and persuade them effectively that it is only by going beyond and beneath contemporary experience into a historical pilgrimage of self-understanding that we can *begin* to comprehend the meaning of the epiphany of man in our time, then the limitations of the author may be forgiven and his efforts and aspirations will have been justified.

Behind these intellectual efforts and aspirations are persons; and here, as author, I must personally acknowledge my indebtedness. Robert Pollock (1901–78), in his legendary lectures at the Graduate School of Fordham University, first suggested the intimate connections between modernity and medieval thought and thus made possible the conception of this project. The interest and questioning of students in "The History of Modern Philosophy" at St. Francis College, Brooklyn, New York, occasioned the emergence of the structure of this work. The Department of Philosophy at

St. Francis College—more than fifteen years of conversations with my colleagues Francis Slade, Joseph Carpino, and Nino Langiulli—constituted the intellectual community that permitted this project to be carried out.

During a period of seven years, Ann Hartle and Joseph Carpino of the Department of Philosophy at St. Francis College were the first to read each chapter as it emerged from the typewriter. Their numerous letters, their advice, and their encouragement showed me that the project could and should be completed.

The comments and suggestions of those who read the completed manuscript—Joseph Carpino, Ann Hartle, Clyde Lee Miller (of SUNY at Stony Brook), John J. McDermott (of Texas A&M University), Michael Keane, and Peter Leonard—significantly contributed to the improvement of the final version. The editing of a very dense section on Hegel by Joseph Carpino must also be acknowledged. And for the support of John J. McDermott and Colin Jones (Director of New York University Press) in bringing the book to publication, I am grateful.

Finally, it was the patience, interest, and conversation of my wife, Sheila, that enabled me to see this work through from its inception to its publication.

I

THE MEDIEVAL CONTEXT
FOR MODERNITY

THE noted medievalist Henry Osborn Taylor was constrained to admit that the Middle Ages appear far distant and "spiritually strange" to the contemporary mind.[1] Yet, despite its strangeness to contemporary man, the medieval past is the vital context for his own more immediate modern philosophical past.

As long as the glory and significance of the Middle Ages are viewed entirely in terms of Scholasticism, and as long as medieval society is viewed as a largely static social hierarchy reflecting only the complete dominance of society by religious dogmas, the meaning of the Middle Ages will be construed largely and perhaps entirely as a mere continuation of classical or ancient experience and categories. Viewed in this fashion, medieval civilization, far from being perceived as the context of modern philosophical thought, will be perceived as the thought and culture against which modern thinkers and reformers reacted. Although this chapter can hardly pretend to settle the issue of which direction the medieval period more decisively leans toward—our Greek and Roman classical past or our modern European past—it can attempt to dispel the view of this period as a mere continuation of the classical past. The interpretation of medieval society as concerned with purely spiritual (at the expense of secular) issues and the interpretation of medieval society as static and homogeneous do not stand up to thoroughgoing examination. Such an examination, as Charles H. Haskins remarks, "shows us the Middle Ages less dark and less static . . . than was once supposed."[2]

Medieval society was frequently in a state of ferment and turmoil, frequently on the brink of chaos, immersed in struggles between secular rulers and popes, between bishops and monasteries—struggles that were productive of the most fruitful kinds of opposition. A case could be made, in other words, for asserting that despite certain profound *intellectual continuities* with classical civilization, the medieval epoch represents an *experiential* or *cultural break* with the classical past. The medieval epoch brings to birth a new society, perhaps even a new beginning for Western civilization and, in doing so, constitutes the fertile loam out of which the categories and culture of modernity would emerge.

The *later* Middle Ages, for example, have been spoken of as possessing their chief glory, not only in cathedrals, epics, and scholasticism, but also in the construction for the first time in history of a highly complex, heterogeneous civilization situated "not on the backs of sweating slaves or coolies but primarily on non-human power."[3] If only in terms of its technology, the roots of the modern era lie in the Middle Ages.

But even the very *beginnings* of the Middle Ages signal experiences that will be highly significant for the advent of modern culture and categories. Far from being simply a continuation of the Roman Empire, early medieval society was a pioneer society, living on a "frontier both geographical and intellectual, and engaged in advancing it."[4] The classical sources of civilization were hopelessly sealed off, and if there was to be a rebirth of Western civilization, society would now have to face the Atlantic, no longer the Mediterranean Ocean.[5] Here, then, was a society primitive in character, largely agricultural, but a society that, because it was "relatively free of binding tradition and intensely empirical," could afford "Christianity the peculiarly powerful form and influence it assumed in Western Europe."[6] Here was a society in which newly emergent forms of technology, primitive as they were by contemporary standards, "responded to the needs and capacities of an impoverished agrarian society."[7]

Such a picture, needless to say, does not demonstrate the *utter* novelty of the medieval venture. What entitles us to call this period of one thousand years the Middle Ages is precisely its mediation of a very difficult to understand classical past and a more accessible modern past. Medieval culture and especially medieval categories have a decided continuity with the classical past, but this continuity is *limited* and, what is more important, must be interpreted within a wider framework than has, all too often, been the custom.

One ought to understand by the term "Middle Ages" a fusion of diverse and astounding forces never before welded together—the forces found in barbarism, Christianity, and the residue of the classical mind—all in some fashion opposed to each other and yet viewed by medieval culture as reconcilable.

Medieval civilization—as this battleground for historical forces, as this unified attempt to reconcile profound oppositions in Western civilization—comes into focus as the necessary context for modern civilization. The agricultural revolution that began the Middle Ages signaled a change in the center of gravity of Western civilization from the South to the North, and it is here that the "distinctive features of the late medieval and the modern worlds developed" and that the tone was set for "the dominant feature of the modern world: power technology."[8] The change that "mattered most for the long term future" was the "rise of a new civilized style of life in northwestern Europe" in the early Middle Ages.[9] So successful was the development of this new style of life that by the early fourteenth century extraordinary progress had been made in Europe toward the replacement of human labor by both waterpower and windpower.[10] At the height of its glory, the medieval mind is usually portrayed as captivated by the building of cathedrals and theologies, but we are often unaware that the closing of the Middle Ages witnessed as well a love affair with the construction of mechanical clocks of astounding intricacy.[11]

The point of these remarks, however, is not that cathedrals and theologies are less important indices of medieval civilization than we have been taught but that cathedrals, theologies, and new technologies, ranging from the moldboard plow to the clock, were inspired by the same profound sensibility. This sensibility, for all the efforts of medieval thinkers to demonstrate its continuity with classical thought, was in the end a fundamental departure from the ancient or classical experience of the world. The extent of this departure is what we must now attempt to suggest.

THE ANCIENT "MYTHOS"

Underlying primitive religion is the division of the world into sacred and profane spaces, the cutting off and preservation of sacred from profane zones. Unlike modern man, who experiences space as homogeneous, primitive "homo religiosus" perceives some parts of space as "qualitatively different from others," so that an opposition exists between "strong, significant space," space that is sacred, "the only real and real-ly existing space," and "all other space, the formless expanse surrounding it."[12] Primitive religion engages in a sanctifying or hallowing that is initiated when "a specific zone is detached from space as whole, . . . distinguished from other zones,"[13] and made secure, no longer subject to change, sacred.

What will be decisive for our purposes is the contention that ancient philosophy, although it is something of an entirely different order from primitive religious experience, nonetheless maintains, on its own peculiar terms, this fundamental bifurcation of space into the sacred and the profane. Underlying the ancient or classical "logos" is a primitive religious "mythos" that divides the world into sacred and profane spaces.

The generalization that logos follows mythos in regard to the most fundamental distinction made by ancient philosophy does have its notable exceptions. Thus, for example, Heraclitus envisages human discourse as a whole, a single fabric whose wholeness is accounted for by what he calls the "Logos." The wholeness of human speech, as he sees it, resembles the very harmony of the cosmos in that it is a harmony of opposed tensions.[14] Nonetheless, the larger and more characteristic traditions of ancient philosophy held that the experience of the wholeness of the world—the singular experience of the world as completely sacred and homogeneous throughout—could not be had by man. The thinking behind this majority opinion in ancient philosophy was that if man could experience the world as entirely sacred it would have to be such that change and mutation would be as sacred and perfect as those parts of nature that were at rest and immutable. That the mutable could be as perfect as the immutable was a prima facie contradiction. Any virtues that might pertain to the notion of the world as a "sacred gestalt" would be outweighed by the unacceptability of a contradiction.

Security as well as logic and, perhaps most important, the very drift of the ancient experience of the world rested with the assumption that change was imperfect and rest was somehow perfect and self-contained. Much as Heraclitus at the beginning of ancient philosophy, the Stoics, at its end, seem to pose the exception. Stoicism conceived of a universe that was continuous and bound together by the force of "Hexis," but this binding force was one that worked to assure the limitedness of the universe, even though the universe was surrounded by an infinite void. But although this void served as a kind of envelope for a very interesting and interconnected world, one that kept the best of men, or the sages, quite busy, it could not engender or sustain a positive notion of the infinite that would qualify this world as completely and homogeneously sacred.[15] The very exceptions in ancient philosophy indicate how prevalent a norm the sacred-profane bifurcation was for that philosophy.

The assumption of sacred and profane space—along with its philosophical corollary of the imperfection of change and the perfection of rest—had a decided impact on ancient cosmology. That which is at rest occupies a space that is more perfect, that is, more self-contained and defined, than that which is in motion or involved in change. Time, too, would have to follow the logic of space; the most perfect kind of time would have to be that which comes closest to being self-contained—that time which falls back upon itself and repeats itself. Thus, time, to the extent that it can be viewed as intelligible, comes to be viewed as an eternal cycle of genesis and destruction.

In essence, then, the demythologizing of ritual and myth by ancient philosophy, while on the one hand involving the loss of ritual salvation and purification and the substitution of rational purification (or inquiry) for salvific gnosis, involves on the other hand the maintenance of the primitive religious and mythic bifurcation between the sacred and the profane. For the ancient mentality, philosophical as well as prephilosophical, "reality manifests itself as force, effectiveness, and duration"; and the "outstanding reality is the sacred," for "only the sacred *is* in an absolute fashion, acts effectively," and makes things endure.[16] On the philosophical level, of course, the bifurcation between the sacred and the profane is translated into the bifurcation between perfection and imperfection. Thus, for Plato there is the space of perfection occupied by the "Eidei," or Forms, and the physical space of imperfection confronted by the realm of opinion; for Aristotle, there is the space of the celestial spheres, that of perfect motion, and the space of imperfection, the home of man, the terrestrial sphere.

Aristotle's cosmology might be said to be the clearest and best indication of the significance of ancient philosophy's assumption of the bifurcation of the sacred and the profane. Thus, in the *Metaphysics* he remarks that

what is passing away must still have something of what has passed away; and of what is coming to be, something must already be. And in general when anything is perishing, something is present; and when anything is coming to be, there must be something from which it comes to be and something by which it is generated, and this process cannot go on to infinity.[17]

As Aristotle sees it, the very existence of change demands the existence of something prior that is in some fashion unchanged. Imperfection requires the prior existence of perfection; the actual is prior to the possible, and the perfect is prior to the imperfect.

In this way, for Aristotle, the cosmological order must be implicitly divided into two distinct realms—one of movement and one of rest. The realm of movement must be the "mimesis," or imitation, of the realm of perfection or rest. A correspondence, however, exists between the realm of perfection or rest and the realm of imperfection or motion; for without the former, the latter could not exist. Thus, the living individual in terms of its movement in the terrestrial sphere corresponds to the circular and perfect movement of the celestial spheres. When this individual reaches its point of maturation, it must pass on its form to "its descendants to be realized in them once again, and so on and on, world without end."[18]

In the Aristotelian cosmology there is in all change an inescapable return to prior contrarieties. To the extent that an old element is transformed into a new element, the old element must be said to possess a quality whose contrary belongs to the new element. A new thing is simply a new contrariety attached to the old thing. The "new," therefore, can never be radical or unconditional novelty but must be a new combination of old elements—a new arrangement of pregiven elements. Change is ultimately consigned to repeating what is already there. If it were possible for change to generate the unconditionally novel, it would then follow that an infinite number of contrarieties would attach themselves to the old or preceding element. And if this were to happen, there would be an "infinite regress" of elements, which would amount to a contradiction in terms, for the universe is inescapably finite and "no sensible magnitude is infinite."[19] For Aristotle, and for ancient philosophy in general, there can be no real question, as William James put it, of whether we are "witnessing in our own personal experience what is really the essential process of creation,"[20] the emergence of radical novelty in being, since all generation is programmed by an unending cyclical repetition.

This basic cosmological model has as its corollary an astronomical model that is representative for the ancient world. The circular movement of the sun is caused by the outermost sphere of the celestial bodies. The sun, in turn, effects the continuous cyclical character of the genesis and destruction of individual entities proceeding apace in the lowest, or terrestrial, sphere of the universe. Insofar as movement is continuous, it is ultimately caused by a cause that is not itself moved or caused but that abides in perfect rest—the unmoved mover. Time is the measure of this continuous movement; consequently, time is cyclical, since

amongst continuous bodies which are moved, only that which is moved in a circle is 'continuous' in such a way that it preserves its continuity with itself through the movement. The conclusion, therefore, is that *this* is what produces continuous movement, namely, the body which is being moved in a circle; and its movement makes time continuous.[21]

A procession of time, for Aristotle, that was vectorial and unrepeatable would imply an unending attribution of contrarieties and consequently a discontinuity of movement within itself. Time, then, in its essence, must be eternal and cyclical in order to fit a world that, in its essence, is finite and limited. This cosmos—which is self-contained (contains within itself the sources of its own meaning), which is underived from anything other than itself (is eternal in the sense of being without beginning or end), and which is finite or limited and bifurcated into zones of perfection and imperfection—is representative of the majority opinion of ancient philosophy.

As a spokesman for this majority opinion, Aristotle holds that coming-to-be occurs necessarily, that in order for the prior to exist, the very future being of the posterior must be assumed to be necessary.[22] A vectorial or rectilinear procession of time that proceeded *ad infinitum* would contain no "arche," or first principle, from which coming-to-be would derive its necessary character. Only cyclical coming-to-be guarantees a connection with necessity and thus with perfection itself. When all is said and done, *motion must be subordinate to a reality that transcends motion.* On this proposition, the majority opinion of ancient philosophy must stand fast. The earth itself must be assigned a position in the cosmos that, although it is at the center, is necessarily inferior. Man abides in the home of imperfection where rationality struggles for momentary victories over an irreducible and irrational substrate. Rationality in the terrestrial sphere is an island in a vast sea of becoming, or as Plato would say, philosophy occurs in the "cave" of hopelessly fluctuating human opinions. Yet, there exists a glimpse of a perfection not of this earth and in essence more-than-human.

The fundamental antithesis of the ancient mythos—the sacred and the profane—thus finds its expression in the ancient logos, particularly in its astronomy. For in this astronomy, as Thomas Kuhn remarks,

the first distinction suggested by the senses is that [of] separating the earth and the heavens. The earth is not part of the heavens; it is the platform from which we view them. And the platform shares few or no apparent characteristics with the celestial bodies seen from it. The heavenly bodies seem bright points of light, the earth an immense non-luminous sphere of mud and rock. Little change is observed in the heavens: the stars are the same night after night. . . . In contrast, the earth is the home of birth and change and destruction. Vegetation and animals alter from week to week; civilizations rise and fall from century to century. . . . It seems absurd to make the earth like the celestial bodies whose most prominent characteristic is that immutable regularity never to be achieved on the corruptible earth.[23]

Both reason and the senses, then, attest to the static, nonplanetary, central, but inferior status of the earth in the universe.

The growth of astronomical reflection around this basic two-sphered model of the universe would consist in adding circles and spheres to the basic model; it would not be conclusively challenged until the time of Copernicus in the sixteenth century. Yet the key—the very context of the Copernican challenge, and thus the very context of modernity itself—is to be found in the time that elapsed in between the genesis of this model and the Copernican challenge. In the Middle Ages is to be found the emergence of an experience of the world quite different from that of the ancients— the emergence of a mythos quite different from that of primitive religion.

THE MEDIEVAL "MYTHOS"

Medieval man's experience of the sacred was decisively different from that of ancient man's. Although ancient man produced the most definitive moments of Western philosophy, he could not free himself from the dualism of the sacred and the profane, from the dualism of celestial perfection and terrestrial imperfection. The burden of primitive religious experience is carried by the ancient world. On the one hand, ancient man

hopes to secure and strengthen his own reality by the most fruitful contact he can attain with hierophanies and kratophanies; on the other, he fears he may lose it completely if he is totally lifted to a plane of being higher than his natural profane state; he longs to go beyond it, and yet cannot wholly leave it.[24]

With the elaboration of the Christian mythos in the Middle Ages, however, the God of Christianity is posited as an infinite and transcendent Being who as He is in Himself is unknown to man but who touches and permeates the natural order. Completely other-than nature, this God is viewed as completely indwelling in nature. God, being "incomprehensible to all reason and all intellect," as the medieval philosopher-mystic, Joannes Scotus Eriugena (c. 810–c. 877), says, "in Himself is incomprehensible," but can be known by being "truly and faithfully denied in all things."[25] The hidden God, "Deus absconditus," is knowable in His unknowableness, since He can be known by His theophany,[26] by His manifestation of Himself in the world. The essence of things is no longer to be found in the unchanging, perfect sectors of the order of nature but rather, as Eriugena tells us, in the mind of God.[27] To reflect upon this God was to challenge the dualism of an exclusively sacred and exclusively profane space and to enter the domain of a new mythos and symbolism. It was from the Pseudo-Dionysius (whose writings were first cited in the early sixth century) that the medievals developed this new symbolism as a way of bridging "the apparently nontraversible gap that the mind perceived" between God and nature, as a way in which "the understanding confronted *transcendence and immanence* held in simultaneous tension," and in a way that was "not without a sense of inward exaltation."[28]

The new symbolic posture toward the sacred, the new mythos, would have its focus in the doctrine of the Incarnation that makes possible a situation where time is no longer a mere cyclical repetition of paradigmatic events—a situation in which God manifests Himself in time. For this new mythos

time begins anew with the birth of Christ, for the Incarnation establishes a new situation of man in the cosmos. This is as much to say that history reveals itself to be a new dimension of the presence of God in the world.[29]

What is important here, however, is not simply that God deigns to take on human flesh but that He creates a world that has ontological potency to receive and show forth His reality. What is of the utmost significance, in other words, is that the Incarnation is a cosmological fact in the medieval mythos—that the very structure of the world is Incarnational. The Incarnation must be visualized as written into the very foundations of Creation before its implications for medieval experience can be fully articulated.

What is perhaps the summit of medieval architecture, the Cathedral of Chartres, is a concrete attempt to purvey the cosmological character of the Incarnation. Here infinity touches the cosmic and natural; infinity attempts to break through the limits of nature. In its essence, Chartres is the embodiment of the attempt to contain the uncontainable, and as such it is a testament to the belief that the finite can no longer be satisfactorily grasped in terms of fixity and perfection. Movement itself must now be supremely important: the infinite spilling over and breaking out of the finite. Far from negating the significance of nature, such an understanding of nature in terms of the infinite cuts away the moorings of the bifurcation of nature into sacred and profane zones. *All nature must be sacred,* for God spills out of it.

Common to the "Masters in the schools, mystics, exegetes, students of nature, seculars, religious, writers, and artists" is this conviction that nature "possessed a *signification* which transcended its crude reality"[30]—a signification which would prompt Alan of Lille (c. 1128–1202) to say that every "creature in the world is, for us, like a book and a picture and a mirror as well" and, before him, Hugh of Saint-Victor (1096–1141) to say that the "entire sense-perceptible world is like a sort of book written by the finger of God."[31] If the world itself is Incarnational, it makes little sense to operate on the ancient assumption that space is divisible into the intrinsically sacred and profane—into the intrinsically perfect and imperfect.

Not only, then, in dialectic but in art as well, the sacredness of all of nature and the cosmic fact of the Incarnation for the medieval mind can be witnessed. Unearthed sarcophagi of the fourth century A.D. depict Odysseus, a key figure in ancient mythology, as prototypal for the Christian "viator," or pilgrim. He is pictured "at the mast, with the great sail-yard, making together with the mast, a pattern in the form of a cross."[32] In the fifth century, Maximus of Turin would observe of this that the "mystery of the wood under the imagery of the Homeric myth" was capable of receiving the mystery of the Lord Jesus who "suffered himself to be fastened to the wood of the cross."[33] Feeding off the medieval mythos, Maximus implied that it was only because of a God-filled world, a theophanic nature, that the Incarnation could occur as an event in the world. Providing this insight with a more dialectical form, Eriugena conceived the essence of God as unchanging in God and yet displayed in creation. The "Divine Essence," he said, manifests itself in the world as multiple and visible "when it is joined to an intellectual creature" (and therefore it is accessible to human understanding), but it remains one, invisible, and inaccessible or "incomprehensible" to man as it is "in itself."[34]

A world that manifests an Infinite God is a world of a single sacred fabric where everything is a "sacramentum," a "sign of an inner reality,"[35] and where nothing "escapes the sacred which extends to man as well as to fauna, flora, and stone."[36] None of the particular things of nature, then, can be profane. The least of sensible things must be sacred, since, as St. Bonaventure (1221–74) remarks, God can be contemplated not only *through* "the mirror of sensible things" but also *in* them "in so far as He is in them," all of them, "by essence, potency, and presence."[37] Symbols can be found everywhere in a world that is interconnected, where one element calls up another, where sacred significations pervade what would otherwise be the most profane and mundane things. Thus, for Dante (1265–1321), the number seven was more than a number, more than an abstraction; it was a powerful symbol laden with the sacred, for "behind it loomed the powers of the seven sacraments" and "the seven gifts of the Holy Ghost,"[38] the power of a nature touched by the infinite.

The perception of the world as one sacred fabric, however, would seem to suggest a world of one substance, a monistic universe. The excesses of medieval symbolism and allegorical interpretation might lead us to draw this conclusion. But a bland monistic universe hardly does justice to the medieval view of a world fraught with tension and conflict. The infinite can be experienced only in time and in the context of opposing tensions that stand in need of unification; in its growth and becoming the world is sacred. Let us recall that the experience of a sacred and sacramental nature fits the medieval experience of a wilderness, of a Europe not yet fully settled. And thus the experience of a God-filled world elicited a commitment to the building up and completing of this world. In the end, medieval man was called upon to contemplate the sacred, not at rest, but in its mutations and oppositions. "Behind the monolithic appearance" of medieval civilization "was a variety of traditions, both co-operating and competing,"[39] and medieval man had to confront the experience of one sacred world in terms of reconciling the force of barbarism, Christian symbols, and a classical or ancient inheritance.

The role of the ancient or classical inheritance in this medieval reconciliation requires further comment. Our emphasis has been on the novelty of the medieval mythos, and it would appear that medieval thinkers were in quest of new symbols, perhaps a whole new discourse, to do justice to this new consciousness. But the only available linguistic vehicle for expressing the novelty of their experience was, in fact, the highly refined language of ancient philosophy. We see this situation aptly illustrated in the language of Scotus Eriugena, as he strains the language of ancient philosophy to its limits in his attempt to articulate a nonclassical conception of the infinite.

Thus, [God] is called Essence, but strictly speaking He is not essence: for to being is opposed not-being. Therefore He is *hyperousios,* that is, super-essential. Again, He is called Goodness, but strictly speaking He is not goodness: for to goodness wickedness is opposed. Therefore [He is] *hyperagathos,* that is, more than good, and *hyperagathotes,* that is, more than goodness.[40]

The philosophical language medieval thinkers inherited from the ancient world was "not primarily regulated by symbolism,"[41] that is, by the medieval experience of nature as entirely sacred. The premise of a bifurcation between sacred, perfect space and profane, imperfect space was built into classical philosophical discourse.

The disquietude and perhaps the very creativity of the medieval intellectual venture may have had a great deal to do with having had to live with a philosophical language that was not entirely suited to the novelty of the medieval experience of the world. The dualism of perfect and imperfect realms of being—what we might call the tacit metaphor of a perfect spatial "up" and an imperfect spatial "down"—to be found in ancient thought was no longer adequate for and possibly no longer relevant to the medieval mythos. Ancient philosophical discourse had to be stretched and pulled in the efforts of medieval thinkers to find new ways of speaking about and naming a theophanic God who, in the words of Saint Anselm (1033–1109), "cannot be conceived except as a unique being, so that nothing else can be conceived to be like Him."[42]

Perhaps the vague expectation of a dialectical language freed from the presupposition of the dualism of the sacred and the profane was harbored by medieval philosophic discourse in its attempt to address this utterly "unique being" to whom Anselm

alludes. But if such an expectation can be said to have been fulfilled, the first harbinger of its fulfillment comes with the closing
of the Middle Ages in the writings of Nicholas of Cusa (1401–64).
Cusanus stands at the gateway to a new philosophical discourse
and a new logic for philosophy—the logic of modernity. Living
as he did in the fifteenth century, he stands before us as the last
great medieval and first great modern mind. As such, he reminds
us of the enduring medieval context for modernity.

NICHOLAS OF CUSA: THE HERALD
OF MODERNITY

The starting point of Cusanus' thought is precisely the medieval
view of the infinite spilling over the finite—the "fusion of the
human and the divine" that "has become reality in Christ who
as this fusion provides man with his measure"[43]—thus far described in this chapter. According to Ernst Cassirer, Cusa

never criticized this picture. Indeed, his whole speculation . . . seems
rather to presuppose it. Nevertheless, the first sentences of the work *De
Docta Ignorantia* give birth to a new thought, and point to a completely
new *total intellectual orientation.*[44]

Although Cusa "stands in the history of philosophy as a con-
tinuer" of the tradition of Pseudo-Dionysius, Eriugena, and St.
Augustine, he is "no mere synthesizer of his predecessors, even
though he appropriates their terminology and utilizes their
motifs."[45]

In what sense, then, does Cusa provide a new intellectual orientation while maintaining a deep-seated continuity with the medieval view of the infinite? In what sense can Cusanus be said to
be the first purveyor of the rudiments of a new philosophical
discourse for the medieval experience of a seamlessly sacred nature? The answer to this question—what makes Cusanus the "first
modern thinker"[46]—is the fact that he saw sharply and clearly
that ancient philosophical categories and language were hopelessly
at odds with the medieval experience of the world.

To Cusanus, Aristotle's logic, based on the principle of the excluded middle, seems precisely for that reason to be merely a logic of the finite, one which must always and necessarily be found wanting when it comes to contemplating the infinite. All its concepts are concepts of comparison; they rest upon the union of the equal and the similar and upon the separation of the unequal and the different. By such a process of comparing and distinguishing, of separating and delimiting, all empirical being splits up into definite genuses and species that stand in a definite relationship of super- or sub-ordination to each other.[47]

What must be established, Cusanus saw, was a new logic, the rudiments for a new philosophical discourse, based not on differentiation and heterogeneity but on harmonization and homogeneity.

How does Cusa go about developing the rudiments of this new language? In keeping with the early medieval outlook on a universe able to be experienced as pervasively sacramental and as the fitting home for genuine change and contrariety, he begins by considering how knowledge and ignorance, for the Christian, are harmonious. He begins by reflecting on the senses in which knowledge is in fact a form of ignorance. Such an identity is, of course, highly reminiscent of the Socratic identification of knowledge with the awareness of one's own ignorance. We find Cusanus saying in *De Docta Ignorantia* that

since the desire in us is not in vain, assuredly we desire to know that we do not know. If we can fully attain unto this [knowledge of our ignorance] we will attain unto learned ignorance. For a man—even one very well versed in learning—will attain unto nothing more perfect than to be found to be most learned in the ignorance which is distinctively his. The more he knows that he is unknowing, the more learned he will be.[48]

Unlike Socrates, however, for whom knowledge as awareness of ignorance was the primary rational response to a cosmos with a fixed finite order, Cusa conceives of his "learned ignorance" as the properly human response to a universe which is through and through sacred and in being such is truly *unlimited*. Cusa takes the decisive step of calling the universe experienced by medieval man a "privatively infinite" universe. He chooses this term to convey the sense that the universe is *infinite*, not in the sense in which God and *only* God is infinite, but in the sense in which the universe is the manifestation or theophany of an Infinite, Incarnating God. The universe taken as a whole can be said to be infinite by virtue of being contained in God *or* by virtue of containing God who is the Absolute Maximum. The universe

is contracted in plurality, and it cannot exist without plurality. Indeed, in its universal oneness this maximum encompasses all things, so that all the things which derive from the Absolute [Maximum] are in this maximum and this maximum is in all [these] things. Nevertheless, it does not exist independently of the plurality in which it is present, for it does not exist without contraction, from which it cannot be freed.[49]

To put Cusanus' case somewhat baldly: God is infinity in unity, the universe infinity in plurality; God is originative infinity, the universe derivative infinity. The universe being a necessary plurality by virtue of the unity of God, the human intellect "never comprehends truth" not only about God but about this universe "so precisely that truth cannot be comprehended infinitely more precisely."[50] Man gains access to the originative infinity of God *only* by gaining access to the privative infinity of the universe. Man is in basic ignorance about infinity—not only the infinity of God but the infinity of the universe. Yet this ignorance is a fruitful darkness—a darkness that discloses itself as a twilight. Man can gain access to the pluralistic infinity of the universe; he can make his ignorance here a form of knowledge and in so doing make his ignorance of God a form of knowledge. But Cusa must add the all-important stipulation. If God can be known by man only by virtue of man's knowing the universe, man can never attain a completed knowledge of this universe. In a privatively infinite universe, all parts will have an infinite resonance; each will "speak" to the other without surcease. Each element of the universe will stand in some sort of relation to every other,

so that from out of all things, there arises one universe and in [this] one maximum all things are this one. And although every image seems to be like its exemplar, nevertheless except for the Maximal Image (which is, in oneness of nature, the very thing which its Exemplar is) no image is so similar or equal to its exemplar that it cannot be infinitely more similar and equal.[51]

The thrust of Cusa's argument constitutes what we might call the decisive turning into the logic of modernity. Medieval thinkers raised a challenge to the ancient presupposition of bifurcated space; they apprehended clearly the force of the notion of infinity. By maintaining the logic of ancient philosophical discourse, admittedly their only alternative, however, they were still burdened with a finite universe. The full force of the experience of the Infinite Christian God demands a privatively infinite universe.

Cusa begins to build the rudiments of a language for such a universe by taking in hand the ancient symbol of circularity—the "kuklos." Applied by the ancients to a circular and eternally repetitive time governing and limiting change in a finite universe, the kuklos is initially applied by Cusa to God, the Absolute Maximum, whom he likens to an

infinite circle, which is eternal, without beginning and end, indivisibly the most one and the most encompassing. Because this circle is maximum, its diameter is also maximum. And since there cannot be more than one maximum, this circle is most one to such an extent that the diameter is the circumference. Now, an infinite diameter has an infinite middle. But the middle is the center. Therefore, it is evident that the center, the diameter, and the circumference are the same thing.[52]

But since God, the Absolute Maximum, "who is everywhere and nowhere," is the "circumference and center" of the universe, it follows, in a manner of speaking, that "the world-machine will have its center everywhere and its circumference nowhere."[53] The kuklos in the end is applied to a privatively infinite universe.

Speaking of circularity in such terms is, of course, contradictory. But Cusa would have us ask whether it contradicts the nature of the universe *or* the understanding of the universe propounded by ancient philosophical categories. Cusanus seems to turn the tables, suggesting that we worry, not about whether our categories contradict Aristotelian logic and Euclidean geometry,[54] but about whether our categories do justice to an expansive, privatively infinite universe. In this way, he pushes the ancient metaphor of circularity to the point where it breaks down as a description of infinite space. By doing so, he breaks the hold of the ancient notion of the eternal circularity of time. The circle must be infinite to meet the demands of the Christian experience of the world. The godly, the Divine, the Absolute Maximum that fills the universe is "incomprehensible"; and in it, as in the universe, "the center is the circumference."[55]

The consequence of this is that there can be nothing to serve, as Cusa sees it, as a limit to the universe; the universe must be "unbounded," for "it is not the case that anything actually greater than it, in relation to which it would be bounded, is positable."[56] Thus, as Jasper Hopkins points out, the universe

is not limited in space by anything physically outside its dimensions. . . . In this sense, something spatial is deemed to be limited only if it is limited by some other spatial thing. But the universe is composed of whatever spatial objects there are. Hence there is not anything external to it which fixes its bounds. Accordingly, it is unlimited by anything else. . . . In being unbounded, it is unlike every other finite thing, that is, it is unlike every object within the universe.[57]

Such a universe has its actual existence limited only by its nature, which is to be a manifestation of God. The only limit on this universe is the fact that it is not, as such, God. Therefore, as Cusa says, "although with respect to God's infinite power, which is unlimitable, the universe could have been greater," nonetheless, "since the possibility-of-being, or matter, which is not actually extendable unto infinity, opposes, the universe cannot be greater."[58] On the one hand, since the existence of the universe is dependent on God, it is a "reflection of God" in a "restricted way."[59] On the other hand, the universe "exists in the best way in which the condition of its nature," which is to be a manifestation of God, "allows."[60]

In effect, then, although matter cannot be infinitely extended, space is an unbounded continuum. This means that Cusa challenges "the Aristotelian conception of space as essentially tied to bodies" and argues instead for a kind of "transcendence of space over bodies."[61] Cusa's privatively infinite universe is thus a spatially unbounded universe.

If Cusa is thus the conclusion to the medieval epoch—a conclusion that constitutes the beginning of a new epoch—as we have so briefly described him, it can be suggested that, in its conclusion, the medieval epoch serves as the repository for the seeds of a radically new cosmology destined to take the place of the ancient cosmology. Cusa himself reveals the seeds. The earth is no longer a terrestrial sphere to be separated from the celestial realm. Instead, "the earth is a noble star" with an "influence . . . different from [that of] all other stars."[62] In so speaking, Cusanus clearly establishes himself as the harbinger of the logic of modernity. As Alexandre Koyré remarks,

In the infinitely rich and infinitely diversified and organically linked-together universe of Nicholas of Cusa, there is no center of perfection in respect to which the rest of the universe would play a subservient part; on the contrary it is by being themselves and asserting their own natures that the various components of the universe contribute to the perfection of the whole. Thus the earth in its way is just as perfect as the sun or the fixed stars.[63]

In Cusanus, then, the medieval experience comes closest to attaining a remarkably new kind of philosophical discourse capable of theoretically rendering, in a manner that earlier medieval thinkers could not, the experience of a seamlessly sacramental universe. Cusa brings the vaguest gropings of medieval alchemists and the most tenuous probings of medieval mystics as well as the more theoretically solid propositions of philosophers like Eriugena into the confines of the rudiments of a promising new dialectical language. In Cusa the mystical attains philosophical stature; the Hermetic maxim,

What is above is as that which is below; what is below is as that which is above; to accomplish the miracles of the one thing,[64]

is afforded a philosophical elaboration. And in providing this elaboration, Cusanus leaves medieval thought on the threshold of the cosmological shift destined to flow from Copernicus and his disciples. The elements of John Dewey's description of the uniqueness of modern science are already clear in the thought of Cusa.

Change in short is no longer looked upon as a fall from grace, as a lapse from reality or a sign of imperfection of being. Modern Science no longer tries to find some fixed form or essence behind each process of change. Rather the experimental method tries to break with apparent fixities and induce change. The form that remains unchanged to sense, the form of seed or tree, is regarded not as the key to knowledge of the thing, but as a wall, an obstruction to be broken down.[65]

Still, it must be said that Cusa provided only the bare rudiments of a new philosophical vocabulary. Rare are the philosophical minds who single-handedly hammer out the entire framework of a new philosophical language and logic. Yet, when we read Cusa as we have done, we are acutely aware of how forcefully he accentuates the medieval context for the logic of modernity. We become all the more aware of the grounds on which Lynn White, Jr., could remark that

modern science is not simply a continuation of the interrupted scientific movement of antiquity: it is something novel, created by the later Middle Ages, having interests, presuppositions and methods alien to the Greeks. It is *this originality* as much as the renewed vitality of science which demands explanation.[66]

Indeed, to suggest that this originality is the province only of the *later* Middle Ages is too timid an analysis of the medieval context for modernity.

We must now examine what was done with the rudiments of Cusa's novel discourse and with the substance of the medieval experience of the infinite in time.

2

THE BIRTH OF THE
MODERN COSMOLOGY

THE birth of the modern cosmology was a fruition of the elements of the medieval Christian experience heretofore described. As such, the birth of the modern cosmology was the beginning of a new philosophical discourse for handling the medieval Christian experience of a sacramental universe—the immediate issuance of the rudiments of that new language provided by Nicholas of Cusa, an issuance that would assume its final shape in the language of what is called modern science. This new cosmology has, not without good reason, been called the Copernican Revolution.

There are, however, certain dangers in labeling the birth of the modern cosmology the Copernican Revolution. For one, it implies that Copernicus was the sole and entire author, whereas in reality Copernicus' contribution makes sense only in terms of his inheritance of the medieval experience and in terms of the development and elaboration of his insights by those who immediately followed him. For another, the term "revolution" implies too sudden a turning; it conveys the idea of a turning without precedent, a turning that amounts to a radical disjunction from the experience preceding it. Given the medieval context for modernity, it would be more accurate to say that historical continuity with—rather than revolutionary overthrow of—long-fermenting patterns of thought characterized the birth of the modern cosmology.

Yet the term "Copernican Revolution" does suggest a basic truth about the birth of the modern cosmology, provided of course that we treat Copernicus as one of a group of intellectual revolutionaries and that we understand the term "revolution" in a more nuanced fashion. Thomas S. Kuhn aptly locates the proper nuance when he says of an intellectual revolution that it

is seldom or *never just an increment* to what is known. Its assimilation requires the reconstruction of prior theory and the reevaluation of prior fact, an intrinsically revolutionary process that is seldom completed by a single man and never overnight. No wonder historians have had difficulty in dating precisely this *extended process* that their vocabulary impels them to view as an isolated event.[1]

The birth of the modern cosmology may justly be called a revolution, for it was *not just* an increment to what was already known in and by the medieval experience of a sacramental universe; it was *also* the transformation of that experience (and of the rudiments of a new philosophical discourse that Cusa supplied) into the language of modern science. Provided, then, that we understand its extended character—occurring not just in the thought and life of Copernicus but throughout the sixteenth and early seventeenth centuries—the birth of the new cosmology can be justly called a revolution. And we are also justified in calling this revolution Copernican by virtue of the figure who stands at its head, whose conclusions triggered the more replete reflections of Kepler, Galileo, and Bruno.

COPERNICUS AND KEPLER: THE CHARTING OF A NEW UNIVERSE

Long before the lifetime of Nicolas Copernicus (1473–1543), even as far back as ancient times, the opinion was held, though not without great criticism, that the earth was not entirely a static body. The theory of the earth's diurnal rotation was propounded by some in classical times, and it can be plausibly assumed that Aristotle's active and extensive attack upon it was an attack upon a significant astronomical hypothesis of his day.[2] Cicero, remarking on those who held this hypothesis, observes that they thought that the earth, "by revolving and twisting round its axis with extreme velocity, produces all the same results as would be produced if the earth were stationary and the heaven in motion."[3]

Nevertheless, this surprising hypothetical quirk could be assimilated only within the parameters of the basically finite two-sphered universe of the ancients. The theory of diurnal rotation of the earth was not strong enough by itself to unseat the appeal of this classical cosmology. As Arthur Koestler remarks, the "three fundamental conceits" of this cosmology were

the dualism of the celestial and sub-lunary worlds; the immobility of the earth in the centre; and the circularity of all heavenly motion . . . the common denominator of the three, and the secret of their unconscious appeal, was the fear of change, the craving for stability and permanence.[4]

Copernicus went much further than to merely react against the common opinion, exemplified in the famous verse of Du Bartas, that the earth was incapable of diurnal rotation.

So far do they from Sense and Reason erre,
Who think the Heavens stand, and th' Earth doth stir . . .
But who hath seen a selfly-turning stone?
How then should the earth turn herself alone?
Let's therefore boldly with old truth affirm,
That th' Earth remains immoveable and firm.[5]

Rather, it was the role of Copernicus, or at least the primary implication of his writing, to challenge the validity of the two-sphered, terrestrial and celestial universe. In highly poetic terms, Copernicus went so far as to dethrone the earth from its position in the center of the universe and to enthrone the sun in that position.

For who would place this lamp of a very beautiful temple in another or better place than this wherefrom it can illuminate everything at the same time? . . . And so the sun, as if resting on a kingly throne, governs the family of stars which wheel around.[6]

Copernicus rejected a geocentric universe in favor of a heliocentric universe. In doing so, he challenged the privileged status of the bifurcation between celestial and terrestrial space.

For Copernicus, the behavior of the planets was incompatible with the classical Aristotelian-Ptolemaic two-sphered universe; he felt that in adding more and more circles his predecessors had simply been patching and stretching the Ptolemaic system to force its conformity with observation.[7] Copernicus attempted to construct a new model, a heliocentric model, with the earth assuming a planetary status.

But the revolutionary character of Copernicus' seminal insights does not stop here. Copernicus dares to incorporate the heliocentric universe within the kind of thinking about the infinite originally proposed by Cusanus. Not only

does the author of the heliocentric universe state plainly to his age his belief in an infinite universe, but he definitely presupposes and employs such a universe in constructing his system of the world.[8]

Relying on mathematics, Copernicus argues for the appearance of an infinite magnitude for the universe.[9]

Taking up Cusa's insight of a privatively infinite universe, then, Copernicus saw to the very heart of the inconsistency between an infinite universe and the Aristotelian-Ptolemaic universe with its finite frame. He saw, in the words of Thomas Kuhn, that

an infinite space has no center; every point is equally distant from all points on the periphery. And if there is no center, there is no preferred point at which the heavy element, earth, can aggregate and there is no intrinsic 'up' or 'down' to determine the natural motion of an element returning to its proper place. In fact, there is no 'natural place' in an infinite universe, for each place is like every other. The whole Aristotelian theory of motion is . . . inextricably bound to the conception of a finite and fully occupied space. The two stand or fall together.[10]

With this in mind, Copernicus sought a mathematical proof for the infinity of the universe, which, he hoped, would in turn verify the minority opinion, handed down from ancient times, of the diurnal rotation of the earth. The pivotal dimension of his so-called revolution was his arguments against classical Aristotelian space and against the Ptolemaic two-sphered universe and his recasting of Cusanus' privatively infinite universe in terms of heliocentrism.

Yet, despite the profound revolutionary implication and aura of his thought, there is a peculiar reserve and almost at times unsureness about Copernicus' statement. Although he had written the work for which he is primarily remembered, *On the Revolutions of the Heavenly Spheres*, some thirty years before its publication in 1543, he was unsure of its soundness. The first printed copy arrived at his bedside a few hours before his death.[11] Furthermore, the dedication of this work to Pope Paul III is hardly redolent of the sure, ringing tones of a revolutionary.

> I can reckon easily enough, Most Holy Father, that as soon as certain people learn that in these books of mine which I have written about the revolutions of the spheres of the world I attribute certain motions to the terrestrial globe, they will immediately shout to have me and my opinion hooted off the stage. . . . For a long time I was in great difficulty as to whether I should bring to light my commentaries written to demonstrate the Earth's movement. . . . Therefore, when I weighed these things in my mind, the scorn which I had to fear on account of the newness and absurdity of my opinion almost drove me to abandon a work already undertaken.[12]

Copernicus had every reason to be unsure of his revolutionary pronouncements, since his heliocentric model was more primitive than the finely reasoned out Ptolemaic system, and he himself could not have been unaware of this.

Retaining the Aristotelian-Ptolemaic celestial sphere, Copernicus argued that, whereas the interior concavity of the sphere was finite, its outer surface was without conceivable bounds. In order to afford the earth both axial and orbital motion, the size of the outer sphere had to be, for all practical purposes, unlimited. Thus, the heavens appear finite to the senses; only the mind can begin to grasp their unbounded extension. This is a very primitive model of the universe when compared with the elaborate epicycles of the Ptolemaic model and the complex considerations that prompted Aristotle to conclude that "the earth does not move, and does not lie elsewhere but at the centre."[13]

The primitive character of the Copernican model and its unsure footing suggest the center and limits of his contribution. Its center is in the medievals and Cusanus: the idea of a positive conception of the infinite now tentatively applied to the cosmos. Its limits lie in the fact that Copernicus in his revolutionary book is scarcely aware of its revolutionary character. Copernicus could not help but be aware of the apparent absurdity of his system, given the testimony of the senses against it and the superior refinement of the Ptolemaic model. Yet, although Copernicus could not objectively afford to be a revolutionary in his lifetime, the implications of his system after his death would gradually crystallize themselves in the minds of others into a revolutionary break with the classical astronomy. *De Revolutionibus Orbium Caelestium*, though it stands within a classical and ancient astronomical tradition, posed an argument for an infinite space and a mobile earth which, despite the primitiveness of its terms and even its mathematics, would eventually shift the direction of a newly nascent scientific thought and give rise to that "rapid and complete break with the ancient tradition"[14] that commentators have with basic correctness, if at times with excessive literalness, associated with the Copernican Revolution.

Astronomically, what Copernicus did was to give the earth a clear axial and orbital motion, make the sphere of the stars outwardly infinite (and thus deprived of a physical function), thereby requiring a vast and, for all practical purposes, unlimited increase in the size of the universe.[15] After Copernicus, it can be said with assurance, the terrestrial and celestial spheres could never again be entirely and absolutely distinct. In doing away once and for all with the immutability of the bifurcation between celestial and terrestrial space, Copernicus challenged the very legitimacy in astronomy of taking the earth as the focal point of reference, as the center of the system. This was the challenge implicit in Copernicus' thought that made him the initiator of an extended process of revolution in spite of his lack of firm systematic footing. It was the challenge perceived by those who were implacably opposed to his ideas. Thus, John Wilkins in 1640 proposes as one of the arguments against Copernican heliocentrism

the vileness of our earth, because it consists of a more sordid and base matter than any other part of the world; and therefore must be situated in the centre, which is the worst place, and at the greatest distance from those purer incorruptible bodies, the heavens.[16]

But this was the challenge also perceived by Copernicus' defenders—those who would solidify this challenge into the foundation of a sophisticated astronomical system capable of rivaling the Ptolemaic model. Unable to shake "the foundations of European thought straight away,"[17] the work of Copernicus required someone like Kepler to translate its thrust into a revolution in cosmology.

The boldness and resolution lacking in Copernicus can be found in Johannes Kepler (1571–1630) who, as he himself put it, wanted to "provide a philosophy or physics of celestial phenomena in place of the theology or metaphysics of Aristotle."[18] A student of philosophy and theology at the University of Tübingen, Kepler was transferred, before attaining a position in the Church, to a teaching post in mathematics and astronomy. Of this, he remarked that since he "wanted to become a theologian," he was restless, but "observe how through my efforts God is being celebrated in astronomy."[19] His aim was to create a philosophical discourse that would raise the Copernican universe into a self-sufficient system—a discourse that would adequately convey the experience of a God who manifested Himself in all of nature.

Kepler had read the works of Nicholas of Cusa "whose geometrical mysticism agreed so closely with his own thinking," and he even began his first work "with considerations which he had taken over from that thinker."[20] Moreover, he was deeply committed to the Copernican system.

I deem it my duty and task to advocate outwardly also with all the powers of my intellect the Copernican theory, which I in my innermost [being] have recognized as true and whose loveliness fills me with unbelievable rapture when I contemplate it.[21]

Yet Kepler saw that Copernicus was far from offering a completed system; the "unexhausted treasure of truly divine insight into the magnificent order of the whole world and of all bodies" contained in Copernicus' work, he believed, must still be completed.[22]

Copernicus had already used mathematics in his argument; Kepler was destined to carry the role of mathematics even further and, with it, the Copernican Revolution. Inescapably, there is a classical Pythagoreanism in Copernicus—a conviction that the universe is literally made up of numbers. Kepler did not merely discern mathematical relations or entities in all objects presented to the senses but argued that all certain knowledge must be knowledge of the quantitative characteristics of things. It is the human mind in its mathematicizing, not the testimony of the senses that for so long was conceived as supportive of the Ptolemaic model, that constitutes the true and proper disclosure of the nature of the universe. In his *Epitome of Copernican Astronomy* he remarks,

So too in man there is the intellect which abstracts universals and forms numbers and proportions, as things which are not outside of intellect; but individuals, received inwardly through the senses, are foundations of universals; and indivisible and discrete unities, of numbers; and real terms of proportions. Finally, memory, divided as it were into compartments of quantities and times, like the sphere of the fixed stars, is the storehouse and repository of sensations. And further, there is never judgment of sensations, except in the cerebrum; and the effect of joy never arises from a sense perception, except in the heart.[23]

In this manner, as Kepler says, to discover harmony in sensible matters is to

uncover, to comprehend, and bring to light the similarity of the proportion in sense matters with a particular prototype of a real and true harmony, a prototype existing inside in the mind.[24]

Perfect knowledge, then, is itself mathematical, for Kepler, and mathematics is the justification of the Copernican universe. The new philosophical discourse, fully adequate for an infinite and sacramental universe, is grounded in mathematical symbols. And this is the case precisely because the structure of the mind of man in its mathematicizing is the same as the innermost structure of the infinite Copernican universe. But Kepler goes even further. It is the theophanic, Infinite God of medieval Christianity that allows for this identity between the structure of the human mind and the innermost structure of the physical universe.

For what is implanted in the mind of man other than numbers and magnitudes? These alone we comprehend correctly, and if piety permits us to say so, this recognition is of *the same kind as the divine*, at least insofar as we in this mortal life of ours are capable of grasping part of it. . . . Geometry is one and eternal, a reflection out of the mind of God. That mankind shares in it is one of the reasons to call man an image of God.[25]

God has not simply created the world in terms of "geometrical relations . . . laid out from His own resources,"[26] but He has created man with a mind that contains these very same relations "in order that man may directly communicate" with Him.[27]

Kepler thus attempts to verify the Copernican Revolution by an appeal to its ultimate mathematical coherence and harmony—its ability to read a mathematical order in what had previously been an inexplicable diversity. The sheer differentiation of the particulars of this universe can now be accounted for in terms of number, and we can speak of qualitative difference only because there is numerical and geometrical harmonization of these differences. Rejecting the Aristotelian arguments for a *finite* universe, arguments that presumed that mathematics was in between metaphysics and physics, and that presumed that quantity was merely one of the predicamental accidents, Kepler argues forthrightly for the *infinity* of the universe in terms of the essentially mathematical character of the way in which the human mind understands nature.

Just as the eye was made to see colors, and the ear to hear sounds, so the human mind was made to understand, not whatever you please but quantity.[28]

After Kepler, the unbounded Copernican universe is established as a *quantitatively* homogeneous, infinite network that is at once an early modern analogate to, and a fruition of, the medieval sacramental world. This is the universe of modern science. Kepler's flight into metaphors to describe this universe recalls, in fact, the metaphors of his medieval predecessors.

There were three things above all others the cause of which I sought without wearying, namely, the number, size, and motion of the orbits. I was induced to try to discover them because of the wonderful resemblance between motionless objects, namely, the sun, the fixed stars, and intermediate space, and God the Father, God the Son, and God the Holy Ghost.[29]

The created universe is thus perceived, as the medievals perceived it, as "an expression of the Creative Trinity," and this universe is now "subjected to the laws of harmony and proportion"[30] that are the groundwork of modern science.

Along with Copernicus, then, Kepler played midwife for the birth of the modern cosmology. But this birth still required a further elaboration of its fruit—an elaboration of modern scientific method itself as the new and adequate discourse, philosophical in its foundations, for the medieval theophanic world. But even with Kepler this further elaboration is intimated.

I consider it a right, yes a duty, to search in cautious manner for the numbers, sizes, and weights, the norms for everything [God] has created. For He himself has let man take part in the knowledge of these things and thus not in a small measure has set up His image in man. Since He recognized as very good this image which He made, He will so much more readily recognize our efforts with the light of this image also to push into the light of knowledge the utilization of the numbers, weights, and sizes which He marked out at creation. For these secrets are not of the kind whose research should be forbidden; rather they are set before our eyes like a mirror so that by examining them we observe to some extent the goodness and wisdom of the Creator.[31]

· Given Kepler's contribution, there are still two questions that must be raised in order to complete the prolonged birth of the modern cosmology: What are the implications of the Copernican universe for man's knowing? What are the implications of this universe for his acting? The attempt to answer the first amounts to the attempt to spell out the nature of scientific method, and we find this effort begun by Galileo. The attempt to answer the second amounts to the more ambiguous effort to spell out the rudiments of a modern ethical theory—an effort initiated by Giordano Bruno.

GALILEO: APOLOGIST FOR THE NEW SCIENTIFIC METHOD

It is difficult to overestimate the importance of Galileo Galilei (1564–1642) in the birth of the modern cosmology. His name, according to Koyré, is

indissolubly linked with the scientific revolution of the sixteenth century, one of the profoundest, if not the most profound, revolutions of human thought since the invention of the cosmos by Greek thought: a revolution which implies a radical intellectual 'mutation' of which modern physical science is at once the expression and the fruit.[32]

Writing of Galileo's role in this radical intellectual mutation, the Renaissance humanist Campanella proclaimed that

These novelties of ancient truths, of new worlds, new systems, new nations, are the beginning of a new era. Let God make haste, and let us for our small part help all we can.[33]

From the very beginning of his thought, Galileo confronted boldly the entrenched classical astronomy, particularly in its defense by significant segments of the institutionalized Church. And he did this as a faithful son of the Church, as the story of the course of his struggles so palpably reveals.

Like Kepler, Galileo challenged the traditional Aristotelian distinction between a mathematical knowledge that dealt with the empirical surface of phenomena and a metaphysical knowledge that dealt with the reality underlying these phenomena. Mathematics, as with Kepler, was the root grammar of the new philosophical discourse that constituted modern scientific method.

Unlike Kepler, however, the significance of mathematics for scientific method, in Galileo's eyes, was mediated by a binding commitment to empirical observation. As Ludovico Geymonat indicates in his masterful biography,

Galileo's own passion for mathematics never became detached from an interest in observation, measurement, and design; from the very beginning, mathematics appeared to him as . . . a key to the translation of natural processes into precisely reasoned propositions that were consistent and capable of rigorous verification.[34]

Furthermore, Galileo's whole approach to mathematics as the core of modern scientific language, again unlike Kepler's purist approach, was linked with an interest in technology. Galileo

almost always considers mathematics as a study connected with technology, not as a pure mathematics in the modern sense.[35]

In Galileo mathematics is found, not in splendid isolation, as in Kepler, but in conjunction with empirical verification and technological instrumentation. It is the "effective guarantee of our having proceeded correctly in our reasoning."[36]

Yet both Kepler and Galileo were in agreement that mathematics when applied to the study of natural phenomena could reveal the underlying reality of the universe—a reality best portrayed by the Copernican account of a heliocentric universe of limitless spaces. Kepler, however, lived as a Protestant in Germany, a land where there was comparatively little control over cosmological thinking in its relation to institutionalized religion. Galileo lived near the very seat of Roman Christianity in a land where institutionalized religion, or at least significant factions in it, still held rather firmly to the connection between the Ptolemaic system and the scriptural sources of Christianity. Despite the inadequacy of classical Aristotelian and Ptolemaic language to describe the experience of a sacramental universe entailed by much of medieval Christianity, the sources of authority in the Church still tended, by and large, to hold on to what they thought to be the sure connection between the Aristotelian-Ptolemaic systems and Catholic doctrines. To grasp this phenomenon, we must remember that the Church was still in the throes of its Counter-Reformation, building its securities against the convulsive changes of the Protestant Reformation. Its predominant posture was inevitably retrenchment—an attempt to minimize further convulsive changes in the face of the Protestant "schism." The overwhelming tendency was to make all further change suspect. Subjected to this atmosphere, Galileo's attempt to defend the new scientific method and to construct an apology for its consistency with the Christian faith of his fathers ran headlong into one of the great controversies of history.

When Galileo, in the fashion of Kepler, argued for the capacity of mathematics (though, for him, in conjunction with empirical observation) to portray the very physical reality of the universe, when he denied the absoluteness of the Aristotelian distinction between mathematical and metaphysical knowledge, he met ecclesiastical resistance. In 1615 Cardinal Robert Bellarmine (1542–1621), a leading theologian and administrator of the Roman Church, was delegated to apprise Galileo of the integrity of the Aristotelian distinction in the eyes of the Church. Bellarmine conceded the plausibility of the Copernican hypothesis but suggested that the appearances of heavenly motion might just as satisfactorily be accounted for or "saved" ("salvare apparentia") by non-Copernican hypotheses. To propose the Copernican system as certain,

Bellarmine insisted, Galileo would have to show that it did more than merely account for the phenomena but that the universe could not, without contradiction, be accounted for by any system other than the Copernican. This had not been done and, Bellarmine implied, could not be done. As Bellarmine put it, Galileo would act "prudently" if he contented himself with

speaking hypothetically and not absolutely, as I have always understood that Copernicus spoke. To say that on the supposition of the Earth's movement and the Sun's quiescence all the celestial appearances are explained *better* than by the theory of eccentrics and epicycles is to speak with excellent good sense and to run no risk whatever. Such a manner of speaking is *enough for a mathematician*. But to want to affirm that the Sun *in very truth* is at the center of the universe and only rotates on its axis without going from east to west is a very dangerous attitude and one calculated to arouse all Scholastic philosophers and theologians but also to injure our holy Faith by contradicting the Scriptures.[37]

Bellarmine thus admonished that Galileo tone down, as it were, his portrayal of the Copernican system and the explanatory power of the new scientific method and offer them as mathematically convenient hypotheses rather than as established truths about the innermost nature of physical reality.

Galileo, it would seem, had three paths open to him in dealing with this admonition. One was to accept outright the admonition, renounce any claim of the method to produce enduring truths about the nature of physical reality, and limit himself to piecemeal research in the hope that he could prudently show the consistency of the Copernican system with that research. The second was to reject outright the admonition and challenge the very authority of the Church to pronounce on these matters. The third was to appear to accept the admonition while writing in such a fashion that he would be able to "educate" the Church and rescue it from its "misconceptions." That Galileo chose the third accounts for the inevitability and peculiarity of the conflict that ensued. Yet he could not bring himself to accept either of the first two paths. Piecemeal research was not sufficient to satisfy his appetite in the realm of the new scientific methodology, and the Church's approbation of the new method was of inestimable value to him. Galileo thus chose to become an apologist for the new scientific method in the public realm of Roman Catholic Christendom. Holding that the new science was not simply a private scholarly activity but a "matter of public interest that was destined to permeate all society," he saw that it was in need of support from those who occupied the highest positions of authority in society, and so he became convinced that "he must try by every means to convert the Church to the cause of science" and therefore to the Copernican theory.[38]

Bellarmine had emphasized the inconsistency of the Copernican theory—when proposed as an incontestable truth about the physical world—with Scripture. Galileo took the fateful step: he ventured into scriptural exegesis, arguing that although Scripture presents an immutable truth, it speaks in many instances in a figurative manner, and when it so speaks it should not be used to "support the opinions of certain fallible philosphers" at the "jeopardy of its authority."[39] Galileo thus proposed a distinction between two kinds of language: an ordinary language, imprecise and at times inconsistent, and a scientific language, always rigorous and exact. In order to make His Word comprehensible to its intended audience, God employed ordinary language, which required writing that the sun revolved around the earth. Since, he remarks,

in many passages the Scriptures are . . . needful of expositions differing from the apparent significations of the words, it seems to me that in physical disputes they should be reserved for the last place.[40]

Galileo's attempt to dissolve Bellarmine's objection amounted, then, to the construction of a sharp differentiation of the new philosophical discourse, that of modern scientific method, from ordinary discourse, the latter of which when guaranteed by divine inspiration produced certitudes about man's relation to God but not about the physical universe. The invincibility of Scripture in regard to the religious and ethical dimensions of reality was paralleled by the invincibility of the new scientific method in regard to the physical dimensions of reality. Faith in the former does not contradict faith in the latter.

Such an explanation was probably offensive to certain powerful ecclesiastics simply by virtue of its being an intrusion into a territory they held proper to trained theologians. Yet, had Galileo limited its promulgation to theologians, he might still have avoided the furor that was to ensue. Unfortunately for religious authority, and fortunately for scientific authority, as some would have it, Galileo perceived an even more promising potential in the new scientific method that dictated that he carry his educative mission to all men of moderate education in Christendom. He explicitly assigned the scientist the function of

raising from ignorance the greatest number of persons. In other words, science is not a matter of restricting the liberating function of reason to some specialists, but of projecting it to all men in order to awaken them, stimulate them, render them ever more conscious.[41]

It was this assumption of a public role, this attempt to educate not only the theologians but the faithful, that became the decisive kindling point in the Galilean controversy with the Church.

In publishing his *Dialogue Concerning the Two Chief World Systems* in 1632, Galileo gave the appearance of taking Bellarmine's admonition to heart, yet he let slip in, not too well hidden, the conviction that the Copernican system was demonstrated by modern scientific method to be the only true system of the universe. And he did this by insisting that

we must not demand that nature accommodate herself to what seems more sensible to us; instead we ought to accommodate our intellect to what nature has done.[42]

It may very well be, Galileo argued, that since God knows infinitely more extensively than man, man can never know everything there is to be known about the universe. But what is known mathematically by man is known no more or less certainly than what is known mathematically by God.

The human understanding can be taken in two modes, the *intensive* or the *extensive. Extensively*, that is, with regard to the multitude of intelligibles, which are infinite, the human understanding is as nothing even if it understands a thousand propositions; for a thousand in relation to infinity is zero. But taking man's understanding *intensively*, in so far as this term denotes understanding some propositions perfectly, I say that the human intellect does understand some of them perfectly, and thus in these it has as much absolute certainty as Nature itself has. Of such are the mathematical sciences alone; that is, geometry and arithmetic, in which the Divine intellect indeed knows infinitely more propositions, since it knows all. But with regard to those few which the human intellect does understand, I believe that its knowledge equals the Divine in objective certainty, for here it succeeds in understanding necessity, beyond which there can be no greater sureness.[43]

Such mathematical certainty, in conjunction with empirical observation, is able to verify the bountiful Copernican universe—a universe that Galileo perceived as congruous with the deepest import of Christianity. It "would be excessive boldness," Galileo says, "for anyone to limit and restrict the Divine power and wisdom to some particular fancy of his own"; it is rather "the magnificent scene which Galileo unfolds," Campanella remarks, "in which the God of wisdom and power and love brings forth his riches."[44]

In keeping, then, with Cusanus' assertion of the planetary character of the earth, with Kepler's assertion of the quantitative homogeneity of the universe, and with other recent observations of such a universe—as for instance, those made by Tycho Brahe in 1572 that seemed to indicate that the stars too could come into being and pass away—Galileo made bold to affirm that the ancient presupposition of separate celestial and terrestrial spheres could in no way serve as a rational postulate for a world system. He claimed on the basis of mathematical verification, and he claimed publicly, the absolute *certainty* of an

open and indefinitely extended entirety of being, governed and united by the identity of its fundamental laws; it determines the merging of the *Physica Coelestis* with the *Physica Terrestris* [and it] enables the latter to use and to apply to its problems the methods, the hypothetico-deductive mathematical treatment—developed by the former; it implies the impossibility of establishing and elaborating a terrestrial physics or at least a terrestrial mechanics without a celestial one.[45]

The distinction between celestial and terrestrial physics could no longer survive; mathematics was the universal language of both and produced certainties in both.

But Galileo went even further. Copernicus and Kepler argued in terms of the certainty of mathematics and the deceptiveness of the senses. For them mathematics was the substitute for defective sense reports. Galileo, as previously suggested, argued in terms of the certainty of mathematics corroborated by empirical observation. He argued for the Copernican universe and its foundation in modern scientific method by appealing to the corroborative power of the senses. By means of the telescope, an extension of the senses "analogous to the extension of reason through mathematics," Galileo argued that objective reality definitely "corresponded to the proportions expressed by numbers."[46] Though Galileo was not the first to view the heavens with the telescope, he was the first to grasp the import of the things he saw with it. Through the telescope he believed that at last he had complete empirical evidence that the "true sky is very different from the sky of Peripateticism, that the world is indeed different. In this way the experience of the senses proved that Copernicus' world was true."[47]

Through the telescope, he discovered blemishes on the sun (the famed sunspots) and mountains on the moon. He saw evidence for the absence of a perfectly symmetrical perfection in the celestial bodies; they too shared the imperfections of the terrestrial. "When we look for incorruption in the heavens," Sir Thomas Browne would say, basing himself on Galileo's observations through the telescope, "we finde they are but like the Earth; durable in their main bodies, alterable in their parts."[48]

Galileo emerged from his observation with supreme confidence in the absolute correctness of the universe of modern science. Since "it has pleased God to concede to human ingenuity an invention" by which "an infinite number of objects which were invisible" have "become visible," we have been enabled to bring "the heavens thirty or forty times closer to us than they were to Aristotle."[49] The ordinary man could now grasp the truth of the Copernican universe without need of his having the mathematical genius of a Kepler. Yet Galileo had to convince his contemporaries of the merits—of the very legitimacy—of the telescope as a mode of empirical observation and verification. The sense observation relied on by Aristotelianism and Ptolemaicism was that of the direct, unaided report of the senses. The first reaction of the skeptics of Galileo's day was that the telescope obfuscated and deceived rather than sharpened the senses. Thus, Galileo's faith in modern scientific method had to be extended to the capacity of the telescope to sensibly verify the new universe.

To believe in the telescope when it is turned toward the sky means to believe in the existence of that which it enables us to perceive, even though in principle there is no way to verify that existence by direct vision. Who can deny that this faith implied a veritable *methodological revolution?*[50]

Indeed, Galileo proclaimed this methodological revolution to all who had eyes to see in this new way. He insisted that astronomical hypotheses had to accord with the teaching of physics, that the theory of celestial movements had to rest on foundations that also supported terrestrial movements. The very course of the stars, the ebb and flow of the seas, the movement of falling bodies and projectiles, all of which he investigated empirically, had to be accounted for by a system of postulates constructed in the single language of mathematics. The distinctions between natural and artificial or violent motion, between celestial perfection and terrestrial imperfection, had publicly and irrevocably seen their day.

It must be conceded, of course, that Galileo placed primary emphasis on the ability of the mathematical language to bespeak the innermost nature of things, and only secondary emphasis on the singleness of the mathematical postulate system. But those who would carry out his task of elaborating the new scientific method would begin with the latter emphasis as primary. If it is the case that the primary impact of his thought in his own time was in terms of the establishment of the Copernican hypothesis as consistent with the innermost nature of things, its primary impact for posterity would be in terms of the establishment of a singular dynamic, holistic discourse (such as that sought for by medieval Christians) that was mathematical in character and able to represent both the movement of the stars and the oscillations of the oceans and the fall of heavenly bodies. If it is true that today, along with Bellarmine and against Galileo, paradoxically, we opt for the hypothetical character of the mathematico-physical system of science, it can be justly said that this is so because of Galileo's efforts.[51]

The universe confirmed by scientific method, according to Galileo, is one where the space of Euclidean geometry must be substituted for the space of Ptolemaic astronomy, one where a homogeneous and abstract space must be substituted for the heterogeneous and physically differentiated space of classical astronomy. The space of this universe is thus mathematicized, with a geometrized infinite nature replacing the hierarchically ordered world structure of the ancient cosmos. In this universe, mathematics is not only the language of science by which, in an Augustinian fashion,[52] man is able to "interrogate nature" in such a way that "nature's reply will emerge . . . clearly and beyond any possible misunderstanding,"[53] but it is also the very language of nature itself, as Galileo indicates.

Philosophy is written in this grand book, the universe, which stands continually open to our gaze. But the book cannot be understood unless one first learns to comprehend the language and read the letters in which it is composed. It is written in the language of mathematics and its characters are triangles, circles, and other geometric figures, without which it is humanly impossible to understand a single word of it. Without these, one wanders about in a dark labyrinth.[54]

Here is the tombstone for an old and the birthstone for a new world—the paradigmatic text, with medieval overtones, for modern scientific method.

The irony in all of this was in the judgment of his work by that religious institution to which Galileo, like his medieval predecessors, was so deeply committed. In 1632 Galileo was called before the Italian Inquisition. On his side, Galileo could have avoided this disastrous confrontation had he not taken so public a stand in his apologetic mission for modern science. On the other side, the narrow-mindedness of many ecclesiastics in authority leads one to suspect that in addition to their concern with scriptural integrity and doctrinal authority, they were also governed by political motives.[55]

That political intrigue played a heavy role on the part of the inquisitors cannot be denied; what also cannot be denied, it appears, is that in defending the reconcilability of the new method with the scriptural foundations of Catholic doctrines, and in so public a fashion, Galileo appeared to many in ecclesiastical authority to be usurping their magisterial office. Galileo had

thrown down the challenge, and now he was going to pay for it. The original challenge went far back in time. He had become a danger when he started writing in Italian and when he decided to bypass the universities and vested intellectual authority and reveal his mind to enlightened public opinion. . . . The scientist as an isolated specialist had not been understood as a social danger. . . . It was Galileo, the Renaissance figure who wanted the scientific awareness spread to the whole advancing front of his civilization, from its expressive and technological capacities and its critical activity to its philosophical reflection, who appeared as a dangerous novelty monger.[56]

Galileo, of course, did not perceive his educative, apologetic function in behalf of the new method as a usurpation of the Church's teaching authority. Are we simply, then, to attribute the response from so many ecclesiastical quarters as that of less intelligent men in the face of a superior mind? Despite the jealousy of Galileo on the part of many clerical intellectuals of the time who secretly held Copernicanism while publicly avowing Ptolemaicism, pettiness and even intrigue do not fully account for the official Church reaction. There were profound kinships between the conception of the new universe and Christian tradition, as our account thus far has labored to make explicit, but the clear perception of these affinities required a single-minded devotion to matters of intellect, a devotion not accessible even to those ecclesiastical administrators who prided themselves on being humanists. One must also remember the toll taken by sheer inertia, the tendency of the clerical powers of the time to build into their decisions a resistance to change in the face of the traumatic changes of the Protestant Reformation. Undoubtedly most of these authorities failed to perceive the full import of the Galileo case; it was for them, "beset as they were by a multiplicity of ordinary and extraordinary business that looked far more important,"[57] a matter of secondary importance.

Galileo's condemnation and the consignment of his *Dialogue* to the *Index Librorum Prohibitorum* have no completely satisfactory explanation to this day. We are left with the pathos of Galileo's abjuration before the Inquisition: "I have not held and do not hold as true the opinion which has been condemned, of the motion of the Earth and the stability of the Sun"[58]—the situation of a man forced to publicly renounce what he had publicly proclaimed. Yet the pathos does not consist in what we today might suspect, the moral degradation of saying what one did not believe; in Galileo's day, everyone knew the difference between a due formality and a substantive expression of one's convictions. Rather, it consisted in the social degradation of being reduced to this formality by the sheer power of ecclesiastical authorities.

Arthur Koestler insists that it "was Galileo's ill-conceived crusade which had . . . precipitated the divorce of science from faith."[59] In doing so he misplaces the significance of Galileo, for the origins of such a divorce are more complex and certainly more problematic. Galileo's significance ought to be placed in the provision of the first articulation of the modern scientific method—a provision which he saw had to be executed in the public realm, for not even the mathematician could claim science as exclusively his own.

Presiding as he did at the birth and death of a world, no frequent thing in the history of civilizations, Galileo was confident of the rightness of the newborn; his judges were not. His confidence blinded him to certain issues. What about the possibility that the "reason and intellect with which we are endowed . . . may sooner or later turn out to be able to handle with scientific rigor those truths which concern the moral disciplines"?[60] For Galileo, science was to be limited to the realm of physical nature; as distinct from the language of Scripture and theology, its province was not that of ethical matters. Galileo never confronted squarely the problem of whether the new universe also entailed a radical revision of not only how man knows nature but how he acts. Others, such as John Donne, faintly glimpsed the problem.

> [The] New Philosophy calls all in doubt,
> The Element of Fire is quite put out;
> The Sun is lost, and th' earth, and no man's wit
> Can well direct him where to look for it.
> And freely men confess that this world's spent,

When in the planets, and the firmament
They seek so many new; then see that this
Is crumbled out again to his atomies.
'Tis all in pieces; all coherence gone;
All just supply, and all relation:
Prince, Subject, Father, Son, are things forgot,
For every man alone thinks he hath got
To be a phoenix, and that then can be
None of that kind, of which he is, but he.[61]

Still others, such as Giordano Bruno, clearly saw such a problem and ventured forthrightly, if not excessively, into the realm of what the new universe entailed for human actions. For Galileo there is, however, a self-imposed limitation of the implications of the new universe to man's knowledge of the physical world; there is, further, a delicate balance of the destructive impulse with the constructive impulse. And for this purpose

a twofold work of destruction and of education is necessary—destruction of prejudices and traditional mental habits and of common sense; creation in their place of new habits, of a new attitude toward reasoning. . . . It is necessary in fact (for Galileo) to educate the reader, to teach him to have faith no longer in authority, in tradition, in common sense. It is necessary to teach him to think.[62]

For Galileo, however, the methodological revolution is carefully limited to knowledge of the physical world; only here is common sense challenged. Only here is privileged authority challenged. "By eliminating one after the other most of the speculative elements of the doctrine of motion, or by treating them in a strictly mathematical way," he opened "to systematic investigation the unlimited *physical* space in which a *privileged* form of motion has no sense."[63]

Despite the condemnation of his work by ecclesiastical authorities, and despite the fact that he did not reach a full understanding, not to mention justification, of the new scientific method, he was still able to make "an enormous contribution to the development of the *methodological* understanding of science."[64] Even an ecclesiastical tribunal might eventually have to recognize this, as Descartes intimated in 1634.

I do not see that this censure has been endorsed by the Pope or by any Council, but only by a single congregation of the Cardinals of the Inquisition; so I do not altogether lose hope that the case may turn out like that of the Antipodes, which were similarly condemned long ago. So in time my World may yet see the day.[65]

One must, nonetheless, admit a justification for the nervousness of ecclesiastical authority, for there were questions, entailed by the method, of which Galileo had not dreamed. What happens to privileged forms of authority and privileged institutions in this new universe? Without a hierarchical universe, what happens to a hierarchical society? Centuries would transpire before these questions would find their full philosophical equals. But they entered already the unequal minds of some—among them, Bruno whose confrontation, even before Galileo, with the authorities was still more tragic. Galileo may in fact have unknowingly "inherited the wind" of this confrontation.

BRUNO: PROBING THE ETHICAL IMPLICATIONS OF THE NEW UNIVERSE

For centuries, Marjorie Nicolson points out, "infinite" had been "God's word, not man's." But now "man was beginning to apply to an expanded universe adjectives and epithets long reserved for Deity, appropriate alone to the Incomprehensible."[66] Even more than Cusa and Copernicus, Giordano Bruno (1548–1600) exults in the new predication of the term.

We insult the Infinite Cause when we say that it may be the cause of a finite effect; to a finite effect it can have neither the name nor the relation of an efficient cause.[67]

Bruno is the most prominent early modern explorer of the ethical implications underlying this new use of the term "infinite." Though he was neither an astronomer nor a theologian in the strict sense, "contemporary astronomical writings contributed to the cosmology that was the passionate faith of his life, and he was led by his cosmology to a new ethic."[68]

Bruno entered the Dominican order in 1563; but in 1576, having been accused of heresy, he left the order and for the remainder of his life restlessly traveled throughout Europe. Unlike Galileo, he indulges in a theological language very much akin to that of Cusa and the medievals.

I call the universe infinite because it has no margin, limit, or surface; I do not call the universe totally infinite because each part that we encounter is finite. I call God all infinite because he excludes from himself every term, and every one of his attributes is one and infinite; I call God totally infinite because all of him is in all the world and in each part of it totally and infinitely.[69]

The mystical language of the medievals returns to speculation on the infinite universe in the thought of Bruno. Yet Bruno is in substantial agreement with the scientific reflections of Copernicus, Kepler, and Galileo. In a truly infinite universe there can be no absolutely privileged position; and as a consequence, Bruno holds, the position of the earth or of any body, for that matter, can be defined or measured only in relation to some other object.

Since measurement of any object requires a relationship to another object, and since comprehension of the meaning of anything requires comprehension of its relations to other bodies in an infinite universe, the combinatorial possibilities involved in knowledge are virtually infinite. Each object has a potentially infinite resonance vibrating to the tune of other objects—calling up virtually every other object in the universe. In this manner, having assimilated the primitive roots of the new science, Bruno recalls the symbolic universe of the medieval alchemists and mystics. He invokes the sacred world of energy of the medievals; once again, in Bruno science comes to be mixed with magic. Rejecting the "contemplation of inert definite essences," Bruno labored for "the convergence of knowledge and action" in a "science which is at the service of a magical transformation of the universe."[70] Using the alchemical language of magic, Bruno attempts to drive the new science to intimations of its ethical import.

Our philosophy reduces to a single origin and refers to a single end, and makes contraries to coincide so that there is one primal foundation of both. From this coinciding of contraries we deduce that ultimately it is

. . . true that there are contraries within contraries, wherefore it is not difficult to compass the knowledge that each thing is within every other—which Aristotle and other sophists [*sic*] could not comprehend.[71]

Even more explicitly than Galileo, Copernicus, and Kepler, Bruno ties up the new cosmology with its roots in the medieval Incarnational experience of nature. Much like the God of which it is a manifestation, the universe does not move itself locally, since there is nothing outside itself to which to transport itself. Like God, it is incorruptible, since there is no other thing into which it could change; like God, the universe has everything in itself. Like the Christ of the medieval alchemists, who was symbolized by the philosopher's stone, the universe comprehends in itself all contrariety in unity and harmony, being neither entirely matter nor purely form. Like the divine, the universe in its wholeness cannot be measured. In sum, Bruno attempts to set forth, not the new method of knowledge for the new universe, but the religious *faith* underlying this new method.

But what of the ethical implications of the new universe Bruno can be said to explicate? In an infinite universe there is an infinity of worlds, each of which is finite like our own. As Bruno remarks,

Infinite perfection is far better presented in innumerable individuals than in those which are numbered and finite. . . . But since innumerable grades of perfection must, through corporeal mode, unfold the divine incorporeal perfection, therefore there must be innumerable individuals . . . whereof one is our earth.[72]

There are, then, as Bruno says, "innumerable suns, and an infinite number of earths revolve around these suns."[73] Any possible inhabitants of these worlds must be in conformity with the peculiar conditions of their own world. Man is not alone in the universe; there is the preeminent possibility of other rational life. Furthermore, in being infinite, the universe is implicated in a limitless progression or buildup from the minimum to the maximum. Individuals in this world have significance only as part of this progression—only in relation to other individuals. The individual in this infinitely progressing universe, consequently, "whether corporeal or incorporeal," Bruno says, "is never completed; and among eternally pursuing individual forms," it never rests content.[74] That which is beautiful in an absolute and definitive fashion cannot be merely individual. Nothing individual can bind absolutely and normatively but only in relation to something else. "Similarly, nothing which attracts is absolutely good but since the universe . . . is composed of contraries, so good is also composed of contraries."[75]

In a universe where individuation is not purely pregiven, not to mention complete, individuality gains significance only in relationality. And so, the goodness of individual action and accomplishment emerges only in relation to other individual action and accomplishment. There can be no privileged individuals, just as there can be no privileged space in this universe. And if there can be no privileged individuals, there can be no privileged individual or institutional sources (for institutions are but complex individuals) of authority.

No institution or law ought to be accepted which does not tend to the highest end: the direction of our minds and reform of our natures so that they produce fruit necessary or useful for human intercourse.[76]

It was precisely the finite and closed universe that served to limit the creative and ethical possibilities of man. Under its sway, the

human spirit was . . . suffocating in the close air of a narrow prisonhouse whence but only through chinks it gazed at the far-off stars. Its wings were clipped so that it was unable to cleave the veiling cloud and reach the reality beyond.[77]

Precisely because it is access to the "reality beyond" that allows man the stretching and expansion of his own inner reality, the breakdown of the old cosmology and the birth of the new suggest new possibilities for the expansion of human interior space in meeting the demands of the infinite external spaces of the universe. The infinite universe must be reflected in the human spirit; the new cosmology of the infinite universe thus becomes for Bruno "an extended inner spiritual experience, filling the infinite need of the soul for infinity."[78] Man, the "great miracle, must now expand himself to receive" the infinite universe.[79]

"Jove," Bruno suggests, now "represents each one of us"[80] in relation to this universe; each of us is now left with the inescapable duty of developing the inherent possibilities of his unique inner-most being. It may, in fact, be his strong emphasis on magic and magical religion that allows Bruno to emphasize the human mind's capacity for the infinite in the face of an infinite universe. Frances Yates points out that the magician "wants to draw the world into himself"; the magical Hermetic writings that so strongly influenced Bruno very likely permitted him to emphasize the reflection of the world in the mind.[81]

Fighting against those who would still treat man as a locus of closed forces and finite potentialities in the new universe, who would treat man as if his universe were still finite, Bruno dreamed of the day when man "would walk like a new Adam in a world of new creation."[82] Those who would "enforce their own prejudices with fire and sword"[83] were in point of fact enemies of the new concept of man that was the fitting complement of an infinite universe.

In a universe where no point could be absolute or definitively binding on the whole, Bruno felt that authority nonetheless bound and deceived in countless ways. He was thus led to proclaim a necessary imperative in an infinite universe: freedom of thought regardless of the consequences of what is thought. "We wish," he said, "this law to be vigorously observed, that reason is as true as it is necessary, and the authority of no man howsoever true and excellent he may be is admissible as an argument."[84] The ethico-cosmological character of Bruno's thought is evident in the public debate to which he summoned the learned doctors of the Collège de Cambrai in Paris in 1586. Here, in presenting articles "on nature and the world against the Peripatetics," he distilled the basic elements of his thought.

We have been imprisoned in a dark dungeon, whence only distantly could we see the far off stars. But now we are released. We know that there is one heaven, a vast ethereal region in which move those flaming bodies which announce to us the glory and majesty of God. This moves us to contemplate the infinite cause of the infinite effect; we see that the divinity is not far distant but within us, for its center is everywhere, as close to dwellers in other worlds as it is to us. Hence we should follow not foolish and dreamy authorities but the regulated sense and the illuminated intellect. The infinite universe is a conception more worthy of God's majesty than that it should be finite.[85]

In 1592 Bruno was incarcerated in the prisons of the Holy Office and was eventually tried by the Venetian Inquisition. At the end of this trial he fully recanted of all the heresies of which he was accused and threw himself in penitence on the mercy of the judges. By law he had to be sent to Rome, however, and in 1599 heretical propositions from his work were drawn up by Cardinal Bellarmine. In the face of these propositions, Bruno suddenly shifted his attitude and obstinately maintained "that he had never written or said anything heretical and that the ministers of the Holy Office wrongly interpreted his views"; he was therefore sentenced as an "impenitent heretic" and burned alive in Rome on February 17, 1600.[86] "Perhaps your fear in passing judgment on me," he was reported to have said to his accusers, "is greater than mine in receiving it."[87] In this way he came to be considered as the first martyr for faith in the new universe. Yet this traditional view does not fully stand up to examination, for the eventual publication of the summary of the trial shows that "little attention was paid to philosophical and scientific questions in the interrogations."[88] It may, more likely, have been his emphasis on magical religion or a combination of his magic and his bold forays into the ethical implications of the new universe that accounted for his fate.

If this is so, his fate was doubly tragic. For in the modern world now dawning, his dream of a blending "of science interpreted as 'natural magic' and religion interpreted as 'divine magic' was obviously doomed to fade."[89] Yet there was a more lasting import to his thought. Much as Galileo provided the foundations for the future elaboration of scientific method, Bruno might be said to have provided the initial tentative exploration of the moral theory of the modern age. Though his influence on his immediate contemporaries, as Alexandre Koyré speculates, appears negligible, he was in his teaching "far ahead of his time," and his influence seems "to have been a delayed one."[90] The primitive seeds of his emphasis on freedom and conscience may very well have come to bloom in the Enlightenment and in the ethical thought of Immanuel Kant where moral autonomy plays such an important, though philosophical, role.

Thus, in the Copernican Revolution of Copernicus, Kepler, Galileo, and Bruno, one finds the birth of the new cosmology including both the development of a new method of knowing and a somewhat primitive ethic for the new universe. The methodology for knowing in this universe—the modern scientific method—is neither the pure source of modernity nor sprung suddenly from the heads of its first articulators. It is an issuance of the thought and experience of a new kind of universe with roots deep in the Middle Ages. The revolution in question is a sudden turning in a movement with a long history; the birth of the modern cosmology is revolutionary only to the extent that it signals very decisively the transition into a new age—that of modernity.

With the completion of the drawn-out birth of the new cosmology, the task of completing the formulation of the new scientific method would fall to minds better known today, such as Descartes, Newton, and Leibniz. Though they be better known, they are no less indebted to the revolutionary breakthroughs of Copernicus, Kepler, and Galileo. And those who would in turn follow them in weaving the fabric of the logic of modernity would find themselves raising the ethical questions and the moral possibilities first presented by the enigmatic Bruno.

3

THE MATURATION OF
MODERN SCIENTIFIC METHOD

PROFOUND forces, as we have seen, were at work in medieval civilization. These forces challenged the ancient mythic bifurcation between the sacred and the profane, as well as the ancient cosmological distinction between privileged and unprivileged spaces and the classical metaphysical bifurcation between an immutable unmoved perfection and a changing sphere of imperfection. These forces began to bear fruit in the first attempts to construct a new philosophical discourse for a universe devoid of the sacred-profane dualism, of the separation of the celestial and terrestrial spheres, and of the distinction between a perfect up and an imperfect and corruptible down. But these first attempts occurred toward the close of what is known as the Middle Ages in Nicholas of Cusa's new mode of thinking about the infinite.

Cusa's notion of a privatively infinite universe found its fulfillment in the Copernican Revolution that marked the birth of a new cosmology to take the place of the Aristotelian-Ptolemaic system. This new universe, articulated by Copernicus and Kepler, issued in the elaboration of a new way of knowing adequate to this universe. The first efforts in elaborating this new way of knowing—this novel discourse for a new universe—can be seen in Galileo. In assuming the role of public apologist for the new scientific method, Galileo, in effect, drew out the venom of entrenched, institutional resistance to the scientific revolution and freed those who would follow him for other tasks. Those who would follow him could assume the task of bringing the new method of knowing to its maturation. Their names, Descartes, Newton, and Leibniz, are known by those with the most casual acquaintance with modern thought. Descartes was destined to provide the philosophical foundations of the method; Newton and Leibniz, working with the Cartesian edifice, were destined to provide important revisions on his method. In Descartes we find the largest and most significant figure in this part of our attempt to verbalize the logic of modernity—the pivotal point in the formulation of modern scientific method: the provision of that method with its metaphysical foundations. For in Descartes we encounter the "early modern mind's reckoning with the conditions of its emergence and the tasks to which it must commit itself."[1]

Before beginning our consideration, there is one further point of an introductory nature worth dwelling upon. Much of the pre-Cartesian thought we have examined was concerned to justify the proposition that the mathematical core of the method, when applied to the study of natural phenomena, could reveal the underlying reality of the universe.[2] This obsession is seen, perhaps, most clearly in the apologist's role assumed by Galileo—in his placing primary emphasis on the capacity of the mathematical essence of the new method to bespeak the innermost nature of reality, and in his secondary concern with the singleness of the mathematical postulate system. In bringing the new method to maturity, Galileo's inheritors will place primary emphasis on the singleness of the postulate system.[3] For Descartes, Newton, and Leibniz, the primary issue is the capacity of scientific method to be the paradigmatic way of knowing, the best available approximation to a singular universal language—a language long sought after by the medievals. Their deemphasis of the issue of the method's access to the innermost nature of things, one conjectures, permits them to develop the method's potentialities to the fullest— as an answer to the question of how man shall know in an infinite universe.

This is not to say that Descartes, Newton, and Leibniz were persuaded that the scientific method was in no way revelatory of the nature of physical reality; rather, it is simply to say that they were no longer impelled or constrained to defend the connection between the mathematical core of the method and the nature of physical reality. Commencing with Descartes, the modern mind appears liberated for the first time to attain a level of thought beyond the celebration or apologetic justification of the infinite universe; it is liberated to examine analytically and critically the foundations of the new kind of knowledge entailed by such a universe.

But, in leading scientific method to its mature formulation— and this applies in the first place to Descartes—it appears that the price that must be paid is a certain alienation of human intelligence from the innermost nature of physical things. Hegel, who accomplishes what might be termed the completion of the logic of modernity, detects this price.

The principle of modern philosophy is hence not a free and natural thought, because it has the opposition of thought and nature before it as a fact of which it is conscious.[4]

An intimation of this price is had in the deemphasis of sensory observation that we have already discerned in the intellectual midwives present at the birth of the modern cosmology—Copernicus and Kepler. Michael Oakeshott's remark is very much to the point in this regard.

The data of scientific knowledge are never mere 'observations'. And an interest in mere observation, in things 'seen' is not, as such, a scientific interest; it belongs rather to the world of natural history—science before it has realized its own character. Science begins only when the world of 'things' opened to us by our senses and perceptions has been forgotten or set on one side.[5]

The maturation of modern scientific method seems to bring in its wake the very real problem of the alienation of thought and consciousness from material things. So real is this problem that it might almost be said that the mature formulation of the method bequeathes a new bifurcation for the logic of modernity—a bifurcation to replace that of the vanquished classical bifurcation between an imperfect down and a perfect up.

Yet, in the end, what makes Descartes, Newton, and Leibniz mature philosophical voices in regard to the new method—residing on a quite distinct level from that occupied by Copernicus, Kepler, Bruno, and even Galileo—is that they are capable of generating philosophical *problems* in regard to the new universe and its proper scientific knowledge. In them we find something quite different from the mystical, prophetic, and apologetic tones of their predecessors; we find a dialectical and critical analysis of the kind of knowledge suitable for an infinite universe—a dialectic that, for all its criticism, is no less rooted in a profound faith in the rightness of the new universe than was the discourse of their predecessors.

DESCARTES: THE METAPHYSICAL
FOUNDATIONS OF MODERN SCIENCE

If Copernicus, Kepler, Galileo, and Bruno can be justly called the prophets of a new universe, René Descartes (1596–1650), to be justly called the Father of Modern Philosophy, must be said to be concerned, not with the prophetic heralding of a new universe, but with the most deep-seated dialectical grappling with the task of rationally justifying and analyzing the philosophical foundations of the knowledge appropriate to this new universe. As Hegel says,

René Descartes is a bold spirit who recommenced the whole subject from the very beginning and constituted afresh the *groundwork* on which Philosophy is based, and to which, after a thousand years had passed, it once more returned.[6]

We have seen that Kepler wanted to provide a philosophy that would replace the metaphysics of Aristotle.[7] Yet, in the end, Kepler was unable to construct a metaphysical foundation for the new method of knowing; though able to decisively exclude the Aristotelian metaphysic, he could not construct an adequate substitute to serve as the underpinning for scientific method. Galileo, too, in his attempt to educate the reader of his time in the method's ultimate cogency, in the hope that he would be able to teach him to think,[8] failed to demonstrate how the new method conforms to the innermost process of thinking itself. And Bruno, also, could do little more than proclaim the primacy of the illuminated intellect over the claims of foolish and dreamy authorities;[9] he was unable to provide a metaphysic justifying the primacy of this intellect in the modern universe.

All of these thinkers, though presiding at the birth of a new universe, were unable to articulate the philosophical foundations of the method on which they relied. In this way, Descartes could criticize Galileo for having "no philosophy," for supposing it "possible to dispense with metaphysics"; he determined that the time was now ripe to construct an authentic metaphysics with which to secure the foundations of scientific knowledge.[10] Galileo explored the objects of the new universe by means of a mathematical method, but according to Descartes he was unable to analyze "the first causes of nature" and so, limiting himself to the explanation of only "certain particular effects," he was fated to build "without foundation."[11]

Descartes perceived that the moment had now come for the great metaphysical foundation-work of the new science. Though the ancient, classical theory of knowledge was outmoded, it had at least this virtue: its foundations were secured by a metaphysic— largely that of Aristotle. The new science was incapable of being founded in this metaphysic; its future would be forever blocked were it to be deprived of an adequate metaphysical foundation. The stakes, as Descartes saw them, were momentous. The provision of a metaphysical ground for scientific method was not just window dressing or even an academic exercise. Just as men needed some kind of ultimate rational foundation for the attainment of their salvation, so they were in need of an ultimate intellectual foundation for the new science if that science would fulfill its promise of bettering their physical welfare on this earth. Thus, the primary shape of his philosophical task took root in Descartes' mind.

How can man, by means of Reason, and for the sake of the independent exercise of Reason, disclose to Reason the foundations of sciences that will find the truths necessary for mundane welfare as Revelation gives men the truths necessary for Salvation?[12]

Yet we would certainly be wide of the mark if we were to presume from Descartes' emphasis on metaphysical foundation-work and rational analysis of scientific method that he was not deeply convinced of the ultimate correctness of the method, for

Descartes' faith in its essential rectitude is as intense as that of Galileo. But the intensity of his faith assumes a form quite different from that of his modern predecessors. In his concern with securing foundations for the method, with providing the method with an adequate and novel metaphysic, his faith in the method is colored, much more than the faith of his predecessors, by the characteristics of great intellectual and dialectical warfare. In order to metaphysically found the new scientific knowledge, Descartes must wrestle with its inner connections and question it from within. Unlike his modern predecessors, he must engage in a questioning and criticism of the very foundations of knowledge. Scientific method itself must be subjected to what Kepler and Galileo never dared to subject it, namely, an unremitting test.

To be practicable, however, this test must limit itself to the decisive claims to knowledge made by a particular scientific investigator. Descartes must begin with his own claims to knowledge.

As soon as my age permitted me to emerge from the control of my tutors, I entirely quitted the study of letters. And resolving to seek no other science than that which could be found in myself, or at least in the great book of the world, I employed the rest of my youth in travel, . . . in collecting varied experiences. . . . But after I had employed several years in thus studying the book of the world . . . I one day formed the resolution of also making myself an object of study. . . . This succeeded much better, it appeared to me, than if I had never departed either from my country or my books.[13]

Unlike his predecessors, doubt would be the starting point for Descartes. "The whole of philosophy as it had been carried on up to this time," Hegel says, "was vitiated by the constant presupposition of something as true."[14] Descartes would dare to make the "abolition of all determinations the first condition of philosophy."[15]

Descartes' metaphysical mission can be traced, surprisingly enough, to a mystical experience during the day and night of November 10, 1619—an experience that supplied the inspiration and the guiding principle for his whole life-work.[16] In the solitude of his heated room he began to review in a skeptical fashion the knowledge he had attained; disunity and uncertainty seemed to characterize this knowledge in the arts as well as the sciences. In mathematics he discovered certainty, but this certainty failed to make his other knowledge any clearer. What was required was

a fresh start, one that would sweep away all systems which had become encumbered with false logic, or, at best, half-truths. The task that gradually took shape in his mind during these long hours of self-confinement was how to arrive at the certainty of mathematics in other fields, which, like philosophy, appeared in a state of chaos. . . . He had been in the process of ridding himself of all his former 'prejudices' or preconceived ideas. How was he to rebuild, to use his own image, the house he had just burned? . . . After many hours of taxing his mind to its utmost, he finally found the method he had been seeking. . . . What he now realized, as if in a blinding flash, was the unity of all the sciences, indeed of all knowledge. . . . He was now in possession of 'everything at once', the 'foundations of a marvelous science' which would replace current confusion and disparity with the unity of an architectural monument.[17]

Elated and exhausted at the end of the day, he retired to sleep and had three dreams. The first was a nightmare in which phantoms appeared and terrified him. He awoke from this dream and turned to his right side, praying that he might be protected from any evil effect of his dream.[18] His second dream consisted solely of his hearing a piercing noise, like a clap of thunder, and he awoke once again in fear. His third dream had nothing terrifying in it;[19] he later saw in the reassurance of this dream a symbol of the "mirabilis scientiae fundamenta," which he had intuited while awake during the day.[20] He was certain "that his intuition, which suggested the possibility of the unity of all sciences, had been divinely inspired."[21]

Taken together with his waking experience of that day, his dreams suggested to him that the "mirabilis scientiae fundamenta," the metaphysical foundations of the sciences, had to proceed from an intuition that the "principle of science must be looked for within ourselves."[22] The waking and sleeping experiences of this day afforded Descartes the basis for a process of thought that proceeded from the negativity of doubt; he would record the completed thought process in his great work, *Meditations on First Philosophy,* first published in 1641. In this work is contained "a complete and perfect demonstration of metaphysical truths" which, when once completed, are completed forever.[23] In regard to the metaphysic transcribed here, he would say that "this is the matter to which I have devoted the most study, and in which by God's grace, I am entirely satisfied."[24]

The very title of this work suggests a certain parallel to the spiritual technique of religious meditation as it was practiced in Descartes' day, especially in the technique of Ignatius of Loyola. This parallel is quite perceptible in the First Meditation.

The purpose of the First Meditation is similar to that of the meditations of the first week of the *Spiritual Exercises* [of Ignatius] on *peccata,* to make the meditator realize the fragility and instability of his ordinary state of mind. We must learn to doubt in order to learn to know. It is for this reason that the most stringent of all tests is introduced: *de omnibus dubitandum.* The master psychologist of Manresa planned to purify his penitent through the negativity of the first week to enable the will to make the unhampered choice between the two Kingdoms. Descartes wishes too to purify the mind of its prejudices, to render the mind free to see the truth, in and through itself. This need for intellectual purity, a mind *sine cera,* is the condition of all metaphysical thinking.[25]

Ignatius' technique aimed at a training of the will, a conditioning of the will out of its ordinary or everyday orientation into sin and vapid concerns; it was a disciplining of the will. Descartes' technique aimed at a training of the mind, a conditioning of the mind away from its tendency to take the ordinary or everyday apprehensions of the senses and human opinion as definitive; it was a disciplining of the mind. Both aimed to purify; whereas Ignatius began with the negative of sin and reflection on sin, Descartes began with the negative of doubt and reflection on doubt. Descartes' methodical doubt, as it has come to be called, is a kind of first or preliminary knowing—a testing procedure for knowing. It discloses itself, however, not as the doubt of radical skepticism bent on finding what cannot be known, but as the metaphysical instrument necessary for the disclosure of those propositions or first principles that unconditionally withstand doubt.

In initiating the building of his intellectual edifice with an all-encompassing doubt, Descartes begins, as Hegel has indicated, with the admission of no pregiven truth or premise. Unlike Galileo and his other modern predecessors, he does not begin with the pregiven truth of modern scientific knowledge itself.

Science . . . cannot establish for itself the legitimacy of its own procedure; methodology cannot of itself demonstrate that the character, connexion, and order of our thoughts exactly represent, correspond point for point, with the character, connexion, and order of independent fact. So if certain knowledge about the ultimate character of parts of reality is to be attained by science, science must be guaranteed by something more radical than can be supplied by inference from its own procedure. Accordingly Descartes plainly intends his Metaphysics to be no mere appendage to his Method or to his Physics. Without a supporting Metaphysic the Method would be no more than an elaborate speculative hypothesis, and it would be foolhardy to place confidence in its capacity to produce knowledge that is certain.[26]

Scientific method requires a support outside itself in the certitudes of a metaphysic; this metaphysic can appeal to no prior proposition taken on faith or even taken as self-evident. This apparently is what Descartes means when he says that what the atheist knows in geometry "cannot constitute true science," for Descartes presumes an atheist to be one who rejects the possibility of an underlying metaphysic—one whose knowledge is not supported by an authentic metaphysic.[27] Yet, not even metaphysics can establish its own certainty; rather, it must "establish with certainty that certainty is attainable both within and beyond its own restricted field."[28]

The starting point of *The Meditations,* then, must be a pervasive doubt applied to everything that offers itself as knowledge. In the First Meditation, Descartes begins by doubting that his senses deliver accurate data; but this first doubt still leaves the new science with its mathematical essence intact. He than proceeds to doubt his ability to truly distinguish between apprehension in a waking state and imagination in a dreaming state; but this doubt still leaves the necessity of mathematical conclusions untouched. As Descartes remarks, "whether I am awake or asleep, two and three together always form five, and the square can never have more than four sides, and it does not seem possible that truths so clear and apparent can be suspected of any falsity or uncertainty."[29] It is only with his third and last doubt—that God, if He exists, deceives him, or that an "evil genius" exists to deceive him, raising the possibility that God "has brought it to pass . . . that I am . . . deceived every time that I add two and three or count the sides of a square"[30]—that Descartes raises a doubt that is seemingly total; for not even the propositions of geometry can resist it. The First Meditation thus ends in a destructive predicament where

order may well be disorder, disorder may well be order. . . . We should be utterly deceived without being able to recognize the tangled web of deceit.[31]

It is with the darkest of doubts that the First Meditation concludes.

The Second Meditation reverses this all-encompassing doubt, disclosing that reason must necessarily affirm its own authority in questioning itself.[32] Even if God deceives me,

He can never cause me to be nothing so long as I think that I am something. So that after having reflected well and carefully examined all things, we must come to the definite conclusion that this proposition: *I am, I exist,* is necessarily true each time that I pronounce it, or that I mentally conceive it.[33]

Since I cannot doubt that I doubt, and since to doubt is to think, I am constrained to affirm the "cogito ergo sum," in which my "thinking and my being are contained, logically inseparable in a single experience"[34] of my selfhood. Far from being a "reasonable *animal,*" this self is a "thing which thinks," a pure "res cogitans."[35] This is the bare minimum of the first metaphysical principle that Descartes discovers; here the Cartesian self, the modern metaphysical subject, "finds existence in the shape of thought and comprehends existence; and conversely it finds in its thought existence."[36]

But, in saying that the existence of the self is the first principle of Descartes' metaphysics, we must be somewhat careful, since it "is a first truth only because found first, not because of a superior intrinsic credibility."[37] It is not the bare *Cogito* but rather the nature of the self as "res cogitans," or the thing that entertains the proposition, which is Descartes' first principle.[38] To make the *Cogito* productive as a proposition, to transform it into the first principle of a metaphysic, Descartes must show that it is the nature of the self that is first known most clearly in all knowledge-claims about the world. He attempts to do this toward the close of the Second Meditation in the example of the wax object. What I know best, what, in fact, I *only* know about this object, is not delivered to me by my senses, not only because they can be deceived, but because the material attributes toward which they are oriented are changeable. All that I can know can only be delivered by my mind; and my mind delivers an idea of an extended substance. What I really know in knowing this object or any other thing in the world is the nature of my mind—the nature of myself as "res cogitans."

I who seem to perceive this piece of wax so distinctly, do I not know myself . . . with much more *distinctness* and *clearness* . . . since all the reasons which contribute to the knowledge of wax, or any other body whatever, are yet better proofs of the nature of my mind![39]

In demonstrating that the self knows itself better than it knows bodies, Descartes does not presume to show that the self has more being than bodies but rather that the ideas it has of bodies assure it of its own existence rather than of the existence of bodies.[40] The existence of the thinking self is thus seen to be the first metaphysical principle in the order of discovery; it has primacy in the order of discovery but not in the order of being, as we shall see shortly. The nature of this self is seen to be pure thought; it is purely a thinking thing. In knowing anything else in the world, the self knows primarily its own nature. Thus, what the wax object brings clearly to the fore is that the efficacy of the *Cogito* consists in its conformity to the criterion of clarity and distinctness of idea; for clarity and distinctness of idea is the necessary condition of all claims to knowledge that are authentic.

Thus, as Descartes emerges from the Second Meditation, he can be said to have presented two propositions withstanding doubt—two first principles for his metaphysic. The first is the intuition of the necessity of the thinker's existence: the necessary nature of the self as thinking thing. The second is that whatever is true is clearly and distinctly perceived as an idea, and that whatever is clearly and distinctly perceived as idea is true. These two first principles are coimplicated. The first is implicated in the second insofar as any clear and distinct perception of "anything what-ever is at the same time the perception of a quality of ourselves."[41] The second is implicated in the first principle, insofar as the first is an implicit claim for the sovereignty of reason; in the exercise of "cogitatio," thought "intuits its functional finality. . . . Thought as thought necessarily claims and exercises sovereignty whenever it is exercised at all."[42] But a court can be supreme and sovereign only to the extent that it "is illuminated by the light of the law. Similarly, Reason, the thinking thing, exists and is what it is in its existence, because it receives the radiance of ideas and in so doing discovers them."[43] Thus, the *Cogito* has the status of a first principle capable of disclosing the unity of being and thought only because it is an exemplification of clarity and distinctness in idea-tion; in this way, the second metaphysical principle is implicitly exercised and thus implicated in the first. The first two meta-physical principles require each other to be principles. Together they will serve as foundations, Archimedean points of leverage, for anchoring the certitude of scientific knowledge.

Like Galileo and Kepler before him, Descartes considers math-ematics to be the paradigm of clear and distinct knowing. But Descartes' procedure is not that of Kepler and Galileo, that of transmuting knowledge into mathematics—making mathematics the language of scientific knowledge and even the very grammar of the world. Given its metaphysical underpinning, the Cartesian procedure will be to articulate how knowledge in science can be characterized by the kind of certitude possessed of knowledge in mathematics. What mathematics gives—certitude—will be the prime characteristic of the way we know when we truly know; but true knowledge need not be purely and literally mathematical. In knowing the necessity of my own existence as a really existent thinking thing, I already have a proposition that, though extra-mathematical, has the same degree of certitude as the mathematical proposition that two plus two equals four.

But though Descartes has, in the existence of the thinking self, a real existent known with the same degree of certitude found in mathematical propositions, but not simply known as a mathe-matical proposition, his metaphysic, relying as it does on the two first principles thus far discovered, is still incomplete from two standpoints. From the first standpoint, it can be said that Descartes' metaphysical venture is an attempt to yield grounds for the certainty of scientific knowledge and as such attempts to begin groundlessly in total doubt. The actual body of the metaphysic is an attempt to reverse or cure this doubt; it is thus a "catharsis for the fear that we do not stand in an organic relationship to reality. The metaphysic ends when this fear ends . . . when a weight of uncertainty has been counterbalanced by a weight of evidence."[44] Do the two first principles, then, end the uncertainty of the doubt, and completely so? It would appear that they do not manage, even together, to dispel the doubt of an all-powerful deceiver. From this standpoint, the Cartesian metaphysic is not yet complete.

But the metaphysic is incomplete from yet another standpoint. The following criticism could be leveled at the Cartesian metaphysical edifice at this point in its development.

The method employed by Descartes in metaphysics is suitable for investigating selected tracts of reality, but not for answering the question: what is the ultimate structure of reality? The result is that Descartes' metaphysics becomes an investigation of the character of a part of the real, namely, the self. Like Geometry it starts by being selective without being able to account for its selectiveness.[45]

From this standpoint, Descartes' metaphysic, as thus far articulated, is incomplete as an underpinning for scientific knowledge, since it has not yet established the existence of the material world. Unless he can come to some kind of metaphysical statement about this reality that is other-than-the-self, his metaphysic will be hopelessly inadequate for modern science.

Is there one further principle, to be derived metaphysically, that is able to complete his metaphysic from both standpoints? Descartes believes that there is such a principle and that it is the proposition affirming the existence of a veracious God. With this proposition, Descartes hopes at once to overcome completely *all* the doubts raised in the First Meditation and to complete the ground or metaphysical foundation for scientific knowledge of the physical world.

Descartes offers three proofs for the existence of God—two in the Third Meditation and the so-called ontological proof in the

Fifth Meditation. The force of the three proofs is aptly summarized in the following passages from Descartes.

I myself at the end of the Third Meditation have expressly said that this idea (of an infinite substance) is innate in me, or alternatively, that it comes to me from no other source than myself. I admit that we could form this very idea, though we did not know that a supreme being existed, but not that we could do so if it were in fact nonexistent, for on the contrary I have notified that the whole force of my argument lies in the fact that the capacity for constructing such an idea could not exist in me unless I were created by God.[46]

And the whole strength of the argument which I have here made use of to prove the existence of God consists in this, that I recognize that it is not possible that my nature should be what it is, and indeed that I should have in myself the idea of a God, if God did not veritably exist—a God, I say, whose idea is in me, that is, who possesses all those supreme perfections of which our mind may indeed have some idea but without understanding them all, who is liable to no errors or defects and who has none of all those marks which denote imperfection. From this it is manifest that He cannot be a deceiver, since the light of nature teaches us that fraud and deception necessarily proceed from some defect.[47]

From the fact that I cannot conceive God without existence, it follows that existence is inseparable from Him, and hence that He really exists; not that my thought can bring this to pass, or impose any necessity on things, but, on the contrary, because the necessity which lies in the thing itself, i.e., the necessity of the existence of God, determines me to think in this way.[48]

Capable of conceiving God as a truly infinite being, but incapable of conceiving Him as nonexistent or as imperfect in any way and, therefore, as lacking in veracity, he must vanquish all the doubts of the First Meditation.

The Cartesian metaphysical edifice is thus completed with the third and final first principle—the existence of a veracious God—and the three first principles might be said to find their expression in the formulation *Cogito ergo sum, ergo Deus est*.[49] I think, and in thinking I must affirm my existence as a "thinking thing" precisely because clarity and distinctness of idea is the very criterion of truth. But in affirming this, I am constrained to affirm the existence of an infinite, perfect substance precisely because this clear and distinct idea could not have been conceived were there not a really existent, infinitely perfect substance, a supreme subject.

If the first two principles are implicated in each other, the principle that prevents their coimplication from becoming a 'vicious circle' or 'petitio principii' is precisely their ground in the third principle. In Descartes' own words,

> *Explicitly,* we are able to recognize our own imperfection before we recognize the perfection of God. This is because we are able to direct our attention to ourselves before we direct our attention to God. Thus we can infer our own finiteness before we arrive at His infiniteness. Despite this, however, the knowledge of God and His perfection must *implicitly* always come before the knowledge of ourselves and our imperfections. For, in reality, the infinite perfection of God is prior to our imperfections, since our imperfection is a defect and negation of the perfection of God. And every defect and negation presupposes that [of] which it falls short and negates.[50]

Having established the three first principles of his metaphysic, Descartes is now in the position to offer corollaries in metaphysics about the natural world or physical being. "I am" and "God exists" are two propositions that "secure for us for all time the possibility of attaining knowledge of innumerable other propositions whose truth is certain."[51]

But the question is: How can Descartes use these metaphysical first principles as a basis for warranting scientific claims about the natural or physical world? How can he get from these principles to the point where he can secure scientific method in a really existent physical world? This is a very real problem, since in no one of these first principles is the world of nature made explicitly secure. The lesson of these principles, after all, is that the "thing that thinks is and can be constrained by nothing beyond itself save an eternal nature."[52] To resolve this problem we must search afield in other of Descartes' works.

Descartes first gropes toward a solution to this problem in an early work, the *Compendium Musicae.* Dated December 31, 1618, at Breda, this work was not to be published until after his death.[53] Along with many in his age, Descartes was intrigued by music precisely because, while having a complex physical structure lending itself to quantitative analysis, it also possessed an equally complex psychological set of effects. The very fact that music had such an important temporal dimension allowed him to deal with its mathematical proportions and harmonies before attempting an exploration of its sounds.[54] In his analysis, he thus attempts to reduce sensory perceptions to a model lending itself to strict quantitative measurement. Yet he insists that the very emotions aroused by music are in harmony with the mathematical proportion characteristic of the physical or mechanical structure of its sounds. Might not man someday be able to measure the harmonious relationship of the psychological complex of emotions and the mathematical complex of sounds? Descartes was quite confident that he would—provided he followed a sure criterion of measurement. Such a sure criterion in regard to music was pleasure. The pleasure derived in listening to music was an infallible criterion of the harmony of its mathematico-mechanical structure and its emotional-psychological effect.

In the *Rules for the Direction of the Mind,* written about 1629, though published after his death, Descartes follows a line of reasoning very similar to that of the *Compendium,* though in regard to scientific knowledge in general and not musical apperception. Just as pleasure cannot deceive, when used as a criterion to measure the relation between mathematical harmony and psychological effect in music, so also intelligence cannot deceive when used to measure the harmony between the nature of the physical universe and the mathematical propositions at the core of the scientific method.

But how is the valid and correct operation of intelligence in the measurement of this harmony secured? As with music, it is secured by eliminating all that is not pure. The *Rules* emphasizes pure thought just as the *Compendium* emphasized pure musical modes. But the elimination of all that is not pure thought entails precisely the elimination of any dependence on bodily or sensory operation—for here the analogy with music breaks down. Yet, just as when we reflect on the mathematical proportions of sound in music, we reflect on an ideal of pure harmony, so also when we reflect upon the workings of intelligence, devoid of all dependence on sensory operation, we are reflecting on an ideal of perfect harmony and clarity in our knowledge.

Whereas pleasure is the ideal for musical apperception, in scientific knowledge the ideal is unmitigated certitude—perfect logical necessity wherein the opposite of what we know cannot hold. But this logical necessity, the very nature of truth, is found, not outside the process of thinking, but within the very process of thought as clear and distinct ideation. Consequently, to reflect upon "the working and logical procedure of the intellect insofar as it follows its own nature in the process of thinking is to reflect upon the *conditions of truth.*"[55]

In its substance, then, scientific method is nothing more or less than pure thought confronting the conditions of its own truth. Mathematics is the clearest and most obvious example of thought confronting the conditions of its own truth. But science uses what is clearly and distinctly exemplified in mathematics in order to harmonize pure thought and the structure of the physical world. Science does not merely replicate a language that is mathematical but rather brings the certitude exemplified in mathematics to the knowledge of the natural world in such a way that it transcends dependence on empirical observation of things in this natural world. Science becomes *like* mathematics *not in becoming* mathematical but in becoming completely independent, for its existence, of the peculiarity of the subject matter with which it deals. Science becomes pure methodology—knowledge knowing itself in its purity. When thought is pure—when thought is uncorrupted by anything that could compromise its undiluted logical necessity— it becomes the "unique action which in acting knows itself, which consequently has immediate certainty of itself through its relation to itself."[56] What assures that thought stays pure is simply its fidelity to its own pure nature. Descartes' statements on scientific method are simply procedural guidelines for the task of thought's remaining faithful to its own pure nature.

It might be objected that what Descartes is saying here, that it is precisely the purity of thought (i.e., its radical independence of sensory perception) that assures its representation of a really existent natural world of physical bodies, is grossly contradictory. But it is his metaphysical first principles, or more specifically the foundation of the first two of these principles in the third, that disclose a profound truth rather than a contradiction in this matter.

Without the third principle, the observation might hold that physics as the body of accumulated claims about the physical world is purely hypothetical. Yet when we know our thoughts in physics to be pure or certain, though

we do not yet know whether the material world exists, we are nevertheless aware that that about which we think by means of clear and distinct ideas of corporeal things is something other than our ideas, namely, independent essences.[57]

In other words, scientific method, operative in a body of ideas like physics, bears within all its claims the fundamental claim that it is thinking about bodies that would exist even if it were not thinking about them. Although Cartesian metaphysics can never *directly* establish the existence of these bodies, since it can establish no existence independently of pure thought—that is, it can directly establish only the existence of the finite thinking self and the perfect infinite substance—it can *indirectly* offer a support for the claim of science to be dealing with physical bodies that have an existence independent of thought. This indirect support is that since a veracious God exists, since the hypothesis of a malignant deceiving spirit and a deceiving God has once and for all been evaporated, this God would not allow science, which is purely necessary thought, to be deceived in its implicit claim.

An assurance of divine veracity is our ultimate and sufficient warrant for asserting the independent existence of things corresponding to those ideas whose character we clearly and distinctly understand, and which we distinctly perceive to have 'existential reference' beyond themselves.[58]

Thus, between the "mathematical domain of essences and the corporeal portions of Nature's substantiality there obtains a correlation. It is there by divine institution."[59]

As long as thought can keep itself pure, then, it need not worry about its correlation to an independently existing physical nature. For this correlation is indirectly guaranteed it by the principle affirming the existence of a veracious God. The pure intellection of the thinking thing comes in contact with the objects of the corporeal or natural world whose existence has to be presupposed as outside us and very much foreign. It does so, not through the mediation of the senses, but through the mediation of the imagination. As Descartes says in the *Rules,* "if the understanding proposes to examine something that can be referred to the body, we must form the idea of that thing as distinctly as possible in the imagination."[60] The role of imagination will later be given a considerably more important role in knowing by Rousseau, as well as by David Hume's attack on Cartesian certitude. For Descartes, however, imagination remains simply a means for the contact of pure ideation with a physical realm of things whose existence, along with the very contact, is inferred from the existence of a veracious God.

With the metaphysical ground of scientific knowledge now complete, Descartes is in the position to elaborate on the method for that knowledge. Most of his contemporaries and many of his successors were more fascinated by his contributions to the method,[61] in fact, than they were by his metaphysic. Descartes was able to spell out the procedural components of this method in a detail that we do not find in Galileo. There are, in the first place, two broad divisions to the method for Descartes. The method starts with given data and proceeds to break down their signification; this is the division known as *analysis.* It then proceeds to build up a knowledge that is not only certain but genuinely *new,* a knowledge not implicitly contained in the data from which it proceeded; this is the division known as *synthesis.*

The first broad division, analysis, begins with a preliminary survey of the problematic phenomena of nature. It then moves to a second substage, that of enumeration, in which the problematic or presently inexplicable phenomena are divided into a sequence of parts. In its third substage, the analytic division of scientific method constructs deductions proceeding from effects to causes. This third substage culminates in an intellectual intuition or clear and distinct perception of what is implicitly though inchoately contained in the signification of the problematic data. Thus, the analytic arm of the method manages to make clear and distinct, within the compass of a single intuition, what was contained inchoately in the data with which it began.

Beginning with this intellectual intuition in its certainty, the synthetic division of the method proceeds from the result of analysis, endeavoring to expose to the mind the deductive links binding together the problematic phenomena. It attempts to reveal these links as a clear and distinct series. Thus, the first substage of the synthetic arm of the method is deduction. The second substage is an enumeration that proceeds to verify each of the steps involved in this prior deduction. With the verification of each of these steps accomplished, there occurs in the third synthetic substage the drawing of a conclusion. Whereas the analytic arm of the method simply *explicates* clearly and distinctly, and therefore certainly, what was apprehended confusedly in the phenomena in the first place, the synthetic arm of the method transmutes this certitude into a knowledge that is not only perfect, in the sense of being certain, but genuinely new. Whereas analysis yields what is imperfectly known (and therefore not properly known at all) as perfectly known, synthesis yields what is perfectly known as what has not been previously known in any way. In its synthetic thrust, the method yields new truths about a universe that is for all practical purposes unlimited in its being. Yet synthesis can function successfully only after analysis has yielded self-evidence and certitude in its intuition; the conclusions of the full method are certain and novel; their novelty is significant only in terms of their certainty.

The end product of the whole method, in its analytic ground-work and synthetic superstructure, is to merge the whole series of elements and links of the groundwork and superstructure into a single articulated vision.[62] Science aims for a single, simultaneous vision of nature, and in doing so it is redolent of the basic theme of the early modern cosmology and its medieval mystico-philo-sophical context—the experience of the world as sacramental, as a single limitless fabric, infinite (or as Descartes would phrase it, "indefinite" or appearing infinite to man) in its extent and novelty. Scientific method, Descartes hopes to have shown, is infinite, too, in the sense that the novelty it can unearth is inexhaustible. More-over, scientific knowledge when authentic—when faithful to its proper methodology—is perfect knowledge, knowledge in its purity, knowledge characterized by logical necessity. Descartes is, in effect, arguing that man, as the modern subject, although inescapably finite, is characterized by an infinite aspiration that is embodied in scientific method. This infinite aspiration does not mean that man knows the totality of things in the universe but that he can know the whole of what he can examine and analyze by this method.

Scientific method assures the wholeness and integrity of knowledge by creating a kind of *habitus* for knowledge in an indefinite universe, so that the mind can pass surely and confidently through the links of demonstration, hold these links up to consciousness, and collect and concentrate these links into a single vision. In this way, scientific method enables human inquiry to be "pure and attentive . . . such that no doubt whatever can remain as to what it is that this mind conceives."[63] Moreover, the single vision contained in the cumulative conclusion of the method is such that it expresses itself in a set of certain and easy rules such that anyone who obeys them exactly will advance by an orderly effort step by step without waste of mental effort until he has achieved the knowledge of everything that does not surpass his understanding.[64] Descartes thus sees scientific method as assuring the full exercise of the human capacity to know the universe, a capacity that has an unlimited range of possibilities, though it be limited in each individual by the defects of his imagination, emotions, and attention. The method can effectively guarantee that each individual, if he is completely faithful to it, will know all that he is capable of knowing about the phenomena he seeks to know. In effect, though it "be granted that Reason is infallible," inquirers "can err, for inquirers are men."[65] The method when followed exactly promises to keep inquiry as faithful as is possible in any given inquirer to the purity of knowing. But the fidelity will vary from individual to individual, as each individual inquires more or less, is more or less influenced by his emotions and biases, is more or less led astray by his imagination. Yet, for all who would scientifically inquire, the method is a discipline of inquiry that is necessary in order that error may be minimized.[66]

Descartes is left, then, with the following logic to his metaphysical-methodological edifice. Metaphysics by the certainty of its first principles grounds the certitude of scientific method; it guarantees the certitudes of the new truths of scientific knowledge. Scientific method as the new and adequate discourse for the modern universe, in turn, guarantees something; but what it guarantees is not an epistemological but an ethical proposition. Here Descartes verges in the direction of ethical reflection, as did Bruno, although this dimension of his thought was never to be as developed as the metaphysical and epistemological dimensions. The ethical dimension of modern scientific method is eminently practical, that is, to "render ourselves," by it, "the masters and possessors of nature," so that we may "enjoy . . . the fruits of the earth" and preserve our health, which is "the foundation of all other blessings in this life."[67]

Yet the ethical dimension and the metaphysical foundations of the mature scientific method, as offered by Descartes, are purchased at a high cost. One can estimate this cost by recalling that in attaining the certitude of the necessity of the existence of the thinker, thought is in fact attaining a confirmation of the purity of its own essence. In one sense, the very purity of the thinking of God, the infinite substance, is had in the human attainment of certitude. However, the purity of divine thought cannot be fully possessed by man, since, in the case of man, who is a finite component of an indefinite universe, to think is *not,* as it is for God, to create. Man's thought in its purity, unlike divine thought, cannot bring reality or being out of strict nothingness. Consequently, the purity of human thought must suffer that which the primal purity of God's thinking does not and cannot suffer—the alienation of thought from the things of nature. Only God can think in such a fashion that thought has access to the innermost nature of physical things, since His thought is in fact a creation of these things. As Descartes says,

The idea which we have of God teaches us that there is in him only a single activity, entirely simple, and *entirely pure.* This is well expressed by the words of St. Augustine: 'They are so because you see them to be so;' because in God seeing and willing are one and the same thing. . . . In God willing and knowing are a single thing in such a way that by the very act of willing something he knows it and it is only for this reason that such a thing is true.[68]

Deprived of a thought that is simultaneously willing, deprived of an activity entirely pure, man can experience a thought that is pure only in the sense that it knows itself. In man, thought in its purity is forever alienated from the innermost essence of things in nature. It can only know its own self-sufficing harmonization and ordering of things.

Scientific method thus produces a perfect knowledge of the pieces of the universe with which it deals only to the extent that it produces a perfect ordering of these pieces. It never attains a knowledge of these pieces in their innermost essences, that is, in their full existence independently of itself. Thought can be said to attain to a knowledge of matter only to the extent that it can identify matter with concept, more specifically, with the concept of extension. The matter known by man is completely identified with extension; and this identification, as far as man is concerned, constitutes its whole essence. The matter that finite mind knows "can undergo all things and only those things that extension undergoes."[69] The result is that physical things *qua* physical things, natural essences as natural, are alienated from finite thought in its purity. Scientific methodology has no access to the essence of things independent of itself. Modern scientific knowledge, in sum, discloses not the essence of natural things but the essence of finite thought—the essence of human thinking.

Descartes thus attains a metaphysical foundation for scientific method as the paradigmatic way of knowing, but only at the cost of the alienation of human thought from the innermost structures of nature. Human thought is fated to deal not with nature-as-nature but with nature-as-thought. Modern science is fated to deal, not with nature as given or pregiven, but with nature as assimilable to the thinking of the finite human subject—nature as quantifiable or mechanical. The price paid for metaphysically founding the new scientific method in strict certitude is thus a *new bifurcation*. The "'terminal dualism' to which Descartes is driven toward the end of the metaphysical train of thought" may be "welcome in that an economical program for physical science is indicated,"[70] but it spells out a new bifurcation—the peculiarly modern bifurcation of mind and matter. The dualism bequeathed by Descartes will come to replace the classical dualism of ancient thought between the perfect *up* and the imperfect *down*. The Cartesian dualism will become the modern dualism between the *inside* of human consciousness and its *outside*.

Descartes thus manages to reveal the problematic dimension of the infinite universe of modern science. For the problem with the divinized infinite world that spawned the method of modern science is that in its naturalness it is alienated from man as knower. He can know it with certitude but only as an extensional complex, as a mechanism, never as it is in itself. Man is provided with a secure method for knowing in an infinitized universe; but he must become like God and act like God, in a certain sense, in his knowledge of this universe. And, like God, he cannot strictly speaking be a part of the universe he knows.

If Cusa, Kepler, Galileo, and Bruno effected the construction of a cosmology in which the world was infinitized, and to this extent made like God, then it might be said of Descartes that man in his knowing must come to be like God in order to be fully adequate to this universe. Bruno before him had perhaps suggested as much.[71] But Descartes was able to expose the problem in all of this: man can no longer confidently take his place as a being of nature—a being hedged in by the limits of nature, a tissue of nature in touch with the pregiven meaningfulness of nature. Science takes man beyond the world of natural things into a new world of his own making—a world fabricated by pure finite, human intelligence. As Michel Foucault remarks,

The sciences always carry within themselves the project, however remote it may be, of an exhaustive ordering of the world; they are always directed too towards the discovery of simple elements and their progressive combination; and at their centre they form a table on which *knowledge* is displayed in *a system contemporary with itself.* . . . Representations are not rooted in a world that gives them meaning; they open of themselves on to a space that is their own, whose internal network gives rise to meaning.[72]

After Descartes the time for prophetic proclamation of the new universe is forever past; the time for sheer mystical celebration of its plenitude can never be again. Instead, the problematic character of the dialectical scalpel of philosophy passes its shadow over the plenitude of this universe; the specter of bifurcation rents the seamless cosmic garment of the medievals. Yet, when all is said and done, the modern bifurcation exists on a different level from that of the classical. For the ancient mind, bifurcation was written into the fabric of nature; for the modern mind, taking its cue from Descartes, bifurcation is not written into nature; rather, it is the consequence of finite or human cognition of nature. This is a considerable difference—one that permits the modern mind to look upon the Cartesian bifurcation as remediable or capable of being overcome—at least to the extent that the Cartesian presentation of finite cognition is capable of correction or revision. For the classical mind the bifurcation of being into the perfect and the imperfect was irremediable, since it was a distinction implied in the very idea of philosophy as the ancients saw it.[73] The classical bifurcation may have been problematic to the medieval tradition we have described, but it was not, by and large, problematic to the ancient mind itself. The bifurcation of matter and mind, of the inside and outside of human consciousness, however, is supremely problematic to the modern mind itself—at least that portion of it that follows in the wake of Cartesianism.

Descartes thus left the infinite universe supremely problematic to the modern mind. His quest for certitude yielded a strange and perplexing fruit. In securing scientific knowledge in a metaphysic, he left modernity and its logic a problem to its very proponents. It is this peculiarity, perhaps, that prompted Jacques Maritain to remark that "the sense of the worth and rights of what is modern, as modern, springs into life with the Cartesian revolution."[74] The company of those who would continue to work out the logic of modernity would be fated to grapple with the problematic aspect of the infinite universe encountered by Descartes.

THE NEWTONIAN REVISION OF MODERN SCIENTIFIC METHOD

John Herman Randall, Jr., has aptly summarized the importance of Isaac Newton (1642–1727) in the history of modern philosophy by arguing that to understand that history in "the direction it has taken and the compromises at which it has arrived, we must turn to the major innovators in scientific thought," the greatest of which was Newton. For a century after Newton, Randall suggests, "nearly all philosophizing, especially in its more technical aspects, was an attempt to come to terms with, to analyze and criticize, and to extend Newton's thought."[75] Alexandre Koyré concurs when he remarks that in the galaxy of first-rate minds produced by the seventeenth century, the two brightest stars are "Descartes, who conceived the ideal of modern science or its dream—the *somnium de reductione scientiae ad geometriam*"—and Newton, "who firmly put physics back on its own feet."[76] Although Newton cannot be placed on the level of Descartes' metaphysical synthesis, his methodological synthesis is comparable to that of Descartes by its transforming previous discoveries into a coherent whole—a synthesis so impressive that it seemed, "with its independent time and three-dimensional space," destined for quite a while to "endure as the permanent framework within which to study the universe."[77]

The impressiveness of the Newtonian synthesis resides largely in a welding together of the two primary strands of seventeenth-century scientific thought: the mathematical rationalism of the Continental tradition and the physico-mathematical experimental learning cultivated by the Royal Society in England.[78] Such a synthesis is reminiscent of the Galilean attempt to conjoin the mathematico-deductive and experimental dimensions of scientific method.[79] But Newton manages to effect his synthesis on a much grander scale because of his access to a much more mature and precisely formulated methodology than that to which Galileo had access, for Newton walked in the path paved by Descartes. Newton was able to agree with the fundamental substance of Cartesian methodology while at the same time adding on to that methodology some decisive dimensions for the future of the method. He was able to agree with Descartes that only deduction of the kind epitomized in the certitude of mathematics affords intelligibility in scientific pursuits, since it is only such deduction that demonstrates why the phenomena of the natural world are as they are.

The Newtonian acceptance of the mathematico-deductive core of the scientific method is illustrated in the remarks of one of his commentators.

Newton's laws of motion were primarily conceptual in origin and . . . were probably derived directly from Cartesian physics. It cannot be

claimed that these laws were originally supported by or derived inductively from detailed experimental work . . . this lack of empirical support
. . . was not just an accidental feature, for no amount of experimental
work could ever establish a principle of natural motion. . . . The reason
for this . . . derives from the concept of a force. Forces exist only to
explain effects. Since we are at liberty to choose to regard whatever
changes or states we please as natural (that is, as not being effects), it
follows that the forces which we should say are operative in nature
depend upon the choices we actually make. For this reason, then, a
principle of natural motion . . . cannot be an empirical principle. Of
course it does not follow that our choice of principles of natural motion
is arbitrary. On the contrary, it . . . is just such choices which govern
the whole course of physical inquiry. The choices we actually make are
always theory-committed.[80]

If this interpretation is basically correct, then neither experimentation nor empirical observation is the prime guarantor of the
principles of the Newtonian system of nature; rather, the basic
principles of this system are, like those in the Cartesian system,
deductively guaranteed and derived. Koyré, too, suggests as much
when he remarks that the Newtonian experiments *"presuppose* in
an axiomatic fashion a mathematical structure of nature."[81]

The traditional translation of the often quoted phrase from
Newton's *Philosophiae Naturalis Principia Mathematica,* first published in 1687—"Hypotheses non fingo" ("I do not *frame* hypotheses")—has generated an interpretation that militates against
the assertion that Newton accepted the fundamentally mathematico-deductive character of scientific method in the footsteps
of Descartes. But Koyré suggests that this phrase might better be
translated "I do not *feign* hypotheses," which would imply the
refusal to use "fictions or false propositions" as premises of scientific explanation,[82] and not the outright rejection of all deductive
hypothetical constructs. If this is so, Newton's position seems to
emerge rather clearly: "the forces he is dealing with are mathematical forces; or else he is dealing with them only insofar as they
are subjected or subjectable to mathematical treatment."[83]

In underlining Newton's allegiance to the Cartesian assertion
of the fundamentally mathematico-deductive core of the scientific
method, we should not lose sight of the equally fundamental way

in which Newton represents a revision of the Cartesian enterprise in modern science. There are two ways in which Newton represents such a revision: the first regards his revision of the Cartesian method itself; the second regards his revision of the relation of metaphysical issues to scientific method and inquiry. Let us first concentrate on his revision of the Cartesian scientific method.

Unlike Descartes and Kepler before him, Newton rejects the capacity of the mathematical deduction to supply in and of itself a logical proof sufficient to establish a scientific conclusion as factual. The basic character of Newton's revision here is illustrated in the following statement from the *Principia.*

To describe right lines and circles are problems, but not geometrical problems. The solution of these problems is required from mechanics, and by geometry the use of them, when so solved, is shown.[84]

The deductive core of the scientific method establishes a certainty but the full solution of its problems is not had until this certainty is shown to be applicable to natural phenomena. This applicability to natural phenomena, or factuality, is demonstrated by the confirmation lent by experiments. In essence, the experimental analysis of individual instances must serve for Newton as the guarantor of the physical reality of what has been demonstrated with mathematical rigor. This, it would appear, is what Newton had in mind when he wrote that

the proper method for inquiring after the properties of things is to deduce them from experiments. . . . The theory which I propounded was evinced to me, not by inferring 'Tis thus because not otherwise,' that is, not by deducing it only from a confutation of contrary suppositions, but by deriving it from experiments, concluding positively and directly.[85]

Effectively, Newton appears to be saying that certainty is the proper product of the mathematico-deductive core of scientific method, but certainty is not enough, since one certainty might be consistent with a number of other certainties, but not all these certainties need be equally applicable to a given natural phenomenon. Though not envisaging experimental verification as the core of the scientific method, Newton does see it as a necessary component of that method, since it is the prime agent for transforming certain knowledge into *real* knowledge. Thus, he says in the *Principia,*

> In mathematics we are to investigate the quantities of forces with their proportions consequent upon any conditions supposed; then, when we enter upon physics, we compare these proportions with the phenomena of Nature, that we may know what conditions of those forces answer to the several kinds of attractive bodies. And this preparation being made, we argue more safely concerning the physical species, causes, and proportions of the forces.[86]

Experiment does not constitute the core of the method, but it is the instrument by which the method is made to operate more securely and safely in regard to natural phenomena. Experimentation does not establish the certainty of a scientific principle or law but, rather, locates the conformity of a previously established certitude to a sufficiently diverse range of natural phenomena. Thus, the solutions provided by modern scientific knowledge must be expressed in terms of both deductive reason, as guarantor of certainty, and experimentation as confirmation of conformity to the behavior of natural phenomena. Even in works other than the *Principia,* such as the *Opticks,* published in 1704, Newton makes clear the character of his revision of the Cartesian methodology that, in fact, colored all his scientific inquiries. "My design in this book is not to explain the properties of light by hypotheses but to propose and prove them by *Reason and Experiment.*"[87]

Yet, it must be emphasized, since experimentation is a confirmation in actuality of a certainty in theory, experimentation is not antithetical to deductive generalization. Rather, experimentation is a necessary adjunct to deductive generalization; its mission is to approach and attain generalizations of a kind. In other words, experimental verification is not opposed to deductive inference as the particular is opposed to the general. On the contrary, experimentation, when itself perfected, takes the generalizations of deductive inference and extends and perfects them.

Furthermore, Newton is quite aware that experimentation is a fallible instrument—that further experiments might very well diminish the reliability of the conclusions of present or past experiments. But experimentation, if sufficiently diverse, continuous or ongoing, and when perfected, is capable of correcting its own conclusions.

And although the arguing from experiments and observations by induction be no demonstration of general conclusions, yet it is the best way of arguing which the nature of things admits of, and may be looked upon as so much the stronger by how much the induction is more general. And if no exception occurs from phenomena, the conclusion may be pronounced generally. But if at any time afterward any exception shall occur from experiments, it may then begin to be pronounced with such exceptions as occur. By this way of analysis we may proceed from compounds to ingredients and from motions to the forces producing them, and in general from effects to their causes and from particular causes to more general ones, till the argument end in the most general.[88]

In experimental philosophy we are to look upon propositions inferred by general induction from phenomena as accurately or very nearly true till such time as other phenomena occur, by which they may either be made more accurate or liable to exceptions. Those which are not yet sufficiently precise must be . . . revised by means of the phenomena of nature more fully and accurately observed.[89]

Far from being a rival of deduction, then, experimentation is its helpmate; far from being a mere addendum to deduction that operates extrinsically, experimentation expands the generality and reliability of deduction by being self-corrective.

The Newtonian revision of Cartesian method is considerable. What Newton does is to expand the Cartesian method of analysis and synthesis by the inclusion of a third movement—that of experimental verification. In this way, mathematico-deductive knowledge is the purveyor of intelligibility in scientific knowledge only to the extent that it issues in an experimental framework capable of verifying certain principles as *real descriptions* of nature in all the variety of its phenomena.

With Descartes, Newton is in clear agreement that analysis and synthesis, in that order, are necessary to scientific method. "As in mathematics, so in natural philosophy, the investigation of difficult things by the method of analysis ought ever to precede the method of composition."[90] But, as Roger Cotes in his preface to the second edition of the *Principia* is careful to point out, Newton does not simply derive "the causes of all things from the most simple principles possible" but goes on to "assume nothing as a principle that is not proved by phenomena."[91] Newton himself points out that after the operation of the analytic-synthetic divisions of the method, there is still need for a final appeal to experience, an appeal not necessitated in the Cartesian scheme, even in regard to the most fundamental trait of matter in the Cartesian scheme, extension.

We no other way know the extension of bodies than by our senses, nor do these reach it in all bodies; but because we perceive extension in all that are sensible, therefore we ascribe it universally to all others also. That abundance of bodies are hard, we learn by *experience*; and because the hardness of the whole arises from the hardness of the parts, we therefore justly infer the hardness of the undivided particles not only of the bodies we feel but of all others.[92]

In this manner, the analytic and synthetic thrusts of the scientific method require an additional impetus to be driven to the completion of the logic of science, and this impetus is a final appeal to experience in the form of experimental verification. In this way, Newton's

method was no less important than his results. The brilliant idea that, in virtue of the principle of actuality, what is true in narrower spheres of experience may be extended to wider is only the first step. The next step is the stringent deduction of the consequences contained in the idea which has been posited. While the third step is the proof that that which is thus found to follow logically from the idea is in agreement with experience.[93]

The second major Newtonian revision of the Cartesian enterprise is his revision of the relation of metaphysical issues to scientific method. Descartes, of course, explicitly saw the need for the construction of a new metaphysical foundation for scientific knowledge to replace the Aristotelian metaphysic. In his mind, the issues of scientific method and its metaphysical underpinning were intimately related; the former could never function securely and live up to its full potential until the latter was completed. Newton, on the other hand, appears concerned to keep the issues of method and the issues of metaphysics and religion distinct, at least up to a certain point. Newton was

a devoutly religious man, and in many ways a mystic, but he did not believe that religion or mystery had anything to do with the mathematical laws of planetary motion, although they had to do with the First Cause.[94]

Whereas Descartes conceived scientific method as presupposing certain metaphysical principles (which could be articulated and demonstrated), Newton saw the method as presupposing no metaphysic for its exercise but as leading up to certain metaphysical and religious realizations. This Newtonian revision of the Cartesian conception of the relation of metaphysics and scientific method is well illustrated in Newton's approach to the existence of God. Whereas Descartes approaches God's existence from the viewpoint of the isolated thinking subject, Newton approaches His existence in a more traditional (almost Scholastic) fashion from the order of nature. Whereas Descartes grounds scientific method in the guarantee provided by God's existence, Newton sees God's existence as the final cause—the very bank upon which the waters of scientific method wash. Thus, Newton remarks in the *Principia,*

In bodies we see only their figures and colors, we hear only the sounds, we touch only their outward surfaces, we smell only the smells and taste the savors; but their inward substances are not to be known either by our senses or by any reflex act of our own minds; much less then have we any idea of the substance of God. We know him only by his most wise and excellent contrivances of things and final causes; we admire him for his perfections; but we reverence and adore him on account of his dominion: for we adore him as his servants; and a god without dominion, providence, and final causes is nothing else but fate and nature. Blind metaphysical necessity, which is certainly the same always and everywhere, could produce no variety of things. All that diversity of natural things which we find suited to different times and places could arise from nothing but the ideas and will of a Being necessarily existing.[95]

One is hardly justified in concluding from this that the existence of God is any less important for Newton than it was for Descartes. That existence simply functions in a different way in their syntheses: in Descartes as the ground of scientific method, in Newton as the outcome of the exercise of scientific method; in

Descartes as the ultimate guarantor of certitude or as the ultimate first principle, in Newton as the final cause of nature. In Descartes God's existence is discovered from the self's encounter with the certitude of its own existence; in Newton God's existence is discovered from the order of nature. Once again, Newton remarks,

It is the dominion of a spiritual being which constitutes a God: a true, supreme, or imaginary dominion makes a true, supreme, or imaginary God. And from his true dominion it follows that the true God is a living, intelligent, and powerful Being; and from his other perfections, that he is supreme, or most perfect. He is eternal and infinite, omnipotent and omniscient; that is, his duration reaches from eternity to eternity; his presence from infinity to infinity; he governs all things, and knows all things that are or can be done. He is not eternity and infinity, but eternal and infinite; he is not duration or space, but he endures and is present . . . and by existing always and everywhere, he constitutes duration and space.[96]

The Newtonian revision of the Cartesian conception of the relation of metaphysics to scientific method amounts, then, to a reversal of the Cartesian elimination of final causality from the universe of modern science. In restoring final causality to nature, Newton manifests a "deep intuition for the limits of the purely mechanical interpretation of nature."[97] The book of nature may be a complex of mechanisms, but it requires the active interference of the more-than-mechanical to be sustained, for it reveals

God . . . who not only had made the world clock, but who continuously had to supervise and tend it in order to mend its mechanism when needed . . . thus manifesting his active presence and interest in his creation.[98]

Yet, in his revision of the Cartesian conception of the relation of metaphysics to methodology, and in restoring a significant status to the sensible largely in the guise of experimental verification—a status largely ignored by Descartes in his reduction of the sensible to the innate idea of extension—Newton is nonetheless unable to overcome the Cartesian alienation of the knower from the innermost essences of nature. Newton, in fact, was quite explicit in pointing out that the scientific method was incapable of probing into the ultimate nature and essence of natural things.

Even in regard to the principle of gravity, he admitted that he had "not been able to discover the cause of those properties of gravity from phenomena."[99] And in a letter to Bentley he observes,

You sometimes speak of gravity as essential and inherent to matter. Pray do not ascribe that notion to me, for the cause of gravity is what I do not pretend to know.[100]

Even in regard to the key principle of Newton's physical system of the natural world, the principle of gravity, the ultimate nature or formal essence of this principle remains forever unknown. Scientific method is capable of attaining perfection of knowledge in regard to gravity but not a completed knowledge of its innermost nature—only a completed knowledge of its behavior.[101] Science affords a perfect description of the behavior of nature, clearly deducible from human experience of nature and experimentally verifiable. But scientific knowledge yields knowledge of nature only as it presents itself to man, that is, in its behavior, in its phenomenal status, and not as it is in its innermost nature and as it exists apart from man's perception of it. In fact, Newton goes so far as to present the natural world apart from the human perceiving apparatus as a purely mechanical and dead world—soundless, scentless, and colorless. It is precisely this Newtonian view that prompted the poet Addison to say that

Things would make but a poor appearance to the eye if we saw them only in their proper figures and motions. And what reason can we assign for their exciting in us many of those ideas which are different from anything which exists in the objects themselves (for such are light and colours) were it not to add supernumerary ornaments to the universe and make it more agreeable to the imagination.[102]

Although intuiting limitations to Cartesian mechanism and restoring final causality to nature, Newton is still unable to heal the breach between the inside and outside of human consciousness—the breach discovered by Descartes. Even in his revision of the Cartesian enterprise, Newton could not escape the basic pull of Cartesian mechanism; human, finite consciousness is still left alienated from the innermost nature of natural things and can know them only in their phenomenal status—their mechanical manifestations. There is something, as Koyré remarks,

for which Newton, or better to say not Newton alone, but modern science in general, can still be made responsible; it is the splitting of our world in two . . . two worlds: this means two truths. Or no truth at all. This is the tragedy of the modern mind which 'solved the riddle of the universe' but only to replace it by another riddle, the riddle of itself.[103]

Despite its inability to completely overcome Cartesian mechanism or Cartesian dualism, the Newtonian revision of the Cartesian edifice represents a considerable advance in the maturation of modern scientific method. Just as in Descartes, the literalness of Galileo's emphasis on a mathematical language for nature is loosened in favor of a thinking characterized by the kind of certitude exemplified in mathematics,[104] so also in Newton the transcending of sensible nature by the Cartesian subject is qualified so as to permit a reference to sensible experience largely in the form of experimental verification. As A. Rupert Hall remarks,

Newton stated explicit principles of scientific method, but not less influential was his implicit exemplification of a way of proceeding in science that was at once theoretical and experimental, mathematical and mechanical.[105]

As such, Newton stands as the inheritor of the mathematically oriented emphasis of Copernicus, Kepler, and Descartes and of the experimental orientation of Bacon, Gilbert, and Harvey. Yet Newton melds and blends these two traditions in such a way that the mathematico-deductive method—if no longer, as in the first tradition, the sole and sufficient condition of scientific intelligibility—is nonetheless, unlike the second tradition, the necessary condition of scientific intelligibility.

The Newtonian revision of Cartesian methodology, the Newtonian reconciliation of the experimental outlook and the mathematico-deductive powers of the human mind, would come to serve as a focal point of interest for many of the philosophers who would follow. One dimension of his thought would be developed by British philosophers from John Locke onward and would reach its apex in the naturalistic empiricism of David Hume.[106] The other aspect would be developed by German physicists like Euler and "led to the imposing critical philosophy of Immanuel Kant, probably the most profound analysis of the assumptions of Newtonian mechanics."[107]

THE LEIBNIZIAN POSTSCRIPT TO
MODERN SCIENTIFIC METHOD

Gottfried Wilhelm von Leibniz (1646–1716) lived through one of the most significant periods in the formation of modern Europe, his active life corresponding with the age of Louis XIV. In many of the great political and social changes of this period he was the adviser of princes, the active diplomat, and the trusted counsellor.[108]

His practical and philosophical interests were not, in fact, unrelated. Relying heavily on the Cartesian formulation of the metaphysical foundations of modern scientific method, he offered suggestions for the construction of a universal artificial language that "would contain the true organon of a general science of everything that is subject matter for human reasoning"[109] and that, he hoped, would further the attainment of peace and order throughout the world. His intellectual interests were thus intimately connected with his practical ventures to reconcile Catholics and Protestants, and later Lutherans and Calvinists.[110] The furtherance of science, he hoped, would aid the cause of peace, and the creation of a universal language for all the sciences would further the advance of scientific method by averting the fragmentation of knowledge.[111]

Yet, like Newton, for all his originality, he chose to articulate the logic of modernity by elaborating on the massive Cartesian metaphysico-methodological edifice. The influence of Descartes on Leibniz dates roughly from his encounter with the intellectual life of Paris in 1672 where he first met Descartes' critic, Antoine Arnauld.[112] Of this influence, Leibniz would say that

I esteem . . . Descartes almost as much as one can esteem any man, and though, there are among his opinions some which seem false to me, and even dangerous, this does not keep me from saying that we owe nearly as much to Galileo and to him in philosophical matters as to the whole of antiquity.[113]

Like Descartes, Leibniz too is determined to "search out that which, as immediately and intuitively certain, forces itself upon the mind as self-evident and by its combinations grounds all derived knowledge."[114] Yet, unlike Descartes, there is in Leibniz a deep-seated sensitivity to and assimilation of the previous history of philosophical thought. As John Dewey remarks in his study of Leibniz,

Descartes was profoundly convinced that past thought had gone wrong, and that its results were worthless. Leibniz was as profoundly convinced that its instincts had been right, and that the general idea of the world which it gave was correct.[115]

James Collins, in fact, observes that there is hardly a page of Leibniz's writings that fails to reveal the "record of his conscientious and thorough reading of other sources in philosophy and theology, mathematical and physical science, political and social theories."[116]

In this way, it might be said, Leibniz signals the point of greatest maturation in reflection on the new scientific method, since he is able to forthrightly recognize and utilize the value of past philosophical sources without compromising the radical novelty of the new method. So much is this the case that of all modern thinkers thus far considered Leibniz appears most open to the value and utility of the ancient philosophers themselves. Unlike virtually all of his modern predecessors, he is no longer in the position of reacting or polemicizing against the ancient philosophers. He is quite clear on this in his description of his earliest encounters with the ancients; speaking of himself in the third person, he says,

But when he passed to the moderns, he felt disgust at the swollen periods of empty talk, or broken patchwork of borrowed opinions . . . there was no grace about them, nothing strong or vigorous, no bearing upon life. . . . But the thoughts of the ancients had been large and manly; they stood out strenuous and commanding, and embraced as it were in a picture the whole field of human life.[117]

Leibniz further specifies the value of the ancient philosophy in terms of the importance of that one ancient philosopher most reacted against by his modern predecessors.

The traditional Aristotelian doctrine of the forms or entelechies . . . was justifiably regarded as puzzling and appeared scarcely to be understood by the authors themselves. Accordingly, we believe that this philosophy, which has been accepted for centuries, is not to be discarded in general, but only stands in need of an elucidation which may make it consistent as far as possible. We shall . . . develop it with new truths.[118]

The influence of Aristotle is most evident in Leibniz's concern with the problem of the living world, in his attempt to bring to consciousness the vital principle itself.[119] Like Aristotle before him, Leibniz emphasizes, along with the category of life, the importance of individual substance.[120] Yet it must be said that his very interest in the ancients is but a sign of his mature confidence in the basic correctness of the logic of modernity. He was, in the end,

prepared eagerly to welcome the new philosophy which was then superseding, though more slowly in Germany than elsewhere, the now debased and exhausted philosophy of the schools. He speaks of the pleasure . . . with which as a young man he read the specimens of better philosophizing furnished by Kepler, and Galilei, and Descartes.[121]

Leibniz is among the first modern philosophers, then, to attempt to harmonize the ancients and the moderns—his attempt rivaled only by that of Baruch Spinoza (1632–77). But their attempted harmonization is largely in terms of further assuring the ultimate truth of the logic of modernity.[122] Given his position, we would expect Leibniz to be in disagreement with certain aspects of the Cartesian formulation and the Newtonian revision of modern scientific method, while at the same time in basic agreement with the major motifs of this formulation and revision. Let us begin by examining some of the more significant differences between the Leibnizian contribution and the Newtonian revision of scientific method.

In Newton's mechanical universe, God is allowed to enter for the task of providentially reforming the system of the natural world when the mechanisms of this world have so far run down as to require reformation. For Newton, God descends into the natural world to become a category alongside of other categories. The world is spoken of as a "sensorium Dei"—a bodily manifestation of God. With space and time metaphorically treated as God's sensorium, the more there is of matter the more opportunities does God have to exercise his infinite power and wisdom.[123] God becomes surety for the correction of rundown in a mechanical universe.

Leibniz objects to the role designated for God by Newton; for him God is what Alexandre Koyré calls the God of the "Sabbath Day"[124] who, having finished His work of Creation and found it good, has no more to act upon it but only to conserve it in being. The

Newtonian world—a clock running down—requires a constant renewal by God of its energetic endowment; the Leibnizian one, by its very perfection, rules out any intervention of God into its perpetual motion.[125]

Unlike the Newtonian revision of modern scientific method, then, there is no substantial need in the Leibnizian contribution to the maturation of this method for the notion of God as a corrective measure for the operation of the universe. For God "calls the world into existence all at once; He does not need . . . to forge chains between the successive parts of it" in order for each part to "follow on that which goes before, when once He has brought the first into being."[126]

Leibniz can argue this way precisely because of one of his major points of disagreement with the Cartesian metaphysico-methodological edifice and one of his major points of agreement with the Aristotelian metaphysic, namely, his emphasis on the organic— on the category of vitality. Living individual substances may depend on God for thier creation, but they do not depend on God in the same degree for their continuance; the organic dimension of nature is given a far greater role in Leibniz than it was given in the reflection of Descartes and Newton. The result is a certain qualified self-sufficiency for the universe as a whole.

How does Leibniz arrive at this idea of organism, of life, which is at the root of his thought[127] and that represents an important modification of the Cartesian foundations and of the Newtonian revision of mature scientific method? His starting point appears to be a rejection of the Cartesian notion of matter as reducible to the idea of extension. As he remarks,

I do not believe extension alone constitutes substance, since its conception is incomplete. . . . For we can analyze it into plurality, continuity, and coexistence (that is, simultaneous existence of parts). Plurality has to do with number, and continuity with time and motion; coexistence on the contrary is the only thing that approaches extension. . . . Hence I believe that our thought of substance is perfectly satisfied in the conception of force and not in that of extension.[128]

Leibniz is thus led to treat the extended not as the root component of matter but as a "phenomenon grounded in that whose nature it is to be active, or display force, but not to be extended."[129] Left with the notion, then, that the real is the active, that substance is activity, Leibniz is driven to the conclusion that the ubiquitous presence of motion in the universe requires, for the correlation and unification of these motions, that there be the guiding presence of life.[130] The unification of the diverse forces in the universe requires the underlying presence of the living; Leibniz tries to capture this idea by the use of the term "monad" based as it is on the Greek work *monas,* meaning "unity" or "what is one."[131] The nature of the monad is life itself, and the monad is a particular, an individual; but its entire content—its objective reality—is the summation of the universe which it represents.[132]

As a unifying concept, the monad allows Leibniz to address himself to nature as a unity; each monad as a vital principle is developing either in a forward direction or in a backward direction. Insofar as it develops backwardly, it is giving "law to new and less developed monads" whose spiritual activity is in "an undeveloped and hence partial and limited condition"; here the monad's development is productive of sensation and the corporeal.[133] Insofar as it develops forwardly or increases its activity and vitality, the monad strives to reach the ultimate point where its activity is turned back upon itself and it becomes not only a mirror of the universe but knows itself as a mirror of the universe; here the monad develops into the soul of man.[134]

Given this viewpoint, Leibniz sees the spiritual and the mechanical as more than merely two opposed kinds of existence—for the mechanical embodiments of the monad in sensation and

matter have within themselves the ideal or the rational in potency.[135] Matter or the corporeal emerges as a revelation of the
inability of substance to realize the full spiritual character of reality.
"It is spirit apprehended in a confused, hesitating, and passive
manner."[136] But this confusion and passivity is necessary for the
universe as it exists, for the monads of this universe are necessarily
involved in linear gradation.[137] John Dewey aptly summarizes the
Leibnizian monadic principle in its most powerful implications.

Every created or finite being may be regarded as matter or as spirit,
according as it is accounted for by its external relations, as the reasons
for what happens in it are to be found elsewhere than in its own explicit
activity, or according as it shows clearly in itself the reasons for its own
modifications, and also accounts for changes occurring in other beings.
The externally conditioned is matter; the internally conditioned, the self-
explanatory, is self-active or spirit. Since all external relations are finally
dependent on organic [relations]; since the ultimate source of all explanations must be that which is its own reason; since the ultimate source
of all activity must be that which is self-active—the final reason or source
of matter is spirit.[138]

Matter is always "correlative to confused ideas," but as these ideas
get clarified, matter, to this extent, diminishes so that "to God
who is wholly reason it must entirely vanish."[139] Attaining this
pure rationality in the soul of man, the monad becomes what
Leibniz calls an "image of God," but even in its confused state
where it is productive of matter, it remains what he calls an "image
of the universe."[140]

Although Leibniz justifies the monadic principle in terms of its
rational consistency, starting from what he takes to be the inadequacy of the Cartesian notion of matter, reduced as that matter
is to the bare idea of extension, he nonetheless held that the principle had certain empirical supports. As Herbert Wildon Carr
remarks,

These principles are based on reason. They are logical deductions which
can be tested at every step by the inner light of intellect reflecting on
experience, guided by the law of contradiction and the principle of sufficient reason. But they are also confirmed by observation and experiment. Leibniz pointed to this as the peculiar triumph of scientific research.

Swammerdam and Leeuwenhoek and others, by the new invention, the microscope, are able to show us worlds within worlds, and there is every reason to infer that with better microscopes this would hold to infinity.[141]

Leibniz thus takes a decisive turn away from his modern predecessors from Copernicus to Galileo; instead of arguing for the infinity and plenitude of nature from its outward and extensive infinity, he argues for it on the basis of its infinite inward complexity and plenitude. Like Galileo, who paid great heed to the experimental verification provided by the telescope, Leibniz pays great heed to experimental verification—but in the form of the microscope. Not accidentally, the telescope appears to disclose a universe that is relatively lifeless—a great mechanical complex; but the microscope seems to reveal a universe that is a teeming inner chain of vital and organic beings. In disclosing worlds within worlds, the microscope confirmed Leibniz in his speculation that all these worlds, "however great or small in relation to our normal world of sense experience, are yet of the same size, coordinated on the same principle, by axes of coordination which are invariable."[142]

The kind of postscript to the mature modern scientific method offered by Leibniz constitutes, then, a new emphasis—one not to be found in the foundation-work of Descartes and in the revisionary work of Newton. The emphasis is on the organic; as Leibniz remarks, "in every particle of the universe a world composed of an infinity of creatures is contained."[143] Leibniz's classic formulation is found in the *Monadology*.

Thus there is nothing uncultured, sterile or dead in the universe, no chaos, no disorder, though this may be what appears. It would be about the same with a pond seen from a distance: you would perceive a confused movement, a squirming of fishes, if I may say so, without discerning the single fish.

Thus every portion of matter can be conceived as a garden full of plants or as a pond full of fish. But every branch of the plant, every limb of the animal, every drop of its humors, is again such a garden or such a pond.[144]

Yet, in calling Leibniz a postscript to that segment of the logic of modernity concerned with the formulation of the methodology of scientific knowledge, the Leibnizian contribution is portrayed, not as a radical overhauling of Cartesianism, but as another alteration, another variation on the Cartesian motif. It would seem that just as Newton, in arguing for the role of experimental verification, remains faithful to the fundamental role of mathematical deduction as the necessary condition of intelligibility in the Cartesian edifice, so also Leibniz, in arguing for the pervasive organic dimensions of nature, remains faithful to the fundamentally mechanical character of the Cartesian universe. "It is a commonplace," remarks Louis Couturat, "to oppose Leibniz's *dynamism* to the *mechanism* of Descartes"; but this distinction cannot be justified, for Leibniz is "as much a mechanist as Descartes." If "he modifies the formulas of Cartesian mechanism, he nonetheless entirely accepts its principle."[145]

It may be, as Dewey says of the Leibnizian synthesis, that the words of Lotze apply to it—that "the mechanical is unbounded in range, but is subordinate in value."[146] Nonetheless, matter is necessarily associated with the mechanical as in Descartes and Newton—despite Leibniz's organicistic sympathies. Effectively, the rational, though correlative to the material in a way just not found in Descartes, still lies at the core of the scientific method, preventing the method's access to natural things *qua* natural, to material things as material. Thus, Leibniz is saddled with the same bifurcation of matter and mind, natural things and human consciousness, as Descartes and Newton. He is left with a material world that can be only indirectly inferred and whose existence must remain as insecure in his synthesis as it did in the metaphysic of Descartes. Leibniz, to his credit, was acutely aware of this.

But it must be confessed that even if we take them all together the marks of real phenomena hitherto adduced are not demonstrative, though they have the highest probability, or, as is commonly said, produce moral certainty; but they do not make a metaphysical certainty, so that the assumption of the contrary should imply contradiction. Therefore it cannot be absolutely proved by any argument that there are bodies.[147]

Since natural things are but momentary collocations of monadic principles, since the material thing *qua* material is unknowable and undemonstrable as to the certainty of its existence, since as Leibniz says "things . . . are not causes but only occasions" that can "only receive but not produce or elicit any change,"[148] Leibniz is fated to repeat the Cartesian conclusion that nature in its givenness is to be translated into the significance of the immaterial stuff of thought and rationality.

Forced back upon the Cartesian proposition that necessity can be had only in thinking, more specifically deductive thinking, Leibniz, though modifying Cartesian mechanism by addressing himself to an organic nature, is nonetheless impelled to treat the organic as a function of pure rationality. The monad, in being the basic unit of life, is also the basic unit of consciousness striving for ultimate clarity or rationality. Life is reducible to the striving for the pure translucence of rationality. And so, like the subatomic particles of present-day atomic theory, which his synthesis fore-shadows in a remarkable fashion, the Leibnizian monadic principle testifies to the demise of the *object* or thinglike character of nature; like the subatomic particle, the monad refuses definition "by its spatial position and outlines" and accepts definition only "by the range of its effects as the centre of energies of infinite circumference."[149]

In this way, the pillars of the Cartesian metaphysical foundations for modern scientific knowledge remain intact, surviving the re-visionism of both Newton and Leibniz: man knows nature as a presentation of his rationality. The Cartesian ground of certitude and the very price for its founding—the alienation of the knowing agent from the innermost essences of nature—remain as inescap-able parameters for the thinking of Newton and Leibniz.

Like Newton, Leibniz would be influential for those who would follow him in the articulation of the logic of modernity, especially for the thought of Immanuel Kant.[150] But with Leibniz, the great Galilean-Cartesian-Newtonian grappling with the question, *How can I know?* in the infinite universe is brought to a close. What would follow Leibniz would not be further wrestling with this question but, rather, encounter with the more modest question, *How much can I know?* in this universe. The philosophers who would entertain this question—Locke, Berkeley, and Hume—could afford to be even more problematic in their stance and less prophetic about the infinite universe and its implications than Descartes. With the metaphysical foundations of the world view of modernity clearly set out, philosophy could afford to look with a less comprehensive but more detailed eye at the philosophical accomplishments of the new age.

4

THE EMERGENCE OF THE MODERN PROBLEM OF KNOWLEDGE

D ESCARTES was aware of the great proportions of his task—
that of laying the metaphysical foundations of modern science—when he likened himself to Archimedes in search of a fixed
fulcrum for moving the earth from its orbit.[1] With the Archimedean task of analytically and critically examining the new kind
of knowledge, entailed by the Copernican universe,[2] now completed, philosophy could afford to shift its focus from the question
of how man knows to the question of the limits of his knowledge
in this universe.[3] The result of this change, of course, will be a
shift from metaphysical system-building to more modest but necessary epistemological chores.

Locke provides the keynote address for a "century of great
epistemologies"[4] that would temporarily relieve philosophy of its
Archimedean labors. In his efforts to tidy up the Cartesian edifice,
he shifts the emphasis from the objective ramifications of scientific
method to the psychological ramifications of the practitioner of
this method. Taking his cue from Locke, Berkeley, by virtue of
his attempt to overcome the Cartesian dualism of mind and matter,
is disposed to rearrange the furnishings of the Cartesian edifice.
And Hume, paring down, as he does, the claims of Cartesian
certitude, is inclined to remove a number of these furnishings.

Yet none of these epistemologists destroys the Cartesian edifice
as such; rather, they attempt to resolve its most problematic aspects in its role as the metaphysical foundation for the modern
universe. Their epistemological work, in fact, serves as a bridge

between the *first* metaphysical foundations (in regard to modern science) provided by Descartes and the *second* metaphysical foundations (in regard to the nature of man) provided by Kant. The work of these epistemologists will prove to be something quite removed from a metaphysical failure of nerve or a depletion of speculative energy in the logic of modernity.

LOCKE: PSYCHOLOGY AS A
MODERN SCIENCE

In the face of such "masterbuilders" as Newton with their "mighty designs" for "advancing the sciences," John Locke (1632–1704) conceived of himself as an "underlabourer" who was content to remove "some of the rubbish that lies in the way to knowledge."[5] Devoting himself to finding out "how far the understanding can extend its view, how far it has faculties to attain certainty, and in what cases it can only judge and guess,"[6] Locke believed that it was of great utility for the sailor to "know the length of his line, though he cannot with it fathom all the depths of the ocean."[7] Not so much a part of philosophy as it is a preliminary to it, Locke's work is intended as an examination of the instrument, that is, the human understanding, whereby we erect the philosophical structure.[8] The prior developments of the logic of modernity impressed upon Locke the great power of, and the "ready submission" demanded by, the ideas in men's minds; and he thought that it was of the utmost importance that "great care should be taken of the understanding, to conduct it right in the search of knowledge, and in the judgments it makes."[9]

By temperament, Locke was averse to "mysticism, enthusiasm, and . . . all private visionary insights,"[10] and inclined toward an "equable commonsense," which is "modest when it is most original"—a kind of "inspired pedestrianism."[11] Yet Locke's style of writing has a complexity that suggests that it is no mere reflection of his temperamental proclivities. Especially in *An Essay Concerning Human Understanding,* first published in 1690, we find "many different tones from a reduced factual style to a loose anecdotal" style; passages characterized by tight formal analysis follow passages of easy exposition; and we even find "interior monologues . . . and self-analyses."[12] This stylistic complexity suggests a certain complexity in his intentions which were not merely reflections of his temperamental inclinations but were also, and more importantly, based on a realization that, by limiting himself to the problem of the extent and limitations of knowledge, he would discover something unrealized by his modern predecessors about "the essential nature of knowledge"[13] itself.

Yet, like these predecessors, Locke has a fervent, although unprotested faith in the revolutionary import of modern scientific method.[14] Among the "first books which gave him a relish of philosophical studies were those of Descartes,"[15] and his early notebooks were filled with "bibliographies of Descartes and the Cartesians, with practical plans for studying Descartes himself."[16] Although, like Newton, Locke was influenced by the "virtuosi" of the British Royal Society,[17] the Cartesian influence is visible in his assumption that "some sort of epistemological credential can be provided for knowledge by tracing it back to its origins," and it might even be said that "there is something alien to empiricism in Locke's whole aim of determining *in advance* the limits of human knowledge."[18] Like Descartes, furthermore, Locke accepts "the antithetical nature of the distinction between consciousness and the phenomena of the external world," arguing that the connection between body and mind is something that we can recognize on the grounds of experience but which we cannot understand.[19]

But, for all of Locke's affinity with the Cartesian venture, he did not seek, as Descartes did, metaphysical surety for the physical sciences, nor did he attempt to examine "by what motions of our spirits, or alterations of our bodies, we come to have any sensation by our organs, or any ideas in our understandings."[20] Instead, Locke attempted

for the first time to work out a theory of knowledge from the standpoint of conscious experience. Instead of adopting the point of view of the conscious subject as a temporary expedient, destined to be superseded as soon as the foundations of his system had been laid, Locke sought to make it the permanent centre from which his survey of the whole contents of knowledge should be taken.[21]

The consequence of Locke's epistemology was thus a transformation of the Cartesian notion of self-consciousness. Descartes had looked for the principle of science within the conscious self or *ego* where thought and existence were conjoined,[22] but he used this conscious self to ground the subject matter of science in terms of this self's knowledge of its own self-sufficing harmonization and ordering of things.[23] Locke, on the other hand, by virtue of his emphasis on sensible experience—a continuation and intensification of the Newtonian emphasis on experiment—made the Cartesian self into the newest object of scientific investigation and method. By directing traditional psychology into the realms of observation, experiment, and the study of sensation, Locke began the process of liberating psychology from its moorings in traditional speculative philosophy,[24] thereby providing the fertile soil for the beginnings of modern empirical or scientific psychology.

Although the *Essay* is not primarily a psychological work, since "Locke's purpose in it is the examination of the . . . extent of human knowledge," Locke can be "rightly regarded as the father of English psychology."[25] Whereas Descartes stopped at the definition of the modern subject as a *thing* that thinks, a "res cogitans,"[26] Locke treated this subject as a source of energy, a *power*. To the extent that the human self or mind can be treated as a power, rather than as a thing, it becomes like the physical universe when it is treated as a power and not simply as a thing or sum of finite things—it becomes visible to the eye of modern scientific method, a newfound object for the exercise of that method. Locke could effect this transformation by viewing reason, not simply as a faculty that "guides action directly through its own power," but as a faculty "operating through the other faculties," when it mixes itself "with the passions in such a way as to show the relative value of the objects towards which they are directed, and thus often succeeds in transforming the passions themselves."[27] Since the human mind "has sympathies and antipathies as well as the body,"[28] there is a sense in which the mind is assimilated to corporeal nature and is thereby capable, like corporeal nature, of being subject matter for the new scientific method.

Furthermore, to the extent that Descartes conceives of rationality as constituting a self that is basically a *thing,* he still persists in thinking of reason as something antecedently given. Locke, on the other hand, to the extent that he conceives of rationality as constituting a self that is basically a *power*, thinks of reason not as antecedently given but as "somehow being slowly, painfully generated" out of man's search for the maximum of security in society—a search by which "man may eventually construct a dominion over nature and himself."[29] Descartes, of course, had implied that modern science takes man beyond the antecedently given status of nature into a new world of his own making, a world fabricated by pure, finite, human intelligence.[30] But in Locke, the very consciousness of the scientific investigator, being no longer in possession of pregiven meaningfulness, joins this new world of man's own making and thus becomes matter for scientific inquiry.

In this way, then, Locke's modest intentions conceal a very radical outcome for his thinking, and his self-imposed limitation to the problem of the limits of knowledge does enable him to discover something, unrealized by his modern predecessors, about the very essence of knowledge. We must now dwell on the details of this underlabourer's epistemology with its radical implications for the extension of modern scientific knowledge.

Locke begins his propaedeutic to philosophy in the *Essay* with a polemic against innate or pregiven ideas in the human mind. In place of innatism, he proposes the only view that enables us to "distinguish the evidence of truth from the mere influence of irrational custom," namely, the "view that knowledge is only to be won by the active employment of our faculties in 'the consideration of things'."[31] Yet, Locke does not initiate this polemic in order to disprove the Cartesian rationalistic system, that is, in order to advance the claims of 'sensationalism', for he makes it quite clear that "sense experience of itself could not provide us with the full truth even about material things."[32] On the contrary, the motive of his polemic is his insistence "upon the necessity for an active appropriation of truth by the individual"[33]—his insistence that the truth is not pregiven but *gained* by individuals and "gained to varying degrees . . . in proportion to their own native endowments, their efforts, and their opportunities."[34]

As with Descartes, the object of man's understanding is ideas and not the pregiven things of nature. But *all* ideas, for Locke, are gained or appropriated—either as anterior, external "ideas of sensation" or as posterior, internal "ideas of reflection" constituted by our perception of the operation of our minds. These twin "fountains of knowledge" are the "windows" by which light is admitted into the dark spaces of the mind—a mind that, like "white paper, void of all characters," comes to be furnished with marks or knowledge only through experience.[35] In this way, whatever can be said about the nature of knowledge must be said in terms of the origin of our ideas—the "question as to what an idea is becomes inseparable from the question as to how the mind comes by it."[36]

But ideas as such are only the elements of knowledge; we come to have knowledge when we know ideas in their connections.[37] Knowledge, Locke says, "thus seems to me to be nothing but the perception of the connexion and agreement, or disagreement and repugnancy of any of our ideas."[38] Knowledge consists neither in the having nor in the gaining of ideas but in the power of perceiving the agreement or disagreement of the ideas we have gained from experience. Locke can thus say that the *"power* of perception is that which we call the understanding."[39] When this power of perception immediately, or without the intervention of other ideas or perceptions of ideas, sees the agreement or disagreement of ideas, we have intuitive knowledge which, as in Descartes, is the ground of certitude. Even in mediated perception of the agreement or disagreement of our ideas—that is, demonstrative knowledge—we require a ground for all our connections in intuitive certainty. Whatever falls short of either intuition or demonstration is faith and can be called opinion, but it cannot be properly called knowledge.

Locke's conception of knowledge as a power of perception entails that knowing is always accompanied by what he calls consciousness, or by "a reflex act by which we perceive or are aware of our thoughts as our own."[40] This reflexive power of perception leaves us with agreements and disagreements, conjunctions and disjunctions that do not belong to nature as such but rather to our own perception. We stand "outside the things of this world, and our ideas of them leave us in ignorance of their essence."[41] Our minds

are not made as large as truth, nor suited to the whole extent of things; amongst those that come within its reach, it meets with a great many too big for its grasp, and there are not a few that it is fair to give up as incomprehensible. It finds itself lost in the vast extent of space, and the least particle of matter puzzles it with an inconceivable divisibility. . . . We shall find that we are sent out into the world furnished with those faculties that are fit to obtain knowledge, and knowledge sufficient, if we will but confine it within those purposes, and direct it to those ends, which the constitution of our nature and the circumstance of our being point out to us.[42]

Thus, knowledge as a power necessarily entails knowledge with very definite limits; and the human mind as a power to perceive the connections and disagreements of the ideas it has acquired entails a mind with very definite limits. Thus, Locke insists that

the mind of man being very narrow and so slow in making acquaintance with things, and taking in new truths, that no one man is capable, in a much longer life than ours, to know all truths; it becomes our prudence, in our search after knowledge, to employ our thoughts about fundamental and material questions, carefully avoiding those that are trifling, and not suffering ourselves to be diverted from our main even purpose, by those that are merely incidental.[43]

In looking at knowledge in this perspective, Locke arrives at a number of specific conclusions about the extent and limits of human knowledge. First of all, we can have no knowledge beyond the ideas we have acquired; we are "of necessity ignorant . . . where we want ideas."[44] We can have no knowledge beyond the limits of our perception of the agreement or disagreement of these ideas. Second, intuitive knowledge cannot certify all of our ideas, nor can demonstrative knowledge extend to the entire range of ideas we possess. We "want certain knowledge and certainty as far as we want clear and determined specific ideas,"[45] and certitude falls short of covering the entire extent of the contents of the human mind. And third, the extent of our knowledge falls short of grasping the innermost reality of the physical things of nature. Thus, the propositions of the natural sciences are able to attain a degree of certitude, but all of these propositions have constituent concepts pointing to real essences in nature that are, nonetheless, not known to us.[46] It will be sufficient for the sciences to realize that their certitudes are examples of real knowledge in order to show that the ideas they propose "can be known to be the ideas of possible existents"; effectively, when we know our ideas to refer to what is "capable of having an existence' in nature," we can be content that we have real knowledge.[47]

In drawing limits on the extent of human knowledge and certitude, Locke thus asserts not only that knowledge has no access to the innermost reality of external nature but that it cannot exhaust the full potential of ideas acquired by the mind. Even more explicitly than Descartes, Locke thus constructs a theory of knowledge in which the object of the mind is not nature as such but its own contents and possessions, that is, ideas in relation to one another. These contents are all derivable from experience, whether that experience be internal or external perception.

In this epistemological perspective, universality (or generality) is not envisaged as a trait of natural reality outside the mind but as one of the several powers of that mind. Universality becomes for Locke simply a reference given ideas initially taken from particular beings in experience. Nature may account for the similarity of *things* in all sorts of ways, and men may use these similarities to classify particular beings into sorts and kinds. "But the arrangements are ours, and, for convenience, they often rest on a few outward and obvious similarities. The aim of this sorting is convenience of communication."[48] The "boundaries of species" are, as Locke says, "as men and not as nature makes them, if at least there are in nature any such prefixed bounds."[49] Abstract ideas that permit of the activity of classification, in being constructs of the human mind instead of "being once for all fixed and rigid," are relative "to the degrees of insight which we have obtained into the phenomena of nature, and must adapt themselves to our growing knowledge."[50] Thus, Locke is led to remark the following.

For since all things that exist are only particulars, how come we by general terms, or where find we those general natures they are supposed to stand for? Words become general, by being made the signs of general ideas; and ideas become general by separating them from the circumstances of time, and place, and any other ideas that may determine them to this or that particular existence. By this way of abstraction they are made capable of representing more individuals than one. . . . It is plain by what has been said that general and universal belong not to the real existence of things, but are the inventions and creatures of the understanding, made by it for its own use, and concern only signs, whether words or ideas. . . . When therefore we quit particulars, the generals that rest are only creatures of our own making; their general nature being nothing but the capacity they are put into by the understanding of signifying or representing many particulars. For the signification they have is nothing but a relation, that by the mind of man is added to them.[51]

As far as Locke is concerned, then, an idea comes into the mind laden with a reference to a particular thing; its universality is only a representative use to which it is put. Locke thus emphasizes the inherent particularity of ideas as much as he does the inherent particularity of the mind or mental agent having the ideas. In his political writings he emphasizes the individual agent in society, especially in terms of "the individual's right to his property as against the arbitrary interference of the state."[52] And just as he made individual agents, "taken apart from their political relations, the original and independent units out of which" the civil state is constituted, so he made "the simple ideas, which are the product of analysis, both chronologically and logically prior to" more complex clusters of ideas that are constructed out of them.[53] This parallel between Locke's political and epistemological thinking reiterates the inherent priority of individuality and particularity over universality.

The implications of Locke's position on this primacy are highly significant. Since universality has no foundation in reality external to the mind, Locke is led to conceive of consciousness, not as a relation between the mind as agent and the external natural thing as object, but rather as a relation between the mind as power and ideas as contents of that mind, operated on by its power. In operating on ideas, the human mind frees them of their immediate particular references and affords them the status of universality in their signification. In generating the universal signification of ideas, the mind can no longer be envisaged as a thing meant to serve as a receptacle for ideas but must be seen as a power transforming ideas acquired in experience. Once more, as in Descartes, but even more explicitly, Locke comes to assert that human consciousness does not mean consciousness of a pregiven reality or an objective structure in the natural world, as it is in itself; rather, it means simply and entirely self-consciousness or reflexive awareness of the contents of consciousness.

Whereas, however, Descartes could be confident in the potential of scientific method to gain certitude to such an extent that a man could come to know everything he is capable of knowing, Locke's analysis, in this regard, is considerably more modest in its conclusions. Locke tends to view certitude as but another power of the mind (or perception); for it is in our power to perceive the conjunction or disjunction of our ideas, in this special power of perception, that he finds the certainty which constitutes knowledge.[54] In the diverse forms of "judgment as distinguished from knowledge," we may presume our ideas to agree or disagree, but we do not actually "perceive their agreement or disagreement."[55] For Locke, certainty (as a power of perception) and knowledge (as a power of perception) are one and the same thing, for "what I know, that I am certain of; and what I am certain of, that I know."[56]

But, for Locke, in contradistinction to Descartes, certainty can never constitute the full story of the powers of the human mind; it can never be coextensive with the full range of the contents of human consciousness; experience, with its twofold source for knowledge, always outreaches knowledge and its certitudes. Locke thus introduces what Descartes never really developed: a doctrine of those powers of human perception that yield the less-than-certain or the probable. Probability or "likeliness to be true" is content with what Locke calls "arguments or proofs to make it *pass* or be received for true," and it is called "belief, assent, or opinion, which is the admitting or receiving any proposition for true, upon arguments . . . that are found to persuade us to receive it as true, without certain knowledge that it is so."[57] The difference between probability and certainty, for Locke, is that in certainty, or knowledge, intuition is always operative.

Each immediate idea, each step has its visible and certain connexion; in belief not so. That which makes me believe is something extraneous to the thing I believe; something not evidently joined on both sides to, and so not manifestly showing the agreement or disagreement of those ideas that are under consideration. Probability then, being to supply the defect of our knowledge, and to guide us where that fails, is always conversant about propositions whereof we have no certainty but only some inducements to receive them for true.[58]

A doctrine of probability must compensate, then, for the limited range of certitudes accessible to man—even those certitudes promised by scientific method. Knowledge or certitude does not exhaust the powers of the human mind. In this way, by limiting certitude and toning down the Cartesian emphasis on certitude, Locke offers, especially in the *Essay*, a reflection on the several and diverse sides of human understanding, not merely a reflection on a privileged mode of understanding. He offers a reflection that, in addition to mixing the rational and the passional, interweaves knowledge, in the sense of certainty, with the diverse degrees of belief and opinion. "To know in the strict certitudinal sense does not exhaust our responsible uses of the understanding, which also judges and assents to probabilities in many scientific areas as well as in everyday life."[59]

But by limiting the range of certitudes and by conditioning certitude by experience, Locke, by virtue of his doctrine of "well-grounded probabilities,"[60] was able to admit a wider range of subject matter than strict certitudes into the domain of modern science. He was able to anchor the free-floating Cartesian *ego,* unanchored in nature, in *experience,* that is, in external and internal perceptions. Insofar as it is anchored in experience, insofar as experience serves as the ultimate parameter for certitude, this *ego* itself can be examined scientifically. It can be studied in this fashion because science as a method, like all knowledge in the true sense, wants the compensatory powers of well-grounded probabilities to fill out the limited range of its certitudes. And insofar as it wants this compensation, scientific method is capable of being extended into those spaces that do not so readily lend themselves to certitudes but largely to the powers of probabilistic understanding. Just as the Newtonian world could be studied only in its behavior by science,[61] so now, the human mind, anchored in experience, is able to be scientifically studied in its behavior.

Locke makes clear how the mind of man could become an object for scientific study, in terms of its behavioral manifestations, by emphasizing the importance of mental *development*. The human mind is not a static and fixed entity found only in the developed reason of the adult; rather, it is itself a development from childhood to adulthood. In various of his works Locke probes the human mind as it is found in the child, an examination largely ignored by his modern predecessors. He is confident that "children whilst very young should be treated as rational creatures."[62] The basic power of perception is already had in children, even though its range, especially in regard to certitudes, is much more limited than in the adult. To the extent that "to sense or be aware in any way is to have some idea, it being one of Locke's principles that 'having ideas and perceiving' are 'the same thing',"[63] the minds of children are in possession of ideas derived from their experience. There is then a certain interiority to the child; he is not simply a bundle of sense perceptions, since it "is certain," as Locke says, "that whatever alterations are made in the body, if they reach not the mind; whatever impressions are made on the outward parts, if they are not taken notice of within; there is no perception."[64]

To study the human mind, then, one must study not just the matured, adult mind but the development of the human mind from childhood to adulthood. To study the human mind, one must study it not simply in terms of its certitudinal powers but in its probabilistic judgments as well. The development of man's mental behavior from childhood to adulthood as well as its sources in experience can be objects for scientific study. What will be studied here is precisely what the human mind as a power, from childhood to adulthood, selects out of experience as ideas relevant to its own needs. The science of nature, both nature external to the human mind as well as the natural powers of the human mind itself, must deal with the qualities selected by that mind out of experience, because the "groupings we select define for us the objects relevant to our needs and interests."[65] Thus, although limiting the range of scientific certitudes, Locke expanded the applicability of Cartesian scientific methodology.

With the claims of certitude, and perhaps even the infinite aspiration embodied in Cartesian scientific method,[66] limited by Locke's theory of knowledge, the Cartesian edifice actually becomes tighter. Yet, with the Cartesian *ego*, in keeping with the Newtonian revision of the Cartesian edifice, given an anchor in experience, scientific method is also expanded in regard to the scope of its subject matter, so that the human subject becomes an object for scientific examination insofar as the human mind develops in a context of experience—an experience that is testable. This consequence of Locke's epistemology will later serve as an occasion for the emergence of a new philosophical penetration of the meaning of man—a new or modern philosophy of man in the Enlightenment and its peculiar consummation, Immanuel Kant.[67]

The two sides of the coin of Locke's epistemology—its modest intentions and radical consequence—disclose the nature of his peculiar contribution. "Philosophy itself," he said, "when it appears in public must have so much complacency as to be clothed in the ordinary fashion and language of the country so far as it can consist with truth and perspicuity."[68] His sympathy for the modest task of the underlabourer, illustrated in his own epitaph, "If you wonder what kind of man he was, the answer is that he was one contented with his modest lot,"[69] conjoined with his conviction that "our state here in this world is a state of mediocrity, which is not capable of extremes, though on one side there may be excellency and perfection,"[70] led him to transmute the basic insights of the Cartesian system into the language of common sense. Content with a modest estimate of the novelty of his own contribution, he could say, "If I have done anything new, it has been to describe to others more particularly than had been done before, what it is their minds do when they perform that action which they call knowing."[71] This modesty, however, was the necessary condition for the *commonsensification* of the modern scientific method that was systematically elaborated by Descartes and qualified by Newton and Leibniz.

After Locke, the world view of modern science would be as much a part of the stock of common sense as the world view of ancient science and the Ptolemaic universe had been the stuff of the ordinary experience of the medievals. Certainly he did not manage to do this singlehandedly; complex factors, other than philosophers themselves, after all, have a great deal to do with the mutation of common sense. Yet, if we are asked for Locke's

main contribution to his age and to subsequent ages we may perhaps best answer in this way: His writings secured for posterity the advances which had been made by the most radical and progressive elements of society in the seventeenth century. He consolidated the advanced positions. He did not accept everything which his radical predecessors had taught. Some of their teaching he considered impracticable. But what he saw to be living and important he retained and in his statement of these matters captured the public ear so completely that it was impossible for his contemporaries and for many subsequent generations to ignore him. . . . It is thus possible to conceive the whole of Locke's work as *consolidation through criticism,* and preparation for future advance.[72]

In a sense, in and after Locke, the modern scientific method could afford to loosen the range of its claims to certitude, precisely because it managed to gain full acceptance in public opinion. Science, furthermore, could afford to extend the geography of its subject matter because of the faith of ordinary experience in its mission.

Yet, despite his consolidation of the Cartesian scientific method into a commonly accepted world view, Locke was unable to overcome the chasm, introduced by Descartes, yawning between the human mind and the natural world of things. Locke was able to give the Cartesian *ego* a ground, but that ground, far from being the natural world of pregiven and fixed essences, was human experience itself. With the Lockean ground of the Cartesian *ego* placed in the mutations of experience, Locke too was destined simply to pass on to posterity the alienation of thought from matter, since the relativity of this ground would not permit a dissolution of the Cartesian bifurcation.

Yet Locke could pass on to his immediate posterity far more. It is a "truism that Locke's general position set the framework within which modern philosophy has developed, or at least defined the point of view from which philosophical thinking had to proceed" through Berkeley to Hume and from Hume to Kant.[73] Berkeley and Hume could in no way avoid taking their cue from

Locke in further elaborating a theory of knowledge for the logic of modernity.

BERKELEY: AN ATTEMPT TO OVERCOME CARTESIAN DUALISM

Locke had concluded that the human mind was of a limited capacity, and so we should not be surprised if some matters forever elude our comprehension. Undoubtedly, the Cartesian dualism of mind and matter was, for Locke, one of these matters, and he quietly resigned himself to its insolubility. Bishop George Berkeley's (1685–1753) attitude if less humble than Locke's is also less resigned, since he argues that a large number of the philosophical problems in which we find ourselves trapped are really our own fault, problems of our own making.[74] As a result, Berkeley conceives of his task in epistemology, "not as that of *replacing* one set of doctrines by another, but as that of *eliminating* certain unnecessary perplexities."[75] What Berkeley persuades his readers to lay aside, then, is the abuse of words and purely verbal controversies.[76] Berkeley was apparently able to see that the Cartesian dualism was not only a consequence of human cognition of nature, and thus capable of being overcome,[77] but was also a consequence of confusion owing to the misuse of language. Berkeley's fundamental purpose was to "inquire into the source of our perplexities," regarding our "perplexities as maladies or ailments which are curable."[78] He was perhaps the first modern thinker to explicitly regard the Cartesian dualism in this light.

But, while Berkeley's criticisms are all concerned with the theory of knowledge, as were Locke's, they are prompted, much more explicitly than in Locke, by religious interests.[79] While having many interests throughout his life, Berkeley had one predominant concern—"his opposition to those whose writings tended to undermine religious belief."[80] As far as he was concerned, the search for truth, when genuine, must finally lead us to a deeper knowledge of God.[81] Thus, in "writing at all, Berkeley was impelled by a desire to bring men to a sense of the immanence of the Deity,"[82] an immanence he apparently perceived as laden in the original message of modernity but obscured by recent developments and tendencies in the explication of modernity made by his contemporaries. From a religious point of view, then, while perceiving an inestimable benefit in the logic of modernity, namely, the "ascendancy of inner experience,"[83] he perceived certain equally potent dangers in recent elaborations of that logic. One danger he perceived was the Leibnizian tendency to conceive of God as a God of the Sabbath uninvolved in the operations of nature.[84] Thus, in his work *Alciphron,* published in 1732, he criticizes those philosophers who imagine that God "left this system with all its parts and contents well adjusted and put in motion, as an artist leaves a clock, to go thenceforward of itself for a certain period."[85] To this view, he opposes his own view that God is "not a Creator merely, but a provident Governor, actually and intimately present, and attentive to all our interests and motions, . . . the whole cause of our lives, informing, admonishing, and directing incessantly, in a most evident and sensible manner."[86]

But another danger Berkeley perceived in the explication of the logic of modernity provided by his contemporaries was the tendency he found in Newton and others to attribute the qualities of God to the infinite universe of modern science, thereby making God obsolescent for anything but a functional and hypothetical role within the system of natural philosophy.

Locke, More, Raphson, etc., seem to make God extended. 'Tis nevertheless of great use to religion to take extension out of our idea of God and put a power in its place. It seems dangerous to suppose extension, which is manifestly inert, in God.[87]

It would seem, then, that much as Leibniz perceived the danger of a purely mechanical, lifeless universe for the realization of the potential of a unified scientific method and discourse, so also Berkeley perceived the danger of the independent existence of external matter for the quality of religious belief in God. "Matter once allowed," Berkeley said, "I defy any man to prove that God is not matter."[88] There appears to be no room in Berkeley's philosophy for both God and matter; matter was dangerous and God was needed.[89] In *Siris,* published in 1744, Berkeley goes so far as to suggest that, though the universe may be a part of God, God cannot be an extension of the universe. If matter existed, it would have to be said that God contained matter within himself, thereby violating the purity of existence essential to the definition of God. A God who contained matter would be a trivialized God, an unfitting object for worship; and worship, after all, is the proper activity of authentic religion. Modern philosophy, dependent in its origins on the authentic God of Christianity, was in danger of losing sight of His authenticity, in danger of phasing out this God. The source of this danger was the modern bifurcation of mind and an independently existing matter, a bifurcation Berkeley perceived as preeminently remediable because it was not rooted in the inherent logic of modernity but only in the verbal confusions of the more recent developers of that logic.

The fundamental principles of Locke's epistemology constitute Berkeley's starting point.[90] Berkeley was of the opinion that Locke had travelled on the right path but that he had not finished the journey; this incompleteness, Berkeley believed, was potentially disastrous and was rooted in Locke's account of what it is to perceive a physical object.[91] Thus, in his *Treatise Concerning the Principles of Human Knowledge,* published in 1710, Berkeley begins his attempt to dissolve the Cartesian dualism—that is, to purge matter or corporeal things of any kind of existence or reality independent of the knowing mind—by at once starting from Lockean categories and criticizing the incompleteness of Locke's reflection on those categories.

If Berkeley's starting with Lockean epistemology nonetheless involves an attack on that epistemology, it is because Locke reveals to Berkeley that there is so little to be said for or about *material substance,* and yet still insists on recognizing its existence.[92] What Locke failed to perceive is a problem in his epistemology—the problem that "if the range of our knowledge is bounded by the limits of pure experience, and at the same time real and substantial objects are supposed to lie beyond the limits of experience," then a "sceptical position is ultimately inescapable."[93] As far as Berkeley was concerned, the supposition that there are unknowable things behind ideas "takes away all real truth and consequently brings in a universal scepticism, since all our knowledge and contemplation are confin'd barely to our own ideas."[94] Without authentic truth, there can be no authentic God; Locke's incompleteness is thus an occasion for irreligion or at least for inauthentic religion.

But if the root of skepticism is to be found in the Cartesian dualism accepted by Locke—in the supposition that material things in their innermost reality are distinct from ideas—then the overcoming of skepticism must rest on the contrary supposition, that ideas and material things are to be completely identified. Berkeley's tactic here involves "pushing the sceptic's case to the limit and denying that there is a material world lying beyond what we actually experience when we perceive."[95] But having done this, Berkeley can deny the need for skepticism, since there is now only one world, a world which our senses apprise us of and which is made up of ideas, and this world is the real world.[96] For Berkeley, the incompleteness and defect of Locke consists in his allowing himself to speak of material substance, admitting that this expression does not and cannot denote any object of anyone's experience, and yet *not* concluding that for this very reason it can be only a meaningless and empty word.[97] Locke involved himself in a needless duplication, namely, the things we actually perceive, called "ideas," and behind these ideas, "completely unobservable counterparts which he regards as the real physical objects"; but Berkeley sees this duplication as unnecessary, since if by "asserting the existence of ideas, we have already brought in everything we actually perceive, then nothing more is required."[98]

Berkeley, then, will have the courage to travel the full extent of the path that Locke walked only partway, proceeding from Descartes. He will deny the independent existence of matter. Locke appeared radical in conceiving of universality as a function of particularity, of universals as particular names stripped of the particularity of their original references. But Berkeley would be more radical by insisting that all reasoning is ultimately about particulars and by insisting on a link between his attack on both abstractionism and universals and his case for the mind-dependence of things.[99] For it is the myth that universals are something different from particulars, the myth that we think universal ideas that refer to unknowable particular material things, that allows us to separate our perception from material things, to separate *esse* from *percipi*.[100] Rejecting matter as the *principium individuationis,* Berkeley contends that the fatal flaw of his predecessors was their abstract and arbitrary distinction between the *percipi,* the act of being perceived, and the *esse,* or act of existing. Existence, Berkeley insists, means either to be perceived or to perceive, and he is convinced that if "men but examine what they mean by the word 'existence', they would agree with me."[101] It is their acceptance of the distinction between perception and things, idea and matter, that leads them to assert that there exist material objects or bodies apart from the knowing subject—objects that are, as they exist in themselves, unknowable.[102]

What Berkeley must attack, then, is the "erroneous conception of matter as the substratum of reality," and it is this attack that is "perhaps the most serious task he ever undertook."[103] If, for a moment, we suppose that *esse* is dissociated from *percipi,* we are supposing that it makes sense to talk of things existing independently of any perceiving mind, and we thus blind ourselves to the immanence of God in the universe of modern science.[104]

Berkeley continues his task of purging the modern philosophical perspective of matter by establishing a clear distinction between the ideas of knowledge and the subject that perceives these ideas, which he calls "mind, spirit, soul, or myself." These latter terms denote an entity entirely distinct from the ideas of knowledge, a thing wherein the ideas exist or "whereby they are perceived."[105] With the existence of an idea meaning nothing more than the idea's being perceived, there can be no things external to the thinking subject that can in themselves be said to be unthinking things. It is impossible for the thinking subject to conceive in his thought any sensible thing distinct from his sensations and perceptions. There is, therefore, no other reality in the universe than that substance or reality that perceives. In this way, Berkeley contends that the so-called "absolute existence of sensible objects in themselves or without the mind" either means "nothing at all" or is a "direct contradiction."[106]

Berkeley is not beyond seeing, however, that his position leads him into certain difficulties. Does it not imply that there can be no distinction between real things and ideas or images of things? He surmounts this difficulty by constructing a further distinction, one very similar to that later to be found in Hume. The distinction between real things and images of things, he contends, is nothing more than the distinction between "ideas of sense" and "images of imagination." Ideas of sense are simply stronger, livelier, and more distinct than ideas of imagination. Ideas of sense have an order and coherence that ideas of imagination, being excited at random, simply do not have. Berkeley accounts for the difference between these ideas in a somewhat contrived fashion by postulating that ideas of sense are imprinted on the mind by the "Author of Nature," that is, God, and that ideas of imagination are simply representations or faint imitations of ideas of sense.[107]

The primary distinction, then, of Berkeley's theory of knowledge is not that between mind and body, the inside and the outside of consciousness, as in the Cartesian system, but rather the distinction between mind, as the indivisible and *only* substance, and ideas as the "fleeting, dependent beings which subsist not by themselves but are supported by or exist in minds or spiritual substances."[108] "All the choir of heaven and furniture of the earth," Berkeley says, "in a word all those bodies which compose the mighty frame of the world, have not any substance without a mind . . . their *being* is to be perceived or known."[109] But Berkeley is careful to add that wherever "bodies are said to have no existence without the mind, I would not be understood to mean this or that particular mind, but all minds whatsoever."[110]

What is somewhat startling, given what he says, is that Berkeley should still insist that it "were a mistake to think that what is here said derogates in the least from the reality of things."[111] In fact, Berkeley preferred to think of himself as on the side of common sense, and he was not beyond saying that "I side in all things with the Mob."[112] It is apparently Berkeley's intention "to recall us from strange 'speculative' theories to common sense and thereby to recall us to theism also."[113] He thus insists that his position is consistent with the received opinion of the reality of things.[114] He is at pains "to show that the statement that sensible things are ideas is *not* equivalent to the statement that sensible things possess no reality."[115] This can only mean, in Berkeley's thinking, that the reality of things is nothing other than the reality of ideas. It would seem, then, that the ultimate significance of Berkeley's criticism of matter lies in his conclusion that since matter is the only conceivable nonspiritual ground of the existence of things, and since matter, "regarded in every possible way, has been shown to be non-existent, the only real ground of the existence of things is spirit."[116] By saying that matter does not exist, he "means actually to *defend* our ordinary convictions against an insidious philosophical blunder," for the question is not "Do trees and chairs and houses really exist?" but is rather "What does it mean to say that they exist?"[117] The answer is that their reality is the reality of mind-dependence or perception. Expelled from the natural world, then, is not, in his view, reality but rather matter. Thus, he can say that it is a

manifest contradiction that any sensible thing should be immediately perceived by sight or touch, and at the same time have no existence in nature, since the very *existence* of an unthinking being consists in *being perceived.*[118]

For Berkeley, in other words, the proposition that *things exist in nature* is identical in meaning to the proposition that *things are perceived.* It is precisely this identity that he uses to exclude the modern Cartesian bifurcation between mind and matter and to hold to the absolute and unqualified identity of the inside and outside of consciousness. As G. A. Johnston remarks, "Berkeley's significance really lies in his suggestion that both external and internal fall within the subject's individual experience."[119] Berkeley's epistemology thus has two sides. "It involves a denial that the real world is forever hidden from us, and an assertion that what we perceive is the real world. But it also involves the claim that the real world is made up of mind-dependent ideas."[120] Effectively, everything in the world falls under the category of the mind-idea or subject-object relationship.[121] The mind-matter bifurcation is replaced by the distinction between mind and its ideas.

But there is a decisive problem in Berkeley's resolution, one that he himself does not seem to recognize. The problem with his identity of mind and matter is whether it is a real identity or simply the reduction of the meaning of the outside to that of the inside, a reduction of complex matter to simple idea. The distinction he wishes to substitute for the modern Cartesian body-

mind dualism is the subject-object distinction, that is, the distinction between *ideas as objects* of mind and *mind as* receptacle or
subject of ideas. Berkeley recognizes that mind and ideas cannot
be identified; ideas cannot be the same as the mind that perceives
them. Because they cannot be the same, one of them has to be
primary in its significance. Since, without the mind, there can be
no perception, it would seem that Berkeley would have to admit
that the mind or subject has primacy over the idea or object. The
act of perceiving, in other words, has primacy as well as priority
over the act of being perceived. The primacy of mind, however,
entails that Berkeley's identity of mind and things, his identity of
the inside and outside of consciousness, is really a reduction of
the significance of the outside to that of the inside. The complexity
of all reality is reduced to one kind of reality, that of mind-per-
ceiving. This may be an attempt to restore the medieval vision
of a divinely unified sacramental world to post-Cartesian modernity, but it does so at the cost of sacrificing the plurality of that
world to the bland monism of a universe with one substance:
mind or spirit. This monism, as we have said, is hardly what the
medieval world, at its best, had in mind.[122]

It would seem, then, that Berkeley's identity of Cartesian mind
and matter is in effect a reduction of matter to the univocal substance of mind. Such a reduction enables him to save the authentic
notion of the Christian God from the usurpation of His attributes
by the universe of modern science. It also manages to save the
authentic immanence of the Christian God in this universe. God
is not an object but a supreme subject, the primary reality; God
is not a hypothetical construct for the correction of rundown in
the universe but is rather the all-perceiving-perceiver. Nothing
can be as self-evident, in Berkeley's perspective, as the being of
God, the supreme subject who allows for the very presence of
ideas to the mind of man.[123] Berkeley is thus drawn to the conclusion that things exist really and completely only as presentations
in God's experience.[124] Sensible things, or what we are inclined
to call sensible things, existed before there were men to perceive
them because there was and is an eternal spirit who had them in
mind.[125] As Berkeley remarks in the *Three Dialogues Between Hylas*

and Philonous, published in 1713,

> All objects are eternally known by God, or, which is the same thing, have an eternal existence in his mind; but when things before imperceptible to creatures, are by a decree of God made perceptible to them; then are they said to begin a relative existence, with respect to created minds.[126]

Thus, the fundamental issue, as Berkeley perceived it, was not whether "things have a *real* existence out of the minds of this or that person" but "whether they have an *absolute* existence, distinct from being perceived by God, and exterior to all minds."[127] In this way, the role of *esse est percipi* in the purgation of matter yields the notion of an immanent God sustaining the world. *Esse est percipi* thus discloses itself to be ultimately *esse est a Deo causari*.[128]

Nonetheless, the cost of the preservation of the supreme importance of the immanent Christian God in the present course of the developing logic of modernity was, for Berkeley, the reduction of thing to idea. It would seem, then, that his attempt to heal the breach between Cartesian mind and matter was, in the end, as much a failure as Leibniz's attempt to overcome the mechanistic character of the universe of modern science. Beneath the Leibnizian organic metaphors there still lurks the world-machine, and beneath Berkeley's attempted resolution there still lurks the unresolved modern dualism, for in Berkeley the dualism is overcome only by effectively being dismissed. His argument appears to "fail in the sense that it does not prove what he thought it did,"[129] namely, a true identity of mind and things that still preserves the reality and rich diversity of things. Finding that Locke had made it appear that the external world, in its innermost reality, was inaccessible to man's knowledge, Berkeley "sought to remove this baffling problem at a single blow"[130] by reducing the very existence of things to the intelligibility of mental constructs and sensible perceptions. But this reduction failed to impress his contemporaries and most of those who would follow him.

Nonetheless, Berkeley's epistemological significance should not be underestimated. He managed to make clear the remediableness of the modern dualism of the inside and outside of human consciousness—the modern dualism of mind and matter. His attempt to overcome this Cartesian dualism in a reductive fashion would not be insignificant for Hegel's efforts to resolve this dualism in a nonreductive manner—for Hegel's completion of the logic of modernity. Nor, for that matter, would Berkeley's fears about the rejection of the authentic notion of the Christian God prove to be entirely groundless in terms of what would come to pass in the Enlightenment and in Nietzsche's struggle with faith in the rightness or soundness of the logic of modernity itself.

HUME: THE BREAKDOWN OF CERTITUDE

The uniqueness of Hume (1711–76) in the company of his modern philosophical predecessors is what first catches our attention. Hume was the "first distinguished man of letters in Britain to make a modest fortune from literature alone"; never "dedicating a work to a patron, never seeking for advance subscriptions," he prospered "simply through the booksellers" and his "broad appeal to the public at large."[131] The novelty of Hume's appeal to a large public, moreover, discloses the peculiar nature of his conception of philosophy; for he regarded "philosophy as part and parcel of literature" and believed that to be "a philosopher is to be a man of letters."[132] "I cannot," he says,

> but consider myself as a kind of resident or ambassador from the dominions of learning to those of conversation, and shall think it my constant duty to promote a good correspondence betwixt these two states, which have so great a dependence on each other. . . . The materials of this commerce must chiefly be furnished by conversation and common life: the manufacturing of them alone belongs to learning.[133]

Yet it must be said that Hume's uniqueness in writing philosophy as a kind of popular literature is somewhat foreshadowed by Locke's equably commonsensical style of writing.[134] Hume, in fact, betrays his similarity to Locke when he says, "I was resolv'd not to be an enthusiast in philosophy, while I was blaming other enthusiasms."[135] Like Locke, Hume attempted to examine the limits of knowledge and was highly sensitive to the philosophical tendency to be overconclusive in regard to what is knowable as certitude in scientific knowledge.

Hume's kinship with Descartes is also evident in terms of the role the latter gives to doubt as the starting point of philosophical reflection. Yet even here, Hume's uniqueness must be asserted; his skepticism is much more intense and pervasive of his entire thought than Descartes' doubt. Unlike Cartesian doubt, Humean skepticism results from the fact that he limits certain knowledge in a rigorous sense to demonstrable mathematical truths. Whatever else we know, and this includes all our significant data, we know only probably.[136] The intensity of Hume's skepticism is not unrelated to his style of philosophical writing as a form of literature for a large public audience, since Hume attempted to destroy the long-standing opinion as to the distinction between "an inferior, everyday kind of knowledge, and a superior god-like kind of knowledge" consisting of the ultimate reasons why things are what they are, alongside which "ordinary knowledge appears as a mixture of error and illusion."[137]

Unlike Descartes, then, the skeptical tendency is not merely an initial method; skepticism is not only Hume's starting point in philosophy but is the persistent and perduring motif of his entire writing.[138] Hume's skepticism, in fact, leads him to a radical attack on Cartesian certitudes.[139] Descartes, we have seen, held that scientific method presumed certain metaphysical principles that could be articulated and even demonstrated. Hume's skepticism is more akin to Newton, who argued that scientific method presumed no metaphysical principles and needed none to be exercised.[140] This is not surprising, given the development of Newton's experimental method by British philosophers, since one of the high points of this development is precisely in Hume.[141] Yet Newton himself did envisage the full exercise of scientific method as issuing in certain metaphysical and religious realizations,[142] and it is at this point that Hume parts company with the person he called the "greatest and rarest genius that ever rose for the ornament and instruction of the species."[143]

Unlike all of his modern philosophical predecessors, in fact, Hume appears driven to the conclusion that every application of reason to the events of nature is devoid of the guidance of an absolute logic. His skepticism, in other words—and in this he is a radical departure not only from Descartes and Newton but from Locke as well—pertains to the very capacity of scientific knowledge, not to mention metaphysical speculation, to yield certitudes. In effect, as Hume puts it, "mankind are almost entirely guided," in these areas, "by constitution and temper, and . . . general maxims have little influence, but so far as they affect our taste or sentiments."[144] When it comes to judgments about real existence, or what Hume calls "matters of fact," we are not so much in the position of knowing why we ought to believe anything as we are in the position of simply knowing what we cannot help believing. There is no "one situation of affairs, in itself, preferable to another. Good and ill, *both natural and moral*, are entirely relative to human sentiment and affection."[145]

Human judgments about morality, nature, and *a fortiori* about religious ultimacy are not founded on certain or immutable principles. Philosophy cannot yield metaphysically certain principles for the grounding of morality, religion, or science. Philosophy's only virtue consists in a certain refinement of temper—a pointing out, as Hume puts it, of "those dispositions which we should endeavor to attain by a constant habit of mind and by repeated habit."[146] With judgments about real existence limited to varying degrees of probability and entirely closed off from logical necessity, there can be no question for Hume of what method we ought to use in order to arrive at the best beliefs, for the best that can be accomplished is an account of how in fact beliefs arise in the human mind.[147] Throughout Hume's writing is the explicit insistence that propositions about real existence are matters of belief and the implicit premise that belief itself is not an object of choice.[148]

Over against both Locke and Berkeley, what counts as primary in Hume's epistemology is not a theory of ideas but the determining influence in human and other kinds of animal life of feeling, not reason or understanding.[149] "Passion" is the term Hume uses "for the instincts, propensities, feelings, emotions, and sentiments as well as for the passions ordinarily so-called; and belief, he teaches, is a passion."[150] Furthermore, whereas Locke in the tradition of Descartes had remained a dualist, and Berkeley had taken "a bold step toward monism, idealistic monism, when he denied that matter as such existed at all by itself," Hume made bold to "reject the real existence of both matter and spirit, and proclaimed consciousness as the sole reality"[151]—the consciousness of sensible experience. Yet Hume owes as much of an intellectual debt to Berkeley as he owes to Locke, for many of the tools forged by Berkeley were also used by Hume to attain a theory of knowledge.[152] Thus, Hume assumes Berkeley's epistemological dictum that the very meaning of a word is nothing other than the idea which it expresses.[153] Whereas, however, in Berkeley the relation between the word and the particular idea was left undefined, in Hume that relation is defined as one of customary association.[154] Thus, according to Hume, the use of a particular idea to stand for other resembling particular ideas consists in its capacity to revive them by association.[155]

Very much akin to Berkeley, Hume wondered what justified us in supposing that bodies have an existence distinct from the mind and perception; he wondered why we attribute a continued existence to physical objects when they are not present to our senses. But, unlike Berkeley, he was not motivated by religious sympathies to engage in an idealistic reduction—a reduction of things to ideas. Rather, he was dominated by a pervasive skepticism, not to be found in the empiricism of Locke and Berkeley, and was led to deal with a highly interrupted, discontinuous consciousness and experience. It might even be said that where "Berkeley saw the glory of God, Hume saw nothing but the weakness and vanity of man."[156] It was not, however, atheism but rather agnosticism as the alternative to theism—an agnosticism emerging out of the interstices of Hume's skepticism—that led him far afield from Berkeley's idealistic reduction. Hume recapitulates, in *The Natural History of Religion,* that agnostic perspective that Berkeley, perhaps, feared most.

What a noble privilege is it of human reason to attain the knowledge of a supreme being; and from the visible works of nature, be enabled to infer so sublime a principle as its supreme Creator? But turn the reverse side of the medal. Survey most nations and most ages. Examine the religious principles, which have, in fact, prevailed in the world. You will scarcely be persuaded that they are anything but sick men's dreams: Or perhaps will regard them as the playsome whimsies of monkeys in human shape, than the serious, positive, dogmatical asseverations of a being who dignifies himself with the name of rational.[157]

In sum, like Descartes, Hume tests the modern world view at the court of doubt, but unlike Descartes, he forsakes the quest for certitude in regard to propositions about real existence. With Locke, Hume examines the understanding in its limitations and embraces the perspective of common sense, but against Locke he discards the primacy of reason and the central position of a theory of ideas. Like Berkeley, Hume starts from the problem of the continued existence of unperceived objects, but unlike Berkeley, he makes no ultimate appeal to the religious world view under-lying the origins of modern science. Yet, in attempting to van-quish from the logic of modernity one of its most fundamental features, up to this point—the quest for certitude in regard to propositions about the natural world—Hume paves the way for a new turning point in that logic: a turning into an absorption with the problem of the meaning of man in the modern cosmos. We must now examine in detail the nature of his contribution to that developing logic.

Hume begins his epistemology with the given of a highly dis-continuous and fragmented human experience. He attempts to account for the process of getting order and intelligibility in this highly fragmented experience by constructing, not a theory of ideas, but a theory of the imagination and passions. Thus, he remarks,

we are placed in this world, as in a great theatre, where the true springs and causes of every event are entirely concealed from us; nor have we either sufficient wisdom to forsee, or power to prevent those ills, with which we are continually threatened. . . . These unknown causes, then, become the constant object of our hope and fear; and while the passions are kept in perpetual alarm by an anxious expectation of the events, the imagination is equally employed in forming ideas of those powers on which we have so entire a dependence.[158]

The process of imagination, Hume suggests, initially overlooks the gaps between the isolated atoms of our perceptual experience, what he calls "impressions." Impressions are "all our more lively perceptions, when we see, or feel, or love or hate, or desire or will," and they are distinguished from our "less lively perceptions" or "ideas" of "which we are conscious when we reflect" on these more immediate and primary perceptions.[159] It is imagination that postulates unsensed particulars or ideas to fill the gaps between our impressions. For Hume, "all ideas are images, and . . . every image is particular, that is, completely determinate."[160]

Hume thus attempts to account for our coherent grasp of perceived things in terms of the operation of a human faculty that is extrarational—the imagination. It is this extrarational faculty that is rightfully, for Hume, the dominant faculty in the animal and human mind.[161] As far as Hume is concerned, our understanding is limited because our imagination is limited.[162] Furthermore, we can imagine only what can be experienced, so that our "knowledge of the existence of something consists primarily in that thing's being an object of present experience."[163] Thus, our imagination is limited because our experience is limited.

The imagination, though limited in Hume's view, has considerable power; and this power is very much a mixed blessing. Hume saw that "all the errors of philosophy arose from the fact that imagination determined men much more than they recognized," and so there could be no secure truth for him until he had examined this aspect of the nature of man.[164] The memory, senses, and understanding of men are all founded on the imagination.[165] This imagination is prone to excesses when its individual exercise is uncontrolled and unlimited. When imagination operates with a fundamental sameness in men, however, it is productive of the stabilizing power of custom. Thus, Hume professes to concentrate his interpretation on a fundamental imagination peculiar to mankind.[166] Custom is the product of this fundamental imagination and, as such, is the "representative within the mind itself of all the ideas of our experience that have taken on relation with each other."[167]

When imagination operates outside the stabilization of custom, it tends to reduce everything to *arbitrary* combinations. And yet, in "children, peasants, and the greatest part of mankind," imagination, in an *ordered* way, manages "to attribute objects to some impressions and deny them to others."[168] Hume accounts for this by appealing to determinate principles for the operation of the imagination: "contiguity, resemblance, and causality." Whenever we catch ourselves believing something beyond our evidence, we "may identify some one or more of these principles in the process of thought."[169] The gentle force of association, operating according to these principles, inclines the imagination to make connections that are uniform and relatively enduring. Although these connections are not inseparable or logically necessary, one idea or impression naturally tends to introduce another. Thus, Hume postulates a kind of universal attraction that has "in the mental world as manifold and as noteworthy effects as gravity in the physical world."[170] As with Newton's treatment of the law of gravity, the effects of this force can be calculated, but its essence cannot be discovered.[171] Hume never explains *why* ideas are associated, but attempts merely to *describe how* they are associated.[172]

As a result of these forces of association, the imagination allows us to find resemblances between our impressions. An unlimited range of resemblances between our impressions is theoretically possible, since the imagination is capable of providing a seemingly unlimited number of relations between impressions. There is, however, a limit placed on the imagination in this activity—the extent to which the impressions themselves will sustain the connections given them by imagination. The ideas imposed by the imagination, in other words, must be consistent with the impressions conjoined; they must acquire a force that they would not otherwise have, so that some of the power of the original impressions is transferred to the associated idea.[173]

The upshot of the Humean emphasis on the principles by which the imagination unifies the isolated impressions of raw experience is that the process occurs in man in essentially the same way as it occurs in other animals.

Any theory by which we explain the operation of the understanding or the origins and connections of the passions in man will acquire additional authority if we find that the same theory is requisite to explain the same phenomena in all other animals. . . . Animals as well as men learn many things from experience. . . . It is impossible that this inference of the animal can be founded on any process of argument or reasoning.[174]

Thus, it is custom alone "which engages animals from every object which strikes their senses to infer its usual attendant, and carries their imagination from the appearance of the one to conceive the other in that particular manner which we denominate 'belief'."[175] By emphasizing the psychological mechanisms of the principles of association as applicable to animal behavior, including that of man, Hume further extends the Lockean liberation of psychology, as a modern science, from the domain of epistemology.

Furthermore, since causality is interpreted as a psychological principle or mechanism, it becomes nothing more than a determinate way in which the human imagination connects the discontinuous impressions of immediate experience. Causality is one of the primary customary transitions of the imagination, determined by repetition of experiences, so that all we mean "when we postulate a causal connexion is that we have observed it to be customary in our experience that event A follows event B; and from this customary association we infer the dependence of the one on the other."[176] We infer one impression from another through the influence of the customary conjunctions built up by imagination operating on our past impressions, but nowhere among the objects of perception themselves do we find a distinct bond of causality, and so nowhere do we find any ultimate rationale for human understanding.[177] Strictly speaking, the causal connection is not a rational inference. The causal inference permits no "evidence, either rational or empirical, in *justification* of our belief that it will continue"; this belief is psychologically, not logically, grounded.[178] With the causal relation a natural relation akin to instinct in man, and not a logical relation,[179] it can be said that even after experiencing cause and effect, the "nature of the connexion between them remains wholly mysterious; it is only their time-relation of priority and succession (and also, when space is involved, their space-relation of contiguity) which lies open to observation."[180]

Hume's point is, then, an emphatic insistence that we do not need to make any cognitive penetration into the real essences of things when we affirm causal connections, nor are these causal connections derived from any such penetration.[181] Not only is the causal connection *not* a logically necessary connection, but no particular kind of causal connection, by contrast with any other kind, is essentially more intelligible. "There are no objects," as Hume says in *A Treatise of Human Nature,*

which by the mere survey, without consulting experience, we can determine to be the causes of any other; and no objects, which we can certainly determine in the same manner not to be the causes. Anything may produce anything. Creation, annihilation, motion, reason, volition; all these may arise from one another, or from any other object we can imagine.[182]

In effect, nothing that we know of real existence is more intelligible than anything else we know. In the end, we are still confronted with a set of bare facts and can have no further access to intelligibility. We are left, as Hume himself is constrained to admit, with two principles: "that all our distinct perceptions are distinct existences" and "that the mind never perceives any real connection among distinct existences."[183]

Incapable of being either an impression or an idea,[184] or, for that matter, a rational inference, causation is best identified as a feeling of necessitation. After experience of constant conjunction, "it is not merely the case that experience of A is always followed by expectation of B, but also, that on experiencing A we *feel compelled* to expect B."[185] Judgments of causal connection express not insight but only belief, and they rest "not on the apprehension of any relation (other than mere sequence)" but only on a feeling or sentiment in the mind.[186] An affirmation of cause-and-effect connection is nothing but a belief that is in turn grounded in a feeling of necessitation or compulsion. Consequently, the best that can be had, even in regard to the model of knowing offered us by modern science, is a causal sequence reducible to the following proportions.

i. The observation of repeated sequences generates in the mind a custom or habit.
ii. This custom generates a feeling of necessitated transition.
iii. Upon the pattern of this feeling of necessitated transition we model our idea of causal connection.

In this way, all "causal reasoning begins with an impression of sensation which is present before the mind and acts as the anchor of the entire process."[187] From there the mind passes from the present impression to an idea related to the impression, and finally we then "repose" a belief in this idea.[188] This belief is imposed upon the idea by a compulsion, that is, an emotion, and not by a rational demonstration or intuition.

Unlike his modern predecessors, then, Hume accepts no rational demonstration or rational intuition underneath the principle of causality. Forsaking entirely a deductive, mathematical ground for the principle of causality, Hume carries the psychological tendency of Locke an important step forward. Causality, as the very paradigm of scientific explanation, is interpreted in a purely psychological fashion, with a cause defined as "an object followed by another . . . whose appearance always conveys the thought to that other."[189] Thus, fire suggests burning and is refractory to any other association. With no strictly logical necessity, but only an emotional, habit-conditioned belief accruing to the causal connection, the implication of Hume's position becomes clear. Modern science itself, as our preeminently intelligible grasp of the phenomena of nature, is accounted for by the operation of imagination on the inherently discontinuous atoms of our immediate sensible experience. The foundations of science are not rational but extrarational. In implying this, of course, Hume confines the term "rational" to what he takes to be the two branches of the understanding: "the tracing of abstract relations of ideas (demonstrative reasoning) and causal inferences to matters of fact (reasoning from experience)."[190] In so reordering the modern treatment of the foundations of science, the uniquely Humean contribution to the logic of modernity may be said to lie in the "extension of sentiment or feeling beyond ethics and esthetics . . . to include the entire realm of belief covering all relations of matter of fact."[191] The corollary of this extension is that philosophy in general, of which science, or natural philosophy, is a species, will never be able, in Hume's words, "to carry us beyond the usual course of experience, or give us measures . . . different from those furnished by reflections on common life,"[192] that is, the commonsense view of the world. Science involves reasonings from experience of some kind; but, as Hume puts it, in "all reasonings from experience there is a step taken by the mind which is not supported by any argument or process of the understanding."[193] Instead, the mind is constrained by custom which "renders our experience useful to us and makes us expect for the future a similar train of events with those which have appeared in the past."[194]

In arriving at an ultimately extrarational foundation for modern science and all matter-of-fact knowledge or knowledge about real existence, Hume does not operate in terms of a dichotomy or conflict between reason and emotion. Thus, he insists,

we speak not strictly and philosophically when we talk of the combat of passion and reason. Reason is, and ought only to be, the slave of the passions, and can never pretend to any other office than to serve and obey them.[195]

When we speak of rational conduct or action, we are in essence talking about "conduct whose ends are fixed by feeling, independently of reason, but where the means to those ends are efficiently chosen in the light of knowledge and reason."[196] What we call reason, Hume asserts, is "nothing but a wonderful and unintelligible instinct in our souls."[197] Underneath the seeming reasons of scientific discourse lurks belief, so that what we call synthetic reason is itself merely generalized belief.[198] This has prompted Norman Kemp Smith to remark that Hume has "ousted reason from all *supremacy* in the domain of matters of fact and existence."[199] Belief is what the scientific venture is all about. Yet belief "takes charge at the point where knowledge ceases; it is not in any degree an extension of knowledge"; rather, it is a substitute for knowledge with virtues and limitations appropriate to " the economy of our human nature."[200] Like religion, so it would seem, science becomes a mode of belief for which there are no ultimately rational foundations. It is, then, Hume's "firm conviction that there is always a wide gulf between any alleged rational basis for religion and the actual origins of religion in human nature and history," so that "hope and fear, unknown causes, imagination" become the "central features in Hume's account of religious origins."[201] The difference between science and religion, one would infer from Hume's account, is not that the former is rationally founded and the latter is a groundless collection of beliefs but that, by and large, the beliefs of science serve as ends whose means are more efficiently chosen in the light of reason and knowledge than the means of religion.

Yet to deprive science of its treasured rational foundations is not, for Hume, to deny the importance of science. It would amount to denying its significance if the happiness and fulfillment of man, which science strives to attain, were attainable largely through the life of reason. But, for all his emphasis on learning and the arts and sciences, Hume appears to reject the notion that happiness as such is to be found in the life of reason. Nothing is quite so futile as the attempt of what Hume calls the "severe philosophers" to produce an "artificial happiness" in which we would be "pleased by rules of reason and by reflection."[202]

But why do I apply to you, proud and ignorant sages, to show me the road to happiness? Let me consult my own passions and inclinations. In them must I read the dictates of nature, not in your frivolous discourses.[203]

With scientific method grounded in experience and not reason, and yet still maintaining a position of great importance, the outcome of Hume's critical and skeptical theory of knowledge is the proposition that all knowledge of the natural world is devoid of certitude. Only mathematics and logic in their splendid isolation—which are not science as such, since they pertain in no direct way to natural phenomena or real existence—provide access to knowledge characterized by rigorous necessity or certitude.

With Hume, then, the modern problem of knowledge, although it does not lead to the destruction of the Cartesian edifice, does lead to the disposal of a number of its key furnishings. For Hume, in the modern "scientific quest, no less than in the rest of life, we have to travel without metaphysical guarantees."[204] In rejecting the quest for certitude in science, Hume is not rejecting the validity of modern science, and so is not bent on producing entirely negative consequences from his skepticism. In asking so radical a question as "What is the foundation of all conclusions from experience?" Hume came to the conclusion that such a question was tantamount to "inquiring what reason there is for insisting that our expectations should be shaped by experience," and he saw that human nature uniformly insisted that its expectations should be shaped by experience, and that therefore there could be "no sense in asking for any further or more ultimate reason why."[205] Thus, the positive impact of his skepticism was to bring forth more fully and explicitly what was only begun in Locke—an emphasis on the passions and the imagination, on the extrarational faculties of man as he situates himself in the modern universe. Hume appears to be the first significant philosopher of the modern age "to suppose that certain knowledge was not only a misleading goal for philosophy but in fact an unobtainable goal."[206] His problem, as well as the problem of many of his successors, would be that of "*demonstrating* that science does not require certain knowledge for its attainments."[207] For Hume, the "certainty of demonstration is limited to the pure realm of ideas (logic and mathematics) and . . . all other sciences concerning matter of fact or existence, which are based upon arguments from cause and effect, are reduced to probability."[208] By shifting the expectations of science from certitude to reliable probabilities, Hume was expanding the scope of science to include the territory of human nature in all its radical complexity and unpredictability. He was securing the Lockean possibility of psychology as a science and in the process shifting modern philosophy into a phase of its logic where it would be primarily concerned with the problem of human existence and meaning.

The domains of religion, philosophy, and science itself were the same territory—that of probability and belief. To be convinced of principles in these domains is to decide on the strength of their influence on our conduct or action. Thus, as Hume says,

all probable reasoning is nothing but a species of sensation. It is not solely in poetry and music we must follow our taste and sentiment, but likewise in philosophy. When I am convinced of any princple, it is only an idea which strikes more strongly upon me. When I give the preference to one set of arguments above another, I do nothing but decide from my feeling concerning the superiority of their influence.[209]

Some probabilities, however, are so likely and so preferable, especially in the domain of science, that they are able to be treated as hypothetical or practical certitudes; scientific method is permitted, in other words, to treat them as if, for all practical purposes, they were certitudes. Thus, Hume very carefully notes that

I never asserted so absurd a proposition as that any thing might arise *without* a cause. I only maintained that our certainty of the falsehood proceeded neither from intuition nor demonstration but from another source. That Caesar existed, that there is such an island as Sicily, for these propositions, I affirm, we have no demonstrative nor intuitive proof; would you infer that I deny their truth or even their certainty? There are many different kinds of certainty; and some of them as satisfactory to the mind, though perhaps not so regular as the demonstrative kind.[210]

Far from attacking our commonsensical tendency to treat certain propositions as if they were certitudes, Hume was objecting to our philosophical or metaphysical contrivances for treating them as logically necessary, demonstrable, or intuitable certitudes.

A good example of a practical certitude is the idea of necessary connection which is, according to Hume, an important component of the relation of cause and effect. This idea is ultimately derived from the determinations of custom and feeling. We have a feeling of being determined by custom to pass from a certain impression to a certain idea. That feeling makes the idea a belief, and that same feeling "makes us call the event represented an effect, and the transition an inference." That same feeling "when it continues, supported by fusion of images, after we have surveyed all the relations of likeness and difference between the present case and the rest of our experience, makes us call the inference probable or reasonable." And it is this "very same feeling which is the impression from which the idea of necessary connexion is derived."[211] In effect, certain of the connections we make in our experience are more reasonable because more probable or more likely of future occurrence. The very feelings underlying these associations are able to be denominated more or less reasonable, depending on the reasonableness of the judgment or opinion accompanying them. This accompanying judgment may indirectly influence the action in two ways, either by discovering the existence of an "object which arouses a passion, or by discovering the causes of some state of affairs which we desire, and so showing us how it can be brought about."[212] What is decisive, however, is that although our controlling feelings may be consistent with certain rational judgments, they are not controlled or determined by these judgments, even in the scientific venture.

What appears rational in science is the attempt of its practitioner to speculate after the scientific formulation on why the formulation was contrived in the way it was contrived. Basically, for Hume, the irrational is given the import of the counterproductive, and the rational the import of the productive. In terms of these imports, science can at best be envisaged as having more rational "props" than religion or metaphysics, but its foundation is inescapably extrarational in the more precise demonstrative-intuitive sense of the term rational.

In his examination of the history of religion, Hume raised the thesis of the essential arationality of human nature which underlies both science and religion and which makes plain that sentiment, emotions, affections precede reason and philosophy in human experience and always remain dominant.[213] The "popular mind is ruled by hopes and fears, and out of these hopes and fears creates a religion of multifarious, outside controlling forces, in short, polytheism" that antedates monotheism but that, "even after the general acceptance of philosophy, still survives in the popular mentality."[214] The primacy of the vulgar consciousness is, then, entailed by the primacy of feelings over reason, and these two primacies hold not only in the realm of religion but in all claims to matter-of-fact knowledge. In fact, the two beliefs that are essential to the vulgar consciousness and determinative of it, namely, "belief in continuance of being and belief that the continuants are causally active," when formulated abstractly, are discovered to be in conflict with each other. This is an indication, for Hume, of the "manner in which the passions operate, as balancing factors in a complex mechanism—the mechanism through which nature has provided for the needs of *animal* consciousness" as well as for the so-called "reasoning processes required in the . . . more complicated conditions of human existence."[215]

The primacy of ordinary over philosophical consciousness, and the primacy of feeling over reason, lead Hume to the doorstep of a conception of man as the total series of his impressions, feelings, and ideas. Human beings, Hume claims, are "nothing but the series of *their own* sensations, feelings, dreams, images, and the rest."[216] Moreover, the primacy of the arational dimensions of human nature, along with the way in which vulgar consciousness programs the philosophical reflections of that nature, can best be visualized, Hume suggests, in reflection on the history of man's actions and the history of man's cognitive and passional mutations. In Hume's words, history is "the great mistress of wisdom," which "furnishes examples of all kinds," and every "prudential as well as moral precept may be authorized by those events which her enlarged mirror is able to present to us."[217]

What Hume has effectively done is to extend a theory of knowledge into a study of history and, by so doing, extend the problem of knowledge into the problem of human nature as such. As far as Hume is concerned, if his theory of knowledge is to be valid it must apply to the sphere of human action as well as to nature. There must be "discernible in history a uniformity and regularity of recurring phenomena similar to that observable in the natural world."[218] This suggests two suppositions: the one that the mind of man is the scene of a uniform play of motives; the other, "that the motives of men in the mass are quantitatively and qualitatively the same for all times and all countries."[219] If both of these suppositions are valid, the course of history can be subjected to causal explanation. In order to subject history to causal explanation, the supposition of the uniformity of nature in Hume's epistemology must be paralleled by the supposition of constancy of human nature in his study of human nature in history.[220] As Hume put it, the "chief use of history" is "only to discover the constant and universal principles of human nature by showing men in all variety of circumstances and situations."[221]

Hume's theory of knowledge, it would seem, has its fruition in reflection on history; his theory of knowledge, skeptically issuing in the breakdown of certitude, is catapulted into reflection on human nature in its extrarational underpinnings. Reflection on human nature must begin with reflection on history. For it is history that is the best example of what stands between common sense and learning—between the arts of conversation and those of the sciences—to which Hume conceived of himself as ambassador.[222] Thus, in his essay "Of the Study of History," Hume remarks,

When a man of business enters into life and action, he is more apt to consider the characters of men as they have relation to his interest, than as they stand in themselves; and has his judgment warped on every occasion by the violence of his passion. When a philosopher contemplates characters and manners in his closet, the general abstract view of the objects leaves the mind so cold and unmoved, that the sentiments of nature have no room to play, and he scarce feels the difference between vice and virtue. History keeps in a just medium between these extremes, and places the objects in their true point of view. The writers of history, as well as the readers, are sufficiently interested in the characters and events to have a lively sentiment of blame or praise; and at the same time, have no particular interest or concern to pervert their judgment.[223]

By mediating the realms of ordinary and philosophical consciousness, history becomes, in Hume's words, "not only a valuable part of knowledge, but opens the door to many other parts, and affords materials to most of the sciences."[224] It opens the door, in effect, to a new turn for the logic of modernity. By allowing extrarational faculties a decisive place in the very execution of the paradigmatic way of knowing in the modern universe—science— Hume could see philosophical reflection on the extrarational dimensions of human nature, as it discloses itself in history, as the ultimate outcome of his skepticism.

This outcome is predicated on the proposition that philosophical reflection rests on vulgar consciousness and is only possible by way of it—that reason does not generate the passions, and so is incapable of governing them, since a "passion can only be opposed by a counter passion, and as no passion is produced by reason, none is controlled by it."[225] And this outcome can be encapsulated in the proposition that the "connexion and necessity which ground our so-called inferences can exist only in *us*,"[226] that is, in the inner extrarational recesses of human nature. The outcome of Hume's skepticism is quite positive. As F. H. Heinemann remarks, Hume's philosophy is

important not only as a mirror of his personality, but as a very modern theory of man, stressing his irrational, unconscious character. He preludes the modern philosophy of life in Nietzsche, Freud, and Bergson.[227]

Hume came to see that the "proper and indispensable task of philosophy," insofar as it can be said to explore the foundations of mathematics and the physical sciences, was to reach "a true understanding of human nature."[228] Since man is the measure of all things, it follows that all knowledge derives from the science of man.[229] Such a science of man, Hume came to see, he himself could not develop, but he never "abandoned the aspiration that this objective might in the fullness of time be achieved."[230] "May we not hope," he said, "that philosophy, if cultivated with care and encouraged by the attention of the public, may . . . discover at least in some degree the secret springs and principles by which the human mind is activated in its operation."[231]

If Locke began the process by which knowledge would become supremely problematic for the modern world view, then Hume began the process by which man himself would become supremely problematic for that view. Perhaps this was already sensed in his own lifetime, as evidenced in the fact that by 1761 Hume had earned a place for all his works on the index of prohibited books of the Roman Catholic Church.[232] Hume himself, however, apparently felt that his contribution would have to be judged by what was done with it by posterity; having given instructions that his tomb should have no inscription, save his name and the dates of his birth and death, he left it to posterity to add the rest.[233] But if posterity was to secure Hume's contribution, Hume's debt to those who preceded him, especially Locke, had already been secured. In psychologizing the Cartesian *ego*, Locke permitted Hume, although he never used the word, to regard his own type of understanding as psychological.[234] And like Locke, the Cartesian dualism is terminal for Hume, for whom we only know what seems to be so and never the real nature of physical things.[235]

Nonetheless, after Hume the way was open for building metaphysical foundations for the meaning of man in the modern universe—the way was open for Kant. After Hume, philosophy was freed to make that turn that Socrates had made in ancient philosophy—the turn into philosophical reflection on human things. Yet Hume had cultivated the ground for this turn as Anthony Flew intimates, when he remarks that it is in "Hume, rather than in Kant, that we find the first suggestion of a 'Copernican

Revolution' in philosophy."[236] For it is Hume who first suggests that "moral philosophy," on the verge of speculating on human nature itself, is in "the same condition as natural [philosophy] with regard to astronomy before the time of Copernicus."[237] Before the metaphysical implementation of this revolution could be provided by Kant, however, the ground Hume cultivated would require further cultivation by a movement of thought that its own participants would dare to call the age of enlightenment. In some senses, Hume was a part of this movement, and Ernest Campbell Mossner may not be indulging in hyperbole when he says that "if Germany had its *Aufklärung*, and France its *Éclaircissement*, Britain had its David Hume."[238]

5

THE ENLIGHTENMENT: MODERNITY MADE SELF-CONSCIOUS

THE seventeenth century, as seen in the work of Descartes, Newton, and Leibniz, provided a "systematic expression and objectified itself in definite forms," whereas the eighteenth century, taking its lead from Locke, attempted to dissolve the fixed forms of this systematic expression.[1] The Enlightenment brings this dissolution to its climax and, in the process, replaces the epistemological platform of Locke, Berkeley, and Hume with an anthropological platform. In the Enlightenment, modern philosophy clearly and conclusively takes man as its proper object.

Locke, however, gave the Enlightenment its cue, insofar as, in shifting the object of philosophy from scientific method and its metaphysical foundations to the problem of the limits of knowledge, he was implicitly announcing the dawning of a "psychological age."[2] By transforming the Cartesian thinking *ego* into a *power*, Locke enabled man himself to become the newest subject matter for the exercise of scientific methodology.[3] Thus, in announcing the Enlightenment, d'Alembert (1717–83) would single out Locke as a herald of the Enlightenment by virtue of his having "reduced metaphysics to what it really ought to be: the experimental physics of the soul," the beginnings of the science of man.[4] Voltaire (1694–1778) likewise would remark that philosophers before Locke, in their attempt to determine the "nature of the soul," had written its "romance," but Locke "had modestly written its history."[5]

Hume, too, is intimately akin to the Enlightenment enterprise; by extending his theory of knowledge into a study of history,

Hume carefully led his epistemological emphasis to the portal of the problem of human nature; his dream of a science of man would, in one sense, become the project of the Enlightenment.[6] In addition to the contributions of Locke and Hume, new information on the culture and behavior of primitive man in the new world was beginning to exercise a marked influence on European ways of thought in the eighteenth century.[7] The time was ripe, as d'Alembert noted, to return philosophy to that study which was "so highly recommended by Socrates"—the study of "the nature of man."[8] The time was ripe for a new and major turn in the logic of modernity, a repetition of that first turn of Socrates into the study of human things, of man *qua* man, but with a form and significance quite different from ancient times.[9]

The Enlightenment, in its taking man as the proper object of philosophy, may be said to pull a thread inserted early on in the garment of modernity, namely, that of the protoethical speculation of Giordano Bruno. The Enlightenment appears to have its vital center in a moral vision of the world,[10] and in this way it can be said to bring to fruition the seed cast by Bruno in his attempt to spell out the ethical implications of the Copernican universe. Bruno was far ahead of his time, and his influence seems to have been a delayed one, destined to bear its fruit in the Enlightenment (and ultimately, in Kant) where moral autonomy would play such an important philosophical role.[11] Bruno spoke, in a mystico-philosophical way, of man's ability to form "other natures" and of his liberty as "the god of the earth."[12] Bruno, in his diatribe against institutional authority and its deceptions, in his plea for freedom of thought, no matter what the consequences, in his insistence that Jove now represents each one of us in relation to the new universe,[13] was destined to be elaborated and expanded upon by the Enlightenment.

The great intellectual revolution known as the Enlightenment was characterized "no less by the energy of its leaders in propagating than by their fertility in creating thought."[14] Among the various strands of the logic of modernity we have thus far examined, the Enlightenment is unique by virtue of the fact that its ideological dimensions weigh as heavily as its philosophical dimensions. From one point of view, the Enlightenment appears to be a "vast engine for the diffusion of . . . new ideas";[15] for the Enlightenment was disseminated to an educated public, and its dissemination was no less important to its proponents than the ideas disseminated. So prolific were the literary productions of the proponents of the Enlightenment, and so obsessed were they with disseminating these productions to as much of the reading public as possible, that one commentator on the times proclaimed the advent of "The Age of Paper."[16] The very nature of what the Enlightenment had to say, it would seem, necessitated its being preached to a wide audience, so that we find in the Enlightenment "a sustained attempt to influence and even to create public opinion."[17]

The proponents of the Enlightenment, moreover, were themselves members of the privileged order of the nobility, and sometimes even of the Church, so that the privilege of aristocracy was behind their dissemination of the new thinking.[18] What was novel about this aristocracy was that the ties of patronage and kinship cut across national lines in Europe, so that a kind of cosmopolitan society emerged that itself offered diverse possibilities for the transmission of information in Western Europe.[19] The transmission of enlightened ideas was consciously intended to be a substitute for the ties of tradition that bound men to Church and state. The enlightened nobility was not revolting against aristocratic privilege per se but against everything in tradition, religion, and government that was inconsistent with what it took to be enlightened thinking; it was bent upon seeing its own ideas assume the power and acceptability of tradition itself. Both as writer and as reformer, the proponent of the Enlightenment required a large audience, free expression, and respectable status, so as to be able to be a preceptor to Europe,[20] to Western civilization itself. It was no accident when the French historian Rulhière told the Académie française in 1787 that the beginning of the Enlightenment marked the beginning of the "empire of public opinion," for, as Voltaire claimed, at the time France was coming to be ruled by public opinion, public opinion was coming to be ruled by the philosophes.[21]

The fact, then, that the proponents of the Enlightenment proudly referred to themselves as philosophes should not blind us to the powerful ideological aspect of their thought. In the midst of the ideological thrust of the movement, however, philosophical insight was being generated and cultivated, although not in a systematic fashion, and the philosophical impact of the movement was destined to be as powerful as its exertions in behalf of enlightening ordinary opinion. The ideological dimension of the movement would, in fact, have a decisive impact on the shaping of its philosophical insights. Since the Enlightenment can be conceived as a new European framework for the communication of ideas, the very accessibility of the ideas communicated, the importance of freedom of thought, the importance of its warfare against tradition and the authority of just about every institution except its own aristocratic inheritance would have a powerful influence on the very content of the ideas communicated and the philosophical insights backing up these ideas. In the Enlightenment, philosophy was consigned to ride an ideological vehicle intended to transform popular opinion, and it would emerge with a very different shape from the one it possessed before its embarkation. The power of—and the power to shape—public opinion were aided by a great increase in population. The population decline of Europe in the seventeenth century reversed itself between 1715 and 1740, and the population increased from 140 to 187 million between 1750 and 1800; European economy thus recovered a good deal of its lost vitality.[22] These and other factors conspired for the ideologizing of the logic of modernity as it had thus far philosophically articulated itself.

The fact that the Enlightenment was neither a purely philosophical nor a purely ideological movement but rather a philosophical movement determined by ideological methods, interests, and aims appears to account in good part for the powerful role of the Enlightenment in the unfolding of the logic of modernity. Insofar as the Enlightenment was ideological, it was determined to transform social consciousness; insofar as the Enlightenment was philosophical, it aimed to intensify the individual consciousness of the exceptional mind. To the extent that the individual consciousness of the thinker was shaped by a program for the remaking of social consciousness, the Enlightenment brought to the individual thinker a social vocation, not usually associated with the philosopher, namely, the task of entirely justifying his thinking in terms of his role as preceptor of society. To the extent that the program for the remaking of social consciousness was dictated by great minds, however, the Enlightenment brought to social consciousness a role not usually associated with common opinion—the role of imitating the critical attitude of the philosopher. For a brief moment in modern Western history, the Enlightenment held together the action-oriented impulse of the common man and the reflection-oriented impulse of the philosopher.

In order to maintain the demands of philosophy and ideology in equilibrium, an intense, unmitigated self-consciousness had to be practiced collectively, a self-consciousness not merely of the import of their individual biographies but of the import of the collective biography of their age that the philosophes were writing. This self-consciousness required a sense of the uniqueness and radical historical insularity of the Enlightenment. Reason itself must be viewed, not as a heritage patiently transmitted through history, but as the Enlightenment's novel acquisition.[23] Freed from the spell of the mythicized and enchanted world of prior ages,[24] the Enlightenment, as Diderot (1713–84) saw it, would assume that

all things must be examined, debated, investigated without exception and without regard for anyone's feelings. . . . We must ride roughshod over all those ancient puerilities, overturn the barriers that reason never erected, give back to the arts and sciences the liberty that is so precious to them.[25]

In its exercise of an omnicompetent criticism, the Enlightenment, for d'Alembert, was to be "the century of philosophy par excellence."[26] The "taste for systems—more suited to flatter the imagination than to enlighten reason—is today," according to d'Alembert, "almost entirely banished from works of merit."[27] In rejecting the speculative dimension of philosophy, the Enlightenment would raise doubts about the value of metaphysics,[28] thereby insulating itself from the philosophical accomplishments of the past, even the relatively recent past of the seventeenth century.

Whatever evil resides in men is the result of their being the prisoners of their heritage from the past,[29] of their being bound

by the follies and errors of their predecessors.[30] History must then
be reinterpreted for them in order to free them from the hold of
its errors. The Enlightenment must utilize its sense of its own
uniqueness and historical insularity as the motive for a reexamination of history. In this reexamination, the majority of philosophes will follow the course of Henry Fielding (1707–54) when
he dismissed the period from the collapse of the Western Roman
Empire to the sixteenth century as "centuries of monkish dullness
when the whole world seems to have been asleep."[31] This must
result in the perception of history as a persistent struggle between
two kinds of mentality—the Christian era presented as an age of
myth, belief, and superstition, and the era of Greece and Rome
presented as an age of rationality, science, and enlightenment[32]
that finds its perfect attainment in the eighteenth century. "We
have admired our ancestors less," Chastellux (1734–88) said, "but
we have loved our contemporaries better, and have expected more
of our descendants."[33] Yet, although the Enlightenment "never
wholly discarded that final, most stubborn illusion"—the illusion
that it was without illusions[34]—it can be said that its perception
of its own historical insularity enabled it to attain the moment of
high self-consciousness it represents in the unfolding logic of
modernity.

Of the Enlightenment, it might be said that "a past bespeaks
a future; a future imperatively demands a past."[35] In order to
justify itself as the promise of a future state of perfection for
mankind, the Enlightenment had to re-create the past. To pick
and choose from the past whatever suits its needs was, for the
Enlightenment, to be free of the past in the very use of that past.
The philosophes held eclecticism to be the school that was not
really a school, and here they found the triumph of criticism over
speculation, the symbol of their philosophical independence.[36] Yet
their need to reinterpret the past in order to establish themselves
as a new beginning could not free them from that past. In the end,
the Enlightenment itself was a part of something larger, a phase
of the unfolding logic of modernity with its medieval origins—
a fact illustrated by the faith in modern science that united the
philosophes.[37] The Enlightenment, in being a heightened aware-

ness of itself and its uniqueness, *is* modernity made self-conscious of its own radical nature, demands, and implications.

In examining the Enlightenment as a raising of modernity to self-consciousness, we shall first analyze its negative starting point, specifically, its anti-Christian polemic. We shall then analyze the positive teaching that emerges: its redefinition of human nature. Finally, we shall examine the social theory the Enlightenment bequeathes, as a philosophical heritage, to the future development of the logic of modernity.

THE ANTI-CHRISTIAN POLEMIC

In keeping with its conception of philosophy as a body of criticism devoid of systematic embodiment, the starting point of the Enlightenment is negative, the creation of a polemic against Christianity. In this way, the Enlightenment confirms the fears Berkeley harbored about the rejection of the authentic notion of the Christian God.[38] Leibniz and Newton epitomized, for Berkeley, the objects of his fears. Leibniz proposed a God who was uninvolved in the operations of nature, whereas Newton envisaged a God who was reduced to a function of a physical system, a being who served to maintain that system.[39] Leibniz failed to adequately recognize the immanence of God; Newton failed to adequately recognize the transcendence of God. Berkeley saw the common root of their failures in the notion of the independent existence of an unknowable matter. Berkeley's failure to overcome the dualism of this matter and mind meant that the options available to modern thinkers would remain those of Newton and Leibniz—now interpreted in a simplistic fashion.

The first of these options would be to emphasize the divine immanence; but this would entail an emphasis on the importance of nature that would, in turn, imply that God was increasingly unnecessary for the operation of nature. Consequently, some thinkers would begin to argue that "Newton had been wrong in assuming that gravitation would not keep the solar system in order without the periodic intervention of its divine Creator."[40] The

second of these options would be to emphasize the divine transcendence; but this would entail a separation of God from the
physical universe that would, in turn, imply a severance of the
Christian God from the modern scientific world view. Consequently, some thinkers would begin to argue for the irrelevance
of Christianity to the modern scientific venture. It is but one more
step to argue from this irrelevance to the conclusion that the Christian God cannot have the same rational credentials as the modern
scientific world view. Bishop Joseph Butler (1692–1752) seems
to indicate that this step had been taken when, in 1736, he remarked that it

is come, I know not how, to be taken for granted by many persons that
Christianity is not so much as a subject of enquiry; but that it is now
at length discovered to be fictitious. And accordingly, they treat it as if
in the present age this were an agreed point among all people of
discernment.[41]

It would seem to be precisely from this assumption—that Christianity is an elaborate superstition—that the Enlightenment
proceeds.

   This assumption is first detected in a clandestine literature that
circulated in France between 1700 and 1750 and that offered the
rudiments of "a coherent method and doctrine which finally became the philosophy of the Encyclopedists."[42] The success of this
literature—which violently assailed Christian dogmas and emphasized the flaws of Christian institutions—in "penetrating the
consciousness of the important writers of the eighteenth century"[43] can be traced, in part, to a growing realization, on the part
of many intellectuals, that Christian faith was neither essential to
public order nor necessary for an adequate understanding of the
world.[44] The success of this literature can also be traced, in part,
to the intense self-consciousness of the Enlightenment, which required a sense of great urgency and a contrived earnestness akin
to religious enthusiasm. Despite the fact that there was more religious feeling in mid-eighteenth-century France than is often supposed,[45] traditional Roman Catholic faith had little of the Enlightenment's sense of timeliness or urgency and was "more casually
held, as an hereditary possession."[46]

Finally, the success of this clandestine literature can also be traced to the peculiar situation of the Church itself in France at this time. As a subterranean element in this Church, the Jansenists emphasized a religion of the heart over against the rational constructs of traditional Scholastic theology. The flourishing of an untutored Jansenism may have contributed to the emergence of the Enlightenment in France, for it meant "that stern morals could henceforth be explained as a product of superstition, and strict living ridiculed as provincial and uncouth."[47] Furthermore, the fact that Jansenism was by and large alienated from the ecclesiastical hierarchy, and yet managed to permeate the thinking of some Church intellectuals, implied that the members of the Church could not present a united front against the anti-Christian polemic of the Enlightenment. It may have meant that the impulse of the Enlightenment failed to be assimilated by the Church, that the Enlightenment's clandestine anti-Christian beginnings failed to be purified by men favorable to orthodox Christian beliefs. There was, after all, a humanistic trend within Catholic theology from the Council of Trent (1545–63) down to the eighteenth century itself that enlarged the boundaries of the human, extended the domain of nature, and circumscribed the realm of grace, so as to "regard man in his mundane and fallen state" as a "legitimate and respectable inhabitant of the universe."[48] This tendency was at odds with Jansenism and consistent with the more modest proclamations of the Enlightenment, but a rapprochement between this tendency and the spirit of the Enlightenment never emerged.

The demand for self-consciousness in the Enlightenment over against the tradition-bound orientation of Roman Catholic Christianity, the presence of certain divisions in the Church itself, the ability in terms of ideology to perceive the Christian God as irrelevant to the modern world view and the modern social order, as well as a subterranean element within the Church that attempted to purify and make even more rigorous the ethic of the Church— all of these may have been factors in the initiation of the Enlightenment in an anti-Christian polemic that equated Christianity with superstition. Although, despite these factors, there might have been a rapprochement between the Enlightenment and Christian orthodoxy, it must be said that if there had been, the Enlight-

enment would have been considerably different from the movement it eventually became. Could it be that the Enlightenment
had to begin with such an anti-Christian polemic in order to assure
the absoluteness of its own self-consciousness as well as its own
nature as an ideologized philosophical mode? In the thirteenth
century it would have been impossible for men of discernment
to reject Christianity because, in rejecting it, they would have
been renouncing organized rationality itself, given the dominance
of the Scholastic theological framework in all areas of knowledge.
But, in the eighteenth century, that Scholastic framework had
retreated to a less significant place in the intellectual culture fos-
tered by the Church; reason was no longer indissolubly connected
with doctrine. In rejecting Christian belief, men were now able
to conceive of themselves as *not* rejecting reason.[49] In rejecting the
Christian God, they were able to conceive of themselves as *not*
rejecting the scientific world view. Is one entitled to say that once
such an attitude became possible then it became necessary? Is this
our real explanation for the peculiar origin of the Enlightenment?

In carrying out their anti-Christian polemic, the philosophes
found a precedent in the ancient philosopher Lucretius. Lucretius'
statement, "such are the heights of evil that religion can urge,"[50]
became a favorite theme for the disseminators of enlightenment.
Voltaire was perhaps the most vociferous disseminator of the polemic, inclined as he was to often repeat the phrase "Écrasez
l'infâme"—the infamous one to be crushed being none other than
the Roman Catholic Church.[51] It is ironic that one of the bases
for the Enlightenment's polemic was precisely the accusation that
Christianity failed to possess that characteristic that the very name
"Catholic" claimed it possessed, namely, universality and a certain
abiding uniformity. As the philosophes perceived Christianity, it
seemed to be but "a sort of local custom of the European people,
and therefore, on that ground alone, it was suspect to those who
were resolved to be rid of all merely local customs."[52] Lacking
in uniformity, and plagued with provincialism, Christianity was
of all religions the most riddled with intolerance. "Neither the
Oriental countries, nor the Romans, nor the Greeks, nor even the
Jews," as they saw it, "practiced religious intolerance," but Chris-

tianity did because it sought "to dominate both the temporal and the spiritual realm."[53]

Having reduced Christianity to superstition, and having predicated the most extreme kind of intolerance of this superstition, it only remained to point out how destructive superstition could be, since it was obvious how destructive intolerance could be. Looking at science, the philosophes could not realistically argue that it was free from errors; but they saw that the errors of science were not destructive, since these errors were corrected by science itself in its immanent progress.[54] But the errors of religion, and especially Christian religion, "do not arise from a mere insufficiency of knowledge but from a perverted direction of knowledge,"[55] since its dogmas are superstitious, and superstition (not mere error) is the enemy of knowledge, since it refuses to be corrected by knowledge. Thus, superstition was the primal enemy of enlightenment, and the fight against superstition was to be the primary and most urgent task.[56] Instead of satisfying man's thirst for knowledge, Christianity offered a set of myths that positively blocked the satisfaction of that thirst and amounted to a massive failure of confidence in man's unaided reason.[57]

Relying on their reinterpretation of history, enlightened thinkers defined medieval Christianity as the soil for the germination of Christian superstition. Thus, for Condorcet (1743–94), the Middle Ages are painted in terms of "theological reveries" and "superstitious impostures," with the result that "Europe, compressed between sacerdotal tyranny and military despotism, awaited in blood and tears the moment when new knowledge would allow it to be reborn to liberty, to humanity, and to virtue."[58] This new knowledge is none other than the scientific comprehension of nature. As d'Holbach (1723–89) put it, it is "for want of being acquainted with the powers of nature, with the properties of matter," that man "has supposed the universe under the empire of an intelligent cause, of which he is, and perhaps always will be, himself the model."[59] The very thrust of the Enlightenment's identification of Christianity with superstition was thus to show that at long last the moment had arrived when Christian religion was finally to be overcome by modern science.

As a group, the philosophes had a vested interest in modern science as a resource in their battle against religion; they assumed that when science advances, superstition retreats.[60] Once again, they found a precedent in Lucretius who, when he "spoke of dispelling night, lifting shadows, or clarifying ideas," meant the conquest of religion by science.[61] In announcing a "siècle des lumières,"[62] the Enlightenment was announcing the imminent conquest of Christianity by the forces of modern scientific thinking that would be applied to that being whom Christianity had enshrouded in "myth": man. In their darkest moments, when enlightenment met the greatest entrenched resistance, the philosophes could always fall back in justifying their "brave new ideas" on the success of natural science.[63]

The conquest would proceed on the basis of the antithesis between superstition and rationality, between myth and criticism. Christianity contained all those elements which were negations of the virtues of science. Whereas science was self-corrective, Christianity was fated to become more and more superstitious; whereas science was tolerant of dissent, Christianity was intolerant. Whereas science was indifferent to personal authority, Christianity was anchored in the authority of persons; whereas science was a unified movement, Christianity was divided and divisive. Everywhere, the Enlightenment found the correctives for the failings of Christianity in modern science. "Every sect of every kind," Voltaire said, "is a rallying point for doubt and error. Scotist, Thomist, Realist, Nominalist, Papist, Calvinist, Molinist, and Jansenist are only pseudonyms," for "sect and error are synonymous."[64] But there "are no sects in mathematics, in experimental physics. A man who examines the relations between a cone and a sphere is not of the sect of Archimedes."[65] Science had proved its success and no longer required apologists; and so, the Enlightenment would elevate science into the force that would demythicize the world view of Christianity. With the category of the supernatural in Christianity reduced to crass superstition, the Enlightenment would replace this category with the natural, and since science was the investigation of the natural world, it was in science that it sought the key to knowledge,[66] and to science that it would appeal for the vanquishment of Christianity. Never for a moment did the Enlightenment allude to the decisive role of medieval Christianity in the inspiration of the change in world views that would generate modern science; thus, never for a moment did the Enlightenment perceive the ultimate irony in the conquest of which it spoke—that the offspring had risen up to murder its mother. But, then again, never for a moment was the question raised of whether science was in actuality conquering Christianity or only acting out this conquest in the fantasy of the Enlightenment's ideology.

The previously mentioned possibility of a rapprochement between orthodox Christianity and the Enlightenment was impossible of attainment; Christian humanism was incapable of digesting the Enlightenment, for the brunt of the anti-Christian polemic was the vision of a secularized society. To be enlightened was to envisage a society where Christian beliefs were in no way determinative. In this, the Enlightenment represents an irreversible turn away from the situation of the seventeenth century that, alike in Catholic and Protestant cultures, was an intensely religious age where "preachers and theologians . . . formed public opinion and were almost the sole channels of popular instruction."[67] It has been clear from our study that the concepts developed by the metaphysical systems of the seventeenth century were still firmly anchored in theological thinking. But, in the eighteenth century, "various fields of knowledge—natural science, history, laws, politics, art— . . . withdraw from the domination and tutelage of traditional metaphysics and theology."[68] This shift is signaled by Locke, protested by Berkeley, confidently proclaimed by Hume, and finalized and given ideological embodiment in the Enlightenment. The consequence is that the concept of God that previously had grounded other concepts, most notably in Descartes and Newton, now assumes the position, at best, of that which requires justification,[69] and, at worst, of that which requires expulsion. Although the Enlightenment may only have been serving its ideological aims in announcing the conquest of Christianity by science, although it may only have been *envisaging* a secular society, it was relying on and intensifying an *actual* secularization of reasoned inquiry. Scientific inquiry, as it was actually pursued, and the Christian God, as actually believed in, had, it would seem, parted company.

Between the seventeenth century and the Enlightenment, it would thus appear, lies a loss of contact with an understanding of the medieval Christian origins of the modern universe, for even Descartes and Newton were still operating in terms of some kind of understanding of these origins. This loss of understanding is not the sole province of the Enlightenment, for it seems likely that by the eighteenth century both unbelievers and believers, by and large, had "lost the key to the symbolic language of medieval Christendom."[70] It wasn't the philosophes alone who detested the Gothic cathedrals, for monks rebuilt their monasteries, and "in their rage for modernity they whitewashed the walls, ripped up medieval tombs, and demolished medieval statuary."[71] The Enlightenment is likely the movement that brings this estrangement from the medieval tradition to intense consciousness by bringing modernity into a consciousness of itself. In doing this, the Enlightenment may be the most powerful among several causes of the actual secularization of Western culture[72] that would follow in the nineteenth century. But, continuous with the prior developments of the logic of modernity, the Enlightenment—its protests to the contrary notwithstanding—bears the same indebtedness which that logic bears to the philisophico-mystical vision that Christianity generated in the Middle Ages. From this point of view, the Enlightenment was "religious in its origin," as Christopher Dawson notes, "although it was anti-religious in its results."[73] Of the Enlightenment, it might be said, in the words of Karl Löwith, that "in consequence of the Christian consciousness we have a historical consciousness which is as Christian by derivation as it is non-Christian by consequence."[74]

Whatever we mean by the Enlightenment's vision of a secularized society, however, we cannot validly talk of a collapse of religious institutions in the age of Enlightenment, nor can we correctly speak of a loss of religious concerns in all sectors of society. The actual secularization proceeding apace with the Enlightenment's vision of a secular society was more like a subtle "shift of attention: religious institutions and religious explanations of events were slowly being displaced from the center of life to its periphery."[75] The slowly expanding vacuum would be filled by a secular view of things, a view that rejected any authoritativeness in a being that transcends nature or experience. Any kind of "transcendental authority," whether "imposed from without by the Church or monarch or from within by innate ideas," had to be viewed as something wholly arbitrary, a "strategem of priests and politicians, a set of philosophical prejudices."[76]

The rejection of all forms of transcendental authority required that the philosopher be accorded the social prestige formerly reserved for the priest. If "you want priests you do not need philosophers," Diderot said, "and if you want philosophers you do not need priests; for the one being by their calling the friends of reason and the promoters of science, the other the enemies of reason and favourers of ignorance, if the first do good, the others do evil."[77] Even the anthropological information coming from the new world was interpreted by the Enlightenment as a proof of the destructiveness of a Christian culture over against the creativity and innocence of a culture that had never known Christianity. Raynal (1713–96), in *The Philosophical and Political History of the Indies*, which was so popular that it ran to fifty-four editions before the end of the century, descried the "corruptions and miseries" imposed upon American primitives by their Christian conquerors, and thus condemned "the artificial and Christian civilization of Europe by contrasting it with the natural virtues of primitive peoples."[78] Even that classical historical work of Gibbon (1737–94), *The Decline and Fall of the Roman Empire*, describes, for the instruction of future ages, the "triumph of barbarism and religion" in the fall of the empire.[79] History and anthropology could serve to enlighten men about the destructiveness of a Christian society and the benefits of the secular society that ought to take its place.

The Enlightenment's vision of a secular society involved not only the rejection of transcendental authority, which had its paradigm in the Christian notion of God, but also the rejection of the corruption of human nature that had its paradigm in the Christian dogma of original sin. "The concept of original sin is the common opponent against which all the different trends of the philosophy of the Enlightenment join forces," and it is for this reason that the philosophes again and again return to that classical seventeenth-century defense of the dogma, Pascal's *Pensées*, and repeatedly test the strength of their criticism on this work.[80] Up until the time of the Enlightenment, Christians were the leading educators; but, as perceived by the Enlightenment, the "most optimistic Christian was not free to assert that education, no matter how thoroughgoing, could ever erase the effects of Adam's fall." The "myth" of original sin had to presume man's fundamental inability to change through his own exertions; education could never do the work of grace.[81] Having rejected original sin and transcendental authority, the Enlightenment had only to appeal for the very expurgation of the word "God," at least in reference to the God of Christianity, from the language. D'Holbach, coming as he did toward the close of the Enlightenment, dared to make such an appeal.

Let us then conclude that the word *God* . . . not presenting to mind any true idea, ought to be banished [from] the language of all those who are desirous to speak so as to be understood.[82]

The final touch to the Enlightenment's vision of a secularized society was the notion of progress. Condorcet, perhaps the best applicator of this finishing touch of the vision, rejecting as he did the working of Divine Providence in history, argued that history would have to be understood in terms of its own inherently progressive impulse. Progress thus became an "autonomous human creation free from divine will or direction." Instead of elucidating a "divinely ordained quality in human history as distinguished from natural history," Condorcet relied on "the complete identification of history with the other sciences," so that even if history were "not a science of absolute prediction, like physics," it could still maintain "the fundamental character of science by calling its findings truth with a high degree of probability."[83] With the notion of an inherent logic of progress for history, a logic completely unrelated to Divine Providence, the Enlightenment completed its vision of a secularized society, for now it could substitute for the love of God the love of humanity, and for the "vicarious atonement the perfectibility of man through his own efforts," and for "the hope of immortality in another world the hope of living in the memory of future generations."[84]

The history that the Enlightenment was necessitated to reinterpret, if it was to sustain its claim to utter historical uniqueness, had to be secularized in order for society to be secularized. The past had to be re-created as a secularized subject matter if the future was to be created as a secularized society. In this way, the philosophes revolutionized the study of history by secularizing its subject matter; for, as long as Divine Providence was taken seriously, the historian had no way of subjecting historical events to his own critical scrutiny.[85] We need only compare that great Christian interpretation of history, *Histoire universelle*, written by Bossuet in the seventeenth century, with the *De la félicité publique*, written by Chastellux in 1772, or the *Esquisse d'un tableau historique des progrès de l'esprit humain*, written by Condorcet in 1793, to perceive how radically the content of historical study had been secularized so as to facilitate the Enlightenment's vision of a secularized society. By rejecting the Old Testament as a literal account of the past, the Enlightenment did not merely extend the timescale of history but left the historian entirely "free to decide for himself what had been the forces of historical change and their manner of operating," thus permitting the philosophy of the historian to be determinative of the "divisions which he introduced into his narrative."[86]

The Enlightenment's anti-Christian polemic began, then, with a reduction of Christianity to superstition and ended with the advocacy of a secularized society, a society operating, not on the Christian premises of transcendental authority, original sin, and Divine Providence, but on the secular premises of the authority of enlightened reason, an uncorrupted human nature, and an inherently natural progress in history. But this anti-Christian polemic, from beginning to end, had a Christian underpinning, much as the Enlightenment's justification of its discontinuity with the past was grounded in an inescapable continuity with the preceding logic of modernity. Furthermore, just as the demands of their ideological methods and aims prevented the philosophes from readily admitting their continuity with the modern past, so also these demands prohibited them from confessing the heritage of

Christianity that grounded their very anti-Christian polemic. The philosophical justification of the Enlightenment's vision of a secularized society required working with Christian categories.

Just as it is true of men that they cannot fight unless they occupy the same ground, so also is it true of ideas; in order to vanquish Christian philosophy, the proponents of enlightenment "had to meet it on the level of certain common preconceptions."[87] But, so vehemently would the philosophes reject revealed religion that the Christian contribution to their thinking had to be subterranean, and they were largely unaware of it.[88] So it was that the Enlightenment's vision of a secularized society came to resemble a new religion modeled on the very motifs of Christianity that were being deposed. Nature took the place of God; Newton's *Principia* became a biblical text; Voltaire became the prophet; and by books and pamphlets, by encyclopedic ventures, newspapers, and journals, and by "serious argument and by witty mockery," a new religion (although it was never called religion) was preached (although it was never called preaching) to the civilized nations of Europe.[89] Christopher Dawson was not exaggerating when, in interpeting "religion as the soul of a culture," he argued that belief in progress, as the motive of the Enlightenment, "arose within a Christian culture and was unlikely to survive it."[90] Nor was Carl Becker guilty of hyperbole when he argued that just as it could be said of "the thirteenth century that it was an age of reason as well as of faith," so also could it be said of the Enlightenment that "it was an age of faith as well as of reason."[91] The philosophes were "nearer the Middle Ages, less emancipated from the preconceptions of medieval Christian thought, than they quite realized or we have commonly supposed."[92]

There may have been a loss of understanding of the symbolic language of medieval Christianity in this age, but the motifs of the belief informing that language subtly buttressed the Enlightenment's vision of a secular society; the secular society was an inversion of Christian society. We do well, then, to speak of "a deep polarity of disbelief and belief in the eighteenth century," a polarity that is to be understood as a dialectical movement.[93] What was, effectively, a new religion emerged, but it could never be explicitly admitted to be such. This new religion was a pretender to the throne of Christianity in the latter's connection with the logic of modernity; this new religion gave a new content to the Christian religion by the discovery and acknowledgment of the historical character of the Christian religion.[94] The Enlightenment's inner transformation of Christian piety "is conditioned by the fact that it frees itself from the domination of metaphysical and theological thinking and secures for itself a new standard, a new norm of judgment."[95] This new standard of judgment is *historicized reason*, for reason is now made to function in terms of history, and history in terms of reason. Consideration of the immutable norms of reason must now go hand in hand with consideration of the manner in which these norms unfold in history.[96]

The crux of the anti-Christian religion that the Enlightenment builds on the skeletal structure of Christian beliefs thus involves the following. For the Christian God will be substituted nature; for the embodiment of the Christian God in Christ, human nature; for the providential plan of God, an inherently progressive human history; for the essentially other-worldly kingdom of God, the this-worldly perfected society of the enlightened only to come in the future. Christianity is negated by constructing a counter-Christian religion that replicates the skeleton of Christianity but that has a different kind of flesh and sinew. Just as original sin had defined what the Christian expected of education, so a perfectible human nature would define what the Enlightenment devotee could expect of education. Just as grace had justified the Christian's actions, so critical reason would justify the enlightened believer's actions. Just as happiness for the Christian consisted in a beatific vision of God, so happiness would lie for the worshiper of enlightenment in the vision of a perfected humanity. All the categories of Christian belief would be inverted and reconstituted from the inside, so that an implicit reliance on the structure of Christian belief would lie at the base of the very polemic against Christian belief. The very motifs that were condemned as superstition would serve as the categorical shells utilized to overcome that superstition, and the dynamism of modern scientific method would presumably fill these shells with the material of a religious claim meant to rival Christianity.

We are thus left with what we might be inclined to call an

enigma. In order for the Enlightenment, in its ideological super-structure, to reject Christianity, it was necessitated, in its philo-sophical substructure, to model itself on Christianity. In order to announce in its ideological discourse that the Christian God was separable from the scientific world view—that Christianity as a complex superstition was antithetical to this world view and that this world view was involved in the expulsion of Christianity from Western culture—the Enlightenment had to use Christian categories as its paradigms, had to philosophically anchor its pro-gram in the bones of Christianity. The Enlightenment had to act as if Christianity were decisive in the emergence of the logic of modernity in order to preach the separability of Christianity and the scientific world view. Christianity could not be dispelled as a "myth" that is dangerous for modernity unless those of its theoretical contents which were formative of modernity were mimicked. But the Enlightenment could never concede this in its ideology; the Christian underpinning of its anti-Christian polemic could function only as a philosophical premise buried far beneath the ever increasing mound of its ideological invective. The phil-osophes were thus "right to think of themselves as modern, secular philosophers" but "wrong to claim that they owed their Christian culture nothing,"[97]

THE REDEFINITION OF HUMAN NATURE

The negative starting point of the Enlightenment—its anti-Chris-tian polemic—begins by identifying Christianity with superstition and ends with a vision of a secularized society. This vision enables the Enlightenment to propose naturalistic humanism as the reli-gious substitute for institutionalized Christian orthodoxy. In this naturalistic humanism is had the beginning of the positive doctrine of the Enlightenment, its redefinition of human nature.

The conception of man's place in the great hierarchy of being created and ruled by God,[98] bequeathed to modernity by the medieval Christian vision, was far from problematic. But given the Enlightenment's equation of Christianity with superstition, man's nature and place in nature became profoundly problematic.[99] The Christian vision, with its teaching on original sin, still exerted an influence; man's heart, Diderot said, was "by turns a sanctuary and a sewer."[100] But now all of man's problems were seen to have natural causes, and so their solutions had to derive from purely natural actions.[101] Submission to institutionalized religion is now a betrayal of man's nature; man, for better or worse, is now on his own.[102] Either the moral law, written in man's nature, is supreme, or an arbitrary Divine will is supreme.

If God conforms to the moral law, he is wise and good; if he obeys his own arbitrary will, he is neither the one nor the other; his distinction between good and evil is determined by mere caprice. On the other hand, if God subjects himself to the moral law, his mediation is superfluous, since man, by his own unaided reason, is capable of distinguishing the duty of complying with the general moral law.[103]

Human moral autonomy must be the essence of naturalistic humanism—and it must be shown to be efficacious—otherwise men will be wont to fall back on the superstition of the efficacity of the grace of God. To show the efficacity of man's moral autonomy, the philosophes had to demonstrate their own moral autonomy and convince their audience that it was productive of moral virtue. They had to do more than merely repeat the ethical proclamation of Bruno; they had to be esteemed men of virtue, precisely because from their opponents' point of view they were enemies of morality and virtue. What good would their attacks on Christian faith and doctrine do if they "were unable to replace the old morality by a new and more solidly based one"?[104]

The philosophes had to leave the impression of their own moral uprightness if their case for the radical self-sufficiency of human ethical autonomy was to be convincing. This could best be done by appealing, not to classical virtues, such as temperance and courage, which they would find difficult to convince the unenlightened that they possessed in a greater degree than their orthodox Christian opponents, but by appealing to the purity of their own intentions and their tolerance, which would shine when compared with the picture they painted of the moral compromise and intolerance of Christians. Bruno had already proclaimed the imperative of moral autonomy: "We wish this law to be vigorously

observed, that reason is as true as it is necessary, and the authority
of no man howsoever true and excellent he may be is admissible
as an argument."[105] The Enlightenment would appear to be
merely repeating his proclamation in its contention that the individual's reason discovers "within and by itself, and in its own
terms, the imperative for goodness."[106] But the Enlightenment's
contention would be illustrated in the exemplarity of the lived
moral autonomy of the philosophes.

Bruno and Socrates testified to their ethical propositions in their
sacrificial deaths; the philosophes would testify to their ethical
proposition in their lives—in their high-minded ideals, in their
tolerance of each other (they would omit mention of their intolerance of their enemies), and in their fraternity. The fraternal love,
which that great light of German enlightenment, Lessing (1729–81),
called for was universal, "the love human beings feel for each
other not as children of God, not as brothers in Christ, but as
fellow men";[107] and it was this fraternity that would be advertised
as visible in the lives of the philosophes. Thus, two more Christian
categories were emptied and given a secular content. Christian
charity was transmuted into fraternity, and the Christian com-
munion of saints was transmuted into the pantheon of secular
sages. In the Enlightenment's pantheon of secular philosopher-
saints would be had ample ammunition for convincing the unenlightened that the Christian ethic could be replaced by an effective,
purely naturalistic ethic of human autonomy constructed on "the
tabula rasa of human nature."[108] Once again, the imitation of
Christian motifs had to be used as a philosophical ground for the
ideological aim of convincing the unenlightened not only that
ethics is "independent from religious dogmas and cult" but that
there is "an essential opposition between them."[109] It would be
no easy task to convince the unenlightened that if "ethics is to
grow out of human nature and tend toward individual and social
good," then it follows that "religion, and Christianity more than
all other religions, has actually perverted ethics."[110] Ideology alone
would have been insufficient to alter the common opinion that
religion and ethics were intimately connected; Christian categories
themselves had to be reworked to make the ethic of naturalistic
humanism appealing.

We are now in the position to perceive the positive contribution flowing from the negative starting point, that is, the anti-Christian polemic, of the Enlightenment. Here again we discover an equilibrium between ideological superstructure and philosophical substructure, with human nature redefined in consistency with ideological aims and methods, while at the same time man *qua* man is made into a new object for philosophical speculation. We shall begin our consideration of the Enlightenment's positive contribution, its redefinition of human nature, by first examining its redefinition of nature itself; from here we analyze how this redefinition permits the Enlightenment to reinterpret the hallowed notion of the immutability of human nature. We shall then examine the important role of the affective or irrational dimensions of human nature, as perceived by the Enlightenment, in this reinterpretation. Finally, we conclude with an analysis of the Enlightenment's view of man, in both its ideological and its philosophical dimensions, as the measure of all things.

In their secular religion of naturalistic humanism, the philosophes had not ceased to worship; they had "only given another form and a new name to the object of worship," since, having "denatured God, they deified nature."[111] But the Enlightenment could not deify the concept of nature as it had thus far been used; nature had to mean something more than merely the cosmic orderliness of the universe. Arthur O. Lovejoy has perceptively illustrated the unconscious confusion of two senses of nature in the Enlightenment. There is the more traditional notion of nature as the "cosmical order and its laws, which are in fact known only empirically," and there is the novel notion of nature as right reason, "a body of universal and intuitively known truths of morals and religion."[112] We have seen that the Cartesian bifurcation of mind and matter was a key element and problem in the post-Cartesian understanding of nature. Instead of trying to resolve or overcome this bifurcation, as did Berkeley, the Enlightenment chose to deemphasize and even ignore it. It was able to ignore this bifurcation by interpreting nature not merely as the infinite unknowable spaces outside of human consciousness, as the early modern cosmologists did, but as whatever man knows purely on the basis of reason alone. Nature came to signify not so much a given group of objects but a certain "horizon of knowledge."[113]

To speak of nature as the horizon of unaided reason required that the Enlightenment view reason as identical in all men, with the result that the life of reason could admit of no diversity in its essence. Differences in opinion must be evidences of error, and "universality of appeal or of acceptance" must be not merely an effect but a "criterion of truth."[114] That which was according to nature had to correspond to the assumption of uniformity, so that the notion of uniformity itself was the principal element in the Enlightenment's redefinition of nature.[115] But this emphasis on uniformity was precisely the link between the novel meaning afforded nature by the Enlightenment and the traditional notion of nature as the orderliness of the universe. The notion of uniformity, in fact, enabled the Enlightenment to use the notion of nature as the horizon of unaided reason and the notion of nature as cosmical orderliness interchangeably, since both the exercise of unaided reason and the cosmical orderliness of the external world were characterized by an irreducible uniformity. The uniformity of the external world could be construed as reflected in the uniformity of authentic reasoning, as illustrated in the following statement of d'Holbach.

It is not then in an ideal world, existing nowhere but in the imagination of man, that he must seek to collect motives calculated to make him act properly . . . it is in the visible world that will be found incitements to divert him from crime and to rouse him to virtue. It is in nature . . . that he must search out remedies for the evils of his species, and for motives suitable to infuse into the human heart propensities truly useful for society.[116]

Man's being "governed according to his nature" and his being educated in the "necessary laws" of nature, for d'Holbach, are two sides of the same coin.[117]

The ideological aims of the Enlightenment required quick movement from the sense of nature as the orderliness of the universe to the sense of nature as the horizon of unaided human reason; they required, at times, that these two senses be treated as one. Beneath the ideological superstructure, however, a certain inconsistency between the two senses protruded as a philosophical problem. Philosophically, although not ideologically, the philosophes could perceive or at least experience a seeming contradiction. On the one hand, "they wanted to integrate man fully into the order of nature, to explain man and all his works in terms of mechanical laws just as they explained the phenomena of physics"; but on the other hand, "as residuary legates of the Western humanist tradition, they were concerned to preserve man's uniqueness as a rational and moral being."[118] In the Enlightenment's ideological superstructure, nature as cosmical order and nature as the laws of right reason were made perfectly harmonious and assimilable to each other; in its philosophical substructure, the Enlightenment's reinterpretation of nature posed a problem.

Precisely because nature is philosophically problematic but ideologically unproblematic to the Enlightenment, Cartesian dualism is ignored or circumvented in its ideological superstructure, while it is implicitly problematic in its philosophical substructure. The Cartesian problem is invisible in the Enlightenment's ideological discourse and visible in the philosophical supports of that discourse. Since science takes man beyond the world of natural things into a new world of his own making, a world fabricated by pure finite, human intelligence, man can no longer confidently take his place as a being of nature;[119] this is the Cartesian problem par excellence. Ideologically, the Enlightenment must confidently treat man as a being of nature, fully in accord with nature when he is morally autonomous. Ideologically, the Enlightenment must assume that "all the best gifts of nature are equally distributed, that there can be nothing of real value in human life which is not in widest commonality spread."[120] Philosophically, the Enlightenment is confronted with the problem of man as that being who, in his advocacy of the modern scientific attitude, must place himself beyond nature. The ideological confidence in man as a perfectly natural being, however, derives, in part, its power to make modernity self-conscious from the philosophical awareness of the problem of man's uniqueness as a more-than-natural being. It is thus no surprise that the discourse of the Enlightenment, while emphasizing the importance of man as a being of nature, subtly intimates that man is the being who bestows significance on nature, as in the following from Diderot.

If man, if that thinking and contemplative being, were banished from the surface of the globe, the spectacle . . . which Nature unfolds would become a silence and a desolation. . . . The presence of Man it is that gives interest and meaning to the existence of living things, and how better could we record the history thereof than by taking this consideration for our guide? Why not give to man in this work the place which is allotted to him in the universal scheme of things? Why not make him the centre round which everything revolves?[121]

It is man's transcendence of nature (hidden by Diderot in calling man the "centre" of the universe rather than the being who stands outside and above the knowable universe in his scientific inquiry) that stands behind the Enlightenment's discourse about the self-sufficiency of nature.

In using two different senses of nature as if they were coextensive in meaning, the Enlightenment's ideological program became "obsessed with the notion that by going back to the origin of things we can explain their nature." There must be a "universal human nature which is prior—logically or historically—to society" and that is indestructible in the social state.[122] The origin of nature is in nature, and so the origin of man is in nature; just as there is something unchangeable about nature, there is something unchangeable about man. Moreover, just as what is unchangeable about nature is what still persists of the origin of nature in the present, so also what is unchangeable about man is what still persists of the origin of man in the present condition of man. Man must be derived, not from a divine being outside nature or above nature, but from below; his origin is in the very origin of nature. Nature "has used only a single and same dough," La Mettrie (1709–51) said, "in which she has merely varied the yeast," and so "natural law establishes a resemblance" between man and the other animals "rather than a difference."[123] The Enlightenment had to argue that "man would have more dignity if he were independent of God and of supernatural directives or sanctions, than he would have if he enjoyed a favored status that made of him a means and not an end." But to argue this, it was ideologically necessary "to integrate man completely into nature, to deprive him . . . of his uniqueness," while simultaneously, in terms of a philosophical sensitivity to the developing logic of modernity, justifying man's superiority to nature.[124]

Perhaps the most successful ideological device contrived by the Enlightenment to prevent the philosophical complexity entailed by its redefinition of nature from impeding the smoothness of the implementation of its ideological aims was a countermyth to the Christian myth of original sin. Diderot affords us the clearest formulation of this ideological device.

There existed a natural man; an artificial man was introduced within this man; and within this cavern a civil war breaks out, which lasts for life. Sometimes the natural man is stronger; sometimes he is felled by the artificial, moral man; and in both cases the miserable monster is plagued, tortured, tormented, stretched on the rack.[125]

There is, in other words, an unchanging human nature locked inside an artificial man fabricated by the collective intolerance of religious and political institutions; or, to put it another way, there is an artificial core of antihuman impulses that lurks inside a human nature that has been corrupted not by sin but by Christianity itself. We have here a perfect parallel to, and perfect inversion of, original sin that enables the Enlightenment to avoid making explicit the inherent philosophical tension between its own notion of man as *of nature* and the notion of man as *beyond nature* bequeathed to it by the preceding developments of the logic of modernity. "Morality in a good man" can now be confidently termed by Diderot as "but another name for nature."[126] By the myth of a natural man locked away in an artificial man, the Enlightenment would render itself comfortable in making an easy and untroubled shift from nature to human nature, and from human nature to human morality, so that there would be no firm line of demarcation between its inquiries into nature and its inquiries into morality, and no firm line of demarcation between its examination of morality and its examination of human nature.[127] The Enlightenment could now, almost casually, pass from a redefinition of nature to a redefinition of human nature.

Relying on the popularity in the Enlightenment of the epigram of the Roman playwright Terence, "Homo sum, humani a me nihil alienum puto," Diderot announced: "I am a man and I insist on causes appropriate to man."[128] Nature might point out in its origin the unchanging nature that was the origin of man, yet causes appropriate to man constituted the content of that unchanging nature. Nature was the replacement for the Christian

God; man was a being of nature derived from below rather than from above, and yet man's nature would contain no significant purposes that could be found in the history of the universe but only purposes that could be found within the life of man himself.[129] Furthermore, the very immutability of man's nature was at odds with the pattern disclosed by the Enlightenment's reinterpretation of history. If in "all that happens, and has ever happened, what is at work is simply the mind of man, unvarying in its laws," how then "account for the changes of modes of action and forms of culture which history shows"?[130] Neither historical mutability nor the immutability of human nature could afford to be rejected by the Enlightenment. Even the more avowedly materialistic philosophes, like Helvetius (1715–71), who "conceived of human behavior and opinions as almost completely modifiable," never doubted the essential identity of all men.[131] If the tension between man as a being of nature and man as a being beyond nature could be ideologically resolved by the creation of the myth of a natural and artificial man, the Enlightenment would have to contrive another ideological device to resolve the tension between historical mutability and an immutable human nature. The device contrived, and utilized by most philosophes, was the notion of an "intrinsically identical intellectual and affective apparatus" in all men that constitutes the true universal human nature on which "reformers can count and which they can manipulate."[132]

This new ideological device enabled the Enlightenment to preserve the distinction that Christian theology had always preserved between what is good and what is bad by nature, without appealing to the eternal law of God as a foundation for natural law, since the difference between the naturally good and the naturally bad would be reduced to the distinction between "those customs that were suited and those that were unsuited to man's nature."[133] Such a device would enable Voltaire to give the impression that there was no philosophical difficulty in affirming that while the fundamental principles of man's nature always remain the same, customs and culture produce different fruits.[134] Such a device permitted d'Holbach to circumvent the tension between historical mutability and the immutability of human nature when he insisted that we "shall always deceive ourselves, when we shall give any other basis to morality than the nature of man; we cannot have any that is more solid and more certain."[135] In sum, such a device permitted the Enlightenment to make the claim that it was not simply reinterpreting man's place in the universe but reinterpreting man himself.[136] By appealing to a uniform, unchanging, cognitive, and affective apparatus in all men, the Enlightenment was able to contend that its rejection of the Christian gnosis was not as such a rejection of the immutable.

In the infinitely varied patterns of external nature there was an underlying immutability that permitted the origin of that nature to be maintained beneath its variations. So also, in the infinitely changing patterns of human history there was an underlying immutability that permitted the origin of human nature to be maintained beneath the transformations of history. The underlying immutability of external nature was given expression in Newton's *Principia*; the underlying immutability of human nature would be given expression in an Enlightenment 'Principia' of the human soul; Locke had, after all, shown that it was possible to have this new kind of 'Principia'. In this manner, all other modes of theoretical and practical cognition will be shown to be in function of a theory of human nature.[137] The Enlightenment perceived itself as the provider of a science of man that would give fitting expression to the immutability of human nature. This science, as Turgot (1727–81) saw it, would be a security against "anti-progressive forces," for it would remove moral problems from "the disputes of the marketplace where they always provoked destructive violence."[138] The Enlightenment itself, however, was not destined to complete this new science, precisely because it could not reconcile itself to a philosophical system, and this scientific philosophical anthropology would require a metaphysical foundation just as modern scientific method required the Cartesian foundations. Yet in the very pretentiousness of its claim to provide this science, the Enlightenment would constitute itself as a heritage for the work of Kant who would dare to reassume the stance of Descartes. Although relying heavily on ideological constructs, such as the myth of a natural and artificial man and the ideological device of an affective and cognitive apparatus identical in all men, the fruits of the Enlightenment would not be merely ideological.

Having transformed a negative starting point into a positive platform, that is, having transformed an anti-Christian polemic into a program for the redefinition of human nature, and having initiated this program with a redefinition of nature, as a propaedeutic to its reformulation of the immutability of human nature, the Enlightenment was now in a position to specify the components of that immutable nature, namely, the cognitive and affective apparatus that was identical in all men. It would specify these components by emphasizing, in a fashion similar to Hume, the dominance of the affective over the cognitive or rational. And it would do this in such a way that its redefinition of nature as the horizon of unaided reason would be neither rejected nor contradicted.

The intensity of the Enlightenment's self-consciousness seems to entail the affirmation of the primacy of enthusiasm, passionate affirmation and denial, and highly emotionalized statement. "The throbs and quivers of romantic sensibility" arose out of a "vague uneasiness in which men not accustomed to doubt hoped to assert their values by the very heat and intensity with which they felt them."[139] The emphasis on the emotional and affective dimensions of man was consistent with the highly emotionalized discourse demanded by the ideological aims of the Enlightenment. From this point of view, the content of the Enlightenment's message might almost be said to follow from the style of its presentation. In addition to this consideration, we should also remember that the Enlightenment's diatribe against systematic philosophy entailed a presumption of a certain reconcilability between reason and affectivity. The presumption of "the universal accessibility and verifiability of all that it is really needful for men to know" entailed the notion that "all subtle, elaborate, intricate reasonings about abstruse questions beyond the grasp of the majority are certainly unimportant and probably untrue."[140]

Philosophical reason, stripped of reference to systematic speculation and left only with its coldly critical mission, almost begs for some kind of complementarity. What better complement for a lonely and isolated criticism than the drive and magic of the passional and affective seat of the human psyche! Furthermore, since the proper object of philosophy is no longer external nature but rather human nature, and since the issues of human nature and conduct do not have their boundaries firmly fixed in the Enlightenment's discourse, reason need not be isolated from passion. "Reason has a part in the conduct of life, but it is an ancillary part," and so pride came to mean to the Enlightenment a kind of "moral overstrain, the attempt to be unnaturally good and immoderately virtuous, to live by reason alone."[141] In this way, the thinkers who were perhaps the most influential in the early and mid-eighteenth century attempted to reduce man's claim to reason to a minimum and to belittle that faculty in human existence,[142] in favor of the importance of passion and emotion. In line with this, as early as 1746, Diderot proclaimed that only "the passions, and the great passions, can raise the soul to great things. . . . Sober passions make common men. . . . Restraint destroys the grandeur and force of nature."[143]

In not a few quarters of the Enlightenment, an excessive adulation of the claims of emotion would seemingly contradict the Enlightenment's redefinition of nature as the horizon of unaided reason. Thus, Vauvenargues (1715–47) wrote,

My whole philosophy has its source in my heart. . . . A natural philosophy which owes nothing to reason cannot submit to laws; my philosophy can tolerate only itself; it consists properly of independence, and the yoke of reason would be more unbearable than the yoke of prejudices.[144]

Vauvenargues' contention could hardly be unqualifiedly accepted by all proponents of enlightenment, yet its basic impetus was quite in accord with the mind of the Enlightenment, which looked upon the passions as "the vital impulses, the real motivating forces which stimulate the mind as a whole and keep it in operation."[145] The more representative voices of the Enlightenment would feel obligated to modify and sublimate Vauvenargues' position. They would agree that reason, far from being the dominating force in man, is "comparable only to the hand that tells the time on the face of a clock." The internal mechanism that moves the hand, the motivating force and "ultimate cause of knowledge, lies in those primary and original impulses" emanating from a completely irrational realm in the human psyche.[146] The passions constitute the foundations of reason, and the "true power of the soul springs from the harmonious balance of the passions, not from their destruction."[147] Passion is the energy for reason and for life itself. "Our passions," as Condillac put it, "return to us again and again, one after another, and wax more and more numerous," so that "we live on only that we may desire, and only in so far as we desire."[148]

If the passions dynamize reason, the errors and misjudgments of man do not proceed from what dynamizes but from what is dynamized. "The passions always inspire us rightly," Diderot says, "for they inspire us only with the desire for happiness," whereas the mind deceives us "and makes us take false roads."[149] Man is deceived, not when passion overcomes reason, but when reason miscalculates how man's desires are to be fulfilled. For La Mettrie, neither wisdom nor virtue is natural to man but only feeling; the "first condition of happiness is to feel."[150] For C. G. Leroy (1726–79) pleasure itself is reducible to "the feeling of existence intensified to a certain degree,"[151] and for the abbé de Saint-Pierre (1658–1743) human motivation itself is reducible to a "weighing of passion against passion, desire against desire, desire against fear."[152] Even Bayle (1647–1709), one of the progenitors of the enlightened attitude, informs us, in line with Hume, that reason is slave to the passions and that, despite the disorder that passions sometimes effect, it is ultimately passion itself and not reason that can prevent anarchy.[153] Voltaire, too, confesses to having "come back to feeling, after getting lost in reasoning."[154]

The collective testament of the Enlightenment, then, would appear to be that the essential component of the immutable apparatus of reason and feeling that constitutes human nature is precisely a fundamental identity in the affective life of all men. Human nature, no longer defined in terms of its relationship to a Creative God (as the eternally immutable source of its finite immutable essence), now has its immutability relocated in an essential sameness in the basic feelings of all men. The Enlightenment could afford to make the case for this newfound immutability rather excessively at times, as with Diderot.

I hate all those sordid little things that reveal only an abject soul; but I do not hate great crimes: first because one makes beautiful paintings and fine tragedies of them; and besides, because great and sublime actions and great crimes have the same quality: energy.[155]

The Enlightenment could also afford to admit, as Diderot did, that the collaboration of reason and passion was at best "uneasy and produced unending tensions, unstable compromises, and unresolvable ambiguities."[156] Excessive statement serves to hinder qualified, philosophical statement, but it does serve to facilitate the aims of ideological method; excessive statement could be tolerated and encouraged, then, as long as the purposes of the Enlightenment's positive contribution to the redefinition of human nature were served. In Christianity the Enlightenment perceived both "unreasonable rationalism" (theology) and "superstitious antirationalism" (Christian preaching and intolerant behavior); and so, a psychology that took as its central object of study not rationality but affectivity as the substrate of rationality was the antidote.[157] In redefining human nature, the Enlightenment could argue, as did Voltaire, that the passions have generated social order, that feelings, like pride were the "principal instrument with which this beautiful edifice of society has been built."[158] In all of this, feeling rather than Christian faith was to be the new consort of reason, just as nature was to occupy the place of the Christian God as the ground of an immutable human nature. Nature for the Enlightenment provided man with his passional inclinations, just as God, for orthodox Christianity, provided man with his inclination for beatific happiness.

It was no grave matter, for the mind of the Enlightenment, that the philosophical problem of man, as transcending nature and yet rooted in nature, remained beneath its program to redefine human nature. The Enlightenment was not about to construct a philosophical system requiring metaphysical foundations, and so, all conflicts need not be resolved. Yet its attitude in the face of this was not the modesty of Locke but the *hubris* of believing itself to be the provision of a new science of man.

In emphasizing feeling, as it did, the Enlightenment furthered that inversion that runs throughout its program: the great individual mind would transform social consciousness and, in turn, be transformed by social consciousness. The great individual would preach reason, virtue, and enlightenment to the society that constituted his audience while taking for himself the unphilosophical characteristic associated with the many—the emphasis on what is felt. The Enlightenment was creating a vision of society in which the many would be in possession of the virtues of their preceptor, the philosopher; and their preceptor would be in possession of the virtues of the many, the common man's honesty about his feelings and his freedom from a fear of acting.

We are now at that point in our examination where the anti-Christian polemic and the reinterpretation of human nature can be seen in their actual unity; for the outcome of the Enlightenment's redefinition of human nature is the justification of the proposition that man is the measure of all things, much as the outcome of the Enlightenment's anti-Christian polemic is its redefinition of human nature. In examining the Enlightenment's justification for this proposition, we will perceive how perfectly consonant with, and appropriate for, its positive contribution is its negative starting point. In perceiving this, we will be able to visualize the remarkable unity of the Enlightenment that enabled it to have the outcome and provide the philosophical heritage that, we shall argue in our final consideration, it had and provided.

Carl Becker in his classical study has aptly stated the essential articles of the religion of the Enlightenment.

    i. Man is not natively depraved.
    ii. The end of life is life itself, the good life on earth instead of the beatific life after death.
    iii. Man is capable, guided solely by the light of reason and experience, of perfecting the good life on earth.
    iv. The first and essential condition of the good life on earth is the freeing of men's minds from the bonds of ignorance and superstition, and of their bodies from the arbitrary oppression of the constituted social authorities. [159]

All of these essential articles are founded on the proposition that man is the measure of all things. This proposition is the logical conclusion of the reasoning found in the philosophical substructure of the Enlightenment's edifice, and it is the single most important philosophical dynamism for the vivification of the Enlightenment's ideological superstructure. In its presence to both the ideological superstructure and the philosophical substructure, it epitomizes not only the Enlightenment's self-consciousness, or consciousness of its own historical insularity, but also the Enlightenment's efficacity in bringing modernity to a consciousness of itself.

As the logical conclusion to the philosophical reasoning of its substructure, this proposition manifests a certain kinship with the philosophical contribution of David Hume. The Enlightenment in general, like Hume in particular, comes to conceive reason in such a way that the Cartesian-Galilean emphasis on the mathematical core of scientific knowing is deflated. Scientific method, loosed from its Cartesian-Galilean moorings in certitude by Hume, is brought by the Enlightenment into a clear philosophical awareness of its own innermost meaning. The Enlightenment recognizes that the real achievement of science lies in the new function which it attributes to the *mind of man*, a function in which "the world ceases to be a *cosmos* in the sense of an immediately accessible order of things"; and the power of reason grounded in affectivity becomes our only access to the infinite, teaching us to place the infinite within measure not in order "to limit its realm but in order to know it in its all-comprehensive and all-pervasive law."[160] For the Enlightenment, the infinity of the modern universe is interpreted to mean the infinite resources of human nature. Human nature must be treated as finite in its articulation in individual human beings but as infinite or unlimited in its possibilities for development. History discloses a finite nature; individuals disclose a finite human nature; but the future promises limitless possibilities for the perfectibility of that nature (provided men are enlightened about the meaning of that nature).

There is, however, a sense in which the term "infinite" departs from the ideological superstructure of the Enlightenment, and this appears to be what Cassirer is really describing when he says of the Enlightenment that

it is no longer a matter, as it had been in the great metaphysical systems of the seventeenth century . . . of resolving the finite in the infinite and thus, so to speak, of eliminating it. What is required is that the finite assert itself in its own character even in the presence of this highest standard; that it preserve its specific nature even while it recognizes this nature as finite.[161]

The ideological demands of the Enlightenment's vision of a secularized society, secularized history, and secularized religion prohibit it from admitting the term "infinity" explicitly into its ideological superstructure. But the force of the term remains in its philosophical substructure, now entirely applicable to the resources of human nature. Human nature must be treated as infinite in the possibilities for its development, and undying or immortal in its underlying, affectively grounded rational structure. The soul of the individual might be temporary, but the "soul of humanity, this something essential to human nature," was certainly "immortal because permanent and universal."[162] Although not suitable terms for the Enlightenment's ideology, 'infinity' and 'immortality', reinterpreted to apply solely to an immutable human nature, are powerful philosophical notions counterbalancing the ideological superstructure of the Enlightenment and rendering the Enlightenment as a heritage something more than mere ideology. They allow the Enlightenment to make explicit the truly radical, implicit claim of the logic of modernity: that the essential meaning of the modern age, of modern science itself, is the new meaning it entails for man as the measure of reality and its intelligibility. The logic of modernity—beginning as it does with the attribution to the external universe of a term (infinity) previously reserved for the God of Christianity—must ultimately predicate that term of the possibilities for the future development of man himself.[163]

Although in effect bringing the implications of modern scientific methodology to their ultimate fruition (the notion of man as the measure of all meaning), the Enlightenment tended to interpret its disclosure of this fruition as a historically unconditioned discovery. Thus, the Enlightenment became obsessed with the conviction that "in the history of humanity the time had now arrived to deprive nature of its carefully guarded secret," to strip it of its incomprehensible mystery,[164] to engage in a "demagification of the world."[165] But the emphasis on its own insularity in perceiving this insight, an emphasis consistently maintained in its ideological superstructure, is counterbalanced by a philosophical logic in its substructure that testifies at once to the Enlightenment's continuity with the preceding developments of the logic of modernity and to the continuity of the Enlightenment's anti-Christian polemic with its positive contribution in redefining human nature. This philosophical logic is roughly as follows. The true meaning of nature is not simply unlocked by, and in terms of, modern scientific method as such. Modern scientific method betrays a meaning deeper than itself; it betrays the meaning of man as the very measure of reality and its intelligibility. Man is no longer the creature of God, midway between the beasts and God, as in the medieval synthesis. Man is no longer the rational animal of nature, directed to know what is the case about nature, as in the ancient philosophical synthesis. Man is now the very locus of the intelligibility of nature itself. Nature, in fact, is nothing else than a description of man's powers operating in complete autonomy, neither in dependence on the Christian God nor in dependence on 'nature' as a set of objective, pregiven, or fixed forms. Modern scientific method is the occasion for the disclosure of the notion that man is the measure of all things; but, in so disclosing, it reveals that science itself is in function of, in service of the validation of this proposition and its implementation in social reform.

In this proposition, then, is to be had the *rationale* for the Enlightenment's anti-Christian polemic in all its excess. In its acceptance of man as the measure, the Enlightenment refused to fit human experience into abstract doctrinal systems. Neither theological, metaphysical, political systems, nor the system of Christian orthodoxy can be accepted as valid, since to do so is to exalt their claim to self-sufficiency and so to subtract from the one exaltation to which the Enlightenment must commit itself, the exaltation of man. Diderot constructs an allegory that depicts man's stubbornness in fully accepting his own exaltation. The misanthrope, residing in his cave, seeks ways to take revenge on the human race. In seeking to devise a concept that men would value more than their individual and common life, he comes out of the cave crying "God." And so men came to despise their common plight, their human condition, their very human nature. Epitomizing the Enlightenment's exaltation of man, Diderot counterpoises himself to the misanthrope, that is, the Christian, by saying, "I confine myself to the present life and I consider . . . a meditation about the Beyond and about death as useless, vain, and depressing."[166] In his exaltation of man as the measure of reality, Diderot saw Christianity as the decisive institution in the perpetuation of human servitude. In doing this, he was constructing a parable for the Enlightenment itself. In making the modern era of Western civilization self-conscious of its absolutization of man, the Enlightenment proceeded in such a way that the historical foundations of Christianity as a ground for the new universe were rejected in its ideological superstructure. As Voltaire would say, "almost everything which goes beyond the worship of a Supreme Being and the submission of one's heart to his eternal commands is superstition."[167] Bruno's distrust of institutions as betrayals of man's ethical autonomy in an infinite universe was thus transmuted into a polemic not found in Bruno—an anti-Christian polemic. In its ideological dimensions, the Enlightenment advertised Christianity as an obstacle to the full autonomy of man, the lesson of which it must indelibly etch on the minds of modern men. But, in its philosophical substructure, the motifs and categories of Christianity were maintained as the material to be transformed in this etching.

All the advantages of traditional systematic Christian theology were obtained by the Enlightenment in its unsystematic appeal to an absolute humanity, for, finding that individual men might be mistaken in their views of right and wrong, it "invoked the judgment of man in general."[168] Ethically, the Enlightenment would insist on man's essential autonomy, appealing to the proposition that man is responsible only to himself, "to his own rational interests, to his self-development, and, by an inescapable extension, to the welfare of his fellow man."[169] But this ethical insistence was grounded in a philosophical logic, which—although it would never be extended into a metaphysic by a movement that abhorred metaphysics—eventually demanded a metaphysical systemization; this was the philosophical logic functioning in support of the conclusion that man is the measure of all things.

Equipped with an ideological superstructure that was built on a philosophical substructure and that was kept in equilibrium with that substructure, the Enlightenment began in a negative polemic against Christianity. This polemic began with a reduction of orthodox Christianity to superstition; it then set forth an ideological vision of the conquest of Christianity by science, and finally issued in a vision of a secularized society. This vision of a secularized society presumed upon the secularization of reasoned inquiry, especially the study of history. Far beneath the entire polemic, however, were the emptied categories of Christianity, the same richly filled categories that were decisive in the emergence of the logic of modernity in the first place. These categories permitted the Enlightenment to propose a naturalistic humanism as the new religion destined to replace institutionalized Christianity. In this way, the negative starting point issued in a positive teaching—the redefinition of human nature. This positive contribution began in a redefinition of the modern notion of nature, equating nature with the horizon of man's unaided reason, while holding on to the older notion of nature as cosmical orderliness. By redefining nature, and by constructing a countermyth to original sin—the myth of an artificial and natural man—the Enlightenment was able to sustain the notion of an immutable human nature without explicit appeal to the theological categories of Christianity. This immutable human nature was located not in a metaphysical category but in a psychological identity, that is, the fundamental identity in all men of their cognitive and affective apparatus. In this apparatus, affectivity became the ground of rationality. The outcome of all of this was an absolutization of human nature, a reinterpretation of an unchanging human nature (in which affectivity has primacy) as the measure of all meaning and reality.

THE ENLIGHTENMENT AS HERITAGE

Such is the unity of the Enlightenment. It is a unity secured in the very tensions operative in the Enlightenment, since the polar opposites of each of the major tensions of the Enlightenment serve to balance each other and thus to secure a positive outcome, the redefinition of human nature as the final measure of all possible intelligibility. Because of this, the ideological superstructure of the Enlightenment is balanced and maintained in equilibrium with its philosophical substructure. The ideological dogma of its own historical insularity is balanced by its philosophical premise of continuity with the preceding developments of the logic of modernity. The anti-Christian polemic is balanced by a tacit philosophical reliance on the basic categories of orthodox Christianity. Its redefinition of nature is balanced by an appeal to the older notion of nature. Its emphasis on the immutability of human nature is balanced by its realization of the historical mutability of human customs, behavior, and thought. The very emphasis on a redefined nature as the horizon of unassisted human reason is balanced by a strongly antirational undercurrent entailing the primacy of affectivity. The enigmas of continuity and discontinuity with the past, of a Christian anti-Christian polemic, of a naturalism that is a humanism, of an antirational rationalism—all function in terms of the philosophical justification and ideological retailing of the proposition that what is fundamentally and unchangingly human is the source and criterion of all intelligibility. It is this proposition that is advertised by the ideological excesses and justified by the philosophical insights of the Enlightenment. It is in this proposition that the full revolutionary thrust of the logic of modernity is made clear to modern man for the first time: the center of gravity of modernity is not an infinitized universe but an absolutized man.

The complex unity of the Enlightenment enabled it to have a complex and unified outcome and to transmit a powerful heritage that was able to generate a more powerful philosophical unity than it itself possessed. In considering the outcome of the unified program of the Enlightenment, we shall examine its dominating optimistic vision of a future state of temporal happiness for mankind as well as the more subtle pessimistic strain underlying this vision. In considering the heritage of the Enlightenment for future ideologies, we shall examine its anti-institutionalistic impulse as well as its underlying tendency to present itself as a new kind of institution. In considering the heritage of the Enlightenment for future philosophy, we shall analyze the importance of its radical individualism for the efforts of Rousseau and its presence to Kant as a heritage that at once required sublimation, correction, and systemization.

The unity of the Enlightenment goes far to suggest that the "strongest intellectual forces of the Enlightenment do not lie in its rejection of belief but rather in the new form of faith which it proclaims, and in the new form of religion which it embodies."[170] The unity of the Enlightenment goes far to suggest that, although in its own view it was stripping modernity of its Christian equipage, it was not stripping modernity of something that resembled Christian belief. What the Enlightenment perceived as at stake in the venture of modernity, although not the soul's redemption, was something that resembled the redemptive vision of Christianity: "the temporal happiness of the whole man and the whole of mankind."[171]

Just as the origins of the very logic of modernity lie in a mystical vision within the parameters of orthodox Christianity, a vision of a sacramental nature that is a fitting expression of the Christian God, so also the very origins of the Enlightenment may very well lie in a mystical vision. The making explicit of this mystical vision would appear to be the outcome of the Enlightenment. This vision amounts to a radical secularization of Christianity and thus to a reduction of the medieval mystical vision of a sacramentalized nature and a theophanic God to a vision of a secular society of perfected men grounded in the absoluteness of man. "Our hopes for the future condition of the human race," Condorcet said, "can be subsumed under three important heads: the abolition of inequality between nations, the progress of equality within each nation, and the true perfection of mankind."[172] The problem is that the Enlightenment's vision does not on the surface look like a mystical vision, since its contrived ideological devices function so strongly in its presentation; in the end, the Enlightenment is lacking in the spontaneity of a rich mysticism. But beneath its equilibrium is the force of mysticism stripped of its anchorage in a theological system, although not stripped of indebtedness to Christian categories. The mysticism is bare, lean, lacking in the richness of medieval symbolism, as illustrated in the following words of Condorcet.

All the causes that contribute to the perfection of the human race, all the means that ensure it, must by their very nature exercise a perpetual influence and always increase their sphere of action. . . . We may conclude, then, that the perfectibility of man is indefinite. Meanwhile we have considered him as possessing the natural faculties and organization that he has at present. How much greater would be the certainty, how much vaster the scheme of our hopes, if we could believe that these natural faculties themselves and this organization could also be improved?[173]

Condorcet could dream of a perfected human society because he could envisage a limitless perfection built upon the very immutable core of human nature. The being of man could be altered so as to intensify and perfect the unchanging aspect of man. The fact that Condorcet was not permitted to actually see the incarnation of a perfected human society could be readily explained. By the close of the eighteenth century, he reasoned, men had discovered "how to learn nature's secrets, and therefore how to be happy," but this knowledge was still confined to a few. Yet man's happiness was within his grasp, for the day would soon come when he could "set up institutions which would give his capacities full scope," since nature had set no limit to progress.[174]

But Condorcet was not alone; there was an Enlightenment *schola* attempting to orchestrate the bare, sparse mystical vision of a perfected future social order. For the truly enlightened philosopher, Diderot wrote, there could be no doubt of a coming civil society that would be a "divinity . . . on the earth," for what "experience shows us every day is that the more reason" people have, the more relied upon they can be "for the common intercourse of life."[175] Civil society was on the verge of a great transformation, and like the early Christians, the philosophes thought the secularized "parousia" imminent. Condorcet believed that he had already, as he put it, "proved the possibility and indicated the means of resolving what is perhaps the most important problem for the human species," namely, the "perfectibility of the broad masses." The problem of rendering an enlightened conscience and a "habitual submission to the rules of humanity and justice, almost universal qualities," had been solved, so that the ordinary man would now be capable of living in a society in which he is "as happy as he is permitted by the pains, the needs, and the losses which are the necessary consequence of the general laws of the universe."[176]

The pared-down, lackluster mystical vision of the Enlightenment was devoid of the cosmic dimensions of the mysticism of the medievals and devoid of the Trinitarian dimension of Christianity; it could, at best, yield another kind of utopia. The utopian dream of perfection, having for so long been identified with the golden age or the Garden of Eden or eternal life in the heavenly City of God, was, in the Enlightenment, "projected into the life of man on earth and identified with the desired and hoped-for regeneration of society."[177] Just as the Christian God justified the medieval mystical vision of a sacramental universe, so, with the Enlightenment, posterity would be "judge and justifier of those virtuous and enlightened ones" who were not of the world of the unenlightened.[178] Thus, Voltaire wrote,

I shall not be a witness to this fine revolution but I shall die with the three theological virtues which are my consolation: the faith which I have in human reason which is beginning to develop in the world; the hope that ministers in their boldness and wisdom will at length destroy customs which are as ridiculous as they are dangerous; the charity which makes me grieve for my neighbour, complain of his bonds, and long for his deliverance.[179]

Posterity, not the God of Christianity, is the validator of these secularized theological virtues. The enlightened scientist, too, would partake of this secularized mysticism. Thus, Joseph Priestley (1733–1804) spoke, in 1768, of how "glorious and paradisiacal," and "beyond what our imaginations can now conceive," the coming perfected society would be, confident that he could justify his expectations scientifically by appealing to the true theory of human nature.[180] The utopian society, after all, would be a society of perfected scientific methodology facilitating the ethical perfection of its citizens. "What science offered as its greatest contribution to the life of man was that it would at last give man a true theory of his own nature and thus enable him to control his own destiny."[181] Descartes had, after all, perceived the ethical promise of scientific method when he entertained the hope that science would make us "the masters and possessors of nature" so that we may "enjoy . . . the fruits of the earth."[182] What Descartes had perceived the Enlightenment would develop into an ethical theory. The modern scientific world view, entailing as it does the absolutization of man, portends a society where scientific knowledge will serve the ethical autonomy and happiness of all men.

In this future utopian society it will at last become evident that, far from being made in the image of God, man is the God of which he has been speaking for so long. "The flower of humanity," Herder (1744–1803) says, "captive still in its germ, will blossom out one day, into the true form of man like unto God, in a state of which no terrestrial man can imagine the greatness and the majesty," and will issue in a "broader culture and humanity."[183] In this future society with its perfect humanistic culture, destined to emerge, as Condorcet puts it, "in the immensity of the centuries which will follow us," will be had "a happiness and an enlightenment about which we cannot today even form a vague and indefinite idea."[184] Yet the prospect of this fully humanized society is enough to justify all the frustrations of the philosophes in the face of the unenlightened of their own age. Living "in thought," as Condorcet says, "with man restored to his natural rights and dignity," the enlightened thinker will forget the "man tormented and corrupted by greed, fear or envy," and he will exist in spirit "with his peers in an Elysium created by reason and graced by the purest pleasures known to the love of mankind."[185] In this future society will at last be found a perfected equalitarianism and thus the social fructification of the Enlightenment's notion of the absolute uniformity of what is unchangingly human. Here will be had the living out of a fully informed ordinary opinion, and here at last will the individually great mind of the Enlightenment be seen to be itself transformed by its own transformation of ordinary opinion. The Enlightenment's absorption in the ideal of uniformity, in its reinterpretation of both nature and human nature, tended to foster a kind of intellectual equalitarianism even in individuals not democratic in their political views—an equalitarianism that implied that if "the light of nature is universal, and if the knowledge which it affords is alone truly requisite for the guidance of life," then "one man's intelligence is literally, for all *practical* purposes, as good as another's."[186] The logic of this equalitarianism would find its perfected embodiment in a utopian society where common sense would be enlightened and all men would be equal in their enlightenment.

The most powerful outcome of the Enlightenment's unified program, then, was an optimistic vision of a perfected utopian society in which ordinary opinion would live continuously and completely in fidelity to the ethical principle of human moral autonomy and to the psychological principle of man as the measure of all meaning. This optimistic vision embodies the latent optimism in the Enlightenment's secularization of the content of history that is anchored in the notion of progress. But there is a complex tension in this outcome, just as there are complex tensions in its starting point and positive contribution. As a secular alternative to Christianity, the Enlightenment bequeathes to posterity the "dogma of a religion of socially immanent salvation,"[187] as a replacement for the Christian dogma of a more-than-natural salvation for the temporal order. In replacing the Christian dogma, it must ape the logic of that dogma's presence to the generation and sustaining of the logic of modernity. When we examine the Christian dogma, we find that its thrust is basically optimistic (history, when finally judged, will be shown to justify the plan of God), but we also find the underlying strain of the pessimistic implications of the doctrine of original sin (it is not man, after all, who will justify history; history will be justified in spite of the sins of its actors). It should be no surprise, then, that in being forced to imitate the logic of Christianity's presence to the development of modernity, the Enlightenment's dogma of a socially immanent salvation, for all its optimism, would conceal a pessimistic strain.

One first perceives this pessimistic strain in a certain social cleavage for which the Enlightenment was, in part at least, responsible. The ideological superstructure of the Enlightenment called for a transformation of the consciousness of society in general; yet, in the end, it was not the consciousness of the lower classes that was altered but the consciousness of the intellectual class and the nobility. While the "courtiers of Catherine II or Joseph II read the latest books from Paris and adopted the fashionable radicalism of cosmopolitan society, their peasant serfs still lived in the world of Baroque Catholicism or Byzantine orthodoxy." There developed, then, "a spiritual cleavage in society which contained the seeds of class conflict and social revolution," since in the old order nobles and peasants had shared a common faith, but now with Christianity only effectively good for the lower classes, the "spiritual foundation of social unity was destroyed."[188] This cleavage in society was itself testament to a certain disparity between Enlightenment rhetoric, which called for a transformation of ordinary opinion or social consciousness in general, and the actual range of influence exerted by the Enlightenment. This disparity, in turn, was testament to a certain disabusal on the part of the Enlightenment in regard to its own high-minded goal—a strain of pessimism that surfaces every now and then in the Enlightenment. Thus, the following admission of Voltaire does not quite square with the basically optimistic thrust of the Enlightenment's ideological superstructure.

I doubt if the populace has either the time or the capacity for education. They would die of hunger before they became philosophers. It seems to be essential that there should be ignorant beggars. . . . It is not the worker we must instruct, it is the *bon bourgeois* of the townsmen. We have never pretended to enlighten shoemakers and servant girls, that is the portion of the apostles.[189]

One of the clearest expressions of this pessimism is found in a sense that the Enlightenment's program had failed to better the human condition for the masses in Europe at that condition's most basic level. As late as 1771 Voltaire could note that more "than half the habitable world is still populated by two-footed animals who live in a horrible condition approximating the state of nature," hardly aware "that they are miserable, living and dying practically without knowing it."[190] That such a pronouncement from the "prophet" himself should come so late in the course of the Enlightenment is itself significant, for it was probably not until the middle of the century that the dominant optimism of the Enlightenment began to be contested.[191] Even in the Enlightenment's fundamental appeal to the affective and passional, we find a subtle sense of disillusionment, for the Enlightenment's growing denunciation of the *hubris* of reason and of the pride of appealing to reason devoid of emotion conceals an expression of a certain disillusionment of man about himself, a phase of "that long and deepening disillusionment which is the tragedy of a great part of modern thought."[192] The Enlightenment, furthermore, was not, at least occasionally, adverse to disillusionment about itself. Tucked away in the *Encyclopédie* one finds an article where the author admits that, although he would not completely deny that this was "the century of philosophy," he would prefer to call it "the century of half-learning."[193] D'Alembert, too, notes a disheartening element in the Enlightenment's venture when he admits that we hardly acquire "any new knowledge without losing an agreeable illusion," since enlightenment seems to come "at the expense of our pleasures."[194]

It would appear, then, that the Enlightenment's optimism was not the one logical consummation of enlightened philosophy and that a pessimism both about the Enlightenment itself and the actual melioration of the human condition, which it proclaimed itself to be effecting, "had its roots deep in the philosophical movement itself."[195] The result was that while the belief in progress grew during the eighteenth century, there were significant counterinfluences, so that if the Enlightenment was "characterized by a heightened sense of earthly destiny, and if it was conscious of progress, so too was it conscious of decadence and historical flux."[196] This underlying but subtle pessimism might be explained away, as some philosophes themselves did, as a growing realization on the part of the Enlightenment as to how difficult enlightenment was. Diderot, for example, wrote that he was of the opinion "that it is a thousand times easier for an enlightened people to return to barbarism than for a barbaric people to advance directly toward civilization."[197] But the pessimistic mood could not so easily be explained; it persisted on other grounds. There was a realization on the part of some philosophes that barbarism and enlightenment tended to succeed each other and that the present Enlightenment might just be subject to a short life span. D'Alembert thus remarks that "barbarism lasts for centuries" and seems to be "our natural element," whereas "reason and good taste are only passing."[198] Raynal, too, remarks,

In all ages to come the savage will advance step by step toward the civilized state, while civilized man will return toward his primitive condition. From this the philosopher will conclude that there exists in the interval between these states a point at which the felicity of the race must lie—but who will establish this point? And if indeed it is established, where will be the authority capable of directing men to it and of halting man's course when it has been attained?[199]

Given the dominant optimistic posture of the Enlightenment, how are we to account for this underlying pessimistic strain? Perhaps there is something suggestive in the following observation, made by Horace Walpole (1717–97), a critic of the Enlightenment. "When all the world was in darkness," he said, "it needed an effort to put oneself above prejudices; but what merit is there now in not having prejudices when it is ridiculous to have them."[200] As the Enlightenment grew, we might speculate, in the successes of its war against superstition, there was less of the enemy to fight and, consequently, less virtue in being free of prejudice and in being enlightened. There may have been a kind of nostalgia for the earlier days when the lines of battle were clearer; with this nostalgia there may have come a certain ennui. Boredom, satiation with diatribe, a reduced sense of the "glory" of enlightening could have, in part, generated this pessimistic strain. In addition to these factors, there may also have been another. The grand illusion of the philosophes "was to suppose that the evil propensities of men would disappear with the traditional forms through which they functioned."[201] There may have been a growing sense on the part of the more philosophically sensitive philosophes that the belief that the evil in men would disappear when Christianity was dethroned was itself illusory.

These explanations, however, are at best partial. The pessimism underlying the dominant optimism of the Enlightenment is part of the complex set of tensions that characterize the Enlightenment's program. One wonders, for example, whether, if the Enlightenment were a purely ideological movement, this pessimism would have been significant. When we look at the Enlightenment as an ideological superstructure accompanied by a philosophical substructure, we come to see that substructure as both justifying and at times calling into question various components of the superstructure. There were momentous events occurring well before 1700, such as the breakdown of the Church (in the Protestant Reformation) as the universal institution of Christian mankind, the growth of a plurality of sovereign states as ultimate political units, the discovery of the new world and the more intimate acquaintance with Asiatic civilizations—all of which suggested the possibility of a non-Christian interpretation of the nature of man. But before 1700 there occurred no comprehensive interpretation of man in society and history that would take into account what these occurrences conceivably suggested. Marshaling both philosophy and ideology and harnessing them together, the Enlightenment constructs a "gigantic effort of interpretation in order to recover for the existence of man in society and history a meaning which could substitute for the lost meaning of Christian existence."[202]

The Christian notion of man had been given a philosophical formulation by such philosophers as St. Augustine and St. Thomas Aquinas who were indebted to classical Greek categories. The situation of the Christian notion of man at the time of the Enlightenment may have been similar to the situation of the classical Ptolemaic astronomy at the time of Copernicus. The time had come for something new to replace the old, but the new could not quite as comfortably replace the old as its proponents hoped; the new was not quite as elaborated, justified, and well founded as the old. Could it be that the underlying pessimism of the Enlightenment is precisely an expression of a gnawing feeling that the new conception of man was not as theoretically founded and refined as the medieval Christian conception of man? If so, the very absence of a systematic thrust for the Enlightenment's redefinition of human nature could be a factor in accounting for the Enlightenment's feelings of dis-ease and pessimism, despite the fact that the Enlightenment consciously rejected the claims of the systematic mode. Perhaps, then, its subtle pessimistic strain is a testament to both the failing and virtue of the Enlightenment: a testament to its failing insofar as it could not explicitly concede its continuity with the past, and could not accept philosophy in its full seventeenth-century integrity as both speculative and critical; a testament to its virtue insofar as it was not merely constructing an ideology but a set of philosophical reasonings beneath ideology and, in the process, opening itself up to a certain degree of disillusionment with its own ideological program.

With the outcome of the Enlightenment secured in an optimistic vision of perfect temporal happiness for mankind, which concealed a subtle pessimism about man and enlightenment, the Enlightenment, as a movement, ended and took on a new existence as a heritage. Its existence as a heritage reflects the complexity of its existence as a movement composed of ideological and philosophical structures. It would serve as a heritage both for the future development of ideology and for the future development of philosophy.

The heritage for the future development of ideology is to be found first of all in the Enlightenment's tendency to institutionalize itself, in its tendency to grow from a clandestine activity into a respected component of society. There were three overlapping, closely associated generations in the Enlightenment. The first, dominated by Montesquieu (1689–1755) and Voltaire, did most of its work before 1750. The second reached maturity in mid-century and, represented by men like Buffon, Franklin in America, Diderot, Condillac, Helvetius, and D'Alembert, fused "the fashionable anticlericalism and scientific speculations of the first generation" into a coherent view. The third generation, represented by men like d'Holbach, Beccaria, Lessing, Turgot, and Jefferson in America, moved into scientific mythology, political economy, legal reform, and in some cases materialism.[203] By the time of the third generation, during the 1770s and 1780s, precisely when the philosophes had become most radical in their program, the movement had achieved a respectable place in their society.[204] The Enlightenment by this time had become an institution, and although fated to live only a few more years as a movement, it bequeathed to the future the novel possibility of institutionalizing a radical critique of traditional institutions. Thus, the Enlightenment stands as the heritage of the Marxist ideology.

Moreover, the Enlightenment also bequeathed the notion of a social significance for innovation and mutability. What was admittedly a by-product for the Enlightenment's ideology—historical mutability—would become an axiomatic principle, a sort of "norm or commandment in the regulation of human society and in the search for individual salvation and happiness"[205] for the future of ideology. Although not consciously giving innovation the central and worshipful role it would occupy in future ideologies, the Enlightenment did manage, as a by-product of its mission, to change the force of the term "innovation" decisively from a term of abuse or indifference to one of praise, since in the end the philosophes "were not primarily interested in stabilizing society but in changing it."[206] This notion of innovation unabashedly applied to the political sphere was to see its first post-Enlightenment fruit in the French Revolution, which not a few of the enlightened as well as their opponents saw coming.[207] Mutability and innovation elevated into social norms, as well as a program of institutionalizing the anti-institutional impulse, became the heritage which the Enlightenment bequeathed to future ideologies. Men like Comte and Saint-Simon, in the nineteenth century, would feed off that heritage when they proclaimed that in order to prevent the disintegration of Western society, it would be necessary "to devise new institutions with an authority equivalent to the authority of the decaying institutions."[208]

The Enlightenment also constituted a heritage of a different kind; in its redefinition of human nature, it would serve as a philosophical heritage for the ongoing development of the logic of modernity. The Enlightenment would serve as a nonsystematic body of reflection on man as the proper object of philosophy—but a nonsystematic reflection capable of inspiring a systematic body of reflection in the work of Kant. But between Kant and the Enlightenment stood a figure, Rousseau, who, although usually interpreted as a key figure of the Enlightenment, isolated his thought in many ways from the movement in which to some extent he participated. Rousseau would treat the Enlightenment, in many ways, as a heritage for his philosophical speculation on man; in doing so, he isolated himself from the ideological superstructure of the Enlightenment in order to articulate its underlying philosophical substructure. Rousseau, in articulating this substructure, would concentrate on the elements of radical individualism within the Enlightenment's positive contribution.

The role of the individual great mind in the Enlightenment,

even when exposed to the demands of transforming social consciousness, accorded a certain primacy to the "inner voice" and
proposed that "society must be changed to make it worthy of the
individual, and not vice versa."[209] Even Voltaire's *Candide* ends
on the enigmatic note of urging men to cultivate their private
selves.[210] The motif of radical individualism, however, is ambiguous in the Enlightenment, since, although comfortably fitted into
its ideological superstructure side by side with the plea for the
transformation of social consciousness, it was part of a philosophical problem in the Enlightenment's substructure. The philosophical problem here presented itself to the Enlightenment insofar as at the same time that the philosophes stood for reform,
they stood for individual freedoms, such as freedom of thought
and speech. Reform and freedom were, in the Enlightenment's
ideological superstructure, "two faces of a single hope: freedoms
were among the reforms to be accomplished, reforms were among
the happy consequences of freedom."[211] In the Enlightenment's
philosophical substructure, however, it was realized that harsh
reality frequently prevented this alliance. "With the overpowering
presence of the illiterate masses and the absence of the habit of
autonomy, freedom and reform were often incompatible."[212] As
the French Revolution would concretely illustrate, the path to the
realization of the program of reform frequently led "through de-
vious and embarrassing detours of repression and manipulation
that were a denial or a mockery" of the world hoped for by the
Enlightenment.[213] The tension between the Enlightenment's emphasis on social reform and its emphasis on individual freedom,
the tension between a transformation of social consciousness and
the individual consciousness of the great mind, would constitute
a philosophical problem. Rousseau, concentrating on the philosophical substructure of the Enlightenment, and demarcating that
substructure from the movement's superstructure, would be able
to isolate and spell out the implications of this philosophical
problem.

Rousseau, furthermore, would perceive the connection between
radical individualism and the Enlightenment's absolutization of
man. The literary images of the Enlightenment were not those
of the prior century and prior ages. We no longer have a Dante

engaged in an ascent to paradise under the tutelage of intellect and grace, nor a Spenserian Arthur molded by a great discipline, nor a Bunyan pilgrim partaking of a mystical journey to a home that cannot be upon the earth. The real literary symbol for the Enlightenment, its real symbolical figure, is Daniel Defoe's Robinson Crusoe, the isolated economic man, "pitting his lonely strength successfully *against* nature in a remote part of the earth, and carrying on a little missionary activity as a side line."[214] The metaphor for the Enlightenment is the radical individual, isolated and aware of his absoluteness as man. Rousseau would penetrate the philosophical significance of this radical individual as well as the philosophical significance of its bearing on the Enlightenment's notion of man as the measure of all meaning. It is no mere accident that Rousseau should speak in his *Confessions* of building for himself "like a second Robinson an imaginary dwelling."[215] While standing inside the Enlightenment movement, Rousseau would be able to stand outside its ideological superstructure and thus render some of the more significant material of its philosophical substructure the stuff of a new systemization in the logic of modernity: the systemization of the modern meaning of man.

But Rousseau would not himself complete this systemization. Kant is the figure who serves as the greatest repository for the philosophical heritage provided by the Enlightenment. Utilizing the rudiments of philosophical anthropology articulated by Rousseau, Kant, unlike Rousseau, would stand completely apart from the Enlightenment and would take upon himself the task of sublimating the ideological excesses of the Enlightenment and providing for its genuinely philosophical insights a systematic expression. Rooted in a metaphysical foundation, this systematic expression would be as thoroughgoing as the systematic expression afforded modern scientific method by Descartes. In its eclecticism, the Enlightenment could be a force for intellectual disorder, while at the same time, in its philosophical insights, it could be the occasion for a new metaphysical order. Because of both of these potentialities, Europe had need of Kant.[216]

But the Enlightenment's existence as a philosophical heritage would also be maintained after Kant. Up until the Enlightenment, mathematics was the prototype of exact knowledge, but, beginning with Hume and climaxing in the Enlightenment, history became the methodological model by which "new understanding for the general task and the specific structure of the abstract sciences" would be had.[217] Although the Enlightenment's "conception of history is less a finished form with clear outlines than a force exerting its influence in all directions,"[218] its influence would be registered in the new significance given history by Hegel in his completion of the logic of modernity.

What, then, by way of summary, is the significance of the Enlightenment in the development of the logic of modernity? Prior to the Enlightenment, the logic of modernity unfolded in terms of the contributions of individual thinkers who were continuous with each other. But the Enlightenment, far from being a label applied to a sequence of thought from historical hindsight, is a designation that a genuinely collective embodiment of consciousness applies to itself. By constituting itself as the *first*, and perhaps last, genuinely collective movement of thought in the unfolding of the logic of modernity, the Enlightenment makes clear that the great individual thinkers involved in the unfolding of that logic are themselves less significant than, and in function of, that logic.

As a collective movement, the Enlightenment is intensely self-conscious; its contributors subserve their individual consciousness to the demands of a collective, enlightened self-consciousness; and, although the best of them still conceive of themselves as great minds, they introduce a dialectic between the individual mind and the social consciousness that is to be reshaped. To maintain its self-consciousness, the Enlightenment had to fashion a refined ideological structure, since ideology, rather than philosophy, epitomizes the mode of a self-consciousness that is collective. But, its ideological aims and methods had to be balanced by the existence of philosophical problems and insights. For every ideological claim to be made, a philosophical problem emerges. The self-consciousness of the Enlightenment can be sustained over more than one generation only if the ideological superstructure is secured on a philosophical substructure—a place where the philosophical problems entailed by ideological claims can be safely deposited so as not to interrupt or slow down the implementation of the ideological aims of the Enlightenment. Philosophy is in the service of ideology.

But ideology is, in turn, in the service of philosophy. By reducing philosophy to its critical function and stripping it of its systematic and speculative function, the Enlightenment had to call upon ideology to replicate the speculative function of philosophy. Ideology becomes a way of maintaining a speculative world view without falling prey to metaphysics and systemization. If the Enlightenment were purely an ideological movement, it could not have been decisive in the unfolding of the logic of modernity— a logic that, though experiential in its origin, is philosophical in its growth. As the body of philosophical insights builds up, the Enlightenment is driven to extend its consciousness of itself into a consciousness of its continuity with the prior developments of the logic of modernity. The Enlightenment's self-consciousness must be transmuted into modernity's self-consciousness. If the Enlightenment had been a purely philosophical movement, it would at best have been decisive in the unfolding of the logic of modernity—one among several decisive moments in that unfolding. By bringing the mode of collective self-consciousness to bear on philosophical consciousness, the Enlightenment was able to bring modernity into a high degree of self-awareness. If the Enlightenment had been a purely ideological movement, it would at best have issued in a movement limited to a high degree of consciousness of itself. Being the peculiar amalgam of ideological program and philosophical insight that it was, it was able to project the intensity of its own self-consciousness onto the logic of modernity itself. It was able to subsume the basic contours of the developing logic of modernity into itself and render that logic aware of its radical implication, namely, that the reinterpretation of the meaning of man was necessitated by the development of modern scientific methodology.

The logical movement of modernity was from a sacramentalized nature, to an infinitized universe, thence to the language of modern science as the proper way of knowing this universe, thence to the rendering problematical of the nature and limits of knowledge as such—and now, finally, to the rendering problematical of man himself who knows, acts, and makes in this universe. The Enlightenment would spell out the outcome of this developmental sequence in its redefinition of human nature. But such an outcome is not simply a further development in the logic of modernity; it is a rendering modernity conscious of what it is ultimately about: the theoretical and practical autonomy of man, the metaphysical and ethical absoluteness of human being.

There was a heavy price exacted of the Enlightenment for this. Its philosophical substructure could not govern the dynamisms of its ideological superstructure. The price was one of tremendous ideological excess that would be reflected in, and intensified by, future ideologies. There was also a heavy price exacted of the logic of modernity for its modification by the Enlightenment. When the Enlightenment was completed, that logic was left to reach its point of completion without the consciousness of the informing vitality of the Christian notion of God; the theophanic role of this God would have to be played by an absolutized human nature. The awareness of the medieval symbolic discourse lying at the *Ursprung* of the logic of modernity would very nearly vanish, even in the great metaphysical effort of Kant. Yet the completion of the logic of modernity would itself require a conscious return to this *Ursprung*, and thus a regained awareness of the informing vitality of the Christian notion of God. But the Enlightenment could not be surpassed by denying its achievement. Even Hegel, completing as he does the logic of modernity, would have to give the Enlightenment its due.

Bruno had joyfully sensed the ethical implications of the modern universe, and so he mystically proclaimed man's autonomy. Berkeley had, in fear, perceived the danger of certain developments in the logic of modernity for the authentically Christian God. It remained for the Enlightenment to celebrate the realization of Berkeley's fears with the joyfulness of Bruno.

6

THE SYSTEMIZATION OF THE MODERN MEANING OF MAN

BOTH Rousseau and Kant function with the Enlightenment as their heritage; both accept the Enlightenment's celebration of the autonomy of man. But, in doing so, both transcend the Enlightenment's antisystematic bias. Thus, Rousseau speaks of his works as an "interconnected system," unlike the works of his day, which are "groups of separate thoughts on each of which the reader's mind can rest"; yet his system is implicit and not explicit, requiring his reader to draw it out painfully.[1] Such an implicit system of philosophical anthropology serves as a rudimentary base for the explicit and finely articulated system of Kant. Kant's system attempts to bridge the gap between the metaphysical and epistemological reflection found in Galileo, Descartes, Newton, Leibniz, Locke, Berkeley, and Hume and the anthropological and ethical reflection found in Bruno, the Enlightenment, and Rousseau. As nexus between the modern view of nature and the modern view of man, Kant strives to provide systematic metaphysical foundations, not simply for scientific discourse (as did Descartes), but for the intelligibility of man as such. Kant thus transcends the Enlightenment's antimetaphysical bias as well.

ROUSSEAU: THE RUDIMENTS OF A MODERN PHILOSOPHICAL ANTHROPOLOGY

Perceiving that the "hopes of the Enlightenment are those of modern man," and thus taking the Enlightenment as his point of departure, Jean-Jacques Rousseau (1712–78) absorbed a good deal from the philosophes, especially in psychology, and made them one of his primary audiences.[2] Although not accepting party membership in its ideological program, Rousseau followed the basic philosophical direction of the Enlightenment, sharing with that movement an unquestioned acceptance of the perspective of modern science as decisive for his thinking.[3]

Yet, although he may have been *of* the Enlightenment in a very fundamental sense, Rousseau was certainly not a representative figure of the Enlightenment, for, unlike the philosophes, he was not criticizing within a society in which he was comfortably integrated; and so it is a matter of dispute whether Rousseau is the logical outcome of the Enlightenment or the "first of a new and different dispensation."[4] Although proceeding from the most basic philosophical premises of the Enlightenment, Rousseau was convinced that that movement failed to produce a satisfactory understanding of human nature by virtue of what he called a "servile and deceptive conformity" in which "every mind has been cast in the same mould," and where never before has there been so much reading and so little learning.[5]

Impelled to distinguish his ideas from the opinions of the Enlightenment, and thus to isolate himself from the ideological superstructure of the Enlightenment in order to articulate and transfigure its underlying philosophical structure—impelled, that is, to stand outside its ideological program in order to stand inside its philosophical underpinning—Rousseau came to see that if the only justification for morality is the "public teaching of a philosophy that attacks all religion in the name of human reason," then "popular morality is certain to be destroyed because the mass of men cannot reason."[6] Popular enlightenment, in this situation, could only be a source of corruption, since it contributed to the weakening of what he called "all the ties of mutual regard and benevolence linking men to society," thereby amounting to the "great philosophic edifice on which such pretty houses of cards are being built today."[7]

If, then, there is a sense in which contemporary self-consciousness discloses the proper direction in which the meaning of human nature is to be found, there is an even stronger sense, resulting in large part from the Enlightenment's ideologizing of the logic of modern science and philosophy, in which that self-consciousness both conceals and distorts human nature.[8] Thus, when in his first *Discourse* (1750) Rousseau condemns modern science as harmful, he does not condemn it absolutely but only in terms of its effects on society. The science and philosophy popularized by the Enlightenment are destructive in their social import; they are permissible or salutary only insofar as they are *not* as such a social factor. Rousseau perceived a fundamental disproportion between the needs of society and the demands of modern science and philosophy; he thus opposed himself to the "thesis of the Enlightenment," which held that the "diffusion of philosophic or scientific knowledge is unqualifiedly salutary to society"—that a natural harmony exists between the requirements of society and those of modern science and philosophy.[9] "What are we to think," Rousseau says, "of those compilers who have indiscreetly broken open the doors of the sciences, and introduced into their sanctuary a populace unworthy to approach it?"[10]

Rousseau was thus forced to renounce the psychological optimism of the Enlightenment, thereby becoming the enemy, the defector, or as Voltaire called him, the "apostate." And although Rousseau was inclined to exaggerate this antipathy, the evidence appears convincing that there was "a systematic attempt on the part of the philosophes to discredit him," for they saw coming from their own ranks a new enemy warning against the dangers of progress.[11] Yet, for all this, Rousseau came to see that the problem did not lie just in the Enlightenment. He came to see that the concealment of human nature in its purity was the product of a long process of evolution, that the problem resided in the nature of civilization itself, insofar as civilized man, and not just modern man, "is born and dies a slave," as he phrased it, and "man's breath" itself, both literally and figuratively, was "fatal to his fellows.[12] Civilization was the shroud hiding human nature from his eyes and those of his contemporaries. "The more I study the works of men in their institutions," he would say, "the more clearly I see that in their efforts after independence, they become slaves, and that their very freedom is wasted in vain attempts to assure its continuance."[13]

It was on the road to Vincennes, on his way to visit the imprisoned Diderot in the summer of 1749, that Rousseau came to this startling realization—that he came to see the true nature of his relation to the Enlightenment and, in consequence, the fundamental problem of the relation between civilization and human nature. This was the occasion for his writing his first *Discourse*, and if it were not for the spark of this occasion, Diderot remarked, Rousseau would have remained "a barrel of gunpowder or gold fulminate which might not have exploded."[14] Rousseau himself described this occasion as a kind of *conversion*.

All of a sudden I felt my mind dazzled with a thousand inspirations . . . if I had ever been able to write a quarter of what I saw and felt . . . how clearly would I have explained all the contradictions of the social system, with what power I would have exposed all the abuses of our institutions, how simply I would have shown that man is good by nature and that only institutions have made men evil.[15]

Reading an announcement in the *Mercure de France* of the subject proposed by the Academy of Dijon for a prize essay—"Has the revival of the arts and sciences done more to corrupt or to purify morals?"—Rousseau recollected that from "the moment I read these words, I beheld another world and became another man."[16] He suddenly realized, he tells us, that he and his contemporaries were "so bound, oppressed, and overwhelmed by institutions, so completely in the hands of others from the very moment" of their birth, that the only freedom left them was freedom of thought, and yet thought itself was the very "slave of public opinion."[17] This experience turned Rousseau to the task of writing, a kind of writing that would prepare the way for a new awareness of human nature and would require the "revitalizing of both language and experience."[18] Rousseau would now take upon himself the task of defining or, more accurately, *disclosing* human nature in its purity—the task of stripping away the layers of civilization concealing the pure essence of man's nature. This task would present itself as an enormously profound problem, a problem that he would first have to devote himself to making clear and explicit.

The first question confronting Rousseau was precisely what it might mean to speak of human nature in its purity. Man in civilization, it would seem, is engaged in an endless task of appropriation—a task in which he strives to assimilate the things of nature into his own being and thereby extend his own being by what he accumulates, makes, and learns. But, of all the things man strives to appropriate (and there is nothing he does not strive to appropriate), "what he strives most eagerly to appropriate," as Rousseau puts it, "is man himself."[19] Man's nature in civilization is somehow foreign to him, as foreign to him as the other things he seeks to appropriate; man's nature, like the rest of nature, is foreign to man in civilization. But what is purely natural among the things that man appropriates? Precisely those beings which are completely at-one with themselves. The human nature that man seeks to appropriate in civilization is, then, a being completely at-one with itself. The "primary idea of man," Rousseau says, "is to become separate from all that is not himself."[20]

Tacitly presupposing the Galilean theme (as well as its sources in medieval philosophy and mysticism) of nature as a book, Rousseau is led to proclaim that there is "one book which is open to everyone—the book of nature"; but this book, far from being written in mathematical language that must be learned first in order to be properly interpreted (as Galileo put it), "speaks to all in a language they can understand" (as Rousseau puts it), so that there is "no excuse for not reading this book."[21] It is, in fact, "The Age of Paper" inaugurated by the Enlightenment, its dissemination of "so many books," as Rousseau says, that leads "us to neglect the book of the world."[22] It is significant that Rousseau returns to the Galilean metaphor precisely because, in returning to it, he transforms both it and its medieval sources. This is not the book of nature written in mathematical symbols, nor is it the book of theophanic nature; it is rather the book of human nature in its pristine condition—human nature completely at-one with itself. It is the book that makes modern scientific ciphers possible and theological symbols unnecessary. Civilization is the force that keeps this book shut, since, with the emergence of civilization, the self discovers a non-self[23] that entails a condition for civil society (as a whole) and even primitive society (in part) that cannot be purely natural.

Human nature in its purity, consequently, is a book that is radically individual in its being. Rousseau tells us that it was only "after having detached myself from social passions and from their dismal throng" that he "refound Nature with all its charms."[24] He was willing, he says, to concede that "society is natural to the human species in the way that decrepitude is natural to the individual," but whereas "old age flows from the nature of man alone," society "flows from the nature of mankind, not immediately," but only "with the aid of certain external circumstances, which might or might not have happened, or at least might have happened sooner or later."[25] The beginning of *society*, then, and not just civilization, though it is as inevitable as old age, cannot be properly or purely natural, since it cannot be completely at-one with itself, nor can it permit man to be entirely at-one with himself. Society, and not just civilization, begins with the *othering* and objectifying of the human self. Human nature in its purity is a book that exists apart from society, a book constituted by a presocial condition, by the experience of a savage who, as Rousseau says, "lives within himself, while social man lives constantly outside himself" receiving the "consciousness of his own existence" from the "judgments of others concerning him."[26] The problem with this book of nature, however, is that we always find it shut, since man as we find him does not and (it would seem) cannot exist entirely apart from some kind of society.

Although a necessary concern for man, society is not a purely natural concern and may be viewed as a product of the evolution of the species, an evolution that amounts to "an artificial progress away from a truly natural condition in which man was an animal or little more than an animal." Society entails a kind of digression or alienation of man from the purity of his own nature; in perceiving this, Rousseau becomes one of the first modern thinkers to have articulated the idea of man's alienation from his original being.[27] Like "the statue of Glaucus," Rousseau tells us,

which was so disfigured by time, seas and tempests, that it looked more like a wild beast than a god, the human soul altered in society by a thousand causes perpetually recurring, by the acquisition of a multitude of truths and errors, . . . by the continual jarring of passions, has, so to speak, changed in appearance, so as to be hardly recognizable.[28]

If man's social condition is like a layer of rust covering up his pure essence, then man as we find him in society is a being of mixed condition, a kind of half-natural and half-social being—a being, as Rousseau says, not of a "dual" but of a "compound" nature, who exists properly neither for himself nor for others, and who combines "the vices of society with the abuses of the natural state."[29]

How, then, can Rousseau read a closed book? He can read such a book only in the sense that he can speculate on its contents. "Oh Man, behold your history," he can proclaim, "such as *I believed it to read*, not in books written by your fellow creatures, who are liars, but in nature, which never lies."[30] His speculation about the closed book of nature tells him that the unity of nature consists in each individual's taking "account of only one person, one will, one system of ends—himself and his own"; the man of nature, the presocial man, he tells us, "lives for himself" as the "unit, the whole, dependent only on himself" and regards his fellows almost as he regards "animals of different species."[31] In his purely natural condition, man's soul "is wholly wrapped up in the feeling of its present existence," deprived of "any idea of the future, however near at hand," so that each man regards "himself as the only observer of his actions, the only being in the universe" who takes "any interest in him, and the sole judge of his deserts."[32] The state of nature is a state of radical independence of the individual; it is, as such, a state of indeterminacy. The purity of man's nature must lie, then, in the freedom of the state of nature and in the absence of limitation, in this state, on what man shall become. Natural man, the savage, is thus "distinguished by having almost no nature at all, by being pure potentiality" with no ends but only possibilities, with the result that human nature in its purity is very nearly a natureless essence that is infinitely malleable.[33]

Rousseau's speculation on the contents of the closed book of nature, then, leads him to make a momentous shift in the course of Western philosophical speculation on human nature. He is led to "replace the classical definition of man as the rational animal by the definition of man as free agent"; and he is led to replace the classical idea of human perfection by that of human perfectibility. Thus, what distinguishes man from the other animals in the state of nature is, first, his freedom of the will, by which he is the only animal in a position to defy nature; and second, it is his perfectibility, by which he is the only animal who "can gradually improve his faculties and pass this improvement on to the whole species."[34] "It is not, therefore, so much the understanding that constitutes the specific difference between the man and the brute," Rousseau says, "as the human quality of free agency."[35] Reason cannot qualify as the "naturally ruling principle in man because it is itself unnatural"; or, as Rousseau tells us, if nature "destined man to be healthy, I venture to declare that a state of reflection is a state contrary to nature, and that a thinking man is a depraved animal."[36]

Now, if the purity of man's nature consists in freedom and not in rationality, and this freedom entails perfectibility, then it is the "faculty of self-improvement," as Rousseau puts it, which "by the help of circumstances gradually develops all the rest of our faculties and is inherent in the species as in the individual."[37] For the ancients, rationality, speech, and life in political society were specifically human traits that man has by nature; but for Rousseau these specifically human traits can only be derivatives of the freedom and perfectibility he possesses by nature. Human nature in its purity, consequently, amounts to a prehuman condition for the emergence of man's humanness, since everything specifically human about man must be derived from perfectibility—the perfectibility entailed by his freedom.[38] Man does not even possess speech by nature, since, as Rousseau says, "a kind of society must already have existed among the first inventors of language," and "if men need speech to learn to think, they must have stood in much greater need of the art of thinking, to be able to *invent* that of speaking."[39] Speech presupposes rationality more than rationality presupposes speech, and both presuppose society, which is already a departure from the primal unity of the state of nature.

Human nature in its radical indeterminacy and freedom, human nature in its purity, is something subhuman to be associated with the state of the brute or pure animality.[40] What is characteristically human, although derived from this pure state of nature, is not coextensive with it. What is characteristically human is in no way "the gift of nature" but only "the outcome of what man did, or was forced to do, in order to overcome or change nature," so that the pure state of nature is precisely that stage in which that which is distinctive of the human as such has not yet manifested itself.[41] "Savage man," Rousseau insists, is a being "with purely animal functions: thus seeing and feeling must be his first condition, which would be common to him and to all other animals."[42] In the state of nature, man is an animal among animals, although distinguished from these other animals by the absence of his dependence on the other members of his species. In society, man is no longer an animal among animals but a being in whom reason serves as the principle of "creativity or mastership over the blind forces of nature" while it is itself an accidental product of those blind forces—man's very humanity is a "product of accidental causation."[43] Reason is properly human but it is not natural; to have human nature in its purity and to have nothing else, paradoxically, is not yet to be man.

But if human nature in its purity is a prehuman being, this prehuman essence is nonetheless good. This goodness flows from the indeterminacy of this essence, that is, from natural man's fundamental capacity for self-determination, from "the absoluteness and independence of natural man's existence" that permits him to exist as a being capable of becoming good or bad.[44] This goodness is manifested in natural man's possession of the untarnished sentiment of pity, a feeling that puts him "in the place of the sufferer," as Rousseau says, and that excites "a natural repugnance at seeing any other sensible being," and particularly any being of his own species, "suffer pain or death."[45] This feeling, in turn, flows from another most simple operation of the human soul that is also "prior to reason"—a feeling deeply interesting him in his "own welfare and preservation," a self-love that amounts to his very first feeling. This is the feeling of his own existence that lies at the bottom of "the condition of infant man."[46]

If, however, "everything specifically human is acquired," man must leave his infant condition and create a kind of second nature, by means of the development of property, law, and the mechanical arts; and in the creation of this new nature there are "no natural obstacles to man's almost unlimited progress" or, for that matter, to his "almost unlimited degradation," so that progress in society will itself amount to a double-edged affair insofar as it will realize "the potential for perfectibility which is inherent in man alone," while at the same time increasing man's unhappiness.[47] As Rousseau remarks in his second *Discourse*,

Man who loses, by age or accident, all that his perfectibility had enabled him to gain, falls by this means lower than the brutes themselves. . . . This distinctive and almost unlimited faculty is the source of all human misfortunes; . . . it is this which, in time, draws man out of his original state, . . . which successively producing in different ages his discoveries and his errors, his vices and his virtues, makes him at length a tyrant both over himself and over nature.[48]

As man determines his primal indeterminate nature, as man creates a second nature for himself, his development is a process, Rousseau tells us, by which the "perfection of the individual" necessitates the "decrepitude of the species," by which, although "man is good, men become wicked," so that man exchanges a situation of unselfconscious animality for the self-conscious frustration of humanity.[49] With every subsequent advance made by the race, Rousseau argues, the race is further removed "from its primitive state," so that the "more discoveries we make, the more we deprive ourselves of the means of making the most important of all," so that "by our very study of man" the "knowledge of him is put out of our power."[50]

Man's progress in moral knowledge in society inevitably entails "a weakening of his animal instinct of sympathy," and man will eventually reach the point where his natural self-love will be corrupted into a selfishness—which, Rousseau remarks, is "always comparing self with others" and "is never satisfied," since "this feeling, which prefers ourselves to others, requires that they should prefer us to themselves, which is impossible."[51] The emergence of this selfishness is the point at which "the strong come to submit to serve the weak" but also the point at which men purchase "imaginary repose at the expense of real felicity"—the point at which *human* faculties become fully developed but also the point at which "to be and to seem become two totally different things." This is the point beyond which the state of nature is destroyed forever as a possibility for most men and beyond which "freedom can no longer be a single or unitary principle" for men.[52] This is the point at which political society emerges from the womb of primitive society—the point beyond which the rate of social change quickens at an ever faster pace, involving "further dislocation and greater hostilities," until the Enlightenment itself is reached as a curse hiding behind a benediction. The Enlightenment thrusts man forward into a position where he can understand his human nature, and yet it further conceals the meaning of that nature. The Enlightenment discloses a possibility, while simultaneously concealing the meaning of that possibility, namely, the possibility that man's history in civil society is a history of what Rousseau calls "human sickness."[53]

Neither in the subhuman condition, where he possesses his nature in its purity, nor in the social condition, where the price he pays for progress is the concealment of that nature and the corruption of the species, can there be said to be a "telos," or end natural to man; consequently, an understanding of human nature in its purity depends not on man's end but on his beginnings.[54] Rousseau's speculation on the contents of the book of nature, then, is in essence a speculation on man's beginnings. This speculation leaves him with only two solutions to the problem of defining or disclosing human nature in its purity. One is to create, at least in speech, the possibility of a kind of new "social counter-will," which will reverse the process of civilization and reattain an optimum point in society midway between the state of nature and the worst excesses of civilization or political society; the other is escape from society and civilization entirely to a kind of "private desert."[55] Rousseau saw clearly the sharp outlines of the solutions confronting him.

What makes humanity unhappy is the contradiction between our condition and our desires, between our duties and our inclinations, between nature and social institutions, between the man and the citizen. Make man one, and you will make him as happy as he can be. *Give him all to the state or leave him all to himself.*[56]

The first solution, Rousseau perceived, required beginning with civilization in its present state, with modernity in its self-consciousness; it required the acceptance of the arts and sciences in their present state as what he called "the steel we must leave in the wound, for fear the wounded man will die if it is extracted."

It required the acceptance of the Enlightenment and its dual emphasis of social reform and individual freedom—its dual emphasis of a transformation of social consciousness and the individual consciousness of the great mind.[57] Effectively, he realized that "having destroyed our capacity for unconscious goodness, we have not created the conditions for conscious virtue," and so he saw that the primary focus for his first solution would be the question, "How can civilized man recover the benefits of the natural man, so innocent and happy, without returning to the state of nature, without renouncing the advantages of the social state?"[58] What is "the social and political order in which men do not acquire the needs and passions which prevent their being happy"—the social order that would quicken men's "faculties without producing in them needs beyond their power to satisfy"?[59] The solution to these questions lies in "finding ways to give to the collective or general interest a *natural* force, that is, one that is reflexive and does not depend on a process of rational reflection"[60]—in finding a way to give public or social interests the force that lies behind the individual's interest in the state of nature.

Rousseau must, in essence, attempt to reconcile the legitimate exercise of freedom in political society with the valid demands of order. If freedom for man in the state of nature is absolute insofar as his independence of other men is absolute, if only the savage is entirely free because he alone entirely "desires what he is able to perform and does what he desires," then freedom can be only a partial and correlative principle for civilized man. Freedom is not "doing what he wished" but rather "*not* doing what he did *not* wish."[61] This *negative* freedom can be construed as essentially self-legislation that, unlike the unconditioned freedom of the state of nature, exists only insofar as man acquires it for himself.[62] Possessed only insofar as it is acquired and constantly reacquired, this freedom becomes something like reason itself, namely, a non-natural being, something that is "not so much either the condition or the consequence of virtue as virtue itself," so that it is not "virtue which makes man free but freedom which makes man virtuous."[63] Freedom in political society can now be construed as a "submission to a strict and inviolable law which the individual erects over himself," what Rousseau calls the "volonté générale," so that the only legitimate authority becomes that which "the principle of legitimacy, *the idea of law as such*, exercises over individual wills"; it is this notion of freedom to which Rousseau accords priority as the basis of political life.[64]

The nature of his first solution requires, then, that Rousseau engage in a political philosophy, not just a moral philosophy as the Enlightenment and Bruno did. But this political philosophy is "but a part of that study of the human heart which he had made his province," and therefore Rousseau must engage in political philosophy as a part of his philosophical anthropology, so that in his political philosophy he will find room for the expression of his feelings and thoughts.[65] The unnatural and negative freedom that stands at the heart of his political philosophy "must prove itself in its independence, in its original autonomy, and take the reins from chance," that is, from the blind forces of nature.[66] As a discipline, this freedom finds its embodiment in the general will, or *volonté générale*, which is nothing more than a "transposition of the most essential individual moral faculty to the realm of public experience," permitting the existence of a community in "which everyone obeys only the general will which he recognizes and acknowledges as his own will."[67] This general will is the collective version, in other words, of what Rousseau calls the conscience or *lumière intérieure*, which he defines as an "innate principle of justice and virtue" in the "bottom of our hearts," by which "we judge our own actions or those of others to be good or evil."[68] It is this conscience that, when universalized for and by the whole community, permits the existence of a society that mediates between the lost state of nature and the present state of civilization.

The best possible condition for man in his humanness, then, is not primitive and not, properly speaking, of nature, but is the "product of art, that is, of a conscious exercise of man's contriving intelligence." It is a combination of virtue and goodness, standing "midway between the goodness of man in the state of nature and the virtue of the citizen in a legitimate regime"—a condition that lies in man's "departing from his natural state, but not too much," a condition in which individuals can remain independent of the will of one another, and where "common life has a solidarity, a simple, vigorous, and unmediated concreteness."[69] In this state a "nearly perfect convergence exists between absolute liberty and social dependence, between nature and social institutions"; and in this state consists the *golden age*, what Rousseau calls "the earliest life of man," that is, of man in possession of his properly human attributes. In this partriarchal, rural life, the most peaceful and the "most attractive to the uncorrupted heart" is had the one state "where one need not seek peace in the wilderness"—a "just mean between the indolence of the primitive state and the petulant activity of our egoism," the "happiest and most stable of epochs" from which men could have departed "only through some fatal accident."[70] Here man has "reached the perfection of childhood"; his "progress has not been bought at the price of his happiness"; he is frozen at the point where the childhood of the race is perfected. Thus, he retains the original principle of his nature and yet exists for others; he is at the same time good for himself and others.[71] The disastrous circumstances that impelled man to leave this point constitute what Rousseau calls the "crisis which forms the bridge between the child and the man," between man having just left the state of nature and man having irrevocably entered civil society.[72] "We are born, so to speak," Rousseau tells us, "twice over, born into existence and born into life, born a human being and born a man,"[73] and the golden age appears to be the point midway between these two births.

Rousseau, however, is perfectly aware that modern man cannot return to this golden age of simple habits, and yet there is still a possibility that "if some men restore part of its unmediated concreteness, they may postpone the conclusive slavery of civilized barbarism."[74] If it is impossible to recover for society that point midway between civilization and the state of nature, it is still possible to attain, partially at least, a point midway between the golden age and modern civilization. This new midpoint is attainable if individuals, at least a few individuals, can do in their moral relations with each other what was done in the social relations holding between all individuals in the golden age. Perceiving a kind of "trichotomy between nature, morals, and politics,"[75] Rousseau envisages the possibility of a small moral society of individuals, constituting a kind of island in the sea of modern civilization, who would learn to preserve their moral relations from the corrupting influence of the political relations of modern civilization. These individuals would learn to act as if they were not political in the very act of being political—as if they were natural in the very act of living out the denaturalized and completed second nature of modern civilization. In order to learn these things, they must act as if the premise of the state of nature, which was still maintained in the golden age, was still operative. The premise of civil society, which is in fact operative in modern civilization, is that our first duties are to others. The premise of the state of nature is that our "first duties are to ourselves," and since "our first feelings are centered on self," "the first notion of justice springs not from what we owe to others, but from what is due to us."[76] Now, to act as if the premise of the state of nature was still operative in modern civilization, the individual must always be able to treat his fellow man as a mere duplication of himself. By treating others as replicas of himself, the individual will be able to act in such a way that he treats his acting justly toward others as simply a matter of acting authentically toward himself. Thus, he identifies himself in the other so that he loves the other as himself, and he generalizes or extends this identification to all, even though all do not live in terms of this generalization or extension.[77]

The new moral, nonpolitical midpoint between modern civilization and the unattainable golden age requires that the individual relate himself to other individuals as abstractions so that he may be estranged from them as particulars, so that he may systematically conceive of his relations to them as relations to himself, so that his action abolishes the other as an other-for-him.[78] By acting in this way, although his nature is definitively denaturalized by modern civilization, his actions will have the force of nature, and although he lives the life of a good citizen in modern civilization, his cititizenship will transcend the corrupting influences of that civilization. Although the independence of nature is completely destroyed in modern civilized society, if that society is to be made tolerable for men, the independence of nature must be re-created in the moral relations of a few men.[79] By not allowing his identity for himself to be engaged in his relations with other men, modern civilized man would be able to "keep his nature intact, at least in essence," and thus be able to "benefit from the enlargement of his powers made possible by the intellectual progress of the human race without being enslaved by the by-products of that progress."[80] Rousseau's first solution amounts, then, to his proposal of an abstract society of morally related individuals modeled on the concrete but unattainable society of the golden age. As an abstract society, imperfectly imitating a concrete society, it involves an abstract encounter with human nature in its purity that imperfectly imitates the concrete encounter with that nature possessed in its perfection by the savage. Thus, in describing his imagined role as the tutor of Émile, Rousseau can say, "it is I who am really Émile's Father; it is I who have made a man of him,"[81] thus implying that the concrete being of nature (fatherhood) has been replaced by the abstract being of his moral relation to Émile (tutor *as if* father). Thus, his first solution—the creation of a kind of new social counterwill—seems to be a realizable possibility.

Yet the first solution, he himself realized, was not sufficient by itself. For, in order to treat others as a mere duplication of one's self, and thus to scrape away, if only in one's moral relations, the accretions covering up the pure essence of human nature, one must be absolutely sure of what this pure essence is, so as to know how much to scrape away. Now, in analyzing the problem of defining or disclosing human nature, Rousseau has speculatively confronted this pure essence; he has only *speculated* on the contents of the book of nature. In order for his first solution to be efficacious, however, he must concretely and with a kind of Cartesian certitude confront the pure essence of human nature so that there can be no doubt as to what it is. He must not merely describe what human nature in its purity *might* look like but experientially encounter what it *must* be. He must himself *read* the book of nature and not merely guess at its contents; he must engage himself in the second and final of his two solutions, namely, a complete retreat from society and civilization to a kind of private desert. But, far from negating the first solution, this second solution permits it to be not merely a solution in speech but a solution in experience.

But how can the pure essence of human nature be concretely uncovered? How can the book of (human) nature in its purity be read? Certainly, civilization as it now stands cannot possibly disclose this essence concretely, since it could not by itself even disclose this essence speculatively. Nor can this essence be concretely revealed in history, since history can speak, at best, only of the point where the essence was beginning to be covered up. Even anthropological inferences about primitive man assume the perspective of civilization. In all of these, we only find the self of civilized man, which is "really a creation of his imagination out of the moments of past and future and out of the opinions of others."[82] Nor can this essence be disclosed either by God or by human reflection on God, since "not even the concept of the Deity can remain immune from the perverting influence" of civilization—in other words, the fall of man in modern civilized society can be said to "have involved the fall of God."[83] Since all values— moral, spiritual, and intellectual—have been perverted by civilization, the authentic thinker has no starting point outside himself to consult for the concrete revelation of human nature in its purity.[84] If it is to be concretely encountered at all, the pure essence of human nature must be found in an exploration of the individual's inner being; introspective psychology must necessarily replace every other possible way of describing human nature. The exploration of inner being must be made inseparable from an analysis of human nature, and this very analysis must be written as a biography of an individual.[85] Realizing that if "anyone sincerely asks the question 'Who am I?', he is asking it not only for himself but also for the whole human race," realizing that the concrete manifestation of man in his natural condition resides within each of us buried under a mass of civilized accretions, and realizing that every individual, theoretically at least, is capable of discovering within himself the original pattern of humanity,[86] Rousseau saw that what was possible for all men theoretically was concretely realized in himself. He could now afford to retreat to a private desert where, detached from all society, he asks, "What am I in myself?" without any "wish to occupy myself any longer save with myself."[87] The book of nature was within Rousseau, and so for Rousseau to read the book of nature was for Rousseau to read Rousseau.

Here we meet the boldest aspect of Rousseau's anthropology,

for he himself claims to be the first and only man who has reached the state of nature.[88]

These traits, so new for us and so true, once traced, still found of course in the depths of men's hearts the attestation of their genuineness, but their presence would never have been revealed if the historian of human nature had not begun by removing the rust that hid them. A retired and solitary life, a love of reverie and contemplation, in the calm of the passions, those primitive traits which have disappeared in the multitude, could alone enable him to rediscover them. In a word, it was necessary that one man should depict himself in order thus to show us primitive man and if the author had not been just as singular as his books he would never have written them.[89]

Rousseau's return to the state of nature is not a turning back in time but a turning within, experienced, as he says, in "these hours of solitude and meditation" when "I am fully myself and for myself, without diversion, without obstacle, and where I can truly say that I am that which nature has designed."[90] In doing this, Rousseau is at once indicating his continuity and more significant discontinuity with the Enlightenment. The Enlightenment was taken by the notion that by going back to the origin of things we can explain their nature.[91] In analyzing the problem of defining or disclosing human nature, Rousseau shares, to a degree, this obsession, but in his final or second solution to this problem he rejects this obsession in favor of an *inward* encounter with human nature. Rousseau is eminently suited to such an inward return to the state of nature, since of all his contemporaries he alone appears to have emerged from nothing, because he "had been both his own master and his own pupil, as if he had had to relive the history of mankind in his own person."[92]

Human nature in its undiluted being is "to be revealed in the process of uncovering, of penetrating, the history, the movements of his soul," of rendering an account, as he says, "to myself of the modifications of my soul and of their successions," of applying "the barometer to my soul."[93] The movements of his soul, moreover, are traceable to one principle, unlike the events of his life, which are "worked by more than one cause"; and when these movements are traced back to their single principle, it is then, he says, that "I am most fully myself, without mixture, and without obstacle."[94] Underneath all his experience, behind his empirical self, there stands a *true self* that contemplates his empirical self and that enables him to put a kind of "distance between himself and his own acts"—a true self that enables him to say that "I know, whatever may be the effect of my act, that I shall none the less have the merit of my good intention," a merit that is always there.[95] It is not, in other words, Rousseau as such, or Rousseau in his experience, that constitutes the state of nature; it is an inner self behind his experience that, when he encounters it, discloses the state of nature and that, when he reads it, enables him to say that he reads the book of nature. Here, once again, Rousseau manifests his continuity and more significant discontinuity with the Enlightenment. For the Enlightenment, human nature must be treated as finite in its articulation in individual human beings but as unlimited or infinite in its possibilities for development; the soul of the individual might be temporary, but the soul of humanity was certainly immortal because permanent and universal.[96] In consistency with the Enlightenment, Rousseau predicates the notion of infinity of man rather than of God or the universe, but, unlike the thinkers of the Enlightenment, what is infinite and unlimited is precisely deep within the *individual*, deep within himself.

In order to claim to be the first and only man who has in this manner reached the state of nature, however, Rousseau must claim "a divine perspective on his life"; he must claim to see his true self, the pure essence of human nature, "from the standpoint of the divinity."[97] If "truly personal existence is the experience of plenitude, the condition of a being that is full of nothing but itself," then the existence of the true self is possessed of something akin to the plenitude that the medieval philosopher-mystics attributed to the theophanic God of Christianity, and the very perspective of this God is required to see or unearth this true self. Rousseau himself, like the medievals, is possessed of a yearning for the infinite, as when he says, "I suffocated in the universe" and "wanted to soar into the infinite."[98] When he delves within himself and finds his true self, he speaks of himself "as undisturbed as God himself," existing "upon this earth as upon a strange planet, whence I have fallen from that which I inhabited"; and he speaks of this true self as judging his empirical self "with perhaps as much severity as I shall be judged by the sovereign Judge after this life."[99] Rousseau's encounter with his innermost being assumes the proportions of the voice of God. Rousseau's selfhood discovers, "within and by itself, and in its own terms, the imperative for goodness," for its own goodness. He places "himself in the unrealizable so that he may breathe and utter himself as God utters Himself in creation."[100] There is, as Rousseau notes, something within himself that "tries to break the bands which confine it," and space is not its measure, nor does the whole universe suffice to contain it, so that the ecstatic sentiment of his own existence "while it lasts is said to make him as self-sufficient as God."[101] Effectively, in order to define his own state, the state of his inner self, Rousseau had to appeal to the definition of the divine eternity as it had been formulated by the Neoplatonists and Church Fathers—an eternity in which, as he says, all truths are "a single idea" just as "all places are a single point, and all times a single moment." Like God, he must see himself at a glance, all at once, and so his personal identity cannot be construed as dependent on his memory.[102]

Now, Rousseau not only concretely encounters human nature in its purity, but he also presents that encounter to his readers; he not only reads the book of nature within him, but he also presents in speech his original reading. Rousseau's articulation of his inward recovery of the state of nature will be made possible by the learning and language he has acquired in the context of society—a learning and language that will have to be skillfully used, most notably in his *Confessions,* to make the reader see him as he sees himself, to enable, as he says, "the outside world to behold a man as he really was in his inmost self," and to provide "the first model for the study of man," that is, the *systematic* study of man "which is certainly yet to begin."[103] In his presentation of his true self to his readers, it is not primarily his memory that he relies on but his creative imagination, "which constructs, which weaves feelings and possibilities," and that is the peculiarly *creative* faculty in man.[104] Although Rousseau confronts his true self without the aid of his creative imagination, he requires this imagination if he is to present that confrontation to his audience. Thus, if he confronts his inner self as something that has the attributes of God, he must, in his imaginative re-creation of the reality of that inner self, relate to it in a manner similar to God, so that in his imagination he becomes like God, namely, alone and master of the universe.[105] Rousseau is, therefore, impelled to *create* a unity for the events of his life, much as the theophanic God of Christianity is impelled to *other* Himself in creation. It is Rousseau's imagination "which allows him to connect the discrete situations of his life in terms of a unitary self which has gone through these situations," so that his happiness will depend not just on his confrontation with his inner self in his reveries but also on how "he cultivates his *faculté consolatrice, imagination.*" Just as modern science, despite its claims to unconditional rationality, really constructs the universe on the basis of creative imagination, so also Rousseau's life when perceived as a unity is his own construct.[106] The self created by his imagination for his readers is inescapably a social self or self-for-others, but it is distinguished from the social selves that his contemporaries present to each other by virtue of the fact that his own conscious, concrete confrontation with his inner self is the conscious precondition for the social self he creates, whereas the imagination of his contemporaries is completely determined by the opinions of others.

In both his reading of the book of nature within himself and his re-creation in speech of this book, Rousseau must read and write as if he were God. But what is required is not the attempt to become one with God by "being raised by God to a participation in his life," as with the medieval philosophers and mystics, but the attempt to absorb or assimilate the divinity into himself.[107] Rousseau is thus operating with the metaphors of the faith underlying the medieval notion of a theophanic God but without the substance of that faith, in a manner similar to the Enlightenment. Unlike the Enlightenment, however, there is no consciously contrived and ideologically retailed anti-Christian polemic, nor is there need of such a polemic. It is Rousseau himself or, by extension, the individual who can concretely confront his own innermost self, who "must become his own savior and, in the ethical sense, his own creator," and in his imaginative re-creation of his life, Rousseau need not look, as he tells us, to God or any other "definite object" but only to a being dwelling "entirely within myself." This is in contrast to those earlier *Confessions* of St. Augustine, who says of his soul that "as it cannot of itself enlighten itself, so it cannot of itself satisfy itself."[108] To the extent that every man can potentially do what Rousseau actually does—read the book of nature within himself—then every man can potentially be what Rousseau actually is, namely, his own Christ; for Rousseau has demonstrated, by "turning himself back into natural man," that "natural man was without sin" like Christ.[109] Sooner or later, Rousseau must "appear to himself as the incarnation of a new conception of redemption," for, as he has the Savoyard priest say in *Émile,* "what is there so absurd in the thought that all things are made for me, when I alone can relate all things to myself?"[110]

In reading the book of nature within himself, then, Rousseau is like the savage in the state of nature, for, despite the gulf which separates them, both he and the savage are isolated and self-sufficient.[111] Yet Rousseau's return to this state, unlike the condition of the savage, involves the experience of his inner self as godlike and Christlike. Thus, as a natural man, Rousseau is "somehow a beast (savage) and a god (in his divine self-sufficiency)." Like the savage, he is at one with himself and not torn in two; but, unlike the savage, his return to nature involves, as long as he maintains it, a freedom from what he calls "the fetters of the body," a freedom like that of God.[112]

At the bottom of his selfhood Rousseau finds a primal certainty, a certainty prior to, and conditional for, what men call logical certainties, a certainty that pertains to "the sentiment of his own existence" and that places him back where Descartes began: *Je pense, donc je suis.*[113] Rousseau is back at the point of Descartes and not entirely back at the point of the savage because both Descartes and Rousseau are conscious not only of their existence (like the savage) but of the radical import of their certainty of their existence (unlike the savage). Like Descartes, then, Rousseau "believes that the thinker must be provided with some primary, intuitive certainty capable of supporting all his subsequent intellectual arguments," but Rousseau probes more deeply than Descartes, holding that this "certainty cannot be reached by mere ratiocination, but is given directly to personal consciousness," and refers, as Rousseau says, "to what I have felt."[114] In starting from the certainty of his own existence, furthermore, Rousseau is like Robinson Crusoe, insofar as his certitude can be applied to his survival, to his conduct (unlike Descartes), so that his certitude permits "operations," as he puts it, that "well directed and for long repeated" will supply him "with results as sure as those of science."[115]

Having come to the most fundamental certitude—that "I cannot be mistaken about what I have felt"—Rousseau demonstrates the existence of an *inner self* to be the pure essence of human nature— a self founded on the primal certainty of the feeling of one's own existence and "grasped in a timeless instant of self-perception."[116] Rousseau must be "entirely given up to the present moment" in order to encounter this inner self, which is "essentially a-temporal and a-social"; he must exist not only in solitude, that is, as society-less, but in expectation of his own imminent death, that is, as time-less.[117] Only in this way can he encounter the bottom of his selfhood, the very ground of human nature. He describes this encounter in detail.

But if there is a state where the soul finds a position sufficiently solid to repose thereon, and to gather together all its being, without having need for recalling the past, nor to climb on into the future; where time counts for nothing, where the present lasts forever, without marking its duration in any way, and without any trace of succession, without any other sentiment of privation, neither of enjoyment, or pleasure nor pain, of desire nor of fear, than *this alone of our existence, and which this feeling alone can fill entirely*; [then] so long as this state lasts, he who finds it may be called happy, not with an imperfect happiness, poor and relative, such as that which one finds in the pleasures of life, but with a sufficing happiness, perfect and full, which does not leave in the soul any void which it feels the need of filling.[118]

The unconditional sentiment of his own existence, encountered in an atemporal and asocial instant, is "experienced only and precisely *as* one's own"; it is "essentially private" and enables Rousseau to "feed myself" on "my own substance." It is the condition of a desert island, not that of a social being, and although Rousseau does not experience it all of the time or even most of the time, it becomes, as he says, the "standard of comparison for all other conditions."[119] When everything "exterior falls away, what is left is something which feels its own existence," a feeling that is unmediated, that is "not experienced through anything other than itself." This feeling permits Rousseau, although pressed on all sides, to remain in equilibrium because he depends upon no one but himself. This feeling enables Rousseau to say, "I did not think, I did not reason, I did not philosophize," but only "felt myself with a sort of voluptuousness."[120]

Although consciously had in Rousseau, this primal affective certitude of personal existence is unrecognized in most men and need not be, and indeed rarely is, directly experienced by most men; in demonstrating its existence in himself, Rousseau is demonstrating its existence as an unconscious precondition for our thinking about ourselves—for the very operation of the imagination in the creation of our social selves.[121] He has demonstrated, in other words, in himself a movement from the exterior, the state of living "in the opinions of others," to the interior, the state of "living within oneself," a movement that, as such, is a reversal of the movement from the interior to the exterior that Rousseau has found in the development of man from the state of nature to civilization.[122]

Rousseau thus claims to have concretely demonstrated in his very interiority the pure essence of human nature as the being of inner selfhood—as the being that "underlies its own history" and that remains when all social contexts have been removed.[123] The book of nature is an inner self that, although closed shut by civilization, has been reopened by Rousseau, and that, when read by Rousseau, reveals that the nature of man is an entirely "private, self-defining impulse, a feeling of self, beyond law, above time, and without limit."[124] In finally reading this book, Rousseau has redeemed the self-consciousness of the Enlightenment by demonstrating the philosophical connection between the Enlightenment's insight into the notion of man as the measure of all meaning and its more tenuous insight into the radical individual.[125] Rousseau, perceiving that his disclosure of human nature in its purity was a further radicalization of the radical insight of the Enlightenment, also saw that the "interiorization of the self is politically dangerous because it allows a man to dissociate himself from his public acts." He saw that a few men, like himself, "will discover their true humanity within them," but the majority of men are best fitted to be citizens and not alter-Rousseaus.[126]

But the greater part of men, agitated by continual passions, know little of this state. . . . It would not even be good in the present state of affairs, that . . . they should be disgusted with the active life, of which their needs always being reborn, prescribe to them the duty.[127]

Rousseau offers his second solution to the problem of human nature, then, not as an exemplar for others, but as a demonstrative ground for his first solution. By showing the actuality of a single man's removal from civilization, he was demonstrating the real possibility of a lesser but more socially beneficial alternative, namely, the creation of an invisible, abstract society of autonomous moral agents as a kind of island within modern civilization. In doing so, he finished the rudimentary base for the systemization Kant was destined to give modern philosophical anthropology.

The manner in which Rousseau can be incorporated by Kant is to be grasped in terms of the manner in which Rousseau himself incorporates the prior developments of the logic of modernity. In the first place, Rousseau reconfronts the logic of modernity with its *systematic* origins in Descartes. Rousseau claimed that a careful study of his "very paradoxical maxims" would serve to disclose his "system."[128] In returning, however, to the Cartesian systematic possibility, Rousseau reaps the benefit of Locke's psychologizing of the Cartesian *ego*, of Locke's emphasis on the notion of reason as emergent in the very development of experience; he returns to Locke's individualism.[129] Whereas, however, "Locke's was the individualism of the strong," Rousseau's is the "individualism of the weak," an individualism discovered in the human weakness in himself, which enabled him to become the "chronicler of the sufferings of victimized man in general," the first philosophical articulator in the unfolding logic of modernity to "feel the problem of human unhappiness in modern society."[130] In proposing what he called a "*sad* and great system," Rousseau saw that men in civilization are "victims of the blind inconsistency" of their hearts who, unable to know how to live, "die without having lived."[131] Yet, for all his weakness, the individual has buried within him, far down, an absolutely unconditioned self-hood that constitutes the locus of the absoluteness of human nature. This was no cause to share the Enlightenment's optimism about the future social order. Rousseau proclaimed that it was "a noble and beautiful spectacle to see man raising himself, so to speak, from nothing, by his own exertions," going "back into himself, there to study man and get to know his own nature." But he perceived the terrible ambiguity of the absoluteness of man, for there now appeared a fresh enemy that man has not yet learnt to conquer, namely, himself.[132] In rejecting the antisyste-matic and uncritically optimistic biases of the Enlightenment while accepting the Enlightenment's divinization of man, Rousseau was able to mediate between the blend of criticism and ideologizing found in the Enlightenment and the blend of criticism and fully explicit systemization found in Kant.

It is not entirely surprising, then, to find Kant himself saluting Rousseau's point of view as "a great discovery of our age," totally unknown to the ancients. Rousseau is the "restorer of the rights of humanity" who brought forth the claims of freedom and au-tonomy in his definition of man and thereby entitled himself to be called "the Newton of the moral world."[133] Having carefully studied Rousseau's *Émile,* Kant believed that Rousseau was wres-tling there with the most imposing problem of the moral life— the education of man as a truly moral being in such a way as to resolve the conflict between man's "moral end and his physical nature with its amoral passions."[134] When Rousseau insisted that apart from conscience he found nothing in himself to raise him "above the beasts"; that the man who "obeys his conscience is following nature" and "need not fear that he will go astray"; that if "good is good, it must be good in the depths of our hearts as well as in our actions," he was providing one of the key rudi-mentary components for the Kantian anthropological system.[135]

Rousseau also suggested a metaphysical component for the Kantian system. The inner self, as Rousseau sees it, is essentially private and thus radically unique. Yet there are traits held in com-mon by the inner selves of all men. In all men the inner self is private, boundless or inexhaustible, atemporal, the only reality capable of making the individual self-sufficient; it is the principle that accounts for the unity of the individual's experience. In effect, the radically unique inner self is possessed of a dimension of universality—a universality rooted not in a common access to the things of nature but in the fundamental sameness of the traits possessed by all inner selves. By appealing to a kind of universality without appealing to the things of nature as such, Rousseau was articulating an insight that would permit Kant to embody radical selfhood in a table of categories built into human consciousness— a table of categories creative, in its entirety, of the intelligibility of nature. If, in other words, the inner self is the book of nature, then it is not the intelligibility of nature that *measures* the truth of human consciousness but the powers of human intelligence that *create* the intelligibility of nature.

But, in proposing what could provide a metaphysical as well as an ethical ground for the Kantian project, Rousseau also and by the same token posed a threat whose explosive potential would have to be defused by the resulting system. The primal attributes of the theologically received God of medieval Christianity— namely, His infinity, eternity, self-sufficiency (or plentitude), and His unconditioned creativity—are transmuted by Rousseau into the powers and perquisites of an inner self that, moreover, is now seen to be coextensive with human nature as such.

This inner self becomes the precondition for an effectively *boundless* exercise of the creative imagination in its construction of the social self—this in accordance with the infinity of the medieval God. Creation *ex nihilo* is paralleled by Rousseau's notion of the self as the precondition for civilized man's self-creation, a creation of what he is not. Corresponding to the self-sufficiency and plenitude of the Christian God, Rousseau's inner self is complete unto itself and the sole precondition for the happiness of the individual. And finally, echoing even the received notion of God's "durée," this new self is as such atemporal and to be perceived in a timeless instant. In applying the divine attributes to the inner self, Rousseau must inevitably imitate (or repeat) the medieval negative-theological dialectics of God's immanence and transcendence.[136]

Like the God of medieval Christianity, the inner self dwells in the world while at the same time existing beyond the world. Like this God, it possesses a kind of "glory" that makes the concerns of men, the very concerns of civilization, "vanity" by comparison. The inner self of the savage is uncivilized in the sense of being pre-civilized, but the inner self encountered by Rousseau is uncivilized in the sense that it transcends civilization as such; there is no civilization to which it can lead. It poses the possibility of a postcivilized essence for man. Human nature, that is, inner self-hood, manifests itself in civilization—as the precondition for civilized man's creation of his self-for-others—but it exists *beyond* civilization, much as the Christian God manifests Himself in nature but exists beyond nature.

It would seem that Rousseau was ever so slightly opening a door destined to be fully opened by Nietzsche—a door that opened not only on the possibility of the end of modernity but on the possibility of the end of Western civilization as such. The problem for Kant, it would seem, was how the civilization-less essence of human nature could be safely secured for Europe and thereby for Western civilization itself.

KANT: THE METAPHYSICAL FOUNDATIONS FOR THE MEANING OF MAN IN THE MODERN UNIVERSE

1. INTRODUCTION

Immanuel Kant (1724–1804) passed his life in a narrow circle: he was born and died in Königsberg and lived the life of a German professor without any exciting crises other than intellectual.[137] His debt to the prior developments of modern philosophy, however, sets the stage for the far-from-narrow scope of his intellectual mission.

Insofar as he shares the Enlightenment's exaltation of man, Kant can be called a man of the Enlightenment. He himself defined the substance of this movement as "man's release from his self-incurred tutelage," that is, his release from his "inability to make use of his understanding without direction from another," and he proclaimed the courage to use one's own reason as the very motto of enlightenment.[138] As to the damaging ideological and polemical aspects of this movement, Kant saw them as "the total dissolution that always precedes the start of a new creation," and that "magnifies my hopes that the great, long-awaited revolution in the sciences is not too far off."[139] Yet, insofar as Kant carries the Enlightenment into a critical and systematic examination of man's newfound stature, the spirit of the Enlightenment is in him "at a point beyond self-satisfaction and rebellion."[140]

In addition to the Enlightenment, Kant is indebted to Leibniz and Hume, Newton and Kepler, whose thought he examined in his lectures, Herder tells us, with as much intensity as he examined the writings of Rousseau, always returning, in the process, to his focus on nature and the moral value of man.[141] Rousseau and Newton certainly epitomized for Kant the two poles of modern philosophical reflection on nature and morality, which Kant joined in his conception of man as an "analogue to the great cosmic order."[142] Thus, Kant says,

I am by disposition an enquirer. I feel the consuming thirst for knowledge, the eager unrest to advance ever further, and the delights of discovery. There was a time when I believed that this is what confers real dignity upon human life, and I despised the common people who know nothing. Rousseau has set me right. This imagined advantage vanishes. I learn to honour men, and regard myself as of much less use than the common labourer, if I did not believe that my philosophy will restore to all men the common rights of humanity. . . . Rousseau is another Newton. Newton completed the science of external nature, Rousseau that of the internal universe or of man. Just as Newton laid bare the order and regularity of the external world, so Rousseau discovered the hidden nature of man.[143]

Rousseau challenged, for Kant, what was assumed by the whole tradition of Western metaphysics—the supremacy of the theoretical life—proclaiming instead the supremacy of the moral or practical life. It was Rousseau who permitted Kant to announce that philosophy is "nothing but the practical knowledge of man."[144]

Yet Kant's path had to diverge from that of Rousseau. While both argue that the goodness of nature consists in its providence for the species but not for the individual, Kant holds that the development of civilization is in accordance with the intents of nature, so that, as Kant says, Rousseau "proceeds synthetically and begins with natural man," whereas "I proceed analytically and begin with civilized man"; the result, for Kant, is that civilization is the essential "setting in which man is to test and prove his freedom."[145] But if Kant diverges from Rousseau's path, it is only to return to that path in a more secure fashion than Rousseau—to transform what was experience in Rousseau into the substance of metaphysically grounded idea.[146] Kant takes up Rousseau's emphasis on freedom as the distinctive feature of man *as* man, as well as his emphasis on conscience as the seat of moral being, and transforms Rousseau's notion of the inner self into the autonomy of the human person as the only end to be chosen unconditionally for its own sake. Kant thereby demonstrates the capacity of the prophetic function of the philosopher, as found in Rousseau, to survive in the domain of metaphysical system.

Subserving Kant's coupling of Newton and Rousseau (nature and freedom) is his coupling of Hume and Leibniz (experience and rationality). Whereas in Hume, Kant was confronted with the position that thought is "merely a practical instrument for the convenient interpretation of our human experience," with no metaphysical validity of any kind, in Leibniz he was confronted with the "self-legislative character of pure thought"; he had to determine how much of Leibniz's position could remain after justice had been done to Hume's damaging criticisms.[147] Kant said that his "recollection of David Hume was the very thing" that first "interrupted my dogmatic slumber and gave my investigations in the field of speculative philosophy a quite new direction"; but he also said that he hoped to "advance further" than the man to whom he owed the "first spark of light," interpreting this Humean spark as the principle of not carrying "the use of reason dogmatically beyond the field of all possible experience."[148] Hume was optimistic that philosophy might someday discover the secret springs of the human mind, intimating that a turnabout in thinking about man similar to that of Copernicus was needed to do this, but these hopes could find their fulfillment in Kant only to the extent that Kant was able to overcome Hume's criticism of the rationality of science while maintaining Hume's insight into experience as constituting the limits of knowledge.[149]

It was in Leibniz that Kant found the instrument for overcoming Hume's criticism from within. Leibniz's rejoinder to the slogan "there is nothing in the soul which does not come from the senses" was "except the soul itself," and Kant interpreted this to mean "except such concepts as are prerequisite for learning anything"; Kant sought, then, to carry on a fundamental discussion with Leibniz, what he called a "real *apologia* for Leibniz."[150] Thus, Kant takes up Leibniz's recognition of the phenomenal character of space and instead of referring it to God's reason, as did Leibniz, refers it to human thought, so that we are enabled to speak of extended things only from the standpoint of man.[151] Experience has conditions that are nonexperiential, and these conditions are human. In transforming Leibniz in order to overcome the Humean critique of rationality, Kant passes beyond both Leibniz and Hume.

Given the metaphysical nature of his thought, Kant's reliance on prior modern philosophy extends backward to the metaphysical venture of Descartes. In perceiving the domination of the object by the subject, Descartes provides Kant, in the *Cogito*, with a starting point; but Hume had taught Kant the importance of experience and thus enabled him to say that "even our inner experience, which for Descartes is indubitable, is possible only on the assumption of outer experience." The result is that inner experience is itself possible only mediately, and "I have no knowledge of myself as I am but merely as I appear to myself."[152] The *I think* is no longer in splendid Cartesian isolation, anchored only in an appeal to the existence of God, but finds its anchor in human experience (as with Locke). In reaching back to Descartes, Kant outreaches Descartes, providing metaphysical foundations, not simply for the nature investigated by modern science, but for man as such.

There is, finally, a Kantian affinity for Berkeley. Like Berkeley, Kant aligns "the active-passive dichotomy with the understanding-sensibility dichotomy," holding that "thinking is something we do while sensing is something which happens to us." Kant thus agrees with Berkeley that space is ideal but rejects Berkeley's assertion that it is learned from experience, arguing instead that space "inheres in us as a pure form of our sensibility before all perception of experience."[153] Like Berkeley, too, Kant is, initially at least, drawn to the task of overcoming the modern dualism, but his attempts in this direction are not reductionistic like Berkeley's. Unlike Berkeley, Kant becomes aware of the impossibility of a resolution and limits himself to a finely articulated reinterpretation of the dualism.

In the Enlightenment, then, Kant retrieves a focus for his philosophy, namely, human autonomy, but situates it in a systematic context. In Newton and Rousseau, he perceives the bipolar logic of modernity—nature and freedom—but situates this logic in a metaphysics of morals that transcends Rousseau and a metaphysics of nature that transcends Newton. In Leibniz and Hume, Kant perceives the dialectic of legislative rationality and experience but situates this dialectic in a more-than-Leibnizian conception of the a priori structure of purely human consciousness and a more-than-Humean conception of experience as made possible by that a priori structure. In Descartes, Kant perceives the starting point of his metaphysical venture but situates this starting point in a more-than-Cartesian awareness of the reciprocity of inner and outer experience. Finally, in Berkeley, Kant perceives the advantages of idealism and the liabilities of dualism but situates them in an awareness of the limits of idealism and the necessity of dualism.

Effectively, Kant's incorporation of the prior developments of the logic of modernity illustrates his conception of philosophical method. Kant holds that philosophy as an unalterable system does not yet exist, and so it cannot be learned as the sciences are learned. One can learn to "philosophize," that is, to "think for oneself," but to do this one must regard the partial philosophizing of the past as a "history of the use of reason" to be used not for eclectic ventures, as in the Enlightenment, but for present philosophizing that aims at the completeness of a system. Working out from the "ruins" of past philosophy, philosophical method in Kant proceeds in a systematic or what Kant calls "scholastic" fashion and strives to be ultimate, that is, metaphysical.[154]

Kant is fully aware that such a conception of philosophical method is not in vogue. The Enlightenment, for all its positive value, has set the tone for "virtually the entire learned world," Kant says, which appears "dead to metaphysics" and to have "lost heart in the investigation of metaphysical truths"; yet for all this, "metaphysics is the genuine, true philosophy," and "I have the fortune to be a lover of Metaphysics." If Kant directs criticisms at the metaphysical systems of the past, he does not reject metaphysics as such.[155] If it is the case, as Kant says, that "there is, as yet, no such thing as metaphysics," it is nonetheless true that "since the interests of common sense are so intimately interwoven" with metaphysical interests, a "new birth" of this "science after a new plan is unavoidable, however men may struggle against it for a while." This new birth is imminent because metaphysics is meant to be a "completely isolated speculative science of reason" in which "reason is indeed meant to be its own pupil"—a science resting "on concepts alone, not, like mathematics, on their application to intuition," a science of "such completion and fixity as to be in need of no further change," since it cannot have as its source "objects and their observation, by which its stock of knowledge could be further increased."[156] In "mathematics and in natural philosophy," as Kant puts it, "human reason admits of limits but not of bounds, namely, it admits that something indeed lies without it, at which it can never arrive, but *not* that it will at any point find completion in its internal progress"; but metaphysics admits of bounds but not of limits, that is, the unknowable is not foreign to it, but internal completion is possible and necessary. Metaphysics "leads us toward bounds in the dialectical attempts of pure reason," in its concern with what the other sciences can never be concerned with, namely, the attitude of our reason toward the "connection of what we know with what we do not, and never shall, know."[157]

On the one hand, then, metaphysics must be a science, and so if the other sciences became sciences by revolution, then it follows that metaphysics would likewise have to be set on the path of science by a total revolution. On the other hand, since reason is "its own pupil" only in metaphysics, it is only in the unique science of metaphysics that reason is capable of giving "an exhaustive enumeration of the various ways in which it propounds its problems."[158] Kant can, therefore, set himself the task of launching metaphysics on the path of science by a revolution, but a revolution that, by virtue of the uniqueness of metaphysics as a possible science, cannot be a mere repetition of the Cartesian-Newtonian revolution.

The content of metaphysics as a possible science, however, since it is the only science in which pure reason is its own pupil, is determinable only upon determination of the object of pure reason. Pure reason, as Kant says, has "two objects, nature and freedom"; therefore, metaphysics must be "either metaphysics of nature or metaphysics of morals," that is, it must first present itself "in two distinct systems," and only later or "ultimately in one single philosophical system."[159] Now, reason can have only two objects because, as Kant says, "there are only two kinds of concepts": "natural concepts," which "render possible theoretical cognition according to principles a priori"; and the "concept of freedom," which furnishes "fundamental propositions which extend the sphere of the determination of the will and are therefore called practical."[160] A twofold metaphysics of morals and of nature, then, is called for, and since metaphysics is, as Kant says, "the full and complete development of human reason," it will constitute "what may be entitled philosophy in the strict sense of the term" that has as its "sole preoccupation" a wisdom which it seeks "by the path of science."[161] Metaphysics is initially twofold in relation to the two objects of pure reason but ultimately seeks a conjunction of these objects and hence a final unity for itself. Consequently, the Kantian philosophical task of launching metaphysics on the path of science by a revolution is, in its immediacy, the laying of foundations for a twofold metaphysics of nature and of morals, and, in its finality, the creation of a unitary metaphysics that—since, as we shall see, neither nature nor morality is possible without man—amounts to a metaphysics of man. The Kantian task in its finality discloses that the fundamental question of philosophy, encompassing all others, remained for him: "What is man?"[162]

Having examined the nature of Kant's incorporation of the prior developments of the logic of modernity, and having examined the nature of the task he proposed for himself, we are now ready to present the body of our interpretation of Kant. In conformity with his task, as we have presented it, we shall first examine Kant's metaphysical foundations for nature. We shall then examine his metaphysical foundations for morality. Finally, we shall examine the conjunction of these two metaphysical foundations and the ways in which this conjunction is manifested in Kant's theory of politics and his theory of religion. Having completed the body of our interpretation, we will be enabled in our conclusion to assess the significance of Kant's unified metaphysics of man as well as the Kantian contribution to the logic of modernity.

2. THE METAPHYSICS OF NATURE

Like Descartes in his effort to establish the metaphysical foundations of modern science, Kant, in his effort to establish the metaphysical foundations of nature, is aware of the enormous proportions of his task. However, unlike Descartes who perceived these proportions as *Archimedean*, that is, as moving a world (science) already in existence, Kant, given the necessity of a veritable revolution as his starting point, perceives these proportions as *Copernican* (establishing a new world). Thus, it is in Kant's re-creation, and not mere repetition of the Copernican Revolution that is to be found the focus of the various strands of thought and the entire problematic of a metaphysics of nature that Kant aimed to resolve.[163] Hitherto, Kant says,

it has been assumed that all our knowledge must conform to objects. But all attempts to extend our knowledge of objects by establishing something in regard to them a priori, by means of concepts, have on this assumption, ended in failure. We must therefore make trial whether we may not have more success in the tasks of metaphysics, if we suppose that objects must conform to our knowledge. This would agree better with what is desirable, namely, that it should be possible to have knowledge of objects a priori, determining something in regard to them prior to their being given. We should then be proceeding precisely on the lines of Copernicus' primary hypothesis. Failing of satisfactory progress in explaining the movements of the heavenly bodies on the supposition that they all revolved around the spectator, he tried whether he might not have better success if he made the spectator to revolve and the stars to remain at rest.[164]

On the surface, it might appear that Kant's revolution is exactly opposite to that of Copernicus, since the latter put an end to the geocentric and therefore anthropocentric character of astronomy and Kant appears to be making philosophy anthropocentric. But Kant intends to say that just as Copernicus argued that the sun's movement around the earth was only an appearance due to our own movement, so he (Kant) is classing as appearance, and thus attributing to ourselves what his predecessors had attributed to external reality. In effect, the Kantian Copernican Revolution asserts that the "ground of the presence or absence of an object in knowledge is to be seen within the nature of the knower." This human knower is not concerned primarily with "the empirical object or with the concept derived from the empirical object by abstraction" but with "its own *act of construction*, with what it puts into the figure" of its perceptions in accordance with its own a priori forms.[165] The key that unlocks the treasure trove of an authentic metaphysics of nature, then, is the proposition that "knowledge must not be regulated by things, but that things as empirical objects must be regulated by the fundamental condition of the faculty of knowledge." As Kant put it, "the question whether anything is or is not a cognizable being is not a question concerning the possibility of things, but of *our knowledge* of them," that is, "we can know a priori of things only what we ourselves put into them." Copernicus had implicitly appealed to this principle, although he was unaware of it, since he recognized, as Kant says, that "viewed from the earth, the planets sometimes move backwards, sometimes forward, and sometimes not at all," but viewed from the sun, an act "which *only reason can perform*," they move "constantly in their regular course."[166]

The Kantian Copernican Revolution heralds a metaphysics of nature and not merely an epistemology, and so the shift signified in this revolution is not primarily epistemological but metaphysical—a shift from the nature of the world as it may be in itself to the positing act of the human knower of the world in which being finds its proper meaning and ground. From this we should infer that it heralds a metaphysics of the subject but not a metaphysics of mere subjectivity, for Kant held that "subjectivity itself has an objective structure which is at the same time the structure of reason itself"; self-consciousness involves an activity in terms of which contents that do not constitute the self are apprehended as existing for the self.[167] The metaphysical (and not just epistemological) import of the Kantian Copernican Revolution, then, is that our knowledge of the objects of nature is possible only if the objectivity of these objects (the constitution of their being) is already manifest beforehand. This entails that the laying of a foundation of the metaphysics of nature must trace the constitutive a priori synthesis that makes nature possible back "to its original sources which permit that synthesis to be what it is," that is, back to that "precursory, experience-free" being that Kant calls "human pure reason."[168] In this tracing we are not simply tracing the laws governing our cognition back to their source; we are tracing the laws "governing and setting the conditions of the possibility of a thing to be, to be present, to come into being within our experiential realm," back to their source. We thus find ourselves concerned with the problem of the nature of being as such—with that core of metaphysical thought that has been termed *ontology*.[169] By calling his founding of ontology "Copernican," Kant situates it in the context of the founding of physics as a modern science in which man's researches into nature conform to what reason has itself put into nature. Kant perceives in the first Copernican Revolution the realization that when we as men look on the phenomenal world we look inward; and he perceives in his own second Copernican Revolution that when we examine the structure of being *qua* being we are examining the ontological structure of human being as such.[170]

The Kantian founding of the metaphysical foundations of nature, then, leaves us with the notion of man, not as the classical Greek *shepherd of being*, but as the *legislator of being,* that is, as the legislator of the intelligibility of the being of nature. As Kant puts it,

The highest legislation of nature must lie in ourselves, that is, in our understanding; . . . we must not seek the universal laws of nature in nature by means of experience, but conversely must seek nature, as to its universal conformity to law, in the conditions of the possibility of experience which lie in our sensibility and in our understanding.[171]

Since man's very inhabitation of the world is "by means of an interpretive, mediating set of concepts and projects," and men

interpretively mold their experience in this world at the very point
of having it, things in nature "look as they do to us because we
are as we are." All we can mean by a thing of nature is that of
"which it is possible to be conscious, that to which it must be
possible to refer what is presented in consciousness," so that, as
far as nature is concerned, Kant says that "we make everything
ourselves."[172] As legislator of nature, however, the being of
human consciousness must have both spontaneity and receptivity,[173] that is, there must be a dialectic in human consciousness
between its receiving a chaotic manifold and its spontaneously
creating this manifold into an order. Kant interprets this dialectic
in terms of a triple orientation of human consciousness, the first
in which receptivity dominates spontaneity, the second in which
spontaneity dominates receptivity, and the third in which pure
spontaneity comes into its own. The first orientation finds its
embodiment in the *sensibility,* the second in the *understanding* (*Verstand*), and the third in *reason* (*Vernunft*).

Sensibility through the pure forms of space and time accounts
for the forms of appearance; understanding through the categories
accounts for the connection of appearances according to law, that
is, for nature; and reason accounts for the whole as a totality of
appearances, that is, for the world.[174] Because reason is unmediated spontaneity or creativity, it requires no principle of connection with understanding; its relation with understanding is immediate. Because understanding is a mediated spontaneity, that
is, a faculty where spontaneity dominates and orders receptivity,
it requires some principle of connection with sensibility; and this
principle is the schematism of the imagination that shares in the
sensibility of the forms of appearance and the intelligibility of the
form of the connection of appearances according to law (found
in the understanding). There are, then, four dimensions or faculties
in human consciousness: sensibility, the schematism of imagination, the understanding, and pure reason. Kant's establishment of
a metaphysics of nature consists in the examination of these four
faculties in their interrelatedness, for their examination establishes
man as the legislator of the being of nature. In examining these
faculties, Kant will capture the very process by which knowing

becomes scientific; demonstrate the foundations of the scientific in this fourfold structure of human consciousness; and thereby make man, by virtue of his legislating consciousness, the object of the metaphysics of nature.

Although, as the bare minimum of human consciousness, sensibility, as Kant says, is "the *receptivity* of a subject by which it is possible for the subject's own representative state to be affected in a definite way by the presence of some object," it is not a faculty of pure or unmediated receptivity, since "objects do not strike the senses in virtue of their form or specificity." There must, then, be a principle of spontaneity in sensibility, namely, what Kant calls a sensible "intuition" containing "nothing but the form of sensibility, antedating in my mind all the actual impressions through which I am affected by objects," which enables me to "anticipate the actuality of the object." Effectively, we can know nothing external to us through the senses, except insofar as it already "stands in relation to ourselves"; and so to perceive at all with our senses we must be able to orient ourselves by "virtue of a subjective ground of distinction."[175] The result is that, although the matter of sensibility is given (accounting for the primacy of receptivity in sensibility), the form must antedate the matter in order to have sense perception. Now, everything that is sensibly perceived is perceived as occupying or correlated to space and as having duration in time. Our "idea of time," Kant says, does not "arise from but is supposed by the senses," for it is only "through the idea of time that it is possible for the things which come before the senses to be represented as being simultaneous or coming after one another." Our "determination of space," far from being the consequence "of the situations of the parts of matter relative to each other," he says, is a precondition of the relations of parts of matter, so that "the possibility of external perceptions as such *supposes* the concept of space and does not create it." Space, therefore, far from being something objective, is subjective and ideal and "proceeds from the nature of the mind by an unchanging law, as a schema for coordinating with each other absolutely all things externally sensed."[176] Space and time become, then, for Kant, not objectively given characteristics of a natural world of fixed meanings, but forms of sensibility within human consciousness that serve as the primal forms of sensible perception in the first place.

As what Kant calls the mere "forms of sensible intuition and so only conditions of the existence of things as appearances," space and time are the "preformative forms in pure intuition," which in their "transcendental ideality" are purely human conditions. Yet, as human conditions, they are "objectively valid so far as all sensuous experience" for all men is concerned, and so they cannot be reduced to or derived from anything else.[177] As primal and irreducible "substrates of the intellect," as Kant calls them, space and time are not given as determined but must first be "infinite space and time" if there is to be in sensation any definite space and time that is "assignable by limiting." As primal and irreducible, they are not mere illusion, for appearances themselves are *real* and not mere illusions or deceptions; and so they must be real human conditions for what Kant calls the "receptivity of our mind—conditions under which alone it can receive representations of objects."[178] In this sense, Copernicus' apprehension of an unbounded universe is transmuted by Kant into the apprehension of a boundless creativity in human consciousness.

If space, as Kant says, "does not represent any property of things in themselves," but is "only in me," yet nevertheless in me as real, that is, the "material of all objects of outer intuition is actually given in this space," it follows that space must be given prior (temporally or logically) to the sensuous manifold, that is, to the material or raw data for sense perception. But, if space must be temporally prior to the bare manifold of sensibility, it follows that its preformativeness is in some way mediated by the preformativeness of time, so that time must be that "formal principle," as he says, "of the sensible world which is absolutely first," the one "subjective condition necessary" for coordinating with "each other by a fixed law whatsoever things are sensible."[179] Now, time has priority over space, not in the sense that it is the form of space but in the sense that it is "the medium through which what is given in space reaches consciousness"; in this sense, the series formed by time is the irreducible minimum of order, and so time must have priority as a point of departure in Kant's laying of the foundations of a metaphysics of nature by an examination of the structure of human consciousness.[180] The consequence of this, for Kant, in sharp contrast to Plato's derivation of the temporal from a timeless order somehow understood by timeless concepts, is that ideas must be brought within the form of time in order to constitute knowledge, since in time alone, as Kant says, as a "necessary representation that underlies all intuitions," is "actuality of appearances possible at all." Time is "nothing but the form of inner sense, that is, of the intuition of ourselves and of our inner state," distinct from space as the form of the outer, yet bound up in the way of identity with the consciousness of a relation to something outside ourselves.[181] Time is "pure affection of itself" and, as pure self-affection, forms the absolutely first condition of subjectivity. The consequence is that if "specific instances of metaphysical knowledge are to be found," what must be looked for, in the first place, is the "temporal property which any thing must have in order for empirical knowledge to be got of it by each of the several categories."[182]

The irreducibility and ideality of space and time, along with the priority of time in relation to space, point to the need for a further dimension of human consciousness beyond sensibility. Space as a pure form of empirical intuition is "something when there is something in it," but with nothing in it, it amounts to an *ens imaginarium*; thus, the pure form of space before its determination in sensible perception leads us to infer that pure intuition apart from sensible perception is essentially pure imagination.[183] Time, unlike space, can and must exist as more than an *ens imaginarium,* since, unlike space, it does not contain any sensible manifold but must be formed by some dimension of human consciousness. To say that pure sensibility lets time spring forth is contradictory, since time is one of the twofold forms of sensibility; understanding cannot generate this pure form, since it requires it in order to organize appearances according to law. It must, then, be the pure imagination as a formative faculty that lets time spring forth, not simply as a being of the imagination, like space, but as a being that permits the imagination itself to exist as a kind of "primordial time" or "original time."[184] Both space and time as pure intuitions point to the existence of a productive imagination that provides schemata or "generalized forms of temporal and spatial existence" that serve as intermediaries between sense and thought, or the forms of *sensibility* and *understanding,* enabling the understanding to generate unified experience out of the presentations of sensibility.[185]

In leaning toward sensibility, the productive imagination "maintains the unity of space and time in our experience and so maintains the unity of the given intuitions in space and time." In leaning toward understanding, the productive imagination enables the appearances given to sense to be combined in such a way that they can be apprehended as objects by the understanding. Since imagination is the "faculty of representing in intuition an object that is not itself present," and since all our intuition is sensible, the imagination belongs to sensibility. But, since the schemata of the imagination are an expression of spontaneity that are "determinative and not, like sense, determinable merely," imagination can be said to belong to the understanding and seems almost to be a "lower manifestation of understanding itself acting directly upon intuitions given under the form of time."[186] There is, therefore, no possibility of understanding's connecting the forms of appearances provided by sensibility according to law apart from an imaginative synthesis which possesses unity; and so imagination is, in Kant's words, "a blind but indispensable function of the soul," of which "we are scarcely conscious," and without which "we would have no knowledge whatsoever"—the "ground of the possibility of all knowledge."[187]

Insofar as the schematism of the imagination brings the "manifold of intuition on the one side into connection with the condition of the necessary unity" of the understanding on the other, it can be called the totality of "pure intuition and pure understanding, united in advance," constituting the free space within which all unified experience can be had, that is, within which all objects can be encountered. Thus, in the immediate perception of this house is contained the "schematizing, preliminary insight into such a thing as a house in general," and it is by means of the re-presentation of this schematism of a house in general that what is "encountered can reveal itself as a house, that is, can present the aspect of a given house."[188] The pure imagination as primordial time and shaper of schemata permits the coming together of the intuitions of the predominantly receptive faculty of sensibility and the categories of the predominantly spontaneous understanding, and thus permits the understanding to constitute an objectification of the subjectivity of human consciousness, that is, permits the understanding to attain knowledge.

The categories of the understanding differ fundamentally from the forms of sensibility. Whereas space and time determine the way in which objects appear, the categories determine the way in which objects are thought. In order to have knowledge, the intuitions of the former must be given as corresponding to the concepts of the latter in such a way that the mind first apprehends the given manifold of sense, then reproduces it in imagination, and finally recognizes or judges it by means of the concept in the understanding. Thus, as Kant says, the given intuition is subsumed under a concept that "determines the form of judging in general relatively to the intuition, connects empirical consciousness of intuition in consciousness in general, and thereby procures universal validity for empirical judgments."[189] Knowledge is thereby constituted as a transition from the primacy of receptivity in sensibility to the primacy of spontaneity in understanding; the concepts are based, as Kant says, "on the spontaneity of thought," whereas the intuitions of sensibility are based "on the receptivity of impressions." Knowledge, in other words, is constituted by the transition from isolated sense perceptions to a unity of experience.[190]

Now, as the third dimension of human legislative consciousness, understanding signifies the sense in which the human self "posits the order, the unity, and the objectivity of phenomena" and, in doing so, posits itself as objective, that is, "objectifies its own unifying functions." The transition from perception to experience is thus the transition from the subjectivity of the forms of space and time to the objectivity of the understanding, but this objectivity is an objectification of subjectivity, and only in this sense does Kant speak of the understanding as transcending the sensibility. In this way, Kant changes the direction of transcending from the ancient *soul-body* or the medieval *God-man* to the modern *subjectivity-objectivity* dialectic in which there are "nonobjective premises of all objectiveness."[191] Transcendence comes to mean in Kant "no object without a subject," insofar as concepts "without content," that is, without intuitions, are "empty"; but it also comes to mean "no subject without an object," insofar as "intuitions without concepts are blind." Effectively, where there is no real self-consciousness, no consciousness of an *ego,* there is no objective idea of the world possible. Thus, self-consciousness and consciousness of a world become correlates in the understanding that mutually condition one another in the understanding's being applied to the sensible manifold and that reveal the understanding to be the human faculty that makes the act of objectification possible.[192]

Insofar as the understanding is the faculty of objectification, it may, Kant tells us, "be represented as a faculty of judgment," since understanding is "a power of knowing by means of concepts"; but to know by means of concepts essentially amounts to uniting our ideas, that is, judging. By a judgment, concepts are not only brought to a unity of consciousness, but one also thinks how these concepts are united; so that every judgment is a kind of act of self-consciousness that brings the intuitions of sensibility under the concepts of the understanding and in doing so allows the understanding to connect the appearances, made possible by the forms of sensibility, according to law.[193] This connection of appearances according to law is precisely the construction of nature—a nature with purposes and ends—but whose teleology "is not a teleology internal to nature itself, but a teleology of the aspirations of the faculty of judgment which sets itself the task of building the science of nature."[194] The nature constructed by the judgmental understanding is subjective in its ground, since the self-consciousness of judgment underlies the objectification of the understanding and since a nature that was nonsubjective in its ground would be a non-rational nature and therefore no nature at all. The understanding, as judgmental, and nature belong together, then, in a promordial way, for the understanding in its judgments is the faculty of positing relations, and nature as a sum total of relations is "nothing but the coming into force of the original potentiality of the understanding."[195] Specifically, the judgmental understanding is productive of mathematics, as the core of the methodology of modern natural science; and so, to say that the relational character of understanding produces the relational character of nature is to say that the latter is the "immediate consequence of the relational character of mathematics." This is consistent with modern assumptions, since Kant means by *nature* neither the existence of the living (as in ancient science) nor the existence of creation (as in medieval science) but the mechanical nature presented in pure mathematical natural science.[196]

Now, the "unity of nature," produced by judgmental understanding, as Kant says, has to be a "necessary one," that is, an "a priori certain unity of the connection of appearances," and such unity could not be "established a priori if there were no subjective grounds of such unity contained in the original cognitive powers of our mind."[197] This is why receptivity is made subservient to spontaneity in the understanding, and this is also why it is not until Kant establishes the reach of human consciousness beyond sensibility and imagination that he can demonstrate the fundamental possibility of a scientific metaphysics of nature. He tells us that such a metaphysics is "properly concerned with synthetical propositions a priori," that is, with propositions whose predicate is not merely implicitly contained in their subject and whose content is not merely derived from experience; the real problem upon which all metaphysics of nature depends is how synthetic propositions a priori are possible. Since metaphysical judgments seek the bounds of pure reason (the relation of the knowable to the unknowable), they cannot be made out to be true in the way in which empirical judgments (judgments derived from experience) can or in the way in which analytic judgments (propositions whose subject implicitly contains their predicate) can, but can only be shown to yield metaphysical knowledge if there is a way of determining whether synthetic a priori judgments are true.[198]

In explaining the possibility of synthetic a priori propositions, Kant shifts his idea of form from that of a *mold* or *filter* (space and time in regard to the bare sensible manifold) to that of a pure, *unspatial,* imageless, *activity* (judgment unifying categories and placing intuitions under them). His line of argumentation here is that "all thinking involves synthesis, that is, involves construction according to a rule and recognition of the unity of the process of constructing," and that the "forms of functions of thought, that is, the unifying principles involved in all our thinking, are responsible for the specific notions," such as cause and substance, which are basic to our theorizing about physical being.[199] Now, if causality is one of the constitutive principles of the synthesizing *form* of the understanding, then it follows that so "far from the causal principle being discovered through experience, experience would be impossible if the principle did not hold a priori of experience." Causality is one of the essential components of the synthetic and constructive *form* of understanding, so that the "same fundamental act, that of construction, which generates the objects of mathematics also generates the objects of natural science." As a result, the "validity of geometry in physics is thereby directly given," and the Humean critique of the rationality of the causal principle is overcome.[200]

Kant's analysis of the activity of understanding as that thinking which unifies all unity is at the same time a hymn to the creative powers of understanding and an elegy on its limitations. As hymn, it signifies that "the understanding with its categories first builds up the empirical" and that it is only because it builds up this world that it "can later gain knowledge of it by conscious investigation"; and so, it signifies the reach of metaphysics into the question of the source of spontaneity or the bounds of pure reason. But as elegy, it signifies the limitation of the subject matter of metaphysical *knowledge* to experience.[201] In all of this, as Kant says, the "synthesizing itself is not given," but "must be done by *us*," and it is because of our synthesizing that we are able in the first place to "communicate with one another."[202] The understanding requires, then, as the final aspect of its activity something to which its synthesizing can be attributed, namely, the "transcendental *ego* or self-in-itself," and something characteristic of the consciousness of this self, namely, a "transcendental unity of apperception," which denotes the way in which the understanding is "affected by its own activity from within."[203]

The ultimate form of thought as it is found in the understanding is for Kant "the unity of apperception, the 'I think' which necessarily accompanies all our ideas of objects."[204] Kant is indebted to Leibniz for the term *apperception,* since Leibniz distinguished between what he called the "perception," which is "the inner state of the monad representing external things," and "apperception which is consciousness or the reflective knowledge of this inner state." But Kant significantly extends Leibniz's use of the term by identifying it not only with self-consciousness but with the self-identity which is presupposed by self-consciousness. This enables Kant to hold that the "original and necessary consciousness of the identity of the self is at the same time consciousness of an equally necessary unity of the synthesis of all appearances in accordance with concepts." The result is that "all appearances so far as they are appearances of an *object* must conform to the necessary unity of apperception," just as "all appearances so far as they are intuitions must conform to the forms of space and time."[205] Space and time are thus the irreducible forms (molds) for sensibility, and the transcendental unity of apperception is the irreducible form (pure activity) for all the synthesizing of the understanding. The transcendental unity of the *ego* to which the transcendental unity of apperception points thus becomes the archetype of all objects of knowledge. But, since the *I think* of the transcendental unity of apperception depends on the exercise of thinking activity, and so "guarantees only the existence of the thought and not the existence of the self-in-itself," the transcendental unity of apperception can only point to, not establish, the transcendental *ego* or self-in-itself as the "correlative of internal phenomena."[206] The transcendental unity of apperception is, then, "the supreme principle of all judgment and thus of all employment of the understanding," a synthetic and not an analytic unity, in terms of which the whole of nature "and not merely each object in it, must be a unity governed by necessary law." But as such, it is an *ultimate unity of experience* and neither is nor establishes a self independent of and behind all experience, although it does suggest such a self as its correlate, that is, it proposes the thinkability but not knowability of such a self-in-itself.[207]

Kant has, thus far, examined three dimensions of human legislative consciousness. The first, sensibility, is predominantly receptive and provides the form of the particularity of sense presentations; the third, understanding, is predominantly spontaneous and provides the form of the generality of categories; the second, imagination, mediates between the first and third. Now, it would seem that just as sensibility requires a more ultimate faculty of consciousness to which it is related by imagination, so also understanding requires a more ultimate faculty. Reason thus becomes for Kant related to understanding as the categories are to sensibility, that is, "just as there would be no sense experience without the categories, there would be no coherent use of understanding without reason."[208] Reason, however, is immediately related to understanding, whereas understanding is only mediately (through imagination) related to sensibility. But how can such an immediate relation ensue? Kant calls understanding the "faculty of rules," and reason the "faculty of principles," which means that reason produces the concept of the conditions for any given conditioned object of the understanding; that is, reason "is directed always solely toward absolute totality in the synthesis of conditions" and "endeavors to carry the synthetic unity" that is thought in the understanding "up to the completely unconditioned."[209] Reason (*Vernunft*) is required as a fourth dimension of human consciousness, then, because understanding can aspire only to the conditioned (i.e., to experience), and for understanding to be a meaningful aspiration to the conditioned, there must be a human aspiration to the unconditioned. As an aspiration to the unconditioned, Kant tells us, reason "never applies itself directly to experience or to any object" but only to understanding; and it never delivers knowledge of "particular objects which lie beyond the field of experience," but rather guarantees "completeness of the use of the understanding in the system of experience."[210]

Insofar as it is an aspiration toward the unconditioned and is related immediately to understanding, reason does not permit the synthesis of the understanding to "come to an end," as Kant says, "until we reach a whole which is not a part, that is to say, a world," a world as the totality of appearances which makes possible the production of nature as a unity of appearances according to law.[211] In the antinomies Kant illustrates the difference between this concept of nature and this concept of world. As the idea of a whole which is not a part, the world cannot have the same existence as things-as-appearances "to which one of every pair of disjunctive properties must be distributed." Unlike nature, for example, which must be conceived as either finite or infinite, the world cannot be conceived as either finite or infinite; so that the world, as a totality of appearances, unlike nature, must be conceived as not *in* space or time at all, in order to prevent reason from being involved in an insoluble contradiction.[212] The fact that reason is inclined toward contradictory alternatives, or antinomies, and can be rescued from these alternatives only by itself, in terms of its *construction* of the notion of world (for it is we ourselves who think the world as a unity), points to the way in which reason positively relates to understanding, namely, as the provider of a whole that is not a part as the condition for the unity of nature. But it also points to the way in which it conflicts with understanding, namely, "understanding always setting a final boundary and conclusion" and "reason always going beyond such a conclusion"—understanding as the human faculty of finiteness and reason as the human faculty of infinity.[213]

But what is it that enables reason to think the idea of world as totality of appearances? Since there can be no faculty "beyond or behind the activity of our own self-critical reason," there must be some kind of idea or ideas, thought by reason, which enables it to produce the idea of such a world. Now, there are two other ideas that reason thinks, namely, "soul" and "God," which underlie the "questions which human nature can never cease to ask," and that amount to the great themes of metaphysics in the past. All three of these ideas can only be "cogitated," that is, they cannot be known, or the objects to which they refer, which are necessarily more-than-appearances, cannot be known. But since they are thinkable, they foster a kind of "dialectical illusion" in reason, that is, the illusion that it can know what it can only cogitate or think; and this dialectical illusion gives rise to the "phantasms" of traditional metaphysics, namely, cosmology, psychology, and theology, all of which are edifices without foundation in Kant's eyes.[214] Although traditional metaphysics is an illusion that can and must be dispelled, the dialectical illusion of reason itself is a necessary illusion of reason, and Kant's foundations of the metaphysics of nature "can prevent the illusion from deceiving us but cannot dispel it."[215]

Now, among the three ideas of pure reason, the idea of God

gives rise to the illusion of metaphysical knowledge in theology.
Kant's metaphysics of nature can overcome this illusion by pointing out that God is a "mere something in idea, of which as it may
be in itself, we have no concept," so that we postulate this idea
in order to view the things in this world "as if they had their
ground in such a being."[216] The function of the idea of God is
to serve as that idea of pure reason, in other words, which primarily makes possible reason's construction of the notion of world
as a totality of appearances for the proper employment of the
understanding. As the primary ground for the idea of world, the
pure idea of God, however, does not operate in isolation but in
conjunction with the other ideas of pure reason in what Kant calls
an "architectonic" of pure reason. By an architectonic or "canon"
of pure reason, Kant says, "I understand the art of constructing
systems," which enables our "diverse modes of knowledge" not
to be a "mere rhapsody" but to "form a system." By virtue of
its architectonic, reason will not be perceived merely as existing
for the completeness of understanding, that is, merely as producing the notion of world, but will be perceived as "in fact occupied
with nothing but itself"—the "unity of reason" as a "unity of
system."[217] The architectonic is thus analogous to the forms of
space and time and the transcendental unity of apperception: all
are irreducible forms of their respective faculties.

  Understanding, then, sees itself "driven from the conditioned to
the conditioning elements, which are themselves conditioned";
and so *reason,* by the necessity of its own nature, is forced to think
the concept of the absolute and put "itself at the standpoint of the
absolute" and, from that point of view, to provide the ground
for the determinations of the understanding. The absolutely unconditioned that reason thinks in its architectonic can never be
met with in experience; nor can *knowledge* of the unconditioned
ever be reached; nonetheless, the duty of *thinking* the unconditioned is prescribed for reason.[218] By assuming the architectonic
of pure reason as the "fundamental source of the laying of the
foundations" of a metaphysics of nature—that is, by assuming
that the "delimitation of the essence of pure reason" is as such the
laying of the foundations of a metaphysics of nature—such a
metaphysics can now securely address itself to the bounds of pure

reason, that is, to the relation of the knowable to what is not and cannot ever be known by man. By the architectonic, metaphysics is able to compare such knowledge as is possible for us, namely, a knowledge limited to experience, with the idea of an absolute, and thereby show that "science is not the final goal of human existence."[219] If reason in its architectonic becomes transparent to itself by inquiring into the conditions of the possibility of the very conflict of reason with understanding and the very dialectical illusion of reason itself,[220] then metaphysics of nature by assuming the architectonic as its core addresses the bounds of pure reason.

In completing his examination of the four dimensions of human consciousness, Kant has thus completed his task of laying the foundations of a metaphysics of nature. All that remains for him is to examine the implications of these foundations. These implications are seen to amount to one overriding consequence, namely, a recasting of the modern bifurcation of the inside and the outside in terms of what Kant calls the *noumenon* and the *phenomenon*.

Kant's conception of the understanding and its relation to pure reason requires that he look upon the categories of understanding as "being objectively valid of phenomena but inapplicable to things-in-themselves." Since modern natural science renounces any knowledge of essence and limits itself to the relational character of nature, it follows, as Kant says, that "pure mathematics as well as a pure science of nature can never be referred to anything more than mere appearances." Thus, nature itself is possible only by means of "the constitution of our sensibility, according to which it is in its own way affected by objects which are in themselves unknown to it and totally distinct from these appearances."[221] Since experience can be only what he calls a "cognition of objects as they appear to us, not as they are (when considered by themselves)," the idea of the independently real must be "an object which is independent of the conditions of knowledge." In place, then, of the sublunar and the supralunar worlds that had gone at the latest by the time of Newton, Kant places the phenomenal knowable order of mere nature and the unknowable noumenal world.[222] Furthermore, since metaphysics of nature "can attain knowledge of anything only in so far as it is a possible object of empirical knowledge," and since "empirical knowledge

cannot supply information about how things are in themselves,"
metaphysics, in attaining knowledge of things in general, cannot
secure knowledge of how they are in themselves. Thus, the speculative metaphysics of the past must be replaced by a metaphysics
of nature that, in its content, is a "metaphysics of experience"
professing to give us "certain and a priori knowledge within the
limits of experience."[223]

The fact that metaphysics of nature takes the architectonic of
pure reason as its essence or source enables it to lead us, as Kant
says, to "the objective boundary of experience, namely, to the
relation to something which is not itself an object of experience
but is the ground of all experience." But the architectonic, and
therefore metaphysics of nature itself, cannot teach us anything
concerning this thing-in-itself. Metaphysics of nature, then, although sharing with natural science a limitation of its content to
the phenomenal, differs from natural science in that its given is
the thinkability of things-in-themselves, whereas the given of science is the knowability of the object of appearance. The result is
that metaphysics of nature confronts us with the true sense of our
limitations—that is, with the realization, as Kant puts it, that "the
domain that lies out beyond the sphere of appearances is for us
empty."[224] The metaphysical dualism of matter (as outside) and
mind (as inside) generated by Descartes is thus, according to Kant,
grasped in its significance when recast as the metaphysical dualism
of a thinkable but unknowable noumenon and a knowable but
real phenomenon.

Now, strictly speaking, since Kant has already defined the notion of world as a totality of appearances, we cannot speak of
phenomenal and noumenal worlds or a "distinction between two
types of entity," but must instead speak of "a distinction between
two alternative ways of talking about the world." As Kant says,
the "object in itself or noumenon is a mere *ens rationis* in the
representation of which the subject posits itself," for it is "not
itself a separate object but only a special relation for the constituting of the self as object."[225] Kant thus internalizes the dualism
in human consciousness as such; moreover, since he aligns the
noumenon with the subject-object distinction and presumes that
if the subject and object were absolutely identical we would be

incapable of knowing anything, he considers this dualism as un-
bridgeable and the problem of overcoming it as having no solution.[226] The modern dualism of the inside and outside is thus for
Kant built into the inside of being, that is, man; this dualism is
the very condition for insidedness, and so there can be no such
thing as man unless there is the thinkability of the phenomenal-
noumenal bifurcation.

There is, for Kant, an enormous advantage in his reinterpretation of the modern dualism—that "no item of experience or
. . . interpretation can be idolized" and implicitly identified with
reality.[227] In being a consciousness with the dimensions of sensibility, imagination, understanding, and pure reason, man is seen
as a being in which, respectively, receptivity dominates, the principle of spontaneity is allowed to be in relation to the principle
of receptivity, spontaneity comes to rule receptivity, and finally
the principle of spontaneity discloses itself in its purity. But man
as such never becomes a being of pure spontaneity or creativity.
Reason thinks pure spontaneity but does not know it in its pure
essence. In thinking the idea of God as ground of the idea of world
as a totality of appearances, man thinks the idea of pure spontaneity, since there is nothing opposed to divine being, realizing
in the process that his own being is receptive as well as spontaneous. God is thus thought as "the creator of things-in-themselves" and man as "the creator of appearances," so that things-
in-themselves "which are works of God we do not know, and
appearances which we know are not the works of God" but of
man.[228] Being is given as dual, as noumenal and phenomenal, as
"eject" of divinity and "object" of humanity; being is in relation
to infinite and finite knowledge. Thus, Kant says that the "phenomenon of a thing is a product of our sensibility" and that "God
is the author of things in themselves."[229] But since the duality of
being is significant only as a duality intrinsic to man, the advantage
of all of this does not lie in the establishment of the existence of
God but in its pointing to a metaphysical realm beyond nature.
The advantage of Kant's refusal to identify any human experiential
perspective with reality as such, in other words, instead of guaranteeing knowledge of God as part of metaphysics, guarantees the
capacity of a metaphysics of nature to point beyond itself to a

metaphysics of morals. Kant is left standing, in other words, on the threshold of his second enormous task: the laying of a foundation for a metaphysics of morals.

3. THE METAPHYSICS OF MORALS

For all the seminal insights of Bruno and the Enlightenment and the potentially systematic insights of Rousseau, moral philosophy, Kant tells us, has "not advanced beyond the ancients," for to do so it must attain what the ancients never attained—a moral philosophy that is the systematic equal of a metaphysics of nature. Only now is this possible because the insights of the moderns, especially Rousseau, are incomplete articulations of moral principles that are really, Kant says, "a dimly conceived metaphysics" inherent "in every rational man's constitution."[230] To lead this dimly conceived metaphysics into the status of a system, or a metaphysics of morals, requires that Kant begin where he left off in his metaphysics of nature, with pure reason.

Kant had established in his metaphysics of nature a twofold orientation of pure reason: into understanding and into itself. He can now point out that insofar as reason permits, as he says, the "legislation through natural concepts" to be carried on "by means of the understanding," it is *theoretical*; and insofar as it thinks the ideas of pure reason purely for its own sake, and thus become its own pupil, it carries on "legislation through the concept of freedom" and thus is *practical*. This implies that reason as theoretical and oriented toward the understanding provides a "constitutive proposition" that describes the sensible world, whereas reason as practical and oriented toward itself provides a "regulative proposition" that does not tell us anything about objects but only postulates what we ought to do, that is, provides imperatives instead of objects.[231] The metaphysics of nature, insofar as it limits speculative reason, shows itself to be, as Kant says, "indeed negative"; but insofar as it removes "an obstacle which stands in the way of the employment of practical reason, nay threatens to destroy it"—the knowability of reality in itself—such a metaphysics has "a positive and very important use," which is to show that the "theoretical limitation of reason finds its counterpart in the practical extension of the same reason," that nature itself takes on a phenomenal aspect for the sake of "the practical extension of reason."[232]

The highest employment of pure reason—the highest use of its architectonic or canon, as Kant puts it—is not in regard to the speculative but rather in regard to "the practical employment of reason": "pure practical laws" are the highest "products of pure reason." In this way, the theoretical field is less radical than the practical field, and the latter is in a sense more rational in demanding from reality more in the way of rational conduct than theoretical reason demands in the way of nature.[233] However, since theoretical reason and practical reason have this in common, namely, neither can furnish, as Kant says, "a theoretical knowledge" of the "thing-in-itself," and since practical reason is a higher use of pure reason than theoretical reason, the tendency of all theory and all speculation is to verge toward the practical.[234] Yet it is "one reason that carries out the same function into two different applications," namely, the function of seeking the unconditioned for all that is conditioned and being unable to find it as an object of knowledge. In this way, both practical and theoretical reason bring a manifold into unity. The principles of practical reason bring the "manifold of desires to the unity of practical reason and give rise to acts and decisions of will." The principles of theoretical reason enable the categories of the understanding to "bring the manifold of intuition to the unity of self-consciousness" or apperception, and thus give rise to judgments of objects of experience. Both unifications appeal to the pure ideas of reason.[235]

Now, if pure reason has two orientations, and if its practical orientation is higher than its theoretical orientation, and if the latter tends toward the service of the former, then the ideas of pure reason (God, soul, world) find their highest application, as Kant says, in terms of the "final purpose of our pure practical reason," not in the theoretical realm where they have been trapped for so long by the prior history of metaphysics. This means that these ideas find their highest use in the regulation or prescription of conduct, not in the possibility of a knowledge of nature; their highest use is outside knowledge but not outside reason in a faith that is rational. "I have therefore found it necessary," Kant says, "to deny knowledge in order to make room for faith."[236] Practical reason is thus what Kant calls "faith," the "moral attitude of reason," the "permanent principle of the mind to assume as true" that which is necessary to presuppose as "condition of the possibility of the highest moral final purpose." The ideas of pure reason have their highest use as "postulates of a practical but rational faith" that are necessary to postulate because without them morality cannot be made fully intelligible.[237] This rational faith finds its manifestation in what Kant calls "conscience," which is "practical reason holding up before a man his duty for acquittal or condemnation," a kind of "internal court of justice within man." Unlike Rousseau, however, Kant holds conscience to be only an empirical manifestation of rational faith. Conscience is not so much what he calls an "obligation and duty" in itself as it is "an inevitable fact" and "instinct" that signifies that pure practical reason is capable of determining "the will by itself and not in the service of inclinations."[238]

In its constitutive employment of the ideas of pure reason, that is, as theoretical reason, reason thinks the idea of God as the "original ground" for its production of the idea of world as a totality of appearances, thus enabling understanding to generate nature and thereby modern natural science. In its regulative employment of the ideas of pure reason—as practical reason—reason thinks the idea of freedom as an "unconditioned causality" that enables it to produce a moral order.[239] Understanding legislates the being of nature by means of reason's production of the notion of world, but reason directly legislates morality in accordance with the notion of freedom. In producing science, understanding perceives man primarily as a knower, whereas in producing morality, reason perceives man primarily as a will, a power of spontaneity, an absolute self-activity, existing not simply for the sake of satisfying desire but for determining action independently of desire.[240] From the standpoint of science, nothing "natural can be other than it is in the particular relations in which it is found," but from the standpoint of morality what ought to be can be other than what is. Thus, for man to be conscious of himself as a will or absolute self activity is for man to be conscious of himself as conforming to a higher law than nature—the law of what ought to be, or the moral law—with the result that a "free will and a will under moral law are one and the same thing."[241]

Kant is thus drawn to the following conclusion. Pure reason is the highest faculty of human consciousness; science is the highest product of understanding in relation to pure reason; and morality is the highest product of pure reason in relation to itself. Since practical reason is the highest employment of pure reason, morality is the highest product of pure reason; therefore, morality is the highest product of human consciousness. Morality is the domain where human reason comes into its own, and we must conclude that the architectonic of pure reason, as discussed in the metaphysics of nature, were it able to be completely given, would be nothing less than "a list of the supreme moral laws."[242] But any attempt to explain how the notion of freedom, which makes morality possible, is itself possible must be excluded, since to explain anything "is to bring it under the laws of nature, especially the causal laws." Thus, Kant's laying of the foundations of a metaphysics of morals must rest content with the proposition that "we know that freedom is possible but we do not know how it is possible." Kant must direct his attention, instead, to elucidating morality in terms of its assumption of the possibility of freedom. Just as experience is the content studied by a metaphysics of nature, morality made possible by freedom—the moral law within man— is the content studied by a metaphysics of morals.[243]

Since morality is the highest product of pure reason in its highest employment as practical reason, it follows that the highest principle of morality is the same as the supreme principle of practical reason; and this principle is the pure idea of freedom according to which practical reason governs. The pure being of freedom or "autonomy" is not an "empirical rule or concept" but the "formal concept of lawfulness in general," and it is this alone that can have "unconditional practical necessity" and thus serve as the supreme "criterion of a genuine moral principle."[244] In knowledge human consciousness is "applying more than the mere concept of law or universality as such," but in morality the human will works only with the form of law or universality in its purity; and so the moral law within man is the concept of lawfulness as such.[245]

This concept of lawfulness as such, operating as a moral law within man, cannot be accounted for as experience; it cannot be accounted for by any evolutionary developments of man. In a strict sense, morality has no history. But, in the history of human experience, there are hints or empirical indicators of practical reason's unmediated production of morality. Kant, then, perceives the "sense of decency," which is an "inclination," he says, "to inspire others to respect by proper manners," and thus "the real basis of all true sociability," as an intimation of practical reason's production of morality. But the actual production of morality is a completely atemporal "last step of reason" that amounts to man's ahistorical "release from the womb of nature."[246] There is also the feeling of "reverence" or respect that has a privileged status in Kant's metaphysics of morals, since it is the only feeling that, as Kant says, is "produced solely by reason" and therefore entitled to be called a "moral feeling." This feeling arises "because I am conscious that my will is subordinated to a law without the intervention of any object of sense." This feeling of wonder with which the metaphysics of morals begins is directed toward the "original moral predisposition itself in us" and seems to be the only experiential component Kant admits into his metaphysics of morals.[247]

If the moral law within man, then, is nothing else than the pure idea of law as such, produced by practical reason in accordance with the pure being of freedom, accompanied but not constituted by the moral feeling of reverence, it follows that the only unqualified good, the only good that is good entirely for itself, and not merely in terms of something else, is the moral law within man. Whereas the medieval Scholastic, Thomas Aquinas, said that "all moral acts are orderable to something else," morality for Kant is not directed to something else and is good without reference to anything else.[248] Whereas in the realm of science man is committed to a procession of higher and higher unifications of his understanding, he is committed in the realm of morality to a life of higher and higher moralization; but science does not serve itself, whereas morality is an end in itself. As the only unqualified good, the moral law must be examined by Kant in his metaphysics of morals under three aspects: as transcending the necessity of nature, as identifiable with the good will, and as manifested in the categorical imperative.

As something ultimate and absolute serving as "the limit and also summit of all human consciousness," morality as a law within man must transcend the necessities of nature; or, as Kant says, man is "entitled to be the lord of nature" only insofar as there is within him a moral law that "can be self-sufficient independently of nature." As completely independent "of all natural or empirical determination," the moral law requires the operation of what Kant calls a "free causality," which is "not determined by any ground in the sensible world," and that enables man to be elevated "above himself as a part of the world of sense" and above his existence "in time."[249] As a timeless, universal, pure lawfulness, of which not even God can be the author, the moral law within man is what leads him to judge that true sublimity "does not reside in anything of nature" but only in ourselves as producing the moral law "insofar as we can become conscious that we are superior to nature."[250]

As "bonitas absoluta," as Kant calls it, the moral law, in consequence of its transcendence of nature, cannot be identified with prudence, which simply "requires a good understanding," but can only be identified with *good will* since what we find, when we consider the goodness of an action in terms of "what constitutes the goodness in and for itself," is precisely the good will. Of this will, it can be said that nothing "in the world—indeed nothing even beyond the world—can possibly be conceived which could be called good without qualification except a good will," a will that is so absolutely good that it cannot possibly be bad.[251] Absolute value can be ascribed to such a will because by it man is raised "above the stream of events which we call nature," and he is no longer at the mercy of his own natural instincts and desires. But such a will is not given to man as are the four faculties of his consciousness—it is "man himself," Kant tells us, who "must make or have made himself into whatever in a moral sense" he is or is to become, so that the "moral quality of the will" must be "completely self-acquired."[252] Kant attempts to describe how such a will is self-acquired by, first of all, distinguishing between what he calls *Wille,* which is the pure notion of will as a legislative function, and *Willkür* which is the determinate executive faculty of man. He presents *Wille* as giving law to *Willkür,* and the moral law is seen as what *Willkür* would command if it were exclusively and entirely rational, that is, completely determined by *Wille. Wille* seems to be identified by Kant with that which is unconditionally worthy of reverence or what he sometimes calls "sincerity in a calm mind accessible to all reasons."[253] This process of *Wille*'s determination of *Willkür* is given more systematic expression by Kant in his description of man's formation of, and obedience to, the moral law within as a categorical imperative.

If the self-acquisition of a good will is identified with the creation of a categorical imperative, such a creation is a purely spontaneous consciousness of the moral law, a consciousness that creates *ex nihilo* what it is aware of in a proposition that is not only synthetic and a priori, like the propositions of a metaphysics of nature, but practical as well, that is, proceeding from reason's pure orientation into itself. Such a proposition must be unconditionally free and yet unconditionally binding; or, as Kant says, it must be "an end" freely set for oneself "which is at the same time a duty," whereby I and I alone "force myself" and where, since I alone force myself, my "force is quite consistent with freedom."[254] As a purely practical, purely spontaneous proposition, proceeding from reason's orientation into itself, the categorical imperative must be a pure expression of lawfulness as such, and so it must function as a universal law. Thus, a categorical imperative must assert as an uncompromising principle that of acting "on no other maxim" or motive "than that which can also have an object itself as a universal law."[255] This means that the categorical imperative is a propositional expression of a will that every one else can act on in similar circumstances, an expression that Kant formulates as follows: "So act that the maxim of your will could always hold at the same time as a principle establishing universal law."[256]

But Kant goes further by reformulating this principle of universalizability: "Act as though the maxim of your action were by your will to become a universal law of nature." Here the categorical imperative is seen as a universalizability that serves as "the basis for the creation of a new world," by implication, better, higher, more real, than the natural world.[257] Kant must now provide these formulations with greater specificity.

The first proposition of morality is that to have moral worth an action must be done from duty. The second proposition is: An action performed from duty does not have its moral worth in the purpose which is to be achieved through it but in the maxim by which it is determined. . . . The third principle, as a consequence of the two preceding, I would express as follows: Duty is the necessity of an action executed from respect for the law.[258]

In these formulations Kant provides, respectively, the form, matter, and the full characterization of moral propositions. Thus, the first formula expresses the form, universality; the second formula expresses the matter, "human beings as beings in whom absolute value may be brought to realization"; and the third formula expresses the complete characterization of moral propositions as a unity of form and matter. The third formula is given greater concreteness by Kant when he offers the following rule: "*Do the most perfect possible by you* is the primary formal ground of all obligation to act."[259]

Taking this reformulation of the third formula together with the implication of the second formula, we see that the "most perfect possible by you" does not refer to the realm of experience, to building bridges or houses, for example, but to the human person as such, that is, to the unknowable transcendental *ego* that Kant alludes to in his metaphysics of nature. It is the absoluteness of the person as transcendental *ego* that is affirmed as the only unconditional value by Kant's formulations of the categorical imperative. Thus, when Kant says that the categorical imperative establishes "a law before which all desires fall silent," he perceives this law as proceeding from "a worth and dignity that will owe nothing to anything or anybody but man himself," man as he is in himself, man as transcendental *ego*.[260] Whereas the metaphysics of nature disclosed human understanding in its transcendental unity of apperception as the legislator of appearances according to law, that is, of nature, the metaphysics of morals discloses the transcendental *ego* in its unknowability as the legislator of morality or pure lawfulness.

We are now in a position to perceive the scope of Kant's re-construction of the Enlightenment's notion of man as an absolute. The metaphysics of nature yields the notion of man as the legislator of nature; the metaphysics of morals yields the notion of man as the legislator of morality. In his legislation of nature man is a being at once spontaneous and receptive; in his legislation of mo-rality man is a purely spontaneous being. In his legislation of nature man creates order out of chaos; in his legislation of morality man creates being out of nothingness, that is, creates the cate-gorical imperative as a manifestation of his transcendental self-hood, much as the medieval Christian God creates the world as a manifestation of Himself. Kant thus goes beyond the Enlight-enment insofar as he metaphysically founds man's independence in an ethical theory raised on "the concept of man as an end in himself," in an ethical theory in which the absoluteness of man as a "moral *ego*" or person is made manifest to itself.[261] In un-swerving fidelity to, and reverence for, the moral law within me, "I submit to myself" and "I am myself in this act of submitting to myself *qua* pure reason"; now, in submitting to myself *qua* reason, "I raise myself to myself as a free being capable of self-determination" and thus disclose my "*ego* in its dignity," in its unconditionalness.[262] Such unconditionalness cannot possibly exist within the world of appearances but can only characterize man as noumenon; the noumenon is thus seen to have a deeper significance than it had at the conclusion to the metaphysics of nature. It refers to the human person as the source of the ethical judgment of value.[263]

The metaphysics of morals, in other words, shows that in being aware of the transcendental unity of apperception, as examined in the metaphysics of nature, I am conscious that there is a real "noumenal self though I can never attain any knowledge of its nature." Practical reason as rational faith discloses "an instance, quite unlike anything in the phenomenal world, where thought of itself alone can create its own object directly," that is, create an idea of what ought or ought not to be in any possible situation conceived by the mind.[264] The metaphysics of morals comes to the conclusion that the thing-in-itself is nothing else but the subject, the "absolute *ego*," revealed in the pure spontaneity of man morally acting.[265] Kant summarizes it best.

Man in the system of nature (*homo phaenomenon, animal rationale*) is a being of little significance and, along with the other animals, considered as products of the earth, has an ordinary value (*pretium vulgare*). . . . But man as a person, that is, as the subject of a morally practical reason, is exalted above all price. For as such a one (*homo noumenon*) he is not to be valued merely as a means to the ends of other people or even to his own ends, but is to be prized as an end in himself. This is to say, he possesses a dignity (an absolute inner worth).[266]

Kant's metaphysics of morals thus reveals that the thing-in-itself is to be identified with the principle of unconditional spontaneity in man—an expression of the constructive genius of man insofar as the activity of the subject proceeds entirely from the pure creativity of practical reason. It is thus only "in man and only in him as subject of morality," Kant says, that "we meet with unconditioned legislation in respect of purposes, which therefore alone renders him capable of being a final purpose to which the whole of nature is teleologically subordinated."[267] Morality requires that behind "our selves as we know them are our selves as they really are" and that the "only point at which we can go beyond the region of appearances is the self-consciousness of freedom." At this point we neither have nor can have any real knowledge; consequently, the ethical objectivity of the thing-in-itself does not disclose itself "as the objectivity of a new object of knowledge" but as the objectivity of the unconditionally good will. Unlike knowledge that is in all its aspects subject to the primordial form of time, "our moral state, with respect to its disposition (the *homo noumenon*)," Kant says, "would not be subjected at all to temporal change."[268] If the metaphysics of nature leaves us with the knowability of being as appearances, but within the limits of human experience, it can be said that it is the unknown that encompasses the Kantian metaphysics of morals, that the *docta ignorantia* of Cusa assumes ethical embodiment in this metaphysics. Immorality itself is now interpreted in terms of the unknowability of the noumenal self, that is, in terms of the "noumenal self's neglecting to act and thus letting phenomenal causes take their course so that the action is determined by desire."[269]

The new ethical status provided the noumenon by Kant leads us to the final conclusion of his metaphysics of morals. In one of his early works, Kant spoke of "the immaterial world as a great whole, as immeasurable but unknown gradations of beings and active natures, by which alone the *dead* matter of the corporeal world is endued with life." Kant can now give this world its final determination, for he can now identify this world not with the idea that theoretical reason produces for the employment of understanding—the idea of a world as a totality of appearances—but with a world that is intrinsically intelligible, that is, purely thinkable but unknowable to man, namely, the totality of things-in-themselves or the "whole of rational beings as things-in-themselves."[270] "I entitle," Kant says, this world

> a *moral world*, insofar as it may be in accordance with all moral laws; and this is what by means of the freedom of the rational being it can be, and what according to the necessary laws of morality it ought to be. . . . This world is so far thought as an intelligible world only.[271]

This notion of world as a totality of things-in-themselves, that is, as a moral totality of noumenal beings, is what Kant equates with a *kingdom of ends*; this equation is made possible by his view that "I ought to treat other persons as ends and not merely means," a duty having its foundation in "my own will rather than in the other person."[272] The idea of a world of things-in-themselves, then, is identifiable with the idea of a multiplicity of absolute morally willing agents whose moral wills are somehow in consonance with one another and thus generate the unity of a world.

Kant was of the opinion that the existence of a "general will," similar to that of Rousseau, shared by a number of individuals was an empirical manifestation of a real connection between this multiplicity of moral wills, and thus a manifestation of an invisible moral society, similar to that of Rousseau, in which the freedom of each individual's will coexists with "the freedom of everyone else in accordance with a universal law."[273] Such an invisible moral society is literally a world in itself, because in it the autonomy of each individual is sacrosanct, and there is no conflict between the individual and society but only a kind of absolute self-sufficiency of community. This world, "in which the highest possible good can be realised with our collaboration," Kant says, is "a necessity experienced by the unselfish will as it rises beyond mere obedience to formal laws and creates as its own object the highest good." This "idea of the totality of all ends" enables man to "see himself as analogous to the divinity," insofar as his unconditionally creative moral autonomy, while it has no subjective need of anything else, is not closed up within itself but exists in a community of morally autonomous persons, much as the Christian God exists in a community of persons—the Trinity.[274] Although the "kingdom of ends is thought of, to some extent, on the analogy of the kingdom of nature," it ultimately differs from the kingdom of nature in that its members are not things as they appear but persons or moral legislators as things-in-themselves. The laws of the kingdom of ends are not "uniformities of sequences," as in nature, but "imperatives enjoining mutual consideration and respect"—pure lawfulness as such.[275]

In the ethical notion of a world as a totality of things-in-themselves, then, is had "a systematic union of rational beings through common objective laws" in which the moral maxims of each agent "can belong to a universal legislation to which he is at the same time also subject." Kant can reformulate the categorical imperative, in terms of this notion, as follows: "Act according to a maxim whose ends are such that there can be a universal law that everyone have these ends."[276] It is significant that Kant chooses to call this world in which the "free will of each being is under moral laws, in complete systematic unity with itself and with the freedom of every other," a *Corpus Mysticum*, for such a world appears to be a highly novel, modern attempt to resituate the Augustinian notion of the "City of God" over against the "City of Man," to resituate the traditional Christian theological notion of the realm of grace over against the realm of nature. A "kingdom of ends," in its "complete moral perfection," as Kant says, "is that which alone can render a world the object of a divine decree."[277] The Christian notion of the Divine Creation of the natural world *ex nihilo* is transmuted by Kant into the notion of the human creation of a moral noumenal world *ex nihilo*. If Kant's metaphysics of nature shows us that the noumenal is one of two ways of talking about the world (and not strictly speaking one of two worlds), his metaphysics of morals shows us that man must, nevertheless, *think* the noumenal (as a world of moral agents) as one of two worlds. With this, the Kantian metaphysics of morals is completed, and we must now examine the unity of the two metaphysics.

4. THE UNITY OF THE KANTIAN METAPHYSICS

The conjunction of the Kantian metaphysics of nature and metaphysics of morals can be glimpsed in terms of a series of bipolarities: phenomenal and noumenal being, theoretical and practical reason, knowledge and rational faith, science and morality. Each of these bipolarities constitutes the "two poles of the human spirit" and discloses a movement from "cosmology to humanity." Each conceals a unity of pure reason in the midst of the difference between its two poles; each finds its symbolic manifestation in Kant's coupling of Newton and Rousseau.[278] Kant signifies this unity in difference.

All the interests of my reason, speculative as well as practical, combine in the three following questions:

1. What can I know?
2. What ought I to do?
3. What may I hope?

The first question is merely speculative. . . . The second question is purely practical. . . . The third question, "If I do what I ought to do, what may I then hope?" is at once practical and theoretical.[279]

This unity in difference is the "I" who knows theoretically, thinks practically and thereby acts, and has ultimate expectations based on what it can know theoretically and think practically—a being whose selfhood has a twofold aspect: the empirical self that legislates nature and the transcendental *ego* that legislates beyond the realm of appearances. It is *man as a whole*—simultaneously "spectator and creator of the sensible world" and "moral being through freedom," simultaneously possessing membership in the sensible and the intelligible worlds—who constitutes the locus of the conjunction of the Kantian metaphysics of nature and of morals.[280] "Man," Kant tells us, is "thus to himself, on the one hand phenomenon, and on the other hand" a "purely intelligible object," and thus regards himself from "two different points of view," as noumenon freely legislating for himself and as phenomenon legislating within the bounds of sense and desire.[281]

Man, however, looks upon himself from two different points of view in such a way that neither point of view violates or usurps the other, so that the intelligible origin in freedom, although it "takes effect in phenomenality," does so by "starting a new causal chain" that it joins simultaneously without a break to "the phenomenon that has resulted from natural causality." Man must always simultaneously exist in both realms of this "two-world metaphysics," for he can achieve intelligible freedom only while he is subject to sensible determinations.[282] Yet the two worlds must be said to be within man; according to Kant, man is the dualism with which modern philosophy is plagued. But if man *is* a dualism that, by virtue of the structure of his consciousness, is unconquerable, it must be said that man *is*, independently of his consciousness, so to speak, a "unity of object and subject, of nature and freedom." This unity is perceived in the realization that it is only because there is man that there is nature, and it is only because there is man that there can be the creation of morality by virtue of his self-subjection to reason, that is, in the realization that it is one being, *man,* who simultaneously goes beyond himself as a phenomenon and yet exists "subsisting and enclosed in the world."[283] It is the unity of man that underlies Kant's approach to any subject matter and that stands behind all the intricacies of his thought.[284] The metaphysics of nature and the metaphysics of morals must be seen to have their unity, not in a third metaphysics extraneous to each of them, but in the sheer fact that the metaphysics of nature points forward to the metaphysics of morals, and the metaphysics of morals points backward to the metaphysics of nature. The first anticipates the second; the second builds on the conclusions of the first. The fact that Kant rarely addressed himself to their unity should not be construed as an admission of their disjunction but only as a kind of confidence that they spoke in and of themselves of their unity.

Yet, there is at least one passage in Kant's writing where he addresses himself, with an uncharacteristic lyricism, to the unity of his lifelong metaphysical venture and, in consequence, to the unity that is man.

Two things fill the mind with ever new and increasing admiration and awe, the oftener and more steadily we reflect on them: the starry heavens above me and the moral law within me. I do not conjecture them merely and seek them as though obscured in darkness or in the transcendent region beyond my horizon: I see them before me, and I associate them directly with the consciousness of my own existence. The former begins at the place I occupy in the external world of sense, and it broadens the connection in which I stand into an unbounded magnitude of worlds beyond worlds and systems of systems and into the limitless times of their periodic motion, their beginnings and their continuance. The latter begins at my invisible self, my personality, and exhibits me in a world which has true infinity but which is comprehensible only to the reason— a world with which I recognize myself as existing in a universal and necessary (and not only, as in the first case, contingent) connection, and thereby in connection with all those visible worlds. The former view of a countless multitude of worlds annihilates, as it were, my importance as an animal creature, which must give back to the planet (a mere speck in the universe) the matter from which it came, the matter which is for a little time provided with vital force, we know not how. The latter, on the contrary, infinitely raises my worth as that of an intelligence by my personality, in which the moral law reveals a life independent of all animality and even of the whole world of sense—at least so far as it may be inferred from the purposive destination assigned to my existence by this law, a destination which is not restricted to the conditions and limits of this life but reaches into the infinite.[285]

The parallelism of this passage to a passage in Aristotle is striking.

It is because of wondering that men began to philosophize and do so now. First, they wondered at the difficulties close at hand; then, advancing little by little, they discussed difficulties also about greater matters, for example, about the changing attributes of the moon and of the sun and of the stars, and about the generation of the universe. Now, a man who is perplexed and wonders considers himself ignorant . . . so if, indeed, they philosophized in order to avoid ignorance, it is evident that they pursued science in order to understand and not in order to use it for something else.[286]

For both Aristotle and Kant philosophy begins in "wonder"; and for both this wonder is at one point directed to the stars. Whereas, for Kant, this wonder begins with the place he occupies in the external world of sense and extends to the stars, and finally returns to himself (but not in the place he occupies in the world of sense but in a life within him independent of all animality), for Aristotle this wonder begins about perplexities close at hand, extends to the lunar, and thence to the celestial spheres. Whereas for Aristotle wonder is depicted in terms of the distinction between the sublunar and the celestial, that is, a distinction between the downward and the upward, for Kant wonder is depicted in terms of the distinction between what lies outward, but not in the "transcendent region beyond my horizon," and what lies inward. The unity that Aristotle wonders at is the unity of being that transcends man but to which he somehow has access insofar as he considers himself ignorant and pursues understanding. The unity that Kant wonders at is the unity of being that does not transcend man, that is, the very unity that man is, insofar as he associates the starry heavens "directly with the consciousness of my own existence." Effectively, for Kant, the awe that the "starry heavens awake in us only indirectly is produced directly by the contemplation of the moral law, sublime in itself, and of the moral agent who embodies this law." In the former Kant perceives man as humbled by the infinite without him, and in the latter he sees man as exalted by the infinite within him. Thus, the "starry heavens seem sublime because man first feels reduced by them to impotency, only to rise above them again" when he comes to realize that his moral being, which proceeds from a reason that permits of their comprehension, "is not subdued but heightened by the magnitude revealed in them."[287]

What Kant discovers, in other words, when he says elsewhere that we are "transported" with "astonishment" when we "behold the infinite multitude of worlds and systems which fill the extension of the Milky Way," and when he says that "the universe by its immeasurable greatness and the infinite variety and beauty that shine from it on all sides fills us with silent wonder," is precisely the transcending reverence with which the soul must regard "its own being when it considers that it is destined to survive" the transformations of the starry heavens.[288] It is no accident that the words "the starry heavens above me, the moral law within me" are inscribed over Kant's grave in the cathedral on the *Stoa Kantiana*. These words not only describe the two poles of his thought—the cosmos that was the object of his youthful love and the moral law that was the "object of the almost mystical enthusiasm of his old age"[289]—but they signify his thought as a unity and in its unity, for they imply that the infinity revealed in the heavens has its source in the noumenal self of man.

The conjunction or unity of the metaphysics of nature and of morals finds its clearest expression in the proposition that the noumenal being of man is the substratum of the phenomenal being of man—that man perceives the universe as infinite because he contains the infinite creativity that produces the moral law. The sheer capability for thinking the "infinite without contradiction," Kant says, requires a faculty of human consciousness able to think the "idea of a noumenon which admits of no intuition, but which yet serves as the substrate for the intuition of the world as a mere phenomenon."[290] It is thus the moral autonomy, the moral absoluteness of man, which permits the natural world to be intelligible to man; and so, it is the "intellectual dignity of man corresponding to his moral dignity which enables the scientist to purify the sensible world so that it can be intelligible in mathematical symbols." The ethical "ideal thus penetrates the theoretical sphere itself" and becomes "its supreme master and interpreter."[291]

It is the existence of the world as noumenal that permits its presentation as phenomenal in man. There is only one world, but that one world is not something outside man in which man is contained. That one world *is* man—the being in whom the knowable is grounded in the unknowable. Like Plato, Kant ends in the unknowable, with moral faith as the Kantian analogue of Platonic myth,[292] but, unlike Plato, the unknowable, for Kant, is a dimension of *human* being—that dimension of human being which enables the knowable dimension of human being to come into existence. If such is the shape of the conjunction or unity of the two Kantian metaphysics, we have only now, in conclusion to the body of our interpretation of Kant, to indicate the manner in which this unity concretely manifests itself in the less developed but nonetheless significant political and religious theories of Kant.

Kant leaves no doubt that, in keeping with the Enlightenment, historical progress is one of the central tenets of his political theory. The course of human history is "not a decline from good to evil, but rather a gradual development from the worse to the better," Kant writes, and if it "seems so senseless to us, perhaps it lies in a poor choice of position from which we regard it." From the perspective of the individual, history seems "complex and chaotic," but from the perspective of the "human race as a whole," it presents itself as a "steady and progressive though slow evolution of its original endowment."[293] This historical progress is, as such, a progress in what Kant calls "cultural matters," that is, the race as a whole is being benefited in the long run by the arts and sciences and the physical benefits procured by their applications. But we are "permitted to assume," he says, by virtue of this cultural progress, that the race is also "engaged in progressive improvement in relation to the moral end of its existence," a progress that "may at times be interrupted but never broken off."[294]

There is thus a sense in which morality is now seen by Kant to require historical progress, yet Kant never elevates this idea of progress to the rank of a pure idea of reason, alongside soul, God, and world, precisely because historical progress is an inherently phenomenal reality for Kant, that is, historical progress is in its essence the overall process by which nature is being legislated by the human understanding. In other words, historical progress is the human legislation of nature viewed from the perspective of the human race. We can thus assume, as Kant puts it, that nature has done something "to favor man's moral purpose," in the sense that what we as individuals neglect to do, in the way of morality, "comes about by itself" for the race, "though with great inconveniences to us" as individuals.[295] There is therefore what Kant calls a "purposive striving of nature to a cultivation which makes us receptive of higher purposes than nature itself can supply," so that the "beautiful arts and the sciences," as man's legislation of nature, "win us" from "the tyranny of sense propensions, and thus prepare men for a lordship in which reason alone shall have authority." Effectively, the "mechanism of nature" operating through man's fear of destruction brings about external compliance with the moral law, but this external compliance is not morality as such but only legality. Historical progress can bring about only a state according to morality but not a truly moral state.[296]

From this point of view, in terms of the human race, historical progress can be said to be a phenomenal manifestation of the noumenal creative process of freedom, a phenomenal "education of the human species," as Kant puts it, in which a "good which man has not intended" preserves and "perpetuates itself." This permits us to be justified in the expectation of finding "a perfectly rational purpose" in the history of mankind without looking for that purpose "only in another world." This rational purpose is what Kant calls the "greatest moral perfection" of the race in accordance with "human freedom." But the rationality we find in history is always a phenomenal manifestation of the noumenal being of man—that is, of the idea of freedom—and this is why Kant says that the "inner principle" of this history "is freedom."[297]

Now, we know that in its most violent form, war jeopardizes the existence of mankind, just as in its most violent form controversy threatens the existence of reason, and so we are permitted to infer that human history as a progress aims at an absolutely conflict-free situation, the rational establishment of eternal peace. But this perpetual peace, as a thinkable phenomenon, must be grounded in the noumenal reality of freedom, and so it must spring from reason itself and be oriented into a worldwide expansion of reason, in such a way that were we to attain it we would "give up no knowledge other than pseudo-knowledge" and "accept no faith other than the rational faith" of practical reason.[298] This "task of establishing a universal and lasting peace" in accordance with reason is the "ultimate purpose" of the phenomenon of human history, Kant tells us; and so "perpetual peace" is the "supreme political good," flowing from the pronouncement of an "irresistible *veto*" by "moral-practical reason within us," namely, "there shall be no war." It is not really "a question of whether perpetual peace is really possible or not," for we "must simply act as if it could really come about" and "turn our efforts towards realising it."[299] The ideal of perpetual peace cannot, however, be elevated into a moral law but can only be the phenomenal manifestation of such a law, or the phenomenal consequence of fidelity to such a law. As Kant says, "Seek ye first the kingdom of pure practical reason and its righteousness, and your end (the blessing of perpetual peace) will necessarily follow."[300] Man finds himself driven by the phenomenal process of history, then, toward external compliance with the inner moral law; man also finds that he can aid and abet this process but only by means of his individual fidelity to his noumenal selfhood. Kant's political theory is thus a concrete illustration of the unity of his twofold metaphysics, witnessing to the noumenal as substrate of the phenomenal. Kant was perhaps aware of this when he said, "I am far from regarding metaphysics itself" to be "dispensable" and "I have been convinced" that the "true and lasting welfare of the human race depends on it."[301]

We have seen in our examination of Kant's metaphysics of nature that the pure idea of God makes possible the idea of world as a totality of appearances that serves as a concept for the employment of the understanding. We have seen in our examination of Kant's metaphysics of morals that the pure postulate of freedom makes possible reason's orientation into itself and thus makes possible the employment of practical reason. In seeing this much, we saw the fundamental difference between the two metaphysics. It is instructive to note that in his political theory Kant engages in something of a turnabout and presents the idea of freedom as the noumenal ground for the phenomenal presentation of a meaningful, progressive history, thereby emphasizing not the difference between the two metaphysics but their unity. We will now see a similar turnabout in Kant's theory of religion where the idea of God will be shown to have an intimate relation to the morally practical, self-legislating reason.

From its very inception, Kant's theory of religion is insistent that we can "reach a perspective for accepting the divine reality" only where we also "recognize the unconditionally demanding duty to act morally in this world and to embody moral purposes in the natural course of events." As Kant says, it is "only the recognition of our duty and of the final purpose enjoined upon us by reason which brings out with definiteness the concept of God," so that "God must be represented not as substance outside me" but as the "highest moral principle in me." Although "fear first produces gods," he says, it is "reason by means of its moral principles that can first produce the concept of God."[302] If the metaphysics of nature disclosed that the pure idea of God makes possible the concept of world as a totality of appearances for the employment of understanding in its legislation of nature, the Kantian theory of religion now discloses that the pure idea of God could not exist without the pure postulate of freedom, that the pure being of freedom makes possible the pure idea of God, and that the idea of God remains pure only insofar as it can be considered as representative of the highest moral purpose in man.

This enables Kant to argue that when the idea of God is maintained in its purity in the worship of God, that is, in religion, such religion becomes a phenomenal manifestation of man's moral duty to his noumenal self, so that whatever "over and above good life conduct," Kant says, "man fancies that he can do to become well pleasing to God is mere religious illusion." There are, in effect, no duties toward God distinguishable from our duties toward man, and when religion is a phenomenal manifestation of morality it is nothing more than "morality applied to the knowledge of God." Morality comes first, and theology, following its lead, is nothing more than "morality," as he says, presenting itself as "the ultimate cause," as an "object of adoration"—nothing more in its essence than "inner religion."[303] The consequence of Kant's twofold metaphysics is the definitive destruction of "the old metaphysical substructure for theological dogmatics," in which God is made the ground of finite being, and the replacement of this substructure by a truly trustworthy support for religious faith, namely, one in which "the incontrovertible fact of the moral self-consciousness" becomes the ground for the very possibility of religion. This trustworthy support is a theology that limits itself to the adequate determination of the concept of God for "the highest practical use of reason."[304]

Now, of all "the public religions which have ever existed," Kant tells us, "the Christian alone is moral"—that is, a phenomenal manifestation of the noumenal selfhood of man—since it alone enjoins us "to become free, 'to be freed from bondage under the law of sin, to live for righteousness'." This is why in speaking of the Gospels, he says that they not only agree "with the speculations of a perfected reason" but shed "new light on the whole field surveyed by that reason" in such a way that they disclose "moral faith" as the essence of Christianity.[305] Kant can thus, in opposition to the Enlightenment, call himself a Christian, but only within the limits of assent to the purest elements of Christianity— those elements which conform to the demands of morality. He is willing to give his assent only to the extent, as he says, that Christianity "contains within itself" a principle of "steadily approximating" to the "pure rational faith" that constitutes practical reason.[306] Thus, the Christian doctrine that we are saved by faith and not by works is perceived by Kant as a phenomenal expression of the universal moral law within us. When St. Paul in his Epistle to the Romans speaks of the conflict of the old and new law, Kant perceives this as an expression of the tension between the law of nature and the law of morality. When Paul says that when the "gentiles who have not the law do by nature what the law requires, they are a law to themselves," and when he speaks of a "real Jew" and "real circumcision" as possible only "inwardly," he is providing an authentic phenomenal expression for the noumenal being of morality. When Paul says that "Israel who pursued the righteousness which is based on law did not succeed in fulfilling the law," because it "did not pursue it through faith, but as if it were based on works," he locates as his principle the dictum: "Do not be conformed to this world, but be transformed by the renewal of your mind," which for Kant is the most perfect phenomenal expression in religion of the noumenal essence of morality.[307] But there are impure elements in Christianity, those that are inconsonant with the idea of religion as a proper phenomenal manifestation of man's noumenal selfhood, such as dogmatism and authoritarianism, and when these are allowed to rule its pure elements, then, as Kant says, "a natural antipathy and insubordination" toward Christianity "would be bound to become the predominant mode of men's thinking."[308] Like Rousseau, Kant transcends the Enlightenment's anti-Christian polemic, but unlike Rousseau, he accounts for the very possibility of that polemic and his transcendence of it.

Kant gives us, then, in his theory of religion a theory of purified religion as a phenomenal manifestation of the noumenal being of man. Whatever religious certainties can be found have their foundation in the ethical certainty postulated by rational faith, that is, by practical reason.[309] In doing this, the Kantian view of religion testifies to the validity of the proposition that the ground of the phenomenal order is found in noumenal moral order and thus confirms the unity of the Kantian metaphysics of nature and of morals. We have thus completed the body of our interpretation of Kant, and have only in our conclusion to address ourselves to a statement of the nature of Kant's accomplishment of his task in its finality, that is, a unified metaphysics of man, and to a statement of how this accomplishment will be incorporated by the completion of the logic of modernity.

5. THE SIGNIFICANCE OF KANT'S PROJECT

In solving the main problem of his intellectual life—in producing a method of metaphysics that provides a unity for the metaphysics of morals and the metaphysics of nature and that yields the "first principles of that which is within the comprehension of human knowledge"—Kant has shown himself to be neither primarily an epistemologist nor an ethician but an "encompassing metaphysician." In demolishing the speculative metaphysics of the past, he rejects the traditional metaphysical interpretation of being *qua* being as a being that exists independently of man and reveals instead that the core of metaphysics, the "internal possibility of ontology," lies in the immanent structure of human being as such. For the first time in Western history, it would seem, metaphysics presents itself as the highest study of our inner nature, with its focus no longer in the "specific things that are" but in the "grounds of their being for us." The result is that the ultimate ontological question of metaphysics is shown to be "equivalent to the question concerning the true nature of man."[310] The problem of being *qua* being is identical with the problem of man *qua* man.

If this be metaphysics in its unity, the tree of which metaphysics is the root must reflect this unity. Philosophy must be unabashedly anthropocentric, striving to bring the "sciences into relation to the highest purposes of humanity." Philosophy can no longer be in the service of theology (as with medieval philosophy) or in the service of science (as with much of prior modern philosophy) but must be in the service of human being, specifically the highest aspect of human being, namely, man's ethical, noumenal being. Because it is in the service of the ultimately unknowable, philosophy must recognize that its concepts are not absolutely definable, as are the concepts of science, but capable of entering into an indefinite number of relations. It must recognize that "knowledge alone" does not make it true philosophy, as Kant says, but that there must be in addition an "insight" into the harmony of its knowledge with "the highest ends of human reason."[311] Furthermore, unlike the sciences, there can only be one philosophy. The singleness of human reason requires that there can be no more "than one true system of philosophy," no matter how "diverse and often contradictory the ways men have philosophized about one and the same proposition," for only in this way can philosophy close the scientific circle and demonstrate the inner order and connection of the sciences in their relation to the highest human purposes that are practically moral.[312] As far as its previous history is concerned, Kant can simply say that prior to this time philosophy has been "a mere idea of a possible science," which nowhere existed *in concreto* but was only approximated by "many different paths" and has now "at last been discovered" in its one true path as the "science of the ultimate ends of human reason." The starting and finishing points of this philosophy are neither God nor world but man, for "man is the area in which all the rest become reality."[313]

The essential questions of philosophy, then, which Kant has set forth—"What can I know?"; "What ought I to do?"; and "What may I hope?"—require, as Kant says, that a "fourth question ought to follow," namely, "What is man?" But in reality "all these questions might be reckoned under anthropology, since the first three questions refer to the last."[314] The first three questions do not have, in other words, a "merely accidental relationship to the fourth" but, according to their essence, must be reducible to the fourth, so that the entire range of the problems of philosophy finds its abode and center in the essence of man. There is no single work of Kant that contains the answer to that fourth question, for nothing less than his critical philosophy as a whole is adequate for answering that question.[315] If "there is any science man really needs," he says, referring to his critical philosophy as a whole, with its metaphysical roots and the manifestation of the unity of those roots in his theory of religion and politics, "it is the one I teach, of how to occupy properly that place in creation that is assigned to man, and how to learn from it what one must be in order to be a man." This is a science that studies man, "not only in the varying forms in which his accidental circumstances have molded him, in the distorted form in which even philosophers have almost always misconstrued him," but in "what is enduring in human nature."[316]

The unity of philosophy in the service of the highest human ends is secured and made possible, then, by the unity of metaphysics. But metaphysics has unity only as an "interrogation of man," that is, as an anthropology, which enjoins man to seek the intelligibility of being neither below nor above himself but in man himself who is, as Kant says, "his own ultimate purpose." Metaphysics belongs to human nature not simply in the sense that man does metaphysics but in the sense that man is the subject matter of metaphysics.[317] In describing the unity of his metaphysics as a "metaphysics of metaphysics,"[318] Kant was implying that he had not only overcome the traditional identification of being *qua* being with a being that exists independently of man (whether the *nature* of the ancients or the *God* of the medievals) and identified this ontological problem with man *as* man; he was also implying that, since the ground of the unity of his metaphysics lay in the noumenal ground of the phenomenal, the ontological problem was to be identified with *homo noumenon* as the ground of *homo phaenomenon*. Being *qua* being is identified with man *qua* man; and man *qua* man is identified with human noumenal being as the ground of human phenomenal being. In its unity, then, Kantian metaphysics is a "metaphysics of metaphysics"—a fundamental ontology that has as its problem an unknown and forever unknowable being as the ground of a knowing and known being. Man is being-as-such, where the known finds its ground in the unknown—where finitude finds its ground in infinity. In thinking freedom, morality becomes possible as the only human encounter with this infinite, unknowable ground, and so the unity of metaphysics has its "model and its echo in the ethical."[319]

For all this, Kant could still say that "I see before me the unpaid bill of my uncompleted philosophy, even while I am aware that philosophy, both as regards its means and its ends, is capable of completion."[320] Nonetheless, the unity of that philosophy—a unity, characterized by Kant himself, in terms of the attempt to see the object of unity "at all times from different directions, and to extend one's range of vision from microscopic observations to a general view," so that one adopts all conceivable standpoints, each of which reciprocally verifies the optical judgment of the other—is evident. The testament to this unity can be found in words Kant applied to someone else but that must be applied to him: the talent of "combining an exceptional acuteness for details with a breadth of vision of the whole."[321]

Kant's admission of the incompleteness of his philosophy, however, suggests that the logic of modernity has not yet been completed, and it further suggests how Kant will be assimilated by this completion. We thus return to where we started in our interpretation of Kant, for the necessary condition for the assimilation of Kant by the completion of the logic of modernity is his assimilation of the prior developments of that logic.

If Descartes provided the first modern metaphysics as a foundation for modern science, Kant radically altered and extended the range of this metaphysics by founding modernity in something more ultimate than science. Although nature in Kant is as mechanical as it was in Descartes, it is legislated by man, and this legislation is made possible by something that transcends the mechanical—by what Kant calls "an *art* concealed in the depths of the human soul, whose real modes of activity" man is "hardly likely ever" to "discover."[322] Man makes the world of natural phenomena out of the raw data of the sensible manifold, and he creates morality *ex nihilo*; man must think the idea of God as pure creativity (God as creator of things-in-themselves) if he is to think the idea of a world as totality of appearances. But, paradoxically, the pure idea of freedom is seen to make the idea of God possible— only the pure creativity of practical reason, not God, can author the moral law. Yet the ultimate unknowability of this creativity, that is, the creativity of noumenal being as such, must be posited. Although at last man is presented as a unity of scientific and ethical legislation, he is still bound by the dualism of the inner and outer, now construed as the dualism of the unknowable and knowable, which is within him, constitutive of his being, and therefore ineradicable.

There is, in other words, a fundamental ambivalence in Kant's philosophy. On the one hand, there is the realization that there can be no such being as man, considered in terms of his consciousness, unless there is the thinkableness of the phenomenal-noumenal dualism. On the other hand, there is the realization that since nature and morality exist only because there is man, man must be, independently of his consciousness, a unity. Thus, it can be said that only because there is man can there be the conceivability of the phenomenal-noumenal bifurcation. Kant never overcomes this ambivalence; it appears to be the unspoken condition of his philosophy. Hegel seems to be cognizant of this unspoken condition, and thus he recognizes the possibility of extirpating in his own thought what is an ineradicable dualism in the Kantian achievement.

In our interpretive weaving of a logic for modernity we have seen the following sequence: first, reflection on an infinite universe; second, reflection on scientific method as the proper way of knowing in this universe; third, reflection on the problem and limits of knowing as such; and, fourth, reflection on the very meaning of man as the ground of this knowing. It remains for Hegel to complete this sequence by returning the logic of modernity to a consciousness of what lies before its starting point, namely, its *Ursprung* in the medieval theophanic world. In this way, Hegel can reconstitute the starting point of this logic—the modern infinite universe. The only path for extirpating the modern bifurcation is not to show, as Kant did, that a mechanical universe can have its ground in a radically unmechanical human creativity, but to show that the modern infinite universe is not properly spatial and mechanical at all, not really nature at all, but is historical, and, in being such, it is the only fitting substitute for the cosmos of fixed natural forms (spatial and atemporal) conceived by the ancients. For Hegel, this will involve the attempt to see the outer as an objectification of the inner, matter as an objectification of mind, and thus, the attempt to see history as the embodiment of the absoluteness of human consciousness. The philosophy of history, which assumed a secondary function in Kant, will assume the primary role in Hegel, enabling the inner and the outer to be perceived as one. In returning the logic of modernity to its sources in medieval thought, Hegel will perceive this logic in the fullness of its antithesis to the ancient mythos and logos, as opposed to Kant who tended to perceive this logic primarily in terms of itself, that is, in terms of its own developments as proceeding from Copernicus.

The Hegelian absolute, or what Kant called the thing-in-itself, is that pure reason which Kant has laid bare, but Kant has not drawn the full consequences of his metaphysical insight; for as Hegel will see it, pure reason, as absolute, undergoes a history, and this history is what is really meant by the modern infinite universe. By ending with the unknowableness of the pure creativity of practical reason, Kant posed a threat to the very supremacy of the *logic* operative in modernity, and thus Hegel would have to identify metaphysics with logic more radically than ever before.[323] It might almost be said that just as Kant ran to fill the breach made by Rousseau's critique of civilization, Hegel will run to fill the breach made by Kant's dissociation of the knowability and creativity of being—by Kant's critique of pure reason. But, if this much can be said, it can be said only because Kant makes possible the Hegelian completion of the logic of modernity.

7

THE COMPLETION OF THE LOGIC OF MODERNITY

IN weaving the garment of the logic of modernity, we have accentuated the following threads: the origin of this logic in the medieval mythos and its radical opposition to the ancient mythos; the initial cosmological presentation of this logic in Copernicus and Kepler; the generation of the rudiments of a scientific methodology (in Galileo) and of a novel ethical viewpoint (in Giordano Bruno); the metaphysical task of laying foundations for scientific methodology in Descartes and the revision of these foundations in Newton and Leibniz; the delineation of a theory of the nature and limits of knowledge-as-such in Locke, Berkeley, and Hume; the process by which modernity is made self-conscious in the Enlightenment; and finally the generation of the rudiments of a philosophy of man in Rousseau and the refounding of the Cartesian foundations in a metaphysics of man in Kant. The Kantian refounding signals the readiness of the edifice of modern philosophy for its own completion. The question, however, as Martin Heidegger formulates it, is: "Where must we seek the completion of modern philosophy?" or "On what does the *telos,* the completion, of modern philosophy depend?"[1]

The answer to this question, as proposed in this chapter, is that this completion requires the complete resolution of the Cartesian alienation of mind and body—of human consciousness and nature. But such a resolution itself requires not merely a return to the Copernican beginnings of modernity but also a return to the very fountainhead of modernity—the medieval mythos and its opposition to the ancient mythos. The fruit of such a return is the reconstitution of the universe delivered by the midwifery of Copernicus and Kepler—the creation of a "cosmos" for modernity in full cognizance of the development of the logic of modernity and of the origins of that development in the medieval mythos. This completion, requiring as it does a return more radical than Kant's return to Copernicus, is to be found in Hegel who perceived that the full import of the world as a creation of God required going beyond Kant,[2] returning to a point to which Kant never returned.

With the completion of the logic of modernity in Hegel, philosophers are left to confront the completed edifice—to evaluate, criticize, accept, reject, or modify it. These, it would appear, are the tasks of contemporary philosophers. Nietzsche, the last modern or first contemporary philosopher, displays what philosophy can be after Hegel. Unlike his modern forebears, Nietzsche is no longer secure in his faith in the positive possibilities of the modern venture; he must struggle with modernity's faith in the propriety of its own venture. Nietzsche is thus a testament to the completion of the modern philosophical edifice; he may thus be fittingly considered as a postscript to its completion.

HEGEL: HISTORY AS THE MODERN "COSMOS"

1. INTRODUCTION

a. The Dualistic Backdrop

Georg Wilhelm Friedrich Hegel (1770–1831) lived through Germany's intellectual and artistic zenith, what he himself called "a time of ferment," a "period of transition to a new era." It was, he said, a period that could not be condemned as irrational because it failed to correspond to "a paradigm taken from the ancient world," but that "is as it ought to be." It only has need of its rationality being *grasped* by a theoretical work (which achieves more than practical work) that will reinstate faith in this present age by casting itself into thinking as into "an ocean without beaches," where it is "as yet unknown where everything leads, where one will end."[3] The division of life, which is the "unfree and given aspect" of this age, which has found its expression in philosophical form in the all-encompassing Cartesian dualism, has need of philosophy as a kind of therapy, a means of salvation, a restoration of harmony, which raises to life again that which has "died the death of dichotomy" in the dualism of the modern world. Since it is only philosophy that has led this age into "this labyrinth of the mind" only philosophy is capable of leading it out and healing its lived alienation.[4] Yet, to resolve the dualism of modern thought, philosophy need only comprehend its own time, since the final unity is already implicit in the *life* of this time; for a "conflict which in one sense is yet to be resolved by thought is in another already resolved in life." Hegel would not have us make "the mistake of regarding the antithesis of subjectivity and objectivity as an abstract and permanent one," which poses the insoluble problem of "how to patch up a relation between a thought and a real object already fatally severed." Instead, he will insist that "the apparent severance between thought and its object" is "in the last resort necessitated by their real identity" because the "reality of opposites and real opposition only happen because of the identity of the opposites." The philosophical comprehension of this age will thus disclose that "there is absolute accordance where it was believed that there was the greatest opposition" and that the "consummation of the infinite end" consists merely "in removing the illusion which makes it seem yet unaccomplished."[5]

The modern dualism was induced by the modern scientific revolution that achieved a pyrrhic victory by rooting its representations in its own internal network rather than in the world. Science can "objectify itself only by forgetting its subjective origins" and solves the riddle of the universe only to replace this riddle by the riddle of the modern mind itself. This dualism is first unearthed in Descartes when he perceives that man's thought, unlike God's, cannot bring reality out of nothingness and so must suffer the alienation of thought from the things of nature, the alienation of the inside from the outside of human consciousness. In Kant, this dualism is built into the inside of being, that is, of man, as the phenomenal-noumenal dualism that is the necessary result of his "formal idealism."[6] Yet, although dualism was ineradicable for the ancients because it was written into the fabric of nature, it is, by virtue of its being a consequence of finite cognition or man's cognition, capable of being resolved for the moderns, and it was Berkeley's virtue to bring this capacity for resolution to the foreground.[7]

Aware of the genesis, nature, and resolvability of this dualism, Hegel saw that philosophy "must give the separation into subject and object its due," must take it seriously, and not simply attempt to nullify one of the opposites and exalt the other into something infinite by "undermining the objectivity of one side of those things which are opposed," as Berkeley had done. Dualism was a necessary moment for modernity, and since it was induced by modern mathematical physics, its resolution can be achieved only by comprehending "the spiritual significance of the struggle which produced that physics," a struggle that required that consciousness create a dualism within itself. Consciousness must now mature "itself inwardly, even when under this barrier, until it overcomes this dualism" and attains its objective reality in the actuality of the present age, an actuality that exists only "through its own re-establishment out of the deepest fission" of the subject and object as identical, so that the impenetrable thing-in-itself and the subjective solitude of the "I" are both superseded—all this without falling into a Berkleyan reductionism premised on a hard-and-fast "opposition between consciousness and its object" where "self-consciousness as individual is alone in question."[8]

b. Preliminary and Prior Attempts at a Resolution of the Dichotomies

Like Berkeley before him, Hegel saw that the continued acceptance of the modern dualism implied the demise of the Christian notion of God, the very notion that made the logic of modernity possible in the first place. But Hegel saw further that although Christianity began with a kind of dualism of its own, namely, that "sense of suffering in which it rends the natural unity of the Spirit asunder, and destroys natural peace," Christianity was able to *overcome* the dualism underlying the ancient logos, namely, the division of the world by the ancient mythos into sacred and profane spaces. Hegel perceived that by virtue of the Christian understanding of the dialectic of divine transcendence and immanence, man must connect the imperishable to the contingent and overcome the dichotomy of the sacred and the secular. For, as St.

Augustine had said, God is "both interior to everything because all things are in Him, and exterior to everything because He is above all things," and as Pseudo-Dionysius had said, "God is known in all things and apart from all things."[9] Even Rousseau was forced to imitate this dialectic in conceiving of his inner self as dwelling in the world while at the same time existing beyond the world.

Hegel realized that just as this dialectic resolved the classical dualism, it was a necessary condition for overcoming the modern dualism, and philosophy would have to perceive anew how the "opposition of self and the in-itself, of immanence and transcendence," was overcome by means of a non-bifurcating interpretation of Christianity that perceives in the Incarnation, with its God that dies in man while raising Himself to the divine through a history, the definitive unity of transcendence and immanence. This perception assures the Christian that "the earth belongs to the Spirit" and insures the definitive resolution of the mind-matter dualism. Hegel further saw that the ground of the Incarnation is the Christian notion of a Trinitarian God in which the "Father 'poses' the world and is reflected within its essence as the Son." The "separation implied by the notion of reflection is overcome with the Spirit or Holy Ghost," thereby making the Trinity the paradigm for the Incarnation and thus the ultimate paradigm for the overcoming of the separation between subject and object.[10]

But if this understanding of the resolution of the modern dualism requires a return to the full import of the Incarnation and Trinity, it also requires a return to the fountainhead of modernity, namely, to the medieval mythos in *its* opposition to the ancient mythos. This must be done in such a way that the very universe constructed by early modern philosophy is radically reconstructed as "a comprehensive system, in which every legitimate source of conflict and division" is incorporated as an organic part of the whole, a reconstruction that fully articulates the change in western man's cosmos, the change in the very being which presents itself to western consciousness.[11] The philosophical comprehension of his age, being identical with the philosophical conquest of modern dualism, requires a grasp of the import of the Incarnation and Trinity, and promises the real understanding of the modern "cosmos."

For the Enlightenment the cosmos is *not* an awe-inspiring reality but simply neutral stuff for man (or the universal scientific consciousness) to dominate intellectually. This human consciousness was the only significant reality, so that the center of gravity of modernity is seen to be an absolutized man rather than an infinitized universe, and the world ceases to be a cosmos in the sense of an immediately accessible order of things. The consequence of this bringing of modernity into self-consciousness, for Hegel, is a "radical homelessness," where "Spirit, so to speak, floats over the waters," in one sense "a god, but more fundamentally an impotent god."[12]

Although the Enlightenment is *not* "enlightened about itself," it makes possible the momentous Kantian shift from a metaphysics of nature to a metaphysics of morals, from cosmology to humanity (a shift Hegel calls a "great and important one," a "great step forward"), since the Kantian philosophy is "the 'illumination' or *Aufklärung* reduced to method." Kant's transition is so important because he perceives that the "comprehending medium is 'I'," and that "whatever I have to do with must allow itself to be forced into these forms of unity" that enable him to see that "reason brings forth ideas."[13] But these ideas are unfolded "in subjective form alone," so that "we know not what things-in-themselves are," and although "reason has certainly the desire to know the infinite," it has not the power to overcome the impassable gulf separating it from the thing-in-itself. Nonetheless, in realizing that man perceives the universe as infinite because he *contains* the infinite creativity that produces the moral law, and in concluding that the world unlike nature must be conceived as not in space or time at all (in order to prevent reason from being involved in an insoluble contradiction), Kant "brought thought to such great heights" that he prepared "the ground for the transcending of his own position." Hegel will accomplish this transcending by means of a reverse movement from humanity back to cosmology, what he calls the "true transition" from the finite mode of human life addressed in Kant to the thought that this world is a *cosmos,* to the restoration of the vanished totality of the whole.[14]

In the beginning of the logic of modernity, Cusa saw that the full force of the experience of the infinite Christian God demanded a universe that was as infinite in its plurality as God was in His unity. Following him, Copernicus argued against the Aristotelian position that no sensible magnitude is infinite and allowed Kepler to argue that the universe was in fact an infinite quantitatively homogeneous whole. But Hegel, following Spinoza who argued that the infinity of the universe does not consist in its configuration or figure, but in its unbounded self-creating dynamism, and accepting Spinoza's rejection of a personal point of view in favor of an impersonal system, expresses dissatisfaction with the conception of the infinite universe found at the beginning of the logic of modernity, calling it a "theme of barren declamation." The question of "the infinitude of space" means "nothing to Reason," because it is only "negative infinitude to which Reason knows itself to be superior."[15]

Pascal's fear of "the infinite immensity of spaces," of the "eternal silence of these infinite spaces," of this "awful desert of the universe," which can be turned into a home only by virtue of "an intimacy with God who fills it," discloses a profound truth, for Hegel, since this universe can become a cosmos (since it cannot understand itself) only through man, that is, through the *ego* in which there is an "infinite likeness of self-consciousness to itself."[16] Like the universe that Bruno saw as "an infinite animal," which fills the infinite need of the soul of man for infinity, and like the infinity of nature which Leibniz argued for on the basis of its inward complexity and plenitude as a teeming inner chain of vital and organic beings, the cosmos that Hegel reconstructs must be a beautiful, living cosmos, analogous to a life-form, and comprehended by "the Aristotelian-derived category of internal teleology." The aim is not to show, as Kant did, that a mechanical universe can have its ground in a radically *un*mechanical human creativity, but to show that the modern infinite cosmos is not properly spatial and mechanical *at all* but organically *historical*; as such it is the overcoming of the modern dualisms of subject and object, inside and outside, vitality and mechanism.[17]

This means a cosmos of the totality of cultural experience, of history itself, predicated on the unity of divine transcendence and immanence, where God is not an entity that subsists apart. It will be a cosmos that in a sense is more akin to the Roman notion of "a *mundus,* a moral spectacle, a thing with a moral government, beautiful because of its moral grandeur," than it is to the Greek notion of the world as a physical cosmos, a pregiven intelligible order of nature. Yet a cosmos that is akin to the Ciceronian ideal of "Studium Humanitatis ac Litterarum" and to the study of great men nonetheless maintains all the Greek emphasis on intelligibility (even though the intelligibility is not pregiven); for the Hegelian *mundus-cosmos* will find its conditions in the normative intelligibility of the Christian notions of Trinity (a true becoming in God), Creation (a true beginning of intelligibility), and Incarnation (the normativity of the particular). By working out the intelligibility of these notions, Hegel will lay bare the true intelligibility of the beginning of the logic of modernity, show that this beginning becomes itself by ceasing to be itself, and demonstrate how this beginning must cease to be itself in its original presentation as infinite spatial nature in order to unfold itself as the cosmos of modernity.[18]

In this way, the philosophical comprehension of his own age, the conquest of modern dualism, and the articulation of the modern cosmos will all be identical. In being identical, they will constitute a completion or "telos" for modernity that will articulate the true import of the beginning of modernity. In this way, Hegel says, the world of modern man will be divested of its "strangeness," and what Hölderlin, Hegel's contemporary and friend, called the "fate of modern man"—to be destined "to find no resting place"—will be overcome in modern man's being at home in his world and thus "at home with his spirit." No longer "stranger to himself," he will be "at home in the objective world" as an intelligent world validated by the power of reason.[19] This is the Hegelian project, and now we must set forth the method he proposes for the execution of this project.

2. THE HEGELIAN METHOD AND ITS LOGIC

The Hegelian method is a dialectic of three realms: *logos* or *logic,* the "science of the idea in and for itself," that is, the bare universal; *natura* or *philosophy of nature,* the "science of the idea in its otherness," or the particular, the sphere of difference; and *Geist* or *philosophy of Spirit,* the "science of the idea come back to itself out of that otherness," that is, the concrete universal or individual as a synthesis of the universal and particular.[20]

As world-spirit (*Weltgeist*), the idea is first in a state of being-in-itself, then in a state of alienation or self-estrangement where it passes into nature, and finally in a state of being-in-and-for-itself where it returns from self-estrangement to itself.[21]

Thus, the Hegelian method is not simply a method of research or of philosophical exposition but claims to be the adequate description of the structure of being, since it is only because the real itself undergoes this dialectic—only because "being matches what thought thinks of it"—that the method is dialectical. Each category in it, unlike the concepts of Kant's *understanding*, is "not a mere necessary rule for possible experience"; on the contrary, our minds constitute their object "only because they are constituted by the activity of universal spirit in them." Unlike the "subjective deduction" of geometry where the content itself does not actually go through the process we follow out in the act of demonstration, the method *is* the self-unfolding notion, so that unlike the "dialectical scrutinizing of all assumptions" that in the ancients only prepares us for actual knowing, dialectic with its negativity becomes the heart of knowing. The consequence of this is that the Hegelian method is simultaneously a system and a language with its own grammar and vocabulary—a language which is simultaneously a world-forming or cosmos-forming process.[22] Descartes had proposed an analytic-synthetic method in which the synthetic method is the reverse of the analytic method, in which the analytic arm of the method starts from the individual and proceeds to the universal, while the synthetic arm proceeds from this universal back to a new explication of the individual; but Hegel raises this method to a dialectical status by transcending Descartes' limitation of the method to the physical sciences.[23]

Hegel's greatest innovation here is to have developed a new doctrine of contradiction and negativity. For the ancients, contradiction is a proof of worthlessness, but it is precisely "the propulsive force of contradiction" that underlies the Hegelian method-system-language and that necessitates both "objectification in the world and alienation of the self," not with the lifeless necessity of a mathematico-deductive system but with a species of necessity characteristic of ideas that live in history and are more living as they are more various in their aspects.[24] Propelled by contradiction, the Hegelian method necessarily "involves a triplicity of stages," for it is only through a triad of syllogisms that a "whole is thoroughly understood in its organization." A triad of being-in-itself or capacity, being-for-itself or negativity, and being-in-and-for-itself or actuality permeates reality itself, in such a way that each member of the triad is a "notional deepening of what has gone before," with the higher containing the lower *explicitly* and the lower containing the higher *implicitly*, with the lower more abstract, and the higher more concrete, and the whole movement taking us from an abstract beginning to a concrete term.[25]

But, in being triadic, the whole process is a development in time where the past is the negated, the present is the negating, and the future is the negation of negation. The negated elements are preserved as reference points for all future activity; the triadic dialectical development—in being a "synthesis or totality which unites thesis or identity with antithesis or negativity"—is propelled by negation, by a "surge towards the future, which negates the now," and that catapults ideas toward new goals that they must first anticipate hypothetically. Ideas are "far less abstractive than prospective" and not only fix what is already known but also maintain an outlook for new and unknown connections.[26]

The temporal character of the Hegelian dialectic will thus be a reflection of the emphasis Christianity places on time and historicity, and the Christian mystical ascent from the senses to contemplation will be a model for a transition in the Hegelian method from "an initial stage of positiveness and stability, characteristic of the understanding, through a stage of contradictory sceptical malaise, characteristic of dialectic proper," or negative reason, to a "stage of accommodation which will reinstate stability and positiveness at a higher level," or positive reason. The understanding "determines and holds the determinations fixed," while negative reason resolves "the determinations of the understanding into nothing," and positive reason "generates the universal and comprehends the particular therein." The dialectic of *Sein* ("pure unqualified, indeterminate being"), *Nichts* ("unqualified nothingness"), and *Werden* ("becoming"), which is operative in actuality, has as its expression in consciousness the dialectic of *Verstand* (the "abstract conceptualization" of understanding), *negative reason* (where opposition is in the process of being overcome), and *positive reason* (where opposition is overcome as the identity of opposites, the "identity of content and form," the identity of universal and particular, and where the "content produces its form from itself").[27]

In Kant, reason or *Vernunft* is the power of understanding the connection between the general and particular, so that *Verstand* is thought in finite relations, whereas *Vernunft* is thought which makes the unconditioned its object. But *Vernunft* never applies itself directly to experience, instead limiting itself to guaranteeing completeness in the use of the understanding in the system of experience, with the result that, as Hegel puts it, "theoretic reason spins cobwebs of the brain" for Kant and "practical reason has to allow its reality to come to an end with its postulates." Kant raised the thinking of contradictions to "a necessary activity of reason," but by "refusing any dialectical character to truth" itself, he fails to evaluate the contradictoriness of reason "positively" and, instead, raises the "ought," which Hegel says is only "the standpoint which clings to finitude," to the highest point.[28] For Hegel, on the contrary, dialectic and contradictoriness enter the heart of truth and being, and reason becomes more than an infinite aspiration—it becomes the power of infinity to actualize itself in reality.

Thus we have the Hegelian project and the method by which it is to be executed; we must now begin the arduous journey of traveling with Hegel the course of its execution from *logos* to *natura* to *Geist* (as each of these shows forth the transition from *being* to *nothing* to *becoming,* which is in turn plotted by the transition from *understanding* to *negative reason* to *positive reason*).

3. HEGEL'S LOGIC AND ITS METHOD

a. Introduction

In the Hegelian sense, logic is the study of *Logos* or the Word of God, since thinking itself in its highest and most comprehensive sense is for Hegel the "Word of God rendered entirely accessible to man." Such a claim implies that the development of God in Himself has the same logical necessity as that of the universe, and that although logic is the abstract beginning, this abstraction as such is not man's work but the work of Spirit itself that, by thinking itself through as *logos*, "logicizes the whole of being" and thereby "acquires the significance which the *logos* had possessed for Greek philosophy."[29]

The Greek *logos* entailed an at-oneness of thought and language, and Hegel too presumes that "language leads us to logic because in logic the categories naturally at work in language are focused on as such," so that "language thus reaches its perfection in the idea of logic, since in the latter thinking goes through all the determinations of thought occurring within itself and operating in the natural logic of language." The forms of thought are thus in the "first instance, displayed and stored in human language," and into "all that becomes something inward for man," into "all that he makes his own, language has penetrated." As the explication of the natural logic of language, logic is the "anatomy of un-embodied, bare intelligibility, pure relational possibilities, and therefore of being itself," the "realm of shadows, the world of simple essentialities freed from all sensuous concreteness." But this shadowy realm "is the absolute culture and discipline of consciousness" and is therefore unassailable and certain in treating the concrete objects of philosophy in their complete abstraction as thought-types. As the "science of the pure idea," logic is "pure knowledge in the entire range of its development," the first manifestation of the "thinking of thinking," and thus is the first "exposition of what alone can be the true method of philosophical science" in its necessary development, the first exposition of the spiritual hierarchy of all the sciences.[30]

In the beginning Hegel must be first a logician who reduces philosophy to logic in order to attain a spiritualization of logic, but this logic is not "the science of the mere form of thought"; rather, it aims at "a return to a fullness of being from a completely emptied being," at a "making explicit of what had been made implicit at the start," so that logic is coincident with metaphysics insofar as it deals with "thoughts accredited able to express the essential reality of things." By including metaphysics in logic,

Hegel can cite Kant as his predecessor, even though Kant ultimately posed a threat to the spiritual significance of logic by the
unknowability of the noumenon. Logic, however, is not the totality of all determinations of thought but simply the *dimension*
that "underlies all posited determinations of thought," so that
logic must focus on "thought drawn out of its immediate unity
with oneself."[31]

Cusa had seen that Aristotle's logic, by being a logic of the
finite, with all its categories resting upon the union of the equal
and the similar and upon the separation of the unequal and different, was hopelessly at odds with the Christian experience of
the world. Bruno, too, had rejected the Aristotelian logic in which
every determination is fixed once and for all. Following their cue,
Hegel claims that Aristotle and the ancients had defined thought
only in its "finite applications and aspects" in their logic and had
failed to recognize "contradiction to be as essential and immanent
a determination of things as is identity."[32] To do justice to the
infinite, Hegel saw, would require that logic attempt to comprehend "what it could mean to approach God," that logic attempt
"to think the thoughts of God after Him." Logic must attempt
to assume the standpoint of "God as He is in His eternal essence
before the creation of nature and of finite spirit." It must try to
understand eternity or how "it was before the times of the creation
of this world," yet it must make this attempt in anticipation of
God's destiny as the God of Creation and, ultimately, of the Incarnation. It is thus the "Hebraic God, that is, religiously absolutized patriarchal intelligence, who is being articulated in Hegel's
Logic," but in anticipation of the Creative Logos articulated in
the philosophy of nature, and the Holy Spirit reconciling God to
man, or the *Logos* which is to be Incarnate, articulated in the
philosophy of Spirit. Hegel is thus reminiscent of Rousseau who
assumes the standpoint of divinity in order to see his true self, but
Hegel attempts to assume this standpoint of a "reality prior to
reality" *not* as identical with his own but as a *cosmic* perspective
that itself presupposes, unlike Rousseau's situation, language in
which thinking has its own abode. God alone "has the absolutely
undisputed right," Hegel says, "that the beginning be made with
him," and it is in this sense that thought must begin with God

in His "emptiness," an emptiness that is "as such the beginning of philosophy."[33]

Like his overall philosophy or method, Hegel's logic has a triadic structure. The first moment is "the doctrine of *being*, which is said to be a theory of thought in its immediacy, of the notion implicit or in-itself," where there "is no diremption into distinct levels, and where all is straightforward and on the surface," where all is immediacy, the presuppositionless, the "zero case of categorization." The second moment is "the doctrine of *essence*, which studies thought in its reflection or mediation, where the deeper being-for-self of the notion is opposed to its surface show," where mediation by another occurs, and where being is regarded as on the way to full disclosure. The third moment is the "doctrine of *notion* which is said to be a study of thought returning to self, and its developed being-by-self," where being in its opposite remains identical with itself, and in that way mediates itself, so that it is the synthesis of being (immediacy) and essence (mediation), the "fulfilled case of categorization, where thought categorizes itself as having enclosed all determination." In this dialectic, essence constitutes the mean and transition from being into notion, so that essence is the outcome of being, and the notion the outcome of essence, but in such a way that the notion is the unity of being and essence. Essence that was "the first negation of being, which has thereby become illusory being," is negated in the notion that, as the negation of the negation found in essence, thereby proves to be "being once more, but being that has been restored to the infinite mediation and negativity of being within itself."[34]

b. The Beginning

Hegel's logic begins with "absolute abstraction," the "characterless," the "unutterable, the inconceivable," the "immediate in general," which (as "abstraction of reference to self," where "there is yet no other," except "pure naught") is "the beginning," a beginning of "immediacy itself." For it lies in the nature of "beginning that it must be being and nothing else," a "completely empty being" that amounts to the "being of beginning" or the "beginning of being." The beginning is made with the absolute, but because "the absolute is at first only in itself, it equally is not the absolute," or is God as an "abstract absolute" who is "the eternal beginning and remains so eternally," but that as beginning is "absolute indifference" and not "the absolute grasped as actuality."[35]

But, if being in its beginning is an empty absolute, it can as beginning be only and merely thought, so that the problem of the beginning of being is precisely the problem of the beginning of intelligibility, or a positing of "being in non-being," since if this positing is absent, and "the absolute separateness of being from nothing" is presupposed, then beginning or for that matter becoming is incomprehensible, as it was for the Greeks who knew nothing of either a beginning of being or of intelligibility. For them, neither the activity of "the ruler nor of the artificer brings anything into being," but simply "weds a form which is eternal to a matter which is given." This act of positing being implies that being in its initial presentation is identical to nothingness, and so the positing of being must refute itself and disclose that being is not only being but nothingness as well, necessitating that being in its immediacy must yield to dialectic and "sink into its opposite, which also taken immediately is nothing."[36]

Like Kant's Copernican hypothesis, the positing act of the knower (with Hegel it is the Divine Knower and not just the human) must be paradigmatic; and as with Cusa, God is presented as "God originating being, not as being who is and then originates other beings of a lower degree." But this originating being, for Hegel, is "nothing, pure nothing," simple "equality with itself," "empty intuition and thought itself," which discloses that nothing is thought of and therefore it is; but it also discloses that being as nothingness is not, however, an existence already *there* outside of thought, but *is* only as a pure thought. The result is that, as with Descartes, pure being is pure thought; but in Hegel, the consequence of this is drawn: pure thought is the same as nothing or *Nichts*. Thought must, consequently, "be an 'other' to being in its fullness insofar as it thinks Being in its emptiness, or as a beginning." Thought is an exhaustive negativity that is the emptying process of being itself; it is the disclosure of the identification of being and nothing at the beginning, the revelation of "a nothing from which something is to proceed," that is, a beginning of a being that eventually removes itself from non-being, sublates it as something opposed to it.[37]

The beginning of logic and the beginning of being are possible only by thought that "is itself and its non-being, and is only itself, in that it is the negative of itself," so that consciousness, far from being "a determinate *Dasein*," is something that goes beyond itself, is always, in fact, beyond itself. The result is that a "transcendental requirement constitutes the nature of consciousness as such," and consciousness betrays the fundamental character of its nature as that of "already being something which all the same it is not yet." For to be conscious means to be in motion, on the way, from an "already" to a "not-yet"—to be conscious means to be the "structure of the absence of essence." Negativity can exist only for thought but thought *really* exists. It is, in fact, Anselm's Ontological Argument, "wherein are identified the process of thought and the process of reality," which becomes the paradigm of Hegel's logic.[38]

Unknown to the ancients, the Ontological Argument, as Hegel sees it, "starts from the notion or conception of God and goes from this to being," so that "being becomes predicate, and the absolute Idea is first of all established as subject, but the subject of thought." The "being of God is immediately and inseparably bound up with the thought of God," for it "lies in the very nature of thought and subjectivity to be inseparable from being and objectivity." It is this "conversion of the absolute concept into existence," Hegel says, that "has constituted the depth of the idea in the modern world." Its importance is not that the argument consists simply in an abstract passage "from a formal concept to reality" but that it presents the realization that "the fully developed concept *is* reality." As St. Anselm says, "no one who understands that which God is, is able to conceive that God does not exist," and "that than which a greater cannot be conceived is not able to be thought not to exist." Phrasing the argument in the negative, Anselm implies that "in so far as a negative existential proposition seems to be about the very object or objects denied existence, it presupposes their existence," and in the case of God the inconceivability of His nonexistence entails the unity of thought and of existence in the infinite.[39] Being as the beginning of logic, then, in its very emptiness, entails, for Hegel, the identity of thought and being as the true beginning, and it is this identity, posited initially as empty (or nothingness) that will be filled out by the two remaining moments of the logic.

If with being "everything is immediate," it follows that in the second moment of the logic, namely, essence, "everything is relative"; for to be out-of-relation is "reserved for essenceless indeterminate being." The German word for essence (*Wesen*), Hegel tells us, is derived from the past participle of the verb "to be" (*sein*); and so essence is an "accomplished being" where the past is not utterly denied but only laid aside and thus at the same time preserved. It is the moment when "knowing inwardizes, recollects itself out of immediate being" and becomes being "reflecting light into itself." Essence is thus the moment when being passes over into appearance, which can only happen as sublated being or the absolute negativity of being, where being preserves itself in essence by virtue of the fact that "negativity is equal with itself." Essence is thus the realm where contradiction is seen to create being, where there ensues a real conflict between being and non-being, where "contradiction is the root of all movement" and "makes something out of nothing."[40]

Where Spinoza formulated the principle that "all determination is negation," Hegel proposes that "all negation is determination" and applies this new principle to the realm of essence by arguing that "being reduplicates itself in such a way that appearance is just as necessary to essence as essence is to appearance." Whatever appears, so long as it really does appear, is real, and this appearance or showing or shining is the characteristic by which essence is distinguished from being. Essence is thus "not something beyond or behind appearance," but just because it is the essence which exists, the existence of that essence is appearance, since "the essence of essence is to manifest itself."[41]

Hegel points out that the word for negating, *aufheben,* means both "to cancel out or annul" and "to preserve or save or store up," and this double usage of language is not an accident, for in the realm of essence "to put a thing aside" is not "to have done with it" but to "keep and preserve it." Essence is the realm of contradiction where being is negated and yet preserved; but since negation arises out of consciousness, and consciousness comes into its own in man, if meaning is to begin in essence, "then the beginning of human-ness is of crucial importance in so much as it would account for the appearance on the scene (or presence in being) of the negative." The moment of essence discloses that the meaning of the negative must somehow be grounded in the being of man, that the "I" of human self-consciousness is not properly speaking a being but is "what for itself negates itself and for itself preserves itself in that self-negation." Man is thus the concept detached from being or, better yet, the "act of detaching the concept from being." Man is the being who "never is what it is and always is what it is not," so that the human ego is the "night of disappearing," and the sense in which essence is the war of being and nothing is precisely the sense in which man is "at war against himself." And as that which first makes essence possible, man is the first point where being comes into its truth.[42]

But if being is sheer immediacy, and essence sheer relationality, if being is empty unity, and essence the conflict of being and nothing as appearance, then the absolute truth of being and essence, the "ground to which the regress of both leads," is the *notion* or the third moment of the logic which "demonstrates itself to be what is mediated by and with itself," that which "in passing outwards into its opposite passes only into itself." The notion is "that absolute unity of being and reflection in which being is in and for itself only in so far as it is no less reflection or positedness, and positedness is no less being that is in and for itself." In the notion "identity has developed into universality, difference into particularity," and opposition into individuality; and the movement from universality to particularity to individuality is becoming or *Werden,* which proves that it is "the dialectical immanent nature of being and nothing" to manifest their unity as their truth.[43]

Becoming contains being and nothing as two unities, "each of which is itself a unity of being and nothing," so that becoming is a double determination in which on the one hand "*nothing* is immediate, that is, the determination starts from nothing which relates itself to being," and this is "coming to be"; and on the other hand, "*being* is immediate, that is, the determination starts from being which changes into nothing," and this is "ceasing-to-be." In becoming, being and nothing have ceased to exist as opposite abstractions and now exist in absorption, in solution, so that becoming is a "being which does not lose itself in nothing." If "the immediate indeterminate being of the beginning (*Sein*) is the result of the most exhaustive abstraction (*Nichts*), then the structure of concrete being must result from their re-combination (*Werden*)," which is the identity of identity and non-identity.[44]

The process, here, is foreshadowed by Kant's notion of synthetic a priori judgments as "an identity which is in its own self an inseparable difference." If the movement of the notion is becoming, this movement is a victory of being over not-being, prefigured by the Christian doctrine of Creation, for although essence is not possible without man, yet it is not man who frames the notion, since the notion is mediated through itself and with itself. The situation is recognized by religion when it says that God created the world out of nothing by a "free creative activity which can realize itself without the help of a matter that exists outside of it." The "absolute notion" is in fact none other than the notion of God, not the empty God of the first moment, but the full reference to self, by which, as Anselm said, "all things were created from nothing and are preserved from nothingness." It is now that Being which is first intimated in the Book of Genesis as the primal overcoming of nothingness, the separator of light from darkness.[45]

The victory of being over nothing in becoming presents itself as pure change by which in striving to maintain themselves, things struggle to overcome their negation. "To be perfect is to have changed often" is an insight endemic to modernity, which no longer looks upon change as a fall from grace, or an imperfection of being, but as what Hegel would conceive as "an accumulation or enrichment of content, made possible by the continuity of negative activity" or the negation of negation found in the notion. The absolute, having transited from sheer immediacy to the status of appearance in essence, thus discloses itself in the notion as the principle that to be is to become. But the vanishing of being and nothing in becoming must finally prove itself to be "the vanishing of becoming or the vanishing of the vanishing itself," so that becoming will be "an unstable unrest which settles into a stable result," so that the "changing of the changeable is the development of the permanent, of the subsisting-in-and-for-itself."[46]

Aristotle had said that "the becoming of becoming" cannot be becoming itself, implying that becoming can be intelligible only in terms of that which does not become, but Hegel argues that the permanent can be intelligible only in terms of becoming, that is, that the becoming of becoming is a becoming that has become and that holds becoming at the very center of its having become. This determinate being or *Dasein* is the individuality or concrete universality that is the term of the development of the notion, an individuality that is not to be understood as the immediate or natural individual but rather as the individual expressly put as a totality, the grounded-ground or concrete reality as a whole in which "each of its constituent functions is the very total which the notion is." It is this totality, or concrete universality, which is the fully developed notion, the infinite in and for itself, which is a consummation and not a pregiven absolute, since it exists only in having transcended limitation, its otherness, as the infinite return into itself. This infinite totality is the absolute divine notion itself by which the things in the world have their subsistence.[47]

The triadic development of the logic, in other words, is the triadic development of the absolute into the fullness of its notion, yielding the notion of cosmos or totality as the truth of the absolute, that is, as the truth of the Christian God who becomes what He is, who is not simply pregiven as what He is. All that Hegel has said thus far in the logic is thus a philosophical explication in abstract terms of the becoming of the Christian God, that is, of the Blessed Trinity, and we must in conclusion to our consideration of Hegel's logic lay bare this explication.

c. Trinitarian Prefigurations

If his logic attempts to comprehend the thoughts of God before creation, it is attempting to grasp the truth of the pre-wordly Trinity, and not merely a God who is only for the first time realized in His creation. For Hegel, the Divine Life is necessarily Trinitarian, produced by the notion, as Augustine put it, that the Godhead itself is "ineffably and inseparably a Trinity" from all eternity "differentiated into the three persons." And it is not Deism, which is "merely the mode in which the understanding thinks God," but Christianity with its Trinitarian God that "contains the rational notion of God."[48] Jacob Boehme, the sixteenth-century mystic whose thought influenced Hegel, held that the Trinity depicts "motion" in God, and Athenagoras, an early Greek Father of the Church, spoke of the Holy Spirit as "an affluence of God, flowing from Him, and returning back again," a kind of self-realization in God. Marius Victorinus, another early Christian thinker, visualized God "as in a continuous process of unfolding and refolding in which the unknowable reveals itself in the Son as image, and in the Spirit the same Godhead knows itself, and so returns back to itself." Hegel, therefore, stands on very orthodox ground when he pictures the Trinity in such a way that the "universal goes out of itself, undergoes self-diremption and engenders the particular." That is: the Father begets the Son before all ages, while the particular nevertheless returns to unity with the universal in the common life of the Holy Spirit. The Fathers of the Church held tenaciously to the real distinctions between the members of the Trinity, which enabled them to conclude that God's unity is not absolute but relative, that God was not to be considered as absolutely alone, that there was a mutual *perichoresis* or interpenetration of persons in God. St. Anselm maintained that "what each is separately, this is all the Trinity at once," for "each separately is none other than the supremely simple unity" that cannot be multiplied. And now Hegel contends that as God is undividedly one and yet three persons, so the notion, although it contains three moments, is yet one undivided notion, for each moment is the entire notion.[49]

Echoing the words of Marius Victorinus who held that the "Son is the form through which the Father defines Himself," and the words of St. Anselm who spoke of the Son as the "knowledge" of the "paternal substance," as the "knowledge of knowledge," Hegel proposes that in "the Son, the Father knows himself," and "The Son is 'I' or self-consciousness," so that the Trinity consists of the essence, of the self-conscious being that knows this essence, and of the knowledge of the former in the latter.[50]

Whereas, as found in Christian tradition, the relationship be-

tween the Father and the Son is that of generation and is a relationship or metaphor taken from vital nature, so that the Son
proceeds by way of a likeness-producing operation, the relation
of the Holy Spirit with the Father and the Son is lifted out of the
natural order and is portrayed as "a product of reflection, an
hypostasized noumenon tacked on the natural family-picture of
father and son," as a "spiration" or breathing-forth. The effect
is that, strictly speaking, unlike the Father and the Son, the Holy
Spirit has no proper name but is a function of God that in being
hypostatized "rounds out the Three and restores the One"; or,
as the Lateran Council said in 1212, "the Father is of none, the
Son is of the Father alone, and the Holy Ghost is of both
equally."[51]

The result is that the Trinity includes what is by nature and
excludes what is by nature, includes negation and excludes negation, includes diremption *and* the restoration of unity, or what
Hegel would call the "negation of negation," the preservation of
particular determinations in unity. This is quite unlike the trinity
of the Hindus, where Siva as the third to Brahma and Vishnu is
only a "wild whirl of delirium." As developed in Christian tradition the Trinity, as an inclusion of difference within unity and
unity within difference, for all its mystical paradoxicality, has as
its primary thrust a fundamentally logical impetus, an interest in
intellectual consistency (although this is not to deny its genuinely
religious function). And in having this impetus, it implies, as
Hegel puts it, that "God exists only for the man who thinks, who
keeps within the quiet of his own mind." Because of this logical
thrust, the truth which receives its philosophical expression in
the Hegelian dialectic is no different from the truth which is articulated by religious imagery in the Christian doctrine of the
Trinity; and thus Hegel can say that to "prove" the "dogma of
the Trinity," this "silent mystery," this "eternal truth," is "the
whole of philosophy." The work of pure theoretical contemplation is to "become aware of the pure Idea of God, to comprehend
the mystery of the Trinity," a mystery that is "the axis on which
the history of the world turns," the "goal and the starting-point
of history."[52]

St. Augustine had said that "each and every nature has been

made by the Father through the Son, and in the gift of the Holy
Spirit," for everything has "these three perfections at once,"
namely, "it exists as a single something," its "own nature sets it
off from other beings," and "it does not deviate from the universal
order of things." St. Bonaventure suggested somewhat later that
the tripartite structure of philosophy that deals with "the cause
of being," the "principle of understanding," and the "order of
living" is simply a reflection of "the power of the Father," the
"wisdom of the Word," and the "goodness of the Holy Spirit."
Now, in keeping with them, Hegel speaks of the Father as the
"universal," the Son or the "other" of God as "infinite particularity, manifestation," and the Holy Spirit as concrete "individuality as such"—the three moments of the logic.[53]

It is the Blessed Trinity, furthermore, that lies concealed for
Hegel in the strands of prior modern philosophy. The full Cartesian *Cogito*—*Cogito ergo sum, ergo Deus est*—with its identity of
thought and being has the Trinity enshrined in it; and the Kantian
categories of modality—possibility, existence, and necessity—
have brought into notice the conception of the Trinity as the
"ground-plan" of thought even though only in an "outward
way." It is also true, of course, that this Trinitarian ground-plan
is missing in other equally significant moments of modern
thought; but in the end, if the conquest of modern dualism requires
an understanding of the reconciliation of divine transcendence and
immanence, it is only the doctrine of the Trinity that can effect
this reconciliation. For it is in this doctrine that we find the first
conception of the unity of the divine and the human, if only to
the extent that Mary, as the instrument of God's birth, became
involved in the Trinitarian drama as a human being, and thus is
to be regarded as a symbol of mankind's participation in the
Trinity.[54]

In the development of the doctrine of the Trinity in Christian
dogma, it was important that the *homoousia* (sameness of substance) formulation should triumph over the *homoiousia* (similarity
of substance) formulation, for otherwise the descent of the Holy
Ghost would not have permitted man to enter into a relationship
of unity with the substance of God. For Hegel the words of God
in Genesis must ultimately signify that man now *is* "one of us,"

and no longer merely *"like* one of us," and that through the
activity of the Holy Spirit "man as spiritual force is surreptitiously
included in the mystery of the Trinity." As Cyril of Alexandria,
an early Church Father, put it, the "Holy Spirit . . . operates in
us, truly sanctifying and uniting us to Himself and by conjoining
us with Himself makes us partakers of the Divine Nature." St.
Augustine said that "with a knowledge of this Trinity propor-
tioned to this life, we can see beyond the shadow of a doubt that
every intellectual, animate, and corporeal creature has its existence" and "its perfectly ordered career from the creative power
of this same Trinity." And Scotus Eriugena had seen that "all
things created by God are created in the image of God and are
therefore trinities consisting of essence, power, and operation,"
so that the doctrine of the Trinity is "the creative schema of the
universe." This schema is alluded to by Kepler, when he depicted
the created universe as an expression of the Creative Trinity. It
is in Hegel that this creative schema is restored to modern philosophy as the starting point of his completion of that philosophy;
this same creative schema will be further elaborated as the structure
of the remaining divisions of Hegel's philosophy: the *Naturphi-
losophie* and the *Geistesphilosophie.*[55] We must now examine the
externalization of *logos* as *natura,* that is, the philosophy of nature.

4. THE PHILOSOPHY OF NATURE

a. Introduction

As the raw material of self-conscious spirit, nature is the exact
antithesis of anything spiritual, the negative of logos, which, as
negative, is an abstraction, but an abstraction that is a real phase
in a real process and not just a mental abstraction. Unlike the
notion, nature cannot be self-posited, and so it must be the "self-
externality of the notion." Externality constitutes, therefore, "the
specific character in which nature, as nature, exists," so that nature
is "the result of intelligibility torn out of itself and hurled into
otherness." Nature is the logos in the form of other-being, where
differences "are allowed to fall apart and to appear as indifferent
to each other" because of the "externality in which the notion
chiefly exists in nature."[56] In nature there is "an impotence" to

"adhere strictly to the notion," and because of this, nature is the
finite, since the finite is what does not correspond to the notion.
This nature is not the *physis* of the Greeks but rather the *natura*
or created nature of the medievals. Hegel is operating with the
Christian notion of God as creating the world out of nothing, a
doctrine that implies that "matter, as such, has no independent
subsistence" and that nature is not "an unfolding of an impersonal
logos." This tradition implies that God's activity is not exhausted
in the theoretical contemplation of the forms but is extended to
the activity of embodying them.[57]

For the ancients, form and matter are eternal, and there can be
no "attribution to God of an omnipotent power over nature"; but
as soon as nature is conceived to be created by God, the contingent
"becomes more than an imperfection in the embodiment of form,"
since the activity of the Creator terminates on the contingent being
of the creature. And if such activity is essential to God, it follows
that the element of contingency is essential to what he creates. In
consistency with Christian doctrine, Hegel holds that this activity
of creation is essential to God, that "creating is the activity of the
absolute idea," and that a "God who could exist without the
world, without an external embodiment" is "God as an abstraction"; for God is a being who, as Anselm said, unlike man never
fails "to express what He conceives."[58]

As the Creator, Hegel says, God is found "in His specific character as the Logos, as the self-externalizing, self-expressing
Word," who, "when He lends existence to the passing stage of
his own show in Himself, may be described as the goodness that
creates a world." Nature as creation is "the idea in the form of
having been posited by Absolute Spirit as the opposite of Spirit,"
but its truth is the Creator Himself. Or, as Anselm put it, "whatever the supreme Substance created, it created through nothing
other than itself."[59] Although what is created is an "other and is
placed at first outside of God," Hegel says, "it belongs to God's
essential nature" to "reconcile to Himself this something which
is foreign to Him, this special or particular element which comes
into existence as something separate from Him." Although in
creation God "distinguishes Himself from Himself," and becomes
"an object for Himself," that is, "an other opposed to Himself"

(so that He is in a sense the "contradiction of Himself with Himself"), yet this separate "existence of the finite must in turn annul itself." For it is God's and must dissolve or cancel its own self and thus vanquish the otherness in God; so that God "maintains Himself for Himself as His own result" by coming to recognize Himself in this otherness.[60]

God both "works and rests," Augustine says, "both controlling and directing His Creation," and yet in "Himself having external repose," so that His rest is identical with his activity. Or, as Hegel would have it, God "in determining Himself remains equal to Himself," for His power is to remain "the self-same Spirit in its externalization." That is, God is what Hegel calls "an absolute movement which is at the same time rest, absolute rest."[61] It is thus of the essence of Creation that it takes place as a temporal counterpart or fulfillment of relations themselves eternal, which are found in the Trinity, and focused on the mediating term of the Trinity, the Logos. It follows, as Hegel says, that "God can be Creator in the true sense only in so far as He is subjectivity, for as such He is free" to be "the subject of the rational necessity which manifests itself in the world." And in creating (or externalizing Himself), and then reconciling Himself with His externalization, He becomes the God who has conquered contradictions. If the logic traces out the relations holding in the Trinity as being, essence, and notion, by focusing on the thoughts of God before Creation, that is, on the thoughts of God as the Father, then the philosophy of nature will trace out the relations holding in the Trinity, in its own dialectic, by focusing on the thoughts of God in the act of Creation, that is, on the thoughts of God as Son. The philosophy of nature will thus seek to answer the question of why and how God has come to create the world.[62]

b. Mechanics to Animality

The first moment of the triadic dialectic of *natura* is called "mechanics" and deals with "the determination of asunderness or mutual outsidedness," which is the stage of "matter and its ideal system," namely, space and time. The second moment is called "physics" and deals with "the determination of particularity," where reality "is posited with an immanent determinateness of form and with an existent difference in it," which is the stage of natural or merely physical individuality. The third moment is called "organics" and deals with "the determination of subjectivity, in which the real differences of form are also brought back to the ideal unity which has found itself and is for itself," and this is the stage of life, both vegetative and animal.[63]

In the first moment of the dialectic of natura all unities are local or spatial at best, and being is all matter where everything is external to everything. At this point, matter is looked upon, much as it was by Leibniz, as a revelation of the inability of substance to realize the entire spiritual character of reality, and thus as spirit apprehended in a confused, hesitating, and passive manner. Just as the logic began with the emptiest and most abstract thought, the philosophy of nature begins with empty space, which, like empty being, is destitute of all determination and differentiation. But space, like being, proves to be only this inner negation of itself, and so the self-sublating of space, which is time, proves to be the truth of space.[64] But time itself, as it is found in nature, is still sheer externality, only it is "the negative unity of self-externality" or of space, so that nature in the first moment of the dialectic proves to be spread out over the externalities of space and time. In space, everything is outside of every other thing; and in time, everything is outside of itself, in a vein similar to Augustine who conceived of time as the disquietude of a consciousness which has not attained itself, which sees its self as outside itself. Space is annihilated by time that causes space to "sink into the nothingness of the past" and that reveals time to be "the purely formal soul of nature."[65]

The first moment of natura, however, can only have its truth in the second, where the notion negates its universality as found in space and time and "projects itself into the externality of individuality." But this physical individuality "by itself does not correspond to its notion," and it is this "limitation of its existence which constitutes the finitude and ruin" of the physical individual; for this individual is merely the "negative unity of individuality" found in the individualization of matter.[66] When this physical individual becomes subject to chemical composition, all its particular properties are eventually brought to destruction; but this chemical composition is itself "an analogue of life," of the "inner restlessness of life," and it is only in the third moment of the dialectic of natura, namely, the organic moment, that the truth of the whole dialectic emerges. For here, in the organic, we are presented, for the first time, with subjectivity and the counter to the externality that dominates the first two moments. While the organic body is still a whole composed of many members external to each other, nevertheless each individual member of the organic individual "exists only in the subject, and the notion exists as the power over these members." The organic individual is the movement of its becoming, not unlike an incarnation and realization of a purely logical possibility.[67]

As for Leibniz before him, the category of life is dominant for Hegel, as it was with Aristotle; but unlike the Greeks, Hegel defines life as the first reflection into self, the initial presentation of subjectivity. And since this life is the truth of nature, insofar as it is the dialectical outcome of natura, Hegel is brought close to the notion of nature as permeated by process. But he does *not* conceive of an evolution from sheer matter to physical individuality to life, or even an evolution from species to species within life; for as he says, the "Mosaic story of creation is still the best." "Man has not developed himself out of the animal, nor the animal out of the plant." Unlike inanimate things, the plant "unfolds and develops itself" and "constitutes and preserves itself in this movement"; and unlike the plant that is still "submerged in the process of the mutually external parts" that make it up, there is in the animal "a duplication of subjectivity" that enables it to consciously preserve itself in its relation with the outer world. (This finds its manifestation in the animal's ability to oppose itself to its place, to rid itself of its place, even though it must posit its place afresh.) In human animal life, we no longer have merely the feeling of the animal but the ability of consciousness now to return some of its own intelligibility back into the world of nature by matter-modifying work.[68]

The living organism is "implicitly the other of itself," for "implicitly it is the universal or kind," and yet, immediately it exists as an individuality. Death emerges as what shows the kind or the universal to be "the power that rules the immediate individual," insofar as the living individual bears within it "the germ of death," containing a "disparity between its finitude and universality." Yet the living being, if it exists only insofar as it contains contradiction within itself, is nonetheless the power to hold and endure the contradiction within it. Although the living individual "proceeds to negation and its grief," it is the first place in nature where matter has become really intelligible; and nothing is alive which is not in some way or other idea. Like Leibniz, for whom life is reducible to the striving for the pure translucence of rationality, Hegel sees life as the breaking forth of rationality in nature, precisely insofar as life is the movement which reduces the other to itself and discovers itself in that other that it has within itself.[69]

Yet Hegel does not hold that rationality emerges from some blind development or evolution in life, for in the end, the kind of self-conscious rationality we find in man is something other than life, pure and simple; it is a new mode of being involving a break with nature. The gross subjectivity of the living organism, especially that of the animal, is "not yet for itself as pure universal subjectivity," is not aware of itself in thought, but (in the animal) only in feeling and intuition. Subjectivity, when it breaks with nature and becomes self-consciousness in man, will be that point at which "life becomes a conscious principle of negativity."[70]

It is, Hegel says, "from the idea of life that the idea of Spirit has issued," insofar as the "idea of Spirit has proved itself to be the truth of the idea of life." Nature is simply the "process of which the transition to Spirit is the ultimate truth," the process by which "Spirit proves itself to be the truth of nature." This is remarkably in keeping with St. Anselm's words, when he says that created things are ever in God, "not what they are in themselves, but what this Supreme Spirit Himself is." And it is not at all far from Leibniz for whom the final reason or source of matter is spirit. Hegel goes on to say that when "the last self-externality of nature has been sublated, and the notion, which in nature is present only in principle, has become for-itself," then "nature has passed over into its truth," that is, concrete universality, which is Spirit.[71]

Here is to be found the answer to the question of why God has come to create the world. God created nature *because* "Spirit wills

to achieve its own liberation by fashioning nature out of itself,"
that is, Spirit wills to relate itself to an outer world in order to
"raise its own implicit reality, this formal truth," explicated in the
logic, "into real truth." It is necessary that the spiritual distinguish
itself from the natural and that the severed life of the natural is
suppressed for the Spirit by its own act in order that Spirit "win
its way to concord again." Thus, the hand of Spirit which inflicts
this wound on itself is also the hand which heals it. Spirit must
other itself as nature in order to be explicitly what it is implicitly;
it is the bounty of Spirit "which gives to this opposite the whole
fulness of its own being," but as separated from itself, in order
to overcome this separation.[72]

God reveals Himself in two different ways," Hegel says, "as
nature and as Spirit," but whereas "nature never gets so far as to
be conscious of its divine essence," Spirit does, but it can do so
only by being the truth of nature. "Because Spirit is presaged in
nature," it attracts us, and because it "seems an alien existence in
which Spirit does not find itself," it repels us; and insofar as it is
both, nature confronts us as a riddle and a problem—precisely as
it confronts modern science. But the goal of the philosophy of
nature is the solution of the riddle, the realization that "Spirit finds
in nature its own essence, i.e., the notion," the comprehension,
as Boehme said, that the "abyss of nature and creation is God
Himself."[73]

"Above this death of nature, from this dead husk," Hegel says,
"proceeds a more beautiful nature, Spirit," for the "notion strives
to burst the shell of outer existence" or nature "and to become
for itself," so that it is "the essential character of nature to sacrifice
itself, to consume itself," as a "burnt offering" in order that the
notion which is enclosed in nature may break through its covering
and absorb this covering, and render this covering transparent,
and for the first time have itself revealed to view. Enclosed in
nature, "Spirit often seems to have forgotten and lost itself; but
inwardly opposed to itself, it is inwardly working ever forward,"
until, grown strong in itself, it consumes the envelope of its existence and does not merely pass into another envelope but comes
"forth exalted, glorified, a purer spirit," after having made war
upon itself.[74]

Natural consciousness thus works off its naturalness and becomes an absolute consciousness freed from any sort of givenness, and the "opaque essence of the universe does not contain any power which can withstand the force" of this absolute consciousness which is Spirit emergent from its enclosure in nature. If Scripture gives us two "beginnings," one in Genesis, the other in St. John, the one cosmological, the other theological, the first describes for Hegel the externalization of *logos as natura,* and the second describes that second creation which came to pass after the first, namely, Spirit's coming into its own out of natura, the mastery of nature not by physics, as in modern science, but by Spirit—a second creation that is begun in Christianity.[75]

As Descartes had held that man knows nature as a presentation of his rationality, Hegel now argues that nature is the complex of presuppositions that Spirit makes for itself. And because nature is this presupposition of Spirit, Spirit is the truth of nature; although nature is the first in point of time, Spirit is its "absolute *prius.*" Spirit as the termination, the "omega," proves to be the true "alpha"; Spirit must alienate itself in nature as its unconscious work; but, having emerged from this nature, it is ready to produce itself as the deeds and life of history, that is, to bring itself to pass with consciousness. But it can do its conscious work only after it has turned itself inside out in nature.[76]

Hegel's basic thesis, which proves to be the culmination of the philosophy of nature, that Spirit can only exist by returning to itself out of its embodiment, that exteriority or alienation is an essential stage in its realization, finds its representation in the Christian premise of original sin. For man's loss of innocence is descriptive of the necessary condition for the immersion of Spirit in its conscious work; man is created as the image of God, but this existence is only natural, and man can become spiritual only through rising above the natural. It is in the narrative of the Fall that Hegel finds, as he tells us, the "advance out of the merely natural life, and the necessity for the entrance of the consciousness of good and evil," which will enable man to be born a second time, spiritually, after having been born naturally, for the Fall is the "eternal mythus of man," the "very transition by which he becomes man."[77]

Just as Rousseau held that what is characteristically human is in no way the gift of nature but is the outcome of what man did in order to overcome nature, so also Hegel argues that man "creates his humanity only by negating himself as animal," for paradise is a "park where only brutes, not men, can remain." Man must make himself the negative of nature (which of itself merely is, unself-consciously) in order that truly human life can appear as of a different order and the necessary conditions for a history be posed. In this way, the "fall of man from God is necessarily also the fall of God into man," and God can say "Adam has become like one of us."[78] Whereas the animal is by nature what it ought to be and its "natural individuality is only a fleeting fact that cannot look back on itself," the doctrine of original sin teaches us that man is "not by nature this particular in which the Spirit of God lives and dwells," but that man "has the power of becoming explicitly what he only is implicitly." The doctrine implies that insofar as man "acts like a creature of nature, his whole behavior is what it ought not to be," that man as he is by nature is not what he ought to be before God. If life itself is the natural hearth of the universe, then it is man who is "the spiritual hearth of the universe," for it is by reason of his being Spirit, that man is man.[79]

c. Dialectic of the Master and the Slave

The import of the Fall is worked out in the dialectic of "master and slave." Man must rise above life, which is nonetheless the condition of his emergence, and by risking his life must free himself from enslavement to life. The master and slave are primarily aspects of human consciousness, and the slave is that aspect that prefers life to liberty but that, in knowing what it is to fear death *and* through labor, "shapes being-as-other, or the objective world, in the form of self-consciousness." The worker-slave finds himself in the product of his work and thus "becomes the master of his master," that is, of the objective world.[80]

Man thus "achieves his true autonomy, his authentic freedom, only after passing through slavery, after surmounting fear of death by work performed in the services of another (who, for him, is the incarnation of that fear)." It is this slavish consciousness that "realizes and reveals the ideal of autonomous self-consciousness and thus its truth." The human ideal born in the master can be realized only in and by slavery, and at its consummation slavery turns into the opposite of what it immediately is.[81]

The dialectic of master and slave reveals in course that if self-consciousness is to become true self-consciousness, then it must stand on its own and find another self-consciousness that is willing to be for-it. For self-consciousness is desire, but what it desires is itself; that is, it desires its own desire, and this is why "it will be able to attain itself only through finding another desire, another self-consciousness," in which it can lose itself and find itself as an other-being. But in doing so, it has superseded the other, since "it does not see the other as an essential being, but in the other sees its own self." The master and slave recognize themselves as mutually recognizing one another, and in this is created "spiritual life—the medium in which the subject is an object to itself, finding itself completely in the other yet doing so without abrogating the otherness that is essential to self-consciousness." It is, however, in work that self-consciousness becomes recognizable by others, that the spatial natural world is temporalized, that man is born and history begins, that the "I" is not merely natural self but the identity of the self with itself.[82]

Man's self-consciousness born in the master-slave dialectic is a break with naive and immediate life that in being so is forced into a reflection upon death, insofar as the slave puts off his death and works out his life by labor. In death is found the necessity of the transition from individuality into universality, but whereas in nature "death is an external negation, Spirit carries death within itself and gives it positive meaning" and makes death into the beginning of the life of the spirit. As long as there is no death within nature, there is no place for newness in the world, but with death appropriated by Spirit and transformed into the possibility of a regenerated life, there rises up a newness that can penetrate into being by taking the place of the being given by nature. As long as nature remains the final revelation of logos, as it does for the ancients, novelty can never be radical or unconditioned newness but merely a new combination of old elements.[83]
We are now at the point where we can begin the last leg of our

journey through the Hegelian system, the exploration of Hegel's philosophy of Spirit.

5. PHILOSOPHY OF SPIRIT

a. Introduction

In keeping with Anselm who said that God's being is "life itself" and with the Christian tradition in general which accentuated the living God by assigning the activity of spiration or breathing-forth to the Holy Spirit, Hegel conceives of *Geist* or Spirit as life itself. This life is a negation of the dying life of nature and thus proves to be the living unity of the dialectic of logos and nature.[84] It "exists only in so far as it brings itself out of itself"; it exists not as natural life but as the state of having been reborn, as "regenerate Spirit."[85] The process of being reborn is "the process in which Spirit becomes what it is in itself," the process by which it makes its actuality adequate to its notion, the process by which it raises itself to its truth. Only this "self-restoring sameness or this re-flection in otherness within itself," and not "an original or im-mediate unity as such," is the true absolute, so that Spirit exists only as a consummation in which it has made itself truly infinite. Beginning as "substance" or the "final unity of essence and being" articulated in the logic, the absolute now becomes Spirit or "sub-stance as subject"—the "self-determining, self-developing, self-articulating Holy Spirit" of Christianity.[86]

In developing itself from substance to subject, Spirit is in its every act only apprehending itself, exhausting its own possibili-ties, revealing "itself completely, going down into its uttermost depths and revealing those depths." The work of Spirit to know itself is none other than the life of the Spirit, for Spirit is the act of apprehending itself. The Christian God as Holy Spirit has con-sciousness only as self-consciousness and reveals that the nature of God as Spirit is to be "Himself the mediation of Himself with Himself."[87] The self-knowing of Spirit, the becoming determined of Spirit, is simultaneously a self-determining, so that in knowing itself Spirit produces itself, exists "only by being its own pro-ducer," making itself "its own deed, its own work." The Christian God "creates Himself within Himself"; this is the true Trinitarian import of the "genuinely synthetic progress" that Kant failed to see.[88]

But insofar as Spirit exists only as self-knowing and self-producing, it exists only "in so far as it manifests itself to itself," accomplishing "its manifestation in its own element, not in an alien material." Spirit is thus not "an essence that is already finished and complete before its manifestation, keeping itself aloof behind its host of appearances, but an essence which is truly actual only through the specific forms," as Hegel says, "of its necessary self-manifestation." Just as "the light of nature is neither something nor a thing, but its being is only its showing or shining," so manifestation for Spirit is self-identical with its absolute actuality. And this manifestation is a discourse in Spirit; or, as Anselm says, the Supreme Being is "nothing else than what its expression is." But to be this manifestation of Himself to Himself, it is necessary that God as Spirit transform the hidden unity of Himself into the other of Himself, in order to overcome the otherness of this other and return back again into Himself. For it is only by manifesting itself in its counterpart, in separating "something from itself in such a way that it relates it to itself," by "self-differentiation into mutually opposing forces, and by victory in and over these oppositions," that Spirit can be subjectivity and thus Spirit.[89]

Spirit, then, as Hegel says, is "nothing but a distinct mode of reducing what is external," namely, its creation of nature, "to the inwardness" of itself, and in this "assimilation of what is external," Spirit remains with itself and for itself in being manifested. Spirit thus proves itself to be infinite not in the sense of being spatially extended ad infinitum, as with the infinite universe of the early modern cosmologists, but in the sense of its being complete (bei-sich), being at home with itself, overcoming its own externalization, recognizing itself in everything that "from eternity has happened in heaven and earth." The "deeper the Spirit goes within itself, the more vehement is the opposition, the more abundant is the wealth without," for the depth is "to be measured by the greatness of the craving with which Spirit seeks to find itself in what lies outside of itself"; and to Spirit alone is it given to "impress the stamp of its own infinity and free return into itself upon its external manifestation."[90]

Spirit is then the "word of reconciliation" that "beholds the pure knowledge of itself" in its opposite, the "identity of identity and non-identity" in which unity exists only as an overcoming of opposition, in which self-accordance exists only because "Spirit is one in the diversity of all its phases," in which the "complexio oppositorum" or union of opposites, symbolized by the Holy Ghost, is to be found. Bruno's coinciding of contraries from which we infer that there are contraries within contraries, and Cusa's theory of the coincidence of opposites in which God is victorious over the opposition of otherness and nothing, in which God is not-other ("non-aliud") to the world and yet is not simply identical with it—these early modern mystical themes (with their medieval sources) are restored by Hegel on the web of a developed modern philosophy, thus elucidating the conditions for the very development of that web, in full cognizance that the "greater the opposition from which Spirit returns into itself, the greater is the Spirit." And the "highest truth, truth as such, is the resolution of the highest opposition and contradiction."[91]

The process by which Spirit struggles to come to itself, to come to unity, to overcome its externalization is, like the triadic development of *logos* and *natura,* grounded in the Trinitarian unfolding of God, but now with its focus, not in the thoughts of God before Creation, not in the thoughts of God in Creation, but in the thoughts of God as the Holy Spirit of reconciliation. In the first moment of the philosophy of Spirit, Spirit is pure self-relation, having "before it all that its notion contains," with its being self-contained and free, that is, *Subjective Spirit,* or Spirit operative in real individual human minds. In the second moment, Spirit realizes itself in a world produced and to be produced by it, that is, Spirit operative in institutional realities, *Objective Spirit.* In the third moment, there occurs the unity of Subjective and Objective Spirit, Spirit having fully attained reconcilation with its externalization, that is, *Absolute Spirit,* realized progressively in art, religion, and philosophy.[92]

b. Subjective Spirit

Kant's great success in articulating the great discovery of modern philosophy, namely, subjectivity, was nonetheless accompanied by a failure to recognize that infinity is not a static absence or denial of limitation but is the "passing beyond limitations, the self-determination of the finite to its truth." Infinity is "the absorption of the finite into its own fuller nature," so that it comes to be "at home with itself in its other." This coming-to-be-at-home with itself by the infinite in the finite was signified by the Incarnation, the birth of Christ, where, as Luther says in one of his hymns, "He whom all heavens' heaven ne'er contained lies now in Mary's womb"—that great turning point in history that stirred depths in the human soul that have not yet been fully discovered.[93]

In the Incarnation, the Divine, which is the depth of an infinity incommensurable with all things finite and human, has "become absolutely commensurate with human selfhood, so radically as to enter into actual human finitude and to suffer actual human death." Thus, it yields "an infinite finite, a finite whose reality is in the infinite," an event whereby human consciousness is given a perfectly free relationship to the infinite in the knowledge of the absolute infinitude of Spirit. This was a knowledge lacking to both Greek religion and Greek philosophy as well as to the Judaic "religion of sublimity" for which the world is sustained by a God who is alien to it, and for which the world is under God's mastery but has no part in God.[94] In the Incarnation, God is no longer the perfect self-sufficient sovereign lord of the universe, but is rather seen to be "dependent on his creation as the medium of his own development, a development which by taking place in the world can be comprehended by the philosopher." Yet Judaism, by depressing nature "to the condition of a mere creature," allows Spirit to occupy the first place. The "utter sublimity of God," as Hegel would have it, "without hope of any union with man, comes ultimately to be lived as pain," a pain that calls for the consolation of "Christian subjectivity," the consolation of the infinite spilling over and breaking out of the finite.[95]

St. Bonaventure had spoken of Christ as "a common speech between God and man," and Maximus the Confessor had said that in the Incarnation human nature has "penetrated through the whole of the divine nature, possessing thenceforward absolutely nothing that is detached or separated from the Deity which is hypostatically united" with it. Now, for Hegel, Christ is "the identity-within-difference" of the divine and human, the reconciliation of "the estrangement between the human and the divine," in which the divine and human natures are now implicitly one. And this unity appears as "seen and experienced in the world" as a certainty that is "universal for immediate consciousness"—not as an ideal humanity but as an individual subject immersed in "the temporal and complete externality of immediate and natural existence." So that, as St. Augustine said, "the sacred assumption of human nature" is no longer merely a matter of "faith believed in the light of the knowledge of the eternal immutability of the Trinity" but is concretely recognized "as fitting in with the mercy which the Supreme God shows to men."[96]

But if the Incarnation is a certitude, Hegel sees, then the propositions that it entails are certitudes; and chief among these propositions is "the infinite value of specific existence," that is, of individual or particular existence, of that "which will never reappear." The Incarnation "transvalues all of sensuous reality, which becomes more profound and reflects itself on itself for consciousness." That is, it "attributes absolute value to particularity, to the here and now," since Christians must believe themselves to be saved not merely by Christ's *teachings* but by the "spilling of his blood upon one particular square yard of ground, outside of one particular city gate during three particular unrepeatable hours."[97] For the ancients, the contingent and particular were found to represent only a defect of being, with the particularity of matter being only the source of the imperfection in the actualization of form. But for the Christian, the particularity of the nature of man, by virtue of the Incarnation, as Anselm said, is "exalted," and so exalted, as Hegel now says, that the "subjectivity which belongs to human nature" must exist in God Himself, so that the human, the finite, frailty, weakness, the negative become a divine moment in God Himself, requiring that the subjective element be "set up as if it were something objective." The Incarnation thus becomes the interpretation of the mind of God, the manifestation of the relationships existing in God, the disclosure of an eternity of fellowship of affection in God, and thus the disclosure of man's inclusion in this fellowship, the disclosure that "man has an infinite worth."[98]

The "right of the subject's particularity," first revealed in the Incarnation, "his right to be satisfied, or in other words the right of subjective freedom," Hegel tells us, is "the pivot and centre of the difference between antiquity and modern times." It has become "the effective principle of a new civilization" and is now the "principle of modern philosophy"; for the "grandeur of the standpoint of the modern world consists in this going down of the subject into itself whereby the finite knows itself to be the infinite and is yet hampered with the antithesis or opposition which it is forced to solve."[99]

In the Reformation, according to Hegel, this modern principle first presents itself as a place in the depths of man's inmost nature where alone he is "at home with himself and at home with God." Then, in Descartes, this principle becomes the subject matter of philosophy in the "affirmation that the truth of thought is to be found in the thinking," an affirmation that is transmuted by empiricism, especially Locke and Hume, into the principle that "man must see for himself and feel that he is present in every fact of knowledge which he has to accept." In Rousseau this affirmation is seen to entail "the sense that man has liberty in his spirit as the altogether absolute"; while in Kant, the principle assumes theoretical embodiment as a knowledge "aimed at freedom," which prepares the ground for "a great new creative movement" centered in "the doctrine of the absolute and infinite self, whose constructive processes shall explain the fundamental laws of the world."[100]

If modern philosophy is a working out of the particularistic implications of the Incarnation, which could not be known to the Greeks (who "knew neither God nor man in their true universality," who could not recognize that man as man was of infinite worth and had "infinite rights"), these implications necessitate that the particular, by "its reflection into itself," has "been equalized with the universal." The "principle of the self-subsistent inherently infinite personality of the individual" dawned in its inward form in the Incarnation, and this principle is not merely the bare-subject that manifests itself in the third moment (organics) of the philosophy of nature, but is the subject aware of its subjectivity, the unity in self-consciousness of "the wholly limitless with determinate limitation," which raises "the individual I to the human I" as a "concrete existence that is itself free."[101]

The first moment of the philosophy of Spirit thus makes clear that the world of created nature no longer can be construed as that which subsists in itself but only as that which subsists in relation to self-consciousness, which is its truth, and that modern philosophy sees as its truth. But if the first moment of the philosophy of Spirit has shown that God, as Idea, is "subjective for what is objective," the second moment of this philosophy will show that God is "objective for what is subjective." For when Subjective Spirit passes over into Objective Spirit, it comes to know "that its subjectivity, in its truth, constitutes absolute objectivity itself," and in so knowing it brings itself forth "as an outwardly existent world of freedom." This world is *not* the world of nature (which is found already existing by Spirit, and from which Spirit is engaged in liberating its notion) but a "world which Spirit creates for itself in order to become objective." This is the world of institutions and is ultimately the whole of human history.[102]

c. Objective Spirit

As Objective Spirit, Spirit is universal self-consciousness, or the movement of the community as self-consciousness, the "I which is we and the we which is I." It is attained not, as with the Greeks, as an intuitive sense of belonging to a community, but is achieved by the moderns "at the cost of a great deal of intellectual effort." As such, this Objective Spirit is the truth of Subjective Spirit, for the "right of individuals to be subjectively destined to freedom is fulfilled when they belong to an actual ethical order, because their conviction of their freedom finds truth in such an objective order."[103] Just as Subjective Spirit had as its condition the Incarnation, the second moment, Objective Spirit, can begin only "when the Incarnation shifts into the past, when its present reality becomes a matter of memory or tradition," that is, when the "dead divine Man or Human God" permits the "coming into existence of God's individual self-consciousness as a universal self-consciousness or as the religious community"—which is to say that the condition of Objective Spirit is the Resurrection that proves Christ's death to be "only the death of death."[104]

The "sensuous and present form" of Christ must be taken up to "the right hand of the Father" (or as Anselm put it, the Son of God must "give his humanity to his divinity"), so that the redemption begun in Christ could be completed in the Holy Spirit by being effected in a community of persons. But if universal self-consciousness begins in the community of Christian believers, it is in the state, that is, the modern nation state, where Objective Spirit finds "its substantive rationality" as the "absolute power on earth." For in the state we have the unity of universal and particular where the interest of the whole is realized in and through particular ends, in such a way that the stictly particular, personal, individual value of each member is recognized by all members. Hegel calls the state "a hieroglyph of the reason which reveals itself in actuality" that has to be "deciphered through a discarding of the accidental and arbitrary" structures of the modern state. When deciphered, it proves that the principle that makes the state the realization of the Christian community is the state's realization of a subjective practical activity or an activity of will that secures the freedom of the subject and gives to the modern principle of the *I will* its appropriate objective existence.[105] The "philosophic proof" of this concept of the state for Hegel is the development of ethical life from its immediate phase in the family where "altruism is limited and particular and does not apply to all and sundry," through a phase of "civil society" or division where "universal egoism" reigns, to the true ground of these phases in "universal altruism" or the "self-conscious ethical substance" of the state. This self-conscious ethical substance works itself out first in the immediate actuality of an individual self-dependent state, then in the relation of one state to other states, or "international law," and finally it gives itself its actuality in the process of world history, and makes world history possible by presenting the subject-matter of such history.[106]

In the second verse of the first chapter of the Book of Genesis, it is said that "the Spirit of God was moving *over* the face of the waters," but in regard to world history, Hegel says, Spirit does not merely brood over it "as over the waters but lives in it and is alone its principle of movement," its fullness, the composer of its events. For Hegel, not only does it make no sense to see reason only in nature and not in history, but nature is only the immediate becoming of Spirit, a "slumbering spirit," that awakens to self-consciousness in world history, in obedience to the absolute command of Spirit to "Know thyself." For world history is the conscious labor that Spirit engages in over some two thousand years in order to attain "a higher consciousness about its thinking and about its own pure essential nature"; this entails that at the summit of the moment of Objective Spirit, Spirit has "become the human subject creating its history, who no longer has the universal outside himself, who is no longer opposed to the universe, but who bears it and absorbs it in himself."[107]

In world history, as Hegel says, the Spirit requires "the complex of human passions" as the woof for its own notion, which is the warp of the "vast arras-web of universal history." The eternity of God, as Anselm had said, contains "even the ages of time themselves." Whereas for the Greeks, history is experienced as a degenerescence with no event occurring once and for all as an indispensable reference point enabling them to give a single irreversible direction to the course of history, the medievals, by virtue of the reference point of the Incarnation and the irrepeatability of the drama of Golgotha, can see history as a "trames recti itineris," a straight line within which Divine Redemption is given and man is educated in that redemption; time comes to have significance for Christianity, Hegel sees, precisely as history, where it is no longer the negative externality found in the philosophy of nature.[108]

For this reason, the course of history "does not show us the becoming of things foreign to us, but the becoming of ourselves and of our knowledge," for it is man, who is "what he is only to the extent that he becomes what he is," who has his true being in history. Thus, the negativity that the logic saw as having its home in man is now seen to have its home in history, since history exists only by action that negates the given of nature. On the other hand, history is equally the course of God coming to his realization as Spirit, the changeless offering itself to becoming, *becoming the mutable,* and receiving new determination, so that history is just as much God's becoming as it is man's. As the becoming of God that is coeval with the becoming of man, world history unites the objective with the subjective, that is, it includes not only what has happened but the narration of what has happened. World history, properly understood, is not just what has happened to man but man's *appropriation* of what has happened and what he has done.[109]

Because of this, human speech is inseparable from the being of history, and the very language-forming process is a historical world-forming process. Because language is "self-consciousness existing for others," it makes history possible, while at the same time presuming history as its ground.[110] But since this history is also the very becoming of God, it follows that God's becoming in history has for its necessary presupposition human discourse as participating in the shaping of history, so that the Word of God or the Logos that has externalized itself in nature, and which now as Spirit returns to itself by entering human history, is a Word which by becoming Spirit requires the human word for its unfolding.

The way to truth of the Hegelian dialectic in logic now discloses itself as a historical process, for man must make the world his own doing if he is to recognize himself for what he truly is; but this doing is at once a knowing, so that the energies of reason are not simply operative as a schematism in individual consciousness, as Kant argued, but are operative as *Weltgeist* or world-spirit, beneath the becoming of being, that is, beneath history. As a result, the Hegelian inclusion of metaphysics in logic is now seen to yield a final transformation of history into ontology, with history conceived metaphysically and metaphysics conceived historically.[111] As at once the articulation of being and the becoming of intelligibility, history is a continuous process of canceling out or annulling the past and yet at the same time preserving its essential in a higher synthesis, in which the "grades which Spirit seems to have left behind it, it still possesses in the depths of its present." This process requires that the truth of history "can only be where it makes itself its own result," so that it requires error as a necessary dynamic element for itself, requires that human discourse preserve error in the very heart of reality in order that every truth emerge as an error that has been corrected. Spirit as Objective Spirit is the living, actual process of overcoming errors made by man in the heart of the becoming of being that is history.[112]

In presenting history as the modern ontology and epistemology, Hegel's primary source is Christianity from which that most un-Greek idea of explaining a thing by its temporal history is derived. But he does have some precedent in modern philosophy. Hume had spoken of history as the great mistress of wisdom, and Hegel notes that Hume's notion of custom is a kind of necessity in shared self-consciousness. The Enlightenment had connected the idea of freedom with the world's history; Rousseau in the *Émile* had argued that the individual's development summarily repeats the development of the species, and thus provided Hegel with a kind of preliminary history of natural consciousness. And of course Kant, especially in his "Idea for a Universal History," is much closer to Hegel than is commonly supposed, although he never elevates historical progress to the rank of a pure idea of reason.[113] But in the end it is Hegel who accomplishes an ontologization of history for modernity, for just as the Greeks had taught that logos or *nous* was the ground of nature in spite of the disorder and irrationality of the sublunar world, it is Hegel alone who now teaches us that reason can be discovered in history despite the contradictoriness and erratic character it seems to display. For just as modern physical science has treated nature as a riddle to be solved, Hegel presents history as a riddle to be solved, arguing, in fact, that it is the riddle of history and not of nature that modernity is ultimately about.[114]

The "history of the world," Hegel says, is the "true *Theodicea*, the justification of God in history"; for what "has happened, and is happening every day, is not only not 'without God' but is essentially His Work," since the plan of Providence is at work in and will be realized in history, and this history will prove to be the "process by which mankind assimilates the significance of the Resurrection of Christ" that is the condition for Objective Spirit. Like St. Augustine before him who said that "by the decession and succession of things the beauty of the ages is woven," and who wondered who "would not be moved to faith by so remarkable an order of events" by which Divine Providence counsels "the entire human race in common," Hegel sees Divine Providence as the ultimate design of a cosmos that is historical. But this Providence, Hegel tells us, stands to this cosmos "in the capacity of absolute cunning"; for "God lets men do as they please with their particular passions and interests"; but the result is "the accomplishment of, not their plans, but His," yet in such a way that the necessity of His Providence is transfigured into freedom. And so the freedom that man progressively attains in history contains this providential necessity "as an unsubstantial element in itself." In this way, the truth of the necessity of Divine Providence is the realization of the freedom of man in history. Thus, for Hegel, in contrast to the Enlightenment, there is no notion of progress in history as an autonomous human creation free from divine will or direction, precisely because history is simultaneously the becoming of God and man.[115]

In its adherents, Christianity has realized "an ever present sense that they are not and cannot be slaves," and this will to liberty is no longer merely an impulse that demands its satisfaction. Rather, this will to liberty has grown into a "non-impulsive nature," meant to develop into "legal, moral, religious, and not less into scientific actuality"; and the history of the world, as the justification of the ways of God, is the process of the consciousness of freedom, a process in which freedom is won only through struggle. The struggle is of such intensity that history must be called the "slaughter-bench at which the happiness of peoples, the wisdom of states, and the virtue of individuals have been victimized," indeed the "way of despair, the way by which consciousness at each moment loses what in it is not yet true." Yet, it is a struggle that, since it is the enormous labor of Spirit itself, aims at a culmination of history in which freedom is realized.[116]

There is, then, to the labor of Spirit in history a triadic dialectic, recapitulating God's coming into awareness of Himself in the Trinity, a dialectic that in its first moment is that of the Oriental world that knows only one man to be free, the despot (and, therefore, it does not really know freedom at all). In its second moment, it is that of the Greek world where there is freedom, but where only some men are free. Its third moment is that of the modern world where the consciousness is attained that man as man is free, that it is "the freedom of Spirit which constitutes its essence." Thus, modern man no longer shuns the barbarians, as did the Greeks, but discovers America; no longer is modern man stopped short by chaos in his quest for order, but rather he seeks to penetrate the infinitude of contingent facts; no longer does he perceive freedom as that which *some* men have by nature, but rather now he affirms that all men are free simply because they are human. This triadic structure of world history, corresponding to the Father in His isolation, the Son differentiating Himself from the Father, and the unity of both in the Holy Spirit, is somewhat reminiscent of the breakdown of history given by Joachim of Flora (c. 1135–1202). Joachim proposed the sequence of a time under the law, a time under the Gospel, and a time when the Holy Spirit "will teach those whom He will fill with all truth."[117]

This dialectic of world history culminating in the present is Spirit's working itself out as Objective Spirit, and Hegel is now ready to chart the entrance of Spirit into its third and consummatory moment, that of Absolute Spirit.

d. Absolute Spirit

i. Introduction.   Only when man has been established both as an individual and as a member of society in the fullest spiritual sense is it possible to proceed to the third stage in the philosophy of Spirit, that of Absolute Spirit, where intelligibility has been fully appropriated by concrete minds that then exist consciously through their social objectification in history. This is the stage of Spirit when it has attained an "actuality which can no longer be otherwise, for its in-itself is not possibility but necessity itself," a necessity in which subject and object are inseparably united, where the object itself is a subject and the objective is itself *ego*. With Absolute Spirit there is absolute certainty that being and thought are simply two poles of the same field like the concave and convex side of the same lens, absolute certainty that every form of being is a form of reason, or as Hegel's famous formulation has it, there is absolute certainty of the truth that "what is rational is actual and what is actual is rational."[118] Previously this was the conviction that "the plain man like the philosopher" took his stand on, and from it philosophy started in the logic and the

philosophy of nature, but now it is established as an absolute
certainty of truth and not just a subjective certitude that the very
reality of the real is its rationality, and the very rationality of the
rational is its reality, that *whatever is intelligible is real, and whatever
is real is intelligible*, and that being itself is meaning, as meaning
is being. One need no longer say with Berkeley *esse est percipi*,
but one must rather say *esse est intelligi*. This identity imposes itself
on a being that is moving in a direction, that is, on that becoming
of being that is history; and because of the dialectic of history he
has articulated, Hegel can now confidently say that "to recognize
reason as the rose in the cross of the present and thereby to enjoy
the present, this is the rational insight which reconciles us to the
actual," a rational insight that now attains its truth in Absolute
Spirit.[119]

But if the actual is through and through rational, then actuality
is now established as the unity of inner and outer, the "coincident
alternation of inner and outer" combined into a single necessity,
the "self-translation of inner into outer and of outer into inner,"
in such a way that the notion spoken of in the logic has come into
full unity with its externalization as an absolute actuality where
the inside and outside of human consciousness, the quintessential
modern dualism, are reconciled because each is seen to presuppose
the other and each passes over into the other. Prior to the stage
of Absolute Spirit, being as exterior was conceived as consisting
of parts, while as interior it was conceived as whole, so that the
notion was taken to mean the inner, and actuality the outer. But
now in the final analysis of Absolute Spirit, the destinies of the
inside and outside of human consciousness prove to be identical,
for the outside of consciousness and being is but the expression
or manifestation of the inside of both consciousness and being,
since reality is as such self-manifesting.[120]

But if the identity of reality and rationality entails the identity
of the inner and the outer, it further implies that speculative reason
as the synthesis of negative reason and understanding is nothing
less than a synthesis of consciousness and self-consciousness, at
once consciousness of the universe and the "I." Its "determinations
are just as much objective, that is, determinations of the essence
of things," as they are determinations of the subject which knows;

Absolute Spirit is thus the stage where self-consciousness no longer has consciousness alongside it but "truly pervades it and contains it dissolved within itself."[121]

Unlike Locke, then, for whom our minds are not made as large as truth nor suited to the whole extent of things, and like Leibniz for whom the monad strives to reach the ultimate point where its activity is turned back upon itself and where it knows itself as a mirror of the universe, Hegel conceives reason as the moment of Absolute Spirit, which reveals itself to be "the certainty of consciousness that it is all reality." In this moment the "certainty of being all reality has been raised to truth," and Absolute Spirit is "conscious of itself as its own world, and of the world as itself," conscious that just as Adam said of Eve that she was of his flesh, it finds in the world "reason that is its own reason." Like Aristotle's *nous* that only thinks itself because it is most excellent, *Vernunft* or positive reason only thinks itself because its self is actuality; but whereas for Aristotle the determination of what is highest must start from *what* is thought, for Hegel the self of thought, true to the logic of modernity, is what is highest and what thought starts with. And while "the self-differentiation of things" is what is primary for Aristotle, the "self-referentiality" of thought is what is primary for Hegel; reason knows all reality because it knows itself.[122]

Absolute Spirit, then, as the identity of the real and the actual, the inner and the outer, consciousness and self-consciousness, is what Spirit has become, and it is thus the vanquishing of the becoming of Spirit. But what Spirit has become or developed into is no less a development than Spirit's development through Subjective and Objective Spirit. As in its prior moments, so in Absolute Spirit, the truth of development holds: the coming to light of what was latent and hidden (so that what a thing is inwardly, that it becomes outwardly also) is still the rule. In this development no more comes out, in one sense, than what is already there in itself; while Spirit is getting further away "from the indeterminate beginning, it is also getting back nearer to it," except that now in Absolute Spirit the "silent ceaseless weaving of the Spirit in the simple inwardness of its substance" is such that it no longer conceals its action from itself. Now it shows itself to be the healer of the wounds that it had inflicted upon itself in its prior development; now it proves that its wounds "heal and leave no scars behind," and that it is "the truth of truth," the truth of the whole. But that whole, the totality, the cosmos, is nothing other than the essence of Spirit itself "consummating itself through its development."[123]

The comprehension of this totality is itself a penetration of the totality which coincides with the development of the totality, with the result that for Hegel the self-movement of the thought content *is* identical with the self-movement of the thinking subject, much as for Eriugena, insofar as "we think rationally, our thought reproduces the process by which the world is formed." The very criterion of the development is in fact the knowledge of the development; that is, we know that there is progress from A to B if A can be grasped or comprehended from B, but B cannot be understood from A.[124]

Accordingly, if development makes the beginning explicit, so that Absolute Spirit is the explication of the beginning in the logic, it is inevitably true that the old adage that "the stream is clearest near the spring" does *not* apply to the work of Spirit, since in this work the stream is "more equable, and purer, and stronger, when its bed has become deep, and broad, and full." And its beginnings are as such no measure of its capabilities, for its beginnings are only explicated in its development, where the goals of that development are made clear. In Absolute Spirit, the all-encompassing goal of the development is now made explicit, for the goal of Spirit is to attain the point where knowledge no longer needs to go beyond itself, where reason in its quest finds only reason itself, where Spirit—like the animal who consumes food as the other of itself and brings forth nothing but itself—brings forth only itself, where Spirit is no longer hidden to itself. In this manner, Absolute Spirit, as Hegel says, may "be compared to the old man who utters the same creed as the child, but for whom it is pregnant with the significance of a lifetime."[125]

If Subjective and Objective Spirit represent the attempt to comprehend the mystery of the Holy Trinity, focusing, respectively, on the mysteries of the Incarnation and Resurrection, Absolute Spirit represents the attempt to comprehend the mystery of the

Holy Trinity by focusing on the Christian notion of the Second Coming, the end of time, the perfection of the work of the Holy Spirit begun at Pentecost. But if Absolute Spirit is fully developed Spirit, and yet, as developed Spirit, has itself a development, that development is composed of the moments of art, religion, and philosophy, the final Hegelian triad; and each of these moments in turn unfolds dialectically.

Art, religion, and philosophy have this in common: they all have originated in wonder where what is perceived simultaneously attracts and repels, excites and frustrates. This wonder leads in art to the form of "intuition and imagery," a form that is external and represents the objective side of Absolute Spirit. In religion, it leads to the form of "feeling and representative thinking," where the form is internal and represents the subjective side of Absolute Spirit. And finally it leads to philosophy, as the "unity of art and religion," in the form of "pure freedom of thought," where the subjective and objective sides of Absolute Spirit are fully united.[126]

ii. Art.   In the first moment of Absolute Spirit (art), the sensuous is something ideal but exists as an external, beautiful thing. Since the beautiful is expressive of the true, the sensuousness of art stands "open throughout in every respect to conceptual thinking." And so art invites us to intellectual consideration, and that not for the purpose merely of creating art again but for the purpose of philosophically knowing what art is. Thus, fine art "only fulfills its supreme task" when it is simply "one way of bringing to our minds and expressing the Divine," when it places itself in the same sphere as religion and philosophy and acts as the first interpreter of religious consciousness.[127]

As such, art itself involves a dialectical development from the visual arts, such as sculpture and painting (which have a determinate character) to music (which contains the principle of "the self-apprehension of the inner life as inner") to their final unity in "poetry, the art of speech." Poetry unites the spiritual inner life and the presentation of the objective world; it completes "art's gradual dematerialization of its means of expression" and is the original presentation of the truth to be found in religion and ultimately philosophy.[128]

Sculpture, with its sightless figures, cannot convey a "concentrated expression of the inner life," whereas painting "opens the way for the first time to the principle of finite and inherently infinite subjectivity," since in painting the "spectator is as it were in it from the beginning." Sculpture is the high point of Greek art, whereas poetry integrated into modern tragedy proves, as the high point of the art of the moderns, to be expressive of the "subjective inner life of the character who is not, as in classical tragedy, a purely individual embodiment of ethical powers."[129]

The opposition between classical and modern art is, however, already prefigured, for Hegel, in the opposition between classical architecture and medieval Gothic architecture. Gothic cathedral architecture "constructs a building which exists as an enclosure for the Spirit" where "spiritual convictions shine through the shape and arrangement of the building and so determine the form both of its interior and exterior." The "interior of the building not only acquires a more essential importance," but glints through the "shape of the exterior and determines its form and arrangement in detail." In Greek temple architecture "the external form is the chief thing and, owing to the colonnades, remains independent of the construction of the interior." Moreover, in Gothic architecture the "building strives upward" and gives the appearance of lifting itself to the sky, converting "load-carrying into the appearance of a free ascending," where in Greek temples there is no upward emphasis, for the whole stretches out directly in breadth and width without any emphasis on rising.[130] In effect, Gothic architecture is dedicated to the "reconciliation of God with the world and therefore with Himself," and this dedication finds its perfection in modern tragedy with its "representation of absolute subjectivity as the whole of truth," whereas Greek architecture is dedicated to the reconciliation of man with nature, and thus draws the height of its edifice from a man's height but increased with the increasing breadth and width of the building. Where the Greeks make a religion of art, a religion of beauty, creating the gods out of the material of their own passions, Gothic architecture casts art in the service of religion, and thus begins the process of art's dematerialization. This dematerialization attains its apex in modern tragedy where the "form of art has ceased to be the supreme need of Spirit." Thus, the whole dialectic of art points toward the significance of religion as a manifestation of Absolute Spirit.[131]

iii. Religion. Although it is the "absolute result" in which consciousness "already raised itself above all that is finite," religion is a manifestation of truth that is "given to man from outside." On this account, man "has humbly to assent to it, because human reason cannot attain to it by itself"; for mankind in general truth is primarily revealed in the form of religion, and Absolute Spirit must exist "in its immediate reality as religion, earlier than it does as philosophy."[132]

There are three components to religion: a representation of God in art or image, "a powerful sense of separation from Him which the believer longs to overcome," and finally a cult that encompasses the way that man strives to overcome this separateness and become conscious of his unity with God's being. Besides having three material components, religion undergoes a dialectical development in regard to its form. There is first the moment of "natural religion," where Spirit knows itself as substance in a natural or immediate shape. Then, in its second moment we have the "art religion" of Greece, where Spirit knows itself "in the shape of a superseded natural existence," rising to "the form of the self through the creative activity of consciousness," by making self-consciousness explicit in an outer shape, that of the gods. By bringing together the gods of all nations in a pantheon that makes possible their mutual destruction, and by representing the divinity in the form of the singleness or particularity of the emperor, Roman religion serves as the supremely important point of transition to the third and final moment. This moment is "revealed religion," or the final religion, Christian religion, where Spirit comes to exist in the unity of consciousness and self-consciousness, in "the shape of being-in-and-for-itself." Here the "mystery of bread and wine" becomes the "mystery of flesh and blood"; here "is revealed what Spirit is, what God is," and here the truth of religion emerges at last.[133]

For the final religion, the "eternal life of the Christian is the Spirit of God itself, and the Spirit of God just consists in self-consciousness of oneself as the Divine Spirit." As the truth of religion, Christianity discloses that religion is simultaneously the portrait that a finite spirit, man, draws of God *and* the knowledge that God has of Himself, the self-consciousness of God, by which it can be said that man knows God only to the extent to which God knows Himself in man. God is God only so far as He knows Himself, but His self-knowledge is a self-consciousness in man, so that religion is in essence God revealing "Himself to Himself in and through the medium (or audience) of man."[134]

On the one hand, religion is not merely a discovery of man but is a "work of divine operation and creation in him." But on the other hand, the content of religion, in order to be what it is, requires man, so that the relationship of God and man in religion is revelatory of both. This becomes manifest, however, only in the final religion, Christianity, where it is known that God has revealed Himself, that "it is the very nature of God to reveal Himself," so that what "is revealed is just that God is the revealed God," that God Himself *is* His revelation, in fine, that all "that God is, He imparts and reveals."[135] This revelation does not stop with Scripture but continues as Christian dogmatics which involves the thinking of man, and here what God reveals to man in thought is as much revelation as what He reveals in Scripture. Ultimately, there cannot be a Divine Reason and a human reason that are absolutely different; it is in man's theological thinking, Hegel says, that "God returns to Himself, and only as this return is He God." In that theological thinking, God reveals that His will in and for itself is to be with us, so much so that without this being with us the Absolute would be completely alone, unable to "rise into unconcealedness"; and without this rising, the Absolute would not be life.[136]

Hegel's interpretation of religion with God as its starting-point and goal harks back to the medieval *Summas* that share this principle. It is also clearly reminiscent of the patristic mode of thought, which regarded the history of man's salvation as the revelation of a process within the Trinity. In harkening back to these sources, the characteristic tendency of Protestantism (especially the Lutheranism on which Hegel was brought up and that he never forsook), namely a kind of "soteriological anthropocentrism," is in some sense superseded to arrive at an older Catholic position of "God in Himself and His Glory," with its union of "invariable principle and detailed contingency," with its union of faith and reason (a contrast that Luther split into a dichotomy), and with its union of Scripture and tradition, and philosophy and theology.[137]

"Formerly," Hegel says, referring to the Middle Ages, "the mind found its supreme interest in knowing God, and searching into His Nature," but "it no longer gives our age any concern that it knows nothing of God." This contemporary situation is epitomized in the Kantian philosophy that claims that the mind "must stop at religion, and religion at faith," an extension of the *sola fide* standpoint of Protestantism that takes up "the same agnostic ground as is taken by the mere Enlightenment of understanding." The "theology of the Middle Ages," he says, in this respect, "stands much higher than that of modern times," for "never have Catholics been such barbarians as to say that there should not be knowledge of the eternal truth, and that it should not be philosophically comprehended."[138] Thus, Hegel agrees with Eriugena in his assertion that the "true philosophy is the true religion," and he lauds the Fathers of the Church for "elaborating the Christian religion in thinking knowledge," and even praises the Scholastics of the Middle Ages for holding that "the science of God is nothing but philosophy"; and, of his own position, he says that "genuine theology is thus at the same time a real philosophy of religion, as it was, we may add, in the Middle Ages." Hegel quotes Anselm's words: "It appears to me great negligence if we are firm in the faith, and do not seek also to comprehend what we believe," and he notes that Abelard followed Anselm by daring to give a philosophic proof of the Trinity in lecturing before a thousand listeners.[139]

In his fidelity to the medieval and, to that extent, Catholic Christian understanding of the union of faith and reason, Hegel holds that faith no more vanishes in thought than does being; on the contrary, the essence of both is thought. And by the same token, "just as the truth of being is in thought—which by no means denies that being is true—so too, the truth of faith is in thought—which does not deny that faith is true, nor that it is faith." Faith, then, as the absolute object of religion in its truth, does not constitute the other of reason, for human reason itself is unconsciously, so to speak, represented in faith, and the "divine right" of faith is really "the right of absolute self-identity or of pure thought."[140]

The very fact, however, that the modern view perceives an opposition between faith and reason conceals a deeper truth about modernity, for "modern philosophical thought cannot be one aspect of a life of which faith is another," since the "very claim to infinity, which makes it modern, makes it hostile to all claims external to it." In this respect, it is unlike Greek thought, which, "falling short of the modern infinity, left room for an historical religious truth external to it, as is illustrated in the medieval use of Greek philosophy." Precisely "because Greek philosophy does not conquer the contingent, the divine incursion into the contingent falls outside it," a fact that "at once allows Greek thought to survive in medieval theology and forces it to become subservient to ecclesiastical authority."[141]

The very claim to infinity of modernity, therefore, forces it into insisting on the antithesis of faith and reason, but there is no other course for modernity, according to Hegel, until the final modern philosophy, the completion of the logic of modernity, comes to recognize that the infinity it claims "presupposes the faith against which it is directed"; and in this recognition, modern philosophy must cease to oppose faith and must recognize itself as the "speculative transfiguration of Christianity." Christian revelation is thus a condition for modernity, and the consciousness of this must be restored to modernity, if the "infinite autonomy of modern moral selfhood" is to be properly comprehended—that is, grasped in reference to Christian truth.[142]

The Enlightenment had proposed feeling in the place of Christian faith as the consort of reason, and in so doing it took its "stand upon the extreme point of freedom," Hegel says, "rejecting authority and faith in general," and in the process driving "faith in like manner to take its stand in an abstract fashion upon itself, and to attempt entirely to free itself from thought." Man, "identifying himself just as man" in the Enlightenment, "hopes to realize the supremacy of reason on earth"; and God is made into "an empty supreme being," the "sapless abstract of immediate knowledge," while the world is stripped of the intrinsic and left vacuous, unordered, and determined only by utility.[143] Because of this, the Enlightenment appears, in the eyes of faith, to be a perversion and a lie, yet faith will not be able in the end "to deny Enlightenment its right," for what the Enlightenment fails to recognize is "that what it condemns in faith is directly its own thought." The Enlightenment fails to recognize that it "repudiates faith through ignorance of its intrinsic identity with what it rejects"; it fails to see that what it "declares to be an error and fiction is the very same thing as Enlightenment itself." The very emancipation of man, which the Enlightenment advocates by negating religious faith, if pushed to its limits, brings about the discovery of man's "true self as vehicle of *Geist.*" When pushed to this point, philosophy must unite with religion and *Aufklärung*, since the modern principle, which asserts that freedom can exist only when man's reason approves as valid the principle upon which he acts, will be shown to be nothing less than an explication of what is implicit in Christian faith. [144]

If Christianity is the absolute religion, the truth of religion, then the expression "faith" is reserved for Christianity as constituting the truth of religion, for "faith knows that in which it believes" not merely "in the sense of having an idea or knowledge from without it, but knows it with certainty," so that it is "in certainty that the nerve of faith lies." The "immediate certitude of faith" is "the identity itself, reason," which, however, does not yet recognize itself and so "is accompanied by the consciousness of opposition." It is in fact "the inwardness of certainty" of faith that underlies the modern philosophical quest for certitude. Thus, Descartes (when he indicated that the intuition that suggested to him the unity of all the sciences had been divinely inspired, and when he appealed to the divine veracity as a warrant for asserting the independent existence of the things of nature) and Rousseau (when he claimed that he could not be mistaken about what he had felt, and when he attempted to assume the standpoint of divinity for himself) were unwittingly appealing to the certitude of faith as a paradigm for the cognitive and affective certitudes they were speaking about. Both Descartes and Rousseau were implicitly appealing to the principle that "God is the beginning of all things, and the end of all things," the beginning as known in faith and the end as spiritually grasped in thought. What was merely implicit in Descartes and Rousseau, as well as in other modern thinkers, Hegel claims to bring to explicitness in his finalization of modern philosophy, an endeavor in which the Anselmian notion of "fides quaerens intellectum" is finally accomplished, in which faith is brought to its full comprehension or "intellectum."[145]

Eriugena had said that faith is "a certain beginning" by which "knowledge of the Creator begins to be produced in the rational nature," by which the "sight of God" can be eventually achieved; and Anselm had said, "I do not seek to understand that I may believe, but I believe in order to understand," for this "also I believe, that unless I believed, I should not understand." Hegel, too, recognizes that faith and revelation must first be a given in order for faith to find its realization in reason, and this is why he sees the medieval proofs for God's existence as having such profound significance. He views them as mappings of what he calls "the elevation of the thinking Spirit to that which is the highest thought, to God," an elevation that is "essentially rooted in the nature of our mind," an elevation that Kant could not grasp when he insisted on the "impossibility of proving God's existence" and effectively took us back "to the Unknown God" of the Athenians that St. Paul had claimed to know. Anselm had already supplied Kant's deficiency when he said that God must of necessity be "whatever it is proper to believe of the Divine substance." The customary Enlightenment formula that argues for a demagification of the world is rejected by Hegel, since for him the myth and symbol surrounding faith "do not cover but rather uncover religious truth"; and philosophy, though it aims to "rise above religious representation," were it simply to destroy such representation, would "reduce itself to emptiness."[146]

Because Christianity is the "revelation of reason," it is the "religion in which religion has itself become objective in relation to itself," which assures that "there will be no further religious revolutions," that there "can never again be a truly new religion" but only further clarification and development of Christianity. But insofar as rational knowledge must be a fundamental characteristic of the Christian religion, this religion must give "development to its content, for the ideas regarding its general subject-matter are implicitly or in themselves thoughts, and must as such develop themselves." The idea of Christianity "will in course of time expand into a multitude of ideas," as Cardinal Newman says, and this revelation once begun, its continuance is but a question of degree.[147] This development *begins* with accepted and unreasoned belief, but Christianity cannot be limited to its first appearance in the words of the Bible. It must unfold itself in a history of developing dogma, that is, developing revelation, or as the Church that is the very development of Christianity as a revelation of reason. Hegel's Christianity is thus the Christian Church as it developed through history, a Church that is necessary for God as Spirit, since without it God cannot be the mind of the Church and without being this mind He cannot be fully God.[148] But the Church "is not merely a religion as opposed to another religion"; it is also at the same time a particular form of secular existence, occupying a place side by side with other secular existences. In other words, the "Church is, on the one hand, the pure Spirit of God, but it is also, secondly, in the world" as "an actuality of the Kingdom of God upon earth" in which the "reconciliation of God with Himself is accomplished in the world," and not merely as a heavenly kingdom that is beyond the world. Because it has a secular existence, however, the Church must eventually be "subjected to inward divisions," and precisely because it is subjected to such divisions in the Protestant Reformation, it permits the emergence of the modern state that, in contrast with particular sects, attains to universality of thought and possesses the spiritual as an element that is no longer foreign to it. Implicitly, the Church is the state, since it is "a contract of each with all and all with each to protect every member of the society in a specific faith and specific religious opinions," but this implicit condition of being state must fall into disunion with itself, so that the modern state is able to emerge as the explicit reality of the Kingdom of God, the "Divine Idea as it exists on earth."[149]

We thus get, in reference to the Kingdom of God, three stages of development. The first is that of immediate naive faith, or the Church in its unity, where this naive faith is informed by reason in doctrinal development. The second is "the position of the understanding," of "Enlightenment," where the Church falls into disunion, and the modern secular state emerges out of the disunion. The third is the "stage of philosophy," that is, the completion of modern philosophy, in which that philosophy comprehends itself. The Kingdom of God that Hegel examines in his philosophy of religion—that is, the Church in its secularization moving into the modern secular state and thus permitting the movement of world history—will thus be seen to have been implicitly what the "intellectual kingdom" of the history of philosophy will prove to be explicitly, since this intellectual kingdom is the understanding of the Kingdom of God, the comprehension of the intelligibility of world history.[150] We have thus come to the consummation of Hegel's philosophical synthesis, to the third moment of Absolute Spirit, and thus to the completion of the development of developed Spirit, to philosophy itself.

iv. Philosophy. Religion is aware of the Divine Spirit as "external to the spirit of man," although it strives to overcome this externality; but philosophy is aware of this Spirit as "internal to man's spirit," so that in philosophy "man raises himself to the divine without resting in the intermediary stage of mere representation" and "accepts only what thought is conscious of as being its own." Nonetheless, philosophy is not contrary to religion but simply grasps religion in concept, for religion is simply "intuited philosophy," and philosophy is simply "cognizant religion," both having the same object, namely, God. The result is that in explicating religion, philosophy only explicates itself, and in explicating itself, it explicates religion.[151]

Properly so called, philosophy, as Hegel sees it, has its beginning only in the West, because only in the West is Spirit "submerged in itself," only in the West does reason come to know itself and deal only with itself, and only in the West was the identity of idea and being explicitly posited. As for Plato before him, philosophy is for Hegel man's highest possession and true reality; but as "knowledge knowing itself," it is impossible for it to have any other content than "the history of philosophy, the account of its continuing self-exposition." Its proper content is an "extant hereditary possession" that "is not assumed merely as given, but is seen and known to warrant itself, because warranted by the free self-evolution of thought."[152]

But if philosophy is the unfolding of itself through its own history, this unfolding is directed into a final shape, a final modern philosophy, whose essence it is to reenact in thought "the divine side of the Christian divine-human relationship" and to attain complete comprehension of the divine idea. This final modern philosophy Hegel calls "Science," which "alone is the theodicy" because it is the comprehension of the theodicy that is world history. In "Science" human thought proves to have taken "on a divine character in thinking the divine," proves that although "philosophy is the supreme achievement of human thought," the condition for "its being adequately human is that it is also divine." Philosophy in its finality thus realizes that faith or belief in the divine is possible only because there is the divine in the believer himself, which divine rediscovers its own nature in what it believes, even if (as faith) it is not aware that what is found is its own nature.[153]

The final modern philosophy thus discloses that the question, "What is it to know God?"—present as the decisive question of the previous moments of Hegel's philosophy—is really the question, "Is there something divine in knowing?"—namely, in man. Long before Hegel, Kepler had held that the numbers and magnitudes implanted in the mind of man are comprehended by man with the same certainty as God comprehends them, and Bruno had insisted that the divine was not far distant but within us. Now Hegel makes explicit this divinity dwelling in man as a condition for modern philosophy, not simply by adding another philosophical system to the logic of modernity, but by presenting a *completion* to that logic which claims to comprehend the history of philosophy and to reproduce the same evolution of thought which is exhibited in the history of philosophy.[154]

All "the various philosophies" that go to make up the history of philosophy, Hegel tells us, are "no blaze of a fire of straw, nor casual eruption here and there, but a spiritual, reasonable, forward advance" of "one philosophy in its development, the revelation of God, as He knows Himself to be." In that development, the philosophers are "nearer to God than those nurtured upon spiritual crumbs" (since they "read or write the orders as they receive them in the original" from Spirit), and the "latest birth" is the "result of all the systems that have preceded it, and must include their principles." Each particular philosophy will have truth insofar as "it includes the negative state and the positive, and reproduces the process of becoming false and then returning to truth," so that each successive philosophy is at once the correction of error of its precedent philosophy and the presentation of a new possibility of error. But with the process in its totality comes the totality of Spirit's development, the revelation of what has been the aim of Spirit throughout its history, the presentation of the world's history in its innermost signification.[155] Although each particular philosopher is like a blind man who is "driven forward by the indwelling Spirit of the whole," and the "shores of those philosophical islands of the Blest that we yearn for are only littered with the hulks of wrecked ships" (a situation that tends to induce an "age which has so many philosophical systems lying behind it" to arrive "at the same indifference which life acquires after it has tried all forms"), the philosophical systems of different epochs are not merely idiosyncratic views but have been and still are necessary, for none of them has passed away and all of them "are affirmatively contained as elements in a whole." None of them has ever been refuted, but all that has been refuted is the assertion that any one of their various principles is absolute in character. And none of them "can make its appearance sooner than it does," since the movement of the whole is "impelled by an inherent necessity" that is implicitly rational.[156]

In the history of philosophy, "the going out of the Idea in course of its development" proves to be "a going within itself, a self-immersion," whereby the progress forward "makes the Idea, which was previously general and undetermined, determined within itself." In the progress forward, nothing is lost, all principles are preserved, so that the whole of the history resembles "a circle of circles," in which the "idea appears in each single circle"; but, at the same time, the whole idea is constituted by the system of these circles, and each circle is a necessary member of the encompassing circle. In its finality, as the completion of modern philosophy, philosophy has become the apprehension of this circle of circles, the apprehension of its own development, which demonstrates that the history of philosophy that it comprehends has "not to do with what is gone but with the living present" that is what it is because the past of that history of philosophy is sublated in it. As the apprehension of the intelligibility of the history of philosophy, the final modern philosophy is thus the apprehension of the spirit of the era in which this final philosophy makes its appearance—the consciousness of what is substantial in this era, "its own time apprehended in thought."[157]

The final modern philosophy thus entails the conclusion of modernity and is comprised of an inverted history of philosophy that begins at the end, in a vein somewhat like those seventeenth-century presentations of history from a supernatural point of view which were written as if the writer had arrived at what the Apocalypse calls the end of time. Hegel claims to understand modernity because he is at its end, an end that he philosophically interprets as the philosophical realization of Christianity's notion of the end of time, and thus the comprehension of Absolute Spirit's having become what it destined itself to become.[158]

The content that the final modern philosophy comprehends—the history of philosophy—has for Hegel a triadic dialectical development. Its first moment consists in Greek philosophy, from Thales, about 600 B.C., to the Neoplatonists, embracing a span of one thousand years. The second moment consists of medieval philosophy, a "period of fermentation and of preparation for modern philosophy," and extends to the sixteenth century, and again embraces a thousand years. The third moment, that of modern philosophy, begins with Descartes and culminates in the final modern philosophy, which comprehends the whole dialectic. The first of these moments "is regulated by thought," and develops thought as "far as the idea"; the second moment falls "into the opposition between existence and formal reflection," apprehending "thought as Spirit"; and the third moment comprehends the "Idea as Spirit" that knows itself.[159]

The "Greek principle is freedom as beauty, reconciliation in imagination," which represents "an idea in sensuous guise," but in its philosophy it "desires to tear itself away from what is sensuous," since philosophy "is the constitution of thought into a totality beyond the sensuous and the imaginary." But it can do this only by proceeding from "the objective as from something given," and thus transforming this objective into abstract thought that is known to it as "universal essence or existence" but "not as subjective thought." Because Greek philosophy is "essentially related to what is natural," subjectivity confronts it as a determination that is still accidental.[160]

Plato begins with what is given by nature but "takes the more determinate content out of sensuous perception" and fails to attain the highest idea attained by Aristotle—that "thought about thought takes the highest place of all" insofar as it spiritualizes all the forms which the universe contains. But the realization of the notion in Aristotle is a "long series of particular conceptions which are external to one another, and in which a unifying principle led through the particular is wanting." In the Stoics we do find the "system" that was lacking in Aristotle, the "attempt to comprehend the world as thought" that presents for the first time the notion as subject in its inwardness—a notion that is also present in Greek Skepticism which inverts Stoicism and attempts to deny all content to the world by virtue of "thought in its pure solitude with itself." It is only with Neoplatonism, however, that the "Absolute is determined as Spirit in a concrete way," that "God is not a mere conception" but a kind of trinity that continues "to emanate more and more." Neoplatonism thus introduces the dialectical principle into philosophy as a principle of development, but this principle is not methodical and occurs only disconnectedly. In doing so, Neoplatonism prepares the ground for Christianity, but Spirit is not yet for it "individual spirit" as in Christianity.[161]

Christianity unleashes the second moment of the dialectic of the history of philosophy, namely, medieval philosophy, which proclaims that "in man has sprung up the consciousness of the truth, or of Spirit in and for itself," that "man requires to participate in this truth," that man must be qualified to have this truth present to him, and that man must be convinced of this possibility. The apex of medieval philosophy is Scholasticism, which locates the actualization of this concrete Spirit in man in another world and not in this and thus focuses its energies on God's unchangeableness.[162]

With the appearance of the Lutheran Reformation, however,

man was called from the beyond into "the presence of Spirit" and was conceived as standing "in a relation to God which involves his personal existence," so that his heart must relate itself to God directly "without mediation, without the Virgin, and without the Saints." Whereas Christianity had implicitly made the "intelligible world of philosophy the world of common consciousness" (so that Tertullian could say, as Hegel quotes him, that even "children in our day have a knowledge of God, which the wisest men of antiquity alone attained to"), the Reformation makes explicit this principle that "thought has come to the consciousness of the world at large as that to which every man has a claim," so that "free thought" is "the duty of every man."[163]

Thus begins the third moment of the dialectic of the history of philosophy—modern philosophy—which announces that philosophy itself is "a matter of universal interest," that "everyone is a thinker from the beginning." It is with Descartes that modern philosophy first comes into its own as "a philosophy which is, properly speaking, independent, which knows that it comes forth from reason as independent, and that self-consciousness is an essential moment in the truth." And here philosophy separates itself from the medieval "philosophizing theology" and attempts to commence from itself in an "I think" that entails "thought as being and being as thought." Here "thought starts from thought as what is certain in itself" and opposes itself to what is "extended, spatial, separated, not at home with itself."[164]

This principle of certainty as the unity of thought and being is extended by Kant into "the consciousness of thought in its subjectivity," so that now "abstract thought as personal conviction is that which is maintained as certain" and an absolute standpoint is raised by which the finite aspires to the infinite. It now becomes clear that as Greek philosophy was the "complete formation of the natural consciousness" that makes itself into a universality, that philosophizes about everything that is by nature, modern philosophy is the coming-into-its-own of the possibility of a more-than-natural consciousness made available by Christianity. For the task of modern philosophy is not simply to set forth the universality immanent in nature but to free "determinate thoughts from their fixity so as to *give* actuality to the universal, and impart

to it spiritual life."[165] The accomplishment of this task is "the
present standpoint of philosophy" where the two sides of that
diremption of the idea that has plagued modern philosophy, nature
and Spirit, are "each of them recognized as representing the totality
of the idea, and not only as being in themselves identical, but as
producing this one identity from themselves," so that thought or
the notion is reconciled with reality or actuality. Pure science is
at last attained, and Spirit in this pure scientific knowledge at last
knows itself as Absolute Spirit, with the result that it "would
appear as if the world-spirit had at last succeeded in stripping off
from itself all alien objective existence, and apprehending itself at
last as Absolute Spirit." The "strife of the finite self-consciousness
now comes to an end." Spirit has fully returned to itself and
completely overcome *logos'* externalization of itself in *natura*, and
this return has its self-consciousness articulated in the final modern
philosophy, which is nothing more than a comprehension of the
dialectic of the history of philosophy—which in turn is a comprehension of the dialectic of world history.[166] Spirit has comprehended its own process of comprehending itself and it has done
this in man.

We have thus completed our journey through the Hegelian
system; we have thus set forth the execution of the Hegelian
project, and we must now contemplate the result of that execution.

6. THE SIGNIFICANCE OF HEGEL'S PROJECT

a. Recapitulation

In the first place, the result of the Hegelian completion of the
logic of modernity is a restoration to that logic of the grand medieval attempt "to see the Christian mysteries in everything whatever, every natural process, every form of human activity, and
every logical transition," a restoration of a language to speak of
God, of a God who intervenes in history, and a language that had
been lost between the seventeenth century and the Enlightenment.
Thus, the great medieval vision of the world as "speculum," a
"mirror" in which God is to be seen, and the great medieval
metaphor of the world as a ladder by which the mind rises to

God—as we find them, for example, in St. Bonaventure—are restored by Hegel in a kind of historical repetition of Dante's *Divine Comedy*, describing "the route that consciousness takes through history in coming to the awareness that as Spirit it could legitimately look into itself in order to find reality." The medieval quest to name God, to contemplate God in His diverse names, is restored by Hegel in an effort to show that the *via moderna* is permeated through and through by the *sensus Christianus*, and that the path of modern philosophy is not a departure from the path upon which medieval thinking set out.[167]

This restoration of the medieval perception of the Christian mysteries in everything involves, for Hegel, an identification of the mystical with the speculative, for as he says, the "truth is just that which has been called the mysteries of religion," for the "perfectly blessed and holy" is what "is imbued with reason and knows the world of reason." Perhaps aware of this identity of the mystical and speculative, Hegel's students, in 1830, on his sixtieth birthday, presented him with a medal with his portrait on one side and, on the other side, a scene containing on the left a male figure seated and reading from a book, behind whom is a pillar upon which an owl perches, containing on the right the figure of a woman holding fast to a cross, and in the middle a naked genius turned toward the seated figure and pointing to the cross on the other side, thus mediating between speculative philosophy, the "owl of Minerva," and the Christian mysteries focused in the Cross of Christ, which Hegel called the "gallows and wheel that have long been hallowed" as "the highest pain and the deepest rejection together with the most joyous rapture and divine honor."[168]

The Hegelian identification of the mystical and speculative implies, as he himself says, that it is the "reestablishment of the doctrines of the Church, reduced to a minimum by the understanding," which is "truly the work of philosophy"; and it is philosophy that at the present time is not "only orthodox, but orthodox par excellence." Like Eriugena for whom philosophy is the interpretation of the Bible, Hegel looks after and honors in his philosophy everything "that seems to give theology its particular splendor and special dignity" and "removes the rose of reason in the midst of the Cross," translating the eyes of faith into the eyes of reason, and the theology of history established by Augustine into a philosophy of history.[169]

By his identification of the mystical and speculative, Hegel proves to be perhaps the first philosopher to have "borrowed the whole cast of his thought from Christianity"; and he may prove to be the last philosopher "whose immense historical sense was still restrained and disciplined by the Christian tradition," for it appears that Hegel encountered the notion of Spirit at Golgotha and Gethsemane and not in Athenian gardens and colonnades. Just as Augustine had invoked the God of Christianity as "the Truth in whom and from whom and through whom all things are true which anywhere are true," Hegel holds that to "think at all is to think God, because to think at all is to rise above the sensible and finite to the infinite." Just as Kepler proclaimed that God was being celebrated in his astronomy, and Berkeley asserted that the search for truth must lead us ultimately to a deeper knowledge of God, Hegel proclaims that the object of philosophy is "eternal truth in its objectivity, God and nothing but God, and the explication of God" as the only *principium essendi and cognoscendi*.[170]

It has been said that Hegel's philosophical system has its roots in the Greek tradition of logos, but this can be so only if, as Hegel says, what the Greek philosophy was in principle became actual in the Christian world. For, as far as Hegel is concerned, the *logos* of the Greeks finds its truth in the Christian *Logos* and ultimately in *Spirit* that properly belongs only in the revealed religion of Christianity. Long before Hegel, Gregory of Nyssa had argued that the Christian conception of God passes in the mean between the polytheism of the Greeks and the monotheism of the Jews, in that it cancels the Hebrew abstract unity of God by "the acceptance of the Word" and by "belief in the Spirit," and it destroys the polytheistic error by "the unity of the nature" it assigns to God. And John of Damascus had argued that in the Christian conception of God we have the Jewish idea of the "unity of God's nature" and the Greek idea of plurality in "the distinction of hypostases" in God.[171] For Hegel, by virtue of the Incarnation, the Christian God is like the Greek gods, since the divine is united to the natural or human. But whereas the Greek gods have "acquired their existent embodiment only through human imagination," the Christian God is an "actuality in flesh and spirit," and whereas the "pagan deities contented themselves with being materialized into statues, the Christian God can appear only as absolute *Geist*" in the nonimmediacy of Spirit's development. And where the pagan gods, when they die, cannot be brought back to life, the Christian God is the Resurrection. Yet, common to the Greek gods and the Christian God is this: that if a "manifestation of God is to be supposed at all, His natural form must be that of Spirit, which for sensuous conception is essentially the human," for no other material form can lay claim to spirituality; thus, if Greek religion errs, for Hegel, it errs not in overanthropomorphizing the divine but in not being anthropomorphic enough since Christianity has presented an Incarnate God who is not simply an individual humanly shaped but an actual, single individual, wholly God and wholly an actual man, drawn into all the conditions of human existence.[172]

Christianity is, then, for Hegel, a reconciliation of Greek polytheism and Judaic monotheism insofar as both are absorbed and overcome: the Christian God is more human than the gods of the Greeks and more divine than the God of Israel (since there is no trace of irrationality in Him). The unity in opposition of Athens and Jerusalem is maintained in Rome. For the Greeks, "man is not ready for reconciliation with the truly universal, so the gods are human at the price of being multiple and particular," whereas the Jews fail to attain the concreteness of Spirit because for them "God essentially exists for thought alone" as a kind of absentee proprietor of a world He has made in order to own. But the "Jewish idea that God essentially exists for thought alone, and the sensuousness of the Greek form of beauty, are equally contained" in the Christian notion of God and, freed from the limitation attaching to them, are taken up into something higher. Just as St. Augustine had woven the temporal and historical sense of the Hebrews with the timeless concepts of Platonic thought under the inspiration of Christian revelation, so also Hegel unites the *logos* that the Greeks had exalted in laying the foundation for their metaphysics with the Creator God of Judaism under the inspiration of the doctrine of the Holy Trinity, and he does so in such a way that nature and history are united, since logos externalizes itself in nature, and Spirit overcomes this externalization in history.[173]

If, in the first instance, the result of Hegel's execution of his project is the restoration to modern philosophy of the medieval ability to see the Christian mysteries in everything—the restoration of the medieval sense of the glory of God—the result of this execution on the second level may be said to be a ratification of modernity's exaltation of man, but now embodied in the majestic significance of philosophy itself. "Spinoza's artlessness," Hegel says, "which makes philosophy begin with philosophy itself," must be properly appreciated, and the day must soon come "when from beginning to end it is philosophy itself whose voice will be heard." The object of philosophy for Spinoza is his own system, and this might also be said of Hegel, except that Hegel insists that the system is not simply his, but the spiritual totality of all viewpoints. In the end, the Hegelian synthesis claims to be a "logic of philosophy," a "philosophy of philosophy," a "science of science," and as such the consummation of modernity.[174]

As the philosophy of philosophy, Hegel's final modern philosophy entails an identity of the truth of the actuality it apprehends with its own truth, with one Spirit pervading both the actual world and philosophical thought. The only distinction that remains is that the character of the actual world or present age "still appears to present itself as accidental," whereas philosophy "as the justification of principles is at the same time the universal peace-bringer and universal reconciliation" that has overcome not only the modern dualism but the dualism between itself and all of life.[175] Hegel's project is the presentation of the unity of thought with both the spiritual and natural universe,[176] in which the spiritual absorbs the natural, and in which the cosmos is no longer a pregiven fixed nature, as it was for the Greeks, nor even a spatially infinite universe as it was for the early moderns, but an unfixed, developing *history* that is a progressive determination of being by consciousness, the becoming of being, the simultaneous becoming of man and God.

In history, mind and matter, thought and reality, the inside and the outside of human consciousness are overcome in their separateness and find their unity in art, religion, and ultimately philosophy, for the dialectic of the history of philosophy establishes itself as the comprehension of *history* as the modern cosmos, and thus as the truth of that cosmos. Philosophy is able to be this comprehension because it is not governed by "subjective idealism" or by the "illusion that ideas exist only in our heads," only for a subject; for Spirit does not "leave the question of its actualization or non-actualization" entirely "dependent on our will," and the final modern philosophy attests to the truth that men "will come to discover their spirituality by the work involved in rejecting it," although Spirit relies on the minds of men for its instruments.[177]

As the comprehension of the modern historical cosmos, the final modern philosophy is "itself a circle in which the first is also the last and the last is also the first." Thus, the sphere of Absolute Spirit ends the Hegelian system; but it is also the absolute foundation, the beginning, where one finds the identity of being and meaning. This Hegelian merging of beginning and end is teleological activity where the consequent is the ground. That is, it is a "becoming of what has become" in which only what already exists comes into existence, and only at the end do "we have in a completed form what constitutes at the same time its presupposition." The result is the same as the beginning, only because the true beginning is the purpose.[178] But if that which is result is also that from which it has resulted, and if "consciousness on its onward path from the immediacy with which it began is led back to absolute knowledge as its innermost truth," then God can be called Spirit only when He is known to be at once the beginning and end, becoming in the end what He posited Himself as being in the beginning. Much as St. Augustine concentrated on the Divine Word as the beginning Who is abiding with us and yet is to be attained only in the future, in eternal life, since this Word is the beginning which we have not yet achieved, so also for Hegel the words of T. S. Eliot are applicable: "The end of our exploring/ Shall be to arrive where we started/And know the place for the first time."[179] The end that proves to be the fully explicated content of the beginning is nothing other than the final modern philosophy, the explication of the beginnings of modernity, that is, of the Christian conditions for modernity.

In radical contrast to Aristotle for whom there can be no science of science or philosophy of philosophy, since there can be no "deduction of all principles from one first principle which certifies itself," Hegel claims "to possess wisdom in a comprehensive and completely discursive sense," as "Das absolute Wissen," for, as he says, "to help bring philosophy closer to the form of Science, to the goal where it can lay aside the title 'love of knowing' and be actual knowing—that is what I have set myself to do."[180] Wisdom is attained in the final modern philosophy only when philosophy realizes that thought is historical, a realization that can come, it would appear, only at the end of history.[181]

But what could such an end of history mean? Does it mean an actual end to history, where the freedom of all is attained, or does it mean an end where man simply realizes the import of historicity, so that now man is for the first time aware that history is the battleground for freedom? If the end of history means the attainment of the freedom of all, then it would seem that this end entails that man must cease to be human or become genuinely divine. But if this end means simply that man has realized his historicity, and Hegel is writing as a man living in an historical world and not outside it, then this end involves an annulment of time only in and for philosophy and not for actuality. Thus, it is philosophy that has overcome the immediacy of time and history and, in comprehending what its realized intelligibility would be, for the first time lets history *be* in anticipation of its realized intelligibility, lets history be as a cosmos. Whichever the case may be, however, the claim of Hegel is that the final modern philosophy is no longer simply a seeking of truth but "is in the truth, and *is* the truth itself."[182]

If in the first place the result of Hegel's execution of his project is the restoration of the medieval sense of the glory of God to modern philosophy as its condition, and if on the second level the result is the ratification of the modern exaltation of man but now in terms of Spirit's production of philosophy through man, the synthesis of these two results is the realization that the self-confidence of modern man is and must be one with confidence in God, a self-confidence imbued "with the entire mystery and majesty of true confidence in God." The ultimate result of Hegel's execution of his project, in other words, is the identification of "religious confidence in an infinite God who, transcendent of the finite world, has fully entered into it and redeemed it," with a "modern secular self-confidence, immanent in the infinite aspirations of modern culture."[183]

The final result is, then, what Hegel called the unity of the "Sunday of life, when man in humility renounces himself, and the working-day, when he stands up independently, is master of himself and considers his own interests." Kant could say that the "mightiest revolution coming from inside of man is his departure from his self-incurred tutelage," and for Hegel, too, "humanity has come to consciousness of itself"—it has become "capable of bearing and generating its own destiny." And so, for modern man, God can no longer be considered apart from the Subjective Spirit, but if modern man loses sight of this identity of self-confidence and confidence in God, loses sight of the archetypal statements of Christianity as ground for his self-confidence, he would be threatened with an unprecedented impoverishment of mind and soul.[184]

Either modernity is "self-confidence, qualified as confidence in God, confidence in God given concrete form as self-confidence," or it is nothing. This is the unity that Hegel represents in his philosophy as no other modern did, and this unity presumes the same faith in the modern world that we find in Hegel's modern predecessors from Bruno and Galileo down to Kant, for Hegel never despaired of the modern world, and thus "never faced up to the effects of such despair upon his thought." I am necessary to God, and God is necessary to me; and where Aristotle said that the "marvelous" thing was that "the manner of God's existence is as good as ours *sometimes* is, but eternally," Hegel says that "letting oneself be determined by God is the same as letting oneself be determined by one's own being, which is essential and not accidental," since Spirit is the Divine in man and "not a spirit beyond the stars, beyond the world."[185]

Hegel once said that the existence of God appears to Hebrew consciousness, "not as a truth but as a command," so that this consciousness is entirely dependent on God; but "that on which a man depends cannot have the form of a truth."[186] The final result of Hegel's execution of his project, therefore, might be expressed in the following terms. Dependence on God (on the part of man) must be overcome; man must prove himself (in his relation to God) as nondependent, and he must work this non-dependency out to the extreme of no longer needing God. But in attaining this extreme he will, in effect, show himself to be more in need of God when he is *not* dependent upon Him than when he was dependent upon Him. In a very real sense, this is what has happened in the logic of modernity. In its beginning, modern scientific method recognized that although it is impossible for us to know everything, we nevertheless know the method by which anything whatsoever can be known; and thus the promise of this method is interpreted by Descartes in terms of the mastery and possession of nature. Later on this promise is given a deeper signification, as in Rousseau who articulates the promise in terms of the nature of man as an entirely private self-defining impulse, and at this point the fears of Berkeley that modernity, dependent in its origins on the Christian notion of God, would phase out this God come into their realization: man appears to stand outside nature, the master of nature, the radical subjectivity, who stands in the place of God.[187] But it is at this point that the ground is broken for modernity to confront its free self-confidence with the condition of it—that is, with Christian confidence in God—and to realize that both stand or fall together, that modern self-confidence is empty without confidence in God, and that confidence in God is powerless without concretization in modern self-confidence.

The way in which Hegel has united modern secular self-confidence and the medieval confidence in God has prompted some of his commentators to say that the "radical and comprehensive fashion in which Hegel achieved the historical self-justification of his philosophy appears overwhelmingly superior to all later attempts," and "nowhere has any thinker arisen of sufficient calibre to absorb and develop Hegel's philosophy as a whole," or for that matter to oppose Hegelianism as a whole, to systematically develop the implied alternatives that he rejected. Hegel, according to Karl Barth, sought to do "for the modern Protestant world what St. Thomas Aquinas" had done "for the Catholic Middle

Ages"; the only question is why, in the eyes of those who followed him, he was never quite recognized as accomplishing for modernity what Aquinas had accomplished for medieval Christianity.[188] As to this, we must, in the conclusion to our conclusion, forswear examining the defects of his successors and focus on the possible or alleged defects of the Hegelian synthesis.

b. An Appraisal

Does the Hegelian synthesis assume what in the end could only be the "incomprehensible synthesis of God"?[189] St. Anselm said that "I do not attempt, O Lord, to penetrate Thy sublimity, for by no means do I compare my understanding with that: but I long to understand in some degree Thy truth, which my heart believes and loves." And St. Augustine had asked, "With what understanding can man apprehend God, who does not yet apprehend that very understanding itself of his own, by which he desires to apprehend Him?"; for "God is more truly thought than He is uttered, and exists more truly than He is thought." For Cusa, too, the names we give God never reach Him, and He is involved in our language, not ultimately "as a possible term of designation, but as its condition and source."[190] This strand of the medieval tradition does not appear to enter Hegel's synthesis, and he has been accused on that account of following the road of that "forceful Lutheran defiance which seeks to take the world and God by storm," and even charged with "a sublimated lust (*concupiscentia*) of the intellect" that strives "to make God captive in the concept and thus to manipulate Him."[191]

But if Hegel tried to do something that could not be done—to present the incomprehensible synthesis of God, and thus the honor due him is only the honor of "having willed something great and having failed to accomplish it," and if all that can be said is that there is "no greater attempt than the Hegelian to unite the God of the philosophers with the God of Abraham, Isaac, and Jacob"—then it follows that the Hegelian reconciliation of Christian faith and philosophy is a failure. But it would be awesomely significant in its very failure, for no similar effort can hope to succeed, and its failure gives "the lie to every attempt to break out of the circle of reflection in which thought thinks itself." If it has failed, its failure could prove to be a "final step before a great turning and break with Christianity," the "end and dissolution of everything Christian in the thought of the modern period."[192]

It was in fact very soon after Hegel's death that his synthesis came to be looked upon by many as already superseded, and in turning away from Hegel the age was acknowledging that, having "reached the summit of its desires and achievements, it was dissatisfied with itself." Yet the "self-confidence of modern man still wanted to assert itself," and the age soon declared "that the inheritance of the Enlightenment must be entered into once again."[193] But a return to the Enlightenment would ultimately not do; to accept the Enlightenment and reject Hegel would be to embrace a "broken self-confidence,"[194] for if Hegel is a failure, then it is not only Christianity that in some sense is vanquished but modernity as well. This is precisely what Nietzsche implied— that if Hegel fails, then Christianity and modernity fail as well.

But there is another possibility. What if the truly incomprehensible thing is that the synthesis of God is comprehensible? What if the reason why Hegel's writings (unlike those of Augustine and Anselm and so many other medievals that are works of prayer and "stand upon a faith that has been given"[195]) never include an addressing of God is that he claims to have arrived at a comprehension of faith in "intellectum," a comprehension that is not "hubris" or the "concupiscentia" of the intellect but that is simply the comprehension that God's synthesis is comprehensible to man? Could it be that the very ambiguities that Hegel leaves intact in his system prevent us from thinking of the concept of the whole as totally determined by his system, and that by virtue of these ambiguities, Hegel, in the end—if not explicitly, at least implicitly—recognized that it would be open to others, as it was not open to him, to criticize his system from the higher vantage-point that philosophy has yet to attain? He may have recognized, in some sense, that he did not complete the enormous task before him and, in an absolute sense, that it cannot be completed. But he may still have been confident that its value consisted in announcing to modern man that his vocation is to continue to strive to comprehend the Divine synthesis. He may have known that the value of the system was to be found in its articulating the notion of absolute knowledge and not its entirety, in its being a "first encounter with the entirety of our history, one such that afterward historical consciousness will never again let us out of its grip."[196]

If this be a viable possibility, then Hegel's failure might be construed to consist in the fact that his philosophy, like all prior modern and medieval philosophy, has not absorbed the entirety of Christian doctrine,[197] a failure that is necessary, for philosophy is still not ready for such a complete absorption. And, therefore, the failure is not substantially destructive of Hegel's synthesis, since this synthesis as well as modernity itself could only be a decisive failure if in fact Christianity is such a failure.

Étienne Gilson has described St. Thomas Aquinas as a man "possessed in an uncommonly high degree" of "two intellectual qualities whose combination in the same mind is rather rare: a perfect intellectual modesty and an almost reckless intellectual audacity," a combination that prevented him, when he undertook the *Summa*, from being the victim of the over-confidence which is convinced that it has given the Christian religion the ultimate and definitive form and prevented him from being a victim of the debilitating fear that the whole structure of Christian thought may be without solid rational foundation.[198] There is much in Hegel that might suggest that he possessed great daring without this kind of modesty. But we should not foreclose the possibility that the modesty is hidden in what he says, that his modesty might be of a more difficult kind to ascertain than the humility of Aquinas, since it is hidden beneath the boldness that dared "to want to invent . . . a key to open every lock" in the logic of modernity—but that became a key that would frighten his successors and tempt them in their fright to lose faith in the orthodoxy of the logic of modernity.[199] Perhaps this fright has something to do with a failure to perceive a hidden modesty in Hegel: his trying to do what he thought *God* had best fitted him to do, however enormous and even impossible the enterprise as a whole might have been.

In any case, it was the logic of modernity, brought to its completion or "telos" in Hegel, that made possible the intellectual world of the twentieth century. In some ways, this world finds it increasingly difficult to daringly believe in the modernity that made it possible. Philosophy itself in this world is frequently inclined to "emphasize the relativity and anthropomorphic character of all knowledge, as well as the all-pervasive ruling power of illusion."[200] Of this world and of the fate of the logic of modernity, Nietzsche was the first sign.

NIETZSCHE: THE STRUGGLE WITH FAITH IN THE LOGIC OF MODERNITY

If Friedrich Nietzsche (1844–1900) is a modern philosopher, he is indeed an incongruous page, a nonsequitur inserted into the standard history of modern philosophy, precisely because the belief in the orthodoxy of the logic of modernity, which we find in philosophers from Cusa to Hegel, is questioned and struggled with by Nietzsche, who speaks of himself as the "incarnate wrestling match," a wrestler who opposes "as has never been opposed," but who is the "opposite of a negative spirit," since he strives to free his hands for a blessing. Nietzsche has wrestled with the angel of faith in the rightness of the logic of modernity, and it is this lonely struggle that conspires, as Nietzsche puts it, "to keep me imprisoned in my abyss"—making of his philosophy a grave where "one does not live with others any more," and making Nietzsche a disinherited child of the modern world to whom belongs neither what has been not what will be.[201] But, if Nietzsche in his wrestling strives to free his hands for a blessing, then what he condemns (his negativity) serves as a foundation for what he affirms (his positivity). The core of his negativity is his critique of modernity (as manifested in his own age) and of Christianity (which he perceives as making modernity possible); surrounding this core is his critique of the intelligibility of history, of the notion of absolute truth and logic, and of metaphysics (with its fundamental distinction between appearance and reality). The outer layers of his positivity are his doctrines of the irrationality of existence, perspectivism, the future (which entails the "overman"), and mental development as a matter of the body. The core of his positivity proves to be his teachings on the will to power, eternal recurrence, and the transvaluation of all values. To chart the course of Nietzsche's struggle to curse in order to bless, we must begin, then, with his critique of modernity (as manifested in his own age).

"Our modern culture," Nietzsche says, "is not a real culture, but a kind of knowledge about culture" from which "no decision as to its direction can come," so that the "whole of modern culture is essentially internal," devoid of a "fixed and sacred primordial site," too "weak and ill organized to provide a form and external expression for itself"; it is a "frivolous deification of the present" that is "doomed to exhaust all possibilities and to nourish itself wretchedly on all other cultures." Propelled by the "coarsest and most vicious forces" of egoism, modern progress can only mean a step-by-step advance into a decadence and wilderness where we shall once again need cloisters, and where all that can be done is to retard this development and thus "gather up degeneration itself, and make it more vehement and sudden." Having lost the "will to tradition, to authority, to centuries-long responsibility," to "solidarity between succeeding generations backwards and for-wards," men will now be inclined to call their living very fast and irresponsibly freedom, and to perceive authority as the "danger of a new slavery."[202]

It is the "disorganizing principles" that give our age its character; that incline man in his present condition to resist "taking anything deeply," to forgive everything because he "understands every-thing"; and that require an "overabundant development of inter-mediary forms," an "atrophy of types," where "traditions break off," where the "ethics of the common man" triumph, and where the "herd man" gives the appearance of being the only permissible kind of man. Thus, the "levelling and diminution" or homoge-nizing of man is today the "great process that cannot be ob-structed," and it entails man's loss of "dignity in his own eyes to an incredible extent," man's loss of reverence for man, the loss of the very "will to man," in the face of the "shaking palsy of current ideas" with their air of unreality, their odor of a lunatic asylum.[203] Nietzsche, in the midst of all of this, must strive to look upon modernity in "as unmodern a way as possible," must circle the values of modernity "very much in the upper air, very much like a bird," and thus resist his whole age and stop it "at the gate to demand an accounting," in order to overcome the supreme measures of value of his time in himself. In this way, he will be able to say that "to explore the whole sphere of the modern soul, to have sat in its every nook" is both his torture and his happiness, which makes him "the first philosopher of the age, perhaps even a little more, something decisive and doom-laden, standing between two millennia."[204]

Yet the wasteland of the present age is not inconsistent with the fact that men still live in the age of moralities and religions, since the democratic movement at the heart of modernity (which is not only a form of the decay of political organization but a form of the diminution of man) is made possible by Christianity which, by means of its notion of the "equality of souls before God," first invited "the individual to play the judge of everything and everyone" and thus passed "deeply into the tissue of modernity." Nothing in "our unhealthy modernity is more unhealthy than Christian pity," and for Nietzsche "to wield the knife here" will be his kind of philanthropy.[205] Nietzsche's critique of modernity in his own age must issue in a critique of Christianity.

After reading St. Augustine's *Confessions*, Nietzsche refers to this work as "vulgarized Platonism"—the adaptation of a "way of thinking which was invented for the highest aristocracy of soul" to "suit slave natures." In seeing into "the guts of Christianity in this book," Nietzsche sees that "Christianity is Platonism for 'the people'," the manifestation of a weariness that wants to reach the ultimate with one fatal leap, the "most prodigal elaboration of the moral theme to which humanity has ever been subjected." Nietzsche sees that modern humanism and its egalitarian ideals are "Christian ideals in disguise."[206] Nietzsche says that he has great respect for the ascetic ideal behind Christianity, so long as "it really believes in itself and is not merely a masquerade"; but since Christianity is "a system, a consistently thought out and complete view of things," if one removes from it its fundamental idea, the belief in God, one "breaks the whole thing to pieces." This is precisely what is happening in his own age—an age where the "practice of every hour, every instinct, every valuation which leads to action" are anti-Christian—and yet Christianity is still needed by most people because they "still believe in grammar" and the "ineluctable, poetic pretension" that is the Christian God. Because he refuses to admit the contradiction of his belief with his practice, modern man is a "monster of falsity" in his shamelessness at being called a Christian.[207]

"All the possibilities," Nietzsche says, "for a Christian life, the most single-minded and the most superficial," have been tried out; and the time has now come when "we have to pay for having been Christians for two thousand years." The time of vast upheaval is approaching, when the multitude itself will discover that "all Christianity is founded on gratuitous affirmations," that the supports and values offered by Christianity are mere fiction. This exposure will "plunge man into a nothingness whose equal has never before been felt in all human history." Having seen what the multitude will eventually see, Nietzsche says, "I pronounce my judgment, I condemn Christianity," for to be a Christian will be hereafter improper. Even today "it is indecent to be a Christian," to adhere to a belief that is "a hangman's metaphysics," that is mankind's greatest misfortune, the one great intrinsic depravity, the "most malicious false-coinage there is for the purpose of disvaluing nature," and the "greatest reproach against existence."[208]

In this way, Nietzsche foresees the coming of the day "when the most solemn concepts which have caused the most fright and suffering," the "concepts of 'God' and 'sin', will seem no more important to us than a child's toy." For, if once men sacrificed human beings to their gods, and then reached the enlightenment of sacrificing instead their own strongest instincts, it will remain for "the generation that is now coming up" to sacrifice God Himself "for the nothings"; and all of us today "already know something of this."[209] Thus, the classic words of the madman in Nietzsche's *The Gay Science*.

'Whither is God?', he cried, 'I will tell you. We have killed him—you and I. All of us are his murderers. But how did we do this? How could we drink up the sea? Who gave us the sponge to wipe away the entire horizon? What were we doing when we unchained the earth from its sun? Whither is it moving now? Whither are we moving? Away from all suns? Are we not plunging continually? . . . Is there still any up or

down? Are we not straying as through an infinite nothing? . . . Is not
the greatness of the deed too great for us? Must we ourselves not become
gods simply to appear worthy of it? There has never been a greater deed;
and whoever is born after us—for the sake of this deed he will belong
to a higher history than all history hitherto'.[210]

This death of God is the "catastrophe, inspiring of respect, of a
discipline in truth that has lasted for two millennia and which now
prohibits the lie implicit in monotheistic belief." For it is Christianity itself, having produced "the will to absolute truthfulness,"
that "must now draw its strongest conclusion, the one by which
it shall do away with itself"; and this shall be accomplished by
raising the question, "What does all will-to-truth signify?" In this
sense, God has died out of "His pity for man," and with His death
a great sadness must descend upon mankind, in which even the
best will grow weary of their works, in which men shall live on
in tombs, in which "the world will be standing on its head."[211]

But, just as after "Buddha was dead, his shadow was still shown
for centuries in a cave," so also there are likely to be caves for
thousands of years in which God's shadow will be seen, and men
will have to vanquish that shadow also. So it is that the "greatest
recent event"—that "the belief in the Christian God has become
unbelievable"—is too great for "the multitude's capacity for comprehension even for the tidings of it to be thought of as having
arrived as yet." In announcing these tidings of great sadness, however, Nietzsche's very opposition to Christianity as a reality will
be inseparable from his tie to Christianity as a postulate; for, as
he says, even we "atheists and anti-metaphysicians" must appeal
to the "metaphysical faith" on which the modern "belief in science
rests," and so we must "light our torches at the flame of a mil-
lennial faith," a faith that "God is truth, and truth divine," even
though this faith is becoming less and less credible and its last day
approaches.[212]

But, with the death of God, there also "disappears the guarantee
for an intelligible world," including the Hegelian understanding
of history as "God's sojourn upon earth." Nietzsche thus contends
that God was "first created by history," that the value we put on
the historical is "merely a Western prejudice," and that history

is merely a "disguised theology." The "very possibility of forming a total vision of world history is of Christian origin," and with the death of the Christian God, the "interpretation of history to the glory of divine providence, as perpetual testimony of a moral order and moral ends," must become a thing of the past. Along with the belief in the God of Christianity, consequently, there must also die "the fundamental faith that would enable us to calculate, to promise, to anticipate the future" in plans of great scope, so that what "will not be built any more, henceforth, and cannot be built any more" is "society in the old sense of that word." We have thus reached the point where man must come to "see through himself and history," but to see in this way is to perceive that "man as a species does not represent any progress compared with any other animal"; thus, Nietzsche can say, "I live as if the centuries were nothing," and "at root, my distrust goes so far as to question if history is really possible at all."[213]

But this means that everything has evolved by chance and that there are no absolute truths. The "world appears logical to us because we have begun by making it logical," since logic applies only to "fictitious entities that we have created," not for the purpose of knowing, but for the purpose of schematization and calculation, as "conditions of life for us." We are "from the beginning illogical," and we can at last recognize this and therefore recognize the illusoriness of the traditional definition of man's nature as reason and spirit. If it is the case that "behind all logic and its seeming sovereignty" there stand valuations or "physiological demands for the preservation of a certain type of life," it follows that "every philosophy also conceals a philosophy" and is a hideout in which every word is also a mask. If we "withhold our faith from the God of the ascetic ideal," then a new problem poses itself, namely, the problem of the value of truth, the questioning of "the will to truth," a questioning that must disclose that all logic, "born of the vital need to lean upon identities," does so despite the fact that "nothing real is reducible to unity or identity." Thus, logic is made possible by a useful and necessary falsification, and the will to logical truth can be executed only after a fundamental falsification of all events is enacted.[214]

The fundamental questionability of logic and absolute truth

entails, furthermore, the radical questionability of metaphysics itself, so that Nietzsche attempts to bring Western metaphysics to an end, to close it off and allow it to turn aside "into its own inessentiality and disarray." Metaphysical thinking "rests on the distinction between that which truly is, and that which by comparison does not constitute true being," that is, on some form of the distinction between appearance and reality; and so the death of God entails that the "suprasensory world is without effective power," that that which "formerly conditioned and determined the essence of man in the manner of purpose and norm has lost its unconditional and infallibly operative power of effective action." The result is that the suprasensory world no longer "quickens and supports life," and we can no longer honestly "believe that truth remains truth when the veils are withdrawn," for we "have lived too much to believe this," we have come to recognize the enchantments and deceptions involved in every strong faith, and as moderns we exercise "the care of the 'burned child'."[215] Having effectively transformed the traditional metaphysical understanding of being into a value, having traced the distinction between the real and the apparent world back to value relations— that is, having contended that mankind has projected the conditions of its preservation "as predicates of being in general"— Nietzsche is led to the conclusion that becoming and the apparent world are the only world. This conclusion, which he proposes as a countermovement to metaphysics, requires that he refuse to readmit God or metaphysics into his thought by the back door by means of "some unverifiable principle which would turn out to be God in disguise."[216]

Thus, neither the modern concept of the self as a subject or as an *ego* (the modern notion of consciousness as an individual attribute), nor the ancient concept of the cosmos can be admitted into Nietzsche's position; for consciousness can no longer be assumed to be the standard and condition of life, and we live and must live "in the age of the atom, of the atomistic chaos," where the world is "to all eternity chaos," where there is no totality, since there is nothing to bring being to order. Unlike Hegel, for whom being is a "subject that passes through various phenomenal stages toward absolute knowledge," and for whom interpretation is a dialectical mediation of the whole, Nietzsche holds interpretation to be a response to a "basic ontological dispersion," with no possibility of "gathering up different particular viewpoints into a superior synthesis," since nature is fundamentally irrational. In this way, Nietzsche's position discloses itself to be a "theoretical work which argues against theory," a position in which *what is said* is necessarily in tension with the *way it is said*.[217] Nietzsche attempts to search a being that cannot be rationally apprehended by dissolving or breaking through reason; he attempts to plumb the irrational nature of existence, of life itself—a life against which the history of philosophy has been "a secret raging." Against this philosophy, which still believes in truth, Nietzsche places "the free spirit," who has "not lost the scent of life," who is not "hostile to life," who loves his senses, who is not willing to "bear false witness about life." Against Christianity, which has brought this philosophy to the common man and infinitely extended its power by virtue of the Christian "will to decline" and "impoverishment of life" (accompanied by a "profound, suspicious fear of an incurable pessimism"), Nietzsche places his "wisdom of disillusion."[218]

The positivity of Nietzsche's philosophy, then, begins with his attempt to disclose the positive meaning or blessing entailed in the seeming negativity of the irrationality of existence, much as the negativity of his philosophy began with his attempt to disclose the negative meaning or curse entailed in the seeming positivity of modernity and Christianity. The absence or destruction of meaning that he finds in modernity and Christianity, furthermore, enables him to discover the positive meaning he finds in the irrationality of existence. This means that the falsehood of modernity and Christianity is a falsehood in which the whole of the human has become deeply sunk, a falsehood that is the only thing that at this time permits man "to enjoy the sight of his soul." This, in turn, implies that prior philosophizing really conceals what Nietzsche now makes explicit about the positive meaning of the irrationality of existence; or, as Nietzsche says, "I learned to view differently all that had hitherto philosophized," fathoming the "hidden history of philosophy, the psychology of its great names," discovering that what has been at stake in this history is not at all truth, but "growth, power, life." Nietzsche discovers that this history has incorporated "only our errors, and that all consciousness relates to errors," that philosophy's love of truth was a refusal to admit the final truth, which the greatest minds could not endure or dare to think—the irrationality of existence.[219]

To have come to this realization is to have perceived how problematic modern science is, to realize that modern science is laying "the road to sovereign ignorance." Spurred on by its powerful illusion of knowledge, modern science "speeds irresistibly towards its limits, where its optimism, concealed in the essence of logic, suffers shipwreck." Science must finally admit "that there is no such thing as 'knowing'," that it was a kind of arrogance to dream of knowing, that "we no longer have the least notion that warrants our considering 'knowledge' even a possibility." Modern science must inevitably lead us to the "era of universal mastery," but it can do so only on the basis of being at bottom nihilistic, for it presumes "the meaning of a world deprived of meaning, a knowledge that ultimately has ignorance as its foundation." Nihilism makes modern science possible, and this means that the human world can be destroyed by modern science, since all seriousness must be increasingly confined to the scientist and to the prodigious power of technology.[220] Our whole modern world, made possible by modern science, has as its ideal "the theoretical man" (made possible by the history of philosophy). But, if the "will to system" found in the history of philosophy is an error and is to be repudiated, so that any great philosophy is only "the personal confession of its author and a kind of involuntary and unconscious memoir" (in which there is not and can never be a pure, will-less, or timeless knower), then it follows that all seeing and all purported knowing (no less modern science than philosophy) is essentially perspective.[221]

Nietzsche's analysis of the irrationality of existence thus leads him to his doctrine of "perspectivism," which asserts that the only "value of the world lies in our interpretations" and that "every elevation of man brings with it the overcoming of narrower interpretations." The world has "become 'infinite' for us all over again, inasmuch as we cannot reject the possibility that it may include infinite interpretations," insofar as we cannot exclude the possibility that all existence is "actively engaged in interpretation," and insofar as we cannot disprove the proposition that there is "no limit to the ways in which the world can be interpreted." But this is the "most extreme form of nihilism," since it must necessarily presume that "every belief, every considering-something-true, is necessarily false because there simply is no true world"; so that all perspective is "perspectival appearance" whose origin lies in us to the extent that "we continually need a narrower, abbreviated, simplified world." There can be no question of a true perspective, but only of "the perspective that prevails"—only a question of perspectives as symptoms of growth or decline. For we presume ourselves to know only in the sense that we assume the perspective of "what has been prearranged to count as knowledge"; and we remain "forever imprisoned within ramified structures which, like spiders, we have produced within ourselves."[222]

Nietzschean perspectivism thus requires the exclusion of the erroneous starting point of modernity, namely, the assertion that there are facts of consciousness and no "phenomenalism in introspection," along with its concomitant assertion that "subjectivity is capable of dominating the totality of being." In place of this erroneous starting point, Nietzsche puts his insistence that every representation of the totality of entities is a falsification and unavoidable humanization that is inexorably pushed into the blind alley of the humanness of its perspective. Yet, if this falsification follows from the death of the Christian God, it nonetheless intimates to us how "many new gods are still possible," how many "new ideals are, at bottom, still possible."[223] Perspectivism thus leads Nietzsche to his doctrine of the future, for although there is no route of escape from falsification, there is the possibility of a route of escape from the negation of the value of life—a negation that is engendered by Christianity and that permeates modernity.

The future was the land of his love, and the care of the coming generation was in his mind, so that Nietzsche could say, "I walk among men as among the fragments of the future"—that future which "I envisage" and that is "but little experienced with respect to its truth" by his contemporaries. Thus, he speaks of himself as among the "children of the future," a "premature birth of the coming century," one who sends out messages into the future, one whose new music will require new ears, and whose vision

of distant things will require new eyes. But he will not be able
to speak of the future of mankind with much confidence, for "ever
since Copernicus man has been rolling down an incline, faster and
faster," into the "piercing sense of his emptiness," and nihilism
must represent the ultimate logical conclusion of modern values
and ideals.[224] Nietzsche's doctrine of the future, consequently,
must be a narration of "the history of the next two centuries" as
the "triumph of nihilism" in the "power realm of the modern
age," the "most terrible and problematical but also the most hopeful of spectacles." Nihilism is that "uncanniest of all guests" who
stands at the door of the future, and stands there as the final result
of "the moral interpretation of the world." For the "destruction
of ideals" will be a "new desert," and we "amphibians" will need
"new arts by means of which we can endure it," new "oecumenical
goals embracing the entire earth." Issuing from our very faith in
the categories of reason, nihilism will provide "more favorable
preconditions for more comprehensive forms of dominion, whose
like has never yet existed," and its spiritual bankruptcy will itself
become our guiding principle.[225]

Yet, Nietzsche speaks of himself as "the first perfect nihilist"
who has "lived through the whole of nihilism to the end," leaving
it behind, outside himself, the philosopher who has seen that the
embrace of nihilism is the necessary condition for the victory over
nihilism, who has seen that "to rule and no longer be God's vassal"
is the very instrument for ennobling man. But such an ennobling
will require not that we seek ourselves or even seek man as such
but that our highest thought be that "man is something to be
surpassed," that the *overman*, and not man, be our "first and only
concern."[226]

Nietzsche's doctrine of the future thus makes way for his doctrine of the overman as the victory over nihilism. Mankind is
merely "the experimental material," the "tremendous surplus of
failures," which is but "an embryo of the man of the future." But
this embryo in its contemporary condition has the power of a
being who is "already beyond man"—a situation that harbors the
greatest danger, for the very development of mankind must be
sacrificed "to help a higher species than man to come into existence." The "dwarfing of man" must thus for a long time count

as the only goal, a dwarfing that shall serve as a broad foundation for the overman who will be the "victor over God and nothingness." The overman will give "the earth its purpose," will replace the God who has died, and will be able to assume the "dominion over the earth as a whole" that is made possible by modern science.[227]

"I am waiting," Nietzsche says, "for a species of men who do not yet exist: the masters of the earth." But "I myself am far" from this 'overman' and "do not desire it at all," but simply recognize that this "new man must come forth"; thus "I call myself the last philosopher because I am the last man." "Man is something that shall be overcome," and "what is great in man is that he is a bridge and not an end," and what "can be loved in man is that he is an overture" to the overman, to a being of a higher body. The "whole of mental development is a matter of the body," and the striving of the organic to rise to yet higher levels, to the overman as a higher organism, points to the uselessness of the traditional distinctions between thing-in-itself and phenomenon, between matter and spirit, for the "realm of the intellect and the sphere of consciousness" are but "symbols to be decoded, symptoms of impulsive" or "bodily movements."[228] The "nonsensuality of philosophy hitherto," its "slander on the empirical and only world," its hatred of the "blood of the empirical reality which was sacrificed and shed" by it will be seen, in the face of the impending overman, to be the "greatest nonsensicality of man." Already, the fear had by prior philosophy of the senses is beginning to be unlearned by Nietzsche's contemporaries, who are increasingly believers in the senses and thereby unwitting bridges to the overman.[229]

It now becomes clear that in his struggle with faith in the orthodoxy of the logic of modernity, Nietzsche represents a break with the substance of this logic, insofar as the substance of this logic presumes a universal validity for reason, the paradigm of the Christian notion of God, and the ideal of the autonomous human self. All of these presuppositions are challenged by Nietzsche, thereby making his break a *ne plus ultra* in comparison with all prior breaks, since, for him, being is no longer synonymous with rational being, we can no longer reach being through reason, and

the Christian notion of God is rejected (along with the autonomous human self) in favor of the overman.[230] In place of these
modern presuppositions, Nietzsche will propose the three doctrines that serve as the core of his positive teaching: the will to
power, eternal recurrence, and the transvaluation of all values.

The overman does not fulfill humanity, but rather that which
in humanity is more primary and original than man himself,
namely, the "will to power." The result is that the overman is
the fulfillment of the essence of life. Furthermore, since being has
worth for Nietzsche only insofar as it is accorded worth as a value,
it follows that being itself is nothing but a "condition posited by
the will to power"; thus, the "criterion of truth resides in the
enhancement of the feeling of power." In the end, nothing is
"given as real except our world of desires and passions," that is,
the reality of our drives, for even thinking itself is nothing but
"a relation of these drives to each other." Thus, the world itself
is nothing but a chaotic "monster of energy without beginning,
without end," a will to power and nothing besides, of which man
himself is a subsidiary will to power and nothing besides. Having
no intrinsic form, a world of wills would be formless, but since
wills are always acting upon one another, form is always being
imposed, and thus the will to power must be construed as a creative principle, the creative principle behind man's perspectival
interpretation of the world.[231] But, although the will to power
must be construed as a creative principle, the world-as-will-to-
power lacks the capacity for eternal novelty, and the "law of the
conservation of energy demands eternal recurrence." "My consolation," Nietzsche says, "is that everything that has been" (i.e.,
every *particular* thing) "is eternal," and the "sea will cast it up
again." Thus, the "totality of entities as will to power must permit
the return of the same, and recurrence of the same must be
eternal"—a recurrence of the particularities in an irrational world
in motion, a recurrence that appears to be Nietzsche's only alternative to the Second Coming.[232]

Nietzsche's doctrine of eternal recurrence, however, discloses
a number of inconsistencies in his position. Whereas the meaning
of a unique irrepeatable process lies in the goal or end of that
process, the meaning of a recurring process lies in *what* recurs; but

since the *what* in question is eternally recurring as the same, Nietzsche is forced to exclude any meaningful becoming in the world, for in the end there can be no genuine passing away but only an eternally frozen mobility. This conclusion is at odds with his emphasis on the apparent world of becoming as the only world. Furthermore, given the fact that creativity in pre-Christian Greek philosophy is only an imitation of nature, where for Nietzsche creativity must be the principle behind the will to power, Nietzsche's notion of a will to power must implicitly appeal to the Christian doctrine of *creatio ex nihilo* as its only model. Yet Nietzsche denies the Christian God and the hypothesis of a created world that he speaks of as a "rudimentary survival from the ages of superstition." For Nietzsche to say that "this life is your eternal life" is to revive the Greek notion of eternal recurrence; yet what recurs is not the universal (as with the Greeks) but particulars. In reviving eternal recurrence, Nietzsche has thus tacitly accepted the Christian emphasis on the normativity of the particular. Unknowingly, Nietzsche had revived the ancient controversy between Christianity and paganism, since eternal recurrence (cyclicality) is at the heart of paganism, and a rejection of this recurrence in favor of a unique creation out of nothing is at the heart of Christianity. Nietzsche's own *contra Christianos* is an exact replica in reverse of the *contra gentiles* of the early Fathers of the Church. In imitating the early Christian *contra gentiles*, however, Nietzsche's *contra Christianos* feeds off the importance Christianity affords to the particular. The very importance that Nietzsche assumes for the will in his will to power along with the emphasis he places on man's distant future are decidedly un-Greek and indebted to Christianity; and they illustrate, once again, how Nietzsche's critique of Christianity is rooted in paradigms borrowed from Christianity.[233]

If the doctrines of the will to power and eternal recurrence are anchored in paradigms borrowed from Christianity, the same anchorage can be seen in the Nietzschean doctrine of the transvaluation of all values, for this doctrine is an imitation of the Incarnation as a transvaluation of all of sensuous reality—a transvaluation that attributes absolute value to particularity.[234] "I know my destiny," Nietzsche says, as a "relentless and underground struggle against everything that human beings till now have revered and loved," and "my formula for this is the 'transvaluation of all values'," a transvaluation that is incarnate in "my own person" and is a "declaration of war and victory over all ancient concepts of 'true' and 'untrue'." This transvaluation entails that "there are no moral phenomena at all, but only a moral interpretation of phenomena," an interpretation that is itself of extra-moral origin. Although this transvaluation begins with nihilism and its proposition that the "highest values devaluate themselves," it ends, not in the "dreadful spectacle" of a world that is valueless, but in the attempt to define anew the "weight of all things." Nonetheless, precisely because Nietzsche's *contra Christianos* was so deeply marked by the Christian conceptions of the will, of creation, of the distant future, and of the will to create it, Nietzsche could not accomplish the transvaluation of Christian (and modern) values in the way that Christianity had (successfully) effected a transvaluation of pagan values.[235]

The teachings at the core of Nietzsche's positivity reveal that Nietzsche's struggle with the angel of faith in the orthodoxy of the logic of modernity had to end in victory for the angel, precisely because Nietzsche was wrestling on the ground of the angel, precisely because Nietzsche had to borrow his philosophical weaponry from this angel. Having examined his position in its negativity and positivity, we are now in a position to step back and assess his position as a whole.

There are, it would seem, fundamental ambivalences permeating Nietzsche's philosophy—ambivalences that may derive from the fact that the modernity and its Christian foundations with which he is struggling serve as the presuppositions for the very position he assumes in the struggle. These ambivalences are to be found in four issues: his closeness to the Greeks (which at once discloses his distance from them), his critique of inquiry and theory (which itself relies on theory), his antipathy to modernity (which at once manifests his location within it), and his polemic against faith (which at once reveals a fundamental faith).

"I am to all that is good and robust," Nietzsche says, "so much closer to the Greeks," and hopeful for a "rebirth of Hellenic antiquity" in the "midst of the desolation and exhaustion of contemporary culture." In the world of antiquity, there reigned a "more lordly morality than today," so that the man of antiquity was a "stronger and deeper man than the man of today" and did not bury his "head in the sand of heavenly things" but bore it freely as an "earthly head" that created a "meaning for the earth." Whoever has gained "wisdom concerning ancient origins," Nietzsche was confident, "will eventually look for wells of the future and for new origins." Placed at the final stage of an evaporated Christianity, Nietzsche hoped to find new sources for the future in classical paganism; yet, it was the death of the Christian God that made him understand the ancient world. It was Christianity that enabled him to generate open enmity between our contemporary culture and antiquity. For all his insistence that the culture of the Greeks could alone justify philosophy, and for all his insistence that Greek religion was higher than the Judaeo-Christian religion, Nietzsche was forced to imitate Christianity's response to the Greeks in his efforts to come close to the Greeks. The transvaluation of values *had already occurred* in Christianity's response to the Greeks, and Nietzsche could only be an imitator (even though he inverted what he was imitating). He was, in effect, attempting to transvaluate a transvaluation, and such an effort would never leave him with the original values of the Greeks but only with the categories of Christianity emptied of Divine Presence. His purported closeness to the Greeks sadly reveals how far distant he was from them.[236]

It appears that "today inquiry itself stands in need of justification," Nietzsche says, and that the "will to truth has been forced to examine itself." This can be seen in the fact that today philosophers themselves "represent in word and deed" the "unbelief in the masterly task and masterfulness of philosophy"; thus, the "dangers for a philosopher's development are indeed so manifold today" that one may doubt, in an era where scholarship "has neither faith in itself nor an ideal beyond itself," whether the fruit of philosophy "can still ripen at all." Nietzsche thus comes close to questioning the very possibility of the mainstream of western philosophy—comes close to a univocal rejection of all prior philosophy—to the extent that he raises the possibility of whether, having seen all perspectives as false, we can continue to inquire.

Nonetheless, Nietzsche himself continued the task of inquiry, in full cognizance of the realization that "every attempt to break out of the circle of reflection in which thought thinks itself" is a lie, and in full cognizance of the deeply disturbing possibility that "what things are called is incomparably more important than what they are." In doing this, his critique of the will to truth could only fashion itself on the truth willed by prior philosophers; it is thus no surprise to find that he admits his affinity to Spinoza "whose tendency like my own" is "to make knowledge the most powerful passion."[237]

Nietzsche excoriates modernity, yet he also says that he is "the most modern of moderns," for, although there is "an element of decay in everything that characterizes modern man," nonetheless, "close behind this sickness stand signs of an untested force and powerfulness of the soul." Nietzsche thus remarks on the "ambiguous character of our modern world," for the "very same symptoms could point to decline and to strength." The very transvaluation of values that he calls for would require men "who possess all the qualities of the modern soul, but are strong enough to transform them into pure health."[238] Nietzsche's wrestling with the angel of faith in the orthodoxy of the logic of modernity is a wrestling with a modernity within himself, which he could neither renounce entirely nor totally accept. His striving to distance himself from modernity thus discloses his closeness to certain of the predicates of modernity.

Finally, there is Nietzsche's ambivalence on the whole matter of faith—his attack on Christian faith and faith in the orthodoxy of the logic of modernity, and yet his appeal to faith for the transvaluation of all values. The "need for faith," he says, for "anything unconditional in 'Yes' and 'No', is a proof of weakness," and all "weakness is weakness of will." However, to "lack faith" is to be "sterile," and for those who are embarking on the sea of the future, for those emigrants who would embark on the transvaluation of all values, the "hidden yes" must be "stronger than all 'No's' and 'Maybe's'" that afflict the present age like a disease.[239] Convinced that he could not operate with Christian faith and Western rationality, Nietzsche was forced to fight a battle in which he could rely only on the energies of Christian faith and

Western rationality. He could win this battle neither on rational grounds nor on the grounds of some kind of secularized faith isolated from reason. His very critique of faith discloses an appeal to a faith in the possibility of a transvaluation of values that Christianity had already accomplished but that he would invert. Nietzsche had conceived of himself as cursing in order to bestow a blessing; but what he did not fully realize, it would seem, was that so much of what he had cursed he would end by blessing, and so much of what he would bless he had already cursed.

Nietzsche attempted to criticize the very foundations of the logic of modernity, namely, the meaningful infinity of God, the intelligibility of a world made by God, and the rational capability of man to know himself, that world, and God. In struggling with the angel of faith in the orthodoxy of the logic of modernity, Nietzsche attempted to dethrone God and reason from the modern pantheon, leaving only the prospect of man's transformation into the more-than-human—into the overman. Nietzsche himself, however, could only assume the perspective of the last man who looks out over the boundary of his humanness into the future where man shall no longer be simply man. In saying "I call myself the last philosopher because I am the last man," Nietzsche was, in effect, confessing that, although he strove to be the first of a new order of thinkers, he could not get beyond being the last of an old line of thinkers. The patriarch Jacob, in his wrestling, had prevailed against his angel; the angel thus bestowed upon him a new name—that of "Israel."[240] Nietzsche could not prevail against modernity, and modernity, consequently, had no new name to bestow on Nietzsche.

Nietzsche could not prevail against modernity because modernity was endemic to his position; nor could modernity overcome Christianity, since the paradigms of Christianity were implicit in modernity. There would be those in the coming century who would reject Christianity while holding on to the fruits of modernity; but Nietzsche had seen too deeply into modernity to be in their company. Despite all his efforts, Nietzsche could not escape the lines of battle that had been drawn for him beforehand by Hegel: either modernity is man's new self-confidence qualified as his confidence in God, his old confidence in God given concrete form as his self-confidence, or it is the most destructive of delusions. More important than what Nietzsche said, it would seem, was what he could not deny. What could not be denied was that modernity, without cognizance of its ground in Christianity, was simply one among many of the "works" and "pomps" of the devil. It was a very old name, "antichrist," that Nietzsche bestowed upon himself and signed his last letters with when the night of insanity first descended upon him.

8

REFLECTIONS ON MODERNITY
AND THE PRESENT AGE

HAVING mapped the logic of modernity as thought by the modern philosophers, we are now in the position to attempt to construct a profile of this logic in its seamlessness. This profile will amount to a kind of phenomenology of the medieval Christian mythos and modern logos *over against* the pagan mythos and ancient logos and will enable us to engage in an exercise in thinking about our present age in the light of this logic.

A PROFILE OF MODERNITY

Unrelated to a more-than-natural holiness, the pagan mythos represents the sacred as perfect self-containment, as that which does not shift about and pass away, and thus as structured and formed space, while it represents the profane as that which is outside itself, as that which never abides, and thus as the formlessness of time. Constituted by mythic events—which are stripped of their temporal character and relocated in an arrested or timeless time into which he is transported by the rituals and altars he establishes to the gods—man has the essence of his family, tribe, and city anchored into sacred places and secured against the successiveness of time, and he is thereby enabled to practice an entirely local, patrimonial, and civic religion. Possessed of dwelling places, their presence and absence a function of space, the gods are entirely circumscribed by nature, evidences of the more primal generosity and perfection of a nature whose indifference to man holds them divided from man, so that their human form points not to subjectivity but to their dwelling in a living cosmos. As does an organism, the living cosmos requires a top and bottom, and the gods occupy the sacred places on high—powerless when they do not proceed from these places. Functions of the above and below (as the fundamental differentiation of space), the gods bring a portion of the perfection of these sacred places to the lower places of the cosmos where the profanity and amorphousness of time obtain. Space is thus inherently discontinuous and heterogeneous (sacred and profane, upward and downward), while time is inherently continuous and homogeneous (always profane, an uninterrupted sequence transcended by the frozen time of myth).

Manifesting the power exercised by thinking on language, the ancient logos distinguishes itself from the pagan mythos that manifests the power exercised by language on thinking. But, far from destroying myth, ancient philosophy begins with the amazement or wonder endemic to myth, discloses the hidden truth of myth, and thus reflects the mythic power of language in the precedence it gives to a secret oral tradition over a public written tradition. Presupposing mythic antipathy to time, philosophy separates itself from history, presents no inherent historical development, and is complete at any of its major points—its positions like the facets of a diamond. The ancient logos translates the mythic dichotomy of the sacred and profane into the dualism of a preeminently real (perfect) being and an imitative (imperfect) being, the context of which is the primacy of heterogeneous space and the subordination of homogeneous time.

The physical science engendered by the ancient logos conforms to the natural cognitions of sacred places found in the pagan mythos. A thing is in the world insofar as it is in its natural place that it will move to if allowed to move by nature, so that place is a kind of container for space, distinct from, and able to be left behind by, the thing occupying it, and determined by the differentiation of the upper and lower; natural place requires an intrinsically finite space occupied by concentric spheres, where higher contain lower places, and where the outermost sphere contains all the lower spheres. Between heterogeneous space (the qualitative aspect of the cosmos) and homogeneous time (the quantitative aspect of the cosmos) is ceaseless motion, a transiting from place

to place, which finds its perfection in circular (as opposed to rectilinear) motion where the thing always returns to its natural place.
The outermost cosmic sphere, which revolves while the thing
appearing to move in it is always at rest, and which is turned with
a finish nothing else can approach, is the paradigm of circular
motion. In this way, motion, as the characteristic fact of nature,
is a striving for the permanence of rest abiding (as the seat of the
divine) at the uppermost sphere. Motion is ultimately a tribute
paid to rest, a proof of the static character of the cosmos.

Consistent with the pagan mythos, where the passage of time
implies an ever greater distance from the perfection of sacred
places, the ancient logos perceives time as a mere numbering of
the before and after of motion, of the departure of things from
their natural places, of a change that removes what is. Like the
ceaseless repetition of mythic archetypes, time is an imperfect
quantification of circular motion (of the perpetuity of coming-to-
be and passing-away caused by the circular motion of the outermost sphere) and is eternally repetitive, without beginning or
end, so that we today are neither strictly before nor after the
civilization of the past. Unlike the definitive up and down of
space, there can be no definitive before and after in time; unlike
the natural places for the physical elements, there can be no primary or natural moments of time. It is precisely the inherent
imperfection of time that registers the perishing of individuals
(the degradation of being) in the lower places of the cosmos over
against the eternal recurrence of their species.

Having an inborn urge to move, the elements of nature, left to
themselves, build up the cosmos by a continuous movement that
is originated from a principle internal to nature. But this cosmos
must be finished and complete, since coming-to-be and passing-
away cannot apply to the whole, and since the countless alterations
in the lower cosmic places keep the cosmos in a steady state (reflective of the stability evidenced by the heavenly bodies). To be
unfinished is to be the backdrop of chaos, the very negation of
cosmos; and so the universe must be a finished order of things
occupying or seeking their proper places, where location constitutes the significance of each thing in inverse proportion to its
distance from the stationary pivot of meaningfulness found in the

outermost sphere, and where the spatially articulated and circumscribed unity of the whole is filtered downward through a series of planes. The higher and lower series are themselves divisible into higher and lower planes, with quaternity (as the number of whatever principles characterize the whole) reflecting the subordination of lowermost manyness and particulars to uppermost unity and universality. The perfection of the universals filters down to particulars, and in the process the perfection of the whole becomes less obvious and more compromised in these particulars. Hierarchy is thus the mode of being of a finished cosmos and entails an eminently visualizable universe, yet one whose picturableness is an exigency of reason (not one which exists *as* a mere picture of reason, as a construct or object of will). The cosmos is the supreme given, the perfect self-containedness that cannot be encompassed by anything higher than itself, the totality of what is from which reason takes its reference.

It is in the totality of what is, as the sum total of conditions for being, as the all-limited (and not as unconditional being), that the divine finds its place in the ancient logos. The gods are metaphors for first substances that encompass the whole of nature as principles of nature's perfection and that are not other than or beyond nature. Divinity is supreme limitedness, the perfection of a whole world, the consciousness of the finishedness and eternity of the world, which exists not as power or will (for, being immanent in nature, it has no absolute power over nature) but as the intelligibility of the whole. The highest manifestation of being *as* being, the thinking of thinking which thinks only itself in absolute solitude, the divine "avoids the destruction of the worlds" crashing beneath it and has "no ear for our prayers and no concern for us."[1] The supreme witness rather than unconditional cause of totality, the divine shares its eternity with matter and time; and its distance from man (although enormous) is finite since both the human and the divine exist by nature. The divine is thus accessible (as a more-than-human but natural purpose for human being) to the few men (at a few moments in their lives) who can attain contemplation of the immanent perfection of nature that constitutes the limitedness of being itself. Beginning in myth, philosophy ends in contemplation, in a purely theoretical activity that distinguishes itself from practical action and making.

If the divine is the immanent perfection of nature, there can be no absolute beginning for the cosmos, and nature must be the final revelation of (the ancient) logos, for there is no being beyond nature of which it could be a revelation. Like an organism, nature is a producer and has parts within parts and proper places for parts, but it is the most consummate of all organisms, self-sustaining in its production as if it were a physician doctoring itself. Appointing to all things their proper limits beyond which they can be of no value, nature is older than man and is the giver of all gifts, the greatest of all beneficences, the measure of man's knowing, acting, and making. Human art is but an imitation of the limits of a nature that is a repository (and no mere code) of meanings, so that (the ancient) logos brings a strictly natural consciousness to perfection in philosophizing about everything that is by nature. Since there is always a part of that which is changing that remains in being after the change, no new being is possible, and the totality can neither be subtracted from nor added to, can neither begin nor cease to be.

If limitation is the supreme principle of the being of nature, and being in no literal sense can be said to grow, the forms that inform the matter of things must be principles of limitation in relation to which time is purely accidental. Far from being temporal careers, individual things are spatial loci for atemporal forms, nodes for the spatial redistribution of being; the particular gains significance by virtue of being informed by a universal, and particularity is ordered to universality just as the individual is ordered to cosmic totality. Given the divine as pure reason confronting only itself, there can be nothing above or higher than reason, but there can be particulars beneath the nobility of reason, such as hair, bones, and clumps of earth that are devoid of sensation and are found in the lowermost center of the universe (the place of imperfection where man finds his home). Insofar as human discourse is rational, it molds itself upon nature as the irreducible, and truth finds it locus in the pregiven unities of nature. If there is an epistemological problem here, it is always *what* is and can be known by man. The known is primary, and man must know the truth before he can begin to love it, so that there is no need for any kind of will or willed belief to precede and condition genuine understanding, but only need for the orientation of understanding into the fixed essences of nature contained by a cosmos that in turn contains its own principles of explanation.

In a cosmos where the totality of being and meaning is unchangeable, without beginning and end, where reason does not reach all particulars but remains powerless before an irrationality evidenced in fate, man is the being who cannot guarantee his own happiness, who can no more witness an ultimate victory for virtue than he can for vice, for nothing new can rescue human being from confrontation with its own limitation. But the other side of this hopelessness is a nobility for man in maintaining the claims of rationality as an island in the sea of particularity constituting his sublunar home. The voice of aristocratism, which speaks in the privileged places and motions of nature, must echo in man's home; and thus activities like philosophy and political action are for the noble few and not for the many. Leadership and the rarity of excellence (as opposed to representation and a leveling of being) must be the outcome of the dialectic of the ancient logos, since knowing one's own limits is an ethical imperative as well as a cosmic principle.

The finitude of human being (and of being as such) permits only a purely negative and potential status for the infinite. Far from being an actual thing which is itself infinite, the infinite is simply a potential limitless divisibility characteristic of time and accounting for time's negation of being (in the lower places of the cosmos) and for its lacking a primary or irreducible part. The infinite can make no actual or positive incursion into the contingency of particulars, so that ancient culture can neither exult in, nor be plagued by, infinite aspirations (which could never be constitutive of what is properly human). Man is the being who gazes into his own finiteness because he himself is looked upon by the finiteness of the cosmic totality. A mean between what is divine and less-than-human in nature, man is preeminently a speaker of being (the divine having no need of speech)—the animal who bespeaks the essences of natural things. To be anything more or less is to fail to be properly human, for man as the measure of all things would negate philosophy as a properly human activity with a more-than-human (but natural) end. Philosophy must take its stand against the dominance of the first person in discourse and against immersion in subjectivity.

The baseline of the metaphysics presented (and brought to its perfection) by the ancient logos is the pregivenness of being. Being *as* being is to be unchanging, to have always been the same, to be the completed wholeness of the totality, to be a divine perfection of nature before which man bows, neither as suppliant nor as one who prays, but as one who admires and contemplates from afar. God is the immanent perfection of being, the eternally silent, purely rational "universal law for evermore" that is "called by many a name" precisely because it is the "all-bountiful" that "pulsates through all that nature brings to light."[2] Metaphysics never gets (nor desires to get) beyond the principled pregivenness of being, for all it would find is nothingness. Both the wonder commencing and the contemplation ending philosophy stand in awe of the fact that something (the totality) is rather than (only) nothingness.

Directed to a more-than-natural holiness, the Christian mythos has its origin in faith, which is at once an assent of the will and an intellectual assent resulting in knowledge, which begins as a willing and loving of a truth that is eventually known as a certainty, and which identifies the way to the truth with the truth itself (the identity being a person who is both God as end and man as way). Faith is thus a new locus for truth, shifting the emphasis from nature to person; the "I believe" of faith is an "I believe you," an assumption of the perspective of a second self that becomes a habitual intuition spread across the passing moments of time. The willed certainty of the believer feeds off the uncertainty and doubt of the natural man remaining in him, enabling faith to remain secure in the very uncertainty of itself, and requiring that faith not entrust itself primarily to the spoken word (a secret oral tradition) but embody itself in the infallibility of a written presentation (a book, a bible). Presupposing a new precedence for public written tradition, the Christian mythos (unlike the pagan mythos and ancient logos which are given all at once) must secure its being in time—must work itself out in a doctrinal development.

If quaternity is the number of reason for the ancient logos, triadism is the number of faith for Christian doctrine. God is a threefold polarity of oneness, oneness self-conscious, and the relation of oneness to self-consciousness—a unity whose nondivision becomes division while remaining nondivision in the becoming. No longer a natural *what* but a supernatural *who*, divine unity is a relation (a kind of democracy) of persons, who are not other in the very other-ing connoted by divine self-consciousness (subjectivity), and who therefore have no distance (space or place) between them. Infinite expressiveness characterizes the triune interior life of God, which assumes for itself the importance formerly attributed to the quaternary natural totality by the ancient logos, and that freely outward-izes itself in the Creation of what is by nature; so that nature has a beginning that is unnecessitated and that exists by virtue of a willing of the Divine Knower. This subordination of the *what* known to the *who* knowing suggests the beginning of a relational tripolar (rather than hierarchical) thinking about nature—the beginning of triadism as an un-pregiven cosmic principle, since God's triune interior life is gratuitously bound up with His career in Creation.

The divine beginning of nature (and therefore of time and space) has nothingness as its only stuff; this means that strictly speaking it has no stuff at all, no preexistent matter. The greatest of all beneficences, consequently, is not nature, which is itself a gift, but the freely willed, un-pregiven divine victory over nothingness in Creation. The divine bridging of the abyss between nothingness and (His own triune) Being engenders a gap between Himself (uncreated Being) and His Creation (created being)—an infinite distance, which is not a function of space, and which is therefore not really a distance at all. God can no longer be conceived as the above within nature, operating from spatial distance, but must be thought of as the absolute *other* to nature, whose presence to nature is His very absence from nature, since to create out of nothingness is to be near His Creation while being withdrawn from it. The other-ness of created nature to God is not that of being outside a determined space but is the otherness of time to an absolutely timeless eternal present who has no need of the timeless time of myth. Far from making the world on a pregiven pattern with specifiable spatial points of reference, God is the beginning who had no beginning for whom space has no primacy and for whom the significance of the higher does not define the significance of the lower. It is time and not space which testifies to the infinite gap between Creator and created nature insofar as time is a kind of divine withholding of nearness to created nature. This withholding entails a continuing Creation, a continual overcoming of a nothingness that remains as a trace in that which is created. From the divine viewpoint, however, this withholding is at-one with His nearness or presence to created nature; and so time must present itself as the creatural apprehension of the (absolutely other) Creator's eternal (absolutely timeless) point of view.

If Creation is the freely willed bridging of the abyss between (divine, triune) Being and nothingness, then the Incarnation is the fullness of a free divine initiative to bridge the gap between uncreated (supernatural) Being and created (natural) being—the gap between the Creator's and the creature's points of view. The Incarnation presents the person who is the way and truth of faith, the being who is at once Creator and creature in the very face of Creation's requiring that God not be a member of His Creation. Yet, if God freely breaks through the barrier of creatureliness, He nonetheless remains remote, a member of no spatial place in created nature, in the midst of His very nearness to every soul and molecule of that nature. The center of God's career in Redemption, this divine initiative to bridge the gap (made manifest by time) between uncreated and created being functions in terms of time, constituting itself as an endowing of a particular temporal event with a maximum of being. It is in a particular, privileged moment of time that the God-man "once and for all at the end of the age" sacrifices Himself in atonement for sin rather than "offer Himself repeatedly" in endless ritual (mythical) reenactment.[3] No mere imperfect imitation of Divine Being but a be-ing of the divine and the human, the Incarnation is a clothing of the supernatural in a unique historical being. The time whose time has come gives meaning to the places in which the God-man dwells, and the ancient mythic landmarks that represent the anchorage of essence in sacred places are replaced by personal holiness as a more-than-natural Being suffusing natural being. Constituted by his imitation of the God-man in the unique time in which he lives, the saint dwells upon the earth as a pilgrim with no need of being secured against the successiveness of time.

The divine career in Redemption and Creation as well as the divine triune essence point to a God who speaks. Divine self-consciousness is the Word, who speaks to nothing as if it were something (enabling it to become something), and who embodies Himself in a speech common to God and man. Man is a creature of speech only because God has first spoken, much as man is a lover of the divine only because God has first loved him; man's highest love is now a love of divine speech. If speech is characteristic of both God and man, the being of God presents itself as an absolute other to whom man can pray. A God who can be called upon (because He has called being out of nothingness and called upon man) must be an absolute divine nearness that is at once an absolute divine absence—an original hiddenness and un-pregivenness to human understanding who is at once a disclosure to human understanding.

The doctrinal development by which the Christian mythos works itself out has philosophical implications for the charting of a new logos, and the first of these implications is an absolute beginning and end for the being of nature, as opposed to the multiple conditioned mythic regenerations of nature (in the pagan mythos) and the eternal cosmos (of the ancient logos). God is the absolute subject of all being, the unconditional "I" of the "I am Who am," the end-without-end who is the beginning-without-beginning calling the "generations from the beginning." The infinite must now be conceived as positive and actual, as a meaningfully infinite Being beyond nature, and this infinite beginning of the finiteness of nature must be gradually absorbed by Western culture, reeducating it in terms of infinite aspirations. The second of these implications is the primacy of time and the subordination of space. No longer a numbering of movement and an eternal succession of nows, time is a measuring of consciousness and an interplay of three dimensions (like the three dimensions of the divine) with a direction. Time gains new significance as the very mode of being of the un-pregivenness and ongoingness of a created nature that does not have its existence as spatially articulated and circumscribed but as a relation of different states of the whole at different moments of its existence.

The third of these implications, consequently, is a new conception of totality—one that does not exist simply as the sum total of conditions for being but one that requires an unconditional subject (of being) other to it; man must now somehow speak of God *and* the totality. Far from being the excellence of being finished with a perfection unknown to anything else, far from being an order of things secured in their proper places, totality must now be an unfinished cosmos created anew at every moment by a supernatural other from whom it derives every fiber of its being. With unfinishedness perceived as the backdrop of an achieved order (rather than of chaos), time must be the most important dimension of a totality that is no mere hierarchy of planes and spacelike sections. And if Divine Creation is the bridging of the abyss between Being and nothingness (the radical derivation of something from nothing), the unfinishedness of the whole does not tell against God, for He is not adverse to calling man as cocreator into the very development (finishing) of the cosmos. The unfolding of totality has something to do with the discovery of its lawfulness and might even be implicated in a (human) system-building that progressively approaches the limits of spatialization and visualization. Time, which does not exist as a whole as soon as it begins, and which does not possess its substance all at once, is the reference point for such a totality; and this means that totality is indeed very fragile, always standing on the brink of a return to the chasm of nothingness from which it was created. Such fragility might even tempt some to use the term "universe" as a mere handy appellation with no literal meaning, should they lose sight of the supernatural stability that prohibits the totality from being perfectly self-contained in its being and meaningfulness.

Unlike the ancient logos (which is complete at any of its major points), the modern logos is developmental and has its being as a gradual assimilation of the philosophical implications of the doctrinal development by which the Christian mythos works itself out. In its beginning, the modern logos assimilates the philosophical significance of inside and outside as a replacement for the ancient metaphor of up and down. The creation of the heavenly bodies precedes the creation of life on earth, but the latter is seen to be superior to the former, so that perfection does not filter downward from the higher to the lower, but the temporal after is a kind of outward-izing of the meaning that was implicit in the temporal before. The metaphor proper to time is the inside and the outside, for time gains its significance, not in terms of the before and after of motion, but in terms of the Being of God as outside nature while present inside every iota of nature's being. If Divine Unity is no longer given spatially but instead freely valorizes time (by privileging certain moments of time as primary), then space can be construed as homogeneous and continuous (characterizing a nonhierarchical universe with no natural places, where every place is like every other), and time can be interpreted as inherently heterogeneous and discontinuous. The inferiority of spatial to temporal being thus initially presents itself to the modern logos as a new dualism of the outside and the inside—of an inferior (spatialized) nature and a superior (temporalized) consciousness.

Having to deal with (and attempting to overcome) this new dualism permits the modern logos to finally give philosophical stature to historicity. The intelligibility of the grand historical drama of Redemption is the context for the intelligibility perceived in the continually created natural world, and this confidence that history is gradually disclosing God's method in creating is appropriated as a constitution of man by history, a fusion of philosophy and history, an ontologization of history and an historicization of the cosmos. Yet, the waves of history wash upon the shores of eternity precisely because God never destroys an individual thing but fixes it in His eternal judgment. God's creative activity is an infinite attention to detail suffusing and defining His production of the whole, so that the particular thing is the terminus of this activity. The modern logos thus perceives the singular thing as alone having actual existence in nature, perceives the universal as having its being *as* the particular, and perceives the singular individual not as the occupant of a spatial place but as a temporal career. The primacy of time is of one piece with that of particularity. Beneath the philosophical valorization of history lies the notion of totality as a function of particularity, so that even the lowliest human life contains the whole of things human, and the noblest life presents no more of a lesson than our own. The forms can no longer be principles of limitation but are in a sense outside themselves, derived from a supernatural source, and even their presence as ideas within the Divine Intellect must prove unacceptable to the modern logos. God needs no forms to contemplate, and man too in his primal condition does not wonder at the perfection of nature (its eternal forms), does not act as spokesman for fixed essences, but names the animals and in a sense (like his Creator) brings forms into being. The contemplation of preexistent forms (which have no history) must vanish to make room for an ontologization of history rooted in particularity as measure.

The implicitly historical and particularistic thrust of the modern logos permits it to assign a new status to nature and novelty itself, thereby assimilating the Christian rejection of nature, as the principle of self-containment, and the Christian affirmation of nature as divine utterance. Taking its reference from temporal sequentiality, nature is like an exquisite poem whose order is achieved by the opposition of contraries, like a book that has its first principle in its author. A code rather than a repository of meanings, nature as a book is transformed into nature as a mechanism, no longer the most consummate organism, the self-sustaining producer, but an outwardly sustained product with parts outside of parts (and place more a matter of economy of operation than of integral order). Nature as a presentation of divine creative activity becomes nature as a presentation of man's rationality. A hierarchyless representative framework set up by man, nature is not older than man and exists *as* a picture of forces meant to be mastered by man's knowledge and production. The representative being of nature, however, takes its cue from the normativity of the particular, for it is the inexhaustible concrete particularity of nature that enables diverse mathematical theorems to prove isomorphic with the forces of nature, and thus permits the modern scientific mathematicization of nature. Creating the particulars of nature in a "certain weight, number, and measure," God does not have His glory reflected better in one place than in another, and (in contrast to the divine indifference to crashing worlds in antiquity) no thing is beneath His infinite concern or lacking in significance, even a sparrow's fall to the ground and the divinely numbered hairs of a man's head.

No less than the Christian mythos that is prepared to "speak at great lengths in praise of the worm" and of "ashes and dung," since everything, "however lowly is justly praised when it is compared with nothingness" (for it has infinite value over against the nothingness out of which it was created), the modern logos realizes that if it could understand a mere "flower in the crannied wall, root and all, and all in all," it should "know what God and man is."[4] If nature abounds with immanent purposiveness for the ancient logos, this purposiveness is not readily discoverable and seems to vanish for the modern logos, precisely because the purposes to which God puts the particulars of His Creation can only be surmised by human reason. Such is the inevitable price for the notion of totality as a becoming-whole, for the notion of cosmos as literally (and not merely figuratively) cosmo-genesis. The deification of the here and now and of that which happens once is really the announcement of a cosmos with abundant novelty, of the emergence of the radically new in being, and of the propositions that to be newer is to be better, that everything can and must be remade from the ground up. And this announcement is itself predicated upon the glad tidings of the new man (of faith) and of the new as the specific sign of creation.

Its notion of nature (as representation of a growing, novelty-engendering being) enables the modern logos to incorporate the Christian confidence that men are "gods" (who could be masters of nature if they are willing to be "sons of God") into the emergence of man as the ground of meaning. As the image of God (who is the beginning-without-beginning), man brings the natural world (which is the beginning-with-beginning) to consciousness in himself, and this consciousness is time which draws the beginning-with-beginning outward (and forward) toward its completion in the beginning-without-beginning (who is the end-without-end). The being whose very being is time, man is no longer a mean between what is divine and what is less-than-human in nature, but is a mean between what is supernatural (the thinking of which constitutes man's mind) and what is natural. It is no longer nature that assigns limits to being, but man who is called by God to fix the limits of nature for himself, so that man can now dare to inhabit the space between heaven and earth (the space proper to the gods of the pagan mythos) as its measure. The ancient foolishness of man as the measure of all things becomes modern wisdom, as man becomes the mean between divinity and nothingness, the being who is the consciousness of the trace of nothingness that remains in creation, the being who steps back from being as a stand-in for nothingness (and thus becomes the relational center of that which is). If man has nothing that he has not received, it is nonetheless the case that everything, even the being he has received, must arise from him. Human art is no longer an imitation of the largesse (at once the limitedness) of nature but an imitation of infinite, divine creative activity.

With all spatial references for man in nature now removed, the Christian sense of the saint as a pilgrim upon the earth is transformed into a modern sense of homelessness, as man attempts to assume an extra-earthly perspective on nature. A divine-human fact, after all, would have divine-human consequences, one of which might be that the truly real is not the finite but the unity of the finite and infinite in man. Man is tempted to be like his Creator, to think that he can guarantee his own happiness, to overthrow and create anew his political traditions, and the cynicism and despair issuing from such infinite aspirations appear far worse than the hopelessness of ancient culture. But the other side of this despair is an anticipation of meaning and novelty, a hopefulness before time and history that are no longer the ancient terrors they once were (even though man's perception of totality in terms of his own rationality threatens to become a new terror).

The emergence of man as the measure of intelligibility at once implicitly justifies and finds its condition in the peculiar epistemological emphasis engendered by the modern logos. Created nature could not have existed unless it had first been known to God, and this un-self-contained-ness of nature is a kind of "groaning in travail" and waiting with "eager longing" to compensate for its own want of knowledge and autonomy by pointing to the knowledge and the autonomy of man. The primacy of the Divine

Knower (which implies that truth is a quality of the Divine Intellect and not of any pregiven unities in nature) is transformed into the primacy of human knowing (like God's knowing). The primacy of the human knower within the representative framework of nature (where universality is a function of particularity) initially presents itself as eminently problematical by virtue of the unconsciousness of the modern logos of its ground in the primacy of the Divine Knower. Symptomatic of the liberation of the modern logos from obligation to Christian revelational truth (in order that man may legislate truth for himself), the elevation of epistemology, nonetheless, never gets anywhere by itself, implying that the modern logos never gets entirely freed from its ground in (and obligation to) that revelational truth. Positing knowledge as that which disposes the knower to go on to further knowledge, positing nothingness as all that remains between the knower and the known, and thus building itself upon a relational rather than essence-oriented logic, modern epistemology unconsciously assimilates the identity of way (method) and truth in faith, the status of nothingness in Creation, and the relational existence of divine (triune) knowing. The very unconsciousness of this assimilation accentuates the high degree of epistemological consciousness (knowledge being problematical in a way it could never be to the ancient logos) that modern physical science at once makes possible and feeds off.

If ancient physical science conforms to the cognitions of sacred place found in the pagan mythos, modern physical science conforms to faith in a God who gave man unerring knowledge of the world's structure and elements, of the beginning, middle, and end of time, that man might partake in the thoughts of God. Perfectly consistent in His creation of nature and man (as His image), God preadapts nature to the human mind, and this divine logic is incorporated by modern physical science, so that, much as God freely adapts Himself to His own methodology in creating (and redeeming), modern science adapts itself to its own results (which become part of its advancing methodology). The modern scientific liberation of quantity from its ancient scientific anchorage in quality presupposes the Christian revolt against a spatialized sacred and a temporalized (quantified) profane. The very treatment of modern scientifically disposed man as if he were an infinite being (mathematicizing nature) in the midst of his finitude takes its hold from the focusing of the infinite in the finite presented by the Creator who has become creature. And if modern science must ultimately confront an irrational core within itself that no scientific intelligence can solve, this itself is but a pale reflection of the nothingness perceived at the center of Divine Creation—a Creation presupposed and made more thinkable by this science. As a symbol-generating abstraction, this science strips away the allegories framed for nature by the ancient logos, removing the arbitrariness, occultness, and fate that remain in this nature, and in the process it renders an Efficient Cause of absolute power and intelligence (for the galaxies and the very subatomic particles) more thinkable.

The diverse ways in which the philosophical implications of a developing Christian doctrine are assimilated by a developing modern logos presuppose and clarify a new conception of philosophy. Unlike the ancient logos where the pursuit of wisdom begins with the wonder before nature endemic to the pagan mythos, wisdom begins for the Christian mythos in "fear of the Lord," in awe before a more-than-natural person whose knowing is at once the most efficient action (that of Creation out of nothingness). This implies the beginning of the end of contemplation, as a purely theoretical activity, as the highest end for man. The disappearance of contemplation occurs simultaneously with the emergence of the modern conception of philosophy that (far from beginning with the prephilosophical and ending in contemplation of the eternal forms by the noble few) begins and ends with itself as the preeminently practical-theoretical activity meant to be accessible to all men. Commencing and concluding with its own being, philosophy can neither operate with a secret oral tradition nor be given all at once, and like Christian doctrine (which is a developmental explication of the subjectively certain knowledge entailed by faith), modern philosophy is a developmental spelling out of (and attempt to make habitual for all men) the intuition of certitude lying at its beginning. This imitation of the habitualization of certitude (over the passing moments of time, and intended for all men) endemic to Christian faith means that the inwardness of certainty of Christian faith underlies the modern philosophical quest to make its own certitude fully explicit.

Nothing less than a developing incorporation of "the truth of Christianity into the certainty of humanity," modern philosophy's declaration of autonomy (its beginning and ending with itself) remains informed by its submission to the faith from which it proceeds as its first principle, even though this faith cannot be generated by man's own intellectual effort, and even when this faith becomes "no more than a pretence" and its "words an empty form."[5] The point is not the depth of Christian faith consciously operative in the modern logos, but the hidden authoritativeness of that faith for the "holiness" attributed to (modern philosophical) human reason, for if the God of Christianity works as effectively by His absence as by His presence, Christian faith must work as a leaven as effectively in those times when it is absent from human consciousness as it does in those times when it is present to this consciousness.

It is, therefore, the submerged belief in the freely willed divine career in Creation and Redemption (rooted in God's triune Being) that charts the course of modern philosophical development. The modern conception of nature as presentation of human reason (implying as it does the impossibility of a pure description of nature independent of man and historicity) builds itself upon the Christian notion of grace that intrudes into, mixes with, and transforms nature in the very act of building on nature. The demand of the modern logos for the certainty and self-security of human reason (as an illumination of nature) imitates the immediacy of grace's penetration of nature that transforms what is by nature an inaccessible limit into an attainable supernatural end for man (thereby illuminating the highest truth for man as a divinely accomplished certainty of salvation). Modern philosophy, therefore, presupposes (and develops, by properly philosophical means, the implications of) the completely un-pregiven, absolutely free, entirely gratuitous preadaptation of created being to a supernatural end that is now attainable. The modern logos is thus a coming into its own of the possibility of a more-than-natural consciousness that philosophizes about a nature that is transformed by grace. Here the modern logos must stand, even when unconscious of its standing—its diverse rejections of its own Christian doctrinal ground themselves pointing to that ground (and requiring that modern culture remain Christian even when it loses its faith).

The baseline of the metaphysics presented (but hardly brought to perfection) by the modern logos is the un-pregivenness of being, exemplified in subjectivity as the unconditional positing that is the original form of metaphysics. Much as the unconditional positing of the Creator does not look to anything outside Himself as a model for what He creates, the unconditional positing act of the human knower does not look to anything outside his own knowing (absolutely confident that being and intelligibility are coextensive—that no thing is above or beneath the reach of reason). The modern metaphysical claim to an unshakable foundation of truth in human reason ("I exist") takes its reference from divine self-knowledge ("I am Who am"). With divine (triune) subjectivity as its hidden condition, philosophical discourse can grow accustomed to the dominance of the first person, much as subjectivity can assume metaphysical significance. A dialectic of representation and a leveling of being, a democratizing of beings, in which the infinite is brought into relation with each and every human subject, begins to find its metaphysical embodiment. The paradigm of this dialectic is a God for whom there are no distinctions in places, as there are no distinctions in races, families, and political orders—a God who requires a religion that is no longer patrimonial, a worship and mythos that are no longer secret but carried to the furthest places and the most indifferent men. And if such a God *really* exists and really has become man while remaining God, then it is not simply the case that man's understanding of being has changed, but it is the case that the very meaningfulness of being, the very being of the preeminently real, has changed.

To be in the most fundamental sense is no longer to be finished and without beginning but is to be unfinished and the beginning of being. Being *as* being is the very becoming of itself, the very coming toward itself, the direction and historicity of itself, and no longer the principled pregivenness of nature. But the metaphysics of unfinished being can neither come to be nor disclose any truth unless the beginning of being is the beginning without beginning, the divine subject of being. No longer bowing before the .eternally silent divine finishedness of nature, as one who admires and contemplates from afar, modern man perceives himself as the relational center of unfinished being precisely because his being is defined by the possibility of prayer to an absolute other. No longer the being who is gazed upon by a finished finite totality, man is the being who works on behalf of the finishing of totality, and therefore is the being whose very autonomy is subject to a judgment that will preside over totality itself. Able to call upon a God who Himself speaks, men will be judged by their words that are meant to display "exercises of Reason" in the "obedience of Faith" for the comfort of God's elect—an elect that grows larger, as the names appropriate to a more-than-natural God steadily diminish.[6]

In this way, the amazement of the ancient logos before the finality and principled pregivenness of nature, before the fact that something is rather than nothing, is transformed by the modern logos into an amazement before the un-pregivenness of being, before the continual, freely willed divine rescuing of being from nothingness. And if modern culture appears adverse to prayer, the possibility of prayer is nonetheless its very condition. The "Father of Lights" who speaks being out of nothingness is the hidden condition of modern man's illumination of the night of nature that descends daily but no longer eternally upon an earth (no longer man's assigned home) where spatial distances are diminished by the human voice. In a cosmos where meaningfulness is not excluded from anything and is grounded in a measure not of this world, even the lightbulb and the telephone have a metaphysical significance.

Our phenomenology of the Christian mythos and modern logos (over against the pagan mythos and ancient logos) leads us to the conclusion that, whatever other aspects of deterioration modernity manifests, its logic is no mere progress of an intellectual disease, for our profile of modernity has made explicit what is illustrated by the preceding chapters of this book, namely, that there are cosmologies (and even societies) that, when confronted by Christian faith, must eventually perish, and that the history of philosophy must be studied very closely to ascertain the kind of cosmos such faith prohibits and permits. Western civilization itself, at this point, would appear to be a historical winnowing of cosmoi—its matter provided by the ancient logos and its form provided by the Christian mythos. Christianity is thus a religion that is more than a religion (a religion that must be either total imposture or total truth), and, therefore, the Christian mythos is more than a mythos, for it is implicitly a transcendence of myth that must be worked out in history. This transcendence becomes explicit in modern self-conscious culture that unconsciously transmits and reshapes Christianity, thereby suggesting a spreading of the Christian message, not simply in terms of an uttered creed (to which individuals assent), but in terms of deep-seated changes in thinking that have now made it impossible to think in the way ancient man was accustomed to think on a whole variety of issues (not the least of which is slavery).

For all this, the peculiar greatness of the logic of modernity may consist in its being of no inherent value in itself but of value only as a transition from the medieval assimilation of (and reaction to) ancient philosophy to a full-fledged Christian philosophy (a perfected metaphysics of a novelty-engendering being) and a truly free Christianity. Trinitarianism, Creationism, and Incarnationism are hardly man's natural way of thinking, and the modern cosmos, which (unlike the ancient cosmos) exists directly through the wills and beliefs of men, may be only the beginning of man's learning to think (beyond the limits of theology) a meaningfully infinite being. If this is so, we today, who are living through the closing of the second millennium of the Christian epoch in a culture (that has been called post-Christian) where the practical implications of the modern logos are becoming fully visible and doing battle, may really be living in a time of "the no-more of the gods that have fled and the not-yet of the God that is coming."[7]

AN EXERCISE IN THINKING ABOUT THE PRESENT AGE IN THE LIGHT OF MODERNITY

On July 20, 1917, the American secretary of war reached into a large bowl and drew the first number of the more than two and one-half million men to be mobilized for the first of the century's

world wars. Twenty-seven years later to the day, a bomb exploded at Adolf Hitler's headquarters but failed to kill the man
who had led the century into the second of its world wars; interpreting his survival as a sign that fate had preserved him for his
mission, Hitler gave the survivors of the explosion a medal on
which appeared his name and the date 20 July 1944. Twenty five
years later to the day, utilizing the rocketry that Hitler had used
for destruction, an American mission landed on the moon, and
Commander Neil A. Armstrong, having walked on its surface,
contrasted its near colorlessness with the "bright and beautiful"
earth looming over the western horizon. The thought that began
modernity, namely, that the earth was a "noble star," was now
a perception, and God's name was pronounced in space. Yet, these
dates mark an age where technology feeds the "predatory lusts"
and "angelic impulses" dividing the heart of the century, and thus
the event of July 20, 1969, could also be perceived as another
instance of "unprecedented power operating in an unprecedented
spiritual vacuum."

We have set ourselves the task of appropriating the modern
history of philosophy as part and parcel of the process of understanding the unique way in which the human manifests itself in
the present age; technology itself would seem to be the unique
way we are seeking to understand. Technology is to be found,
of course, in the ancient world, but its primary source of energy
there is slavery. The beginning of what would be modern power
technology lies in the later Middle Ages where the energy of
animals, running water, and wind replaces the energy of slaves.
What is unique about the present age is that modern power technology has become less revolutionary, man has grown accustomed
to it; it has become man's way of being in the world, so that he
is not at all surprised when he finally gets to the moon. Our task
is to begin to think about the innermost nature of technology as
the distinctive characteristic of man's ordinary experience in the
twentieth century.

Technology as such is a release of man from some given aspect
of nature. Thus the alphabet releases him from the magical overtones of the spoken word, the clock from complete obedience to
seasonal rhythms and recurrence, the telegraph from the necessity

of a human messenger, and the lightbulb from obedience to the cycle of night and day. This release from natural givens is both intensified and speeded up in the twentieth century. Thus, with the telephone someone who is not bodily here has his voice called up and made to be here, while with the tape recorder a man hears his own voice while he is no longer speaking, and with the television his vision is not simply extended but he sees through walls; the movie camera contracts and rolls up space and time on a spool and translates them onto a screen, while the airplane rolls up the ground into itself and becomes a self-contained transportation permitting man (in jet travel) to very nearly transcend the experience of the act of traveling; and the rocket, projected beyond the earth, permits man to go where he could not otherwise go. All forms of technology are modes of storing experience, of translating one kind of knowledge into another, of getting at one thing through another, and of informing, extending, and enhancing man's senses; but these modes are intensified and knit together into an encompassing human environment in the twentieth century—an environment that creates its own world of demands, that radically extends the sheer physical influence of each man, that is capable of exerting psychic action (and even of simulating human consciousness), and that can maximize its power with less and less hardware. If modern power technology transforms toolmaking into the unlimited fabrication of tools to make tools, and if it transforms the imposition of an idea on matter by the craftsman into the objectification of the idea (altering the matter) in the machine, this unlimited fabrication and concrete conferring of objectivity by the human subject are made in the twentieth century into an encompassing program, a veritable *environment*, a centralizing institution to which all other institutions must adjust. No longer requiring the self-conscious justification found in the nineteenth century, modern power technology is secured as man's *ordinary* way of being in the world, and it can now be said that the question of being itself is the question of the essence of technology.

Technology in the present age is the very mode of man's presence and absence to physical things and (increasingly) to other human subjects; presence and absence, no longer mediated by

what is given by nature, are mediated by man as the very being
who is present to and absent from, so that technology becomes
a way of presencing and absencing in which man himself is presence-er and absence-er, in which man no longer waits for nature
to mediate the other's presence to him but takes this presencing
upon himself without question or doubt. Technology becomes
a network that is an objectification of human consciousness, a web
of relationships binding together all things and spun out of human
subjectivity—the practical outcome of the modern mode of self-
consciousness, of the modern interpretation of nature as representation of human consciousness. The modern philosophical
tendency to recast contemplation as a form of power, to affirm
the self-referentiality of thought, to perceive being as the very
coming toward itself (as that which already is what at the same
time it is not yet) finds its institutional embodiment in twentieth-
century technology as the forum for the concretization of the
thought of power, as the real "will to power," as the unprecedented unification of power over nature (including human nature).
The centuries of modern knowing in the mode of making
("knowledge is power") appear to be the apprenticeship for the
century where man makes most if not all of what he wants to
know (power is knowledge), and this seems to lead all too readily
to a conclusion where unprecedented power is seen to function
in a near spiritual vacuum.

All that remains of diverse traditions and civilizations other than
Western must meet the terms laid down by the man-made forms
that constitute the contemporary concretization of the thought-
world of modernity. All of us today either live or will soon live
in a world where we will confront more of man and his consciousness than we will of nature and its givens. Yet the very logic
of technology's release from the givens of nature indirectly pro-
motes the preservation of certain of these givens, so that man
seeks to protect nature from his own creation of technological
forms. It is not, of course, the essences of nature in themselves
(the tree-ness of the tree, for example) that are preserved but rather
the things of nature as resting places for human consciousness.
The logic of contemporary man's programmatic concretization
of modernity could, in the final analysis, very well point not to

a completely denaturalized nature but to some kind of cultivation of nature for human consciousness. The climactic event of the contemporary world of technological forms, in fact, enables man to be amazed by the earth as he views it from the moon, so that ancient wonder before the heavens is now amazement before the planet earth.

The human movement into the space beyond the earth is not simply the greatest form (combining so many other forms) of the contemporary technological world but may very well be the beginning of a process that will make clear the proper focus for technology. Modern science creates a single (mathematical) physics for the earth and heavenly bodies, and it does this by attempting in thought to treat the observer as outside the earth (assuming an extraterrestrial perspective on the earth), so that man carries the Archimedean point in his own mind (within himself) and is freed from the human condition of being an inhabitant of the earth. This permits the emergence of an accelerated modern power technology, insofar as the nature of the earth can now be viewed as a kind of representation on man's part of the forces of nature, and these forces can be seen as a framework to be controlled and mastered. As long as man does not or is not able to bring himself bodily into the space outside the earth, then science itself is entirely limited to assuming the perspective of mastery of the earth as material for consumption and production. But once man actually (physically) attains a point in outer space, he attains a point of leverage from which he can perfect the focus of technology; the focus need no longer be the total transformation of the earth into a man-made world but can instead be the making of the universe outside the earth into the object to be transformed by his technology. For the first time, technology can now have limited aspirations on earth precisely because it has begun to discover that its infinite aspirations lie in outer space. Technology can now preserve the beneficial aspects of earthly nature in their integrity and might even be able to transpose a portion of these aspects into the organically dead worlds in the immediate vicinity of the earth or into artificially created worlds around the planets. The space outside the earth would become the primary object and no longer simply the perspective of technology; instead of looking down upon the earth as the productive engineer, man would now be able to look to space as the material for his engineering while he looks to earth as the garden of his delights—his true home (once again) because it is his home base in creating his technological environment. This is hardly to suggest a technology-free earth but only to suggest that the earth will no longer be the sole object for the infinite aspirations of power technology but will instead be a realm where a less and less visible technology (the machines having receded into the walls) exists.

"The essence of technology," says Martin Heidegger, "is by no means anything technological," and "all that is merely technological never arrives at the essence of technology."[8] The contemporary world of technological forms appears as a manifestation of unprecedented power functioning in a spiritual vacuum precisely because technology hides (and has thus far been necessitated to hide) its essence—the spiritual fountain from which it drinks. It is only in its attempt to get away from its conditions on earth, and thus in a sense to get away from itself, by casting man into the "magnificent desolation" of outer space, that technology enables man to begin to wonder at its own essence. The piecemeal marvels of technology distract man from the marvel of technology itself, from being amazed at the essence of technology itself, so that technologizing hides from us the wellspring of the being of technology itself. But in the movement into outer space the more-than-technological essence of technology begins to disclose itself.

In modern power technology man stands forth and challenges the being of nature to be *for* him; in challenging the forces of nature to be for him, man stores up and transforms the energies of nature, redisposing these energies and making them available in ways they could not have been if they had been left at peace in the womb of nature. In doing this man proves that nature can be *for* him, proves that nature is not a beneficence but a transformation point in his own consciousness. Nature is a field of forces to be transformed rather than an inherent context of meaningfulness itself. Man unlocks the hidden meaning of which nature is but a code, and he subjects this meaning to the transformations enacted by his own consciousness. He thus becomes an encompassing predator upon a nature that serves his willing, and nature is reduced to the amorphous material for man's transformative willing.

But this willing that wills itself in technology does not exhaust the meaningfulness of technology's essence. The human willing that wills itself here is impossible without a deep, historically developed, philosophical context, namely, the logic of modernity, and this context is embroiled in the claims of a more-than-natural consciousness rooted in revelational categories. In being a concretization of the modern thought-world, the contemporary world of technological forms leans not only on the primitive beginnings of modern power technology in the late Middle Ages but also on the medieval thought-world that made the modern thought-world possible. For the medieval thought-world, nature possesses a significance that transcends its immediate reality; all things are trinities of essence, power, and operation—of the power of the Father, the wisdom of the Word, the goodness of the Holy Spirit—and the world is invested with such an intense (triune) relationality that its essence is seen to be in every one of its parts, in every individual (the being of which is inexhaustible). At once absolute movement and absolute rest, Divine (triune) Being creates nature as at once near and withdrawn, infinitely beyond and yet a kind of infinite abyss (or within) of nature.

This medieval thought-world that presents divine power and divine presence and absence to a particularized nature is itself built around a spirituality that claims to be a divine calling of man to relate to God as an equal in the very face of the fact that by nature man can never be such an equal. It is this spirituality and its claim that, in being the hidden condition for the thought-world of modernity, must also lie hidden beneath technology as contemporary man's mode of being in the world. Kierkegaard glimpses the world-unifying otherworldliness of this spirituality.

When the seed of the oak is planted in earthen vessels, they break asunder; . . . what must happen when the God implants Himself in human weakness, unless man becomes a new vessel and a new creature. But this becoming, what labors will attend the change, how convulsed with birth pangs! And how rapt in fear; for it is indeed less terrible to fall to the ground when the mountains tremble at the voice of the God, than to sit at table with Him as an equal; and yet it is the God's concern precisely to have it so. . . . . If this fact came into the world as an absolute paradox, nothing that happens subsequently can avail to change this. The consequences will in all eternity remain the consequences of a paradox and hence in an ultimate view will be precisely as improbable as the paradox itself. . . . The advantage of the consequence would seem to lie in a gradual naturalization of this fact.[9]

The realm of infinite aspirations for power found in contemporary technology, a realm now beginning to extend beyond the earth, finds the condition of its own paradoxicality in the paradoxes of Scripture. For it is Scripture that speaks of faith not in "the wisdom of men but in the power of God," of hope proceeding from the "power of the Holy Spirit," of a God whose Kingdom "does not consist in talk but in power," of a God who endows men "with strength like His own," and of a world the very "form" of which is "passing away." Technology as man's way of being in the world, while being the world-making of man, is yet no mere human doing, and in it is to be found the "lightning flash of being" in which "roots and thrives the saving power"—a more-than-human power. The unnatural or denaturalizing thrust of this technology is preconditioned by the thinking of the possibility of a more-than-natural being, and ultimately by a spirituality that claims world-shattering implications flowing from an absolute otherworldliness. And in this way, the hidden saving power submerged in the essence of technology as man's mode of being in the present age is rooted in the claims of this spirituality. The human will to willing does not, therefore, exhaust the essence of technology as man's mode of being in the world, but rather this willing of willing itself hides the thinking of a divine knowing that is at once a divine willing. The hiddenness of such thinking begins to disclose itself as man bodily pushes himself into the space of the pagan gods, the space beyond the earth, and begins to wonder at the earth from an entirely new and unprecedented physical perspective, a perspective more like God's than ever before.

The coming-into-its-own of the technological way of being of contemporary man (i.e., its finding its proper focus in the space beyond earth) would thus be the beginning of the coming into its own of the disclosure of the possibility of a divine more-than-natural condition as technology's own condition for being. Contemporary technology as a new way in which things are present and absent to man—by virtue of man as presence-er and absence-er—would thus be a new mode of the presencing and absencing of being itself—a mode that derives its possibility from God's manner of presencing and absencing Himself from His Creation. No longer present and absent to nature spatially but through time itself, God's mode of presence and absence is the primal condition for the thinking and realizing of the possibility of a technological presencing and absencing of nature to and by man (not in a spatial but in a temporal fashion). Modern power technology, with its beginning in the late Middle Ages (and here the invention of the mechanical clock appears to be decisive), presupposes a developing awareness of a new value for time (with its instants perceived as dissimilar, heterogeneous, but able to be uniformly marked)—a value that itself presupposes abrupt increments of novelty in being. And contemporary technology programmatically strives to overcome space (on earth and in the heavens) while developing its novel forms (one building upon the other, the later encompassing and subsuming the earlier) in a temporal sequence. Contemporary technology is a programmatic implementation of a temporal way of being in the world, the fruit of a philosophical consciousness of time that is in turn the fruit of a thinking of a Divine Being who mediates His presence and absence to Creation temporally and valorizes temporal particulars.

To speak, then, of contemporary technology as a manifestation of unprecedented power in an unprecedented spiritual vacuum is to speak about the way in which this technology presents itself by hiding the very spiritual well-spring from which it drinks. Man leaves the earth as a predator upon nature—this is true—and he physically usurps what was once only the mythical space of the gods, and he arrogates to himself the angelic impulse that Christianity presents, while remaining a predator upon nature. But he enters the spaces beyond earth to pronounce the name of God and to begin to stand in amazement before his own planet. His very entrance into the space beyond earth must have ramifications for the very name of God he pronounces. Ultimately the coming into un-hiddenness of the hidden spiritual condition of

contemporary technology intimates the possibility of a new presencing of God. For Scripture has not testified to, and God has not
yet pronounced man's "dominion over the luminaries of heaven
or over the secret heaven itself," and the hidden spiritual condition
of technology as man's mode of being in the world (no less than
the hidden condition of the logic of modernity that makes possible
this mode) cannot remain forever hidden.

To speculate on the possibility of a new divine presencing to
man is, needless to say, to speculate in the most speculative of
terms. It is to speculate on how Christian philosophy can be the
philosophical being to which the logic of modernity is but a
bridge, and it is to speculate on how the possibility of prayer to
a more-than-natural divine other (as the hidden condition of such
a logic) might become un-hidden and actualized. The God making
possible such an actualization is no mere cosmic principle for a
principled and finished nature but is the infinite speaker of being
out of nothingness. This God who has spoken of old in "many
and diverse ways," this God "Almighty who was and is and is
to come," reigns as the "King of the Ages" over and through and
in time, making "all things new" and constantly drawing men to
knowledge of themselves by drawing them to knowledge of Himself, even though it does not "yet appear" to men "what we shall
be." Having made the sun (the explosions of which man now
replicates on earth at his own peril) and the moon (which now
preserves man's footprints and is no longer simply the object of
his myth-making) as "two great lights, the greater light to rule
the day, and the lesser light to rule the night," God can now be
prayed to as the speaker of being out of absolute nonbeing who
shows forth His glory to man in yet other lights, the Father of
innumerable lights, who draws man toward the very stars man
once thought to be divine and that he now knows to be among
the particulars that God has crafted.

Absolutely free in showing forth His glory, God will still show
that glory at His will and not man's, but the possibility of this
showing can now be prayed for in ways that it could not before
contemporary technology thrust man into the spaces beyond the
earth. And if God's willing has opened itself to and embraced
man's willing, even man's willing of willing in technology (and

his willing of a dominion not yet suspected by Scripture), the possibility of a new presencing of God, of a God who is *to come* (at once the God who was and is) must have something to do with man's knowing and willing—with how intently man will pray (and prepare his mind) for this new presencing.

In this way, such a presencing of God will have something to do with the hidden condition of the logic of modernity, namely, faith, becoming unhidden and conscious. Man's autonomy itself must, in the end, be judged by a higher standard (the glory of God), but the fact of man's autonomy will remain and will not be negated by God, much as nature is to be judged by a higher standard (man's consciousness); but, in the end, nature will remain and will not be negated by man. God is the Creator of nature; man is the creator of a technologized world; God and man are the co-creators of history. History is the context of God and man's respective creations. And God is hidden in all, making technology no merely human thing even in its being created by man.

The way in which one interprets the significance of the present age and the way in which one speculates about the future to which it might lead come down in the final analysis to the significance one sees in the world-unifying otherworldliness of Christianity. If Christianity is the "ineluctable poetic pretension" or if man now and for the future is cut off from the will to will the truth of Christianity, then technology (as man's mode of being in the world) as well as the diverse forms of madness in the present age constitute the breaking of the sacred limits of nature by a being who is meant to be defined by these limits. The modern notion of man as the measure of all things would then be supreme foolishness—having now come home in the present age to stew in its own juices. The madness of our times would not be the corruption of something wonder-full but would only be what it all too readily appears to be: angelic aspirations with purely animal outcomes, man becoming a beast in striving to be a god. The present age would consequently be purely and simply an "irreligious time" of decline, a century of purely "extensive" possibilities and effectiveness, of purely technical possibilities operating in a spiritual vacuum, where the assimilation of ideas into the technical framework renders them "materially effective" but

"spiritually worthless," where men are increasingly unable to
move in the realm of the invisible, and where men are increasingly
able to act in common only by virtue of their "commonest and
lowest nature." A boundless individuality interpreting all things
in reference to a self functioning on the lowest levels of experience
would become the symptom of a demise of civilization that itself
presses on to a technological world order where men will be
conditioned to a well-adjusted but spiritually impoverished animality. In 1920 William Butler Yeats poetically framed the vision
in "The Second Coming"—having seen the spiritual exhaustion
signaled by the first of the century's world wars. "Things fall
apart; the centre cannot hold; / Mere anarchy is loosed upon the
world / . . . and everywhere . . . / The best lack all conviction,
while the worst / Are full of passionate intensity." Yet he also
saw that the significance of these times inevitably, if distortedly,
pointed to the significance of Christianity, for ". . . what rough
beast, its hour come round at last, / Slouches towards Bethlehem
to be born?"

If Christianity, however, has become ineluctable but is far more
than a poetic pretension, and if man has not definitively lost the
will to will Christianity, the massive failings of the present age
could be the subversion of the greatness of its own paradoxical
being (which is a consequence of an even greater paradox), making
its own greatness turn against itself. And these failings could be
part of the trampling of the path to the power realm of spirituality
through the power realm of technology—a proving of the mettle
of spirituality in the trial by fire that attempts to disprove spirituality. But if this is to be, we today cannot simply will the
presence of the God of Christianity into being; we can "at the
most only wake the readiness for the expectation" of such a God;
we can only "through thinking and writing prepare to be prepared
for the manifestation" of such a God. The task of making human
consciousness ready for the presencing of the truly Cosmic God
(who is no member of the cosmos) may very well be the most
important philosophical task that remains for the present age—a
preparation for the age of Christian philosophy in which the truth
of the logic of modernity will become manifest. Long ago St.
Augustine suggested a possibility whose full realization may re-

quire the cosmic perspective of man's departure into the spaces beyond the earth: "Now if wisdom is God who made all things, as is attested by the Divine authority and truth, then the philosopher is a lover of God."[10] If the logic of modernity is what it is presented to be in this book, and if this logic is to lead to the fullness of its meaning beyond itself, this may be the only way open to the philosopher. There may be no possibility of returning to the *nous* of Greek philosophy, and the only other alternatives may be the absorption of philosophy by the sciences or the end of philosophy as such.

In the final analysis—if this exposition of the logic of modernity is substantially correct—the twentieth century is the distillation of that logic into the realm of common sense or ordinary experience; and whatever truth is to be found in that logic is a transmission and articulation of the theoretical content of Christianity. In the end, of course, this book falls short of its aim, namely, to verbalize in full what was unsaid but presupposed by the modern philosophers; it is, furthermore, only the *beginning* of a philosophical reflection on the meaning of the present age. And so, one can *hope* for a return of philosophy in the late twentieth century to its critical and speculative grandeur: a reflection on the innermost intelligibility of the present age by means of a reflective reappropriation of philosophical modernity and its medieval Christian sources.

LIST OF WORKS
FREQUENTLY CITED

BH   Becker, Carl L. *The Heavenly City of the Eighteenth-Century Philosophers.* New Haven: Yale University Press, 1932.

BT   Berkeley, George. *A Treatise Concerning the Principles of Human Knowledge.* With critical essays, edited by Colin Murray Turbayne. Indianapolis: Bobbs-Merrill, 1970.

CN   Carpino, Joseph. "A Study of Negation in Hegel." Doctoral dissertation, Department of Philosophy, Fordham University, 1960.

CP   Cassirer, Ernst. *The Philosophy of the Enlightenment.* Translated by Fritz C. A. Koelln and James P. Pettegrove. Boston: Beacon Press, 1955.

DP   Descartes, René. *The Philosophical Works of Descartes.* Translated by Elizabeth Haldane and G. R. T. Ross. Two vols. London: Cambridge University Press, 1911 (reprinted 1977).

DU   Dewey, John. "Leibniz's New Essays Concerning the Human Understanding." In *The Early Works of John Dewey, 1882–1898.* Volume I: 1882–1888. Edited by Jo Ann Boydston et al. Carbondale, Ill.: Southern Illinois University Press, 1969.

GE   Gay, Peter. *The Enlightenment: An Interpretation.* Vol. I: *The Rise of Modern Paganism.* Vol. II: *The Science of Freedom.* New York: Alfred A. Knopf, 1967, 1969.

HC   Hartle, Ann. "Rousseau on the Nature of Man in *The Confessions.*" Doctoral dissertation (listed under McArdle, Ann), Department of Philosophy, City University of New York, 1976.

HH   Hegel, G. W. F. *Hegel's Lectures on the History of Philosophy.* Translated by E. S. Haldane and Frances H. Simson (1892). Three vols.

London: Routledge and Kegan Paul; New York: Humanities Press (reprinted 1955).

HL   Hegel. *Hegel's Logic* (Part One of the *Encyclopaedia of the Philosophical Sciences*). Translated by William Wallace. Oxford: At the Clarendon Press, 1975.

HP   Hegel. *Phenomenology of Spirit*. Translated by A. V. Miller. Oxford: At the Clarendon Press, 1977.

HR   Hegel. *Lectures on the Philosophy of Religion*. Translated from the second German edition by E. B. Speirs and J. B. Sanderson. Three vols. London: Routledge and Kegan Paul; New York: Humanities Press, 1962 (reprinted 1974).

HS   Hegel. *Hegel's Science of Logic*. Translated by A. V. Miller. London: George Allen and Unwin; New York: Humanities Press, 1969 (reprinted 1976).

HY   Hyppolite, Jean. *Genesis and Structure of Hegel's 'Phenomenology of Spirit'*. Translated by Samuel Cherniak and John Heckman. Evanston, Ill.: Northwestern University Press, 1974.

KC   Kant, Immanuel. *Critique of Pure Reason*. Translated by Norman Kemp Smith. Unabridged Edition. New York: St. Martin's Press, 1965.

LW   Locke, John. *The Works of John Locke*. Ten vols. London, 1823. Reprinted by Scientia Verlag Aalen, 1963.

MP   Masters, Roger D. *The Political Philosophy of Rousseau*. Princeton: Princeton University Press, 1968.

NW   Nietzsche, Friedrich. *The Will to Power*. Translated by Walter Kaufmann and R. J. Hollingdale. New York: Random House, Vintage Books, 1968.

RI   Rousseau, Jean-Jacques. "A Discourse on the Origin of Inequality." In *The Social Contract and Discourses*. Translated by G. D. H. Cole. New York: E. P. Dutton, 1950.

TB   Tipton, I. C. *Berkeley: The Philosophy of Immaterialism*. London: Methuen, 1974.

NOTES

PREFACE

1. *Hegel's Philosophy of Right*, trans. T. M. Knox (New York: Oxford University Press, 1969), Preface, p. 11.
2. James Collins, *Interpreting Modern Philosophy* (Princeton: Princeton University Press, 1972), p. 406.
3. Edmund Husserl, *The Crisis of European Sciences and Transcendental Phenomenology*, trans. David Carr (Evanston, Ill.: Northwestern University Press, 1970), p. 71.
4. Ibid., p. 70.
5. See *HL*, # 19, p. 25; *HS*, Preface to Second Edition, p. 31.
6. Husserl, p. 73.
7. Friedrich Nietzsche, *The Gay Science*, trans. Walter Kaufmann (New York: Random House, Vintage Books, 1974), # 343, p. 279.
8. Ludwig Feuerbach, *Principles of the Philosophy of the Future*, trans. Manfred H. Vogel (Indianapolis: Bobbs-Merrill, Library of Liberal Arts, 1966), # 18, p. 30.
9. Leo Strauss, "Jerusalem and Athens: Some Introductory Reflections," *Commentary*, June 1967, p. 45.

CHAPTER ONE

1. Henry Osborn Taylor, *The Medieval Mind: A History of the Development of Thought and Emotion in the Middle Ages*, 2 vols., 4th ed. (Cambridge: Harvard University Press, 1925), Vol. I, p. xi.
2. Charles H. Haskins, *The Renaissance of the Twelfth Century* (New York: Meridian Books, 1957), p. v.
3. Lynn T. White, Jr., "Technology and Invention in the Middle Ages," *Speculum*, 15 (1940), p. 156. See also White's "The Significance of Medieval Christianity," in George F. Thomas, ed., *The Vitality of The Christian Tradition* (New York: Harper and Brothers, 1945), p. 91.
4. Williaam Carroll Bark, *Origins of the Medieval World* (Stanford: Stanford University Press, 1958), p. 27.

5. Kenneth Clark, *Civilization: A Personal View* (New York: Harper and Row, 1969), p. 7.

6. Bark, p. 62.

7. Ibid., p. 82.

8. Lynn T. White, Jr., *Medieval Technology and Social Change* (Oxford: At the Clarendon Press, 1962), p. 78.

9. William H. McNeill, *The Shape of European History* (New York: Oxford University Press, 1974), p. 85.

10. White, *Medieval Technology*, pp. 87–88.

11. Ibid., p. 124.

12. Mircea Eliade, *The Sacred and the Profane: The Nature of Religion*, trans. Willard R. Trask (New York: Harper Torchbooks, 1959), p. 20.

13. Ernst Cassirer, *The Philosophy of Symbolic Forms*, trans. Ralph Manheim, 3 vols. (New Haven: Yale University Press, 1953), Vol. II, pp. 99–100.

14. Cf. Heraclitus, Fragments # 45, 46, in Milton C. Nahm, ed., *Selections from Early Greek Philosophy*, 3d ed. (New York: Appleton-Century-Crofts, 1947), p. 91.

15. See S. Sambursky, *Physics of the Stoics* (New York: Macmillan, 1959), pp. 21–80; and Margaret E. Reesor, "The Stoic Categories," *American Journal of Philology*, 78 (1957), pp. 63–82.

16. Mircea Eliade, *Cosmos and History: The Myth of the Eternal Return*, trans. Willard R. Trask (New York: Harper Torchbooks, 1959), p. 11.

17. Aristotle, *Metaphysics*, trans. Richard Hope (Ann Arbor, Mich.: University of Michigan Press, Ann Arbor Paperbacks, 1960), 1010a, 18–22, p. 79.

18. George Boas, "Aristotle's Presuppositions about Change," *American Journal of Philology*, Vol. 68, p. 411.

19. Aristotle, *Physica*, trans. R. P. Hardie and R. K. Gaye, in W. D. Ross, ed., *The Works of Aristotle* (Oxford: At the Clarendon Press, 1930), Vol. II, 207b, 15–20.

20. William James, *Some Problems of Philosophy: A Beginning of an Introduction to Philosophy*, (1911) (New York: Greenwood Press, 1968 reprint), pp. 214–215.

21. Aristotle, *De Generatione et Corruptione*, trans., H. H. Joachim, in Ross, Vol. II, 337a, 31–34.

22. See ibid., 337b, 15–35.

23. Thomas Kuhn, *The Copernican Revolution: Planetary Astronomy in the Development of Western Thought* (New York: Vintage Books, 1959), p. 43.

24. Mircea Eliade, *Patterns in Comparative Religion*, trans. Rosemary Sheed (New York: Meridian Books, 1963), pp. 17–18.

25. Joannes Scotus Eriugena, *Periphyseon* (*De Divisione Naturae*), *Books One and Two*, trans. I. P. Sheldon-Williams with the collaboration of Ludwig Bieler, 2 vols. (Dublin Institute for Advanced Studies, 1968, 1972), Bk. I, ch. 39 (482a, 25–26), ch. 10 (451b, 5–6), ch. 66 (510b, 31–33), in Vol. I, pp. 127, 59, 191.

26. See Henry Bett, *Johannes Scotus Erigena: A Study in Medieval Philosophy* (New York: Russell and Russell, 1964), p. 24.

27. "Nihil enim est aliud omnium essentia, nisi omnium in Divina Sapientia

Cognitio." Eriugena, *Periphyseon*, in J. P. Migne, *Patrologiae Cursus Completus*, Series Prima, Latina, Vol. 122, col. 559b.

28. M. D. Chenu, *Nature, Man, and Society in the Twelfth Century*, trans. Jerome Taylor and Lester K. Little (Chicago: University of Chicago Press, 1968), p. 131 (italics mine).

29. Eliade, *The Sacred and the Profane*, pp. 111–112.

30. Chenu, p. 102.

31. Alan of Lille, *Rhythmus alter* (Migne, Vol. 210, col. 579a); Hugh of Saint-Victor, *De Tribus Diebus iii* (Migne, Vol. 176, col. 814b); quoted in Chenu, p. 117.

32. Hugo Rahner, *Greek Myths and Christian Mystery*, trans. Brian Battershaw (New York: Harper and Row, 1963), p. 381.

33. Maximus of Turin, *Homilia* 49 ("De Cruce Domini"), in Migne, Vol. 57, col. 339, quoted by Rahner, p. 382.

34. Eriugena, *Periphyseon*, Bk. I, ch. 10 (450b, 31–33), in Sheldon-Williams, vol. I, p. 55. See also Bett, p. 92.

35. Chenu, p. 120.

36. Marie-Madeleine Davy, "The Symbolic Mentality of the Twelfth Century," *Diogenes* (Winter 1963), pp. 97–98.

37. St. Bonaventure, *The Mind's Road to God*, trans. George Boas (New York: Bobbs-Merrill, Library of Liberal Arts, 1953), ch. 2, # 1, p. 14.

38. Harry Levin, *Symbolism and Fiction* (Charlottesville: University of Virginia Press, 1956), pp. 30–31.

39. Alexander Murray, *Reason and Society in the Middle Ages* (Oxford: At the Clarendon Press, 1978), p. 402.

40. Eriugena, *Periphyseon*, Bk. I, ch. 14 (459d, 31–35), in Sheldon-Williams, Vol. I, p. 77.

41. Levin, p. 21.

42. St. Anselm, "De Casu Diaboli" (The Fall of Satan), ch. iv, in Jasper Hopkins and Herbert Richardson, ed. and trans., *Truth, Freedom, and Evil: Three Philosophical Dialogues by Anselm of Canterbury* (New York: Harper Torchbooks, 1967), p. 156.

43. Karsten Harries, "The Infinite Sphere: Comments on the History of a Metaphor," *Journal of the History of Philosophy*, 13, no. 1 (January 1975), p. 14.

44. Ernst Cassirer, *The Individual and the Cosmos in Renaissance Philosophy*, trans. Mario Domandi (New York: Harper Torchbooks, 1963), p. 10.

45. Jasper Hopkins, *A Concise Introduction to the Philosophy of Nicholas of Cusa* (Minneapolis: University of Minnesota Press, 1978), p. 7.

46. Cassirer, *The Individual*, p. 10. Against this view, see Hopkins, *A Concise Introduction*, pp. 15, 41.

47. Cassirer, *The Individual*, p. 12.

48. Cusa, *De Docta Ignorantia*, Bk. I, ch. 2, # 4, in Jasper Hopkins, *Nicholas of Cusa on Learned Ignorance: A Translation and An Appraisal of De Docta Ignorantia* (Minneapolis: The Arthur J. Banning Press, 1981), pp. 50–51. See also Plato, *Apology*, 21.

49. Cusa, *De Docta Ignorantia*, Bk. I, ch. 2, # 6, p. 51.
50. Ibid., ch. 3, # 10, p. 52.
51. Ibid., ch. 11, # 30, p. 61.
52. Ibid., ch. 21, # 64, p. 76.
53. Ibid., Bk. II, ch. 12, # 162, p. 117.
54. See Martin Davis and Reuben Hersh, "Nonstandard Analysis," *Scientific American*, 226 (June 1972), p. 78.
55. Cusa, *De Docta Ignorantia*, Bk. I, ch. 21, # 64, p. 76.
56. Ibid., Bk. II, ch. 1, # 97, p. 90.
57. Jasper Hopkins, *A Concise Introduction*, p. 31.
58. Cusa, *De Docta Ignorantia*, Bk. II, ch. 1, # 97, p. 90.
59. Tyrone Lai, "Nicholas of Cusa and the Finite Universe," *Journal of the History of Philosophy*, 11, no. 2 (April 1973), p. 162.
60. Cusa, *De Docta Ignorantia*, Bk. II, ch. 1, # 97, p. 90.
61. Harries, p. 15.
62. Cusa, *De Docta Ignorantia*, Bk. II, ch. 12, # 166, p. 118.
63. Alexandre Koyré, *From the Closed World to the Infinite Universe* (New York: Harper Torchbooks, 1958), p. 21.
64. Cited by H. Stanley Redgrove, *Bygone Beliefs* (London: W. Rider and Sons, 1920), pp. 129–130. Cf. Fragment # 69 of Heraclitus in Nahm, *Selections from Early Greek Philosophy*, p. 92.
65. John Dewey, *Reconstruction in Philosophy*, Enlarged Edition (Boston: Beacon Press, 1957), p. 113.
66. Lynn T. White, Jr., "Natural Science and Naturalistic Art in the Middle Ages," *American Historical Review*, 52 (1947), p. 422.

CHAPTER TWO

1. Thomas S. Kuhn, *The Structure of Scientific Revolutions* (Chicago: University of Chicago Press, Phoenix Books, 1964), p. 7 (italics mine).
2. Grant McColley, "The Theory of the Diurnal Rotation of the Earth," *Isis*, 26 (1937), p. 394. See also McColley, "Humanism and the History of Astronomy," in Robert M. Palter, ed., *Toward Modern Science*, 2 vols. (New York: Farrar, Straus, and Cudahy, 1961), Vol. II, p. 149.
3. Cicero, *Academica*, II, 123, in Cicero, *De Natura Deorum, Academica*, trans. H. Rackham, Loeb Classical Library (London: William Heinemann, 1933), p. 627.
4. Arthur Koestler, *The Sleepwalkers: A History of Man's Changing Vision of the Universe* (New York: Grosset and Dunlap, 1963), pp. 75–76.
5. Du Bartas in *Complete Works (and Translations) of Joshua Sylvester*, ed. Grossart, II, 87, quoted by McColley, "The Theory," p. 399.
6. Nicolaus Copernicus, *On the Revolutions of the Heavenly Spheres*, trans. Charles Glenn Wallis, in *Great Books of the Western World* (Chicago: Encyclopaedia

Britannica, 1952), Vol. XVI, Bk. I, ch. 10, pp. 526–527. See also Edgar Zilsel, "Copernicus and Mechanics," in Philip P. Wiener and Aaron Noland, eds., *Roots of Scientific Thought: A Cultural Perspective* (New York: Basic Books, 1957), pp. 276–277.

7. Kuhn, *The Copernican Revolution*, p. 76.

8. Grant McColley, "Copernicus and the Infinite Universe," *Popular Astronomy*, 44 (1936), p. 525.

9. Ibid., p. 526.

10. Kuhn, *The Copernican Revolution*, p. 89.

11. Koestler, p. 119.

12. Copernicus, *On the Revolutions of the Heavenly Spheres*, p. 506.

13. Aristotle, *De Caelo*, trans. J. L. Stocks, in Ross, Vol. II, 296b, 25.

14. Kuhn, *The Copernican Revolution*, p. 135.

15. Ibid., p. 90.

16. John Wilkins, "Discovery of a New Planet," in *Philosophical and Mathematical Works* (1802), I, 190, quoted by Arthur O. Lovejoy, *The Great Chain of Being: A Study of the History of an Idea* (New York: Harper Torchbooks, 1960), p. 102.

17. Herbert Butterfield, *The Origins of Modern Science: 1300–1800*, rev. ed. (New York: The Free Press, 1957), p. 67.

18. Kepler, letter to Johann Brengger, Oct. 4, 1607, quoted by Gerald Holton, "Johannes Kepler's Universe: Its Physics and Metaphysics," in Palter, *Toward Modern Science*, Vol. II, p. 202.

19. Kepler, letter to Mästlin, Oct. 3, 1595, quoted ibid., p. 215.

20. Max Caspar, *Kepler*, trans. and ed. Doris Hellman (London: Abelard-Schuman, 1954), p. 44.

21. Kepler, quoted ibid., p. 384 (Caspar provides no footnotes for his quotations from Kepler).

22. Kepler, quoted ibid., p. 61.

23. Kepler, *Epitome of Copernican Astronomy*, trans. Charles Glenn Wallis, *Great Books of the Western World*, Vol. XVI, Bk. IV, Pt. I, ch. 1, p. 856.

24. Kepler, quoted by Caspar, p. 269.

25. Kepler, quoted ibid., p. 93 (italics mine).

26. Caspar, p. 185.

27. Holton, p. 213.

28. Kepler, *Astronomi Opera Omnia*, ed. Charles Frisch (Frankfurt and Erlangen, 1858), Vol. I, p. 31, quoted by E. A. Burtt, *The Metaphysical Foundations of Modern Science* (New York: Doubleday, Anchor Books, 1954), p. 68.

29. Kepler, *Mysterium Cosmographicum*, in *Gesammelte Werke*, ed. Van Dyck, Caspar, and Hammer (München, 1938–1959), Vol. I, p. 9, quoted by Alexandre Koyré, *The Astronomical Revolution*, trans. R. E. W. Maddison (Ithaca: Cornell University Press, 1973), p. 138. See also Kepler, *Epitome of Copernican Astronomy*, Bk. IV, Pt. I, ch. 1, in *Great Books*, Vol. XVI, pp. 853–854.

30. Alexndre Koyré, *The Astronomical Revolution*, p. 362.

31. Kepler, *Epitome*, quoted by Caspar, *Kepler*, p. 381.

32. Alexandre Koyré, "Galileo and Plato," *Journal of the History of Ideas*, 4, no. 4 (October 1943), p. 400.

33. Campanella on the publication of Galileo's *Dialogue* in 1632, quoted by Giorgio de Santillana, *The Crime of Galileo* (Chicago: University of Chicago Press, 1955), p. 187.

34. Ludovico Geymonat, *Galileo Galilei: A Biography and Inquiry into His Philosophy of Science*, trans. Stillman Drake (New York: McGraw-Hill, 1965), p. 7.

35. Ibid., p. 198. See also p. 18.

36. Ibid., pp. 169–170.

37. Bellarmine, letter to Fr. Paolo Antonio Foscarini, *Ed. Naz.* xii, 159–160, quoted by de Santillana, p. 99 (italics mine).

38. Geymonat, pp. 61–62.

39. De Santillana, pp. 40–41.

40. Galileo, letter to Castelli, *Edizione nazionale delle opere di Galileo Galilei*, ed. Antonio Favoro (Florence, 1890–1909), Vol. V, pp. 282–283, quoted by Geymonat, p. 68.

41. Geymonat, p. 71.

42. Galileo, reply to Cesi, quoted by Eugenio Garin, *Science and Civic Life in the Italian Renaissance*, trans. Peter Munz (New York: Doubleday, Anchor Books, 1969), p. 142.

43. Galileo, *Dialogue Concerning the Two Chief World Systems—Ptolemaic and Copernican*, trans. Stillman Drake, 2d ed. (Berkeley: University of California Press, 1967), Dialogue on the First Day, p. 103.

44. Ibid., Dialogue on the Fourth Day, p. 464. Thomas Campanella, *The Defense of Galileo*, trans. Grant McColley, Smith College Studies in History, XXII, nos. 3–4 (April–July 1937), ch. 3, p. 24 (see also ch. 3, p. 32).

45. Alexandre Koyré, "Galileo and the Scientific Revolution of the Seventeenth Century," *Philosophical Review*, 52, no. 4 (1943), p. 333.

46. Garin, pp. 142, 141.

47. Ibid., p. 142.

48. Sir Thomas Brown, quoted by Marjorie Hope Nicolson, *Mountain Gloom and Mountan Glory: The Development of the Aesthetics of the Infinite* (New York: W. W. Norton, 1959), p. 104 (no footnote provided).

49. Galileo, *Dialogue Concerning the Two Chief World Systems*, Dialogues on the Third and First Days, pp. 335, 56.

50. Geymonat, p. 50 (italics mine). See also Galileo, *Dialogue Concerning . . . World Systems*, Second Day, p. 263.

51. See J. Brodrick, *The Life and Work of Blessed Robert Francis Bellarmine, S.J.* (1928), Vol. II, p. 360, quoted by de Santillana, p. 101, note.

52. See St. Augustine, *The Confessions*, Bk. X, ch. vi.

53. Geymonat, pp. 184–185.

54. Galileo, *The Assayer*, in Stillman Drake, ed. and trans., *Discoveries and Opinions of Galileo* (New York: Doubleday, Anchor Books, 1957), pp. 237–238. For medieval precedents, see *supra*, p. 11.

55. See, for example, de Santillana, pp. 194, 290.

56. Ibid., p. 205.

57. Ibid., p. 282.

58. Galileo, quoted ibid., p. 256 (no footnote provided).

59. Koestler, p. 495.

60. Geymonat, p. 69.

61. John Donne, "An Anatomy of the World," *The Complete Poetry and Selected Prose* (New York: Modern Library, 1952), p. 191.

62. Alexandre Koyré, *Études Galiléenees* (Paris, 1939), III, 202–203, quoted in Geymonat, p. 133.

63. Leonard Olschki, "Galileo's Philosophy of Science," *Philosophical Review*, 52 (1943), p. 352 (italics mine).

64. Geymonat, p. 186 (italics mine).

65. Descartes, letter to Mersenne, April 1634, in Anthony Kenny, ed. and trans., *Descartes: Philosophical Letters* (Oxford: At the Clarendon Press, 1970), pp. 26–27.

66. Marjorie Hope Nicolson, *The Breaking of the Circle: Studies in the Effect of the "New Science" on Seventeenth Century Poetry*, rev. ed. (New York: Columbia University Press, 1962), p. 175.

67. Bruno, *De Immenso*, I, 9 (*Opera Latina*, I, 1, 242), quoted by Lovejoy, p. 117.

68. Dorothea W. Singer, "The Cosmology of Giordano Bruno," *Isis*, 33 (June 1941), p. 187.

69. Bruno, *Opere Italiane*, I, 291, quoted by Sidney Greenberg, *The Infinite in Giordano Bruno* (New York: Columbia University, King's Crown Press, 1950), p. 17.

70. Garin, p. 163.

71. Bruno, *Opere Italiane*, I, 409–410, quoted by Singer, p. 192.

72. Bruno, *On the Infinite Universe and Worlds*, First Dialogue, in Dorothea W. Singer, *Giordano Bruno: His Life and Thought with an Annotated Translation of his Work "On the Infinite Universe and Worlds"* (New York: Henry Schuman, 1950), p. 257.

73. Ibid., Third Dialogue, p. 304.

74. Bruno, *De Immenso*, I, 1 (*Opera Latina*, I, 1, 204), quoted by Singer, ibid., p. 75.

75. Bruno, *Opera Latina*, III, 637, quoted by Singer, ibid., p. 159.

76. Bruno, *Expulsion of the Triumphant Beast*, quoted by Jack Lindsay in his introduction to Giordano Bruno, *Cause, Principle and Unity*, trans. Jack Lindsay (New York: International Publishers, 1962), p. 39.

77. Bruno, *The Ash Wednesday Supper*, Second Dialogue, quoted by Lindsay, pp. 7–8.

78. Frances A. Yates, *Giordano Bruno and the Hermetic Tradition* (New York: Vintage Books, 1969), p. 311.

79. Ibid., pp. 318–319.

80. Bruno, *The Expulsion of the Triumphant Beast*, trans. and ed. Arthur Imerti (New Brunswick: Rutgers University Press, 1964), Explanatory Epistle, p. 79.
81. Yates, p. 454.
82. Bruno quoted by Lindsay, p. 8 (no footnote provided).
83. Ibid., p. 9.
84. Ibid.
85. Yates, p. 299.
86. Ibid., p. 349.
87. According to Gaspar Schopp in Spampanato, *Documenti della vita di G.B.,* cited by Lindsay, p. 12, and Imerti, p. 64.
88. Yates, p. 355.
89. Ibid., p. 396.
90. Alexandre Koyré, *From the Closed World*, pp. 54–55.

CHAPTER THREE

1. Albert G. A. Balz, *Descartes and the Modern Mind* (Hamden, Conn.: Archon Books, 1967 reprint), p. 4.
2. See *supra*, pp. 31–32.
3. See *supra*, p. 38.
4. *HH*, III, 161.
5. Michael Oakeshott, *Experience and Its Modes* (Cambridge: At the University Press, 1966 reprint), p. 186.
6. *HH*, III, 220–221 (italics mine).
7. See *supra*, p. 27.
8. See *supra*, p. 42.
9. See *supra*, p. 47.
10. Descartes quoted (no footnote) by S. V. Keeling, *Descartes*, 2d ed. (London: Oxford University Press, 1968), p. xvii, note.
11. Ibid., p. 132, note.
12. Balz, p. 55.
13. Descartes, *Discourse on Method*, I, in *DP*, II, 86–87.
14. *HH*, III, 227.
15. Ibid., 224.
16. Burtt, p. 105.
17. Jack R. Vrooman, *René Descartes: A Biography* (New York: G. P. Putnam's Sons, 1970), pp. 54–55.
18. Ibid., pp. 56–57. Vrooman's account is based on that of Adrien Baillet, *La Vie de Monsieur Des-Cartes* (Paris: Chez D. Horthemels, 1691), Vol. II, pp. 81–86.
19. Ibid., p. 57.
20. Ibid., p. 62.

21. Ibid., p. 60.

22. Jacques Chevalier, *Descartes* (Paris: Plon-Nourrit, 1921), p. 46, cited by Vrooman, ibid.

23. *Oeuvres de Descartes*, ed. Adam and Tannery, 13 vols. (Paris: Cerf, 1897–1913), Vol. I, 144, 12–14, quoted by Marthinus Versfeld, *An Essay on the Metaphysics of Descartes* (Port Washington, N.Y.: Kennikat Press, 1969 reprint), p. 7.

24. Ibid.

25. L. J. Beck, *The Metaphysics of Descartes: A Study of the Meditations* (Oxford: At the Clarendon Press, 1965), p. 294.

26. Keeling, p. 81.

27. Descartes' Reply to the second set of Objections against the *Meditations*, in *DP*, II, 39. See also Versfeld, p. 16; Keeling, p. 83.

28. Keeling, p. 85.

29. Descartes, *Meditations on First Philosophy*, I, in *DP*, I, 147.

30. Ibid., pp. 148, 147.

31. L. J. Beck, pp. 73–74.

32. Balz, p. 124.

33. Descartes, *Meditations*, II, in *DP*, I, 150.

34. Descartes, *Discourse on Method*, IV, in *DP*, I, 101. L. J. Beck, p. 86.

35. Descartes, *Meditations*, II, in *DP*, I, 150, 153.

36. Hegel, *The Phenomenology of Mind*, trans. J. B. Baillie (New York: Harper Torchbooks, 1967), p. 802.

37. Versfeld, p. 57.

38. Ibid., pp. 61–62.

39. Descartes, *Meditations*, II, in *DP*, I, 156–157 (italics mine).

40. Versfeld, p. 69.

41. Ibid., p. 97.

42. Balz, p. 106.

43. Ibid., p. 107.

44. Versfeld, p. 51.

45. Ibid., p. 85.

46. Descartes, Reply to Objections, II, in *DP*, II, 33.

47. Descartes, *Meditations*, III, in *DP*, I, 170–171.

48. Descartes, *Meditations*, V, in *DP*, I, 181.

49. L. J. Beck, p. 106.

50. *Descartes' Conversation with Burman*, trans. John Cottingham (Oxford: At the Clarendon Press, 1976), # 19, p. 13.

51. Keeling, p. 121. See also Balz, p. 484.

52. Balz, p. 180.

53. Vrooman, p. 49. See Descartes, *Compendium of Music*, trans. Walter Robert (Rome: American Institute of Musicology, 1961).

54. B. Augst, "Descartes' 'Compendium on Music,'" *Journal of the History of Ideas*, 26 (1965), pp. 120 ff.

55. L. J. Beck, *The Method of Descartes: A Study of the "Regulae"* (Oxford: At the Clarendon Press, 1952), p. 31.

56. Karl Jaspers, *Three Essays: Leonardo, Descartes, Max Weber*, trans. Ralph Manheim (New York: Harcourt, Brace and World, 1953), p. 68.

57. Versfeld, p. 136.

58. Keeling, p. 129.

59. Balz, p. 233.

60. Descartes, *Rules for the Direction of the Mind*, XIII, in *DP*, I, 39–40. See also Jacob Klein, *Greek Mathematical Thought and the Origin of Algebra*, trans. Eva Brann (Cambridge: The M.I.T. Press, 1968), pp. 202–203.

61. Cf. Jaspers, p. 94.

62. L. J. Beck, *The Method of Descartes*, p. 93.

63. Ibid., p. 112.

64. Cf. Descartes, *Rules*, IV, in *DP*, I, 9–14.

65. Balz, p. 323.

66. Ibid.

67. Descartes, *Discourse on Method*, VI, in *DP*, I, 119–120. See also Versfeld, p. 25.

68. Descartes, letters to Mesland (May 2, 1644) and Mersenne (May 6, 1630), in Anthony Kenny, ed. and trans., *Descartes: Philosophical Letters*, pp. 151, 13–14 (italics mine). See St. Augustine, *The Confessions*, Bk. XIII, 38.

69. P. H. J. Hoenen, S.J., "Descartes' Mechanicism," in Willis Doney, ed., *Descartes: A Collection of Critical Essays* (New York: Doubleday, Anchor Books, 1967), p. 356.

70. Balz, p. 306.

71. See *supra*, p. 46.

72. Michel Foucault, *The Order of Things: An Archaeology of the Human Sciences*, trans. of *Les Mots et les choses* (New York: Vintage Books, 1973), pp. 74, 78 (italics mine).

73. Cf. Leo Strauss, *Natural Right and History* (Chicago: University of Chicago Press, 1953), pp. 11–12.

74. Jacques Maritain, *Three Reformers: Luther, Descartes, Rousseau* (New York: Thomas Y. Crowell, 1970), p. 84. See also Hiram Caton, *The Origin of Subjectivity: An Essay on Descartes* (New Haven: Yale University Press, 1973).

75. John Herman Randall, Jr., "What Isaac Newton Started," Introduction to H. S. Thayer, ed., *Newton's Philosophy of Nature: Selections from His Writings* (New York: Hafner, 1953), pp. xiii, xiv.

76. Alexandre Koyré, *Newtonian Studies* (Chicago: University of Chicago Press, Phoenix Books, 1968), p. 53.

77. H. D. Anthony, *Sir Isaac Newton* (London: Abelard-Schuman, 1960), p. 209.

78. Randall, p. ix.

79. See *supra*, p. 31.

80. Brian Ellis, "The Origin and Nature of Newton's Laws of Motion," in

Robert G. Colodny, ed., *Beyond the Edge of Certainty: Essays in Contemporary Science and Philosophy* (Englewood Cliffs, N.J.: Prentice-Hall, 1965), p. 65.

81. Alexandre Koyré, *Newtonian Studies*, p. 43 (italics mine).

82. Ibid., p. 35. See *Sir Isaac Newton's Mathematical Principles of Natural Philosophy*, a revision of Andrew Motte's trans. by Florian Cajori, 2 vols. (Berkeley: University of California Press, 1934, 1971), Bk. III, Vol. II, p. 547.

83. Koyré, *Netwonian Studies*, pp. 151–152.

84. Newton, Preface to First Edition, Cajori, Vol. I, p. xvii.

85. Newton, letter to Oldenburg, July 1672, in Thayer, ed., *Newton's Philosophy of Nature*, p. 7.

86. Newton, Bk. I, Prop. LXIX, Theorem xxiv, Scholium, Cajori, Vol. I, p. 192.

87. Newton, beginning of the *Opticks*, 4th ed. (1730; reprinted N.Y., 1931), quoted by E. N. da C. Andrade, *Sir Isaac Newton* (London: Collins Clear-Type Press, 1954), pp. 101–102 (italics mine).

88. Newton, *Opticks*, 4th ed., Bk. III, in Thayer, p. 178.

89. Newton, *Regulae Philosophandi*, Rule IV, trans. Alexandre Koyré, *Newtonian Studies*, pp. 270–271.

90. Newton, *Opticks*, 4th ed., Bk. III, in Thayer, p. 178.

91. Roger Cotes, Preface to Second Edition, Cajori, Vol. I, p. xx.

92. Newton, Bk. III, Rule III, Cajori, Vol. II, p. 399.

93. Harald Höffding, *A History of Modern Philosophy: A Sketch of the History of Philosophy from the Close of the Renaissance to Our Own Day*, trans. B. E. Meyer, 2 vols. (New York: Dover, 1955), Vol. I, p. 409.

94. E. N. da C. Andrade, pp. 42–43.

95. Newton, Bk. III, General Scholium, Cajori, Vol. II, p. 547.

96. Ibid., pp. 544–545.

97. Koyré, *Newtonian Studies*, p. 19.

98. Ibid., p. 21. See also Francis Oakley, "Christian Theology and the Newtonian Science: The Rise of the Concept of the Laws of Nature," *Church History*, 30 (1961), pp. 433–457.

99. Newton, Bk. III, General Scholium, Cajori, Vol. II, p. 547.

100. Newton, letter to Bentley, Jan. 1, 1692/3, in Thayer, p. 53. See also Newton's letter to Bentley, Feb. 25, 1692/3, in Thayer, p. 54.

101. See Burtt, p. 226.

102. Addison, *Pleasures of the Imagination*, quoted by Marjorie Hope Nicolson, *Newton Demands the Muse: Newton's Opticks and the Eighteenth Century Poets* (Hamden, Conn.: Archon Books, 1963), p. 145.

103. Koyré, *Newtonian Studies*, pp. 23–24.

104. See *supra*, p. 61.

105. A. Rupert Hall, *The Scientific Revolution, 1500–1800: The Formation of the Modern Scientific Attitude*, 2d ed. (Boston: Beacon Press, 1966), p. 270.

106. Randall, p. xiv.

107. Ibid. See also John Herman Randall, Jr., "Newton's Natural Philosophy: Its Problems and Consequences," in F. P. Clarke and M. C. Nahm, eds., *Phil-*

osophical Essays in Honor of Edgar Arthur Singer, Jr. (Philadelphia: University of Pennsylvania Press, 1942), pp. 335–357.

108. Herbert Wildon Carr, *Leibniz* (New York: Dover, 1960), pp. 8, 4.

109. Leibniz, "On the Universal Science: Characteristic," XV, in Leibniz, *Monadology and Other Philosophical Essays*, trans. and ed. Paul and Anne Martin Schrecker (New York: Bobbs-Merrill, Library of Liberal Arts, 1965), p. 19.

110. William Kelley Wright, *A History of Modern Philosophy* (New York: Macmillan, 1941), p. 118.

111. William and Martha Kneale, *The Development of Logic* (Oxford: At the Clarendon Press, 1962), pp. 327, 330.

112. *DU*, pp. 261–262.

113. Leibniz, letter to Philipp, Jan. 1680, in L. E. Loemker, ed., *G. W. Leibniz: Philosophical Papers and Letters* (Dordrecht: Synthese Historical Library, 1969), p. 273.

114. Wilhelm Windelband, *A History of Philosophy*, trans. James H. Tufts, 2 vols. (New York: Harper Torchbooks, 1958), Vol. II, p. 398.

115. *DU*, p. 274.

116. James Collins, *Interpreting Modern Philosophy*, p. 157.

117. Leibniz, *Gul. Pacid. Plus Ultra*, G, VII, 52, quoted by H. W. B. Joseph, *Lectures on the Philosophy of Leibniz* (Oxford: At the Clarendon Press, 1949), p. 8.

118. Leibniz, "Specimen Dynamicum," Part One of *Essay on Dynamics*, 1695, in Philip P. Wiener, ed., *Leibniz: Selections* (New York: Scribner's, 1951), p. 121.

119. Carr, p. 139.

120. See Leibniz, "What Is Nature? Reflections on the Force Inherent in Created Things and in Their Actions," in *Monadology and Other . . . Essays*, p. 103.

121. H. W. B. Joseph, p. 9.

122. For Spinoza see Leo Strauss, *Spinoza's Critique of Religion*, trans. E. M. Sinclair (New York: Schocken Books, 1965), p. 15.

123. See *supra*, pp. 81–82.

124. Koyré, *From the Closed World*, p. 240.

125. Ibid., p. 272. See also p. 276.

126. Joseph, p. 185.

127. *DU*, p. 277.

128. Leibniz, letter to De Volder, March 24/April 3, 1699, in Philip P. Wiener, ed., *Leibniz: Selections*, p. 158.

129. Joseph, p. 61.

130. *DU*, pp. 281, 283.

131. Carr, p. 86.

132. *DU*, pp. 288–289, 293.

133. Ibid., pp. 323–324, 319.

134. Ibid., p. 298.

135. Ibid., pp. 324, 353.

136. Ibid., p. 350.

137. Lovejoy, p. 144.

138. *DU*, p. 354.

139. Ibid., p. 419.

140. Leibniz quoted by *DU*, p. 424 (no footnote).

141. Carr, p. 68.

142. Ibid., p. 98.

143. Leibniz, *Opuscules et Fragments*, ed. Couturat (1903), p. 522, quoted by Lovejoy, p. 182.

144. Leibniz, *Monadology and Other . . . Essays*, # 69, 67, p. 159.

145. Louis Couturat, "Sur la Métaphysique de Leibniz," *Revue de Métaphysique et de Morale*, 10 (1902), trans. R. Allison Ryan, in Harry G. Frankfurt, ed., *Leibniz: A Collection of Critical Essays* (New York: Doubleday, Anchor Books, 1972), pp. 40–41.

146. *DU*, p. 427.

147. Leibniz, "De Modo Distinguendi Phaenomena Realia ab Imaginariis," quoted in Joseph, p. 63.

148. Leibniz, "What Is Nature?" in *Monadology and Other . . . Essays*, p. 103.

149. *DU*, p. 360.

150. See *DU*, p. 434. See also F. S. C. Northrop, "Leibniz's Theory of Space," *Journal of the History of Ideas*, 7, no. 4 (October 1946), p. 441.

CHAPTER FOUR

1. See Descartes, *Meditations, II, DP*, I, 149.

2. See *supra*, pp. 51–52.

3. See *supra*, p. 93.

4. Lewis White Beck, in Lewis White Beck, ed., *Eighteenth Century Philosophers* (New York: The Free Press, 1966), p. 7.

5. Locke, *An Essay Concerning Human Understanding*, in *LW*, I, p. L.

6. Ibid. Bk. I, ch. 1, Introduction, # 4, p. 3.

7. Ibid. # 6, p. 5.

8. Richard I. Aaron, *John Locke*, 2d ed. (Oxford: At the Clarendon Press, 1965), p. 74.

9. Locke, *Of the Conduct of the Understanding*, # 1, in *LW*, III, pp. 205–206.

10. Maurice Cranston, *John Locke: A Biography* (London: Longmans, Green and Co., 1957), p. 163.

11. S. Alexander, *Locke* (Port Washington, N.Y.: Kennikat Press, 1970 reprint), pp. 22–23.

12. Rosalie Colie, "The Essayist in His Essay," in John W. Yolton, ed., *John Locke: Problems and Perspectives, A Collection of New Essays* (London: Cambridge University Press, 1969), p. 239.

13. James Gibson, *Locke's Theory of Knowledge and Its Historical Relations*

(Cambridge: At the University Press, 1917), p. 9. On the moral and religious dimension of Locke's interest in the problem of knowledge, see Cranston, pp. 140–141, and Richard Ashcraft, "Faith and Knowledge in Locke's Philosophy," in Yolton, p. 197.

14. See Sterling P. Lamprecht, "Locke's Attack upon Innate Ideas," *Philosophical Review*, 36, no. 2 (March 1927), p. 160.

15. Lady Masham, quoted by Cranston, p. 100.

16. Collins, p. 113.

17. Cranston, p. 265.

18. Cranston, p. 265. See also C. S. Ware, "The Influence of Descartes on John Locke: A Bibliographical Study," *Revue Internationale de Philosophie*, Paris (April 1956), pp. 1–21; Gibson, pp. 209–210; and Descartes, *Rules*, VIII, *DP*, I, 26.

19. Gibson, p. 54.

20. Locke, *An Essay*, Bk. I, ch. 1, Introduction, # 2, *LW*, I, p. 2.

21. Gibson, p. 223.

22. See *supra*, pp. 56–59.

23. See *supra*, pp. 71–72.

24. See Henryk Misiak, *The Philosophical Roots of Scientific Psychology* (New York: Fordham University Press, 1961), p. 71. See also p. 67.

25. Aaron, p. 128.

26. See *supra*, p. 59.

27. Sterling P. Lamprecht, *The Moral and Political Philosophy of John Locke* (New York: Russell and Russell, 1962), p. 118.

28. Locke, Journal entry, "Study," March 6, 1677, in Lord Peter King, *The Life of John Locke with Extracts from his Correspondence, Journals, and Commonplace Books*, 2 vols., new edition (London: Henry Colburn and Richard Bentley, 1830), Vol. I, pp. 185–186.

29. Francis Slade, "Review of *Locke on War and Peace* by Richard H. Cox," in *SCN, Seventeenth Century News*, New York University, 19, no. 3 (Autumn 1961), p. 37.

30. See *supra*, p. 73.

31. Gibson, pp. 36–37.

32. M. V. C. Jeffreys, *John Locke: Prophet of Common Sense* (London: Methuen, 1967), p. 47.

33. Gibson, p. 37.

34. Hans Aarsleff, "The State of Nature and the Nature of Man in Locke," in Yolton, p. 100.

35. Locke, *An Essay*, Bk. II, ch. 1, # 2, *LW*, I, pp. 82–83.

36. Gibson, p. 49.

37. Alexander, p. 43.

38. Locke, *An Essay*, Bk. IV, ch. 1, # 2, *LW*, II, p. 308.

39. Ibid., Bk. II, ch. 21, # 5, *LW*, I, p. 239.

40. Gibson, p. 114.

41. Locke, *An Essay*, quoted by D. G. James, *The English Augustans: The Life of Reason—Hobbes, Locke, Bolingbroke* (New York and London: Longmans, Green and Co., 1949), p. 91 (no footnote provided).

42. Locke, Journal entry, Feb. 8, 1677, in King, pp. 161–162.

43. Locke, *Of the Conduct of the Understanding*, # 43, in *LW*, III, p. 281.

44. Locke, *An Essay*, Bk. IV, ch. 18, # 1, *LW*, III, p. 137.

45. Ibid.

46. R. S. Woolhouse, *Locke's Philosophy of Science and Knowledge: A Consideration of Some Aspects of "An Essay Concerning Human Understanding"* (New York: Barnes and Noble, 1971), p. 136.

47. Gibson, p. 130. Locke, *An Essay*, Bk. IV, ch. 5, # 8, *LW*, III, p. 6.

48. J. D. Mabbott, *John Locke* (Cambridge, Mass.: Schenkman Publishing, 1973), p. 49.

49. Locke, *An Essay*, Bk. III, ch. vi, # 30, *LW*, II, p. 230.

50. Gibson, p. 201.

51. Locke, *An Essay*, Bk. III, ch. 3, # 6, 11, *LW*, II, pp. 168, 172.

52. Paschal Larkin, *Property in the Eighteenth Century with a Special Reference to England and Locke* (Port Washington, N.Y.: Kennikat Press, 1969), p. 65.

53. Lamprecht, *The Moral and Political Philosophy*, p. 131.

54. Gibson, p. 123.

55. Ibid., p. 124.

56. Locke's Reply to the Bishop of Worcester's Answer to his Letter, *LW*, IV, p. 145.

57. Locke, *An Essay*, Bk. IV, ch. 15, # 3, *LW*, III, pp. 97–98 (italics mine).

58. Ibid., # 3, 4, p. 98.

59. Collins, p. 117.

60. Ibid.

61. See *supra*, p. 83.

62. Locke, letter to Clarke, Jan. 28, 1688, in Benjamin Rand, ed., *The Correspondence of John Locke and Edward Clarke* (Cambridge: Harvard University Press, 1927), pp. 285–286.

63. John W. Yolton, *Locke and the Compass of Human Understanding: A Selective Commentary on the Essay* (Cambridge: At the University Press, 1970), p. 111.

64. Locke, *An Essay*, Bk. II, ch. 9, # 3, *LW*, I, p. 130.

65. Yolton, *Locke and the Compass*, p. 104.

66. See *supra*, p. 69.

67. See Gibson, p. 311.

68. Locke, *An Essay*, Bk. II, ch. 21, # 20, *LW*, I, p. 247.

69. Cranston, p. 481.

70. Locke, letter to Denis Grenville, 1678 (Fox-Bourne, I, p. 390), quoted by D. G. James, pp. 79–80.

71. Locke's Reply to the Bishop of Worcester, *LW*, IV, pp. 143–144.

72. Aaron, pp. 302, 307.

73. Lamprecht, "Locke's Attack," p. 164.

74. G. J. Warnock, *Berkeley* (Harmondsworth: Penguin Books, 1969), p. 61.

75. Ibid., p. 62.
76. *BT*, Introduction, # 21, 23, pp. 242, 243. See Warnock, p. 79.
77. See *supra*, p. 74.
78. Colin Murray Turbayne, "Berkeley's Two Concepts of Mind," in *BT*, p. 148.
79. H. S. Thayer, *Meaning and Action: A Critical History of Pragmatism* (New York: Bobbs-Merrill, 1968), p. 500.
80. *TB*, p. 2.
81. *TB*, p. 7.
82. *TB*, p. 295.
83. Windelband, Vol. II, p. 469.
84. See *supra*, p. 88.
85. Berkeley, *Works*, ed. Luce and Jessop, IV, 14, quoted in *TB*, p. 298.
86. Ibid.
87. Berkeley, *Philosophical Commentaries*, # 82, Editio diplomatica, ed. Luce (1944), quoted in John Wisdom, *The Unconscious Origin of Berkeley's Philosophy* (London: Hogarth Press, 1953), pp. 137–138.
88. Ibid., # 625.
89. Wisdom, ibid.
90. *TB*, p. 69.
91. *TB*, p. 19.
92. *TB*, p. 44.
93. *TB*, p. 48.
94. Berkeley, *Philosophical Commentaries*, # 606, quoted in *TB*, p. 52.
95. *TB*, p. 53.
96. Ibid.
97. Warnock, pp. 81–82.
98. Ibid., p. 101.
99. *TB*, pp. 154, 157.
100. *TB*, p. 157.
101. Berkeley, *Philosophical Commentaries*, # 604, quoted in Warnock, p. 22.
102. See Richard H. Popkin, "Berkeley and Pyrrhonism," in *BT*, pp. 112–113.
103. G. A. Johnston, *The Development of Berkeley's Philosophy* (London: Macmillan, 1923), p. 170.
104. *TB*, p. 301.
105. *BT*, # 2, p. 246.
106. *BT*, # 24, p. 257.
107. *BT*, # 33, p. 261.
108. *BT*, # 89, p. 293.
109. *BT*, # 6, p. 248.
110. *BT*, # 48, p. 269.
111. *BT*, # 91, p. 293.
112. Berkeley, *Philosophical Commentaries*, # 405, quoted in *TB*, p. 11.
113. Warnock, p. 125.

114. See *BT*, # 91, p. 293.

115. Frederick Copleston, *A History of Philosophy* (New York: Doubleday, Image Books, 1964), Vol. 5, Pt. II, p. 31.

116. G. A. Johnston, p. 178.

117. Warnock, p. 213.

118. *BT*, # 88, p. 292.

119. G. A. Johnston, p. 8.

120. *TB*, p. 56.

121. G. A. Johnston, p. 183.

122. See *supra*, p. 12.

123. See *BT*, # 149, p. 326.

124. G. A. Johnston, p. 191.

125. *TB*, p. 347.

126. Berkeley, *Three Dialogues Between Hylas and Philonous*, ed. Colin M. Turbayne (Indianapolis: Bobbs-Merrill, Library of Liberal Arts, 1954), III, p. 100.

127. Ibid., III, p. 82.

128. Wisdom, pp. 137–138.

129. *TB*, p. 172.

130. Warnock, p. 233.

131. Ernest Campbell Mossner, *The Life of David Hume* (Oxford: At the Clarendon Press, 1970 reprint), p. 4.

132. Ibid., p. 63.

133. David Hume, "Of Essay Writing," in David Hume, *Of The Standard of Taste and Other Essays*, ed. John W. Lenz (New York: Bobbs-Merrill, Library of Liberal Arts, 1965), pp. 39–40.

134. See *supra*, p. 96.

135. Hume, letter to Henry Home, Dec. 1737, quoted by Mossner, p. 111.

136. Robert Ackermann in Robert Ackermann, ed., *Theories of Knowledge: A Critical Introduction* (New York: McGraw-Hill, 1965), p. 183.

137. A. H. Basson, *David Hume* (Harmondsworth: Penguin Books, 1958), pp. 20–21.

138. See S. N. Hampshire, "Hume's Place in Philosophy," in D. F. Pears, ed., *David Hume: A Symposium* (New York: St. Martin's Press, 1966), pp. 4–5.

139. See *supra*, p. 68.

140. See *supra*, p. 81.

141. See *supra*, p. 84.

142. See *supra*, p. 81.

143. Hume, *History of England* (Edinburgh, 1792), Vol. VIII, p. 334, quoted in Mossner, p. 75.

144. Hume, "The Sceptic," in Hume, *Of the Standard of Taste*, p. 128.

145. Ibid., pp. 127–128 (italics mine).

146. Ibid., p. 130.

147. Basson, p. 72.

148. Ibid., p. 78.

149. Norman Kemp Smith, *The Philosophy of David Hume: A Critical Study of Its Origins and Central Doctrines* (London: Macmillan, 1949), p. 11.

150. Ibid.

151. Misiak, p. 70.

152. Basson, p. 159.

153. Ibid., p. 43.

154. D. G. C. Macnabb, *David Hume: His Theory of Knowledge and Morality*, 2d ed. (Hamden, Conn.: Archon Books, 1966), p. 36.

155. Ibid.

156. Ibid., p. 159.

157. Hume, *The Natural History of Religion*, ed. H. E. Root (London: Adam and Charles Black, 1956), p. 75.

158. Ibid., pp. 28–29.

159. Hume, *An Inquiry Concerning Human Understanding* (1748), ed. Charles W. Hendel (New York: Bobbs-Merrill, Library of Liberal Arts, 1955), II, p. 27.

160. Kemp Smith, p. 257. See Hume, *An Inquiry*, II, p. 27.

161. Kemp Smith, p. 493.

162. Basson, p. 26.

163. Ibid., p. 29. See Hume, *An Inquiry*, II, p. 27.

164. Charles W. Hendel, *Studies in the Philosophy of David Hume* (New York: Bobbs-Merrill, Library of Liberal Arts, 1963), p. 25.

165. Ibid., p. 117.

166. Ibid., p. 196.

167. Ibid., p. 127.

168. Hume, *A Treatise of Human Nature* (1739) (New York: Doubleday, Dolphin Books, 1961), Pt. IV, sec. II, p. 176.

169. Hendel, *Studies*, p. 98. See Hume, *An Inquiry*, III, p. 32.

170. Kemp Smith, p. 257.

171. See *supra*, p. 83.

172. Ackermann, p. 180.

173. Basson, p. 52.

174. Hume, *An Inquiry*, IX, pp. 112–113.

175. Ibid., p. 114.

176. J. B. Black, *The Art of History: A Study of Four Great Historians of the Eighteenth Century* (1926) (New York: Russell and Russell, 1965), p. 94.

177. Hendel, *Studies*, p. 218.

178. Kemp Smith, p. 392. See also p. 375.

179. Hendel, *Studies*, p. 147.

180. Kemp Smith, p. 393.

181. Macnabb, p. 61.

182. Hume, *A Treatise*, Bk. I, Pt. 3, sec. 15, p. 158.

183. Ibid., Appendix, p. 560.

184. Basson, p. 74.

185. Ibid., p. 77.

186. Kemp Smith, p. 44.

187. Robert Paul Wolff, "Hume's Theory of Mental Activity," *Philosophical Review*, 69, no. 3 (July 1960), pp. 295–296. See also Kemp Smith, p. 112.

188. Wolff, p. 296.

189. Hume, *An Inquiry*, VII, ii, p. 87.

190. Macnabb, p. 160.

191. Mossner, p. 76.

192. Hume, *An Inquiry*, XI, p. 155.

193. Ibid., V, i, p. 55.

194. Ibid., p. 58.

195. Hume, *A Treatise*, Bk. II, Pt. iii, sec. iii, p. 375.

196. Basson, p. 92.

197. Hume, *A Treatise*, Bk. I, Pt. iii, sec. xvi, pp. 163–164.

198. Kemp Smith, p. 85.

199. Ibid., p. 446.

200. Ibid., p. 400.

201. H. E. Root, in "Introduction" to Hume, *The Natural History*, pp. 11–12.

202. Hume, "The Epicurean," in Hume, *Of the Standard of Taste*, p. 100.

203. Ibid., p. 102.

204. Anthony Flew, *Hume's Philosophy of Belief: A Study of His First Inquiry* (London: Routledge and Kegan Paul; New York: Humanities Press, 1961), p. 150.

205. Ibid., p. 89.

206. Ackermann, p. 177.

207. Ibid.

208. Mossner, p. 175.

209. Hume, *A Treatise*, Bk. I, Pt. iii, sec. viii, pp. 94–95. See Kemp Smith, p. 447.

210. Hume, letter to Gilbert Stuart (ca. 1738–1739), in John Hill Burton, ed., *Life and Correspondence of David Hume*, 2 vols. (Edinburgh, 1846) (New York: Burt Franklin, reprint), Vol. I, pp. 97–98.

211. Macnabb, pp. 103–104.

212. Ibid., p. 163.

213. Mossner, p. 333.

214. Ibid.

215. Kemp Smith, p. 543.

216. Terence Penelhum, "Hume on Personal Identity," *Philosophical Review*, 44, no. 4 (October 1955), p. 575.

217. Hume, *The History of England*, Vol. VII, p. 150, quoted in Mossner, p. 317.

218. J. B. Black, p. 95.

219. Ibid.

220. Ibid., p. 96.

221. Hume, *An Inquiry*, VII, i, p. 93.

222. See *supra*, p. 118.

223. Hume, "Of The Study of History," in Hume, *Of the Standard of Taste*, pp. 98–99.

224. Ibid., p. 97.

225. Kemp Smith, pp. 126, 143.

226. Ibid., p. 137 (italics mine).

227. F. H. Heinemann, *David Hume: The Man and His Science of Man*, (Paris, 1940), p. 63. See also D. B. Klein, *A History of Scientific Psychology: Its Origins and Philosophical Backgrounds* (New York: Basic Books, 1970), pp. 598–599.

228. P. L. Gardiner, "Hume's Theory of the Passions," in Pears, p. 31.

229. Mossner, p. 74.

230. Flew, p. 94.

231. Hume, *An Inquiry*, I, p. 24.

232. Mossner, p. 228.

233. Kemp Smith, p. 519.

234. P. L. Gardiner, p. 32. See also Flew, p. 78.

235. Basson, p. 145.

236. Flew, p. 213.

237. Hume, *A Treatise*, Bk. II, Pt. i, sec. iii, p. 256.

238. Ernest Campbell Mossner, "The Enlightenment of David Hume," in Robert Mollenauer, ed., *Introduction to Modernity: A Symposium on Eighteenth Century Thought* (Austin: University of Texas Press, 1965), p. 43.

CHAPTER FIVE

1. Herbert Dieckmann, "An Interpretation of the Eighteenth Century," *Modern Language Quarterly*, Vol. 15 (1954), pp. 296, 299.

2. *GE*, I, 408.

3. See *supra*, pp. 98–99.

4. D'Alembert, *Preliminary Discourse to the Encyclopedia of Diderot*, translated with introduction by Richard N. Schwab (New York: Bobbs-Merrill, Library of Liberal Arts, 1963), Pt. II, p. 84.

5. Voltaire, *Lettres philosophiques*, Vol. I, lettre xiii, pp. 168–169, quoted by *GE*, II, 167.

6. See *supra*, pp. 133, 135.

7. Norman Hampson, *A Cultural History of the Enlightenment* (New York: Random House, Pantheon Books, 1968), p. 19.

8. D'Alembert, *Preliminary*, Pt. I, pp. 25–26. See also *GE*, I, 81.

9. See *supra*, p. 135.

10. *GE*, I, 179.

11. See *supra*, p. 48.

12. Bruno, *The Expulsion of the Triumphant Beast*, trans. and ed. Imerti, Third Dialogue, Pt. I, p. 205. See also Paolo Rossi, *Philosophy, Technology, and the Arts*

in the Early Modern Era, trans. Salvator Attanasio, ed. Benjamin Nelson (New York: Harper Torchbooks, 1970), p. 79.

13. See *supra*, pp. 46–47.

14. Preserved Smith, *A History of Modern Culture*, Vol. II: *The Enlightenment, 1687–1776* (New York: Henry Holt and Co., 1934), p. 273.

15. Ibid.

16. Henry Vyverberg, *Historical Pessimism in the French Enlightenment* (Cambridge: Harvard University Press, 1958), p. 94. See also Preserved Smith, p. 293.

17. Émile Bréhier, *The History of Philosophy*, Vol. V: *The Eighteenth Century*, trans. Wade Baskin (Chicago: University of Chicago Press, 1967), p. 73. See also Paul Hazard, *European Thought in the Eighteenth Century: From Montesquieu to Lessing*, trans. J. Lewis May (New York: Meridian Books, 1963), p. 167.

18. Hampson, p. 141. See also p. 155.

19. Ibid., pp. 71, 143.

20. *GE*, II, 57–58.

21. *Oeuvres de Rulhière, de l'Académie française* (Paris, 1819), II, 24, quoted in Arthur M. Wilson, *Diderot: The Testing Years, 1713–1759* (New York: Oxford University Press, 1957), p. 95. *GE*, II, 83.

22. Hampson, pp. 44–45. Frank Manuel, *The Age of Reason* (Ithaca: Cornell University Press, 1951), p. 10.

23. *CP*, p. 13.

24. *GE*, I, 145–146.

25. Diderot, "Encyclopedia," article in *Encyclopédie*, ed. Diderot (1751–1765), Vol. V, in Peter Gay, ed., *The Enlightenment: A Comprehensive Anthology* (New York: Simon and Schuster, 1973), pp. 288–289.

26. D'Alembert, "Éléments de Philosophie," in *Mélanges de Littérature, d'Histoire, et de Philosophie* (Amsterdam, 1759), Vol. IV, pp. 3–6, quoted by *CP*, p. 3.

27. D'Alembert, *Preliminary Discourse*, Pt. II, p. 94.

28. *GE*, I, 132.

29. Louis I. Bredvold, *The Brave New World of the Enlightenment* (Ann Arbor: University of Michigan Press, 1961), p. 97.

30. *BH*, p. 93.

31. Henry Fielding, quoted in Hampson, p. 149 (no footnote provided).

32. *GE*, I, 34. See also *BH*, pp. 105–106.

33. Chastellux, *De la félicite publique*, II, 71, quoted in *BH*, pp. 129–130.

34. *GE*, I, 27.

35. Peter Stansky, review of George Dangerfield, *The Damnable Question: A Study of Anglo-Irish Relations*, in *The New York Times Book Review*, July 25, 1976, p. 2.

36. *GE*, I, 160.

37. Kingsley Martin, *French Liberal Thought in the Eighteenth Century: A Study of Political Ideas from Bayle to Condorcet*, ed. J. P. Mayer (New York: Harper Torchbooks, 1963), p. 93.

38. See *supra*, p. 118.

39. See *supra*, p. 110.

40. Hampson, p. 90.

41. Bishop Joseph Butler, *The Analogy of Religion, Natural and Revealed, to the Constitution and Course of Nature*, new edition (London: George Bell and Sons, 1889), "Advertisement," p. 37.

42. Ira O. Wade, *The Clandestine Organization and Diffusion of Philosophic Ideas in France from 1700 to 1750* (Princeton: Princeton University Press, 1938), p. 269.

43. Ibid., pp. 271, 274–275.

44. Robert R. Palmer, *Catholics and Unbelievers in Eighteenth Century France* (Princeton: Princeton University Press, 1939), p. 8.

45. Ibid., pp. 179–180.

46. Ibid., pp. 21–22.

47. Ibid., p. 27.

48. Ibid., pp. 38–39.

49. See ibid., p. 220.

50. "Tantum religio potuit suadere malorum," Lucretius, *De Rerum Natura*, I, 101, quoted in *GE*, I, 101. See Lucretius, *On Nature*, trans. Russel M. Geer (New York: Bobbs-Merrill, Library of Liberal Arts, 1965), I, 80–82, p. 6.

51. Repeated by Voltaire in many of his letters, cited by Frederick C. Green, "Voltaire's Greatest Enemy," in Frederick C. Green, *Eighteenth Century France: Six Essays* (New York: Frederick Ungar, 1964), p. 131.

52. Arthur O. Lovejoy, "The Parallel of Deism and Classicism," in Arthur O. Lovejoy, *Essays in the History of Ideas* (New York: George Braziller, 1955), pp. 81–82.

53. Bréhier, p. 151. See *GE*, I, 166.

54. *CP*, p. 161.

55. Ibid.

56. Ibid.

57. *GE*, I, 230–231.

58. Condorcet, *Esquisse* (Genoa, 1798), p. 129, quoted in Frank Manuel, *The Prophets of Paris* (Cambridge: Harvard University Press, 1962), p. 70.

59. Baron d'Holbach, *The System of Nature or Laws of the Moral and Physical World*, trans. H. D. Robinson (1868) (New York: Burt Franklin, 1970 reprint), Vol. I, ch. 5, p. 38.

60. *GE*, II, 163. See also p. 124.

61. *GE*, I, 103.

62. Ibid.

63. Thomas L. Hankins, *Jean d'Alembert: Science and the Enlightenment* (Oxford: At the Clarendon Press, 1970), p. 132.

64. Voltaire, "Sect," in Voltaire, *Philosophical Dictionary*, trans. H. I. Woolf (London: Allen and Unwin, 1924), in Crane Brinton, ed., *The Portable Age of Reason Reader* (New York: The Viking Press, 1956), pp. 279, 282.

65. Ibid., p. 283.

66. Hankins, p. 234.

67. Christopher Dawson, *The Gods of Revolution* (New York: New York University Press, 1972), p. 11.

68. *CP*, pp. 158–159.

69. *CP*, p. 159.

70. *GE*, I, 352.

71. *GE*, I, 352–353.

72. Dawson, pp. 14–15.

73. Ibid.

74. Karl Löwith, *Meaning in History* (Chicago: University of Chicago Press, 1970), p. 197.

75. *GE*, I, 338.

76. Bréhier, p. 14.

77. Diderot, "Discourse of a Philosopher to a King," in Jonathan Kemp, ed., *Diderot: Interpreter of Nature, Selected Writings* (New York: International Publishers, 1963), p. 214.

78. *BH*, pp. 110–111.

79. *BH*, pp. 117–118. Edward Gibbon, *The Decline and Fall of the Roman Empire* (New York: Modern Library, 1932), Vol. III, ch. lxxi, p. 865.

80. *CP*, pp. 141, 144.

81. *GE*, II, 511.

82. D'Holbach, *The System of Nature*, Vol. II, ch. 4, p. 242.

83. Manuel, *The Prophets*, p. 64.

84. *BH*, p. 130.

85. *GE*, II, 385–386.

86. Hampson, p. 232.

87. *BH*, pp. 122–123.

88. *GE*, I, 326.

89. Preserved Smith, p. 21.

90. James Oliver, "Christopher Dawson: An Appreciation," in Dawson, *The Gods*, p. xiv.

91. *BH*, p. 8.

92. *BH*, p. 29.

93. Dieckmann, pp. 301–302.

94. Ibid.

95. *CP*, p. 182.

96. *CP*, p. 183.

97. *GE*, I, 24.

98. *GE*, II, 168.

99. Ibid.

100. Diderot, letter to Falconet, May 15, 1767, *Correspondance*, ed. G. Roth (1955), VII, p. 59, quoted in *GE*, II, pp. 169–170.

101. *GE*, II, 171.

102. Ibid.

103. Hazard, p. 60.

104. *BH*, pp. 80–81.

105. See *supra*, p. 47.

106. Waldo Frank, *The Rediscovery of Man: A Memoir and a Methodology of Modern Life* (New York: George Braziller, 1958), p. 134.

107. *GE*, I, 333. See Lessing, *Schriften*, XIII, 13–15.

108. Dawson, p. 23.

109. Lester G. Crocker, *An Age of Crisis: Man and World in Eighteenth Century French Thought* (Baltimore: The Johns Hopkins University Press, 1959), p. 393.

110. Ibid.

111. *BH*, p. 63.

112. Arthur O. Lovejoy, "Herder and the Philosophy of History," in Lovejoy, *Essays*, p. 176, note.

113. *CP*, p. 39.

114. Lovejoy, "The Parallel of Deism and Classicism," in Lovejoy, *Essays*, pp. 79–80.

115. Ibid.

116. D'Holbach, *The System of Nature*, Vol. I, ch. 14, p. 130. See also ch. 1, p. 11.

117. Ibid., ch. 14, p. 131.

118. Isabel F. Knight, *The Geometric Spirit: The Abbé de Condillac and the French Enlightenment* (New Haven: Yale University Press, 1968), p. 111.

119. See *supra*, p. 73.

120. Lovejoy, "The Parallel," pp. 83–84.

121. Diderot, article "Encyclopedia," in the *Encyclopédie*, quoted in Hazard, p. 208.

122. Crocker, p. 181.

123. La Mettrie, *L'Homme machine, suivi de L'art de jouis*, ed. M. Solovine (1921), pp. 99–100, 142, quoted in Crocker, pp. 80–81.

124. Crocker, p. 85.

125. Diderot, "Supplement to Bougainville's Voyage," IV, in Kemp, ed., *Diderot: Interpreter*, p. 187.

126. Diderot, article "Leibnizianisme," in the *Encyclopédie*, quoted in Hazard, p. 162.

127. *GE*, I, 185.

128. Diderot, "Réfutation d'Helvétius," in *Oeuvres complètes*, ed. Assézat and Tourneux (1875–1877) (Paris: Garnier), Vol. II, quoted in Crocker, p. 359. See *GE*, I, 128.

129. Crocker, p. 451.

130. Lovejoy, "Herder," p. 172.

131. Crocker, p. 189.

132. Ibid.

133. *BH*, p. 108.

134. *GE*, II, 381.

135. D'Holbach, *The System of Nature*, Vol. II, ch. 7, p. 277.

136. Crocker, p. 454.

137. Bredvold, p. 149.

138. Manuel, *The Prophets*, pp. 43–44.

139. Palmer, pp. 150–151.

140. Lovejoy, "The Parallel," p. 85.

141. Lovejoy, "'Pride' in Eighteenth Century Thought," in Lovejoy, *Essays*, p. 67. See also Arthur O. Lovejoy, "The Indictment of Pride," in Arthur O. Lovejoy, *Reflections on Human Nature* (Baltimore: The Johns Hopkins University Press, 1961), p. 221.

142. Lovejoy, "'Pride,'" p. 68.

143. Diderot at the beginning of his *Pensées philosophiques*, ed. R. Niklaus (Genève, 1950, 1957), quoted in Palmer, p. 186.

144. Vauvenargues, letter to Mirabeau, March 1, 1739, quoted in Bréhier, p. 118.

145. *CP*, p. 355.

146. *CP*, p. 107.

147. *CP*, p. 108.

148. Condillac, quoted in Hazard, p. 363 (no footnote provided).

149. Diderot, quoted in Hampson, p. 192 (no footnote provided).

150. Lester G. Crocker, *Nature and Culture: Ethical Thought in the French Enlightenment* (Baltimore: The Johns Hopkins University Press, 1963), p. 238.

151. Ibid.

152. Abbé de Saint-Pierre, *Projet pour rendre la paix perpétuelle en Europe*, II, 104, quoted in Crocker, *An Age of Crisis*, p. 222.

153. Crocker, ibid., p. 221. See Bayle, *Dictionnaire historique et critique*, IV, 442–443.

154. Voltaire, letter to Helvetius, 1738, in Th. Besterman, ed., *Voltaire's Correspondence* (Genève, 1953 ff.), quoted in Crocker, *An Age of Crisis*, p. 158.

155. Diderot, *Salons*, II, 144, quoted in *GE*, II, 281.

156. *GE*, II, 283.

157. Ibid., pp. 189, 187.

158. Voltaire, *Traité de métaphysique*, ed. H. Temple Patterson (Manchester: Manchester University Press, 1937), p. 53, quoted in Crocker, *An Age of Crisis*, p. 307.

159. *BH*, pp. 102–103.

160. *CP*, pp. 37–38.

161. *CP*, p. 353.

162. *BH*, p. 87.

163. See *supra*, pp. 43, 73.

164. *CP*, p. 47.

165. Hans Georg Gadamer, "On the Problem of Self-Understanding," in Hans Georg Gadamer, *Philosophical Hermeneutics*, trans. and ed. David E. Linge (Berkeley: University of California Press, 1976), p. 51.

166. Diderot, quoted by Lester G. Crocker, *The Embattled Philosopher: A Biography of Denis Diderot* (New York: The Free Press, 1966), p. 308. The allegory is given by Diderot in a letter to Damilaville, 1765, quoted by Crocker, p. 309.

167. Voltaire, "Superstition," *Philosophical Dictionary*, ed. and trans. Peter

Gay, 2 vols. (New York: Basic Books, 1962), Vol. II, p. 473, quoted in *GE*, I, 396.

168. Palmer, p. 191.
169. *GE*, II, 398.
170. *CP*, pp. 135–136.
171. Knight, p. 265.
172. Condorcet, *Sketch for a Historical Picture of the Progress of the Human Mind*, trans. June Barraclough (New York: The Noonday Press, 1955), Tenth Stage, p. 173.
173. Ibid., p. 199.
174. Kingsley Martin, p. 291.
175. Diderot, quoted in ibid., p. 92 (no footnote provided).
176. Condorcet, "Fragment de l'histoire de la xe epoque," in *Oeuvres*, VI, 595, quoted in Manuel, *The Prophets*, pp. 96–97.
177. *BH*, p. 139.
178. *BH*, pp. 140–141.
179. Voltaire, letter to Comte de Leninhaupt, Feb. 13, 1768, quoted in Kingsley Martin, p. 146.
180. Joseph Priestley, quoted by Bredvold, p. 105.
181. Bredvold, p. 105.
182. See *supra*, p. 71.
183. Herder, *Outlines of a Philosophy of the History of Man* (1784–1791), trans. Churchill (London, 1800), quoted in Bredvold, p. 109, and in Lovejoy, "Herder," p. 169.
184. Condorcet, *Vie de Turgot*, pp. 276–277, quoted in Manuel, *The Prophets*, p. 50.
185. Condorcet, *Sketch*, trans. Barraclough, Tenth Stage, p. 202.
186. Lovejoy, "The Parallel," p. 84.
187. Eric Voegelin, *From Enlightenment to Revolution*, ed. John H. Hallowell (Durham, N.C.: Duke University Press, 1975), p. 52.
188. Dawson, p. 30. See also p. 29.
189. Voltaire, letter to Damilaville, Dec. 6, 1757, quoted in Dawson, p. 29.
190. Voltaire, "Homme," in *Questions sur l'Encyclopédie, Oeuvres*, XIX, 384, quoted in *GE*, II, 4.
191. Hampson, p. 113.
192. Lovejoy, "'Pride,'" p. 65.
193. Vyverberg, pp. 77–78.
194. D'Alembert, quoted in Vyverberg, p. 129.
195. Vyverberg, p. 1.
196. Ibid., pp. 230–231.
197. Diderot, letter to the Princess Daskoff, April 3, 1771, quoted in Vyverberg, p. 189.
198. D'Alembert, *Preliminary Discourse*, Pt. II, p. 103.
199. Raynal, *The Philosophical and Political History of the Indies*, quoted in Vyverberg, pp. 147–148.

200. *Letters of Horace Walpole*, ed. Toynbee (1770), Supplement, I, 184, quoted in Preserved Smith, p. 359.

201. *BH*, p. 160.

202. Voegelin, p. 5.

203. *GE*, I, 17. See Henry F. May, *The Enlightenment in America* (New York: Oxford University Press, 1976).

204. *GE*, I, 19.

205. Bredvold, p. 97.

206. *BH*, p. 97. See also *GE*, II, 3.

207. See, for example, Green, "Voltaire's Greatest Enemy," pp. 129–130.

208. Voegelin, pp. 110–111.

209. Hampson, pp. 207–208.

210. *GE*, I, 202.

211. *GE*, II, 497.

212. Ibid.

213. Ibid.

214. Basil Willey, *The Eighteenth Century Background* (Boston: Beacon Press, 1961), p. 17.

215. *The Confessions of Jean-Jacques Rousseau* (New York: Modern Library), Bk. XIII, p. 670.

216. Hazard, pp. 307–308.

217. *CP*, pp. 200–201.

218. *CP*, pp. 198–199.

CHAPTER SIX

1. *Oeuvres complètes de Jean-Jacques Rousseau*, ed. Gagnebin and Raymond, Bibliotèque de la Pléiade (Paris, 1959–1970), Vol. I, 930, 932, quoted in Ronald Grimsley, *The Philosophy of Rousseau* (New York: Oxford University Press, 1973), p. 7, and in *MP*, p. v. See Ernst Cassirer, *The Question of Jean-Jacques Rousseau*, trans. and ed. Peter Gay (Bloomington: Indiana University Press, 1963), p. 40.

2. Allan Bloom, "Jean-Jacques Rousseau," in Leo Strauss and Joseph Cropsey, eds., *History of Political Philosophy* (Chicago: Rand McNally, 1963), p. 515. Judith N. Shklar, *Men and Citizens: A Study of Rousseau's Social Theory* (Cambridge: At the University Press, 1969), pp. 221, 222.

3. *GE*, II, 552. *MP*, p. 115.

4. *GE*, II, 529, 552. J. H. Broome, *Rousseau: A Study of His Thought* (London: Edward Arnold Publishers, 1963), p. 4. Alfred Cobban, *In Search of Humanity: The Role of the Enlightenment in Modern History* (New York: George Braziller, 1960), p. 147.

5. Rousseau, *A Discourse on the Moral Effects of the Arts and Sciences*, Pt. I, in Cole (see *RI*), p. 149. Rousseau, *Émile*, trans. Barbara Foxley, Everyman's Library (London: Dent, 1974), Bk. V, p. 414. See also *MP*, p. 112.

6. Shklar, p. 108; *MP*, p. 89.

7. *MP*, p. 233. Rousseau, Preface to his play *Narcisse*, (*Oeuvres complètes*, II, 959), quoted by Mario Einaudi, *The Early Rousseau* (Ithaca: Cornell University Press, 1967), p. 109. Lester G. Crocker, *Jean-Jacques Rousseau: The Quest (1712–1758)* (New York: Macmillan, 1968), p. 302. See also F. C. Green, *Jean-Jacques Rousseau: A Critical Study of His Life and Writings* (Cambridge: Cambridge University Press, 1955), p. 117.

8. See Grimsley, p. 20.

9. Leo Strauss, "On the Intention of Rousseau," in Maurice Cranston and Richard S. Peters, eds., *Hobbes and Rousseau: A Collection of Critical Essays* (New York: Doubleday, Anchor Books, 1972), pp. 267, 287.

10. Rousseau, *A Discourse on the Moral Effects of the Arts and Sciences*, Pt. II, in Cole (see *RI*), p. 172.

11. Cassirer, *The Question*, p. 104. Einaudi, p. 55. Crocker, *Jean-Jacques*, pp. 346–347. Bertrand de Jouvenel, "Rousseau's Theory of the Forms of Government," in Cranston and Peters, pp. 485–486.

12. Rousseau, *Émile*, Bk. I, pp. 10, 26.

13. Ibid., Bk. V, pp. 435–436.

14. Diderot, quoted in Jean Guehenno, *Jean-Jacques Rousseau*, trans. John and Doreen Weightman; Vol. I: 1712–1758; Vol. II: 1758–1778 (London: Routledge and Kegan Paul, 1966), Vol. I, p. 217 (no footnote provided).

15. Rousseau, second letter to Malesherbes, Jan. 12, 1762, quoted in Cobban, p. 149.

16. *The Confessions of Jean-Jacques Rousseau* (New York: Modern Library), VIII, p. 361.

17. Favre ms. of *Émile*, Annales Jean-Jacques Rousseau, VIII, 271 (not retained in final version), quoted in Guehenno, Vol. II, p. 18.

18. Ronald Grimsley, *Rousseau and the Religious Quest* (Oxford: At the Clarendon Press, 1968), p. ix. See also Robert J. Ellrich, *Rousseau and His Reader: The Rhetorical Situation of the Major Works* (Chapel Hill: University of North Carolina Press, 1969), p. 107.

19. Favre ms. of *Émile*, quoted in Guehenno, Vol. II, p. 18.

20. Rousseau, *Correspondance générale*, ed. Th. Dufour, III, 369, quoted in Georges Poulet, *Studies in Human Time*, trans. Elliot Coleman (New York: Harper Torchbooks, 1959), p. 166.

21. Rousseau, *Émile*, Bk. IV, p. 270. See *supra*, pp. 11, 39.

22. Rousseau, *Émile*, Bk. V, p. 414.

23. Poulet, p. 162.

24. Rousseau, *The Reveries of a Solitary*, trans. John Gould Fletcher (London: George Routledge and Sons, 1927), Eighth Promenade, p. 170.

25. Rousseau, letter to Philopolis, addressed to Charles Bonnet, 1755 (*Oeuvres complètes*, III, 230–236), quoted in F. C. Green, *Jean-Jacques*, pp. 284–285; and quoted in Einaudi, p. 154.

26. *RI*, Second Part, p. 270.

27. Joseph Carpino, "Reader's Commentary," on a paper "Rousseau on Rous-

seau: the Individual and Society," delivered by Ann Hartle (listed under Ann McArdle) at the Annual Meeting of the American Political Science Association, The Palmer House, Chicago, Illinois, September 2–5, 1976, p. 6. Roger D. Masters, "The Structure of Rousseau's Political Thought," in Cranston and Peters, p. 431. *MP*, p. 105. Grimsley, *The Philosophy of Rousseau*, p. 22.

28. *RI*, Preface, p. 189.

29. Shklar, p. 5. Favre ms. of *Émile*, quoted in Guehenno, Vol. II, p. 18.

30. *RI*, p. 198. The italicized portion is taken from the translation by Roger and Judith Masters, *Rousseau, First and Second Discourses*, ed. Roger D. Masters (New York: St. Martin's Press, 1964), pp. 103–104.

31. John Charvet, *The Social Problem in the Philosophy of Rousseau* (Cambridge: Cambridge University Press, 1974), p. 145. Rousseau, *Émile*, Bk. I, p. 7. *RI*, First Part, pp. 223–224, note.

32. *RI*, First Part, p. 211; p. 223, note.

33. Bloom, p. 519. *MP*, p. 298.

34. Strauss, "On the Intention," p. 289. Bloom, p. 519.

35. *RI*, First Part, p. 208.

36. *MP*, p. 104. *RI*, First Part, p. 204.

37. *RI*, First Part, pp. 208–209.

38. *MP*, p. 149.

39. *RI*, First Part, pp. 214–215 (italics mine).

40. Leo Strauss, *Natural Right and History*, p. 271. Lovejoy, "The Supposed Primitivism of Rousseau's *Discourse on Inequality*," in Lovejoy, *Essays*, pp. 18, 24.

41. Strauss, *Natural Right*, p. 274. Lovejoy, "The Supposed Primitivism," pp. 26–27.

42. *RI*, First Part, p. 209.

43. Strauss, *Natural Right*, pp. 273, 272.

44. Cassirer, *The Question*, p. 104. John Charvet, "Individual Identity and Social Consciousness in Rousseau's Philosophy," in Cranston and Peters, p. 465. Strauss, *Natural Right*, p. 271.

45. *RI*, First Part, p. 225; Preface, p. 193. See *MP*, p. 145.

46. *RI*, Preface, p. 193; Second Part, p. 235. Rousseau, *Émile*, Bk. IV, p. 173.

47. Strauss, *Natural Right*, p. 271. *MP*, p. 203. Einaudi, pp. 273–274.

48. *RI*, First Part, p. 209.

49. *RI*, Second Part, p. 243. Rousseau, letter to Christophe de Beaumont, quoted in William Pickles, "Time in Rousseau's Political Thought," in Cranston and Peters, p. 382. Broome, p. 28.

50. *RI*, Preface, p. 190.

51. Lovejoy, "The Supposed Primitivism," p. 21. Rousseau, *Émile*, Bk. IV, p. 174.

52. *RI*, p. 197; Second Part, p. 247. Masters, "The Structure of Rousseau's Political Thought," p. 432.

53. Shklar, p. 11. *RI*, First Part, p. 204.

54. *MP*, p. 5.

55. Shklar, p. 74.

56. Rousseau, quoted in Crocker, *Jean-Jacques*, p. 279 (italics mine; no footnote provided).

57. Ibid., p. 272.

58. Shklar, pp. 212–213. Lanson, "L'unité de la pensée de Jean-Jacques Rousseau," *Annales de la Société Jean-Jacques Rousseau*, VIII (1912), 16, quoted by Peter Gay in his "Introduction" to Cassirer, *The Question*, p. 19.

59. John Plamenatz, "Ce Qui Ne Signifie Autre Chose Sinon Qu'on Le Forcera D'être Libre," in Cranston and Peters, p. 327.

60. Lester G. Crocker, *Rousseau's Social Contract: An Interpretive Essay* (Cleveland: The Press of Case Western Reserve University, 1968), p. 10.

61. Grimsley, *The Philosophy of Rousseau*, p. 160. Rousseau, *Émile*, Bk. II, p. 48. Rousseau, *The Reveries of a Solitary*, Sixth Promenade, p. 132.

62. Strauss, *Natural Right*, p. 281. Cassirer, *The Question*, p. 105.

63. Strauss, *Natural Right*, pp. 278, 281.

64. Cassirer, *The Question*, pp. 55, 59. Grimsley, *The Philosophy of Rousseau*, p. 91.

65. Judith N. Shklar, "Rousseau's Images of Authority," in Cranston and Peters, p. 365. Shklar, *Men and Citizens*, p. 219.

66. Ernst Cassirer, *Rousseau, Kant, and Goethe: Two Essays*, trans. James Gutmann, Paul Oskar Kristeller, and John Herman Randall, Jr. (New York: Harper Torchbooks, 1963), p. 5.

67. Shklar, *Men and Citizens*, p. 184. Cassirer, *The Question*, p. 76.

68. Broome, pp. 121–122. Rousseau, *Émile*, Bk. IV, p. 252.

69. Lovejoy, "The Supposed Primitivism," p. 31. *MP*, p. 95. Stephen Ellenburg, *Rousseau's Political Philosophy: An Interpretation from Within* (Ithaca: Cornell University Press, 1976), p. 168.

70. Ellenburg, p. 201. Rousseau, *Émile*, Bk. V, p. 438. *RI*, Second Part, p. 243.

71. Rousseau, *Émile*, Bk. II, p. 126. Charvet, *The Social Problem*, p. 89.

72. Rousseau, *Émile*, Bk. V, p. 378.

73. Ibid., Bk. IV, p. 172.

74. Ellenburg, pp. 202–203.

75. *MP*, p. 352.

76. Rousseau, *Émile*, Bk. II, p. 61.

77. Charvet, *The Social Problem*, p. 145. Charvet, "Individual Identity and Social Consciousness," p. 475.

78. Charvet, *The Social Problem*, pp. 146, 145.

79. Ibid., pp. 2–3.

80. Ibid., p. 116. Hilail Gildin, "Revolution and the Formation of Political Society in the *Social Contract*," *Interpretation: A Journal of Political Philosophy*, Vol. 5, no. 3 (Spring 1976), p. 258, note.

81. Rousseau, *Émile*, Bk. V, p. 369.

82. Ann Hartle, "Rousseau on Rousseau," paper, American Political Science Association, 1976, p. 8.

83. Broome, p. 112.

84. Grimsley, *The Philosophy of Rousseau*, p. 17.

85. Shklar, *Men and Citizens*, pp. 9, 53–54. Grimsley, *Rousseau and the Religious Quest*, p. 45. See also Grimsley, *The Philosophy of Rousseau*, p. 9; and Rousseau, *The Reveries of a Solitary*, Third Promenade, p. 59.

86. Grimsley, *Rousseau and the Religious Quest*, p. 45. F. C. Green, *Jean-Jacques*, pp. 121–122. Cassirer, *The Question*, p. 124.

87. Rousseau, *The Reveries of a Solitary*, First Promenade, pp. 31, 38.

88. Ann Hartle (listed under Ann McArdle), "Rousseau on Rousseau: The Individual and Society," *Review of Politics*, 39, no. 2 (April 1977), p. 254.

89. Rousseau, *Rousseau juge de Jean-Jacques*, quoted in F. C. Green, *Jean-Jacques*, pp. 258–259.

90. Hartle, in *Review of Politics*, p. 256. Rousseau, *The Reveries of a Solitary*, Second Promenade, p. 43.

91. See *supra*, p. 162.

92. Guehenno, Vol. I, p. 213.

93. *HC*, p. 57. Rousseau, *The Reveries of a Solitary*, Tenth Promenade, p. 40.

94. *HC*, p. 58. Rousseau, *The Reveries of a Solitary*, Tenth Promenade, p. 194.

95. Crocker, *Jean-Jacques*, p. 187. Rousseau, *The Reveries of a Solitary*, Sixth Promenade, p. 126.

96. See *supra*, p. 172.

97. *HC*, p. 141.

98. Grimsley, *The Philosophy of Rousseau*, pp. 150, 147, Rousseau, *Correspondance*, VII, 73, quoted in Poulet, p. 173. See *HC*, pp. 141–142.

99. Rousseau, *The Reveries of a Solitary*, First and Fourth Promenades, pp. 37, 84.

100. Waldo Frank, p. 134. Maritain, *Three Reformers*, p. 125.

101. Rousseau, *Émile*, Bk. IV, p. 242. Gildin, p. 258, note.

102. Poulet, p. 171. Rousseau, *Émile*, ed. Garnier, p. 335, quoted by Poulet, p. 171. *HC*, p. 201.

103. Carpino, "Reader's Commentary," p. 3. Ellrich, p. 69. *The Confessions of Jean-Jacques Rousseau*, Bk. X, pp. 534–535. Rousseau, Prefatory Note to *The Confessions*, translated by *HC*, p. 40.

104. *HC*, p. 157. See also Irving Babbitt, *Rousseau and Romanticism* (New York: Houghton Mifflin, 1919), p. xv, note.

105. *HC*, p. 159. See Rousseau, *The Reveries of a Solitary*, Sixth Promenade, p. 129.

106. *HC*, p. 175. F. C. Green, *Jean-Jacques*, p. 360.

107. Maritain, *Three Reformers*, p. 153.

108. Cassirer, *The Question*, p. 76. *The Confessions of Jean-Jacques Rousseau*, Bk. VI, p. 234. *St. Augustine's Confessions*, trans. William Watts, 2 vols., Loeb Classical Library (London: William Heinemann, 1912), Bk. XIII, ch. 16, Vol. II, p. 409.

109. Broome, p. 145. Guehenno, Vol. II, p. 141.

110. Broome, p. 173. Rousseau, *Émile*, Bk. IV, p. 240.

111. *HC*, p. 217, note.

112. *HC*, p. 217, note. Rousseau, *Émile*, Bk. IV, p. 257.

113. *MP*, p. 289. F. C. Green, *Jean-Jacques*, pp. 214–215.

114. Grimsley, *Rousseau and the Religious Quest*, pp. 44–45. *The Confessions of Jean-Jacques Rousseau*, Bk. VII, p. 284.

115. Ellenburg, p. 300. Rousseau, *The Reveries of a Solitary*, First Promenade, p. 40.

116. *HC*, p. 226. See also p. 108.

117. Rousseau, *The Reveries of a Solitary*, Second Promenade, p. 48. Hartle, "Rousseau on Rousseau," paper, American Political Science Association, 1976, p. 5. *HC*, p. 230. See also *HC*, p. 138.

118. Rousseau, *The Reveries of a Solitary*, Fifth Promenade, p. 113 (italics mine).

119. *HC*, p. 234. Rousseau, *The Reveries of a Solitary*, Eighth Promenade, p. 158. Rousseau, *Émile*, Bk. III, p. 147.

120. *HC*, p. 232. Rousseau, *The Reveries of a Solitary*, Eighth Promenade, p. 160. Rousseau, letter to Malesherbes, quoted in Poulet, p. 172.

121. *HC*, p. 234.

122. *HC*, pp. 223–224. Hartle, in *Review of Politics*, p. 278.

123. *HC*, p. 231.

124. Ibid.

125. See *supra*, p. 189.

126. Hartle, "Rousseau on Rousseau," paper, American Political Science Association, 1976, p. 11. Carpino, "Reader's Commentary," p. 6.

127. Rousseau, *The Reveries of a Solitary*, Fifth Promenade, pp. 113–114.

128. Rousseau, *Rousseau juge de Jean-Jacques*, in *Oeuvres complètes*, Pléiade, I, 932, quoted in *MP*, p. vi.

129. See *supra*, pp. 98–99.

130. Shklar, *Men and Citizens*, pp. 41, 44. Crocker, *Rousseau's Social Contract*, p. 184.

131. Rousseau, Preface to second letter to Bordes, in *Oeuvres complètes*, III, 103–107, quoted in Einaudi, p. 103. Rousseau, *Lettres Morales*, 349–350, quoted in Shklar, *Men and Citizens*, p. 39.

132. Rousseau, *A Discourse on the Moral Effects of the Arts and Sciences*, Pt. I, in Cole (see *RI*), p. 146. Rousseau, *Émile*, Bk. V, p. 407.

133. Kant, *Werke*, II, 326, quoted in Cassirer, *Rousseau, Kant, and Goethe*, pp. 21, 13. Cassirer, *The Question*, p. 39.

134. Cobban, p. 147.

135. Rousseau, *Émile*, Bk. IV, pp. 254, 249–250. See Hampson, p. 213, and Cassirer, *Rousseau, Kant, and Goethe*, p. 48.

136. The thesis in this and the preceding paragraph is that of *HC*, to which the treatment of Rousseau in this chapter is heavily indebted.

137. Friedrich Paulsen, *Immanuel Kant: His Life and Doctrine*, translated from

the second edition (1899), J. E. Creighton, Albert Lefevre (New York: Frederick Ungar, 1963), p. 25.

138. Karl Jaspers, *Kant*, trans. of part of *Die grossen Philosophen* I, Ralph Manheim (New York: Harcourt, Brace and World, Harvest Books, 1962), p. 8. Kant, "What Is Enlightenment?" in Immanuel Kant, *On History*, ed. Lewis White Beck; trans. Lewis White Beck, Robert E. Anchor, Emil L. Fackenheim (New York: Bobbs-Merrill, Library of Liberal Arts, 1963), p. 3.

139. Kant, letter to J. H. Lambert, Dec. 31, 1765, in Kant, *Philosophical Correspondence, 1759–99*, ed. and trans. Arnulf Zweig (Chicago: University of Chicago Press, 1967), p. 49.

140. Karl Barth, *From Rousseau to Ritschl* (London: SCM Press, 1959), pp. 152–153.

141. Herder, *Briefe zur Beforderung der Humanitat*, 79th Letter, quoted in Hans Saner, *Kant's Political Thought: Its Origins and Development*, trans. E. B. Ashton (Chicago: University of Chicago Press, 1973), pp. 342–343.

142. Saner, pp. 208–209.

143. Kant, "Fragmente aus dem Nachlasse," *Werke*, Hartenstein, VIII, 624, quoted in Norman Kemp Smith, *A Commentary to Kant's 'Critique of Pure Reason'*, 2d ed. (London: Macmillan, 1930), p. lvii, and in Herman J. de Vleeschauwer, *The Development of Kantian Thought: The History of a Doctrine*, trans. A. R. C. Duncan (London: Thomas Nelson and Sons, 1962), pp. 39–40.

144. De Vleeschauwer, p. 42. Kant, "Fragmente aus dem Nachlasse," quoted in de Vleeschauwer, p. 40.

145. Kant, *Fragments*, VIII, 613, quoted in Cassirer, *Rousseau, Kant, and Goethe*, p. 22. Cassirer, ibid., p. 42.

146. Cassirer, ibid., p. 35.

147. Kemp Smith, *A Commentary*, pp. xxxii, xxx, xxxiii.

148. Immanuel Kant, *Prolegomena to Any Future Metaphysics*, ed. and trans. Lewis White Beck (New York: Bobbs-Merrill, Library of Liberal Arts, 1950), Introduction, p. 8; Conclusion, # 58, p. 108.

149. See *supra*, pp. 135–136.

150. Leibniz, *New Essays Concerning Human Understanding*, trans. Alfred Gideon Langley (La Salle, Ill.: Open Court Publishing, 1949), II, i, 2, p. 111. Jonathan Bennett, *Kant's Analytic* (London: Cambridge University Press, 1966), p. 98. Gottfried Martin, *Kant's Metaphysics and Theory of Science*, trans. P. G. Lucas (Manchester University Press, 1955), pp. 7–8. Kant, "Polemic against Eberhard," vii, 250, quoted by Martin, ibid.

151. Martin, p. 28.

152. Thomas Langan, "Foreword," to Martin Heidegger, *Kant and the Problem of Metaphysics*, trans. James Churchill (Bloomington: Indiana University Press, 1962), p. x. *KC*, B275, p. 244; B277, p. 246; B158, p. 169.

153. Bennett, p. 55. Colin Murray Turbayne, "Kant's Relation to Berkeley," in Lewis White Beck, ed., *Kant Studies Today* (La Salle, Ill.: Open Court Publishing, 1969), p. 113.

154. Kant, *Introduction to Logic*, in *Kant's "Introduction to Logic" and His "Essay*

on the Mistaken Subtility of the Four Figures," trans. Thomas Kingsmill Abbott (New York: Philosophical Library, 1963), III, 188, p. 16. Kant, letter to F. H. Jacobi, Aug. 30, 1789, in Kant, *Philosophical Correspondence,* ed. Zweig, p. 157.

155. Kant, letter to Moses Mendelssohn, Aug. 16, 1783, in Zweig, p. 105. Kant, *Introduction to Logic,* IV, 196, p. 23. Kant, quoted by Josiah Royce, *The Spirit of Modern Philosophy: An Essay in the Form of Lectures* (1892) (New York: W. W. Norton, 1967), p. 120 (no footnote provided).

156. Kant, *Prolegomena,* Introduction, pp. 4, 5; "Solution of the General Question," p. 115. *KC,* Bxiv, p. 21.

157. Kant, *Prolegomena,* Conclusion, # 57, pp. 101, 102, 103.

158. Saner, p. 16. *KC,* Bxiv, p. 21; Bxxiii, p. 25.

159. *KC,* A840-B868, A841–B869, pp. 658, 659.

160. Immanuel Kant, *Critique of Judgment,* trans. J. H. Bernard (New York: Hafner, 1951), Introduction, I, p. 7.

161. De Vleeschauwer, p. 97. *KC,* B878–A850, p. 665.

162. Jaspers, *Kant,* p. 8.

163. Charles M. Sherover, "Heidegger's Ontology and the Copernican Revolution," in *Kant Studies Today,* p. 456.

164. *KC,* Bxvi, p. 22.

165. A. C. Ewing, *A Short Commentary on Kant's "Critique of Pure Reason"* (Chicago: University of Chicago Press, 1938), p. 10. Sherover, p. 457. H. J. Paton, "Kant's So-Called 'Copernican Revolution,'" *Mind,* 47 (1937), p. 366.

166. Ernst Cassirer, "Kant" article, *Encyclopedia of Social Sciences* (1935 ed.), p. 539. Kant, *Critique of Judgment,* # 91, p. 319 (italics mine). *KC,* Bxviii, p. 23. Kant, "An Old Question Raised Again: Is the Human Race Constantly Progressing?" in Kant, *On History,* p. 141 (italics mine).

167. Charles M. Sherover, *The Human Experience of Time: The Development of Its Philosophic Meaning* (New York: New York University Press, 1975), p. 111. Collins, *Interpreting Modern Philosophy,* p. 313. Sherover, "Heidegger's Ontology," p. 457. John E. Smith, "The Question of Man," in Charles W. Hendel, ed., *The Philosophy of Kant and Our Modern World* (New York: Bobbs-Merrill, The Liberal Arts Press, 1957), p. 10. Kemp Smith, *A Commentary,* p. 251.

168. Heidegger, *Kant and the Problem of Metaphysics,* pp. 17, 22, 42, 27.

169. Sherover, "Heidegger's Ontology," p. 459.

170. H. J. Paton, p. 367. Waldo Frank, p. 346.

171. Kant, *Prolegomena,* Pt. II, # 36, p. 66.

172. Richard F. Grabau, "Kant's Concept of the Thing-in-Itself: An Interpretation," *Review of Metaphysics,* 16 (1963), pp. 778–779. N. Lawrence, "Kant and Modern Philosophy," *Review of Metaphysics,* 10 (March 1957), p. 453. T. D. Weldon, *Kant's Critique of Pure Reason,* 2d ed. (Oxford: At the Clarendon Press, 1958), p. 100. D. P. Dryer, *Kant's Solution for Verification in Metaphysics* (Toronto: University of Toronto Press, 1966), p. 349. Kant, *Opus Postumum,* ed. Adickes, p. 648, quoted in Kemp Smith, *A Commentary,* p. 627.

173. Martin, p. 204.

174. Ibid., p. 57.

175. Kant, "On the Form and Principles of the Sensible and Intelligible World" (Inaugural Dissertation, 1770), in *Kant: Selected Pre-Critical Writings and Correspondence with Beck*, trans. G. B. Kerferd and D. E. Walford (Manchester: Manchester University Press, 1968), pp. 54, 55. Kant, *Prolegomena*, Pt. I, # 9, p. 30. Kant, "Concerning the Ultimate Foundation of the Differentiation of Regions in Space," in *Kant: Selected Pre-Critical Writings*, p. 38. Kant, "What Does It Mean to Orient Oneself in Thinking?" (1786), quoted in George Schrader, "The Philosophy of Existence," in *The Philosophy of Kant and Our Modern World*, p. 31.

176. Kant, "On the Form and Principles," pp. 63, 68, 70. Kant, "Concerning the Ultimate Foundation," p. 43.

177. *KC*, Bxxv, p. 27. Kant, *Reflexionen*, Erdmann, II, 408, quoted in Heidegger, *Kant and the Problem*, p. 149. Martin, pp. 38–39. H. J. Paton, *Kant's Metaphysics of Experience: A Commentary on the First Half of the 'Kritik der Reinen Vernunft'*, 2 vols. (London: George Allen and Unwin, 1936), Vol. I, pp. 143, 144, 153.

178. Kant, "On the Form and Principles," pp. 72–73. Martin, p. 155. *KC*, A77, p. 111.

179. *KC*, A26-B42, p. 71; A375, p. 349. Christopher Browne Garnett, Jr., *The Kantian Philosophy of Space* (Port Washington, N.Y.: Kennikat Press, 1965 reprint), p. 233. Kant, "On the Form and Principles," pp. 68, 65–66.

180. Nathan Rotenstreich, *Experience and Its Systematization: Studies in Kant* (The Hague: Martinus Nijhoff, 1965), pp. 31–32.

181. Sherover, *The Human Experience of Time*, pp. 115, 112. *KC*, A31, pp. 74–75; A33, p. 77; Bxl, note, pp. 34–35.

182. Heidegger, *Kant and the Problem*, p. 194 (see also p. 54). D. P. Dryer, p. 338.

183. Garnett, p. 219. Heidegger, *Kant and the Problem*, p. 150.

184. Heidegger, *Kant and the Problem*, p. 192. William J. Richardson, *Heidegger: Through Phenomenology to Thought* (The Hague: Martinus Nijhoff, 1963), p. 145.

185. Kemp Smith, *A Commentary*, pp. 267, 263. H. J. Paton, "Kant's Analysis of Experience," *Proceedings of the Aristotelian Society*, N.S. 36 (1935–1937), p. 187.

186. H. J. Paton, "Kant's Analysis," pp. 187–206 passim. H. W. Cassirer, *Kant's First Critique: An Appraisal of the Permanent Significance of Kant's 'Critique of Pure Reason'* (London: George Allen and Unwin), p. 91. H. J. Paton, *Kant's Metaphysics*, Vol. I, pp. 536–537.

187. H. J. Paton, *Kant's Metaphysics*, Vol. I, p. 443, *KC*, A78, p. 112; A118, p. 143.

188. Kant, *Critique of Pure Reason*, A124, quoted in Heidegger, *Kant and the Problem*, pp. 88–89. Heidegger, ibid., pp. 81, 106 (see also pp. 138, 108, 86).

189. Robert Paul Wolff, *Kant's Theory of Mental Activity: A Commentary on the Transcendental Analytic of the "Critique of Pure Reason"* (Cambridge: Harvard

University Press, 1963), p. 95. *KC*, Bxxvi, p. 27. H. J. Paton, *Kant's Metaphysics*, Vol. I, p. 354. Kant, *Prolegomena*, Pt. II, # 20, p. 48.

190. *KC*, B93, p. 105.

191. De Vleeschauwer, p. 189. Karl Jaspers, *Philosophy*, trans. E. Ashton, 3 vols. (Chicago: University of Chicago Press, 1969), Vol. I, p. 79.

192. Jaspers, ibid., p. 82. *KC*, B75–A51, p. 93. Paulsen, p. 176. Kemp Smith, *A Commentary*, p. 263. Heidegger, *Kant and the Problem*, p. 78.

193. *KC*, B94, p. 106. H. J. Paton, *Kant's Metaphysics*, Vol. I, p. 248. D. P. Dryer, pp. 120–121.

194. De Vleeschauwer, p. 130.

195. Richard Kroner, *Kant's Weltanschauung*, trans. John E. Smith (Chicago: University of Chicago Press, 1956), p. 71. Martin, p. 125.

196. Martin, pp. 90–91, 67.

197. *KC*, A125, p. 147.

198. Kant, *Prolegomena*, "Preamble," # 2, p. 19; # 5, p. 23. D. P. Dryer, p. 85.

199. T. D. Weldon, p. 138.

200. John Kemp, *The Philosophy of Kant* (New York: Oxford University Press, 1968), p. 37. Martin, p. 36.

201. Martin, p. 126. Jaspers, *Kant*, p. 24.

202. Kant, letter to J. S. Beck, July 1, 1794, in Zweig, p. 216.

203. Wolff, *Kant's Theory*, pp. 312–313. H. J. Paton, *Kant's Metaphysics*, Vol. II, p. 416.

204. Paton, ibid., Vol. I, p. 207.

205. Leibniz, *Principles of Nature and Grace*, # 4, quoted by John Kemp, p. 25. H. J. Paton, *Kant's Metaphysics*, Vol. I, pp. 414–415, 420.

206. De Vleeschauwer, pp. 74, 104.

207. John Kemp, p. 26. H. J. Paton, "Kant's Analysis," p. 206. A. C. Ewing, p. 127. See *KC*, A114, p. 140; B136, B137, pp. 155–156.

208. A. C. Ewing, pp. 261–262. See Immanuel Kant, *Education*, trans. Annette Churton (Ann Arbor: University of Michigan Press, Ann Arbor Books, 1960), ch. IV, # 68, p. 71.

209. *KC*, B356, p. 301; B383, p. 318.

210. *KC*, B359, p. 303. Kant, *Prolegomena*, Pt. III, # 44, p. 80.

211. Kant, "On the Form and Principles," p. 47. Martin, p. 57.

212. Martin, pp. 58, 59, A. C. Ewing, pp. 222–223.

213. Martin, p. 59, and passim, pp. 59–67.

214. H. J. Paton, *The Categorical Imperative: A Study in Kant's Moral Philosophy*, 5th ed. (London: Hutchinson, 1965), p. 29. Martin, p. 129. Jaspers, *Kant*, p. 54.

215. Jaspers, ibid. See *KC*, A792–B820, p. 627.

216. Kant, *Critique of Pure Reason*, A697–B707; A681–B709, quoted in Stanley G. French, "Kant's Constitutive-Regulative Distinction," in *Kant Studies Today*, p. 381.

217. Kant, letter to Marcus Herz, Nov. 24, 1776, in *Kant: Selected Pre-Critical Writings*, p. 123. *KC*, A832-B860, p. 653; A680-B708, p. 556.

218. Paulsen, p. 209. Kemp Smith, *A Commentary*, p. 507.

219. Heidegger, *Kant and the Problem*, pp. 27, 19. Paulsen, p. 211.

220. H. J. Paton, *The Categorical Imperative*, p. 29. Saner, p. 221.

221. T. D. Weldon, p. 70. Martin, pp. 91, 92. Kant, *Prolegomena*, Pt. II, # 30, p. 60; # 36, p. 65.

222. Immanuel Kant, *Anthropology from a Pragmatic Point of View*, trans. Victor Lyle Dowdell; rev. and ed., Hans H. Rudnick (Carbondale: Southern Illinois University Press, 1978), Pt. I, Bk. I, # 7, Remark, p. 25. Wolff, *Kant's Theory*, p. 313. Cassirer, "Kant" article, *Encyclopedia of Social Sciences*, p. 539.

223. D. P. Dryer, pp. 495, 519. H. J. Paton, *Kant's Metaphysics*, Vol. I, pp. 72, 82.

224. Kant, *Prolegomena*, Conclusion, # 59, p. 110. De Vleeschauwer, p. 55. Jaspers, *Philosophy*, Vol. I, p. 82. *KC*, A255, p. 272.

225. T. D. Weldon, p. 321. Kant, *Opus Postumum*, Adickes, p. 654, quoted in Kemp Smith, *A Commentary*, pp. 625–626.

226. Kroner, p. 280. Saner, p. 58. Martin, p. 191.

227. Grabau, p. 778.

228. Martin, pp. 204, 205.

229. Heidegger, *Kant and the Problem*, p. 37. Kant, *Reflexionen*, 4135, quoted in Martin, p. 186.

230. Kant, *Introduction to Logic*, IV, 196, p. 23. Kant, *The Metaphysical Principles of Virtue* (Pt. II of *The Metaphysics of Morals*), trans. James Ellington (New York: Bobbs-Merrill, Library of Liberal Arts, 1964), Preface, # 376, p. 32.

231. Kant, *Critique of Judgment*, Introduction, II, pp. 10–11. French, p. 376. Kant, *Introduction to Logic*, Appendix, 264, p. 77. See *KC*, A509-B537, p. 450; A510-B538, p. 451.

232. *KC*, Bxxv, p. 26. De Vleeschauwer, p. 124. Kroner, p. 95.

233. *KC*, A797-B825, p. 630; A800-B828, p. 632. Rotenstreich, p. 37.

234. Kant, *Critique of Judgment*, Introduction, II, p. 11. Kant, *Introduction to Logic*, Appendix, 264, 265, pp. 77–78.

235. Lewis White Beck, *A Commentary on Kant's Critique of Practical Reason* (Chicago: University of Chicago Press, Phoenix Books, 1963), pp. 50, 239, 143.

236. Kant, *Critique of Judgment*, # 88, p. 306. *KC*, Bxxx, p. 29.

237. Kant, *Critique of Judgment*, # 91, p. 324. L. W. Beck, *A Commentary*, p. 28.

238. Kant, *Metaphysical Principles of Virtue*, Introduction, # 400, p. 59; "Elements of Ethics," Pt. I, # 438, p. 100. Kant, *Lectures on Ethics*, trans. Louis Infield (New York: Harper Torchbooks, 1963), "Conscience," p. 129. Kant, *Critique of Practical Reason*, trans. Lewis White Beck (New York: Bobbs-Merrill, Library of Liberal Arts, 1956), Introduction, Theorem II, Remark # 1, pp. 23–24.

239. Kant, *Critique of Judgment*, # 76, p. 251.

240. George Schrader, "The Philosophy of Existence," p. 41. Martin, p. 175. H. J. Paton, *The Categorical Imperative*, p. 94.

241. Kemp Smith, *A Commentary*, p. 515. Paton, ibid., p. 212.

242. T. D. Weldon, p. 247. A. C. Ewing, p. 265.

243. H. J. Paton, *The Categorical Imperative*, p. 273. Martin, p. 175.

244. John Kemp, p. 61. Kant, letter to Kiesewetter, April 20, 1790, in Zweig, p. 161.

245. H. J. Paton, *The Categorical Imperative*, p. 143.

246. Kant, "Conjectural Beginnings of Human History," in Kant, *On History*, pp. 57, 59.

247. Kant, *Critique of Practical Reason*, Bk. I, ch. 3, p. 79. H. J. Paton, *The Categorical Imperative*, p. 64. Kant, *Religion Within the Limits of Reason Alone*, trans. Theodore M. Greene, Hoyt H. Hudson (New York: Harper Torchbooks, 1960), Bk. I, "General Observation," p. 44.

248. "Omnes autem operationes morales sunt ordinabiles ad aliquid aliud," S. Thomae Aquinatis, *Summa Contra Gentiles* (Turin: Marietti, 1927), Bk. III, ch. 34, p. 254.

249. Kroner, p. 23. Kant, *Critique of Judgment*, # 83, p. 281. John Kemp, p. 63. Kant, letter to Kiesewetter, April 20, 1790, in Zweig, pp. 161–162. Kant, *Critique of Practical Reason*, Bk. I, ch. 3, p. 89.

250. H. J. Paton, *The Categorical Imperative*, p. 270. Kant, *Lectures on Ethics*, "The Lawgiver," p. 51. Kant, *Critique of Judgment*, # 28, p. 104.

251. Kant, *Lectures on Ethics*, "The General Principle of Morality," pp. 17, 18. Kant, *Foundations of the Metaphysics of Morals*, trans. Lewis White Beck (New York: Bobbs-Merrill, Library of Liberal Arts, 1959), First Section, p. 9; Second Section, p. 55.

252. H. J. Paton, *The Categorical Imperative*, p. 77. Kant, *Religion Within*, Bk. I, "General Observation," p. 40. John R. Silber, "The Ethical Significance of Kant's *Religion*," in Kant, ibid., p. cxi.

253. L. W. Beck, *A Commentary*, p. 202. Kant, from his literary self-portrait of the 1760s, quoted in Saner, p. 79.

254. T. C. Williams, *The Concept of the Categorical Imperative: A Study of the Place of the Categorical Imperative in Kant's Ethical Theory* (Oxford: At the Clarendon Press, 1968), p. 111. H. J. Paton, *The Categorical Imperative*, p. 128. Kant, *The Metaphysical Principles of Virtue*, Pt. II, Introduction, # 382, p. 39.

255. Alfred Hoernle, "Kant's Concept of the Intrinsic Worth of Every Rational Being," *The Personalist*, 24 (1943), p. 144.

256. Kant, *Critique of Practical Reason*, Bk. I, ch. 1, # 7, p. 30.

257. Kant, *Foundations of the Metaphysics of Morals*, sec. II, p. 39. Oscar W. Miller, *The Kantian Thing-in-Itself or the Creative Mind* (New York: Philosophical Library, 1956), pp. 62–63.

258. Kant, ibid., sec. I, p. 16.

259. Sir David Ross, *Kant's Ethical Theory: A Commentary on the 'Grundlegung zur Metaphysik der Sitten'* (Oxford: At the Clarendon Press, 1954), pp. 57–58.

Kant, "Enquiry Concerning the Clarity of the Principles of Natural Theology and Ethics," in *Kant: Selected Pre-Critical Writings*, p. 32.

260. Kant quoted in Jaspers, *Kant*, pp. 67–68 (no footnote provided).

261. Kroner, pp. 36–37. Claude Sumner, *Eight Types of Ethical Theory* (Addis-Ababa, Ethiopia: The University College Press, 1962), p. 77. Heidegger, *Kant and the Problem*, pp. 164–165.

262. Heidegger, ibid., p. 165.

263. John Kemp, p. 63. Oscar W. Miller, p. 32.

264. A. C. Ewing, p. 126. T. C. Williams, p. 109.

265. Kroner, pp. 98–99. Martin, pp. 174–175.

266. Kant, *The Metaphysical Principles of Virtue*, "Elements of Ethics," Pt. I, # 434, 435, pp. 96–97.

267. Oscar W. Miller, p. 32. De Vleeschauwer, p. 189. Kant, *Critique of Judgment*, # 84, p. 286.

268. Ross, *Kant's Ethical Theory*, p. 75. Martin, p. 180. Kroner, p. 93. Kant, "The End of All Things," in Kant, *On History*, p. 78.

269. Saner, pp. 53–54. A. C. Ewing, p. 235.

270. Kant, *Dreams of a Spirit Seer, Illustrated by Dreams of Metaphysics* (1766), trans. E. F. Goerwitz (London: Swan Sonnenschein, 1900), p. 57. H. J. Paton, *The Categorical Imperative*, p. 268.

271. *KC*, A808-B836, p. 637.

272. George A. Schrader, "Moral Autonomy," *Journal of Philosophy*, 57 (1960), p. 768. See Kant, *Lectures on Ethics*, "Duties to Oneself," pp. 117–118; Kant, *Education*, ch. vi, # 96, 103, pp. 103, 108–109; and Kant, *The Metaphysical Principles of Virtue*, "Elements of Ethics," Pt. I, # 14, pp. 103–104.

273. T. D. Weldon, p. 65. Cassirer, "Kant" article, *Encyclopedia of Social Sciences*, p. 541. Hans Reiss, "Introduction," in Hans Reiss, ed., *Kant's Political Writings*, trans. H. B. Nisbet (Cambridge: Cambridge University Press, 1970), p. 22.

274. Kant, "On the Common Saying: 'This May Be True in Theory, but It Does Not Apply in Practice,'" in Reiss, ed., *Kant's Political Writings*, p. 65, note.

275. Ross, *Kant's Ethical Theory*, p. 61.

276. Kant, *Foundations of the Metaphysics of Morals*, sec. II, pp. 52, 54. Kant, *The Metaphysical Principles of Virtue*, Introduction, # 395, p. 54.

277. *KC*, A808-B836, p. 637. Kant, *Religion Within*, Bk. II, sec. 1, p. 54.

278. De Vleeschauwer, p. 124. Jonathan Bennett, *Kant's Dialectic* (London: Cambridge University Press, 1974), p. 187. H. J. Paton, *The Categorical Imperative*, p. 162.

279. *KC*, A805-B833, pp. 635–636.

280. Kemp Smith, *A Commentary*, pp. 270, 271. De Vleeschauwer, pp. 192, 193.

281. *KC*, A546-B574; A547-B575, p. 472. H. J. Paton, *The Categorical Imperative*, p. 267. Ross, *Kant's Ethical Theory*, pp. 75–76.

282. Saner, pp. 47, 58. Theodore M. Greene, "The Historical Context and Religious Significance of Kant's *Religion*," in Kant, *Religion Within*, p. liv.

283. Fritz Medicus, "On the Objectivity of Historical Knowledge," in Raymond Klibansky and H. J. Paton, eds., *Philosophy and History: Essays Presented to Ernst Cassirer* (1936) (New York: Harper Torchbooks, 1963), p. 139. Rotenstreich, pp. 127, 171–172.

284. John E. Smith, "The Question of Man," pp. 10–11.

285. Kant, *Critique of Practical Reason*, Conclusion, p. 166.

286. *Aristotle's Metaphysics*, trans. with commentaries by Hippocrates G. Apostle (Bloomington: Indiana University Press, 1966), 982b, 14–21, p. 15.

287. L. W. Beck, *A Commentary*, p. 282.

288. Kant, *Universal Natural History and Theory of the Heavens*, trans. W. Hastie (Ann Arbor: University of Michigan Press, Ann Arbor Books, 1969), Pt. I, p. 65; Pt. II, ch. 7, pp. 135, 155.

289. Paulsen, p. 53.

290. Kant, *Critique of Judgment*, # 26, p. 93.

291. Kroner, pp. 69, 84. See Kant, ibid., Introduction, IX, p. 33.

292. Kroner, p. 117.

293. Kant: "Conjectural Beginnings of Human History"; "An Old Question Raised Again: Is the Human Race Constantly Progressing?"; "Idea for a Universal History from a Cosmopolitan Point of View" in Kant, *On History*, pp. 68, 141, 11.

294. Kant, "On the Common Saying," in Reiss, pp. 88–89.

295. Kant, "Perpetual Peace," in Kant, *On History*, pp. 111, 113.

296. Kant, *Critique of Judgment*, # 83, pp. 283, 284.

297. Saner, pp. 47–48. Kant, *Anthropology from a Pragmatic Point of View*, Pt. II, # E, pp. 245, 246. Kant, "Idea for a Universal History," p. 11. Kant, *Lectures on Ethics*, "The Ultimate Destiny of the Human Race," p. 252.

298. Saner, pp. 234, 252.

299. Kant, *The Metaphysics of Morals*, Pt. I, in Reiss, pp. 174–175, 173–174.

300. Kant, "Perpetual Peace," p. 125.

301. Kant, letter to Moses Mendelssohn, April 8, 1766, in Zweig, p. 55.

302. James Collins, "A Kantian Critique of 'The God is Dead' Theme," in *Kant Studies Today*, p. 429. Kant, *Critique of Judgment*, # 91, p. 334. Kant, *Opus Postumum*, Adickes, p. 827, quoted in Kemp Smith, *A Commentary*, p. 640. Kant, *Critique of Judgment*, # 86, p. 297. See also Étienne Gilson, *The Unity of Philosophical Experience* (New York: Charles Scribner's Sons, 1937), p. 239.

303. Kant, *Religion Within*, Bk. IV, Pt. ii, # 2, p. 158; Preface to First Edition, p. 7. Kant, *Education*, ch. VI, # 105, pp. 111, 112. Kant, *Lectures on Ethics*, "Natural Religion," p. 83.

304. Paulsen, pp. 207–208. Kant, *Critique of Judgment*, # 91, p. 339.

305. Kant, *Religion Within*, Bk. I, "General Observation," p. 47; Preface to Bk. III, p. 85. Kant, letters to Heinrich Jung-Stilling, after March 1, 1789, and to J. C. Lavater, April 28, 1775, in Zweig, pp. 131, 80.

306. Kant, *Religion Within*, Bk. IV, Preface, p. 140.

307. H. J. Paton, *The Categorical Imperative*, p. 196. Gilson, *The Unity of Philosophical Experience*, p. 238. St. Paul, Epistle to the Romans 2:14; 2:28, 29; 9:31, 32, Revised Standard Version (New York: Thomas Nelson, 1952).

308. Kant, "The End of All Things," in Kant, *On History*, p. 84.

309. Cassirer, *Rousseau, Kant, and Goethe*, p. 49.

310. De Vleeschauwer, p. 135. Heidegger, *Kant and the Problem*, pp. 9, 10. Saner, p. 54. H. J. Paton, *Kant's Metaphysics*, Vol. I, p. 72. Carl H. Hamburg, *Symbol and Reality: Studies in the Philosophy of Ernst Cassirer* (The Hague: Martinus Nijhoff, 1970), p. 143. Heidegger, *Kant and the Problem*, p. 17. Sherover, "Heidegger's Ontology," pp. 466, 467–468. *KC*, A703-B731, p. 570.

311. Paulsen, p. 39. Saner, p. 23. Kant, *Introduction to Logic*, III, 188, p. 16.

312. Saner, pp. 203–204. Kant, ibid., III, 189, p. 17.

313. *KC*, A838-B866, p. 657. Kant, *Introduction to Logic*, III, 185, p. 14. Jaspers, *Kant*, pp. 92–93.

314. Kant, letter to C. F. Staudlin, May 4, 1793, in Zweig, p. 205. Kant, *Introduction to Logic*, III, 186, 187, p. 15.

315. Heidegger, *Kant and the Problem*, pp. 224, 219. John E. Smith, "The Question of Man," p. 13.

316. Kant, *Werke*, Hartenstein, VIII, 624 f., quoted in Smith, ibid., p. 24. Kant, *Werke*, II, 326, quoted in Cassirer, *Rousseau, Kant, and Goethe*, p. 21.

317. Heidegger, *Kant and the Problem*, p. 213. Cassirer, ibid., p. 23. Kant, *Anthropology from a Pragmatic Point of View*, Introduction, p. 3. Heidegger, *Kant and the Problem*, p. 135. Rotenstreich, p. 50.

318. Kant, letter to Marcus Herz, ca. May 11, 1781, in Zweig, p. 95. See also Jaspers, *Kant*, p. 91.

319. Jaspers, *Kant*, p. 90.

320. Kant, letter to Christian Garve, Sept. 21, 1798, in Zweig, p. 251.

321. Kant, letter to Marcus Herz, Feb. 21, 1772, in *Kant: Selected Pre-Critical Writings*, pp. 114–115. Kant, letter to J. H. Lambert, Dec. 31, 1765, in Zweig, p. 48.

322. *KC*, A141, B181, p. 183.

323. Heidegger, *Kant and the Problem*, p. 252.

CHAPTER SEVEN

1. Martin Heidegger, *What Is Philosophy?*, trans. William Kluback and Jean T. Wilde (New York: Twayne Publishers, 1958), p. 89.

2. Gottfried Martin, p. 205.

3. G. R. G. Mure, *An Introduction to Hegel* (Oxford: At the Clarendon Press, 1940), p. ix. Shlomo Avineri, *Hegel's Theory of the Modern State* (Cambridge: At the University Press, 1972), pp. 64, 68. *HP*, # 12, p. 7. Raymond Plant, *Hegel* (Bloomington: Indiana University Press, 1973), p. 65. G. W. F. Hegel,

Philosophy of History, trans. John Sibree (New York: P. F. Colier and Son, 1902), "Introduction," p. 84. *HH*, III, p. 43. Hegel, *Berliner Schriften*, ed. Johannes Hoffmeister (Hamburg: Meiner, 1956), quoted in Emil L. Fackenheim, *The Religious Dimension in Hegel's Thought* (Boston: Beacon Press, 1970), p. 15.

4. Werner Marx, *Hegel's Phenomenology of Spirit: Its Point and Purpose—A Commentary on the Preface and Introduction*, trans. Peter Heath (New York: Harper and Row, 1975), p. 101. Hegel, *The Difference between Fichte's and Schelling's System of Philosophy*, trans. H. S. Harris and Walter Cerf (Albany: State University of New York Press, 1977), pp. 89, 91 (note 10), 195. Walter Kaufmann, *Hegel: A Reinterpretation* (Notre Dame: University of Notre Dame Press, 1978), pp. 86, 49. *HY*, p. 452. Hegel, letter to Windischmann, May 27, 1810, quoted in Kaufmann, p. 329. *CN*, p. 130, note 1.

5. Fackenheim, pp. 209, 207. *HL*, # 194, Zusatz 1, p. 261. Mure, p. 167, Hegel, *The Difference . . . Philosophy*, p. 158. *HR*, I, pp. 47–48. *HL*, # 212, Zus., p. 274.

6. Stanley Rosen, *G. W. F. Hegel: An Introduction to the Science of Wisdom* (New Haven: Yale University Press, 1974), p. xvi. Hegel, *Faith and Knowledge*, trans. Walter Cerf and H. S. Harris (Albany: State University of New York Press, 1977), p. 78.

7. See *supra,* pp. 74, 117–118.

8. Hegel, *The Difference . . . Philosophy*, pp. 156, 155. Plant, p. 83. Rosen, p. 137. *Hegel's Philosophy of Right*, # 187, Remark, p. 125. Hegel, *The Difference . . . Philosophy*, pp. 91, 155. *HY*, p. 228. *HH*, III, pp. 368, 442.

9. *HR*, I, Introduction, p. 17. *HY*, p. 48. Quentin Lauer, *Hegel's Idea of Philosophy* (New York: Fordham University Press, 1971), p. 158, note i. St. Augustine, *De Genesi ad litteram*, VIII, xxvi, 48, in Erich Przywara, ed., *An Augustine Synthesis* (New York: Harper Torchbooks, 1958), pp. 106–107. Pseudo-Dionysius, *On the Divine Names*, in *Dionysius the Areopagite on the Divine Names and the Mystical Theology*, trans. C. E. Rolt, 2d. ed. (London, 1940), ch. 7, # 3.

10. *HY*, p. 483. Plant, p. 55. Jean Hyppolite, *Studies on Marx and Hegel*, trans. John O'Neill (New York: Harper Torchbooks, 1973), p. 31. Karl Löwith, *From Hegel to Nietzsche: The Revolution in Nineteenth-Century Thought*, trans. David E. Green (New York: Doubleday, Anchor Books, 1967), p. 31. Clark Butler, *G. W. F. Hegel* (Boston: Twayne Publishers, G. K. Hall, 1977), p. 135. Rosen, p. 47.

11. J. Glenn Gray, "Introduction," in J. Glenn Gray, ed., *G. W. F. Hegel: On Art, Religion, Philosophy* (New York: Harper Torchbooks, 1970), p. 2. *CN*, "Defense Outline," p. 5.

12. Charles Taylor, *Hegel* (Cambridge: Cambridge University Press, 1975), p. 180. Rosen, p. 151.

13. *HP*, # 565, p. 344. *HH*, III, pp. 429, 444, 426, 437.

14. *HH*, III, pp. 472, 444. *HL*, # 60. Zus., p. 94. Taylor, p. 531. Hegel, *Samtliche Werke*, Glockner, XVI, 538, quoted in Gustav E. Mueller, "Hegel's Absolute and the Crisis of Christianity," in D. C. Travis, ed., *A Hegel Symposium*

(Austin: The University of Texas, Department of Germanic Languages, 1962), p. 104. Löwith, *From Hegel to Nietzsche*, p. 163.

15. Stuart Hampshire, *Spinoza* (New York: Penguin Books, 1951), pp. 53, 171. Henry Alonzo Myers, *The Spinoza-Hegel Paradox* (New York: Burt Franklin, 1974 reprint), p. 58. *HL*, # 94, Zus., p. 138. *Hegel's Philosophy of Nature* (Pt. II of the *Encyclopaedia of the Philosophical Sciences*), trans. A. V. Miller (Oxford: At the Clarendon Press, 1970), # 254, Remark, p. 29; # 268, Zus., p. 62.

16. Blaise Pascal, *Pensées*, trans. A. J. Krailsheimer (Harmondsworth: Penguin Books, 1966), # 68, p. 48; # 201, p. 95. Robert F. Horton, *The Trinity* (London: Horace Marshall and Son, 1901), p. 33. *Hegel's Philosophy of Nature*, # 275, Zus., p. 88.

17. *HH*, III, p. 124. Haym, quoted by Kaufmann, *Hegel: A Reinterpretation*, p. 112. Taylor, p. 88.

18. Kaufmann, ibid., p. 119. Hegel, *Faith and Knowledge*, p. 169. John Herman Randall, Jr., *Hellenistic Ways of Deliverance and the Making of the Christian Synthesis* (New York: Columbia University Press, 1970), p. 90.

19. *HL*, # 194, Zus. 1, p. 261. Plant, p. 78. Löwith, *From Hegel to Nietzsche*, p. 172. J. Glenn Gray, *Hegel and Greek Thought* (New York: Harper Torchbooks, 1968), pp. 5, 85. *HH*, III, p. 546.

20. *HY*, p. 583. *HL*, # 18, p. 23. W. T. Stace, *The Philosophy of Hegel: A Systematic Exposition* (New York: Dover, 1955), p. 231.

21. Franz Wiedmann, *Hegel: An Illustrated Biography*, trans. J. Neugroschel (New York: Western Publishing, Pegasus, 1968), p. 50.

22. Alexandre Kojève, *Introduction to the Reading of Hegel: Lectures on the "Phenomenology of Spirit,"* assembled by Raymon Queneau; ed. Allan Bloom; trans. James H. Nichols, Jr. (New York: Basic Books, 1969), pp. 259, 199. Klaus Hartmann, "Hegel: A Non-Metaphysical View," in Alasdair MacIntyre, ed., *Hegel: A Collection of Critical Essays* (New York: Doubleday, Anchor Books, 1972), p. 108. Fackenheim, p. 27. G. R. G. Mure, p. 100. *HR*, I, pp. 105, 59. Hans Georg Gadamer, *Hegel's Dialectic: Five Hermeneutical Essays*, trans. P. Christopher Smith (New Haven: Yale University Press, 1976), pp. 6, 105. *HS*, p. 838. Joseph Carpino, "An Introduction to Hegel," Lecture delivered to the Honors Program at Boston College, February 13, 1967 (unpublished), p. 16.

23. *HL*, # 228, Zus., p. 286.

24. Rosen, p. xvii. Gadamer, *Hegel's Dialectic*, p. 16. Herbert Marcuse, *Reason and Revolution: Hegel and the Rise of Social Theory* (Boston: Beacon Press, 1960), p. 11. Hyppolite, *Studies*, p. 78. J. N. Findlay, *The Philosophy of Hegel: An Introduction and Re-Examination* (New York: Collier Books, 1962), p. 67. John Henry Cardinal Newman, *Essay on the Development of Christian Doctrine* (1845), (London: Sheed and Ward, New Ark Library, 1960), ch. II, sec. i, # 1, p. 41.

25. J. N. Findlay, p. 66. *HL*, # 198, p. 265. *HH*, I, pp. 20–21. J. N. Findlay, "The Contemporary Relevance of Hegel," in Alasdair MacIntyre, p. 12. W. T. Stace, p. 108. Lauer, p. 27. Henry Alonzo Myers, p. 62.

26. Michael Kosok, "The Formalization of Hegel's Dialectical Logic," *Inter-*

national Philosophical Quarterly, 6, no. 4 (December 1966), pp. 614, 605. *Hegel's Philosophy of Nature*, # 259, p. 37; # 259, Zus., p. 39. Kojève, p. 143, note. *HY*, p. 98, note. Ernst Cassirer, *The Philosophy of Symbolic Forms*, Vol. III, p. 306.

27. *HY*, p. 524. Findlay, *The Philosophy of Hegel*, p. 66. *HL*, # 79, p. 113. *HS*, Preface to First Edition, p. 28. Lauer, p. 24. Marcuse, p. 47. *Hegel's Philosophy of Mind* (Pt. III of the *Encyclopaedia of the Philosophical Sciences*), trans. William Wallace; Zusätze trans. A. V. Miller (Oxford: At the Clarendon Press, 1970), # 467, Zus., p. 226.

28. *HH*, III, pp. 444, 473. Rosen, p. 20. *HY*, p. 482. Gadamer, *Hegel's Dialectic*, p. 5. *HS*, p. 136.

29. Rosen, pp. 33, 274. *HR*, I, p. 114. *HY*, p. 583. Werner Marx, p. xxi.

30. Gadamer, *Hegel's Dialectic*, p. 92. *HS*, pp. 31, 58, 34, 69, 53. Carpino, "An Introduction to Hegel," p. 22. Hegel, "Philosophical Propaedeutics" (Logic), trans. W. T. Harris, in J. Loewenberg, *Hegel Selections* (New York: Charles Scribner's Sons, 1929), # 1, p. 99. *HL*, # 24, Zus., p. 37; # 19, p. 25; # 24, Zus., p. 40.

31. Rosen, p. xiii. *HY*, p. 575. *HL*, # 19, Zus., p. 28; # 24, p. 36. *CN*, p. 138. Hegel, letter to Niethammer, Oct. 23, 1812, in Kaufmann, *Hegel: A Reinterpretation*, p. 336. Gadamer, *Hegel's Dialectic*, p. 95. *HS*, p. 37.

32. *HH*, III, p. 137; II, p. 211. J. N. Findlay, *The Philosophy of Hegel*, p. 195.

33. Hegel, letter to Schelling, Aug. 30, 1795, quoted in Kaufmann, *Hegel: A Reinterpretation*, p. 305. Horton, p. 81. Rosen, p. 106. *HS*, p. 50. Jacob Boehme, *Six Theosophic Points and Other Writings*, trans. John Rolleston Earle (Ann Arbor: University of Michigan Press, Ann Arbor Books, 1958), pp. 10–11. Clark Butler, pp. 88, 87. Gadamer, *Hegel's Dialectic*, p. 94. *HS*, p. 78.

34. J. N. Findlay, *The Philosophy of Hegel*, p. 153. W. T. Stace, p. 223. Klaus Hartmann, p. 105. *HS*, pp. 391, 601, 596.

35. *HS*, pp. 479, 70, 72, 75, 829, 527, 383. *HL*, # 107, Zus., p. 157; # 86, Zus., p. 125. Hegel, "Philosophical Propaedeutics" (Logic), # 9, p. 104. *CN*, p. 104. Jacob Boehme, p. 190.

36. *HL*, # 86, Zus., pp. 125, 126. Hegel, *The Difference . . . Philosophy*, p. 93. *HS*, p. 104. *CN*, p. 3. M. B. Foster, *The Political Philosophies of Plato and Hegel* (New York: Russell and Russell, 1965), p. 183. *HY*, pp. 590, 87.

37. Luis Martinez Gomez, S.J., "From the Names of God to the Name of God: Nicholas of Cusa," *International Philosophical Quarterly*, 5, no. 1 (February 1965), p. 99. *HS*, pp. 82, 101, 73, 74. Gadamer, *Hegel's Dialectic*, p. 90. Rosen, pp. 207–208. *CN*, p. 139.

38. *HS*, p. 402. *HY*, p. 16. *HP*, # 80, p. 51. Martin Heidegger, *Hegel's Concept of Experience*, a translation of "Hegel's Begriff der Erfahrung" in *Holzwege* (New York: Harper and Row, 1970), p. 116. Rosen, p. 121. *CN*, Abstract of Dissertation, pp. 1–2. Quentin Lauer, S.J., "Hegel on Proofs for God's Existence," *Kant-Studien*, Band 55, Heft 4 (1964), p. 455.

39. *HR*, III, p. 353. *CN*, pp. 241–242. *HH*, III, pp. 63, 66. *HL*, # 64, p. 99. *Hegel's Philosophy of Right*, # 280, Remark, pp. 184–185. Lauer, ibid., p. 455. "Nullus quippe intelligens id quod deus est, potest cogitare quia deus non est"

(St. Anselm, *Proslogion* IV, 20, 21), and "Non igitur potest cogitari non esse, quo maius nequit cogitari" (St. Anselm, "Reply to Gaunilo," III, 19, 20), in F. S. Schmitt, ed., S. Anselmi, *Opera Omnia* (Edinburgh: Thomas Nelson, 1946), Vol. I, pp. 103, 133. Eric Toms, *Being, Negation, and Logic* (Oxford: Basil Blackwell, 1962), p. 72.

40. *HL*, # 111, Zus., p. 161; # 112, Zus., p. 163; # 112, p. 162. *CN*, p. 90. Rosen, pp. 106–107. *HS*, pp. 389, 499, 394, 397, 439, 479. Taylor, *Hegel*, p. 342. Toms, ibid., p. 121. Boehme, p. 141.

41. W. T. Stace, pp. 32–33. Jean Hyppolite, *Studies*, p. 181. R. G. Collingwood, *The Idea of Nature* (New York: Oxford University Press, Galaxy Books, 1960), p. 129. *HL*, # 131, p. 186. *HY*, p. 125.

42. J. Glenn Gray, "Introduction," p. 14. *HL*, # 96, Zus., p. 142. W. T. Stace, p. 106. *CN*, p. 164. *HY*, pp. 155, 150, 568 (note). Kojève, p. 144, note. Boehme, p. 111.

43. *HL*, # 159, p. 221; # 83, Zus., p. 122. W. T. Stace, p. 222. *HS*, pp. 578, 615–616, 105.

44. *HS*, pp. 105–106, 74. W. T. Stace, p. 107. *HL*, # 88, Zus., p. 132. *CN*, p. 145.

45. *HS*, p. 209. *CN*, pp. 196, 147. Nicolas Berdyaev, "Unground and Freedom," in Boehme, p. xxxi. *HL*, # 163, Zus., p. 228. *HR*, III, p. 355. "Per quod omnia facta sunt de nihilo et servantur a nihilo" (St. Anselm, *Monologion*, LXV, 30, 31), in Schmitt, ed., *Opera Omnia*, Vol. I, p. 76. Genesis 1 : 3; Gospel of John 1 : 5.

46. *HP*, # 160, p. 99. Taylor, *Hegel*, p. 239. Cardinal Newman, *Essay on . . . Doctrine*, ch. I, sec. i, # 7, p. 30. Rosen, p. 110. Michael Kosok, p. 625. *HS*, p. 106. *HY*, p. 110. See also Carl J. Friedrich, "The Power of Negation: Hegel's Dialectic and Totalitarian Ideology," in D. C. Travis, ed., *A Hegel Symposium*, pp. 23–24; *HL*, # 89, Zus., p. 134.

47. Aristotle, *Physica*, in W. D. Ross, ed., *The Works of Aristotle*, Vol. II, 226a, 15–16. *HS*, pp. 110, 817, 157, 158, 707. *HL*, # 163, p. 227; # 160, p. 223; # 213, Zus., p. 276. Rosen, p. 116. *CN*, p. 93.

48. Fackenheim, p. 205. *HY*, p. 564. Horton, pp. 46, 6. St. Augustine, *Epistolae*, 120, iii, 13, quoted in Harry Austryn Wolfson, *The Philosophy of the Church Fathers*, Vol. I: *Faith, Trinity, Incarnation*, 3d ed. (Cambridge: Harvard University Press, 1970), p. 353. *HL*, # 182, Zus., p. 246.

49. Boehme, p. 203. Athenagoras, "Supplicatio pro Christianis," x, 24, quoted in Wolfson, ibid., p. 302. Marius Victorinus, "Adversus Arium," I, 60, quoted in Edmund J. Fortman, *The Triune God: A Historical Study of the Doctrine of the Trinity* (Philadelphia: Westminster, 1972), p. 136. Wolfson, ibid., p. 349. "Quod autem est singulus quisque, hoc est tota trinitas simul, pater et filius et spiritus sanctus; quonium singulus quisque non est aliud quam summe simplex unitas et summe una simplicitas, quae nec multiplicari nec aliud et aliud esse potest" (Anselm, *Proslogion*, XXIII, 16–19), in Schmitt, ed., *Opera Omnia*, Vol. I, p. 117. W. T. Stace, p. 511.

50. Marius Victorinus, "Adversus Arium," III, 7, cited by Fortman, ibid.,

p. 135. "Sicut filius est intelligentia et scientia et sapientia et veritas paternae substantiae, ita est intelligentia intelligentiae, scientia scientiae, sapientia sapientiae, veritas veritatis" (St. Anselm, *Monologion*, XLVII, 5–7), in Schmitt, ed., ibid., p. 63. Hegel, "Introduction to the History of Philosophy," Hoffmeister-Niccolin ed., translated in Lauer, *Hegel's Idea of Philosophy*, p. 112. *HH*, III, p. 205. J. N. Findlay, *The Philosophy of Hegel*, p. 140.

51. Hegel, "Introduction to the History of Philosophy," ibid. Fortman, p. 234. C. G. Jung, "A Psychological Approach to the Dogma of the Trinity," in C. G. Jung, *The Collected Works* (Princeton: Princeton University Press, 1958), Vol. XI: *Psychology and Religion: West and East*, pp. 132, 159, 131, 135, 146. "Respondeo dicendum quod, cum sint duae processionis in divinis, altera earum, quae est per modum amoris, non habet proprium nomen" (St. Thomas Aquinas, *Summa Theologica*, Prima Pars, Qu. 36, art. 1), in S. Thomae Aquinatis, *Summa Theologica* (Matriti: Biblioteca De Autores Cristianos, 1961), Vol. I, p. 259.

52. Clark Butler, p. 59. *HR*, II, pp. 24, 15; III, pp. 13, 11. Randall, *Hellenistic Ways of Deliverance*, p. 182. M. B. Foster, *The Political Philosophies*, p. 139. Gustav E. Mueller, p. 83. Hegel, *Philosophy of History*, pp. 408–409.

53. St. Augustine, *De Vera Religione*, 7:13, in Vernon J. Bourke, ed., *The Essential Augustine* (Indianapolis: Hackett Publishing, 1974), p. 210. St. Bonaventure, *The Mind's Road to God*, ch. 3, # 6, p. 26. *HR*, III, p. 25.

54. J. N. Findlay, *The Philosophy of Hegel*, p. 140. *HH*, III, p. 439. *HR*, III, pp. 32–33. C. G. Jung, p. 161.

55. C. G. Jung, pp. 194–195, 161. Rosen, p. 9. Cyril of Alexandria, "Thesaurus on the Holy and Consubstantial Trinity," 34.597, quoted in Fortman, p. 90. St. Augustine, *De Vera Religione*, 7:13, in Bourke, p. 210. George Bosworth Burch, *Early Medieval Philosophy* (New York: Columbia University, King's Crown Press, 1951), p. 12. Henry Bett, *Johannes Scotus Erigena: A Study in Medieval Philosophy*, p. 109. Plant, p. 134.

56. J. N. Findlay, *The Philosophy of Hegel*, pp. 273, 272. *Hegel's Philosophy of Nature*, # 248, Zus., p. 19; # 247, p. 14; # 249, Remark, p. 20. R. G. Collingwood, p. 130. *HR*, I, p. 181. *HS*, pp. 608, 805. Carpino, "An Introduction to Hegel," p. 21.

57. *Hegel's Philosophy of Nature*, # 250, Remark, p. 24. *HR*, III, p. 358. M. B. Foster, "The Christian Doctrine of Creation and the Rise of Modern Natural Science," *Mind*, N.S., 43 (October 1934), pp. 464 (note), 462. *HL*, # 128, Zus., p. 185. Luis Martinez Gomez, p. 98. See also *HR*, II, p. 177.

58. M. B. Foster, ibid., pp. 459, 456, 464. *Hegel's Philosophy of Nature*, # 247, Zus., p. 15. Taylor, *Hegel*, p. 100. J. N. Findlay, *The Philosophy of Hegel*, p. 271. "Nam non ut homo non semper dicit quod intelligit" (St. Anselm, *Monologion, XXIX, 22)*, in Schmitt, ed., *Opera Omnia*, Vol. I, p. 47.

59. *HR*, III, p. 31. *HL*, # 131, Zus., p. 187. G. W. F. Hegel, *Aesthetics: Lectures on Fine Art*, trans. T. M. Knox, 2 vols. (Oxford: At the Clarendon Press, 1975), Vol. I, p. 92. "Quidquid summa substantia fecit, non fecit per aliud quam per semetipsam" (Anselm, ibid., XII), p. 26.

60. *HR*, III, p. 1; II, p. 327; I, pp. 198–199.

61. St. Augustine, *De Genesi ad litteram*, IV, xiii, 221, in Przywara, *An Augustine Synthesis*, p. 489. *Hegel's Philosophy of Nature*, # 247, Zus., p. 14. *HP*, # 805, p. 490. Hegel, "Introduction to the History of Philosophy," p. 80.

62. Louis George Mylne, *The Holy Trinity: A Study of the Self-Revelation of God* (London: Longmans, Green, and Co., 1916), p. 106. *HR*, II, p. 181. Taylor, *Hegel*, p. 102. Josiah Royce, *The Spirit of Modern Philosophy*, p. 216. *HL*, # 136, Zus., p. 195. *Hegel's Philosophy of Nature*, # 246, Zus., p. 13.

63. *Hegel's Philosophy of Nature*, # 252, p. 25.

64. Carpino, "An Introduction to Hegel," pp. 21, 22. R. G. Collingwood, p. 126. W. T. Stace, p. 311. *Hegel's Philosophy of Nature*, # 257, Zus., p. 34.

65. *Hegel's Philosophy of Nature*, # 258, p. 34. R. G. Collingwood, pp. 129, 126. *HY*, p. 579. Kojève, p. 137. *Hegel's Philosophy of Nature*, # 261, Zus., p. 43. See Augustine, *Confessions*, Bk. XI, ch. xxix.

66. *HS*, p. 661. *HL*, # 213, p. 275. *Hegel's Philosophy of Nature*, # 276, Zus., p. 93.

67. *Hegel's Philosophy of Nature*, # 336, Zus., p. 271; # 326, Zus., p. 236; # 248, Zus., p. 18; # 337, Zus., p. 275. Carpino, "An Introduction to Hegel," p. 23.

68. Gadamer, *Hegel's Dialectic*, p. 29. Collingwood, p. 132. *Hegel's Philosophy of Nature*, # 339, Zus. 2, p. 284; # 344, Zus., p. 305; # 350, Zus., p. 351; # 353, Zus., p. 356; # 344, Zus., p. 307; # 337, Zus., p. 277. Marcuse, p. 8. Carpino, ibid.

69. *HL*, # 92, Zus., p. 137; # 221, Zus., p. 282. *Hegel's Philosophy of Nature*, # 375, p. 441. *HS*, p. 440. Hegel, *Aesthetics: Lectures on Fine Art*, I, p. 97. Carpino, ibid. *Hegel's Philosophy of Right*, Addition to Paragraph 1, p. 225. *HY*, p. 153.

70. Hyppolite, *Studies*, pp. 24, 30. *Hegel's Philosophy of Nature*, # 350, Zus., p. 352. See also *HP*, # 167, p. 104; *Hegel's Philosophy of Mind*, # 400, Zus., p. 75.

71. *HS*, p. 780. *HR*, I, p. 109. "Semper in ipso sunt, non quod sunt in seipsis, sed quod est idem ipse" (Anselm, *Monologion*, XXXIV, 24), in Schmitt, ed., *Opera Omnia*, Vol. I, p. 53. *Hegel's Philosophy of Nature*, # 376, p. 443.

72. *Hegel's Philosophy of Nature*, # 376, Zus., p. 444. *HS*, p. 783. *HL*, # 24, Zus., p. 43. Hegel, *Aesthetics: Lectures on Fine Art*, I, p. 92.

73. *Hegel's Philosophy of Nature*, # 246, Zus., p. 13; Introduction, Zus., p. 3. *HL*, # 140, Zus., p. 198. Boehme, p. 194.

74. *Hegel's Philosophy of Nature*, # 376, Zus., p. 443; # 251, Zus., p. 25. *HR*, I, pp. 109–110. *HH*, III, p. 547. Hegel, *Philosophy of History*, p. 127.

75. Werner Marx, p. 83. Hegel, *Berliner Schriften*, p. 8, quoted in Shlomo Avineri, p. 118. *CN*, p. 150. *HH*, III, p. 22. Rosen, p. 12.

76. *Hegel's Philosophy of Mind*, # 381, Zus., p. 14; # 381, p. 8. *Hegel's Philosophy of Nature*, # 248, Zus., p. 19. *HH*, III, p. 552. *HY*, p. 154.

77. Taylor, *Hegel*, p. 174. Rosen, p. 224. *HH*, III, p. 6. *HR*, II, p. 203; III, p. 127. Hegel, *Philosophy of History*, pp. 411–412. See also *HP*, # 560, p. 342.

78. Kojève, p. 225. Hegel, *Philosophy of History*, p. 411. *CN*, p. 12. *HY*, p. 170. Rosen, p. 224. Hegel, "Introduction to the History of Philosophy," p. 133.

79. *HH*, III, pp. 5, 9, 10. *HL*, # 24, Zus., p. 44. *HY*, p. 543, note. *HR*, I, p. 2.

80. *HY*, pp. 170, 176. Rosen, p. 162. Hyppolite, *Studies*, p. 29.

81. Kojève, pp. 27, 30, 47. *HP*, # 193, p. 117.

82. Gadamer, *Hegel's Dialectic*, p. 62. *HY*, pp. 160, 166. *HP*, # 179, p. 111; # 184, p. 112; # 803, p. 489. Hyppolite, *Studies*, p. 166. Kojève, pp. 145, 43.

83. Hyppolite, *Studies*, pp. 24, 9. *Hegel's Philosophy of Nature*, # 374, Zus., p. 441. *HY*, p. 18. Kojève, p. 223.

84. "Hoc esse ipsam vitam" (Anselm, *Proslogion*, XIV, 10), in Schmitt, ed., *Opera Omnia*, I, p. 111. *HY*, p. 603.

85. *HR*, III, 127. Hegel in his Preface to Hinrich's "On Religion in An Inner Relationship to Scholarship," quoted in Franz Wiedman, p. 74.

86. *HP*, # 802, p. 487; # 18, p. 10. *Hegel's Philosophy of Mind*, # 379, Zus., p. 6; # 386, Zus., p. 24. *HS*, pp. 829, 555. *HY*, p. 152. Clark Butler, p. 56.

87. *HY*, p. 534. *Hegel's Philosophy of Mind*, # 377, Zus., p. 1. Hegel, "Introduction to the History of Philosophy," p. 80. *HH*, III, p. 547. Werner Marx, p. 57. *HL*, # 147, Zus., p. 211. *Hegel's Philosophy of Nature*, # 357a, Zus., p. 382. *HR*, III, p. 176.

88. Hegel, "Philosophical Propaedeutics" (Phenomenology), # 23 in J. Loewenberg, ed., *Hegel Selections*, pp. 73–74. Hegel, "Introduction to the History of Philosophy," p. 68. Hegel, *Philosophy of History*, p. 127. *HR*, II, p. 176. *HS*, p. 789.

89. *Hegel's Philosophy of Mind*, # 383, Zus., pp. 17–18, 16; # 378, Zus., p. 3. *HS*, pp. 554, 782. Kojève, p. 212. "Non sit aliud quam quod est sua locutio" (Anselm, *Monologion*, XXIX, 2), in Schmitt, ed., *Opera Omnia*, I, p. 48. *HH*, III, p. 6. Heidegger, *Hegel's Concept of Experience*, p. 90. Josiah Royce, *The Spirit of Modern Philosophy*, p. 213. *Hegel's Philosophy of Nature*, # 247, Zus., p. 14.

90. *Hegel's Philosophy of Mind*, # 381, Zus., p. 11; # 377, Zus., p. 1. Hegel, "Introduction to the History of Philosophy," p. 110. *HH*, I, p. 23; III, pp. 545–546. Hegel, *Aesthetics: Lectures on Fine Art*, I, p. 154.

91. *HP*, # 670, p. 408. Taylor, *Hegel*, p. 67. G. R. G. Mure, pp. 169–170. C. G. Jung, p. 186. Luis Martinez Gomez, pp. 88, 93–94. *HY*, p. 198. Hegel, *Aesthetics: Lectures on Fine Art*, I, p. 38.

92. *Hegel's Philosophy of Mind*, # 385, p. 20. Carpino, "An Introduction to Hegel," p. 19.

93. Lauer, "Hegel on Proofs for God's Existence," p. 451. *HL*, # 45, Zus., p. 73; # 94, Zus., p. 137. Luther, cited by Hegel, "Fragment of a System," in Hegel, *Early Theological Writings*, ed. and trans. T. M. Knox (Philadelphia: University of Pennsylvania Press, 1971), p. 315. C. G. Jung, p. 163.

94. Fackenheim, p. 56. Lauer, ibid. *Hegel's Philosophy of Mind*, # 378, Zus., p. 3. *HR*, II, p. 220. Hegel, "The Spirit of Christianity and Its Fate," in Hegel, *Early Theological Writings*, p. 187.

452 NOTES

95. Plant, p. 137. Hegel, *Philosophy of History*, p. 268. Taylor, *Hegel*, p. 498. *HL*, # 147, Zus., p. 210. *HY*, p. 191.

96. St. Bonaventure, *The Mind's Road to God*, ch. 6, # 6, p. 42. Maximus the Confessor, "Ambiguorum Liber," quoted in Harry Austryn Wolfson, pp. 424–425. Rosen, p. 177. Löwith, *From Hegel to Nietzsche*, p. 45. *HH*, III, p. 4. *HR*, III, pp. 73, 72. Hegel, *Aesthetics: Lectures on Fine Art*, I, p. 435. St. Augustine, *De Vera Religione*, 8:14, in Bourke, ed., *The Essential Augustine*, p. 210.

97. *HY*, pp. 200, 210. Kojève, p. 66. Dom Gregory Dix, *Jew and Greek: A Study in the Primitive Church* (Westminster, England: Dacre Press, 1953), p. 5.

98. M. B. Foster, "The Christian Doctrine of Creation," pp. 463, 455. St. Anselm, *Cur Deus Homo*, trans. in S. N. Deane, ed., *St. Anselm: Basic Writings*, 2d ed. (La Salle, Ill.: Open Court Publishing, 1962), ch. viii, p. 191. *HR*, III, pp. 71, 98. Hegel, "The Positivity of Christian Religion," in Hegel, *Early Theological Writings*, p. 143. Horton, pp. 81, 14. Louis George Mylne, p. 12. Hegel, "Introduction to the History of Philosophy," p. 130.

99. *Hegel's Philosophy of Right*, # 124, Remark, p. 84. Hegel, "Introduction to the History of Philosophy," p. 134. *HR*, II, p. 351.

100. *HH*, III, pp. 149, 402. Lauer, *Hegel's Idea of Philosophy*, p. 64. *HL*, # 38, p. 61. Josiah Royce, *The Spirit of Modern Philosophy*, p. 201.

101. *HL*, # 163, Zus., p. 227. *Hegel's Philosophy of Right*, # 7, Remark, p. 23; # 185, p. 124; Addition, paragraph 35, p. 235. *HY*, p. 41. *HS*, p. 583.

102. *HY*, p. 158. *HR*, I, p. 66. *Hegel's Philosophy of Mind*, # 444, Zus., p. 188. W. T. Stace, p. 374.

103. *HP*, # 781, p. 473. *HY*, p. 69. Plant, p. 111. *Hegel's Philosophy of Right*, # 153, p. 109.

104. J. N. Findlay, *The Philosophy of Hegel*, p. 139. *HP*, # 781, p. 473. *HR*, III, pp. 91, 92. Fackenheim, p. 56. See also Rosen, pp. 226–227.

105. *HH*, III, p. 15. *HR*, III, p. 91, note. St. Anselm, *Cur Deus Homo*, ch. xviii(b), trans. in S. N. Deane, pp. 282–283. Fackenheim, p. 146. J. N. Findlay, ibid., p. 99. *Hegel's Philosophy of Right*, # 331, p. 212; # 270, Addition, p. 283; # 279, Addition, p. 288. Kojève p. 58. Shlomo Avineri, p. 177. M. B. Foster, *The Political Philosophies*, p. 131.

106. *Hegel's Philosophy of Right*, # 256, Remark, p. 155; # 259, p. 160. Shlomo Avineri, p. 134. *Hegel's Philosophy of Mind*, # 535, p. 263. Hegel, *Philosophy of History*, p. 112.

107. *Hegel's Philosophy of Mind*, # 549, p. 281. Shlomo Avineri, p. 64. Hegel, "Introduction to the History of Philosophy," p. 86. *HP*, # 807, p. 492; # 803, p. 488. Clark Butler, p. 65. *HH*, III, p. 7. *HS*, p. 51. *HY*, p. 494.

108. Hegel, *Philosophy of History*, p. 69. "Tua aeternitas continet etiam ipsa saecula temporum" (Anselm, *Proslogion*, XXI, 7, 8), in Schmitt, ed., *Opera Omnia*, I, p. 116. Henri-Charles Puech, "Gnosis and Time," in Joseph Campbell, ed., *Man and Time*, trans. Ralph Manheim ("Papers from the Eranos Yearbooks," Vol. III; New York: Pantheon Books, 1957), pp. 49–50, 43, 52. Gilles Quispel, "Time and History in Patristic Christianity," in *Man and Time*, p. 98.

109. *HH*, I, p. 4. Kojève, p. 38. Erich Przywara, "St. Augustine and the

Modern World," trans. E. I. Watkin, in M. C. D'Arcy et al., eds., *Saint Augustine* (New York: Meridian Books, 1957), p. 285. Hegel, *Philosophy of History*, p. 112.

110. Carpino, "An Introduction to Hegel," p. 16. *HP*, # 652, p. 395.

111. Marcuse, pp. 99–100, 95, 163. J. Glenn Gray, "Introduction," p. 11.

112. J. Glenn Gray, ibid., p. 15. Hegel, *Philosophy of History*, p. 134. *HL*, # 212, Zus., p. 274. Kojève, p. 187. Gustav E. Mueller, p. 108.

113. M. B. Foster, *The Political Philosophies*, p. 166. *HH*, III, pp. 372–373, 374, 385. *HY*, pp. 39, 11. William A. Galston, *Kant and the Problem of History* (Chicago: University of Chicago Press, 1975), p. 5.

114. Gadamer, *Hegel's Dialectic*, p. 105. Emile Bréhier, "The Formation of Our History of Philosophy," in *Philosophy and History: Essays Presented to Ernst Cassirer*, p. 168.

115. Hegel, *Philosophy of History*, p. 569. *Hegel's Philosophy of Mind*, # 549, p. 277. Rosen, p. 222. St. Augustine, *De Genesi ad litteram*, I, viii, 14, in Przywara, *An Augustine Synthesis*, p. 121. St. Augustine, letter to Marcellinus, 137, 4.15, and *De Vera Religione*, 25:46, in Bourke, *The Essential Augustine*, pp. 225, 31. *HL*, # 209, Zus., p. 273; # 158, Zus., p. 220.

116. *Hegel's Philosophy of Mind*, # 482, p. 240; # 431, Zus., p. 172. Hegel, *Philosophy of History*, pp. 63–64, 66. Heidegger, *Hegel's Concept of Experience*, p. 146. *HP*, # 29, p. 17. Clark Butler, pp. 41, 183 (note). See also *HP*, # 808, p. 493, and *HY*, p. 528.

117. Shlomo Avineri, p. 228. Hegel, *Philosophy of History*, pp. 63, 62. Rosen, p. 45. *HH*, III, p. 57. Fackenheim, p. 175. Edmund J. Fortman, pp. 197–198.

118. Lauer, *Hegel's Idea of Philosophy*, p. 6. Carpino, "An Introduction to Hegel," pp. 20, 13. *HS*, p. 550. H. S. Harris, *Hegel's Development: Toward the Sunlight, 1770–1801* (Oxford: At the Clarendon Press, 1972), p. 293. Hegel, *The Difference . . . Philosophy*, p. 157. Marcuse, p. 24. *Hegel's Philosophy of Right*, Preface, p. 10.

119. *Hegel's Philosophy of Right*, Preface, pp. 10, 12. Lauer, ibid., p. 32. Carpino, ibid., p. 14. Hyppolite, *Studies*, p. 171. *HY*, p. 110.

120. W. T. Stace, p. 211. *HL*, # 147, p. 208. *HP*, # 795, p. 483; # 262, pp. 159–160. *HS*, pp. 529, 525. J. N. Findlay, *The Philosophy of Hegel*, p. 209. George Armstrong Kelly, "Notes on Hegel's Lordship and Bondage," in Alasdair MacIntyre, p. 200. Taylor, *Hegel*, p. 279.

121. *HY*, p. 68. Hegel, "Philosophical Propaedeutics" (Phenomenology), # 40, in Loewenberg, *Hegel Selections*, p. 78. *Hegel's Philosophy of Mind*, # 425, Zus., p. 166.

122. *HP*, # 233, p. 140; # 438, p. 263. *Hegel's Philosophy of Mind*, # 440, Zus., pp. 179–180. Gadamer, *Hegel's Dialectic*, pp. 28–29, 30.

123. W. T. Stace, p. 25. Hegel, "Introduction to the History of Philosophy," p. 77. *HS*, pp. 841, 824. *HP*, # 546, p. 332; # 669, p. 407; # 20, p. 11.

124. Hyppolite, *Studies*, p. 3. Karl Barth, *Protestant Theology in the Nineteenth Century: Its Background and History* (Valley Forge, Pa.: Judson Press, 1973), p. 401. George Bosworth Burch, p. 9. Kojève, p. 87, note 3.

125. Cardinal Newman, *Essay on . . . Doctrine*, ch. i, sec. i, # 7, p. 30. *HP*,

80, p. 51; # 258, p. 157. Lauer, *Hegel's Idea of Philosophy*, p. 33. *HL*, # 237, Zus., p. 293.

126. Henry Paolucci, "The Poetics of Aristotle and Hegel," in Frederick G. Weiss, ed., *Hegel in Comparative Literature*, Review of National Literatures, St. John's University, N.Y., 1, No. 2 (Fall 1970), p. 181. *Hegel's Philosophy of Right*, # 341, p. 216. Hegel, *Aesthetics: Lectures on Fine Art*, I, p. 104. *Hegel's Philosophy of Mind*, # 572, p. 302.

127. Hegel, *Aesthetics*, I, pp. 38, 91, 11, 7. Paolucci, ibid.

128. Hegel, ibid., II, pp. 960, 973. Paolucci, p. 187.

129. Hegel, ibid., II, pp. 797, 806, 1223.

130. Hegel, ibid., II, pp. 687, 689, 674.

131. Hegel, ibid., I, pp. 530, 103; II, p. 674. J. Glenn Gray, *Hegel and Greek Thought*, p. 45.

132. *HR*, I, p. 54. *HH*, I, p. 71. Hegel, letter to Duboc, quoted in Plant, p. 198. *Hegel's Philosophy of Mind*, # 552, p. 289.

133. Taylor, *Hegel*, p. 482. Hegel, "Introduction to the History of Philosophy," pp. 105–106. *HP*, # 683, p. 416; # 748, p. 453; # 724, p. 438. *HR*, I, p. 84; II, pp. 317, 320, 322.

134. *HR*, II, pp. 57, 327. *HY*, p. 541. *Hegel's Philosophy of Mind*, # 564, p. 298. Rosen, p. 14.

135. *HR*, I, p. 33; III, p. 366; II, p. 335. Lauer, *Hegel's Idea of Philosophy*, p. 56. *HL*, # 140, Zus., p. 198.

136. Lauer, "Hegel on Proofs for God's Existence," p. 465. *HR*, I, pp. 33, 200. Heidegger, *Hegel's Concept of Experience*, pp. 40, 148.

137. Przywara, "St. Augustine and the Modern World," pp. 272, 271. J. N. Findlay, *The Philosophy of Hegel*, p. 100. Löwith, *From Hegel to Nietzsche*, p. 19.

138. *HR*, I, p. 36. Hegel, Berlin Inaugural Lecture, quoted by Franz Wiedmann, p. 69. *HL*, # 136, Zus., p. 196. *HH*, III, p. 67.

139. *HH*, III, pp. 60, 10, 40, 62, 68. *HL*, # 36, Zus., p. 57.

140. Lauer, "Hegel on Proofs for God's Existence," p. 446. *HY*, p. 435. *HP*, # 563, p. 343.

141. Fackenheim, p. 177.

142. Ibid., pp. 189–190, 119, 67.

143. *HR*, III, p. 161. Taylor, *Hegel*, p. 505. *HL*, # 63, p. 98. Hyppolite, *Studies*, p. 53.

144. *HP*, # 564, p. 344; # 563, p. 344; # 565, p. 344; # 549, p. 334. Rosen, p. 183. Taylor, *Hegel*, p. 505. J. Glenn Gray, *Hegel and Greek Thought*, p. 66.

145. *HR*, III, pp. 157, 178; I, p. 2. Hegel, *The Difference . . . Philosophy*, p. 100. Lauer, "Hegel on Proofs," pp. 460–461, 445. Przywara, "St. Augustine and the Modern World," p. 251.

146. Eriugena, in Migne, *Patrologiae Cursus Completus*, Latina, Vol. 122, cols. 516c, 290b, translated in George Bosworth Burch, p. 7, and Étienne Gilson, *History of Christian Philosophy in the Middle Ages* (New York: Random House, 1955), p. 114. "Neque enim quaero intelligere ut credam, sed credo ut intelligam.

Nam et hoc credo: quia nisi credidero, non intelligam" (Anselm, *Proslogion*, I, 18, 19), in Schmitt, ed., *Opera Omnia*, I, p. 100. *HY*, p. 562. *HR*, III, p. 164. *HH*, II, p. 475. "Et id ipsum esse quidquid de divina substantia oportet credere" (Anselm, Reply to Gaunilo, x), in *Opera Omnia*, I, p. 139. Fackenheim, p. 161.

147. *HL*, # 36, Zus., p. 57. *HR*, II, p. 330; I, p. 18. Clark Butler, pp. 182 (note), 128. Cardinal Newman, *Essay on . . . Doctrine*, ch. II, sec. i, # 1, p. 41; sec. ii, # 10, p. 62.

148. *HL*, # 82, Zus., p. 120. *HR*, I, p. 28. *HH*, III, p. 20. Clark Butler, p. 137. Karl Barth, *Protestant Theology in the Nineteenth Century*, p. 420. See *HR*, I, p. 46.

149. Hegel, *Philosophy of History*, pp. 423, 171, 87. W. T. Stace, p. 514. *HH*, III, p. 21. *Hegel's Philosophy of Right*, # 270, Remark, p. 173. Hegel, "The Positivity of the Christian Religion," p. 105. Plant, p. 122.

150. *HR*, III, p. 149. Löwith, *From Hegel to Nietzsche*, p. 46.

151. Lauer, *Hegel's Idea of Philosophy*, pp. 53, 57. Hegel, "Introduction to the History of Philosophy," pp. 148, 117. Baron Boris d'Uxkull, quoted in Franz Wiedmann, p. 59. Löwith, ibid., p. 327.

152. Hegel, "Introduction to the History of Philosophy," p. 128. Hegel, *The Difference . . . Philosophy*, pp. 87, 112. *HH*, II, p. 22. Barth, *Protestant Theology in the Nineteenth Century*, p. 400. Hegel, letter to Niethammer, Oct. 23, 1812, quoted in Kaufmann, *Hegel: A Reinterpretation*, p. 338. *HL*, # 99, Zus., p. 146.

153. Fackenheim, p. 202. Hegel, *Philosophy of History*, p. 84. Hegel, letter to C. G. Zellmann, Jan. 23, 1807, quoted in Kaufmann, ibid., p. 321. Lauer, *Hegel's Idea of Philosophy*, p. 144. Lauer, "Hegel on Proofs," p. 448.

154. Lauer, "Hegel on Proofs," pp. 443–444. *HL*, # 14, p. 19.

155. *HH*, III, p. 547; II, p. 453. *HL*, # 13, p. 19. Marcuse, p. 100. Lauer, *Hegel's Idea of Philosophy*, p. 38.

156. *HH*, III, p. 553; I, pp. 37, 36. Hegel, *The Difference . . . Philosophy*, pp. 87, 85, 89. Hegel, "Introduction to the History of Philosophy," p. 88.

157. *HH*, I, pp. 28, 27, 39; III, p. 546. *HL*, # 15, p. 20. J. Glenn Gray, *Hegel and Greek Thought*, p. 15. Hegel, "Introduction to the History of Philosophy," p. 95. *Hegel's Philosophy of Right*, Preface, p. 11.

158. Bréhier, "The Formation of Our History of Philosophy," p. 168.

159. Hegel, "Introduction to the History of Philosophy," p. 135. *HH*, III, pp. 1, 549; I, pp. 109, 101.

160. *HH*, II, p. 451; III, p. 548; I, p. 153.

161. *HH*, II, pp. 452, 229; III, pp. 548, 1, 2; II, p. 229.

162. *HH*, III, pp. 2, 42–43.

163. *HH*, III, pp. 146–147, 149, 150, 8, 217, 218.

164. *HH*, III, pp. 218, 217, 224, 228, 232, 244.

165. *HH*, III, pp. 423, 424. *HP*, # 33, pp. 19–20.

166. *HH*, III, pp. 545, 552, 551.

167. J. N. Findlay, *The Philosophy of Hegel*, p. 130. Taylor, *Hegel*, p. 180. St. Bonaventure, *The Mind's Road to God*, ch. i, # 2, p. 8, and p. 7 (Boas's

note). Hyppolite, *Studies*, p. vi. Lauer, *Hegel's Idea of Philosophy*, pp. 3–4. Luis Martinez Gomez, p. 95. M. B. Foster, "The Christian Doctrine of Creation," p. 448, note. See also *HY*, p. 535.

168. *HL*, # 82, Zus., p. 121. *HH*, I, p. 79. *Hegel's Philosophy of Mind*, # 441, Zus., p. 181. Löwith, *From Hegel to Nietzsche*, p. 13. Hegel, "Who Thinks Abstractly?" trans. in Walter Kaufmann, ed., *Hegel: Texts and Commentary*, trans. Walter Kaufmann (Notre Dame: University of Notre Dame Press, 1977), p. 117. A photograph of the medal appears as frontispiece in *Hegel in Comparative Literature*.

169. *HR*, I, p. 32; II, p. 345. George Bosworth Burch, p. 7. Barth, *Protestant Theology in the Nineteenth Century*, p. 396. Löwith, ibid., p. 17. Löwith, *Meaning in History*, p. 59. See *Hegel's Philosophy of Right*, Preface, p. 12.

170. Lauer, "Hegel on Proofs," pp. 445, 454. Löwith, *Meaning in History*, p. 57. J. N. Findlay, *The Philosophy of Hegel*, p. 132. St. Augustine, "Soliloquies," I, 3, in Bourke, *The Essential Augustine*, p. 144. *HR*, I, p. 19. Hegel, "How Common Sense Takes Philosophy, Shown through an Analysis of the Works of Herr Krug," in Kaufmann, *Hegel: A Reinterpretation*, p. 60.

171. Werner Marx, p. 56. *HH*, I, p. 55. Gregory of Nyssa, "Oratio Catechetica," iii, and John of Damascus, "De Fide Orthodoxa," i, 7, quoted in Harry Austryn Wolfson, p. 363.

172. *HH*, III, p. 6. Hegel, *Aesthetics*, I, pp. 505, 435. Daisy Fornacca Kouzel, "The Hegelian Influence in the Literary Criticism of Francesco De Sanctis," in *Hegel in Comparative Literature*, p. 218. Rosen, p. 221. Hegel, *Philosophy of History*, p. 329.

173. Hegel, *Philosophy of History*, p. 329. Taylor, *Hegel*, p. 176. *HR*, II, p. 255. Randall, *Hellenistic Ways of Deliverance*, p. 229. Gadamer, *Hegel's Dialectic*, p. 104.

174. Hegel, *The Difference . . . Philosophy*, pp. 105–106, 83. Rosen, pp. 32, xiv. Hyppolite, *Studies*, p. 176. Lauer, *Hegel's Idea of Philosophy*, p. 9.

175. *HR*, I, p. 47. Fackenheim, p. 229.

176. *HH*, III, p. 546.

177. R. G. Collingwood, p. 123. *HL*, # 142, Zus., p. 201. Rosen, p. 219. See Cardinal Newman, *Essay on . . . Doctrine*, ch. I, sec. i, # 5, p. 29.

178. *HS*, pp. 71, 748. W. T. Stace, p. 517. Hyppolite, *Studies*, p. 172. Löwith, *From Hegel to Nietzsche*, p. 37. *HR*, III, p. 2. *HP*, # 22, p. 12.

179. *Hegel's Philosophy of Nature*, # 337, Zus., p. 275. *HS*, p. 71. *HL*, # 74, p. 108. Hyppolite, *Studies*, p. 178. *CN*, p. 159. T. S. Eliot, "Little Gidding," in *The Complete Poems and Plays of T. S. Eliot* (New York: Harcourt, Brace, 1934), p. 145.

180. Rosen, p. xiv. Kojève, p. 75. *HP*, Preface, # 5, p. 3.

181. Allan Bloom, "Editor's Introduction" to Kojève, p. x.

182. Gadamer, *Hegel's Dialectic*, p. 101. Rosen, p. 279. Kojève, p. 122. J. N. Findlay, *The Philosophy of Hegel*, p. 146. Hegel, "Philosophical Propaedeutics" (Logic), # 7, Loewenberg, *Hegel Selections*, p. 103.

183. Barth, *Protestant Theology in the Nineteenth Century*, p. 395. Fackenheim, p. 12.

184. *HH*, I, p. 92. Kant, *Anthropology from a Pragmatic Point of View*, Pt. I, Bk. I, # 59, p. 129. *HY*, p. 597. *HR*, I, p. 101. C. G. Jung, p. 200.

185. Barth, *Protestant Theology in the Nineteenth Century*, pp. 397, 420. Fackenheim, pp. 212, 234. *Aristotle's Metaphysics*, trans. Hippocrates G. Apostle, 1072b, 25, p. 205 (quoted in the Greek at the conclusion to *Hegel's Philosophy of Mind*, # 577, p. 315). Hegel's Preface to Hinrich's book, cited by Wiedmann, p. 74. *HR*, I, p. 33.

186. Hegel, "The Spirit of Christianity and Its Fate," p. 196.

187. Rosen, p. xiv.

188. Gadamer, *Hegel's Dialectic*, p. 104. G. R. G. Mure, p. vii. Fackenheim, p. 10. Barth, *Protestant Theology in the Nineteenth Century*, p. 384.

189. Barth, ibid., p. 417.

190. "Non tento, domine, penetrare altitudinem tuam, quia nullatenus comparo illi intellectum meum; sed desidero aliquatenus intelligere veritatem tuam, quam credit et amat cor meum" (Anselm, *Proslogion*, I, 15–18), *Opera Omnia*, I, p. 100. St. Augustine, *De Trinitate* V, i, 2; VII, iv, 7, in Bourke, *The Essential Augustine*, pp. 138, 139. Luis Martinez Gomez, p. 95.

191. Przywara, "St. Augustine and the Modern World," pp. 257, 277.

192. Kierkegaard, quoted in Plant, p. 184 (no footnote provided). Fackenheim, pp. 240, 224–225. Gadamer, *Hegel's Dialectic*, pp. 101–102. Löwith, *From Hegel to Nietzsche*, p. 38.

193. Barth, *Protestant Theology in the Nineteenth Century*, pp. 384–385, 388, 408, 386.

194. Ibid., p. 408.

195. *CN*, p. 132.

196. Gadamer, *Hegel's Dialectic*, pp. 110, 82, 101. J. N. Findlay, *The Philosophy of Hegel*, p. 332. See *HP*, # 12, p. 7.

197. M. B. Foster, *The Political Philosophies*, p. 192.

198. Étienne Gilson, *Reason and Revelation in the Middle Ages* (New York: Charles Scribner's Sons, 1938), p. 71. E. L. Mascall, "Theology and History," An Inaugural Lecture, King's College, London, October 23, 1962 (Westminster, England: The Faith Press, 1962), pp. 6, 16.

199. Barth, *Protestant Theology in the Nineteenth Century*, pp. 406, 408.

200. Nietzsche, "The Philosopher: Reflections on the Struggle Between Art and Knowledge" (1872), # 41, in Daniel Breazeale, trans. and ed., *Philosophy and Truth: Selections from Nietzsche's Notebooks of the Early 1870's* (Atlantic Highlands, N.J.: Humanities Press, 1979), p. 13.

201. Arthur C. Danto, *Nietzsche as Philosopher* (New York: Macmillan, 1965), p. 21. Nietzsche, letters to Franz Overbeck, Summer 1883, and to George Brandes, Dec. 2, 1887, in Christopher Middleton, ed., *Selected Letters of Friedrich Nietzsche* (Chicago: University of Chicago Press, 1969), pp. 214, 280. F. A. Lea, *The Tragic Philosopher: A Study of Friedrich Nietzsche* (London: Methuen, 1972),

p. 221. Löwith, *From Hegel to Nietzsche*, p. 187. Cf. Rainer Maria Rilke, *Duino Elegies*, trans. J. B. Leishman and Stephen Spender (London: Hogarth Press, 1957), Second Elegy, p. 33; Seventh Elegy, p. 73.

202. Nietzsche, *The Use and Abuse of History*, trans. Adrian Collins (New York: Bobbs-Merrill, Library of Liberal Arts, 1957), pp. 24, 26. Nietzsche, *The Birth of Tragedy*, in *The Birth of Tragedy and the Case of Wagner*, trans. Walter Kaufmann (New York: Vintage Books, 1967), pp. 135, 138. Nietzsche, *Thoughts Out of Seasons*, III, 4, and letter to Rohde, quoted in F. A. Lea, pp. 88, 49. Nietzsche, *Twilight of the Idols*, in *Twilight of the Idols and the Anti-Christ*, trans. R. J. Hollingdale (Harmondsworth: Penguin Books, 1968), pp. 96–97, 93–94.

203. *NW*, pp. 43, 47, 48, 478, 16. Nietzsche, *The Anti-Christ*, in *Twilight of the Idols and the Anti-Christ*, p. 115. Nietzsche, *Beyond Good and Evil, Prelude to a Philosophy of the Future*, trans. Walter Kaufmann (New York: Vintage Books, 1966), pp. 117, 111. Nietzsche, *The Genealogy of Morals*, in *The Birth of Tragedy and the Genealogy of Morals*, trans. Francis Golffing (New York: Doubleday, Anchor Books, 1956), pp. 169, 177, 295, 258.

204. Nietzsche, letters to Brandes, Feb. 19, 1888, and von Deydlitz, Feb. 12, 1888, in *Selected Letters*, pp. 284–285. Nietzsche, *The Gay Science*, trans. Walter Kaufmann (New York: Vintage Books, 1974), pp. 198, 343. *NW*, p. 532.

205. Nietzsche, *The Gay Science*, p. 74; *Beyond Good and Evil*, pp. 117, 116; *The Anti-Christ*, p. 119. *NW*, p. 401.

206. Nietzsche, letter to Overbeck, March 31, 1885, in *Selected Letters*, pp. 239–240. Nietzsche, *Beyond Good and Evil*, p. 3. Nietzsche, *Thus Spoke Zarathustra*, trans. Walter Kaufmann (New York: The Viking Press, 1966), p. 31. Nietzsche, *The Birth of Tragedy* (New York: Vintage Books), p. 23. Karl Jaspers, *Nietzsche and Christianity*, trans. E. B. Ashton (Chicago: Henry Regnery, Gateway Editions, 1961), p. 39.

207. Nietzsche, *The Genealogy of Morals*, p. 294; *Twilight of the Idols*, pp. 69, 38; *The Anti-Christ*, p. 150; *The Gay Science*, pp. 287, 351.

208. Löwith, *From Hegel to Nietzsche*, p. 323. *NW*, pp. 20, 377. F. A. Lea, p. 19. Jaspers, *Nietzsche and Christianity*, p. 15. Nietzsche, letter to Deussen, Sept. 14, 1888, in *Selected Letters*, p. 311. Nietzsche, *The Anti-Christ*, pp. 186, 149, 150; *Twilight of the Idols*, pp. 53, 101.

209. Nietzsche, *Beyond Good and Evil*, pp. 69, 67.

210. Nietzsche, *The Gay Science*, p. 181.

211. Nietzsche, *The Genealogy of Morals*, pp. 296, 297; *Thus Spoke Zarathustra*, pp. 90, 133; Nietzsche, letter to Fuchs, Dec. 18, 1888, in *Selected Letters*, p. 335. Jaspers, *Nietzsche and Christianity*, p. 49.

212. Nietzsche, *The Gay Science*, pp. 167, 279; *The Genealogy of Morals*, p. 288; *The Anti-Christ*, p. 187. Jaspers, ibid., p. 6.

213. Michael Haar, "Nietzsche and Metaphysical Language," in David B. Allison, ed., *The New Nietzsche: Contemporary Styles of Interpretation* (New York: Dell Publishing, Delta Books, 1977), p. 14. Jaspers, ibid., p. 49. Nietzsche, *The Use and Abuse of History*, pp. 52, 11, 49; *The Genealogy of Morals*, p. 297; *The*

Gay Science, pp. 303, 304. *NW*, pp. 44, 363. Nietzsche, letters to Overbeck, Nov. 1880, Feb. 23, 1887, in *Selected Letters*, pp. 174, 261.

214. Nietzsche, *Human, All Too Human*, I, 2, 32, and *The Will to Power*, 521, quoted in F. A. Lea, pp. 117, 123–124, 126. *NW*, pp. 280, 278, 277. Werner Marx, p. 103. Nietzsche, *Beyond Good and Evil*, pp. 11, 229; *The Genealogy of Morals*, p. 289. Michael Haar, p. 17.

215. Martin Heidegger, "Who Is Nietzsche's Zarathustra?" trans. Bernd Magnus, *Review of Metaphysics*, 20, no. 3, Issue # 79 (March 1967), p. 428. Martin Heidegger, "The Word of Nietzsche: 'God Is Dead,'" in Heidegger, *The Question Concerning Technology and Other Essays*, trans. William Lovitt (New York: Harper Colophon Books, 1977), pp. 53, 61, 98, 99. Nietzsche, *The Gay Science*, pp. 38, 337.

216. Heidegger, "The Word of Nietzsche: 'God Is Dead,'" pp. 102, 61. *NW*, pp. 276, 319. R. J. Hollingdale, *Nietzsche: The Man and His Philosophy* (Baton Rouge: Louisiana State University Press, 1965), pp. 200–201.

217. Joan Stambaugh, *Nietzsche's Thought of Eternal Return* (Baltimore: The Johns Hopkins University Press, 1972), p. 73. Arthur C. Danto, p. 119. *NW*, pp. 376, 378. Nietzsche, *Thoughts Out of Seasons*, III, 4, quoted in F. A. Lea, p. 89. Nietzsche, *Die Fröhliche Wissenschaft*, 109, quoted in R. J. Hollingdale, *Nietzsche: The Man*, p. 201. Jean Granier, "Perspectivism and Interpretation," in *The New Nietzsche*, p. 193. Werner J. Dannhauser, *Nietzsche's View of Socrates* (Ithaca: Cornell University Press, 1974), pp. 113, 80.

218. Karl Jaspers, *Nietzsche: An Introduction to the Understanding of His Philosophical Activity*, trans. Charles F. Wallraff and Frederick J. Schmitz (Chicago: Henry Regnery, Gateway Editions, 1965), p. 211. F. A. Lea, p. 170. *NW*, pp. 253, 434. Jaspers, *Nietzsche and Christianity*, pp. 44–45. Nietzsche, letter to Meysenbug, Jan. 14, 1880, in *Selected Letters*, p. 171. Nietzsche, *The Birth of Tragedy* (New York: Vintage Books), p. 23. Nietzsche, *Beyond Good and Evil*, p. 71. Nietzsche, *The Use and Abuse*, pp. 27–28.

219. Arthur C. Danto, p. 79. Nietzsche, *Beyond Good and Evil*, p. 250. *NW*, p. 536. Nietzsche, *The Gay Science*, pp. 35, 85.

220. Nietzsche, *The Birth of Tragedy* (New York: Vintage Books), pp. 18, 97. F. A. Lea, p. 124. *NW*, p. 328. Maurice Blanchot, "The Limits of Experience: Nihilism," in *The New Nietzsche*, pp. 122–123.

221. Nietzsche, *The Birth of Tragedy* (New York: Vintage Books), p. 110; *Twilight of the Idols*, p. 25; *Beyond Good and Evil*, p. 13; *The Genealogy of Morals*, p. 255. Nietzsche, *Philosophy in the Tragic Age of the Greeks*, trans. Marianne Cowan (Chicago: Henry Regnery, Gateway Editions, 1962), p. 23.

222. *NW*, pp. 330, 326, 14, 15. Nietzsche, *The Gay Science*, p. 336. Arthur C. Danto, pp. 77, 100.

223. *NW*, pp. 263, 534, 535. Jean Granier, "Perspectivism and Interpretation," p. 190. Richard Lowell Howey, *Heidegger and Jaspers on Nietzsche* (The Hague: Martinus Nijhoff, 1973), p. 91.

224. Thomas Mann, "Nietzsche's Philosophy in the Light of Contemporary

Events," in Robert C. Solomon, ed., *Nietzsche: A Collection of Critical Essays* (New York: Doubleday, Anchor Books, 1973), p. 370. Nietzsche, letter to Rohde, quoted by F. A. Lea, p. 52. Nietzsche, *Thus Spoke Zarathustra*, p. 139. Heidegger, "The Word of Nietzsche: 'God Is Dead,'" p. 54. Nietzsche, *The Gay Science*, pp. 338, 279, 131. Nietzsche, *Beyond Good and Evil*, p. 145. Nietzsche, letter to Rohde, May 24, 1881, in *Selected Letters*, p. 175. Nietzsche, *The Anti-Christ*, p. 114. Nietzsche, *The Genealogy of Morals*, p. 291. *NW*, p. 4.

225. *NW*, pp. 3, 7, 331, 13, 504. F. A. Lea, p. 293. Heidegger, ibid., pp. 62–63. Nietzsche, *The Genealogy of Morals*, p. 298. R. J. Hollingdale, *Nietzsche: The Man*, p. 145. Erich Heller, *The Disinherited Mind: Essays in Modern German Literature and Thought* (New York: Farrar, Straus, and Cudahy, 1957), p. 196.

226. *NW*, p. 3. Jaspers, *Nietzsche: An Introduction*, p. 158. Jaspers, *Nietzsche and Christianity*, p. 65. F. A. Lea, p. 199. Nietzsche, *Thus Spoke Zarathustra*, p. 287.

227. *NW*, pp. 380, 365, 458, 475. Blanchot, "The Limits of Experience: Nihilism," pp. 123–124. Jaspers, *Nietzsche: An Introduction*, p. 167. Martin Heidegger, *What Is Called Thinking?* trans. J. Glenn Gray and F. Wieck (New York: Harper Torchbooks, 1968), p. 65.

228. Jaspers, *Nietzsche: An Introduction*, pp. 273, 268, 56. Nietzsche, *Thus Spoke Zarathustra*, pp. 12, 15. *NW*, p. 358. F. A. Lea, p. 330. Michael Haar, p. 10.

229. *NW*, p. 538. Dannhauser, p. 225. Nietzsche, *Philosophy in the Tragic Age of the Greeks*, p. 80. Nietzsche, *The Gay Science*, p. 332.

230. Jaspers, *Nietzsche: An Introduction*, pp. 441, 336.

231. Michael Haar, p. 26. Heidegger, "The Word of Nietzsche: 'God Is Dead,'" p. 103. *NW*, pp. 290, 550. Nietzsche, *Beyond Good and Evil*, p. 47. Arthur C. Danto, p. 232.

232. *NW*, pp. 547, 548. Richard Lowell Howey, p. 91. Erich Heller, p. 87.

233. Joan Stambaugh, *Nietzsche's Thought of Eternal Return*, p. 26. Arthur C. Danto, pp. 211, 213. Löwith, *Meaning in History*, pp. 222, 214, 215, 220, 221. *NW*, p. 548.

234. See *supra*, p. 311.

235. F. A. Lea, p. 314. Nietzsche, letters to von Seydlitz, Feb. 12, 1888, and to Brandes, Feb. 19, 1888, in *Selected Letters*, pp. 283, 285. Nietzsche, *The Anti-Christ*, pp. 123, 117. Nietzsche, *Beyond Good and Evil*, p. 85. *NW*, pp. 149, 9, 13. Nietzsche, letter to Overbeck, May 21, 1884, quoted in Erich Heller, p. 160. Löwith, *Meaning in History*, p. 221.

236. Nietzsche, letter to Maier, July 15, 1878, in *Selected Letters*, p. 168. Nietzsche, *The Birth of Tragedy* (New York: Vintage Books), p. 123; *Thus Spoke Zarathustra*, pp. 32, 211; *Philosophy in the Tragic Age of the Greeks*, pp. 6, 33. *NW*, pp. 503, 537. Nietzsche, *Werke in drei Bänden*, ed. Karl Schlechta (München, 1954 ff.), III, 329, quoted in Cowan, "Introduction" to Nietzsche, *Philosophy in the Tragic Age of the Greeks*, p. 6. See also J. P. Stern, *A Study of Nietzsche* (Cambridge: Cambridge University Press, 1979), pp. 210–211.

237. Nietzsche, *The Genealogy of Morals*, pp. 288, 297; *Beyond Good and Evil*,

pp. 123, 124, 284; *The Gay Science*, p. 121. Dannhauser, p. 85. Martin Heidegger, "Nietzsche as Metaphysician," in Robert C. Solomon, p. 113. Arthur C. Danto, p. 78. Nietzsche, letter to Overbeck, July 30, 1881, in *Selected Letters*, p. 177.

238. Nietzsche, *The Gay Science*, p. 341. *NW*, pp. 68, 69, 480.

239. *NW*, pp. 505–506. Nietzsche, *Thus Spoke Zarathustra*, p. 120; *The Gay Science*, p. 340.

240. Genesis 32 : 24–30.

CHAPTER EIGHT

1. Seneca, *On Benefits*, IV, 19. In regard to the ancient mythos, see Walter F. Otto, *The Homeric Gods* (Boston: Beacon Press, 1964), pp. 3, 131, 160–161, 236–237; Mircea Eliade, *Myth and Reality*, trans. Willard R. Trask (New York: Harper Colophon Books, 1963), pp. 12, 51, 139, 141; Numa Fustel de Coulanges, *The Ancient City* (New York: Doubleday, Anchor Books, 1956), pp. 62, 63, 141, 151. In regard to the cosmos presented by the ancient logos, see Aristotle, *Physics*, Bk. II (199b), Bk. III (204a, 205a, 205b), Bk. IV (208b, 210b, 211a, 221a, 221b), Bk. VI (232b, 239a), Bk. VIII (251b, 253b, 264b, 265b); *De Caelo*, Bk. I (278b), Bk. II (287b, 289b, 296a), Bk. III (301b); *De Generatione et Corruptione*, Bk. I (318a, 323a), Bk. II (338b); *Metaphysics*, Bk. Lambda (1074b); *Nicomachean Ethics*, Bk. X (1177b); *De Anima*, Bk. III (435a 11–435b 4); *Problemata* XVII, 3 (see Henri-Charles Puech, "Gnosis and Time," p. 42).

2. Cleanthes, "Hymn to Zeus," in Whitney J. Oates, ed., *The Stoic and Epicurean Philosophers* (New York: Modern Library, 1940), pp. 591–592.

3. St. Paul, Hebrews 9 : 25–26. In regard to Christian faith, see the Gospel of St. John 14 : 6–7; St. Paul, Hebrews 11 : 1; John Henry Cardinal Newman, *An Essay in Aid of a Grammar of Assent* (New York: Doubleday, Image Books, 1955), pp. 156, 163, 170, 180, 193, 302. For the significance of time in Creation and Incarnation, see Jean Mouroux, *The Mystery of Time: A Theological Inquiry*, trans. John Drury (New York: Desclée, 1962), pp. 31–48; the Gospel of St. John 7 : 6, 8 and 12 : 23; Anton-Hermann Chroust, "The Metaphysics of Time and History in Early Christian Thought," *New Scholasticism*, 19, no. 4 (October 1945), pp. 322–352.

4. St. Augustine, *Of True Religion*, trans. J. H. S. Burleigh (South Bend, Ind.: Gateway Editions, 1959), xli, 77, 78, pp. 74, 75. Alfred Lord Tennyson, "Flower in the Crannied Wall." In regard to absolute beginning, see Isaiah 41 : 4 and Exodus 3 : 14. For nature as an "exquisite poem" see St. Augustine, *The City of God*, Bk. XI, 18; and on particularity, see Matthew 10 : 29–30.

5. Martin Heidegger, "Metaphysics as History of Being," in Heidegger, *The End of Philosophy*, trans. Joan Stambaugh (New York: Harper and Row, 1973), p. 22. M. B. Foster, "The Christian Doctrine of Creation and the Rise of Modern Natural Science," p. 450. *HH*, I, pp. 8–9. In regard to the emergence of novelty

in being, see St. Paul, 2 Corinthians 5 : 17, Ephesians 4 : 22–24, Colossians 3 : 9, 10. For the emergence of man as the measure of meaning, see Psalm 82 : 6–7, St. Paul, Galatians 3 : 25–26, and St. Augustine, *Of True Religion*, xxxv, 65, p. 62. In regard to the un-self-contained-ness of nature, see St. Paul, Romans 8 : 19–22, and St. Augustine, *City of God*, Bk. XI, 10, 27. As to modern science and Christian theism, see the Wisdom of Solomon 7 : 15–22 and 11 : 20; Stanley L. Jaki, *The Road of Science and the Ways to God* (Chicago: University of Chicago Press, 1978), esp. pp. 330–331; M. B. Foster, "Christian Theology and Modern Science of Nature," in *Mind*, N.S., 44 (1935), pp. 439–466, and 45 (1936), pp. 1–27; Eugene M. Klaaren, *Religious Origins of Modern Science: Belief in Creation in Seventeenth Century Thought* (Grand Rapids, Mich.: William B. Eerdmans Publishing, 1977), esp. pp. 122–123, 124, 190–191. On the beginning of wisdom see Sirach 1 : 14 and Aristotle, *Metaphysics*, Bk. Alpha, 982b, 12–28.

6. John Henry Cardinal Newman, "Prayer to the Father of Lights," in James Collins, ed., *Philosophical Readings in Cardinal Newman* (Chicago: Henry Regnery, 1961), p. 411. See also St. Paul, 1 Timothy 2 : 3–4 and Titus 2 : 11.

7. Martin Heidegger, "Hölderlin and the Essence of Poetry," in Martin Heidegger, *Existence and Being*, ed. Werner Brock (Chicago: Henry Regnery, Gateway Editions, 1949), p. 289. In regard to the uniqueness of Christianity as a religion, see Jacques-Albert Cuttat, *The Encounter of Religions: A Dialogue between the West and the Orient*, trans. Pierre de Fontnouvelle with Evis McGrew (New York: Desclée, 1960), pp. 72–81. As to the peculiar way in which the Gospel is being spread, see St. Paul, Philippians 1 : 18. On modern philosophy as a transition to a full-fledged Christian philosophy, see Joseph J. Carpino's review of Frederick D. Wilhelmsen's *Christianity and Political Philosophy*, in *Interpretation: A Journal of Political Philosophy*, 8, no. 2/3 (May 1980), pp. 219–220. The entire profile of modernity presented here is heavily indebted to Joseph Carpino, "Three Cosmologies," *Interpretation: A Journal of Political Philosophy*, 6, Issue 1 (Fall 1976), pp. 48–64.

8. Heidegger, "The Question Concerning Technology," and "The Turning," in Heidegger, *The Question Concerning Technology and Other Essays*, pp. 4, 48. On the first moon landing, see *New York Times*, July 21, 1969, pp. 1, 3, and note especially Eugene Ionesco's reference to the perception of the earth as a "beautiful star" and Arthur Koestler's reference to "unprecedented power" on pp. 6–7. The terms "predatory lusts" and "angelic impulses" were used by William James (see Ralph Barton Perry, *The Thought and Character of William James*, 2 vols. [Boston: Little, Brown, 1935], Vol. II, p. 313). On technology in the Middle Ages, see Friedrich Klemm, "The Spiritual Bases of Technical Development," in *Man and Technology*, "German Opinion on Problems of Today," ed. Walter Leifer, Nr. II/1963, (München: Max Hueber Verlag, 1963), pp. 7–11. On the characteristics of technology in general and contemporary technology in particular, see Marshall McLuhan, *Understanding Media: The Extensions of Man* (New York: McGraw-Hill, 1965), pp. 8, 52, 56, 59, 60, 67–68, 89, 94, 101, 155, 182, 304, 342. On man's carrying the Archimedean point within

himself, see Hannah Arendt, *The Human Condition* (New York: Doubleday, Anchor Books, 1959), p. 259.

9. Sören Kierkegaard, *Philosophical Fragments or a Fragment of Philosophy*, trans. David F. Swenson, with a revised translation by Howard V. Hong (Princeton: Princeton University Press, 1967), pp. 42–43, 118–119. On man as called to become God's equal, see St. Augustine, *On Free Choice of the Will*, trans. Anna S. Benjamin and L. H. Hackstaff (New York: Bobbs-Merrill, Library of Liberal Arts, 1964), III, ch. 10, # 108, 109, pp. 111–112. The term "magnificent desolation" was used by one of the astronauts in reference to the lunar landscape (see *New York Times*, July 22, 1969, p. 46).

10. St. Augustine, *The City of God*, trans. Marcus Dods (New York: Modern Library, 1950), Bk. VIII, ch. 1, p. 243. The scriptural allusions (beginning with "the wisdom of men but in the power of God") are from 1 Corinthians 2 : 5, Romans 15 : 13; 1 Corinthians 4 : 20, Sirach 17 : 2–3, and 1 Corinthians 7 : 31. The allusions to technology as no mere "human doing," etc., are from Martin Heidegger, "The Question Concerning Technology," and "The Turning," pp. 19, 49, 29. The reference to Scripture's not having testified to man's "dominion over the luminaries of heaven" is from St. Augustine, *The Confessions*, Bk. XIII, ch. 23. The scriptural allusions beginning with "many and diverse ways" are from Hebrews 1 : 1–2; Revelation 4 : 8, 15 : 3, 21 : 5; First Letter of St. John 3 : 2; and Genesis 1 : 16. The references to the present age as one of decline and purely "extensive" possibilities are from Oswald Spengler, *The Decline of the West*, trans. Charles Francis Atkinson; abridged, ed. Helmut Werner (New York: Modern Library, 1962), pp. 31, 34. The references to "materially effective," etc., are from Jacques Ellul, *The Technological Society*, trans. John Wilkinson (New York: Vintage Books, 1964), pp. 425, 93. The reference to "at the most only wake," etc., is from Heidegger's interview in *Der Spiegel*, trans. David Schendler, "Only a God Can Save Us Now: An Interview with Martin Heidegger," *Graduate Faculty Philosophy Journal* (New School for Social Research, New York), 6, no. 1 (Winter 1977), p. 18.

INDEX

Abelard, Peter, 327
Académie française, 139
Adam, 47, 152, 305; and Eve, 321
Addison, Joseph, 83
Agnosticism, 121–122
Alan of Lille, 11
Alchemy, 19, 44, 45, 47
Alembert, Jean Le Rond d', 137, 138, 141, 183–184, 186
Alienation, 198, 276, 282, 304; of thought and nature, 52, 72, 73, 93, 97, 108, 274, 276
Analysis and synthesis, 68–69, 79, 80, 222, 239, 282
Ancient philosophy, xii, 4, 7–8, 13, 86, 370, 372–373, 374–375
Anselm of Canterbury, 13–14, 294, 307, 308, 315, 327, 330, 347, 348; Ontological Argument, 289
Anthropocentrism, 228, 269, 326
Aquinas, Thomas, 185, 250, 346–347, 349; *Summa Theologica,* 349
Archimedes, 61, 95, 148, 227, 393
Aristotle, 6–8, 22, 25, 32, 37, 45, 54, 80, 280; and Hegel, 280, 293, 301, 321, 336, 344, 345; and Kant, 260–261; and Kepler, 27, 53; and Leibniz, 86–87, 88; *Metaphysics,* 6
Armstrong, Commander Neil A., 390
Arnauld, Antoine, 85
Art, 309, 323, 324–325, 342–343, 373, 383
Astronomy, 7, 8; Copernican, 9, 26, 32–33, 136, 227–228; Ptolemaic, 23–24, 25, 26, 28, 32, 39, 50, 107, 185
Atheism, 58, 121, 354
Athenagoras, 294
Athens, 330, 340; and Jerusalem and Rome, 341

Augustine of Hippo, 14, 39, 71, 185, 400–401; *Confessions,* 214, 352; and Hegel, 277–278, 299, 311, 340, 343, 347, 348; and Kant, 257; and Nietzsche, 352; and Rousseau, 213–214
Authority, 42, 43, 46, 47, 59, 138, 157–158, 205, 351; and the Enlightenment, 140, 148, 151, 152, 153, 187, 328
Autonomy of man, xiii, 205, 218, 262, 305, 328, 383, 388, 399; in the Enlightenment, 138, 157–158, 174, 180, 181, 192, 193, 224

Bacon, Francis, 84
Barbarism, 151, 183–184, 206, 319
Barth, Karl, 346–347
Bayle, Pierre, 168
Beccaria, Cesare Bonesana, 186
Becker, Carl, 154, 170
Becoming, 281, 291–293, 315–316, 318, 320, 342, 356, 363
Beginning: of being, 287–290, 304, 343, 373, 378, 387–388; new, 2, 142
Being *qua* being, 372, 375, 387, 391; for Hegel, 282, 288, 320, 356; for Kant, 229, 268, 270; and Nietzsche, 356–357, 361–362
Bellarmine, Cardinal Robert, 32–33, 34, 38–39, 48
Bergson, Henri, 134
Berkeley, George, xiii, 94, 95, 137, 274; *Alciphron,* 110; and the Enlightenment, 118, 143, 149, 159, 192; and Hegel, 118, 277, 320, 340; and Hume, 113–114, 120–121, 122; and Kant, 193, 223–224; and Locke, 108–109, 110, 111–112, 117; mind and ideas, 113, 114, 115; mind-dependence, 112, 114–115; *Siris,* 110–111; *Three Dialogues Between Hylas and Philon-*

Berkeley, George (*Continued*)
  ous, 116–117; *Treatise Concerning the Prin-ciples of Human Knowledge,* 111; unthink-ing things, 113, 115
Boehme, Jacob, 294, 303
Bonaventure, Saint, 12, 296, 310, 338–339
Bossuet, Jacques-Bénigne, 153
Brahe, Tycho, 36
Browne, Sir Thomas, 37
Bruno, Giordano, 22, 52, 53, 205, 274; and Descartes, 53, 71, 73; and the Enlight-enment and Kant, 48, 138, 157–158, 174, 192, 193, 246; and Galileo, 30, 42, 43, 44, 45, 48; and Hegel, 280, 286, 309, 333, 345; on Jove, 46, 138
Buddha, Gautama, 354
Buffon, Georges-Louis Leclerc, Comte de, 186
Bunyan, John, 189
Butler, Bishop Joseph, 144

Cambrai, Collège de, 47
Campanella, Tommaso, 31, 36
Carr, Herbert Wildon, 90–91
Cassirer, Ernst, 14, 171–172
Cathedral, medieval, 2, 3, 10–11, 150, 324
Catherine II, Empress of Russia, 181
Catholicism, Roman, 32, 33–34, 85, 135, 144, 145, 146, 326–327, 346–347
Causality, 123–124, 125–127, 133, 238, 259; final, 82
Celestial and terrestrial spheres, 6, 23, 26, 36, 37, 38, 50, 261
Certitude, 171, 385–386; in Descartes, 58, 61–62, 66, 74, 104; in Hegel, 311, 319, 320, 321, 329–330; in Hume, 95, 118–119, 122, 129, 130–131; in Kant, 268, 337; in Locke, 100, 101–102, 104, 105, 106; in Newton, 77–78; in Rousseau, 214–215
Change, 5, 7, 15, 19–20, 292, 293, 371, 373
Chastellux, Marquis de, 142, 153; *De la félicité publique,* 153
Childhood, 106, 206
Christianity, xii, 389, 399, 400; and the En-lightenment, 144, 146–150, 151, 153–156, 158, 169, 174, 175, 176, 177, 184, 185, 328–329; and Hegel, 277, 278, 283, 304,

317, 318, 325–327, 328, 329, 330–331, 336, 340, 341, 347–348; and Kant, 266–268; and Nietzsche, xiv, 350, 352–353, 354, 355, 357, 359, 363–364, 365, 366–367
Christ, Jesus, 45, 155, 214, 310, 311, 314, 317, 339
Church, 31, 32, 33–34, 35, 40, 139, 145, 146, 151, 185, 331–332, 339
Cicero, Marcus Tullius, 22, 281
Clock: mechanical, 3, 167, 390, 397; world as, 82, 88
Collins, James, 86
Commonsense, 107–108, 114, 119, 122, 127–128, 131, 133–134
Comte, Auguste, 187
Condillac, Étienne Bonnot de, 168, 186
Condorcet, Marquis de, 147, 152, 177–179, 180; *Esquisse d'un tableau historique des progrès de l'esprit humain,* 153
Conscience, 48, 178, 205, 218, 222, 248
Consciousness, 100, 103, 104, 121, 230, 231–232, 277, 304, 361; and the negative, 289, 290–291
Contingent, 277, 298, 311, 319, 327, 374
Copernican Revolution, 21–22, 26, 50; and Cusa, 19, 21, 22, 24, 25, 27, 50; and Kant, 135–136, 227–229, 288; and Kepler, 27–29; and the Middle Ages, 9, 18–19, 21, 48–49
Copernicus, Nicolas, 9, 21, 22–27, 48, 49, 50, 52, 53, 91, 185, 274–275, 280; and Bruno, 43, 44, 45; and Galileo, 32–33, 37; and Hume, 136; and Kant, 222, 227–228, 232, 273, 275; and Newton, 84; and Nietzsche, 360; *On the Revolutions of the Heavenly Spheres,* 24–25, 26
Cosmology: and anthropology, 258, 279; modern, xiii, 18–19, 69
Cosmos: ancient, 273, 370, 371–372, 373, 374, 389, 461n. 1; Hegelian, 278, 279, 280, 281, 318, 342–343, 344; modern, 275, 278, 280–281, 379, 388, 389; and Nietzsche, 356
Cotes, Roger, 79–80
Council of Trent, 145
Counter Reformation, 32
Couturat, Louis, 92
Creation, Doctrine of, 376–377, 380, 381–382, 385, 386, 397; in Anselm of

Canterbury, 292, 298, 302; in Hegel, 275, 281, 286, 292, 293, 298–299, 302–303; and Kant, 252, 254, 257, 271–272; in Kepler, 30; and Nietzsche, 363; and Rousseau, 212, 213, 219

Cusa, Nicholas of, 21, 36, 43, 44, 50, 73, 288, 309, 347, 350; *De Docta Ignorantia*, 14, 15; learned ignorance, 15, 255; as medieval and modern, 14, 19; privatively infinite universe, 15, 16, 17, 18, 24, 50; unity and plurality, 279–280

Cyril of Alexandria, 297

Dante Alighieri, 12, 188–189; *Divine Comedy*, 339

Dasein, 289, 293

Dawson, Christopher, 150, 154

Death, 215, 301–302, 303, 306, 314

Defoe, Daniel, 189

Deism, 294

Descartes, René, 49, 51, 52, 94, 95, 137, 149–150, 179–180, 274, 335, 346; clarity and distinctness, 60, 67; *Cogito*, 59, 60, 61, 63, 223, 296; *Compendium Musicae*, 64, 65; divine inspiration of, 56, 329; existence of material world, 62, 66; and Hegel, 53, 55, 282, 288, 312, 329–330, 337; idea of extension, 60, 72, 82, 88–89; and Kant, 95–96, 165, 193, 223, 224, 227, 244, 271; and Leibniz, xiii, 85–86, 87, 88–89, 91–92, 93; and Locke, 97, 98–100, 102, 104, 105, 107, 108; *Meditations on First Philosophy*, 56, 58; and Newton, xiii, 75, 76–77, 79, 80–82, 83–84; *res cogitans*, 59, 60, 98; *Rules for the Direction of the Mind*, 65, 68

Dewey, John, 19–20, 86, 90, 92

Diderot, Denis, 141, 151, 157, 161–162, 163, 167, 168–169, 173–174, 178, 183, 186, 196

Dijon, Academy of, 196

Donne, John, 41–42

Doubt, 55, 56, 57–59, 60, 62, 119

Dualism: of imperfect and perfect, 4–5, 50, 74; of matter and mind, 72, 74, 92, 95, 108, 109, 111, 114, 115–116, 117–118, 143, 159, 161, 244, 278, 342–343; of up and down, 13, 24, 50, 52, 72, 261, 353–354, 371, 380

Du Bartas, Guillaume, 23

Earth: ancient view of, 8, 22–23, 25, 373; modern view of, 19, 24, 25, 278, 353, 361, 388, 390, 393–394, 396

Eclecticism, 142, 189

Ego, 280, 291, 319; Cartesian, 98, 105, 108, 135, 137, 217; Transcendental, 238, 239, 253, 254–255, 258

Eighteenth century, 137, 142, 144, 145, 146, 149, 150, 154, 178

Eliot, Thomas Stearns, 343

Empiricism, 97, 312

Enlightenment: anti-Christian polemic of, 143, 145, 146, 149, 153–154, 155, 156, 166, 174, 213, 268; anti-institutional impulse of, 176, 186, 187; as collective consciousness, 190–191; *Encyclopédie*, 183; enigma of, 155–156, 176; epithets for, 139, 141, 148, 183, 197; and Hegel, xiii, 190, 192, 279, 318, 327, 328–329, 330, 331–332, 338, 348; and Kant, xiii, 165, 176–177, 187, 189, 193, 220–221, 224–225, 246, 254, 263, 267–268, 279; as moral vision, 138, 157–158; and naturalistic humanism, 156, 157, 158, 159, 175; and ordinary consciousness, 141, 169–170, 180, 181, 182, 187–188; origin and dissemination of, 138–139, 144; pessimism in, 176, 182–186; and Rousseau, 176–177, 187, 188, 189, 193–196, 197, 203, 204, 205, 210, 211, 213, 216–217, 218. *See also* Ideology

Epistemology, 71, 95, 96, 97, 103, 109, 111, 120–121, 122, 125, 133, 137, 228; ancient and modern, xiii, 102, 373–374, 383, 384

Equality, 177, 180–181, 352, 395–396

Eriugena, John Scotus, 9, 10, 11, 13, 14, 19, 297, 322, 327, 330, 339

Essence, 100–101, 125; in Hegel, 287, 289, 290–291, 294, 299, 320; in medieval thought, xii, 10, 297, 377–378

Euler, Leonhard, 84

Evolution: biological, 301, 302; historical, 198, 263; philosophical, 332, 333

Existence: in Berkeley, 113, 115, 117; in Descartes, 59, 63; in Hume, 120, 126, 128
Experience: in Hume, 122, 123, 124, 125, 128, 129–130; in Kant, 222, 223, 235, 238, 239, 240, 243–244; in Locke, 100, 102, 104, 105, 106, 107, 111; in Newton, 80
Experiment, 75–76, 78–79, 80, 98

Faith: and certainty, 329–330, 375, 385–386; Christian, 144, 169, 347, 366, 375, 376, 377, 385–386, 388, 399, 461n. 3; and the Enlightenment, 154, 169, 177, 213; in modernity, 48, 53, 275, 345, 349–350, 361, 364, 366, 367; in modern science, 54–55, 97, 108, 142, 354; and Nietzsche, 355, 356, 361, 364, 366–367; and Kant, 247–248, 254, 262, 264, 267, 268; and reason, 327–328, 330, 339–340
Fathers of the Church, 212, 294, 297, 326, 327, 363
Feeling: in the Enlightenment, 168, 169–170, 328; in Hume, 120, 128, 130, 131–133; in Rousseau, 201, 202, 205, 215, 216
Fielding, Henry, 142
Flew, Anthony, 135–136
Foucault, Michel, 73
Franklin, Benjamin, 186
Fraternity, 158
Freedom: in Bruno, 47, 48, 138; in the Enlightenment, 140, 188; in Hegel, 312, 313, 314, 318–319, 344; in Kant, 222, 226, 248, 249, 252, 258, 259, 264, 265, 266, 272; in Rousseau, 195, 196, 199–200, 202, 204–206, 218, 222, 312
French Revolution, 187, 188
Freud, Sigmund, 134
Future: for the Enlightenment, 142, 152–153, 155, 176, 177, 178; for Nietzsche, 350, 355, 359–360, 363, 364, 365, 366, 367

Galileo Galilei, 22, 48, 49, 52, 193, 274, 345; as apologist, 33–34, 40, 50; and Descartes, 42–43, 53, 54–55, 58, 61, 68, 73, 84; *Dialogue Concerning the Two Chief World Systems*, 35, 40; educative mission of, 33, 35, 42, 53; and Leibniz, 85, 87, 91; and Newton, 75; and Rousseau, 197
Genesis, Book of, 292, 296, 304, 314
Geocentrism, 23, 227–228

Geometry, 27, 28, 36, 58, 59, 62, 75, 77, 238, 282; Euclidean, 17, 39
Gethsemane, 340
Geymonat, Ludovico, 31
Gibbon, Edward, 151; *The Decline and Fall of the Roman Empire,* 151
Gilbert (Gylberde), William, 84
Gilson, Étienne, 349
God: for the ancients, 298, 375; in Berkeley, 109–111, 114, 116–117, 118, 277, 346; the Christian, 192, 293, 307, 340–342, 353, 354, 355, 359, 361, 362, 365, 376–377, 378, 386, 400; in Cusa, 17, 18, 309; in Descartes, 58–59, 62–64, 67, 68, 71, 73, 81–82; in the Enlightenment, 146, 149–150, 152, 154, 155, 157, 159, 173; as "Father of Lights," 388, 398; the Hebraic, 286, 310, 340, 341, 345, 347; in Hegel, 286–287, 299, 303, 308, 324, 325–326, 330, 333–334, 338–339, 340–341, 343, 344–345, 347; in Kant, 241–242, 245–246, 265–266, 271–272; in Leibniz, 88, 110, 143; in Newton, 81–82, 87–88, 143; in Nietzsche, 352–355, 356, 361–362, 367–368; in Rousseau, 209, 211–214, 219–220, 286, 329; the theophanic, 13, 28, 177, 192, 211, 213
Gods, 324, 325, 340–341, 353, 359, 372, 389; men are, 138, 354, 382; space occupied by, 369–370, 383, 396
Golgotha, 315, 340
Grace, 57, 145, 152, 155, 157, 257, 386
Gravity, 83, 124, 143
Gregory of Nyssa, 340

Hall, A. Rupert, 84
Happiness: in the Enlightenment, 155, 168, 177, 178, 180, 186–187; in Hume, 129; and unhappiness in Rousseau, 201–202, 203, 206, 217
Harvey, William, 84
Haskins, Charles H., 1
Hegel, Georg Wilhelm Friedrich: Absolute Spirit, 298, 309, 319, 320, 321, 322, 323, 325, 332, 335, 338, 343; dialectical method of, 281–282, 283–284, 295; and Greek thought, 310, 312, 313, 317, 324, 328, 335–336, 340–342; and Kant, xiii, 272–273, 275, 276, 279, 280, 282, 284, 285–286,

307–308, 309–310, 312, 317, 327, 330, 337, 345; master-slave dialectic, 305–306; and medieval sources of modernity, xiii, 272, 273, 278; negation in, 282–284, 287, 288–289, 290–291, 292, 295, 300, 302, 315; on the notion, 287, 291–292, 293, 297, 299; Objective Spirit, 309, 313, 314, 315, 317, 319, 321, 322; philosophy of nature, 297, 299, 300, 303, 315, 320; philosophy of Spirit, 307, 309, 313, 319; Subjective Spirit, 309, 313, 321, 322, 345

Heidegger, Martin, 274, 394, 461n. 5, 462n. 7

Heinemann, F. H., 134

Heliocentrism, 23, 24, 25, 26, 32

Helvétius, Claude-Adrien, 164, 186

Heraclitus of Ephesus, 4, 5

Herder, Johann Gottfried von, 180, 221

Hinduism, 295

History: in the Enlightenment, xiii, 141–142, 152, 153, 155, 165, 189–190, 317; for the Greeks, 315; in Hegel, xiii, 272–273, 295, 304, 305, 306, 313, 315–319, 338, 342–343, 344, 348–349; in Hume, 133–134, 189–190, 317; in Kant, 250, 263–265, 273; and modern dualism, 342–343, 380; in Nietzsche, 350, 354–355; of philosophy, 332–335, 337, 357–358

Hitler, Adolf, 390

Holbach, Paul-Henri Thiry, Baron d', 147, 152, 160, 164–165, 186

Hölderlin, Johann Christian Friedrich, 281

Hopkins, Jasper, 18

Hugh of Saint-Victor, 11

Human nature: for the Enlightenment, 143, 153, 156–157, 159, 163, 164–165, 166–167, 168, 170, 171, 172, 175, 176, 211; for Hume, xiii, 130, 132, 133, 134, 136; for Rousseau, 194–198, 199–202, 203, 207–209, 210, 211, 212, 215, 216–217, 219, 220

Hume, David, 94, 95, 274; and Descartes, 68, 119, 120, 122, 135; and the Enlightenment, 137–138, 149, 166, 168, 171; and Hegel, 312, 317; impressions and ideas, 122–123, 124, 125, 126, 127, 132–133; and Kant, 135–136, 193, 221, 222, 238; *The Natural History of Religion,* 121–122; and Newton, 84, 119, 120, 124; on the power of custom, 121, 123, 125, 317; "Of the Study of History," 134; *A Treatise of Human Nature,* 126

Husserl, Edmund, xi

Ideology, 153–154, 158, 165, 166, 186–187; and philosophy, 138, 139–140, 141, 146, 156, 159, 160–161, 170–171, 172–173, 174–176, 184–185, 186, 187, 188, 189, 190–191, 192, 194

Ignatius of Loyola, 57; *Spiritual Exercises,* 57

Imagination: in Berkeley, 114; in Descartes, 67–68; in Hume, 68, 122, 123–124; in Kant, 230, 233–235; in Rousseau, 209, 212–213, 219

Immanence, xii, 109–110, 113, 116, 372, 373, 375; and transcendence, 9, 10, 143–144, 219, 277–278, 296

Incarnation, Doctrine of, 10, 315, 377; in Anselm of Canterbury, 311, 314; in Bruno, 45; in Hegel, 278, 281, 286, 310–313, 322, 341; and Nietzsche, 363

Index Librorum Prohibitorum, 40, 135

Individual: in Bruno, 45–46; in Kepler, 28; in Locke, 103; in Rousseau, 204, 207, 209, 211, 218–219

Infinite: for the ancients, 7, 280, 374; for the medieval mind, 10–11, 12, 14, 20, 289, 310; for the moderns, 43, 69–70, 171–172, 211, 260, 261, 262, 279, 293, 308, 344–345, 358, 378, 383, 384–385, 387

Infinity, xii, 172, 211, 219, 367; in Bruno, 46, 280; in Hegel, 308, 309–310, 328; in Kant, 262, 271

Innate ideas, 99, 100, 151

Innovation, 186–187

Inquisition, 39, 41, 43, 48

Inside and outside, Bifurcation of, 73–74, 83, 117–118, 342–343, 379–380; and Berkeley, 114, 115–116; in Descartes, 72, 276; and Hegel, 273, 320; in Kant, 243, 244, 245, 261, 272

Intolerance, 146–147, 148, 157

Irrational, 132, 159, 167, 275, 341, 385; and the ancients, 8, 374; and Nietzsche, 134, 350, 357, 358, 362

Israel, 267; and Jacob, 367

James, William, 7, 462n. 8
Jansenism, 145, 148
Jefferson, Thomas, 186
Joachim of Flora (Fiore), 319
John of Damascus, 340
John, Saint, Gospel of, 304
Johnston, G. A., 115
Joseph II, Emperor, 181
Judgment: in Hume, 120, 126, 131–132; in Kant, 235, 236–237, 239; in Locke, 104

Kant, Immanuel, xiii, 192, 274; antinomies, 240–241; architectonic, 242–243, 244, 247, 249; categorical imperative, 251, 252–253, 257; the constitutive and regulative, 246–247, 248; on Hume and Leibniz, 222–223; 224; "Idea for a Universal History," 317; ideas of pure reason, 241–242, 247–248; legislation of nature and morality, 229, 231, 253, 254, 255, 258, 259; moral law, 249, 250, 251, 252, 254, 257, 260, 261, 262, 267, 272, 279; on Newton and Rousseau, 218, 221, 224, 258; practical reason, xiii, 246–247, 248, 249, 254, 255, 264, 265, 267, 268; synthetical apriori propositions, 237, 252, 292; teleology of nature, 236, 255; transcendental unity of apperception, 238–239, 254
Kepler, Johannes, 22, 27–30, 44, 45, 48, 49, 50, 52, 274, 275; and Descartes, 55, 61, 73; Epitome of Copernican Astronomy, 28; and Galileo, 31–32, 37; on God and astronomy, 27, 340; and Hegel, 333, 340; and Kant, 221; and Leibniz, 87; and Newton, 77, 84
Kierkegaard, Sören, 395–396
Kingdom: of ends, 256, 257; of God, 155, 331–332, 396
Knowledge: for Descartes, 64, 65; for Kant, 227, 228, 235, 243–244; for Locke, 97, 100, 101–102, 104, 105; modern question of, 93, 95, 384; for Nietzsche, 358, 359; and power, 392
Koestler, Arthur, 23, 41
Königsberg, 220
Koyré, Alexandre, 19, 30, 48, 75, 76, 84, 88
Kuhn, Thomas, S., 8, 22, 24

La Mettrie, Julien Offray de, 162, 168
Lateran Council, 295
Leeuwenhoek, Anton van, 91
Leibniz, Gottfried Wilhelm von, 49, 50–51, 52, 107, 137, 274; and Berkeley, 110, 117, 143; and Hegel, 280, 300, 301, 302, 321; and Kant, 93, 193, 221, 223, 238–239; Monadology, 91; on nature of life, 87, 91, 93, 302
Leroy, C. G., 168
Lessing, Gotthold, 158, 186
Locke, John, xiii, 94, 95, 274; and the Enlightenment, 107, 137, 149, 165, 169; An Essay Concerning Human Understanding, 96, 98, 99, 105; and Hegel, 312, 321; and Hume, 108–109, 118–119, 120, 121, 122, 127, 130, 135; ideas of sensation and reflection, 100; and Kant, 107, 108, 193, 223; as "underlabourer," 96, 99, 107
Logic: in Aristotle and Cusa, 15, 17, 286; in Hegel, 284–288, 289–290, 293, 299, 300, 307, 316, 319, 350; in Nietzsche, 355–356, 358
Logic of modernity, xi–xii, xiii, xiv, 49, 52, 74, 87, 91–92, 93, 96, 108–109, 275, 346, 369, 388, 398, 399; and Berkeley, 110, 111, 118, 277; and Christian philosophy, 389, 398, 400, 462n. 7; and Cusa, 17, 279–280; and the Enlightenment, 138, 140, 142, 143, 150, 153, 154–155, 156, 162, 163, 172–173, 175, 176, 181, 187, 190–192; and Hegel, 192, 273, 277, 281, 328, 333, 338, 349; and Hume, 122, 127; and Kant, 224, 226, 227, 268, 271, 273; and Nietzsche, xiii–xiv, 275, 350, 361, 364, 366, 367; and Rousseau, 189, 217; sequence of, 191–192, 272, 274
Logos: ancient, 4, 273, 277, 369, 370, 371, 372–373, 374, 375, 376, 378, 379, 384, 385, 388, 389; modern, 369, 378, 379, 380, 381, 382–389
Lotze, Rudolf Hermann, 92
Louis XIV, King, 85
Lovejoy, Arthur, 159
Löwith, Karl, 150
Lucretius (Titus Lucretius Carus), 146, 148
Lutheranism, 85, 326, 336, 347
Luther, Martin, 310, 327

Magic, 44, 47, 48

Man: for the ancients, 369, 373–375; in the Enlightenment, 137, 138, 159, 161–162, 163, 169, 173–174, 182–183, 185, 328, 329; in Hegel, 290–291, 301, 304, 305, 306; in Hume, 122, 124, 132–133, 134, 135; as image of God, 28, 90, 180, 304, 382, 384; in Kant, 226, 227, 254, 255, 258–259, 262, 268, 269–272; as measure of all things, 159, 170–171, 172, 173, 174, 175, 176, 181, 189, 216, 375, 383, 399; for the moderns, 191–192, 382–383; in Nietzsche, 351, 355, 360–361; in Rousseau, 196–197, 198–206, 212, 216, 218, 346

Maritain, Jacques, 74

Marius Victorinus, 294

Marxism, 186

Mary, Virgin, 296, 310, 337

Mathematics, 31–32, 38, 119, 127, 129, 130, 135, 148, 171, 189, 381; in Descartes, 58, 61, 66, 84; in Galileo, 31–32, 33, 35–37, 38–39; in Kant, 225, 236–237, 243, 262; in Kepler, 27–29; in Newton, 75, 76, 77, 78

Matter, 361, 372; in Berkeley, 110–111, 112–113, 143; in Hegel, 299, 300, 301, 302; in Leibniz, 89, 90, 302

Maximus of Chrysopolis (the Confessor), 310–311

Maximus of Turin, 11

Mercure de France, 196

Metaphysical foundations: Cartesian and Kantian, 95–96, 135, 165, 189, 193, 223, 226–227, 271; for modern science, 51, 54, 56, 58, 71, 95, 97, 120, 127, 137

Metaphysics: ancient and modern, 375, 387–388; and the Enlightenment, 141, 155, 169, 173, 174, 191, 193; in Hegel, 285–286, 316, 317; in Kant, xiii, 221, 222, 223, 224–226, 227, 228–229, 238, 242–243, 245–246, 258–259, 262–263, 265, 268–269, 270–271; and Nietzsche, 350, 355–357; of unfinished being, 379, 387–388

Middle Ages, 1–3, 9, 12, 20, 50, 346–347; and the Enlightenment, 142, 147, 149, 150, 154, 185; and Hegel, 327, 338–339; and technology, 2, 3, 390, 395, 397, 462n. 8

Milky Way, 261

Mind See Dualism; Spirit

Modern culture, 344–345, 351, 387, 388, 389

Modernity, 49, 74, 94, 109–110, 203, 271, 274, 275, 388, 392; and Christianity, xii, 156, 343, 346, 350, 352, 357, 367–368, 401; and the Enlightenment, xiii, 142–143, 150, 171, 176, 177, 181, 191–192, 274, 279; and Hegel, 278, 281, 292, 317, 328, 335, 342, 343, 345; and Nietzsche, xiii–xiv, 350, 351–352, 357, 359, 364, 366, 367–368

Modern philosophy, xi, 111, 130, 259, 274, 385–386; and Christianity, xiv, 328, 333, 337, 386–387; and Hegel, 52, 309, 312–313, 329–330, 333, 335, 337–338, 339, 343, 344

Modern Science, 19, 20, 22, 73, 99, 213, 276, 358; and Christian faith, 69, 144, 384–385, 462n. 5; and Descartes, 56, 66, 69–70, 72, 346; and the Enlightenment, 147–149, 161, 171, 172, 173, 179–180, 191, 194–195; and Galileo, 30, 41, 50, 51; and Hume, 127–128, 129, 130, 132; and Locke, 105–106, 107, 108; and Newton and Leibniz, 51, 52–53, 88

Monad, 89–90, 93, 239, 321

Monism, 12, 116, 120–121

Montesquieu, Charles Louis de Secondat, baron de, 186

Moon, 390, 393, 398

Morality, 70–71, 157, 163, 194; in Kant, 221, 248, 249, 250, 251, 253, 254, 255, 259, 263, 264, 266, 267

Moral philosophy, 30, 43, 136, 205, 246

More, Henry, 110

Mossner, Ernest Campbell, 136

Motion: for the ancients, 8, 24, 370–371; in Galileo, 38, 42; in Leibniz, 89; in Newton, 76

Mutability, 186–187, 315; and immutability, 4, 159, 164–165, 166, 175, 176

Mysticism, 27, 44, 55, 73, 96; and the Enlightenment, 177–179; and Hegel, 283, 309, 339–340

Myth, 262, 330, 370, 372, 377, 389, 398; and the Enlightenment, 148, 152, 156, 163, 175

Mythos: ancient, pagan, 4, 273, 274, 277,

Mythos: (*Continued*)
278, 369, 370, 371, 375–376, 378, 383, 384, 388, 461n. 1; Christian, medieval, 9, 274, 275, 278, 369, 375, 378, 379, 382, 385, 388, 389

Nature: for the ancients, xii, 237, 298, 369, 370, 371, 372, 373, 374, 375; as a book, 11, 39, 82, 197–198, 199, 203, 208–209, 211, 216, 219, 381; in Descartes, xiii, 72, 73; in the Enlightenment, 159–162, 173; in Hegel, 297–298, 299, 300, 301, 302, 303–304, 305, 306, 307, 308, 315, 338; as internal and external, xiii, 106, 221; in Kant, 219, 229, 230, 236–237, 240–241, 243, 250, 251, 258, 259, 263–264, 271; in Leibniz and Newton, 76, 83, 88, 89, 93, 280; mastery and possession of, xiii, 71, 99, 179–180, 201, 346, 381, 393; as mechanism, 72, 83–84, 92, 237, 271, 381; in medieval thought, xiii, 11, 237, 298, 376–377, 395; for the moderns, xiii, 39, 52, 381–382, 383, 386, 394; and modern technology, 392–393, 394–395; and pre-givenness, 72, 73, 99–100, 108, 342, 373, 375, 378–379, 384; in Rousseau, 197–199, 200–201, 202, 203, 204, 205, 206, 207, 208, 210, 211, 212, 213, 214, 216, 305
Neoplatonism, 212, 335, 336
Newman, Cardinal John Henry, 331, 462n. 6
Newton, Isaac, 49, 50–51, 52, 93, 274; and Berkeley, 110, 143; concept of force, 76, 78; and the Enlightenment, 137, 154, 165; idea of extension, 80; and Kant, 84–85, 193, 243; and Leibniz, 85, 87–88, 91, 92; and Locke, 84, 96, 97, 98, 105–106, 107; *Philosophia Naturalis Principia Mathematica*, 76, 77, 78, 79, 81, 154, 165; *Opticks*, 78; rationalism and experimentalism in, 75, 84
Nicolson, Marjorie, 43
Nietzsche, Friedrich: and Berkeley, 118; eternal recurrence, 351, 362–363; *The Gay Science*, 353–354; and Greek thought, 363, 364–365; and Hegel, 348, 354, 356–357, 367–368; and Hume, 134; as "last philosopher," 361, 367; negativity and positivity of, 350–351, 357, 364;

"overman," 350, 360–361, 362, 367; perspectivism, 350, 358–359, 362, 365; and Rousseau, 220; transvaluation of values, 351, 362, 363–364, 365, 366; and the twentieth century, xiv, 275, 349–350, 352, 367
Nihilism, 358, 359, 360, 364
Nineteenth century, 150, 187, 391
Novelty, 306, 362, 382; and Aristotle, 6–7, 373; and Descartes, 68, 69; and the moderns, 381, 382, 383, 389, 397

Oakeshott, Michael, 52
Odysseus, 11
Opposites, 276; coincidence of, 44–45, 46, 309
Original sin: and the Enlightenment, 151–152, 153, 155, 157, 162–163, 175, 181; and Hegel, 304–305

Particularity, 29, 112–113, 239, 291, 362, 363, 372, 373, 374, 380–382, 384; in Hume, 121, 123; and the Incarnation, 281, 311, 312–313; in Locke, 102–103, 112; and the Trinity, 294, 296
Pascal, Blaise, 152, 280; *Pensées*, 152
Passion: in the Enlightenment, 166–168, 169; in Hume, 120, 122, 128, 130, 131–132, 134; in Locke, 98
Paul, Saint, 330; Epistle to the Romans, 267
Paul III, Pope, 25
Peace, 85, 342; perpetual, 264–265
Pentecost, 323
Perfectibility, 152, 178, 199–200, 201–202
Phenomenon and Noumenon, 243–245, 254–256, 257–258, 259, 262, 263, 264, 265, 266–267, 268, 270, 271, 272, 276, 361
Philosophes, 139, 142, 154, 156, 157, 158, 159, 160, 164, 178, 184, 186, 187, 188, 194, 195
Philosophy: as comprehension of its own time, xi, 276, 278, 281; for the Enlightenment, 143, 166; for Hegel, 275–276, 295, 323, 330, 332–334, 339, 340, 342–343, 344; for Hume, 118, 120, 127–128, 130, 134, 135; for Kant, 221, 224–225, 226, 269–270, 271
Physics, 67, 75, 229, 238, 393; and the En-

lightenment, 148, 152, 160–161; and Galileo, 36, 38; and Hegel, 277, 299–300
Pity, 201, 352, 354
Plato, 5–6, 8, 341; and Hegel, 332, 336; and Kant, 233, 262
Pleasure, 65, 66, 168
Political philosophy, 103, 205, 206–207, 263, 265
Prayer, 348, 372, 375, 378, 388, 398, 399
Present age, xi, 275, 277, 342, 351, 352, 369, 390, 399, 401
Pride, 167, 169
Priestly, Joseph, 179
Probability, 104–105, 130–131
Progress, 201–202, 318, 351, 355; for the Enlightenment, 152–153, 154, 155, 181, 183, 195; for Kant, 263–264, 317
Protestantism, 32, 85, 326–327, 346–347
Providence, Divine, 152, 153, 155, 317–318, 355
Pseudo-Dionysius, 10, 14, 278
Psychological: age, 137; description in Rousseau, 193–194, 209; optimism, 195; science, 95, 98, 125, 130; understanding in Hume, 125, 127, 135
Public opinion, 108, 139, 140, 149, 196
Pythagoreanism, 27

Quantity, 72, 78, 371; in Kepler, 27–28, 29, 36, 280; and quality, 29, 133, 370, 384

Randall, John Herman, Jr., 74–75
Raphson, Joseph, 110
Raynal, abbé Guillaume, 151, 184; The Philosophical and Political History of the Indies, 151
Reason: in Descartes, 70; in the Enlightenment, 141, 146, 155, 158, 166–168, 169; in Hegel, 273, 280, 316, 317, 320, 321, 326, 327–328, 339; in Hume, 119–120, 128–129; in Kant, 224, 225, 226, 229, 230, 240, 242–243, 246–248, 249; in Locke, 98, 99, 217; in Nietzsche, 355, 357, 361–362; in Rousseau, 200, 201, 204
Reformation, Protestant, 32, 185, 312, 331, 336–337
Religion: in Berkeley, 109–110, 112; in the Enlightenment, 146–147, 154–155, 170, 181, 194; Greek, 310, 325, 340–341; in

Hegel, 323, 324, 325–327, 332, 342–343; in Hume, 121–122, 128–129, 130, 132; Judaic, 310, 340, 341; in Kant, 265, 266–268; Roman, 325
Resurrection, Doctrine of, 313–314, 317, 322, 341
Robinson Crusoe, 189, 215
Rousseau, Jean-Jacques, 274, 346; and civilization, 195–197, 198, 203, 204, 206–207, 208, 209, 216, 217, 220, 273; Confessions, 189, 212; conversion of, 195–196; and Descartes, 68, 214–215, 217; Discourses, 195, 196, 202; Emile, 214, 218, 317; on the golden age, 206, 208; and Hegel, 278, 286, 305, 312, 317, 329–330; and Kant, 217, 218–219, 220, 221–222, 246, 256, 267–268, 273; and Locke, 217; on Rousseau, 189, 193, 209–210, 212, 215, 216; on the savage, 198, 199, 201, 204, 208, 214; on the statue of Glaucus, 198; volonté générale, 204–205
Royal Society of London, 75, 97
Rulhière, Claude Carloman de, 139

Sacred, 12; and profane, 3–4, 5, 8, 10, 13–14, 50, 277, 369, 370, 371, 384
Saint-Pierre, abbé de, 168
Saints, 158, 377, 378, 383
Saint-Simon, Claude-Henri de, 187
Salvare apparentia, 32
Salvation, 54, 181, 187, 276
Scholasticism, 1, 33, 81, 145, 146, 224, 250, 327, 336
Scripture, 34, 326, 327, 396, 398, 399
Second Coming, 323, 362
Secularization, 149–151, 152, 153–154, 175, 181, 331, 332
Self, 98, 400; in Descartes, 59–60, 61, 98; in Hegel, 306, 310, 312, in Kant, 219, 228–229, 254, 255–256, 258, 260, 267; in Nietzsche, 356, 361, 362; in Rousseau, 198, 209, 211–214, 215, 216, 218–220, 222
Seventeenth century, 137, 141, 149, 150, 153, 171, 185–186, 335, 338
Sin, 57, 214, 267, 353, 377
Sixteenth century, 22, 30, 142, 294, 335
Skepticism, 57, 111–112, 336; in Hume, xiii, 119, 120, 129, 130, 134

Slavery, 305–306, 318, 351, 389, 390
Smith, Norman Kemp, 128
Socrates, 15, 135, 138, 158
Space, 50, 212; in Aristotle and Cusa, 18, 24; in Bruno, 44, 46; in Hegel, 299, 300; homogeneous and heterogeneous, xiii, 370, 380; in Kant, 223–224, 230, 231–232, 233–234, 235, 239, 241, 242; mathematicizing of, xiii, 39, 381
Species: human, 198, 201, 202, 203, 361; in nature, 102, 199, 371
Speculative: philosophy, 98, 141, 185–186, 191, 222, 339; reason, xiii, 246, 247, 320
Speech, 200, 203, 212, 284–285, 316, 323, 374, 378
Spenser, Edmund, 189
Spinoza, Benedict (Baruch), 87, 280, 290, 342, 366
Spirit, 121, 355, 361; in Berkeley, 114–115, 116; in Hegel, 277, 278, 279, 298, 299, 302–310, 313–319, 321–322, 325, 332–338, 340–344; in Leibniz, 90, 300, 302
Spirituality, 395, 396, 400
State, 139, 185, 203, 314, 331–332
Stoa Kantiana, 262
Stoicism, 5, 336
Subjectivity, 346, 359, 369–370, 375, 376, 387, 392; and Hegel, 276, 289, 299, 301, 302, 308, 310, 311, 324, 336; and Kant, 228, 233, 235, 309
Substance, 116, 238, 298, 307, 325, 330; in Leibniz, 87, 88, 89, 300
Superstition, 142, 144, 147, 148, 153, 156, 157, 174, 184, 363
Swammerdam, Jan, 91

Taylor, Henry Osborn, 1
Technology, 358, 390–395, 397–398; essence of, 394, 396; and Galileo, 31; as a way of being in the world, xii, xiv, 390, 391, 396, 397, 398, 399
Telescope, 37–38; and microscope, 91
Terence (Publius Terentius Afer), 163
Tertullian, Quintus Septimius Florens, 337
Thales of Miletus, 335
Theology, xiv, 86, 241, 242, 266, 354–355, 389; and the Enlightenment, 146, 149, 155, 164, 169, 174, 175; and Hegel, 326, 327, 328, 337, 339, 340

Theophany, 9–10, 15–16
Theoretical: life, 221; man, 358; work, 275, 357
Thirteenth century, 146, 154
Time: ancient view of, xii, 5, 7, 369, 370, 371, 372, 373, 374; in Augustine of Hippo, 300, 317, 341; and Creation, 376–377, 378–379, 461n. 3; in Hegel, 283, 299, 300, 344; and the Incarnation, 377–378, 461n. 3; in Kant, 230, 231–234, 235, 239, 241, 242; modern view of, xii, 378–379, 380–381; and nature, 376–377, 381
Trinity, Doctrine of: in Augustine of Hippo, 293–294, 295–296, 297; and Creation, 299, 395; generation and spiration in, 294–295, 307; in Hegel, 278, 281, 293–297, 307–308, 309, 318, 319, 322–323, 326, 327, 341; homoousia in, 296; and the Incarnation, 278, 296–297, 311–312; and Kant, 257, 296, 307–308; in Kepler, 29, 297; and modern philosophy, 296, 297
Truth: for the ancients, 373–374; in Berkeley, 109, 112, 340; in Cusa, 16; in Descartes, 66; in Hegel, 291, 302, 303, 304, 307, 309–310, 313, 316–317, 325–326, 340; in Locke, 99, 101, 321; in Nietzsche, 350, 354, 355, 356, 357, 362, 365, 366
Tübingen, University of, 27
Turgot, Anne Robert Jacques, 165, 186
Twentieth century, xiv, 349–350, 390, 391, 392, 401

Understanding, 35–36, 125, 200, 374, 378; in Hegel, 283–284, 331–332; in Kant, 230, 234–235, 236–237, 238, 239–240, 241, 242, 248, 249, 282; in Locke, 96, 99–100
Universality, 219, 372, 384; in Hegel, 302, 306, 331, 337; in Kant, 249, 253; in Locke, 102–104, 112
Universe: Copernican, 29, 30, 36, 95, 138, 232; finite, 17, 25, 46; indefinite, 69, 70; infinite, 24, 44, 47, 73, 74, 110, 171, 272, 273, 279, 280, 342; in Leibniz, 88, 321; mechanical, 110, 272–273, 280; riddle of, 84, 276, 303, 317; sacramental, 11–12, 15, 19, 29, 32, 69, 179

Unmoved mover, 7
Utopia, 179, 180–181

Vauvenargues, Luc de Clapiers, marquis de, 167
Vincennes, 195
Voltaire (François-Marie Arouet), 139, 146, 148, 154, 164, 168, 169, 174, 179, 182, 186; *Candide,* 188; on Locke, 137; on Rousseau, 195

Walpole, Horace, 184
White, Lynn T., Jr., 20
Wilkins, John, 26
Will, 199, 372, 374, 375, 394–395, 396, 398; in Kant, 226, 248–249, 251–252; in Nietzsche, 350, 362, 363, 364

Wonder, 260–261, 323, 370, 375, 381, 385, 393, 394, 396
World: for the ancients, 370, 372; for the Enlightenment, 171, 172, 279, 328, 330; history, 314–315, 316, 317, 318–319, 332, 334, 338, 355; in Kant, 230, 240–241, 242, 244, 245, 248, 256–258, 260, 262; -machine, 17, 117; the new, 138, 151, 185; Roman notion of, 280–281; sacramental, 13, 116; as *sensorium Dei,* 87–88; as will to power, 362
Worlds: rational life on other, 45; within worlds, 91

Yates, Frances, 47
Yeats, William Butler, 400; "The Second Coming," 400